Living in the Great Circle

Bill Soderberg
In honor of our people

June Olson

12-17-2012

Gathering of Grand Ronde people taken at Fairground in Salem, Oregon, 1895c.

1. Frank Quenel
2. John Basile "Mose" Hudson
3. Marion Hudson, little girl being held by Mose Hudson
4. Hattie Sands-Hudson holding baby Pearl Hudson
5. Martha J. Sands
6. Isaac Stevens
7. Peter Menard
8. Amanda Menard
9. David Leno
10. Elizabeth Menard

Living in the Great Circle
Grand Ronde Indian Reservation
1855–1905

June L. Olson

Kalapuya Descendant

Confederated Tribes of the Grand Ronde

A. Menard Publications

Despite a most painstaking effort to avoid mistakes in this work, a certain amount of human error should be expected given the mass of information the author has attempted to organize. Added to this problem, is the fact that records often disagree on such things as name spellings and birth and death dates. While the author believes that the information herein is fundamentally accurate, anyone discovering errors in this edition is invited to call them to the attention of the publisher for reference in compiling the next edition.

Design by Meadowlark Publishing Services, Corvallis, Oregon

Cover and frontispiece photo courtesy of Confederated Tribes of the Grand Ronde Community of Oregon

ISBN 9781-4675-0260-3

Manufactured in the United States of America.

A. Menard Publications
12042 SE Sunnyside Road, Suite 322
Clackamas, Oregon 97015
www.grandrondebooks.com

Published 2011

This book is dedicated to the memory of my grandmother, Adeline Menard-Haller, and written specifically for the benefit of my grandchildren: Dylan, Jason, and Annie Page and Adeline Moreland. I thank the Creator daily for sending them to bless my life.

Born on the Grand Ronde Reservation, Adeline Menard-Haller was the great granddaughter of Joseph Shangaretta (Kalapuyan and Iroquois), Nancy Pisk (Lower Chinook and Métis), Pierre Menard (French Canadian), and Josephte Ute (Paiute). After her parents died, Adeline was raised by her grandfather, William Neal, and her step-grandmother, a native woman from Applegate Creek in Southern Oregon who was known by the English name Lucy Johnson-Tom.

Adeline Menard-Haller (1905-1990)

Contents

Preface

I t is the author's hope that this book might be beneficial to educators in teaching Oregon history. As such, *Living in the Great Circle: The Grand Ronde Reservation 1855–1905* was written to promote

- An awareness about the traditional practices of the various native tribes and bands who occupied western Oregon
- Understanding about the reasons behind the discord that developed between the advancing white race and the native people who occupied the land
- A perspective about the changes that began occurring in native tribes as soon as they were forced on reservations
- A portrait of the native men and women who through their leadership helped their people endure the emotional pressure and physical hardship that were forced upon them
- An awareness about the native families that managed to survive this era and whose descendants form the tribe's membership today
- Incentive to celebrate with pride our native people and the ideas they shared in regard to the land and to the circle of life

To clearly identify the different native groups assigned to the Grand Ronde Reservation, the introduction provides a brief description of their removal. This is followed by a family directory that includes any personal history known about each person listed. To aid the reader, individual tables contain tribal affiliation, parent information, and all known native and English names. When individuals are mentioned outside their own profile, their names are typed in **bold** for ease in tracking them.

The indigenous languages of western Oregon contain many sounds unfamiliar to English-conditioned ears; these require time and practice to learn to pronounce correctly. For those native names recorded in the field notes of Melville Jacobs, Leo J. Frachtenberg, Albert S. Gatschet, and Philip Drucker, Dr. Henry Zenk has provided a standardized English spelling. Dr. Zenk has also provided a respelling of each of these names using the Confederated Tribes of Grand Ronde Chinuk Wawa alphabet, which he and Tony A. Johnson developed in order to accurately represent the phonetic systems of local native languages. Less exact English approximations are also given using a nontechnical alphabet. An asterisk (*) next to the native name is used to distinguish these names from those found in other sources.

The following is a combined key to the technical and nontechnical alphabets developed by Dr. Zenk.

English approximations	CTGR alphabet symbols	Approximate values
A, I, U	á, í, ú	as in "f<u>a</u>ther," "mach<u>i</u>ne," "fl<u>u</u>ke"
a, i, u	a, i, u aa, ii, uu	as in "m<u>a</u>chine," "pumpk<u>i</u>n," "p<u>u</u>lsation" as in "f<u>a</u>ther," "mach<u>i</u>ne," "fl<u>u</u>ke"
E, O, e, o	é, ó, e, o	as in "m<u>e</u>t," "n<u>o</u>te"
E	ɜ	as in "l<u>u</u>ck"
e	ə	as in "logic<u>a</u>l" (the obscure vowel)
b, d, f, g, h, k, l, m, n, p, s, t, w, y	b, d, f, g, h, k, l, m, n, p, s, t, w, y	as in English
ch, sh, ts	ch, sh, ts	as in "<u>ch</u>urch," "<u>sh</u>ip," "si<u>ts</u>"
p, t, k	p̱, ṯ, ḵ	as in "s<u>p</u>in," "s<u>t</u>uck," "s<u>c</u>oop"
k, g	q, g, ġ	like k, ḵ, g, but pronounced farther back in the throat
h	x x̣	like German "i<u>ch</u>t" like German "Ba<u>ch</u>," but pronounced farther back in the throat
hl	ɬ	a voiceless hissed "l": try setting the mouth to say "leap," but instead of saying the word, just blow gently
tl	tɬ	nearly "tl," said as it would be in English
p, t, tl, ts, ch, k, q	p', t', t'ɬ, t's, c'h, k', q'	like p, t, tl, ts, ch, k, q, except sharper
	ʔ	the catch in the throat heard between the first and second "oh" of English "oh–oh"

The family directory itself was compiled by using the 1860[72] Grand Ronde Indian Census (GRIC) for the core list of names.[1] The 1872 GRIC is important not only because it is the earliest known record of the individual native families at Grand Ronde, but because, in this document, individuals are listed under their tribal band with both their English name and any native name known to the recording agent.

Its importance is further enhanced by the fact that there is no known record of another GRIC until 1885. To help identify families omitted in error from the 1872 GRIC and track those who were listed, the Catholic Church records at St. Paul and Grand Ronde were extremely helpful.

Until the latter part of the nineteenth century, government officials did not individually identify people on the GRIC. However, around 1872, as the terms of

---

1   After crosschecking the names and ages of individuals on the 1860 GRIC with church records, the year of this census was corrected to 1872.

the treaties were about to expire and allotment land was being issued, more effort was made in this regard.

From the reservation, Chikhyan made this comment in 1905 about the government process of identifying Indian people:

> I am told that my name on the census is Peter Cheekee. The name the white people gave me was Peter and the name my father gave me was Chafean [Chikhyan]. Now, one name was all I needed until they wanted to allot land to me and then I told the surveyors that my Indian name was Chafean [Chikhyan], but I guess they couldn't pronounce it, so they put it down the way they could spell it and pronounce it themselves.[2]

Chikhyan was not alone in this experience. When first dealing with Europeans, many Indian people only used an English first name, but as legal issues began to develop, it became apparent that they also needed to take surnames.

They acquired surnames in several ways. Women often assumed the name of their village or tribe, as in the case of Josephte Utes and Lizette Chinook. In other cases, the English first name that a male head of household used became the surname as well. Subsequently, as in American society, the man's wife or wives and children were given the surname assigned to the husband. Kitty Tom, Rose Dick, and Sallie Bob are good examples of this method of naming people.

In other cases, a man's native name, such as Lhkailhkai, Kayakach, Yachka-wa, Kilmanukh, Wachinu or Selkya, became the surname for his family and was spelled phonetically a number of different ways in English.

Sometimes a man would acquire the name of a prominent white citizen. At Grand Ronde, one Kalapuya man took the name Ben Harding very likely out of respect for the American attorney and politician Benjamin F. Harding, who was elected to the Oregon state legislature in 1858–1860. General Louis Cass of the Umpqua Nation took the name of the United States secretary of state 1857–1860, Lewis Cass. Another Kalapuya man took the name of Luther Elkin, a Linn County Democrat and member of the Oregon State Senate in 1860.

Additional families were identified using the 1885, 1886, 1887, and 1888 GRIC. Both the 1886 and 1888 GRIC provided lists of family assets in addition to the usual information. However, the agent stated that the 1886 GRIC was less accurate than the 1887 GRIC because the Indians had been anxious for him to include family and friends returning to the reservation, but when they did not come back, he removed them the following year.[3]

Like the 1872 GRIC, the 1887 GRIC recorded both the English and any known native name of the individual. The 1888 GRIC gives the tribal affiliation of the

---

2 O. Applegate, *Roll in Regard to Sale of Surplus Land on the Grand Ronde Reservation, 1905.*

3 *Annual Report Commissioner*, 1887, J. B. McClane, 184.

individual head of household.

GRIC reports from 1889 through 1905 were examined for any new families or individuals who may not have been recorded earlier. These people were added to the family directory. Treaty documents and assorted tribal records for 1856, 1857, and 1862 were useful in tracking the prominent leaders of the various tribal bands.

Additionally, allotment and estate records were used to further identify individuals. These records were useful because they often provided additional names for different people and established additional family relationships, birth dates, and death dates.

Finally, historical material from other sources was used to help create a brief profile for as many individuals as possible. Sometimes no material could be found; in other cases there was so much information about the individual it could not all be included.

Some of the most important material was found in the linguistic work of Melville Jacobs, A. S. Gatschet, and L. J. Frachtenberg held by the University of Washington in Seattle, the National Anthropological Archives, Smithsonian Institution in Washington, D.C., the unpublished Joel Palmer papers held by the University of Oregon in Eugene, and the work of Joel V. Berreman and Henry Zenk held by the Confederated Tribes of the Grand Ronde Community of Oregon. The Hudson's Bay Company archives in Winnipeg, Manitoba, National Archives and numerous libraries across Oregon and Washington all provided additional resource material.

Such material, much of it new, not only provides an intimate profile of the individual families on the reservation, but gives a rich glimpse of history from the native point of the view. Although the information and stories taken from the native language informants about their friends and family are not verbatim, they were, as much as possible, kept in their own words.

I would like to acknowledge at this time the following scholars and professionals: Jed Schrock for providing access to important archival materials, my daughter, Tracy Moreland, Dr. Catharine Mason, Donald Haller, Cindy Gulledge, and Linda Murphy for their critical review and editing of chapters prior to publication. I would like to express my appreciation to Dr. Henry Zenk for his linguistic contribution. Also, I would like to credit my uncle Donald Haller and the late Merle Holmes for their great contribution to the preservation of tribal history. Donald Haller's interest in this project and his continued support have been invaluable.

Chronology of History in Oregon Territory 1805–1855

1805—The Lewis and Clark expedition reached the mouth of the Columbia River.

1806—On March 23, Lewis and Clark started back up the Columbia.

1811—The Northwest Fur Company of Montreal sent an expedition overland that reached Astoria in July. One component of the Wilson Price Hunt expedition arrived via the *Tonquin*. Upon arrival, the captain of the *Tonquin* blatantly insulted a native chief attempting to trade with him. In retaliation, the ship was attacked and most of the crew killed. Gunpowder was ignited on board and the ship blew up. Besides twenty-three members of the ship's crew, some two hundred villagers were killed as a result of the incident. Partners of the Pacific Fur Company built Fort Astoria, the first permanent American settlement west of the Rocky Mountains.

1813—The partners of the Pacific Fur Company sold Fort Astoria to the Montreal-based Northwest Fur Company. Fort Astoria was renamed Fort George.

1818—The United States and Great Britain agreed to joint occupancy of the Oregon Country.

1821—Northwest Fur Company and the Hudson's Bay Company merged.

1824—In the spring, Dr. John McLoughlin was appointed chief factor of the newly reorganized HBC and assigned to the Columbia District.

1825—McLoughlin moved the trapping headquarters from Fort George farther up the Columbia River. He named the new headquarters Fort Vancouver.

1827—England and the United States renewed the terms for joint occupancy in Oregon Country.

1829—Hudson's Bay Company met in council with native tribes to negotiate a peace treaty. Chief Kiyasnu (Cassino) rallied his tribe in support. After a demonstration of Scottish bagpipes, the tribes pledged their friendship and agreed to sell their furs to HBC.

1830—An Indian epidemic of "fever" and "ague" struck the tribes of Oregon Territory, killing thousands along the Columbia and Willamette rivers.

1834—The Methodist missionary Jason Lee arrived and opened a mission school in the Willamette Valley ten miles north of present-day Salem.

1839—The Catholic missionary Father François Blanchet arrived, blessed the church at French Prairie, and celebrated the first mass south of the Columbia River.

1840—Reinforcements to the Methodist mission arrived in the Willamette Valley.

1842—Fearful of violating the joint occupancy treaty of 1827, Dr. Elijah White was appointed sub-Indian agent for the United States government. It was hoped White's appointment would provide protection for American settlers while not offending the spirit of the treaty. The Methodist Board in the states ordered Marcus Whitman to vacate the Waiilatpu Mission and take up his missionary work with Perkins and Ellis where the natives were more receptive to the missionaries' work. Whitman ignored the order.

1843—American settlers in the Willamette Valley began meeting at Champoeg in the hopes of forming an American government. The largest wagon train yet, carrying seven to eight hundred people, reached Oregon.

1844—Over the course of the year, fourteen hundred new settlers arrived and three thousand more were on their way. While some went on to California, the majority stayed in Oregon.

1845—The Hudson's Bay Company officially recognized the provisional government. Two thousand settlers were now residing in the Willamette Valley.

1846—The United States and Great Britain agreed to divide the Oregon Country at the forty-ninth parallel. Hudson's Bay Company headquarters were moved from Fort Vancouver to Fort Victoria on Vancouver Island. McLoughlin resigned as HBC's chief factor.

1847—An epidemic of measles struck the native people living in Oregon Country; particularly hard hit were the Cayuse. The Cayuse blamed Marcus Whitman. On November 29, a party of Cayuse attacked the Waiilatpu Mission, killing the Whitmans and a number of other people. This action ignited a war between the Cayuse and the United States. At year's end, the United States military leader, Colonel Gilliam, was accidentally shot to death, the Cayuse were divided, and their leaders were in exile.

1848— President Polk signed a bill creating Oregon Territory.

1849—The provisional government convened in Oregon City. By this time there were more than ten thousand settlers in western Oregon.

1850—The Donation Land Act was passed. On February 21, five of the Cayuse believed to have been involved in the killings at the Whitman mission "turned themselves in" at Oregon City. After they were tried and convicted, they were marched on June 3 to a break in the bluff south of Fourth Street in Oregon City and hanged. The Indian Treaty Act was passed and commissioners were appointed to get western Oregon Indian people to agree to move to the unsettled areas east of the Cascade Mountains. Gold was discovered in the Rogue River Valley in southern Oregon Country, leading to a sudden influx of people into that region.

1851—Leaders of the various Indian tribes and bands in western Oregon met with representatives of the Unites States to negotiate for the purchase of their land.

1853—A treaty was made that established Table Rock as an Indian reserve.

1854—Joel Palmer began negotiating a new round of treaties with western Oregon Indian tribes and bands after Congress refused to ratify the treaties submitted earlier.

1856—A large-scale removal of Indian people from their homes in western Oregon to the reservation was implemented by the American government.

Postwar Hostilities

Conditions of the Indians · cultural differences · legal position of the Indians and settlers · the American Indian War

Before contact with Europeans, Indian people in western Oregon flourished in their way of life. Everything they needed was found living in the wild. The meadows were full of camas. The rivers were thick with fish. Their grandfathers' hillsides were stocked with game. The sight and sound of children playing could be heard in every village, and people were quick to laugh and sing.

All this began to change with the coming of the white man. The trading ships and the pioneers driving wagon trains across the great "Western Frontier" brought with them diseases never before encountered by the native population. Without any natural immunity to these illnesses, sometimes whole villages of people died within a matter of days.

During this time, the Clackamas tribe was warned of a deadly epidemic that would soon come to the people. In hearing the news, one man coughed, then laughed, and jokingly made the remark that perhaps he had the illness. Not much later, the disease struck and this man was the first to die. It killed suddenly. Sometimes children would be running about in the full bloom of health, then begin coughing and fall to the ground dead. Many people died.[1]

After a time, someone among the Indian people predicted another epidemic was coming. When this new sickness struck, the closer a sick person got to the fire, the colder he would become. His whole body would shake for a time. Then the fever would come and he would try to make it to the river. Some died before they got to the water. Others died on the bank after swimming. So many died that the river banks were littered with Indian bodies.[2]

In 1838, Charles Wilkes reported,

> I satisfied myself that the accounts given of the depopulation of this country are not exaggerated; for places were pointed out where dewilt [dwelt] whole tribes, that had been entirely swept off; and, during the time of the greatest mortality, the shores were shrewd with dead and dying. This

---

1   Frachtenberg, Kalapuya Ethnology, 2. Jacobs, Field Notebook 69, *Texts Ethnology Clackamas & Jargon*, 68–88: as told by Wacaut, wife of Chief Wachinu.

2   Ibid.

disease, it is said, occurs semi-annually, and it is the cause of foreigners, it is more mild at each succeeding attack. [3]

As to the ague and fever that killed so many Indians, Wilkes wrote, "the Indians fully believe, to this day, that Captain Dominis introduced the disease in 1830." Dr. John McLoughlin's son David described the Indian desolation as being caused by "mountain fever." He said,

> Once there were villages along the Columbia all the way from the sea to the Cascades. All these plains were covered with tepees and warriors came dashing down the hills. Then typhoid malaria came shortly after the first plowing of fields at Fort Vancouver and the Indians died by the hundreds and by the thousands. A quietness came over the land. No more Indians shouts, halloos and games of ball. No more Indians came to the fort with furs. There was a stench from all the waters, buzzards hovered in the sky. The bones of the Indian were corded up like wood and burned in great funeral pyres. The streams were filled with Indian bodies floating out to sea, for always in fever the natives leaped into the cold Columbia and never lived to reach shore.

The exact number of casualties was undetermined, but after returning to the Willamette Valley, one fur trader reportedly lamented, "Where, oh where, are our friends the Kalapuya once ten thousand strong?"

During this time, **Charlotte Wacheno** (Wasusgani), a young Cascades-Klickitat woman and one of the wives of the Clackamas chief, Wacheno (Wachinu), told of a white doctor living at Oregon City who treated some of the Indian people. According to Wasusgani, soon people noticed that anyone who went to this doctor died and it was rumored that at least one illness originated at Fort Vancouver where native people were given poisoned blankets.[4]

The stories that circulated against the Americans were not isolated to the Willamette Valley. Sometime earlier, William H. Gray, while still with the Marcus Whitman missionaries, had planted a garden near the Waiilatpu mission. In it Gray had several prize melons that the Cayuse children had their eyes on. After a couple of melons disappeared, he decided to inject some of those remaining with ipecac, a drug used to induce vomiting. Two young Cayuse boys stole the melon and became deathly ill.[5]

Gray's action, and a rumor that Marcus Whitman was threatening to return from one of his trips to the East with a disease he intended to use against the Cay-

---

3   Wilkes, *U. S. Exploring Expedition*, 140.
4   Jacobs, Field Notebook 69, *Texts and Ethnology*, 68–88.
5   Johansen and Gates, *Empire of the Columbia*.

use, served to support the Indian theory that the Americans intended to poison them in order to steal their land. When a new measles epidemic broke out in 1847, killing half the Cayuse population, the Cayuse saw it as biological warfare and proof that the rumors were correct.

Accounts given by a Delaware Indian and a few Iroquois reinforced the idea that the Americans intended to steal their land. In sharing their experience, they told how the American missionaries had once visited their people to teach them religion, and that soon the missionaries were followed by other Americans who took away their land.

In addition to these warnings, a few Oregon natives were having strange dreams of a future peril, but preoccupied with grief and mourning the loss of loved ones from the sickness that was everywhere, their leaders could summon little interest. Even when the Cayuse invited them to join together against the Americans, they could not face the prospect of war. If there was a time when this action might have saved their way of life, the opportunity slipped quickly away.

From the beginning, the relationship between the Americans and western Oregon Indians did not fare as well as those that had developed between the Indians and the men of the Hudson's Bay Company. Like the Americans, most of the Europeans associated with the Hudson's Bay Company did not believe an Indian was equal to a white man, but they respected their rights as human beings and adopted their way of life. Even more importantly, almost all the Hudson's Bay men became "blood brothers" by marrying into local Indian families. This practice allowed them to travel safely where the Americans could not go.

Creating a far greater disadvantage for the Americans was the fact that the Hudson's Bay Company had large established settlements at Fort Vancouver and French Prairie (north of present day Salem) before the Americans ever arrived in any real numbers. Given this presence, the United States government was reluctant to violate its treaty with Britain by declaring this region part of the United States. Until the question of joint occupancy was resolved, the American settlers, not sure of their legal rights, frequently hesitated when they were challenged and turned to the Hudson's Bay Company for help. For this reason, Indian people often laughed and called them women.

Adding to the differences between them was the fact that Congress had passed the Donation Land Claim Act, which granted settlers from 160 to 640 acres of land wherever they chose to locate it, without first clearing the Indian title. As a result, for years the settlers put their life's blood into land claims that were still owned by the local Indian people who believed God had created the land especially for them, along with all the natural resources necessary to sustain their lives. They could see no difference between a settler's garden vegetables and the wild berries in the forest. Indeed, even the homes the American settlers lived in belonged to the Indians.

Respect for Americans diminished even further in the eyes of Indian people after Congress failed to ratify the treaty agreements made in 1851. When the authority of the United States treaty representatives was compared with the power of the Hudson's Bay Company and Indian leaders, the Americans simply came up short. Still, most of the western Oregon Indians did not want trouble with the Americans. While some of the bands in the southern region had earned the name of "rogues" or "rascals" from their earliest contact with Europeans, the majority of native people in the Willamette Valley had remained on friendly terms with them.

Even as the number of conflicts with the Americans grew, most Willamette Valley Indians saw no benefit in going to war. They believed they were a dying race and wanted only to spend their last days living peacefully with their families. Other tribes in the surrounding regions held their hostility in check for a time, out of a sense of respect for the Hudson's's Bay men. But ultimately, war was inevitable.

It was in the southern region of western Oregon, where American-Indian relations were the weakest, that a serious problem first developed. Gold was discovered there, attracting large numbers of Americans who hoped to strike it rich. This increasing American presence, combined with their general disrespect for the Indian and total disregard for the native culture, was enough to escalate the number of criminal acts perpetrated between them.

Many of the offenses that occurred violated matrimonial custom and involved the mistreatment of Indian women. In response, Indian law required sufficient payment to offset the crime. For murder, Indian law demanded "an eye for an eye" and held not just the perpetrator but his whole family responsible for the act. If restitution was not made for the death, the victim's relatives were honor bound to retaliate in kind. However, most Americans were not interested in Indian law. Some miners did not even bother with their own legal system of "due process." If they believed an Indian had committed a wrong against them, they often simply shot or hanged him.

Fearing that the increased violence would soon spark an Indian war, some of the settlers called for military protection. United States troops under the command of General John E. Wool and American volunteers called by the governor of Oregon Territory responded, but there was an important difference between the two military forces. The territorial governor, influenced by his constituents' cries for the extermination of the Indians, wanted an aggressive campaign marshaled against the hostile bands of Indians, but General Wool believed it was the role of the army to simply keep the peace.[6]

Almost immediately, bad feelings began to grow between the two military forces. These hostilities were aggravated by Oregon press accounts highlighting the role of the volunteers and, from the army's point of view, "withholding a

---

6   Glisan, *Journal of Army Life,* 326–28.

proper share of the praise for the regular soldiers." At the same time, Oregon newspapers were full of rumors and accounts of exaggerated Indian attacks that kindled more violence.[7]

7   Ibid.

Indian Removal

Wasusgani and Chief Wachinu hastily prepare to leave their home country • Wagayuhlen, a busy medicine doctor and the hayash (high) wife of the Molalla chief, Gwayakiti, is forced to depart from Oregon City • Selecting the site for their new home with the Tualatin chief Kayakach • The council on the Umpqua reserve • A treaty with the southern Molalla

Determined to save the Americans the cost of a war and to protect the Indians from extermination, Superintendent of Indian Affairs Joel Palmer, already at work negotiating new treaties in Oregon Territory, stepped up the process. His plan was to move all the Indians in Western Oregon to a coastal reservation as soon as he could get the treaties signed.

Palmer had replaced Anson Dart as Superintendent of Indian Affairs in March 1853. As superintendent, his job was not only to negotiate treaties with all the Indian tribes and bands in Oregon Territory but to maintain a peaceful coexistence between them and the settlers until the Indians were removed to reservations.

The idea of small Indian colonies or land reserves within the boundaries of the United States had been adopted many years earlier by the government because it was generally believed that Americans and Indians could never live side by side within the same community. From the American standpoint, the Indians had to be either placed on reservations or exterminated.

Congress had not approved previous treaties made in Oregon Territory primarily because they allowed a number of small bands of Indians to reserve tracts of land within their home countries. With this in mind, Palmer pursued the new treaties with the idea of settling the tribes and small bands of Indians on a single reservation in western Oregon.

Early in October 1855, Palmer got word that Major Haller of the United States Army had left The Dalles with a hundred men en route to the Snake River, only to be attacked by Yakama and Cascade Indians about twenty-five miles out. Surrounded, he was pinned down on a hill with a ravine and thicket all around it. Under constant fire, his men and animals were without water for more than forty-eight hours, but he managed to get a messenger past the Indians sometime during the third night.[1]

The messenger reached Fort Dalles on Monday, October 8, at 8 p.m. with a request from Major Haller for a large reinforcement of troops. From the fort, a requisition was sent to the governors of Oregon and Washington territories asking for volunteers, and the few remaining troops from the fort left to offer im-

---

1   Glisan, *Journal of Army Life,* 326–28.

mediate aid. However, Major Haller and his troops made it to Fort Dalles before they could join him. Pursued all the way, Haller lost five men and his howitzer in the fight.[2]

Hostilities against the Americans extended to several tribes, and all the tribes east of the Cascade Mountains had been invited to join together in a war against them. The Indian victory over Major Haller further encouraged their efforts and caused an American soldier to declare that the situation "bid fair to become the greatest Indian war we have had for many years."[3]

In preparation for the next attack, the Oregon and Washington territorial governors called out a thousand volunteers. In addition, there were three hundred men in the regular army and five hundred more were preparing to take to the field within a matter of weeks.[4]

Meanwhile, in the Rogue River region an organized band of Americans laid plans to kill every Indian in the valley regardless of age or sex. After professing a desire for peace with the Rogue River people a few days earlier, they set out on the morning of October 8, 1855, burning Indian homes and killing families in different parts of the valley.[5] Jake's Band, on their way to the Table Rock Reserve, was one of those attacked. Between twenty and thirty men, women, and children from his band alone were slaughtered by Americans on this murderous rampage that lasted several days.[6] At the same time, a group of United States soldiers under the command of Major Fitzgerald had an encounter with the Indians from Northern California and the upper Rogue River Valley. Fitzgerald lost ten soldiers. After the Oregon volunteers reported a second encounter with the same Indians, the Americans acknowledged that they were now engaged in a second Indian war.[7]

In the Rogue River region, the Shasta bands were the leading spirits behind the war. In addition, **Chief John** (Tecumtum) had secured the assistance of the Grave Creek and many of the Umpqua and Cow Creek, as well as the Klamath and surrounding tribes, to join them in a combined effort to drive out the Americans.[8]

Tecumtum was a man with strong fight power. Among the Clackamas, men who were resistant to the arrows and knives commonly used in battle were called

---

2   Ibid., 256–58.

3   Ibid., 260.

4   Ibid., 256–58.

5   John Beeson, Letter to the Editor of the *Oregon Statesman*, October 8, 1856, (BIA, *Letters Received by the Office of Indian Affairs, 1824–1880*, National Archives, Washington DC).

6   Joel Palmer to the Commissioner, April 27, 1856, (BIA, *Letters Received by the Office of Indian Affairs, 1824–1880*, National Archives, Washington DC, Microcopy 234, Roll 609 (excerpt), NADP Document D36).

7   Glisan, *Journal of Army Life*, 259.

8   George Ambrose to Joel Palmer, October 20, 1855, (BIA, *Letters Received by the Office of Indian Affairs, 1824–1880*, National Archives, Washington, DC).

ituixyal.[9] Surely, the word describes the nature of Tecumtum, who would survive his wounds and return to fight time and time again.

To save the peaceful Indians from being caught in the middle of these two divisions, Joel Palmer had no choice but to begin an emergency evacuation even though it was the dead of winter and no preparation had been made for the thousands expected to soon occupy the new Pacific Coast Indian reserve.

Given the volatile nature of the situation, Palmer knew he would need the cooperation of the Indian people in order for an evacuation of this scale to work successfully. At some point he must have shared his plan with the leaders of the various tribes and bands, but how much his plan changed from the time it was first discussed to the time it was put into effect is another matter. For many of the Indian people, the day of their removal caught them completely by surprise.

Charlotte Wacheno (Wasusgani) learned that the white soldiers were coming the day before they arrived. After trading for some time with a local "Boston" woman, they had become friends.[10] During a visit with her, the woman told Wasusgani that soon the American military would be coming to take the Indian people away. She advised her to begin preparing for the trip immediately and warned her not to leave anything behind.[11]

Knowing that Wasusgani's husband, Chief **Daniel Wacheno** (Wachinu), had a canoe that would be difficult to transport, the woman thought they should hide it or ask someone to take care of it. Besides, the woman reasoned, when they returned to Willamette Falls each season to fish, their canoe would already be there.[12]

By the time Wasusgani got home, the news had also reached Wachinu. He had already "broken up" their canoe and was busy with other things.[13] Following his lead, Wasusgani quickly began tying up their personal possessions before night set in.[14]

When the American soldiers arrived the following day, they divided the people into two groups: one was to travel overland and the other was to be taken by riverboat to the town of Dayton on the Yamhill River.

Like Wasusgani, **Wagayuhlen Gwayakiti,** a busy medicine doctor and the hayash wife of the Molalla chief, remembered the day of removal as beginning in the usual way.

Unaware of the advancing military, on that particular morning she packed a horse with food for her relatives. Riding one horse and leading the other, she rode

---

9   Jacobs, Field Notebook 59, *Texts and Ethnology*, 130.

10   "Boston" was a Chinook Jargon term for the American settlers.

11   Jacobs, *Clackamas Texts*, Part 2, 550–52.

12   Ibid.

13   Ibid.

14   Drucker, Clackamas Notes, n.p: Wachinu "had a canoe named *isxana*—meaning fox (it was fast) and one named *igriL hamate*—meaning deer head decoy." A canoe maker would ask what kind the buyer wanted and then carve the figure on the prow.

into Oregon City just as the military arrived to take the people away. Stopped by the soldiers, she was forced to leave her horses where they stood and join the people being taken by riverboat.[15]

When they reached Dayton, Wagayuhlen saw many people from different tribes, but the Santiam band of Molalla were not among them. The soldiers collected the people in groups and put one man in charge of each group. At this time the various bands of native people spoke a surprising number of Indian dialects. In addition, Chinook Jargon was widely used for intertribal communication. However, Wagayuhlen did not understand the dialects being spoken and could not speak Chinook Jargon or English. Consequently, she could not communicate with either the group leader or the soldiers. Frightened, she waited for the rest of the Molalla.[16]

All around her the landscape was dotted with army tents hastily set up by the military as shelter for the people. With winter setting in, the tents were poor substitutes for the lodges they had been forced to leave. To make matters worse, the soldiers had allowed little time for the people to pack their store of native provisions, and many of them could not eat the American rations of beef and pork. Some elders left the rations right where the white distributors had unloaded them.[17] They would not touch it. To them the meat of cattle was bad and the meat of a pig was even worse.[18]

Wasusgani was somewhat better off, as she had learned from her Boston friend how to prepare American food and had even eaten it in the past. Hungry and set on survival, she now put that training to work. She fried the pig and stored all the grease. When other people threw their meat away, she took it. She dried the beef, sacked the sugar, and used everything the whites had distributed.[19]

From the American military standpoint, it was important to keep the peaceful Indians separate from the hostile bands to prevent them from joining the war. Therefore, Palmer issued instructions to keep the people still waiting to be evacuated separate from the hostile bands, even if that meant feeding them.[20]

In planning the evacuation, Palmer had divided western Oregon into a number of districts, assigned Indian agents to each region, and instructed the agents to take a roll call of all the adult men and boys over twelve years of age after they had been collected. No Indian was to be permitted to leave his assigned encampment without a written permit from the local agent. These provisions and others in his October 13 public announcement were intended, in part, to inform as well as calm the white settlers.

Indian Agent Lott Whitcomb, who had been assigned to remove the people in

---

15   Drucker, *Clackamas Notes,* n.p.
16   Ibid.
17   Jacobs, Field Notebook 69, *Texts Ethnology Clackamas & Jargon,* 95.
18   Jacobs, *Clackamas Texts,* Part 2, 550–52.
19   Ibid.
20   Glisan, *Journal of Army Life,* 271.

the Portland and Fort Vancouver area, wrote Palmer on November 9, 1855:

I have collected all the Indians on the south side of the Columbia River between the mouth of the Sandy and the Willamette River…There are about one
hundred in number, all quiet and friendly. No fear of outbreaks… They are providing for themselves. No expenses for provisions as yet.[21]

The following day he addressed another note to Palmer:

Since writing you yesterday, I have correctly asurtained that all the Indians at Ft. Vancouver, about 150, on Friday night, no doubt intended to join
the enemy. … Much excitement present here. All Indians are in danger.[22]

Palmer, in turn, notified his superior on November 12 that the Indians of the
Willamette Valley and the southern part of Oregon Territory were all "in a state of
suspense and alarm." He wrote:

Intense excitement pervades the white population of the entire country;
in the remote districts the people have congregated in blockhouses and
forts erected for their protection; messengers are seen hurrying from
settlement to settlement; alarming reports are everywhere current; night
watches are stationed; and the peaceful as well as the hostile bands of
Indians are measured with extermination.[23]

The situation was growing desperate, but before Palmer could evacuate any
more people, he needed to locate a permanent site for the peaceful Willamette Valley bands and begin constructing winter shelters for them. With this purpose in
mind, he selected a small search party.[24] Sometime earlier, Palmer had expressed
to his superiors the importance of obtaining the goodwill of the Tualatin people.
He reported that, in his opinion, not only did the Tualatin live on the most valu-
able land in the Willamette Valley, but the example set by their chief would affect
the entire course of Indian negotiations in Oregon Territory.

The Tualatin chief was a man named **Kiakuts** (Kayakach), who in the past
had twice successfully defended the Tualatin right to the land in United States
district court. The first complaint against the Tualatin, in 1851, was brought before a grand jury by an American settler named Donald McLeod. Kayakach was

---

21 Lott Whitcomb to Joel Palmer, November 9, 1855, *Correspondence and Personal Papers
of Joel Palmer*, Special Collections, Knight Library, University of Oregon.

22 Lott Whitcomb to Joel Palmer, November 10, 1855, *Correspondence and Personal Papers
of Joel Palmer*.

23 Joel Palmer, November 12, 1855, *Correspondence and Personal Papers of Joel Palmer*.

24 Jacobs, Field Notebook 69, *Texts Ethnology Clackamas & Jargon*, 95–97.

charged with criminally trespassing upon McLeod's property and destroying timber that McLeod had prepared for a structure he was planning to build.

After Kayakach and another Tualatin man named Guyani (Kuyapi) were arrested and placed in the jail at Hillsboro, the judge who heard the case found in favor of Kayakach and the Tualatin people. It was determined that since the land had never been purchased from them, the Tualatin had a right to destroy any timber that grew on it and no action for trespass could be made against them.[25]

When a second case charging trespass against Kayakach was brought before the same court, Kayakach once again defended the Tualatin right to the land. This incident occurred when a settler named Bridgefarmer built a fence across a road opened by the Tualatin. The Tualatin, under Chief Kayakach's direction, broke down the fence and used the road as usual. Again, the court found in favor of Kayakach and the Tualatin people.[26]

So, when Palmer put together a party of men to help him select a site for the new Indian reserve, the highly respected Chief Kayakach and a Tualatin sub-chief called **James Shiliqua** (Shilikwa) were two of the men who rode with him.[27] In remembering this occasion, Shilikwa said that, at first, Palmer directed their attention to a place in the main valley near the present-day town of Sheridan, but Chief Kayakach thought it was best to be further away from white people so there would be less danger of getting whiskey.[28]

In 1851, the Indians of Oregon reportedly consumed, on a whole, less liquor in proportion to their number than any other Indian people in the United States, and white men marveled at "so few drunken Indians."[29] However, by 1855 bootleg whiskey had become a major problem for Chief Kayakach. Just a short time earlier, a quarrel had developed between him and several other prominent Tualatin men, including LeMedicine and **Dave Yachkawa**, after Yachkawa had been drinking. The violence that followed not only threatened Kayakach's life but en-

---

25 J. R. Browne, Published in *Executive Documents*, 8: Browne references a court case between McLeod and the "Klickitat" confusing the name "Kayakach" with "Klickitat." However, his report of the incident matches the Tualatin version regarding the arrest of Kayakach given by Peter Kenoyer in (Gatschet, Frachtenberg, and Jacobs, *Kalapuya Texts*, Part 3, 165–66) with two exceptions. In Peter Kenoyer's version, even though the court found in favor of Chief Kayakach, he was fined $200, which he agreed to pay in kind with four horses.

26 During treaty negotiation with John Gaines in 1851, Chief Kayakach objected to two men by the name of Dixon and Bridgewater being allowed to retain their claims on the Tualatin reserve. Kayakach accused one man of being a great liar and the other of, ill treating his people and whipping the women and children of his tribe. The man named "Bridgewater" and the man J. Ross Browne identified as "Bridgefarmer" are very probably the same man.

27 Palmer, *Pocket Diary*, 5: an entry for March 26, 1856, "Started to Grand Ronde with Henry Sawyer and 5 Indian chiefs to examine reservation and assigned tracts of land to Indians."

28 O. Applegate, Testimony of James Siliqua.

29 *Annual Report Commissioner of Indian Affairs*, Letter 68, 1851, 211.

dangered the leadership of the Tualatin people at a time when all their attention needed to be focused on the Americans.

The disagreement was over three horses that Joel Palmer had sent the headmen as gifts after the signing of the treaty. When the horses arrived, Kayakach did not give Yachkawa the one he wanted. Under the influence of whiskey, Yachkawa angrily mentioned in the presence of an old man named **Wankhpa** that he intended to kill Kayakach. At some point, LeMedicine and Yachkawa fought and Yachkawa cut LeMedicine with the blade of his knife.[30]

Wankhpa brought the news of Yachkawa's discontent to Kayakach. After listening, Kayakach said that Wankhpa and Shilikwa must kill Yachkawa before Yachkawa could kill him. Wankhpa and Shilikwa agreed, knowing that if they did not kill him, almost assuredly, Yachkawa would indeed murder Kayakach.[31]

The plan was to lie in wait for Yachkawa in a thicket along the trail. When he passed by, Shilikwa would shoot him. One man, most likely a man who later took the English name **George Sutton,** was told to sweat with Yachkawa and then bring him by the thicket at a certain time.[32] Soon the date and time of the ambush arrived, but as Yachkawa passed by the thicket where the ambushers were hiding, his companion inadvertently interfered with Shilikwa's line of sight.[33]

After the first shot, Yachkawa ran. Shilikwa shot again, hitting Yachkawa in the leg. Before Shilikwa could fire a third shot, Yachkawa called upon his whirlwind spirit power. A great storm arose.[34] It was said that once Yachkawa got in his whirlwind no one could kill him, so it happened that Yachkawa escaped and fled to Joel Palmer's house in the town of Dayton.[35]

About two weeks later, Palmer sent a man to ask Kayakach and his men to come to see him. Kayakach agreed to leave early the following morning, but he told his men to watch and listen carefully in case Palmer intended to harm him.[36]

When Kayakach and his men arrived at Palmer's house, Palmer asked Kayakach why he had tried to kill Yachkawa. Kayakach explained that after a dispute over a horse, Yachkawa had threatened to kill him. Palmer listened to Kayakach and LeMedicine. Then he talked with them and Yachkawa.[37] Finally, after receiving payments for restitution from Yachkawa and pledging abstinence from whis-

---

30 Gatschet, Frachtenberg and Jacobs, *Kalapuya Texts*, Part 3, 169–70. Joel Palmer, Agreement of April 4, 1855, between LeMedicene, Dave Yatzkawa, and Chief Kayakach of the Tualatin band, as mediated by Joel Palmer, *Correspondence and Papers of Joel Palmer.*
31 Gatschet, Frachtenberg, and Jacobs, *Kalapuya Texts*, Part 3, 169–70.
32 Gatschet, *Texts, Sentences, and Vocables*, 132.
33 Gatschet, Frachtenberg, and Jacobs, *Kalapuya Texts*, Part 3, 169–70.
34 Gatschet, *Texts, Sentences and Vocables*, 4.
35 Jacobs, Field Notebook 79, *Texts and Ethnology Santiam*, 16.
36 Gatschet, Frachtenberg, and Jacobs, *Kalapuya Texts*, Part 3, 169–70.
37 Ibid.

key, Kayakach agreed to help Yachkawa regain the confidence of the Tualatin people.[38]

Most certainly this experience and others like it were paramount in the chief's mind when he rejected the first location. Next, from the main valley, they came up the Yamhill River to look at another site at the mouth of the Willamette, but Chief Kayakach also objected to this place because the valley was too narrow and plough land too scarce. From there they came over into the Grand Ronde Valley, where they thought the mountains would be fine for hunting. They also saw camas, *wipan* (wild celery), *it'uba* (wild rhubarb), and a variety of other things that were familiar to them as food, so it was decided that this place would be their new home.[39]

After directing the Indian agent to begin constructing the necessary buildings at the selected location, Palmer started out for the Umpqua Valley, riding through one of the worst storms ever experienced by the Americans in this region. He and his interpreters reached their destination on December 17 and reportedly found nearly three hundred Umpqua, Yoncalla, Cow Creek, and Molalla under the charge of Indian Agent Theophilus Magruder. These were the Cow Creek people treated with on September 19, 1853, and the Umpqua and Yoncalla band of Kalapuya treated with on November 29, 1854, along with the mountain Molalla, who as yet had no treaty with the United States.[40]

Chief Halo (Hilu), the principal chief of the Yoncalla band of Kalapuya, had not signed the treaty and was not present. In Chinook Jargon, as translated by a family of early settlers named Applegate, Hilu told the Indian agent he had always lived at peace with the white man and had not expected to die by their hands, but he would not leave the land of his father.[41]

After the Applegate brothers assumed personal responsibility for him, Chief Hilu was allowed to stay in the Yoncalla Valley, but the chief's band, including his wives and children, were among the people now waiting on the Umpqua Reserve to be moved to Grand Ronde.[42]

Like Chief Hilu, all the people now gathered on the Umpqua Reserve had always been committed to peace with the Americans, but they wanted to stay in their home country. Palmer knew he would need a strong advocate speaking on his behalf to convince them to do otherwise.

In treaty council, the Umpqua had elected an English-speaking Indian origi-

---

38 Ibid. Joel Palmer, 1855 Agreement between the Tualatins.

39 O. Applegate, Testimony of James Siliqua. Field Notebook 69, *Texts Ethnology Clackamas and Jargon*, 97. Jacobs, Field Notebook 55, *Texts and Ethnology*, 85. Jacobs, Field Notebook 53, *Texts and Ethnology*, 9.

40 Joel Palmer to Commissioner, January 9, 1856, Microcopy M-234, Roll 609, fr. 382-88, *Letters Received by the Bureau of Indian Affairs*, RG 75, National Archives, Washington, DC.

41 Kruse, *The Halo Trail*, 11.

42 O. Applegate, Testimony of Jacob Fern.

nally from Eastern Canada called **Louis Napesa** to act as their headman. Napesa's father had journeyed to Oregon Territory with the Hudson's Bay Company. Knowing that Napesa had great influence among the people, Palmer decided to use him to get the Umpqua to give up their homes.[43]

In order to gain Napesa's cooperation, Palmer offered him special consideration. He promised Napesa he would be paid the full value of his farm in Umpqua country. In addition, he promised that Napesa would be given a tract of land on the reserve equal to the old farm in value, and that the government would build new improvements of the same value on this new tract of land.

After getting Napesa to agree to the arrangement, Palmer wrote:

> It is unnecessary here to give the reasons for thus promising Louis beyond any other of this tribe, but they were such as, in my opinion, justified even a much larger reward.[44]

As far as the rest of the tribe was concerned, Palmer told them there was no time for them to collect their property. Even if there were time, he said, it would be impossible to take it all with them. He promised that he would have someone collect and deliver it to the new reserve or they would be paid an equivalent value for it.[45]

At this point, Palmer learned that many people were suffering from illnesses that he blamed on exposure to the elements and the sudden change in their diet. More precisely, they were starving because the native roots and seeds they normally harvested had significantly declined and big game had also become scarce as a result of increased farming and the unusually severe winter.[46]

The snow was eleven inches deep and the weather was exceedingly cold. Due to the weather and the sickness among them, the chiefs wanted to wait to move the people until spring or at least until the streams and roads were in better shape.[47] After discussing the situation, it was decided that they could stay where they were for the time being, but Palmer instructed Agent Robert Metcalf to remove them at the earliest possible moment.

Once arrangements for the evacuation of the Umpqua had been made, Palmer took the time to talk treaty terms with the chief and headmen of the Molalla people, whose home country was in the Cascade Mountains of Southern Oregon. In addition to selling their lands, the treaty with the Molalla made on December 21, 1855, stated that due to the existence of hostilities between whites and a portion of the Indian tribes in Southern Oregon and Northern California, the Molalla would

---

43 Cawley, *Indian Journal*, 39, 53.
44 *Annual Report Commissioner of Indian Affairs*, 1857, Letter 149, Miller, 363–64.
45 Ibid.
46 *Annual Report Commissioner of Indian Affairs*, 1854, Letter 87, Palmer, 463.
47 Joel Palmer to Commissioner, January 9, 1856, Microcopy M-234, Roll 609, fr. 382–88, *Letters Received by the Bureau of Indian Affairs*, National Archives, Washington, DC.

relocate with the bands on the Umpqua Reserve whenever they were moved to the Coast Reservation.[48]

On January 27 Palmer made a bad political blunder. He wrote Major General Wool in San Francisco in regard to the poor conduct of some of the settlers and military volunteers and their resistance to his receiving United States troops to escort the Umpqua to Grand Ronde.[49] In the same correspondence, Palmer enclosed a copy of a letter written by Father Eugene Cherouse of Walla Walla that described the conduct of the military volunteers as "without discipline, without order, and similar to madmen" and begged General Wool to send in the regular troops.[50] Palmer added that he thought the letter had merit and should receive immediate attention.

---

48   Kappler, *Indian Laws and Treaties*.
49   *Annual Report Commissioner of Indian Affairs, 1856, Letter 77*, Palmer, 195.
50   Ibid.

The Rogue River War

Open conflict • removal of Table Rock refugees while under attack • Yakama and Cascade Indians attack the American settlement in the area presently known as Cascade Locks • Chief Chenoweth's execution • the council at Oak Flat

By the end of January, twelve hundred regular army soldiers and volunteers were reportedly attacking Indians along the Rogue River. In organizing against them, the Rogue River bands had several factors in their favor. First, they knew all the best fighting positions in the mountainous terrain of their home country. Further, they were good marksmen and used a style of fighting that the Americans were not trained to match.

Sketch of "Volunteers on the March in Rogue River." Photo courtesy of Oregon Historical Society (OrHi 101436).

By February, Tecumtum was planning another attack on the Americans. This time the targets were a group of volunteers camped at the Big Bend on the Rogue River and one particularly hated Indian agent named Ben Wright.

Indian agent Benjamin Wright, Photo courtesy of Oregon Historical Society (OrHi 1711).

Since the provisional legislature had passed a law prohibiting the sale of firearms and ammunition to Indians, Tecumtum found it necessary to implement inventive wartime strategies.[1] In preparation for their attack, an Iroquois named Enos Thomas, who frequently acted as a guide for the American army, approached the local white settlers with the story that Captain Poland, who was in charge of volunteer soldiers camped at Big Bend, had sent him for ammunition. The settlers sold him sixty dollars' worth of gunpowder, not realizing Enos was a spy for Tecumtum's band of Rogue River.[2]

---

1   *Annual Report Commissioner of Indian Affairs,* 1854, Letter 87, Palmer, 463.
2   Glisan, *Journal of Army Life,* 282. Bancroft, *History of Oregon,* 239: The Rogue River tribes belonged to the Shasta Nation. Enos Thomas was associated with Chief John, who was the leader of the band in Scott Valley. Chief Jo and Chief Sam were leaders of the band in the Rogue River Valley. Scarface and Bill were the leaders of the band

Meanwhile, Palmer's letter to General Wool had added fuel to the campaigns of those who were set upon, using the situation to further their political interests. Perhaps many Americans thought as Palmer did, but relatively few voiced their objection to the conduct of the volunteers and the treatment of the peaceful Indians. The louder American cry by far was for the extermination of all Indian people.

In this political climate and without military escort, Agent Metcalf began moving the sick and poorly clothed Indians from the Umpqua Reserve. They arrived at the Grand Ronde Agency on February 2, 1856, to join the twenty-one members of the Luckiamute Band of Kalapuya who had arrived some two weeks earlier, on January 19.

When the Luckiamute arrived, Agent Joseph Jeffers immediately issued them their rations and put some of them to work. Later he reported to Palmer that he had put up a temporary building twenty-six by twelve and divided the building into two rooms designed for one family in each room because more of their people were yet to come.[3]

The arrival of the Umpqua was quite different from that of the Luckiamute. Witnessing their condition caused Jeffers to write, ". . . sympathy for them almost overran my better judgment," as many of them were sick and suffering from the cold. Already, three coffins had been built for them and he was working on another.[4]

In Palmer's report to Commissioner of Indian Affairs George Manypenny, he wrote that during the trip ten people had fled, but other members of the bands had joined the group over the course of the journey. In the end, 390 Umpqua arrived safely at their destination.[5]

On the evening of February 6, 1856, about ninety people from the Mohawk and Spores band of Kalapuya arrived at Dayton on the steamer *Enterprise* from Corvallis.[6] A few days later, Palmer notified Manypenny that both the Luckiamute and the Yamhill bands of Kalapuya were at Grand Ronde and that the remaining bands of the Willamette Valley were now camped at Dayton. Arrangements were being made to move them to the reservation within a few days.[7]

Palmer reported that the removal of these Indians and the appointment of agents to watch over them had quieted the fears of some of the American settlers. However, he was convinced that if the military campaign in Washington Territory and Middle Oregon failed, "it will be impossible to save the Willamette Valley Indians from the fury of the settlers." He believed "their guilt or innocence would not be the subject of inquiry," but the very fact that they were Indians would be

in Shasta Valley.

3   Joseph Jeffers to Joel Palmer, January 19, 1856, *Correspondence and Papers of Joel Palmer*.

4   Joseph Jeffers to Joel Palmer, February 7, 1856, *Correspondence and Papers of Joel Palmer*.

5   *Annual Report Commissioner of Indian Affairs*, 1856, Letter 77, Palmer, 195.

6   Palmer, *Pocket Diary*, 2.

7   Ibid.

enough for the settlers to kill them. He wrote that they would "be slain not for what they have done, but for what they might do if so disposed." Further, he announced, "the war is upon us" and "I am well satisfied of the necessity of the immediate removal of the friendly Rogue River Indians."[8]

Even as he penned these words, news came that several hundred Indians had attacked the volunteers at Big Bend. Outnumbered and caught by surprise, almost all the Americans were killed. The Indians had also burned and destroyed all the houses and property in that area except for the fort, and Enos Thomas had killed Ben Wright.[9]

While the Rogue River war chiefs celebrated their success, the American soldiers worked to put their posts in good condition in anticipation of the next attack. As for Palmer, he ordered the immediate removal of the friendly bands of Rogue River people from the Table Rock region.

Like the Umpqua, the peaceful Rogue River people were "excited and unsettled."[10] Difficulties they had experienced with the Americans during the past summer had prevented them from storing their usual quantities of food, and they had not received their government payment of annuities. Starvation and sickness from exposure to the harsh weather had killed nearly 20 percent of those residing on the reserve. To gain greater security against the Americans, many had fled to the mountains. Others were preparing to go. Of those remaining, only a few had shoes to make the trip.[11]

Despite concerns that the eight teams of horses he had secured to haul the thirty-four sick, aged, and infirm people were not enough and the knowledge that his party of Indians would probably be pursued by those who fully intended to kill everyone in his charge, Agent George Ambrose started out with 325 people from the Table Rock Reserve and its surrounding area on Saturday, February 23, 1856.

Like Ambrose, the chiefs had a lot to consider as they moved their people and a herd of about eighty horses toward the reservation.[12] Predictably, five days into the trip, one man went in search of a horse that had strayed during the night and was murdered. Eight pregnant women gave birth along the trail. Eight Indians died, including the man who was murdered. Finally, after thirty-three days and 263 miles, they arrived at the Grand Ronde Indian Reservation on March 25.[13]

---

8   Ibid.

9   Douthit, *Between Indian and White World*, 417. Glisan, *Journal of Army Life*, 282–85.

10   *Annual Report Commissioner of Indian Affairs*, 1854, Letter 87, Palmer, 463.

11   *Annual Report Commissioner of Indian Affairs*, 1854, Letter 87, Palmer, 463. George Ambrose to Joel Palmer, April 14, 1855, United States, Office of Indian Affairs, *Letters Received by the Office of Indian Affairs*, 1824-1880, National Archives Microcopy 234, Roll 608 (excerpt), NADP Document D26.

12   Palmer, *Pocket Diary*, 3.

13   Beckham, *Trail of Tears*, 18-21.

Table Rock in Southern Oregon. Photo courtesy of Oregon Historical Society (OrHi 1722).

The Table Rock refugees had barely arrived when Palmer received news of another Indian uprising. A party of Yakama and Watlala (Cascade) Indians had attacked the American settlement in the area presently known as Cascade Locks.

On March 27, 1856, the Americans sent Second Lieutenant Philip Sheridan and forty soldiers to reinforce the forty-seven whites who were fighting from a blockhouse there. Seventeen of their number had already been killed and as many wounded.

Armed with a howitzer, Sheridan captured nine men, including Chenoweth, chief of the Cascade Tribe. Even though the Indians owed no allegiance to the United States government, they were all charged with treason. Hearing their sentence, Chief Chenoweth offered each of the white officers ten horses and two women in exchange for his life. The offer was refused and he was taken with the other prisoners to the scaffold to be hanged. There, as the hangman kicked the barrel from beneath his feet, Chief Chenoweth greeted death with the now famous war whoop of the Pacific Northwest Indians.[14]

This battle renewed the old fear among the Willamette Valley settlers that Indian people might join together to kill them in their sleep. To discourage any action along these lines, the tribes and bands on the Grand Ronde Reservation were

---

14 Fuller, *A History of the Pacific Northwest,* 232–36. Schlicke, *General George Wright,* 119–23. Richards, *Isaac I. Stevens,* 291–93. Knudsen, *Warrior of the Mist,* 235–37.

ordered on April 6 to surrender their guns and ammunition. Reluctantly, **Chief Yelkas, Chief Quaiquaty** (Gwayakiti), **Chief Wacheno** (Wachinu) and other leaders of the Willamette Valley bands and tribes followed the directive to surrender their weapons, but **Chief Sam Wilder** (Toquahear)'s band of Rogue River, concerned about being caught defenseless in the face of an attack, refused. Palmer wrote Wool that he would leave immediately for the Grand Ronde Reservation to personally investigate the situation and "take such steps as may be advisable."[15]

Finally, it was agreed that Chief Sam Wilder (Toquahear) and his band would be exempt from the order of April 6 as they "needed their guns to defend themselves against the Shasta and other Rogue River bands who had sworn vengeance against Toquahear for not joining them in the war."[16]

After resolving the issue of weapons on the Grand Ronde Reservation, Joel Palmer met with the hostile Rogue River bands on May 21, 1856, at Oak Flat where all the war chiefs except Tecumtum agreed to surrender.

In opposition to the terms the Americans offered, Tecumtum said:

> You are a great chief, so am I. This is my country; I was here when these trees were very small, not higher than my head. My heart is sick with fighting, but I want to live in my country. If the white men are willing, I will go back to Deer Creek and live among them as I used to; they can visit my camp and I will visit theirs, but I will not lay down my arms and go to the reservation, I will fight.[17]

After Tecumtum walked away, the Americans stationed Captain Andrew J. Smith and a company of soldiers armed with rifles and a howitzer at Oak Flat. Tecumtum and his men attacked at eleven the following morning. The forces fought continuously for more than six hours; then, by American estimates, another two hundred to four hundred men from other bands joined Tecumtum's war party. Captain C. C. Augur's company arrived a short time later to support Smith.[18]

Before the engagement began, Chief Elijah's band of approximately a hundred men, women, and children were escorted to Grand Ronde Reservation to join Toquahear and his people.[19] However, **Chief George** (Chocultah) and Limpy's bands remained in the area and soon rejoined Tecumtum's war party.

To convince them to surrender, Palmer directed Metcalf to pick up two Indians from the Grand Ronde Reservation to act as messengers. Metcalf was to take them with him to the Rogue River valley where, if possible, they would talk with

---

15 Joel Palmer to Major General John Wool, April 14, 1856, MSS 114, Folio, Oregon Historical Society: 2.
16 Letter to the Editor, *Oregon Statesman*, January 10, 1857, *Matters on the Indian Reserve*.
17 Booth, *Until the Last Arrow*, 397.
18 Ord, *Ord's Diary*, 15.
19 1856 GRIC.

Oak Flat, Council Site in 1856.

the war chiefs.[20] Palmer further instructed Metcalf to go from there to the Illinois Valley to talk with Tecumtum. However, before Metcalf and his messengers could get there, a battle broke out. It lasted thirty-six hours. Seven white soldiers and one Indian ally were killed, and eighteen more white soldiers were wounded by the time Palmer arrived. Captain Augur's company, who arrived with Palmer, made several additional charges against Tecumtum's warriors, which ended with two soldiers killed and three wounded.

On the reservation, excitement raced through the people as news of Tecumtum's stand against the Americans raised both their hopes and fear. Whether they agreed with him or not, each and every one of them had a stake in the outcome of the war.[21]

20　*Annual Report Commissioner of Indian Affairs,* 1857, Letter 91, June 23, 1856, 212–20.
21　Cris Taylor to Joel Palmer, June 9, 1856, *Correspondence and Papers of Joel Palmer.*

The Surrender

The final days of the war in southern Oregon · conditions for surrender · the military escort to the Grand Ronde Reserve

Approximately ten days later, on the morning of May 30, one of the Indian messengers from the Grand Ronde Reservation, Chief Napesa, was sent to Chocultah, Limpy, and Tecumtum's camp to ask them to surrender.[1] That evening, Chocultah and Limpy, described by the Americans as a hard-looking set, came into the American camp with their people and gave themselves up. They told Palmer they had not fought in the recent engagement and said "they would have been in sooner, but Tecumtum threatened that if they attempted it, he would shoot them."[2]

After surrendering eighteen to twenty good rifles, they were held under guard in a camp just below that of the American military.[3]

On May 31, Major Lutshaw, with 150 volunteers, reached the Big Bend from the meadows, where they remained until June 1. Major Lutshaw had taken prisoner a number of women and children from Chocultah and Limpy's bands, but he refused to turn them over to Joel Palmer even though Palmer now held the two war chiefs in his camp. Further, Lutshaw vowed if they tried to escape or if his company was fired upon by any Indians, he would execute them all.[4]

On June 5, an Indian the Americans called Sambo returned to the American camp to report that twenty-four men and their families were not far behind him. They were carrying in their wounded chief as fast as they could through the rough terrain. In response to questions about Tecumtum, Sambo simply said that Tecumtum was in a strong place awaiting the Americans' next attack.[5]

On June 7, General Lamerick, "a spunky little fellow" in command of fifty volunteers, arrived at Big Bend accompanied by Agent Metcalf and the two Indian messengers from Grand Ronde. The Americans reported that the presence of the two men created "quite an agreeable excitement" among the Rogue River people who crowded around them and "ask any quantity of questions."[6]

---

1 *Annual Report Commissioner of Indian Affairs,* 1857, Letter 92, June 23, 1856, 212–20. Cawley, *Indian Journal,* 52.
2 *Annual Report Commissioner of Indian Affairs,* 1857, Letter 92, June 23, 1856, 212–20.
3 Ord, *Ord's Diary,* 16.
4 *Annual Report Commissioner of Indian Affairs,* 1857, Letter 92, June 23, 1856, 212–20.
5 Edward Otho Cresap Ord, *Ord's Diary,* 16.
6 Ibid.

Chief Tecumtum or Rogue River John. Photo courtesy of Oregon Historical Society (OrHi 4355).

General Lamerick also brought with him the women and children previously held by Major Lutshaw. On his arrival, he turned the prisoners over to Metcalf, who immediately placed them under the care of Colonel Buchanan with other prisoners who numbered by this time 265 people.[7]

That night, from within the American military camp, a dozen or more Rogue River warriors formed a circle and, dancing shoulder to shoulder, sang their war songs. The sound of their singing blended with the wail of mourning songs coming from their women inside makeshift shelters only a few yards away.[8]

Over the next few days, a number of Rogue River refugees, mostly old women, children, and the infirm, came into the camp to surrender to the Americans. After seeing some of them, General Edward O. C. Ord remarked, "[...] just to

7   *Annual Report Commissioner of Indian Affairs*, 1857, Letter 92, June 23, 1856, 212.
8   Ord, *Ord's Diary*, 17.

think of collecting such people for a long journey through an unknown land—no wonder the men fought so desperately to remain."[9]

It was June 25, 1856, before Palmer could report the Rogue River war was finally over. He wrote:

> All of the hostile bands with the exception of that of Chief John, who had about thirty warriors left, and the Chetco and Pistol River group numbering perhaps fifty, have come in to unconditionally surrender themselves as prisoners of war. Old Chief John had sent in two sons, asking the retention of the tribes at Port Orford until he could get there; he was tired of war and would submit to go on the reservation.[10]

As the number of prisoners grew in the American military camps, the soldiers began to quarrel over whether they should be killed. General Ord considered resigning, but then received word that he was to rendezvous with Tecumtum.[11]

On June 29, Chief Tecumtum and his men were finally spotted in the distance. After stopping to talk at the top of the hill, the Rogue River men, "in paint and feathers each with a fine rifle," walked down the hill in single file.[12] In the lead was a "stern and hard-faced old man wearing only a light shirt and a small rimmed old hat" for protection from the cold.[13] The American general easily recognized him as Tecumtum and walked to meet him. Shaking his hand, Ord led Tecumtum and his men to his camp, where one by one they laid down their rifles, some with looks of defiance. Once they were disarmed, General Ord invited Tecumtum into his tent.[14]

In the final count, 183 men, three hundred women, seventy-two boys, seventy-one girls, and 103 infants, totaling 729 Rogue River people, were labeled prisoners of war. In addition to the large number of children present, a number of the adults were too old or too sick to travel by land.[15] Palmer thought the best plan for transporting them would be to take them on foot to the coast and from there by steamship to Portland. From Portland, he planned to take them by riverboat to Dayton; from there they were to be marched by teams of department employees to the Grand Ronde Agency.[16]

One of the women counted as a prisoner of war really belonged to Chief Toquahear's peaceful band of Rogue River. Known by the English name **Betsy Lily Smith**, she and her two sons had been missed during the earlier evacuation of the

---

9   Ibid.
10 *Annual Report Commissioner of Indian Affairs,* 1857, Letter 91, June 23, 1856, 211-212.
11 Ibid.
12 Ord, *Ord's Diary,* 23.
13 Ibid.
14 Ibid.
15 *Annual Report Commissioner of Indian Affairs,* 1856, Letter 93, 220.
16 Ibid.

Table Rock people. While her young niece, **Kitty Tom** (Acattycon), was deemed one of the more able bodied and was transported overland by wagon, Betsy Lily with her young sons traveled to Grand Ronde by steamship with Chocultah and Limpy's bands and the remainder of the Lower Rogue River people.[17] The journey, whether by land or sea, was miserable and degrading.

From Rogue River, Chief Tecumtum and his men were escorted to the Yaquina Agency, but Tecumtum was far from beaten. Within a short time he led another revolt. After it also ended badly, Tecumtum and his son, Adam, were transferred to the federal prison at Alcatraz.

More than eight months had passed since Palmer's plan to relocate the western Oregon Indians had first been set in motion. During that time, more than two thousand people had been moved to Grand Ronde.

---

17 O. Applegate, Testimony of Applegate Jack, Kitty Tom, and Andrew Smith. Robert C. Buchanan to Joel Palmer, July 8, 1856, *Indian Affairs in the Territory of Oregon,* Letter 94.

The Grand Ronde Reservation

Palmer's removal from office · failed treaty obligations · conditions on the reservation and hatred between the races

With the war behind him and aware that his removal from office was inevitable, Joel Palmer sent a letter to the governor of Oregon Territory, George Curry, defending statements he had made in his earlier letter to General Wool about the conduct of some of the Americans in southern Oregon.

The next day Palmer received a note from C. M. Walker reporting that the Indians on the reservation were sick and dying and wanting to know if Palmer was leaving, and if so, why.[1] In a second letter just a few days later, Walker expressed relief that Palmer was not coming to the reservation. He advised him to go home, cross his legs comfortably, and thank God he was "out of the reach of the lick-spittles of this damnable Oregon."[2]

The Indian people at Grand Ronde were accustomed to a political system that was very different from that of the Americans', and did not understand the decision-making process of the American government. Palmer's removal from office not only puzzled them, but raised questions among them as to whether the American government could be trusted to honor agreements made by its representatives once they left office.

Chief Toquahear, in addressing these concerns to the Americans some months later, summarized the thoughts of many Indian people in saying:

> We have waited and waited because the agents told us to be patient that it would be all right by-and-by. We are tired of this. We believe Uncle Sam intends to cheat us. Sometimes we are told there is one Great Chief and sometimes another. One superintendent tells us one thing and the Great Chief removes him. Then another superintendent tells us another thing, and another Great Chief removes him. Who are we to believe? Who is your Great Chief, and who is to tell us the truth? We do not understand the way you act. With us we are born chiefs; once a chief, we are a chief for life. But you are only common men, and we never know how long you will hold your authority, or how soon the Great Chief may degrade you or how soon he may be turned out himself. We want to know the true

---

1   C. M. Walker to Joel Palmer, August 9, 1856, *Correspondence and Papers of Joel Palmer.*
2   Ibid.

head; that we might state our condition to him. Let him come here himself and see us. So many lies have been told him that we think he never hears the truth, or he would not compel us to suffer as we do...[3]

On November 11, 1856, eighty-five more Rogue River people arrived on a steamer at Oregon City and were escorted to Grand Ronde.[4] Another seventy-five were discovered by settlers in the Rogue River valley around the middle of January. After the settlers shot and killed all the men, Indian Agent John Miller made arrangements for the remaining women and children, approximately sixty in number, to be brought to the reservation.[5]

During and immediately after the war, hatred went both ways between some of the whites and Rogue River people. The assassination of the Rogue River men by settlers was only one example of the treachery that stemmed from this hatred. At Grand Ronde, the Rogue River people focused their anger on all the Rogue River children fathered by white men.

Andrew Smith, the three-year-old son of the Rogue River woman Betsy Lily, was one of the children targeted by this misplaced hostility. From the moment of his birth, his mother had to guard him very closely or he would have been killed. Finally, Agent Miller made a special arrangement for his protection. To show his good intentions, Miller gave Betsy Lily a pony and offered to have his brother, William Miller, take the child and raise him off the reservation. Years later, Andrew returned to the reservation. Blind in one eye and with only limited sight in the other, he married Jane, the soft-spoken daughter of a Clackamas woman and **Peter Menard.** They raised a family, and Andrew cared for his mother and grandmother until they died.[6]

During the winter of 1856, Grand Ronde was described by Agent Miller as bearing the impression of destitution, ruin, and starvation. The whole valley was covered in water. There was not even a blade of grass for the animals. Food for the people had to be brought in from the Willamette Valley settlements using seven or eight yoke of oxen because the roads were impassable by any other means.[7]

In April of 1857, the people at Grand Ronde learned that Enos Thomas, after being imprisoned by the American military for over eight months, had been tried and executed.[8]

Although the Americans considered Enos a traitor, he was not tried in military court for war crimes. Rather, he was tried in a civilian mock court and found

3   Browne, *Indian Affairs in the Territories of Oregon and Washington,* 27.
4   A. F. Hedges to George Manypenny, November 11, 1856, BIA, Letters Received by the Office of Indian Affairs, 1824–1880, National Archives Microcopy 234, Roll 609, NADP Document D47.
5   *Annual Report Commissioner of Indian Affairs,* John Miller, July 20, 1857, 361–62.
6   O. Applegate, Testimony of Andrew Smith.
7   *Annual Report Commissioner of Indian Affairs,* 1859, Letter 194, Miller, 429.
8   Nathan Douthit, *Between Indian and White World,* 426.

Battle Rock, site of the hanging of Enos Thomas. Photo courtesy of Oregon Historical Society (OrHi 1011439).

guilty of desertion from the Gold Beach Volunteer Company and for the murder of Ben Wright. After the trial, he was sentenced to be hanged and taken to Battle Rock near Port Orford.[9]

Throughout the whole ordeal, the spirit power of Enos Thomas kept him strong. After he hanged for an hour and a half, the Americans finally had to cut him down and shoot him, as he refused to die.[10]

The execution and exile of their war leaders must have alarmed not just the Rogue River and Shasta, but all Indian people. Fear and anxieties must have been magnified for those waking each morning to the sight and sounds of the American military at Fort Yamhill. Despite their apprehension, the high death rate among them soon drove people to openly complain about conditions on the reservation. At Grand Ronde they had lost twice the number of people they had while engaged in the war.[11] In 1856 alone, five hundred Indians (25 percent of the Indian population) died. Given the numbers of their people who were dying every day, they wondered what they had to lose by returning to their original homes.

This kind of talk worried the Americans, who tightened their control over a large portion of Rogue River and Shasta people by moving them to the Siletz Agency. At this location, they were farther away from the main population of

---

9   Ibid.

10   Ibid.

11   J. W. Nesmith to Commissioner of Indian Affairs, May 5, 1857, BIA, Microfilm M-234, Roll 610, Frs. 518-529, RG 75, National Archives, Washington, DC.

Willamette Valley settlers, with the Pacific Ocean acting on one side as a natural barrier to their escape.[12]

Although Indian Agent Metcalf insisted the Indians had plenty to eat, in truth all the tribes were struggling to find food.[13] Superintendent A. F. Hedges expressed concern that the people at Grand Ronde might be forced to leave the reservation and murder and rob just to survive. To avoid this possibility, he requested immediate subsistence funds from the American government.[14]

Conditions on the reservation, when contrasted with the promises made during treaty negotiations, caused the hearts of many people to turn bad. Even Toquahear, the chief of the previously peaceful band of Rogue River, threatened to take his people back to their home country. In a speech made in council with such American leaders as J. Ross Browne, Joe Lane, James Nesmith, and others, Toquahear confronted them with the following words:

> The government has not kept its promise. This is a bad country. It is cold and sickly. There is no game on the hills and the people are dying. There will soon be none of us left. The graves of my people cover the valleys. We are told that if we go back we will be killed. Let us go then, for we might as well be killed as die here.[15]

Soon it was rumored that some of the headmen of the remaining Rogue River people were counseling the Tualatin chief, Kayakach, in the hope of convincing him to join them in war. Chief Kayakach declined and remained firm in his commitment to peace, even to the extent of reportedly asked the Indian agent to have the Rogue River people "removed from his vicinity or otherwise disposed of."[16]

At this time, the various bands of Umpqua were living at different locations just south of present-day Grand Ronde Road and Highway 22. A Rogue River band was situated just south of the Umpqua. The Willamette Valley Indians were organized in three bands of Kalapuya, a band of Molalla, and the Tualatin. They were located in small villages that formed a ring on the north side of the Yamhill River.[17]

---

12 Annual Report Commissioner of Indian Affairs, 1857, Letter 149, 361.

13 *The Oregon Statesman*, Grand Ronde Agent to the Editor, January 21, 1857.

14 A. F. Hedges to George Manypenny, January 7, 1856, BIA Microfilm M-234, Roll 610, Frs. 239–42, National Archives, Washington, DC.

15 Browne, *Indian Affairs in the Territories of Oregon and Washington*, 27.

16 *The Oregon Statesman*, Grand Ronde Agent to the Editor, January 21, 1857.

17 Michelle, *Just a Memorandum*, 3: all the Umpqua, Chasta, and Rogue River, lived across from the place they call new Grand Ronde today (1956). Jacobs, Field Notebook 69, *Texts Ethnology Clackamas & Jargon*, 99: They moved some across from where new Grand Ronde is now. Cow Creek, Shastas, Rogue River, and Umpqua went to new Grand Ronde. Molale, Clackamas, Cascades, Klamath, and Kalapuyas stayed at old Grand Ronde.

The Native Experience

Corruption and slow government payments · escape · the native children of former Hudson's Bay employees · American politics prevent the collection of resources from off-reservation lands

After treaty negotiations in 1851, western Oregon Indian people suffered a great deal of ill treatment at the hands of white men. The treaty the Americans had claimed would protect their rights had not been ratified. In addition, a Supreme Court decision based on a case of assault against a Clackamas Indian woman denied Indians the right to give testimony against any white person in American courts.[1]

All of this made the new round of treaty negotiations in 1855 more difficult. Finally, Palmer had to make the Tualatin people a promise that he had not made to any other western Oregon tribe: a reservation near their own country.

Further, Palmer denied rumors the Tualatin had heard regarding what would happen to them if they decided to sign the treaty. Palmer told the Tualatin people:

> I understand some persons have told you that if you sell your country, you would be driven away into some strange land perhaps on an island where you would all starve—now you know this is all a lie...[2]

Lie or no lie, it would be years before the tribes and bands assigned to the Grand Ronde Reservation would have legal papers that proved they owned the land. And hunger was a reality for most of them from the moment of their removal.

Even the Umpqua people were destitute. Although their property had been collected from their former homes in the Umpqua Valley and Agent Magruder had created an inventory that showed the government owed them approximately three thousand dollars, the American government ignored repeated requests for payment.[3] Further, the Indians reaped little real financial benefit from the land cession treaties. Some of the problem was due to fraudulent activities after the money was appropriated by Congress, but the government's slowness in setting aside treaty payments in a timely fashion only made the situation worse.

---

1 *Annual Report Commissioners of Indian Affairs*, 1851, Letter 68, Nelson, 210–13.
2 Treaty of March 25, 1854 between the Chiefs of the Tualatin Band of Kalapuya, *Correspondence and Papers of Joel Palmer*.
3 *Annual Report Commissioner of Indian Affairs*, 1857, Letter 149, Miller, 364.

In 1861, the superintendent of Indian Affairs for Oregon called attention to the fact that Congress had failed to pay the twenty-five hundred dollars agreed to in the second article of the treaty with the Umpqua and Yoncalla Kalapuya for the past two years. He also complained that he had not yet received the money Congress had appropriated the previous year to operate the Grand Ronde Agency.[4]

After 1851, treaty negotiators in Oregon Territory insisted on making payments to Indian people in merchandise rather than cash, expressing the fear that otherwise, corrupt individuals would in all probability try to take the money from them. In the end, it mattered little, as the promised merchandise never made it into the hands of the people any better than the cash owed to other tribes. One soldier at Fort Yamhill wrote that the merchandise paid to the Indians could be found in the sutler's store and if the people wanted it, they had to pay for it twice.[5] Moreover, the merchandise substituted for the items intended as annuity payments were of poor quality and of little use to the people. **Chief Joseph Hutchins** (Yalkama) told Meacham some of the blankets were "like sail-cloth muslin."[6] The American J. Ross Browne described the blankets given to Indians as "so transparent both sides could be seen at the same time."[7]

At Grand Ronde, some of the chiefs "had a long talk" with the Indian agent and asked "some hard questions" regarding the quality of the merchandise, but apparently, the agent blamed the president and nothing changed.[8] In this manner, once they were confined to the reservation the payment Indian people should have received for their land was stripped from them by corrupt American officials. The fact that it was occurring was no secret. The corruption was so apparent that American officials frequently discussed the large amount of money annually appropriated by Congress that ended up "feeding white men and starving Indians."[9]

During treaty negotiations the people had been told that they would not be confined strictly to the reservation, but could return seasonally to their usual hunting and fishing areas to harvest enough food to get their families through the long cold winters. Given the promise of off-reservation harvesting and the threat of starvation, the people had every right to expect the Americans to comply with their request for passes. Even the Indian agent believed an off-reservation status was absolutely necessary if the Indians were going to survive.[10] However, passes

---

4   *Annual Report Commissioner of Indian Affairs*, 1861, Letter 57, Rector, 158–60.
5   Barth, *All Quiet on the Yamhill*, 183–84. The sutler was a civilian storekeeper who was authorized to operate a general store on or near a military fort. He purchased and sold a variety of goods that were not supplied by the army.
6   Meacham, *Wigwam and War-Path*, 101–38.
7   Browne, *The California Indians*, 7.
8   Barth, *All Quiet on the Yamhill*, 132.
9   Browne, *The California Indians*, 7.
10 Amos Harvey to J. W. Perit Huntington, June 27, 1867, BIA Microfilm M-2 Roll 24, Letter No. 15, National Archives, Washington, DC. Amos Harvey to J. W. Perit Huntington, July 15, 1867, BIA Microfilm M-2, Roll 24, National Archives,

were not always given.

In 1863, all the white settlers but one signed a petition complaining about the Indian presence around Oregon City. As a result, the request of three Clackamas Indians to have their passes extended for the fishing season was denied.[11] More importantly, this petition questioned the legality of an off-reservation status for Indians. As a result, more passes were denied and more and more Indians were forced into a runaway classification.

Given the failed promises of the treaties and conditions on the reservation, Chief Yelkas's niece, **Molalla Kate** (Muswi), and her family planned their escape around 1860. Despite the presence of the military, they slipped by the guards late one night and traveled east to Molalla Prairie. There they were able to live as fugitives for a number of years. Other Indian people followed suit, and as time went by the numbers increased.

Muswi's Molalla people were brought back to the reservation for the first time around 1863. Since they had been absent for such a long time, their farms and gardens had been taken over by other Indian people. The agency farmer asked the agent's permission to break more ground for them and replace the old wagons, ploughs, and farm implements they were expected to use to prepare the ground for planting. He also noted that the land he had recently cleared for the Umpqua and Yoncalla band of Kalapuya, like that of the Willamette Valley tribes, was "inferior in many respects."[12]

Of the 69,120 acres that made up the reservation, only about four thousand acres were tillable land and, as the agency farmer indicated, the soil on this was extremely poor.[13] Still the Americans were convinced that if they could force the Indian men to learn farming and ranching, the men could produce enough to provide for the current population of more than a thousand people.

Getting Indian men to farm was not an easy task. Among Indian people, it was the women who scratched the earth, harvesting the roots and seeds that grew there. Indian men, depending upon which tribe, were either hunters or fishermen. When some of them objected to being asked to farm, calling it women's work, it incensed more than a few American men, who then decided the real problem was that Indian men were lazy.

As far as Indian men were concerned, ranching was a far more agreeable venture. Some of them had been raising Indian ponies and cattle for a number of years prior to removal and had brought a few with them when they came to the reservation. However, building productive farms and profitable ranches was a long-term goal and at the moment the people were starving.

Washington, DC. A. B. Meacham to E. S. Parker, July 7, 1871, BIA, Microfilm 234, Roll 616, Frs. 690–92, National Archives, Washington, DC.

11 J. W. Perit Huntington to J. B. Condon, June 24, 1863, *Correspondence and Papers of Joel Palmer.*

12 *Annual Report Commissioner of Indian Affairs,* 1863, Letter 27, Sanders, 88.

13 *Annual Report Commissioner of Indian Affairs,* 1875, Letter 58, 346.

Just to survive, some Indian people worked off the reservation as house servants or laborers for white settlers. Others escaped to their home country with the thought of harvesting the same natural resources that had sustained them in the past.

Even as Indian people fled the confines of the reservation, a number of French Indians and Iroquois, most of them the sons and daughters of former Hudson's Bay Company employees, hung around the agency hoping to be allowed to stay. They had become displaced for a multitude of reasons, but most were from French Prairie, where the great flood of 1861 had washed away their family farms.

Since the Hudson's Bay Company had closed its post and moved its remaining employees to British Columbia, the families of those men who had retired to farm at French Prairie now leaned heavily upon the alliances they had formed with the families of their native wives.

Unlike Americans who use direct blood lines in labeling family relationships, the native sense of family was much more expansive. Brothers and sisters to Indian people included those people whom Americans called cousins, and "family" included all the people who lived with them, fought with them, died with them, and were buried beside them. In many cases, people unrelated by blood became members of the family after living among them for a long period of time.

In keeping with the Indian view of family, several men from the French Prairie settlement were adopted into various tribes at Grand Ronde, including Peter Menard, **Frank Quenel, Sam Chantelle,** and **Charlie Petite**.

Peter Menard, a French and Paiute descendant, arrived at Grand Ronde around 1864 with his Clackamas wife. After she died, leaving him with an infant, he married Chief Joseph Shangaretta's oldest daughter.[14]

It was **Chief Joseph Shangaretta** who went with some of the other chiefs to the Indian agent to make sure that Peter's adoption by the Mary's River band of Kalapuya was officially acknowledged and that Peter was placed on the Indian roll with the rest of the band.[15]

Frank Quenel arrived a short time later. Like Peter, several of the chiefs took him to the Indian agent to make sure he was adopted. Since he wanted to marry Chief Louis Napesa's daughter, Frank was adopted into the Umpqua tribe.

The children of a French Canadian named Amable Petit and an Indian woman named Susanne Tawakon were adopted in much the same way by the Clackamas tribe.[16]

Susan Tawakon's father was Thomas Tawakon, an Iroquois boute (the skilled position of bowsman in a canoe or boat), trapper, and steersman, first with the Northwest Company and then with the Hudson's Bay Company from 1815 to 1845. Her mother was "a woman of the country, Chinook" and although only

14 O. Applegate, Testimony of Peter Menard.
15 O. Applegate, Testimony of Peter Menard and Frank Quenel.
16 O. Applegate, Testimony of Captain Frank Quenel.

distantly related" to the Clackamas, their son, Charlie Petite, was adopted by the Oregon City Tumwater. Thereafter, he and his siblings always drew annuities under the treaty with the Clackamas.[17]

Frank, Thomas, and **Mary Norwest,** the mixed-blood children of a Hudson's Bay Company Iroquois known as Jean Baptiste Tyikwarhi and a native woman called Judith Walla Walla, although not related to any of the treaty tribes at Grand Ronde, also wanted to live on the reservation.

Tyikwarhi's son Frank Norwest was a young man when he arrived at Grand Ronde. Both Frank's brother, Thomas, and his sister, Mary, soon followed him to the reservation. Eventually, all of them were adopted by different bands of the Kalapuya.[18]

In addition to these families, Indian people did not object to the Iroquois doctor **Louis Vasselle** and **Marshall Laferte** of the Nez Perce receiving treaty benefits at Grand Ronde because both men "had lived among them for so long."[19]

At the same time, **John Wacheno** (Tsinwalh), son of the Clackamas chief, fought for treaty rights on the reservation for Indian slaves and the descendants of slaves. He believed the slaves should have the same rights as any other tribal member. He reminded the Americans that their slaves had been bought when they were children. Since they were lost to their own people, they had no place else to live and would very likely die at Grand Ronde.[20]

Eventually, it was agreed that in order for people to be enrolled on the GRIC and receive treaty annuities, they had to be accepted by one of the tribes or bands assigned to the reservation and their status had to be approved by the Indian agent.

---

17 Ibid.
18 Michelle, *Just a Memorandum,* 1.
19 O. Applegate, Testimony of Dave Leno. Michelle, *Just a Memorandum,* 8.
20 O. Applegate, Testimony of John Wacheno.

The American Plan

*Ban on traditional marriage ceremonies and the practice of
taking multiple wives · failure of a new economic opportunity ·
the Indian legislature · collectors · violators of the dead ·
how the spirit power of Liham and Igaksdak fought back*

Over the years, Congress had received a number of reports regarding the Spanish missionaries' success with their reservation system. Supporters of that system pointed out that the Indians were learning more civilized habits while providing the missionaries with very profitable establishments. The missions in California had all been built with orchards, vineyards, gardens, and healthy herds all cultivated and tended by Indian labor.

Taking a similar reservation model, Superintendent of Indian Affairs Alfred B. Meacham began making plans for Oregon. After visiting each reservation, he selected Grand Ronde as the site for implementing a new program, since in his opinion the people there were already well advanced in civilization and, on the whole, were peaceful and well behaved. Not only were many of them already farming successfully, but some had built houses that were "better than that of the agent."[1]

In promoting his new reservation system, Meacham explained in a meeting with the various tribes and bands at Grand Ronde that in five years the terms of the treaty would expire. When that time came, he told them, they would need to be ready to show that they could be good American citizens. Toward this end, they had to give up their old ways.

Meacham asked them to choose between the Catholic and Protestant religions in hopes that, like the priests at the California missions, the missionary they selected would teach them to live like the white race. To assist in this process, he placed a ban on the traditional practice of gaining consent to marry by giving many gifts to the bride's parents, the custom of taking multiple wives, traditional burial practices, and traditional religious ceremonies.

In place of their traditional marriage ceremony, Meacham showed them how to marry in the Christian way, complete with a preacher and the father giving away the bride. According to Meacham, some of the parents bemoaned the absence of the bride's price, but on the whole, the people accepted the new wedding ceremony.

The ban on multiple wives was more difficult to get the people to agree to because in addition to outlawing the practice, Meacham demanded that the men

---

1   *Annual Report Commissioner of Indian Affairs,* 1869, Letter 20, Lafollett, 169.

who were already married to more than one woman choose one wife and give up the rest. At that time, there were more women than men on the reservation and few arrangements had been made for the displaced wives. Which wives were the men to abandon? Where would the women live and who would look after them? None of these questions were completely resolved in council. However, shortly after Meacham's mandate, Rev. Robert Summers, a private collector of Indian heirlooms and a frequent visitor on the reservation between 1873 and 1881, described a home he visited at Grand Ronde that may have been created as a result of this ban on multiple wives. Summers wrote:

> A little distance off, over a fence, in a pasture, was a poor miserable little hut with a roof projecting wide on one side. In that side, a foot from the ground, there was a small opening, over which hung a filthy curtain. We crawled through and there, in the middle of the little room, over a heap of coals and ashes, crouched the oldest looking and most withered human being I ever saw—almost beyond belief.[2]

Rev. Summers said a young woman at the lodge told him that she and several others took care of three older women like this one who all lived in the house.

Although Meacham's plan created a number of social problems such as this, he also offered the people two important opportunities. The first was intended to boost the economy of the reservation. On the Klamath Reservation, Meacham had noticed a successful lumber mill that was furnishing several thousand dollars' worth of lumber to the Military Department and local Americans through an agreement made between them and the Indian Department. While the mill at Grand Ronde was in terrible condition, Meacham was convinced that after it was rebuilt it could be equally profitable.

In addition to the new mill and lumber agreement, Meacham gave permission for the people to establish an Indian legislature with a court system based on the state model. The Indian court system was very successful. In his annual report for 1874, Agent Patrick Sinnott praised the Grand Ronde people for the capacity they exhibited in managing their local government.[3]

Two years later, François Mercier, a Belgian cardinal of the Roman Catholic Church and visitor at Grand Ronde, also mentioned the court. He wrote:

> The Indians of Grand Ronde have designed their own civil code. On the model of the White people, they also established a court, where anyone is invited to make a claim or defend one's cause, with more or less emphasis depending on one's oratory talent. Judges, sitting gravely, listen to them as seriously as our own magistrates. A sheriff fulfills the duties of chief

---

2   Cawley, *Indian Journal*, 28.

3   *Annual Report Commissioner of Indian Affairs*, 1874, Sinnott, 317.

Ft. Yamhill Blockhouse that later served as reservation jail . Photo courtesy of Salem, Oregon, Public Library, Salem Public Historic Photograph Collection MSC001.

of police. All these dignitaries are elected by popular vote. The old block-house, built originally by the army as a refuge in case of an attack by the Savages, is now used as a prison for those who violated the law.[4]

It may have been Meacham's intention that the new court would eventually eliminate the traditional social structure of the various tribes and bands by re-placing the role of their customary chiefs with elected government officials. If so, it did not completely succeed, as most of the representatives elected to serve on the legislature were the chief's sons or others in line for the chieftainship.

Judging from some of the laws passed, there can be no doubt that both the Indian agent and the Catholic priest influenced the legislature's work and the court's decisions from time to time. However, compared to the protection Indians received off the reservation, this system was a welcome opportunity for potential justice and the people received it enthusiastically.

With the sawmill and the new Indian court on hand, the people began to plan a community that would meet with the approval of the American govern-

---

4   Fremaux, *Memoires D'un Grand Brainois,* 57.

ment. They began building their own houses with lumber from their own mill and maintained their own roads. Despite their widespread poverty, they passed a self-imposed tax system that paid for court services, funded short-term loans to those who were willing to farm, and met other economic needs. With only a few exceptions for the very old and disabled, every adult male on the reservation was required to work on the roads and every adult man and woman judged capable of paying fifty cents a year to the reservation treasury was required to pay the tax.[5]

As far as the mill went, it was only a few months before Agent Sinnott violated the agreement by taking away the profits. However, after the matter was turned over to higher authorities he claimed great embarrassment and excused his actions by claiming it was all a misunderstanding. In his defense, he wrote that "it was entirely impracticable" for the Indians to sell lumber on the open market as "it would necessarily involve disputes and great annoyances."[6]

In response, Meacham wrote:

If these Indians are ever to manage themselves, why not begin with these lessons while they have or are supposed to have an agent whose duty is to stand between them and the stronger white race with whom they are to mingle and associate? I repeat that these Indian men own the mills and are entitled to the proceeds and that it was and is the agent's duty to transact such business as the Indians would themselves. What if it did require labor and care to prevent confusion? The agent was paid for his time, his business talent, and if he was unwilling or incompetent, he was not in a proper position [...][7]

A short time later the mill fell into ill repair and the enterprise began to fail. The Grand Ronde Indian legislature that Meacham helped establish fared somewhat better. It was not disbanded until a new federal rule replaced it with a court of Indian offenses some thirteen years later. In the new system, the federal government made the laws and the court was appointed by the agent.

At first Sinnott argued against making the change at Grand Ronde, pointing out that it was an additional expense to the government that had been paid for over the preceding twelve years with Indian tax dollars and court revenue. Finally, after all his reasoning was ignored, he wrote in 1883 that he had followed departmental instruction and selected three intelligent and impartial Indians to act as judges of the Indian court and one additional man to act as sheriff.

He wrote he had not set up a police force because one was not needed on the Grand Ronde Reservation. He went on to say that he had decided to pay the new court judge's salaries from department funds appropriated for police officers, be-

---

5   *Annual Report Commissioner of Indian Affairs,* 1881, Sinnott, 143.

6   *Annual Report Commissioner of Indian Affairs,* 1872, Sinnott, 367.

7   Meacham, *Wigwam and War-Path,* 120-124.

Grand Ronde Indian Court of Offenses, 1894. Left to right: police officers Foster Wacheno, Robert Metcalf, and James Foster; Judge Joseph Shangaretta (seated center); police officers Isaac Stevens, Dave Leno, and Lieutenant Frank Quenel. Photo courtesy of Oregon Historical Society (OrHi 94458).

cause in the previous court, judges had been paid.[8]

The following year, Sinnott complained again about the loss of the Indian legislative system. Apparently, he had not been able to use the funds appropriated for the wages of Indian police officers. He wrote that he had filled the court with judges who were willing, however reluctantly, to serve without pay, but he still refused to implement the police force.[9]

Finally, defeated, he wrote in 1885:

> For the last fourteen years local civil officers have been elected bi-annually by the Indians of this agency who have executed such local laws as were enacted by the legislative assembly which were likewise elected by the Indians. The Indians had become thoroughly accustomed to the operations of the local laws and proceedings of their own court officers. Owing to this state of affairs I had much trouble in inducing the Indians to accept the judges of the court of offenses and the rules governing the court. But during the year I nominated a police force of five men, one a lieutenant and chief judge of the court, two privates and associate judges, two other privates, one to act as sheriff, the other prosecuting attorney; and by us-

8   *Annual Report Commissioner of Indian Affairs,* 1883, Sinnott, 126-127.
9   *Annual Report Commissioner of Indian Affairs,* 1884, Sinnott, 142.

ing much time and patience I have succeeded in getting the police force in good working order and the Indians to adopt this court in lien of their old court.[10]

In August 1886, J. B. McClane, a new Indian agent assigned to Grand Ronde, wrote that he believed the court of Indian offenses had been a great benefit to the reservation. He submitted two reports from the court. The first showed that the judges had loaned out all the court revenue for 1883 and 1884 in return for payments in the form of wheat and oats. The second stated that since the new agent had arrived, he had settled all the difficulties with the Indians. Only four trials were held and all the fines were paid in work.[11]

By forcing inmates to work off their fines, Agent McClane substantially reduced the Indian court treasury that had been in operation for years and providing loans to Indian people when times were bad. Not just the farmers but the whole Indian community must have felt the economic loss of this revenue.

Still McClane was not through making changes in the court system. While he praised the performance of the police force, admitted that the people had a great respect for the Indian court, and readily acquiesced to their decisions, by July 1887 he had abolished any formality of justice on the Grand Ronde Reservation by eliminating the whole legal process. In his next report, he wrote:

> If there is any dispute among the Indians, instead of bringing them up before the court, I send one or more of them [Indian police] to the Indians, and they settle it nine times out of ten. It saves much expense and has a good effect upon them [...]"[12]

After some time had gone by, a few people again raised the issue of whether the agency police force could be selected by popular vote rather than by appointment. Agent McClane acknowledged their request in his annual report along with his response. He wrote:

> There were a number of Indians who would like to have all the present police force removed so to get their places for themselves and friends, but I think different.[13]

Around this time, a member of the Umpqua band whom the Americans called Whiskey Jim Pierce brought a large group of Grand Ronde people into the town of Dallas (about twenty miles southwest of the reservation) to have their cases heard in the courthouse there. **James Pierce** (Clamarchnet) had arranged

---

10 *Annual Report Commissioner of Indian Affairs, 1885,* Sinnott, 161–62.

11 *Annual Report Commissioner of Indian Affairs, 1886,* McClane, 209–10.

12 Ibid. *Annual Report Commissioner of Indian Affairs, 1887,* McClane.

13 *Annual Report Commissioner of Indian Affairs, 1889,* McClane, 270.

ten lawsuits and was prepared with all the witnesses for each case. Although Dallas officials did not have jurisdiction to hear the cases, the incident is noteworthy because it shows how determined the people were to have their disputes settled through a court system.[14]

In 1891, a new Indian agent by the name of Lamson took a different position in regard to the Indian court of offenses. He found that the court relieved him of "much annoyance in trivial matters and aided materially in the more important cases."[15] His replacement, John Brentano, continued to give more freedom to the court and commended the Indian judge, Joseph Shangaretta, for his earnest attempts to achieve justice in the courtroom.[16]

The people were aware that their legal problems were not entirely the fault of the Indian agent, but generally stemmed from an overall lack of civil protection for Indians.

In a council held at the agency buildings with Commissioner Felix Brunot, A. B. Meacham, and Rev. Parrish, two reservation leaders, **Chief Joseph Hutchins** (Yalkama) and **Billy Williamson** (Hosanunda), brought up the issue of Indian people being falsely arrested when off the reservation. They asked specifically about two men from Grand Ronde who had recently been incarcerated in the Salem penitentiary. Billy Williamson told the government officials,

> Some Indians here have been shot and whipped by white men for nothing. Two of our people are in Salem penitentiary. We want to get them out. They have done nothing. White men gave them whiskey and got them drunk, and now they have them in the penitentiary.[17]

Without the same civil rights afforded American citizens, Indian people were made to suffer every kind of violence. Perhaps the worst was an 1868 directive from the United States Army surgeon general instructing American military officers to collect Indian crania. After many museums and teaching institutions across the country began participating in the endeavor, Indian communities were not only bombarded by collectors, but the privacy of their homes was invaded and their graves looted.

For years, people around the world had been exhibiting a strange curiosity about the American Indian. This interest had stimulated a profitable worldwide market for Indian things. At Grand Ronde, even Agent Sinnott's wife attempted to fill orders for Indian artifacts, although without much success since she was willing to accept the common response that "there were no more old things left."[18]

---

14 Lampson, *Some Visitors from the Grand Ronde*, 20–31.
15 *Annual Report Commissioner of Indian Affairs*, 1891, Lamson, 371.
16 *Annual Report Commissioner of Indian Affairs*, 1893, Brentano, 266–67.
17 *Annual Report of the Commissioner of Indian Affair*, Minutes of A Council with Grande Ronde Indians at their Reservation, Oregon, September 14, 1871, 151–52.
18 Cawley, *Indian Journal*, 21.

On the other hand, some people, such as the Rev. Summers, were far more aggressive in their hunt. Summers had no trouble forcing his way into Indians' homes in search of artifacts. While most Indian people ignored his rudeness, the wife of **Klickitat Dick Hall** organized her friends and followed him from house to house laughingly chastising his poor behavior.[19]

While the violation of their privacy was bad, the trauma they faced from the desecration of their dead was a far greater injury. Feeling powerless against the Americans, many people came to believe that while justice for them might never be found on earth, things were different in the spirit world.

They told of **Tom Hutchins** (Liham), third chief of the Santiam band of Kalapuya, who had the power of a three-legged coyote. Men with coyote power were smart but mean, and were feared by everyone. After Liham died, his grave was looted and a Willamette University professor got his body. When the professor fell ill with a shaking disease a short time later, many Indian people said his illness was brought on by the force of Liham's spirit power when the professor cut open his corpse.[20]

Another man, an Indian doctor, had carved different figures representing his powers into a board about three feet high. After he died, he was buried in the Indian cemetery and the carving was placed on his grave. In time, an American took the carving to use as a table even though the people warned him against it. That very night the American went insane. It was said he recovered his sanity only after he returned the board.[21]

In July 1871, Joel Palmer, who was now working on the Siletz Reservation, reported to Meacham that he had changed the native burial customs. In place of the old Indian way, he had started furnishing a coffin and "suitable apparel" for the deceased. To ensure that the items were used, he and agency employees attended the burial services and the bodies were buried in areas Palmer had designated.

The Americans were fully aware that religious beliefs were fundamental to the native way of life. Recognizing the importance of the native doctors in keeping the ancient religion strong among the people, the Americans sought to stop these men and women from holding religious ceremonies. To this end, **Dr. John Smith** (Dushdaq), a medicine doctor, was brought up on charges before the Grand Ronde Indian court where he and a few of his followers were tried "as promoters of dissatisfaction and disturbance." At the same time, a new law was written forbidding any future gathering for native dances, festivals, or ceremonials of any kind.[22]

As the people decided whether or not to obey the new law, they kept their

---

19   Ibid., 30.
20   Jacobs, Field Notebook 83, *Texts and Ethnology*, n.p.
21   Jacobs, Field Notebook 54, Texts and Ethnology, 10.
22   Cawley, *Indian Journal*, 27–28.

Oregon City, 1857. Photo courtesy of Oregon Historical Society (OrHi 21079).

eyes on Dushdaq and recalled such men as Igaksdak.[23]

Igaksdak was a powerful Clackamas doctor who had a mean power that caused him to kill people. When he approached someone he wanted to kill, he would twist a rod of hazel while chatting with the person. His power would wrap the hazel around the person's neck and strangle him.

With his power, he stole slaves, horses, and property without fear since the people were helpless. They could not shoot him, as arrows did not penetrate his flesh. If they tried to shoot him with a rifle, the rifle would misfire.

According to the people who remembered him, it was the whites who eventually waylaid and killed him. However, one night as Igaksdak slept, he saw what was about to take place. After he woke up from dreaming of his murder, he went to Oregon City determined to die fighting.

After he killed many white people, others smashed him to death with their rifle butts. Even with his skull smashed and his body left for the night, he came to life again. Sitting there, holding his head, he began to sing his power song. He sang his power song over and over until the white people returned and smashed him again. This time they smashed him for good.[24]

Despite their strong faith, as time went on and pressure upon their way of

23   Jacobs, Field Notebooks 54, *Texts and Ethnology,* 74: his name was the same as that of a supernatural being who could not be killed.

24   Ibid.

life increased, many Indian people grew very discouraged.[25] They talked about how not one new Indian doctor had returned from the mountains since they were moved to Grand Ronde. Some thought perhaps all the most powerful spirits had fled from the Americans to the deepest parts of the Pacific Ocean, never to return. Stripped of their supernatural spirits, many people thought perhaps they needed the protections Meacham promised. Others decided to outwardly go along with the desires of the Americans but quietly continue the old practices.

---

25 Cawley, *Indian Journal*, 44.

Fulfilling the Final Terms of the Treaty

Allotting land · the new dream religion · slowness of the government to issue title · accepting the Salmon River and Nehalem people · the Dawes Act · the Burkes Act · the Surplus Land Agreement · and the power of Indian agent

After the land survey of 1872, Agent Sinnott received instructions to begin allotting Indian land.[1] It was understood that a land title would be issued to each head of household and advanced to his heirs forever. Further, it was understood that these land titles could only be transferred among Indian people.[2]

Also around this time, a new dream dance was carried to Grand Ronde by **Bogus Tom,** a Shasta Indian from California.[3] The dance brought renewed hope to the people that God might restore their old ways.[4] It frightened the Americans because part of the dance prophecy foretold the death of all white people. Immediately a federal ban was placed on the dance, but among some of the people it was secretly continued until the Indian agent and the Catholic priest at Grand Ronde sent the Umpqua chief, Louis Napesa, and a Yakama medicine man to steal the power that an Umpqua man called **Jim Scroggins** had placed in the poles that held up the dance structure.[5] Chief Napesa's resistance to the new dream dance philosophy and the death of Jim Scroggins so soon after his encounter with the Yakama medicine man caused people to lose faith in the new religion, but in its place grew the popular belief that there must be an Indian heaven separate from that of white people.

By 1875, Indian people began hearing rumors from the local white community that the Grand Ronde Reservation, established as a temporary reserve in 1857, might soon be opened for white settlement, and that the current deeds to their allotments could at any time be annulled or canceled and hence were worthless.[6]

The settlers were probably referring to a news article in the *Morning Oregonian* published September 2 that told of a visit by O. A. Brown and Special Commissioner Simpson to the Nestucca reserve. In summing up the event, the reporter concluded by writing:

---

1   *Annual Report Commissioner of Indian Affairs*, 1872, Letter 77, Sinnott, 368.
2   *Annual Report Commissioner of Indian Affairs*, 1866, Letter 7, Huntington, 78.
3   Du Bois, *The 1870 Ghost Dance*, 30.
4   *Annual Report of the Commissioner of Indian Affairs*, 1877, Sinnott, 169–70.
5   Du Bois, *The Ghost Dance*, 31.
6   *Annual Report Commissioner of Indian Affairs*, 1877, Sinnott, 170.

The number of the various tribes is rapidly decreasing, and the land now claimed by them is largely in excess of what they really need. Should these schemes prove successful a large area of public lands will soon be open to settlers.

During a Fourth of July celebration held at Grand Ronde that year, there was more discussion surrounding the possibility that the government would remove all the Indians and throw open the reservation to white settlement. Rev. Summers wrote that the only reason he had heard for opening up the Grand Ronde Reservation was that the land was one of the best tracts in all Oregon and too fine to be given to Indians.[7]

In defending his native right to the land at Grand Ronde, a young man told all the Americans celebrating their independence on this occasion that his people

… gave no man any trouble. They committed no crimes; they did not disgrace their land by drunkenness or shameful carousing; they sought to live orderly and peacefully among themselves and towards the whites; but they loved their homes, just as the white man did his and desired to live and die here and not be taken by force and conveyed to some distant point against their will.

He reminded them that

… when they first gave everything they had to the United States and accepted these homes at Grand Ronde in place of their former possessions, it was upon the government's pledge that these little farms should be theirs forever; that they should be protected in their rights as owners, just as all other subjects were; and, while they meant to be peaceable still and not troublesome, yet they were men and not dogs. They should not be driven hither and thither like cattle, not having done anything to deserve such treatment![8]

On the coast just west of the Grand Ronde Reservation, the Salmon River and Nehalem band of Tillamook along with a few Clatsops were having similar problems. The United States had just opened their homeland to white settlement, making it necessary for Congress to pass an act authorizing their removal through the efforts of Special Commissioner Simpson and Agent Sinnott, who negotiated a treaty with them.

They were relocated to a tract of land north of the Salmon River with assurances that their children would be able to attend school at Grand Ronde. They

---

7   Cawley, *Indian Journal*, 90.

8   Ibid.

were also promised that any disputes among them could be heard in the Grand Ronde court and that they could make use of the Grand Ronde lumber and grist mill. It was further agreed that every effort would be made to have the Salmon River Reserve attached to the Grand Ronde Agency.[9]

Panoramic view of the Grand Ronde Agency taken in late 1890s. In this view the boys' home is listed as building 1. Building 2 is the girls' home, or in other reports, the nuns' living quarters. The boarding school and church complex are pictured as buildings 3 and 4. The agent's house can be found in the panoramic view, listed as building 5. The Indian courthouse and agent's office are identified as 6. The blockhouse or jail is unnumbered and on the far right. Photo courtesy of Oregon Historical Society (OHS 0222582)

During August 1876, a delegation of the Salmon River and Nestucca Indians met with the Grand Ronde agent. They wanted the Americans to honor treaty promises Special Commissioner Simpson had made to them. During their visit, they complained bitterly about giving up their homes for white settlement only to be sent to a place on the south side of the Salmon River where they had neither food nor shelter.

Two years later, the agent reported that a few Salmon River and Nestucca families were living at Grand Ronde and many other people from the Salmon River Reserve were making the eighteen-mile trip to Grand Ronde almost weekly to take advantage of the Indian services offered there and to barter their fish, hides, and berries for other supplies.[10]

In 1885, after the Indian agent at the Siletz Agency stopped a memorial passed by the Oregon legislature asking Congress to open the Salmon River Reserve for sale to the highest bidder, the Siletz Agency was placed in charge of the Salmon River Reserve.[11]

In 1886, virtually all of the Salmon River and Nestucca families listed the previous year on the Grand Ronde Indian census were dropped from the roll. When

9   *Annual Report Commissioner of Indian Affairs*, 1875, Sinnott, 346.

10 Gatschet, in *Texts, Sentences, and Vocables*, 96, estimated that there were about twenty Nestuccas at Grand Ronde. He wrote that the Tillamook had never lived at Grand Ronde. He described the Tillamook band as thirty to forty people with nothing and living at the Salmon River.

11 *Annual Report Commissioner of Indian Affairs*, 1886, Wadsworth, 215.

the Dawes Act was passed in 1887, only two families from the Salmon River Reserve were living on the Grand Ronde Reservation.

Under the Dawes Act, in exchange for renouncing their tribal holdings, Indians could become United States citizens and receive individual land grants in the amount of 160 acres to each head of family and eighty acres to single adults. Full ownership was granted after the expiration of a twenty-five-year federal trust.

By the time the news of the Dawes Act reached Grand Ronde, there were only about 361 Indian people still living on the reservation.[12] Poor sanitary conditions largely contributed to their high mortality rate, and with each death more and more Indian farms fell idle.

Reservation sidewalk leading from St Michael's Catholic Church to the Grand Ronde Agency. Photo courtesy of Oregon Historical Society (OHS 85529)

The agent readily recognized the health risk of having a sewer pass within fifteen feet of a well that was the main water source for the reservation. In assessing the full scope of the problem, he had found that there were other wells, but they were only suitable for collecting surface water.[13] The people were not only forced to drink stagnant water, but were subject to a high safety risk in the event of fire.[14]

While the agent's request for a tower and waterworks at Grand Ronde was finally approved in 1895, it was recalled within weeks without explanation.[15]

---

12 *Annual Report Commissioner of Indian Affairs*, 1891, Lamson, 369.
13 *Annual Report Commissioner of Indian Affairs*, 1893, Brentano, 266–67 and 1895, Brentano, 267.
14 *Annual Report Commissioner of Indian Affairs*, 1891, Lamson, 370.
15 *Annual Report Commissioner of Indian Affairs*, 1895, Brentano, 267.

Among the people, it was common knowledge that each year more children were buried than were placed in the cradle.[16] It was impossible not to notice the low survival rate of children, as most of the old and middle-aged women no longer had children living with them.[17] Hoping to maintain their population, young girls were marrying, in some cases even before becoming of age.

In addition to illnesses commonly found in communities with poor sanitation, tuberculosis was prevalent among the people. For treatment, the people called openly upon Dr. Kershaw, but night after night the sounds of their medicine dances also echoed across the reservation.

Believing, like other agents before him, that this practice caused the people to lose confidence in the legitimate healing practices offered by the agency physician, Agent Brentano threatened the Indian doctors, telling them if they continued he would not issue them any of the government supplies sent for the benefit of the people.[18]

The agent's actions frightened the people. Now many of them only danced the spirit dances after much urging from Indian doctors, and then only to save a life. They realized that soon they would have to rely completely on the white physician as more and more of the old medicine doctors were dying without anyone to take their place.

As an increasing number of Indian people became property owners, the Indian agent explained to them the Americans system for inheriting property. Many Indians, particularly the old people, wanted to continue the old custom where everyone who was a member of their tribe was equally entitled to their property. In forcing them to comply with state probate laws, Agent Brentano found the native custom of living together, and although unrelated, using the same surname, presented problems, as it sometimes made it difficult to identify the deceased's lawful heirs.[19]

From Brentano's concerns grew more questions. Some Americans wondered whether Indian marriages were even legal since Indian couples had typically been married by the church or by traditional ceremony without a license from the state. If Indian marriages were not legal, should the state even recognize their natural children as heirs?

Subsequently, a great deal of authority was left in the hands of the Indian agent, who in many cases made the final decision as to who was eligible to receive an allotment and how large that allotment would be. Further, each Indian estate was handled through two separate litigations. According to federal law, Indian agents managed the transfer of Indian real property. State probate court made decisions in regard to personal property, but it did not have jurisdiction over

---

16 Cawley, *Indian Journal*, 44.
17 *Annual Report Commissioner of Indian Affairs*, 1888, McClane, 206. Cawley, *Indian Journal*, 44.
18 Annual Report Commissioner of Indian Affairs, 1895, Brentano, 268.
19 Ibid.

matters deciding the heirs of allotment land. As a result, the total cost in fees and expenses for administrating Indian estates was very high.[20]

When they were issued the title for their allotment, Indian people automatically became United States citizens. Despite all the publicity to the contrary, Indian citizenship did not impact the state in the way the larger white community feared. Although saloonkeepers could now legally serve Indians alcohol, the agent reported that most of the Indian people at Grand Ronde remained "opposed to drunkenness and deplore the crimes that were committed in consequences."[21]

Nor did citizenship immediately improve the lives of Indian people the way they probably imagined. On paper, Indian people had new legal rights and could have their cases heard in American courts; however, the county did not want to pay for prosecuting cases involving Indians and, as a rule, prosecutors did not bring charges in these cases. As a result, when crimes were committed against Indian people, the offenders generally went unpunished.[22] Nevertheless, the Indian Department closed the Indian court of offenses on the reservation. In final tribute, the agent wrote that the court had the support of the better class of Indians and had been of great assistance in the punishment of crime.

After all the allotments had been made, the Grand Ronde Reservation contained twenty-six thousand acres of surplus grazing and timber land that might have been used to establish a viable community and otherwise benefit the people, but the United States government labeled the land surplus and sent out a representative to make yet another agreement with the Grand Ronde people.

On June 27, 1901, James McLaughlin, a United States Indian inspector, negotiated the sale of this land with some of the Grand Ronde people. Afterward, the decision to sell or not to sell was put to a vote.

At this time women, regardless of their race, were not legal voters. None of the sixty-eight Indian women holding allotments in their own name on the reservation were allowed to participate in this decision. Only men over the age of eighteen were allowed to cast a ballot.

The census that year showed 111 men over the age of eighteen living on the reservation. Included in this count were at least five men who did not belong to the Grand Ronde Reservation: Charles Russie, **Peter Lafferty, John Pichette, John E. Jeffries,** and **Peter Arquette.** None of these men were members of any tribe assigned to Grand Ronde; nor had they been adopted. Four of the five men, Charles Russie, Peter Arquette, Peter Lafferty, and John Pichette, were the husbands of women who belonged at Grand Ronde. John E. Jeffries' wife did not belong at Grand Ronde, but her father had been adopted by one of the treaty tribes and she had inherited his allotment.

Since McLaughlin gave the total number of eligible male voter as 106, it ap-

---

20 Supreme Court Decision, *McKay, et al vs. Kalyton*, 204 U.S. 458 (1907).

21 *Annual Report Commissioner of Indian Affairs*, 1894, Brentano, 260. *Annual Report Commissioner of Indian Affairs*, 1895, Brentano, 266.

22 *Annual Report Commissioner of Indian Affairs*, 1895, Brentano, 267.

pears that these five men were not given the opportunity to vote on behalf of their wives. In the end sixty men from forty-seven Indian families sold back more than twenty-six thousand acres of land to the United States government. Many of the votes came from elderly men who had no means of supporting themselves and no relatives to look after them. These were men between the ages of sixty-four and ninety-six who had outlived all their children.

It could be argued that six of the sixty men voting to sell, not yet being twenty-one years old, were too young to make such an important decision. Another man who voted yes to the sale of the surplus land was committed to the Salem insane asylum the following year.[23]

Sealed bids for the sale of the land on the Grand Ronde Reservation were received at the Oregon City land office from 9 a.m. on Monday, August 1, 1904, until 11 a.m. on Monday, August 8, 1904. The total area of the reservation offered for sale was 26,021.54 acres, divided into 181 tracts of approximately 160 acres each. Three hundred thirty-five bids were received.

The sale was considered very satisfactory, as it was anticipated that over sixty thousand dollars would soon be divided among the Indians at Grand Ronde. In reality, after looking forward to the money for almost three years, the people ended up receiving only forty-four thousand, or $204 each; even this reduced amount was not paid until 1906.[24]

That same year, the Burke Act amended the Dawes Act, giving the secretary of the interior the power to issue a patent in fee simple to an Indian allottee classified as competent and capable. These competent allotees could have their land taken out of trust so it could be sold.

Many Indian people did not fully understand the impact that this act would have on their community. Seeing that it could relieve some of the pressure they were experiencing from prolonged poverty, they did not realize that it held serious consequences as well. Often Indian people were not informed when their land status changed from trust land to a fee patent. Under a fee patent land was taxed, and after a period of delinquent taxes the land was sold without the owners' consent.

By the turn of the century, most of the people who could remember their former way of life were dead or dying, their original reservation land was melting away, and the poverty that had blanketed the people for more than fifty years was still widely prevalent.

---

23 Report of School Superintendent in Charge of Grande Ronde Agency, August, 26, 1901, 341 and H.R. Report No. 175, 57th Cong. 1st Sess., 1901, Agreement with the Indians of the Grand Ronde Reservation in Oregon containing copy of signed agreement with a letter from Commissioner, W. A. Jones and U.S. Indian Inspector, James McLaughlin.

24 Annual Report Commissioner of Indian Affairs, 1906, Kershaw, 329.

Directory of Families
Living on the Grand Ronde
Indian Reservation

A

Adams, John (1826c), Rogue River/Shasta	Native Name: None known by author
Alias: None known by author	Allotment: None known by author
Mother: Unknown to author	Father: Unknown to author

In 1872, John Adam was living with his wife, Lucy, and a woman named Ann who was further identified as the "mother-in-law of Annetta Gilat."

In 1886, John was single and living with a woman called Shasta Kate (1841c). Also living with them was Shasta Kate's two children, Annie (1880c) and Minnie (1883c). Their living situation was recorded as "all poor." John and his family were not listed after that year.

Allen, Augustin, (1869c–77), Molalla, Clackamas, Shasta	Native Name: Katamsh /ka-TAMSH/ (k'atámsh)*[1]
Alias: None known by author	Allotment: None known by author
Mother: Shasta	Father: Moses Allen, Molalla, Clackamas

In 1872, Augustin (Katamsh) was living with his father, **Moses Allen** (Shkayinch). When he died at the age of twelve, Augustin spoke only Chinook Jargon. Although his mother was Shasta, he was identified as a Molalla because his father was largely of that tribe.

Allen, Moses (1832c–1905), Molalla Clackamas[2]	Native Names: Shkayinch /SHKA-yinch/ (shkáyinch),* Khanatksh /ha-NATKSH/ (xanátksh),* Sawitas /SA-wi-tas/ (sáwit'as),* Yakhitalts /YA-hi-talts/ (yáaxit'alts)*[3]

---

1   Jacobs, Field Notebook 68, *Texts Ethnology Clackamas & Jargon*, 84: name possibly Clackamas.

2   Jacobs, Notebook 53, *Texts and Ethnology*, 76: V. Howard's mother's brother was part Molale, part Clackamas. Melville Jacobs, Notebooks 59, *Texts and Ethnology*, 40: V. Howard's uncle died about 1905. St. Michael's Catholic Church Burial Records, 1905: Mose Allen, V. Howard's uncle, died Feb. 16, 1905.

3   Melville Jacobs, Notebook 52, *Texts and Ethnology*, 42: Victoria Howard stated shkayinch was the Molalla name of her Molalla uncle, who for a short time was husband of Mary Mundi. Jacobs, Notebook 69, *Texts, Ethnology, Clackamas & Jargon*, 48: V. Howard's mother's brother, a Molalla; he understood Clackamas and was

Alias: None known by author	Allotment 4
Mother: Wagayuhlen, Clackamas	Father: Chief Quaiquaty, Molalla

Moses Allen (Shkayinch) was the son of **Quaiquaty** (Gwayakiti), the Principal Chief of the Molalla band of Molalla. As was the custom for upper class Molalla men, Moses had his nose pierced like his father. Both men used a yellowhammer feather or dentaliam shell that could easily be pulled through.[4]

In his youth, Moses speared all sorts of fish from a small fishing hole in the mountains of Grand Ronde. The reservoir had so many water creatures that his parents thought maybe that was where the *kitsimanis* kept all the water things long ago.[5]

A kitsimani looked just like a human woman, but she had the power to kill people. She would coerce a headman into becoming her husband by threatening to kill his people. When she grew tired of him, she would induce all the women from the village to come with her under the pretext that she would show them a fine camas patch. Then she would kill and bake them for her Grizzly husband. Her Grizzly husband would eat them on a stick like a shiskabob.[6]

Eagle spirit power gave Moses Allen all the skills of a great hunter and the general ability to accumulate a significant amount of wealth with ease.[7] Where other hunters were frequently scared in the woods, Moses became frightened only once. On this particular trip, he heard what sounded like the cry of a doe. Walking slowly and cautiously toward the sound, he stepped up on a log to get a better look. From this position, he saw a strange spotted creature lying just on the other side. It looked like a young deer except it had the body of a snake. Only its head and paws were that of a deer. If the creature had seen him, Moses felt sure it would have pursued him, but fortunately it was facing away from where he stood. Although Moses returned to the same place on later hunting trips, he never saw the creature again nor did anyone else ever report seeing it.[8]

In addition to eagle power, Moses had the power of rattlesnake.[9] He could pick one up, put it in his pocket, and it would not bite him. In the beginning the power made him wild. It made him eat rocks, but a man who had danced five years for rattlesnake power could cure snakebite, extract teeth, and send snakes to bite people. When he poisoned someone, only a person with the power of brown

named xanátksh, a Clackamas name. Frachtenberg, *Molala Ethnology*, 30 gives the additional Indian names Sawitas and Yakhitalts.

4   Jacobs, Notebook 52, *Texts and Ethnology*, 26.
5   Melville Jacobs, Notebooks 64, *Texts and Ethnology*, n.p.
6   Melville Jacobs, Notebook 56, *Texts and Ethnology*, 118.
7   Jacobs, Notebook 59, *Texts and Ethnology*, 38. Jacobs, Field Notebook 53, *Texts and Ethnology*, 76.
8   Jacobs, Field Notebook 59, *Texts and Ethnology*, 40. Jacobs, *Clackamas Chinook Texts*, Part 2, 559, 661.
9   Jacobs, *Clackamas Chinook Texts*, Part 2, 661. Jacobs, Field Notebook 53, *Texts and Ethnology*, 76.

eagle who ate rattlesnake could cure his victim, but Moses' rattlesnake power was never that strong.[10]

Still, Moses had yet another spirit power. His power for gambling told him to lie in wait for the morning stars on a bald hilltop near Grand Ronde. When the morning stars sprayed sparks on the ground, he would collect the grass and green leaves from the places they had touched and place them with his gambling sticks, which he kept safely hidden in his secret place in the woods.[11]

Although Moses never doctored, he had an uncle on his mother's side of the family called **Polk Scott** (Puk) who had the power to heal. **Tualatin William Wishikin**'s wife, **Sarah Gwayakiti**, was Moses' sister.[12] Another woman named **Jane Hubbard** was listed for a number of years as a "sister" to Moses, but was more likely a cousin. She and her daughter, **Josephine Hubbard**, lived with Moses, along with an aunt named Sarah (1827c–98c).

In 1872, Moses Allen was with his wife, Lucy (1844c–87c) and his son, **Augustin Allen** (Katamsh). Also living with the family was a woman named Mary Ann Jones and her daughter, Leni Baker. Their relationship to him was not recorded.

Photo passed down to descendants of Victoria Howard; identified only as "Molalla" but very likely Victoria's uncle, Moses Allen. Photo courtesy of the Barbara Danforth Private Collection

Mary Ann Jones may have been the woman better known as Mary Mundi who was said to have been Moses's wife for a short time.[13] After Mary's brother,

---

10 Jacobs, Field Notebook 51, *Texts and Ethnology*, 10. Drucker, *Clackamas Field Notes*, n.p.

11 Jacobs, *Clackamas Chinook Texts*, Part 2, 508–09.

12 Jacobs, *Clackamas Chinook Texts*, Part 2, 512: V. Howard said, "After a long time my mother's older brother (Moses Allen) arrived,"…and "might our mother's brother the shaman (Polk Scott) come to see you?" Jacobs, Notebook 68, *Texts and Ethnology*, 61: Jacobs again identified Polk Scott as Sarah and Mose Allen's mother's brother. Jacobs, *Clackamas Chinook Text*, Part 2, 492–93, and 647, Note 426: stated Sarah and Moses Allen had the same mother.

13 Jacobs, Field Notebook 51, *Music and Ethnology*, 2: Mary Mundi was also listed as the wife of a Klickitat man named Joe Hunt. She recorded a Molalla love song and part

Joe Susap, refused to go to the reservation, the Americans allowed him to remain in his home overlooking Willamette Falls for a number of years. It was said that Joe could remember having lived another life long before being reborn in his present body.[14]

In addition to his son, Augustin Allen, Moses Allen had a number of other children: Delphine (1873c), Henry (1876c), Charlotte (1876c–79), Carola (1876c–85), Raymond (1878c–88), Cecelia (d.1883c) and Julia (1886c–88), but all of them died young.[15]

In 1879, Moses represented the people living in the eastern region of the reservation at the Eighth Annual Session of the Grand Ronde Indian Legislature along with **John Pratt** (Gwaimit) and **Peter Kenoyer** (Kinai). After the Legislative Assembly appointed Moses road supervisor, he was assigned to repair the reservation road leading from **Dave Leno**'s place to Litchfield's Bridge as far as **Peter Wheeler** (Kutskait)'s and from the agency to **Jo Shangaretta**'s place. He resigned this appointment May 20, 1880.[16] Then he served on the Grand Ronde Police Force from 1891 to 1893.[17]

Around 1895, he married **Henry Kiki** (Lhkailhkai)'s widow, Sarah. They lived together until Sarah died in November of 1904. Moses died in February the following year.

In probate, his estate was valued at six hundred dollars. Since all of his children had died, his sister's daughter, **Victoria Wishikin (Kinishi)** was his sole heir.[18]

Allen, Nellie (1882c–92c), Kalapuya	Native Name: None known by author
Alias: None known by author	Allotment 3
Mother: Margaret	Father: English[19]

Father Croquet found Nellie critically ill on January 13, 1889. She survived,

---

of a Klamath bone gamble song she remembered from Oregon City for the Museum of Natural History.

14 Jacobs, Notebook 58, *Texts and Ethnology*, damaged last page: Joe Sosap was Mary Mundi's brother.

15 Harriet Munnick and Stephen D. Beckham, Catholic *Church Records of the Pacific Northwest—Grand Ronde* (Portland, OR: Binford & Mort, 1987): Register I, p. 111, S-5, p. 131, S-5, p. 127, S-15, Register II, p. 43, S-11, p. 43, S-14.

16 National Archives, Seattle, Grand Ronde/Siletz, Land and Enrollment Program records, Field Notes and Land Survey 1875–1898, Land Description Book 1878, Box 115; Grand Ronde Justice Court.

17 Grand Ronde Agency Ledger Book, Records of Employees at Grand Ronde July 1883–September 1907, Cultural Resource Department Archives, Confederated Tribes of the Grand Ronde Community of Oregon.

18 *Heirs of Deceased Indians*, Allotment Record, 4: Moses Allen received 76.13 acres.

19 1900 Federal Census, District 812, Grand Ronde Indian Reservation.

but never fully recovered. In poor health, Nellie lived with her father until she died January 23, 1892.[20]

Nellie also received an eighty-acre allotment that **Robert Allen** inherited as her sole heir.[21]

Allen, Nelson (1841c–88c), Tualatin band of Kalapuya	Native Name: None known by author
Alias: None known by author	Allotment: None known by author
Mother: Unknown to author	Father: Unknown to author

In 1886, Nelson Allen was living with his wife, Sarah (1846c) and daughter, Stephanie (1872c). Perhaps because he was one of those who did not farm, the Indian agent noted that he was "poor," and "no account."

By 1887, Nelson had married **Lucinda Metzgar.** Living with them was Lucinda's two children by **Moses Apperson** (Wannexke), Louise and **Norris Apperson,** along with an unidentified baby. The baby was probably Nelson's daughter, Elizabeth Sallianne, who was born January 3, 1887.[22]

In 1888, Nelson moved his family in with his father-in-law, **Antoine Metzgar** (Tamulch). The following year, their children were still living with their grandparents, but Nelson and Lucinda were not listed on the GRIC. By 1892, Lucinda Metzgar was the wife of **Levi Bob.** The children were still listed with their grandparents. Nelson was not listed on any GRIC after 1888.

Allen, Robert (1850c–1918), Kalapuya	Native Name: None known by author
Alias: None known by author	Allotment 1
Mother: Kalapuya	Father: English[23]

In 1887, Robert's wife, Margaret, had recently died, leaving him with their young daughter, **Nellie Allen.** On the 1889 GRIC, Robert was listed with **Sarah Howard,** Sarah's daughter, **Stephanie Howard** (Lhimiki), and another unnamed daughter, probably Nellie. At that time, he had forty fenced acres and five tons of hay.

Stephanie lived with her mother and her stepfather, Robert Allen, until she married **Frank Wheeler** (Aiwai) on November 3, 1890.

After his wife Sarah died, Robert married **Jennie Sansousee,** widow of **Umpqua Bill Condon,** Frank Stanton, and **Fred Harney** consecutively. In 1891,

---

20 Munnick and Beckham, Catholic *Church Records—Grand Ronde,* Register I, p. 64, M-3, Register II, p. 76, S-1.

21 *Heirs of Deceased Indians,* Allotment Record, 3.

22 Munnick and Beckham, Catholic *Church Records—Grand Ronde,* Register II, p. 36, B-47.

23 1900 Federal Census, District 812, Grand Ronde Indian Reservation.

Robert received a 299.86 acre allotment. His wife, Jennie, received an eighty-acre allotment in her own name. After Jennie's death in 1903, her heirs, **Robert Allen** and **Lillie Josephine Condon,** sold forty acres of her allotment to D. S. Bentley.[24]

On July 30, 1904, Robert married **Thomas Orton's** widow, **Eliza Johnson** (Sy-ilsha), who was approaching eighty.[25] Eliza had inherited her sister, **Mary Johnson's,** estate, which included funds from a 140-acre allotment sold to D. S. Bentley October 29 of the previous year.[26] After moving into Eliza's home with her, Robert refused to work or contribute anything toward their support. Eliza supported both of them until her health turned bad in November 1904.[27]

Finally, seriously ill, Eliza asked Robert to help her, but he refused to care for her. Instead, "he left home frequently for days at a time without providing any fire wood for the home or leaving anyone to care for her." After he abandoned her completely in March of 1905, Eliza divorced him. In the divorce decree, Eliza asked to be allowed to keep all rights to the allotment property that was in her name. The court granted her request.[28]

On June 21, 1909, Robert married Mary (Skampup), the former wife of the Yoncalla man called **Calapooia Billy Williamson** (Hosanunda).[29] After they had been married a few years, in December 1914, his wife, Mary Williamson-Allen worked with Leo Frachtenberg, providing him with vocabulary from the Yoncalla language.

After Robert died, Mary inherited his estate, which was valued at $827.50. **Cephas Tipton** paid taxes on Robert's land until it went through probate.[30]

Alpokal (1791c–1861), Cow Creek band of Umpqua	Native Name: None known by author
Alias: None known by author	Allotment: None known by author
Mother: Unknown to author	Father: Unknown to author

Alpokal died and was buried at Grand Ronde January 26, 1861.

Amos, Jack (1868c–96), Yamhill band of Kalapuya	Native Name: Shaklu /Shak-lu/ (sháklu)*[31]

24 *Heirs of Deceased Indians*, Allotment Record 27, 28.
25 Oregon State Archives, 1896, Polk County, Estate File 976, Thomas Orton.
26 Oregon State Archives, 1902, Polk County, Estate File 990, Mary Riley.
27 Oregon State Archives, 1905, Polk County Divorce, Eliza Allen vs. Robert Allen.
28 Ibid.
29 Jacobs, Field Notebook 36, *Santiam Kalapuya Text*, 192: "skampup, Yoncalla woman (Mary Allen)."
30 National Archives, Salem, Oregon, 1916, Polk County, Estate File 1594.
31 Jacobs, Field Notebook 51, *Music and Ethnology*, 45: Jack's Indian name was listed as "Caklu."

Alias: George Amos, Joseph George Amos[32]	Allotment 5
Mother: Unknown to author	Father: Amos Kilya, Yamhill

Jack Amos (Shaklu) married **Lucy Sampson,** the daughter of a Tillamook doctor. By 1888, he and Lucy had an infant daughter named Alice, but the baby only lived a few months.[33]

Shortly after Alice died, on July 1, 1889, Jack Amos and Lucy were married in the Catholic Church. Lucy's sister, Josephine Samson and **Frank Wheeler** (Aiwai) witnessed the ceremony.[34] Around this time, Jack received a 140-acre allotment next to his father and began making his own home.

On January 27, 1893, Jack and Lucy had a little girl they named Emergence. In 1894, they had a son, Louis Amos, but he only lived a few months.[35]

Perhaps because Jack had rattlesnake power, all his children died before him. Jack died a young man on August 14, 1896.[36] His widow, Lucy, married Moses Lane at Siletz. Jack's heirs were Perry Battise, Harriet Klamath, Louise Klamath, L. D. Klamath, and Nellie Lane from the Siletz agency.

In 1929, **Victoria Wishikin (Kinishi)** recorded one of Jack's power songs for Melville Jacobs.[37]

Andrew, Frank (1866c), Molalla	Native Name: Cliluc /Cli-luc/[38]
Alias: None known by author	Allotment: None known by author
Mother: Unknown to author	Father: Unknown to author

In 1886, Frank Andrew (Cliluc) was single and living with **Sam Beaver Trapper** (Shayum) and his wife, Liza. In 1888, Frank was living alone. His name does not appear on any GRIC after 1892.

Antoine, Long Tom band of Kalapuya	Native Name: Luckamafoo /Luck-a-ma-foo/
Alias: Chief Antoine	Allotment: None known by author
Mother: Unknown to author	Father: Unknown to author

Antoine (Luckamafoo) signed the Treaty with the Kalapuya, Etc., 1855 as Principal Chief of the Long Tom or Chelamela band of Kalapuya with Second

---

32 Michelle, *Just a Memorandum,* 6.
33 Munnick and Beckham, Catholic *Church Records—Grand Ronde,* Register II, p. 49, S-21.
34 Ibid., p. 54, M-5.
35 Ibid., p. 104, S-11.
36 Jacobs, Field Notebook 51, *Music and Ethnology,* 45-47.
37 Ibid.
38 1887 GRIC gave Frank's native name as "Cli-luc."

Chief, Charley (Hootil).[39] There were a total of sixteen Chelamela at Grand Ronde the first year. The following year, the band was listed without a chief. In 1865, they were listed with the Mary's River band and their total number was counted at twenty-six. Around this time, **Joseph Shangaretta** became their chief.

Apperson, Joseph (1839c–89), Tumwater band of Chinook	Native Name: Washamsh /wa-SHAMSH/ (washámsh)*[40]
Alias: Oregon City Joe	Allotment 7
Mother: Unknown to author	Father: Chief John Kawache, Tumwater band of Chinook

Joe Apperson (Washamsh) was the oldest son of **John Kawache,** Chief of the Tumwater band of Chinook. At Grand Ronde, Joe Apperson was elected by popular vote to represent all the Oregon City Tribes at the Fifth Annual Session of the Grand Ronde Indian Legislature in 1876.[41] By 1886, Joe had two houses and a barn, eighty fenced acres with seventy acres cultivated, four horses, and a small orchard. Next to **James Winslow,** who was cultivating eighty acres, Joe was the second largest producer on the reservation at that time.

His first wife was one of **Chief Daniel Wacheno** (Wachinu's) daughters. By her, he had a daughter, **Stephanie Apperson.**[42] Later, Joe married Susanne Klickitat. By Susanne, he had Julia (1867), Augustine (1873), and **Matthew Apperson.**[43]

In addition to his own children, he adopted his half brother, **Homer Hoffer** (Tamaguin)'s three-year-old daughter, Mary Ann, in 1874. His father, who was living with him at that time, had insisted that the adoption take place. Chief John believed the adoption was necessary in order to preserve treaty rights for Homer's family on the Grand Ronde Reservation.[44] **Mary Ann Hoffer** paid the price for these rights. Joe was very strict with her. If she failed to respond immediately when he asked her to do something, he beat her with a buggy whip.[45]

In 1887, Joe married Nancy (Tunishni), the widow of **Peter Kenoyer** (Kinai). His son, Mathew, was still living at home when Joe's new wife came to live with them, bringing her twenty-year-old son, **Louis Kenoyer** (Pakhawatas), and six-year-old daughter, **Caroline Kenoyer.**

The increase in Joe's reported assets in 1888 surely reflect some of what Tun-

39 Kappler, *Treaty with the Kalapuya, Etc., 1855,* 668.

40 Jacobs, Notebook 52, *Texts and Ethnology,* 56. Michelle, *Just a Memorandum,* 4.

41 National Archives, Seattle, Grand Ronde/Siletz, Land and Enrollment Program records, Field Notes and Land Survey 1875–1898, Land Description Book 1878, Box #115; Grand Ronde Justice Court.

42 Michelle, *Just a Memorandum,* 11: Mary Ann wrote that John Wacheno was Stephanie's uncle.

43 Munnick and Beckham, Catholic *Church Records—Grand Ronde,* Register I, p. 52, B-83, p. 80, B-6, p. 100, B-25.

44 Michelle, *Just a Memorandum,* 11.

45 Jacobs, Notebook 53, *Texts and Ethnology,* 56.

ishni brought with her when they were married. In 1888, he was listed with three houses and two barns, a large harvest, eleven horses, eight cows, eighteen hogs, and a family garden.

Joe Apperson received a 210-acre allotment that was in still in trust status in 1919. His son, Matthew Apperson, received a forty-acre allotment. Their allotment land was west of the agency on the south side of Hebo road. Their neighbors on the north side of Hebo road were **John Warren** and **Julius Mercier.**[46]

After Joe's death, October 13, 1889, his personal estate was divided between his heirs who were listed as his widow, **Nancy Kenoyer** (Tunishni), his nieces, Mary Ann Hoffer and Edna Hoffer, and his nephews Harry, Ernest, Frederick, and **Andrew Hoffer.**[47]

Heirs to Joseph's allotment were recorded as distant relatives at Yakama named Frank and Smiscon So-Happy, **Macasca Sitton**'s daughter Clarinda Sitton, and Pauline Sutton's daughter Zelda Catherine Sutton.

Apperson, Matthew (1876–91), Tumwater band of Chinook, Klickitat	Native Name: None known by author
Alias: Moses Dolphin[48]	Allotment: 8
Mother: Susanne Klickitat	Father: Joe Apperson, Tumwater band of Chinook

Matthew died when he was sixteen. His heirs were recorded as distant relatives at Yakama, Frank and Smiscon So-Happy, **Macasca Sitton**'s daughter Clarinda Sitton, and Pauline Sutton's daughter Zelda Catherine Sutton.

Apperson, Melinda (1882c–98), Tualatin band of Kalapuya, Tumwater band of Chinook, Klickitat, Yakama	Native Name: None known by author
Alias: Linda Apperson	Allotment: 123
Mother: Lucinda Metzkar, Tualatin band of Kalapuya, Klickitat	Father: Moses Apperson, Tumwater band of Chinook, Yakama

Melinda Apperson received an eighty-acre allotment. Her heir was her brother, **Norris Apperson.**

Apperson, Moses (1859c–86), Tumwater band of Chinook, Yakama	Native Name: Wannexke[48]

---

46 Original Blueprint of Grand Ronde Allotments, Cultural Resource Department Archives, CTGR.

47 Oregon State Archive, Salem, Oregon, 1910, Yamhill County, Estate Joseph Apperson.

48 1872 GRIC.

Alias: Moses Dolphin[49]	Allotment: None known by author
Mother: Yakama	Father: Chief John Kawache

Moses Apperson (Wannexke) was the youngest son of the chief, **John Kawache**. Like his brother, **Joe Apperson** (Washamsh), Moses served for a time on the Grand Ronde Indian Legislature. When the Seventh Annual Session convened, November 4, 1878, the assembly elected Moses Apperson, Court Clerk. May 9, 1881, the tenth annual session of the Grand Ronde Indian legislature re-elected him.[50]

Moses had five children by a Tualatin woman named **Lucinda Metzkar**: Melinda, Moses, Norris, Louise Minnie, and another little girl, but only **Melinda** and **Norris Apperson** survived.[51]

Shortly after the death of their youngest child, on May 8, 1884, at the age of twenty-five, Moses was committed to the Hawthorne Asylum in Salem where he died.[52]

Apperson, Norris (1880), Tumwater band of Chinook, Tualatin band of Kalapuya, Klickitat, Yakama	Native Name: None known by author
Alias: None known by author	Allotment: 122
Mother: Lucinda Metzkar, Tualatin band of Kalapuya, Klickitat	Father: Moses Apperson, Tumwater Chinook, Yakama

Norris Apperson spent his later years on the Yakama Indian Reservation.[53]

Apperson, Stephanie (1863c–82), Clackamas, Tumwater band of Chinook	Native Name: None known by author
Alias: None known by author	Allotment: None known by author
Mother: Chief Wacheno's daughter, Clackamas	Father: Joe Apperson (Washamsh), Tumwater band of Chinook

Stephanie was the granddaughter of **Chief Daniel Wacheno** (Wachinu) and **Chief John Kawache.** She embarrassed her father, **Joe Apperson** (Washamsh), by getting pregnant before she was married. She had her son, **Isadore Kilmonie,** in

---

49 1872 GRIC.

50 National Archives, Seattle, Grand Ronde/Siletz, Land and Enrollment Program records, Field Notes and Land Survey 1875–1898, Land Description Book 1878, Box 115; Grand Ronde Justice Court.

51 Munnick and Beckham, Catholic *Church Records—Grand Ronde,* Register I, p. 114, M-12, p. 118, B-5, p. 125, B-11, Register II, p. 116, S-2, p. 103 conf.

52 National Archives, Salem, Oregon, Apperson, Moses, no. 858, May 8, 1884, Commitment Polk County, Hawthorne Asylum, File 029.

53 Zenk, *Chinook Jargon,* 267.

July 1879. After her father disinherited Isadore, Stephanie's uncle, **John Wacheno** (Tsinwalh) let Stephanie and the baby stay with his family until she married **Alexander Toto**, a half brother of **Wallen Kilmonie** (Kilmanukh).[54]

When Alex and Stephanie were married, Alex already had one wife, **Susan Beagle,** whom he had married in March 1879. Stephanie became second wife to Alex Toto. Their plural marriage just further enraged Joe Apperson .[55]

A short time later, Alex found himself dying of tuberculosis. Since Stephanie had also contracted the disease, they needed to find a home for Stephanie's son, Isadore. Wallen Kilmanukh, Alex Toto's half brother, had raised him after his father died. Therefore, Alex turned to Wallen for help. Wallen agreed to take the child.[56]

Alex died in 1880. Stephanie died in September of 1882. Isadore lived with Wallen Kilmanukh until he was old enough to attend Chemawa Indian School in Salem.

Arquette, Peter (1852c), Iroquois, Walla Walla	Native Name: None known by author
Alias: Peter Arcouet	Allotment: None known by author
Mother: Mary Norwest, Iroquois, Walla Walla[57]	Father: Amable Abraham Arquette, Chinook, French Canadian

Peter Arquette was listed on the GRIC between 1889 and 1893 with his wife, **Lucinda Metzkar.** Around 1894, Peter Arquette married Jennie, the widow of **Yoncalla Tom Johnson**. They had no children.

At Grand Ronde, in 1905, Peter Arquette told Oliver Applegate that his wife, **Jennie Johnson,** was an Umpqua and had rights on the Grand Ronde reservation. However, he said, "I have an allotment on the Umatilla Reservation and I claim my rights there."[58]

Avery, David, Mary's River band of Kalapuya	Native Name: None known by author
Alias: Old David	Allotment: None known by author
Mother: Unknown by author	Father: Unknown by author

In 1872, David was living alone.

---

54 Michelle, *Just a Memorandum*, 11.
55 Ibid.
56 Ibid.
57 1888 GRIC: listed his tribe as the Santiam band of Kalapuya. Michelle, *Just a Memorandum*, 1: Mary Ann wrote "the Norwest family" was adopted by the Grand Ronde Tribes.
58 O. Applegate, Testimony of Peter Arquette.

B

Babcock, Jack (1856c–74), Rogue River/Shasta	Native Name: None known by author
Alias: Backok, Jack	Allotment: None known by author
Mother: Unknown to author	Father: Unknown to author

"Jack Backok" married **Emma Kellogg** at Grand Ronde in April 1872. Both were recorded as "non-Catholics." They had a daughter, Caroline, in 1873.[1]

Babtiste, Oregon, Tualatin band of Kalapuya	Native Name: None known by author
Alias: None known by author	Allotment: None known by author
Mother: Unknown to author	Father: Unknown to author

In 1872, Oregon Babtiste was living with his wife, Susan, and adopted daughter, Nancy. He does not appear on any GRIC after this year.

Baker, John (1854c–70), Yamhill band of Kalapuya	Native Name: Shikshik /Shik-s/hik/
Alias: None known by author	Allotment: None known by author
Mother: Unknown to author	Father: Unknown to author

On December 12, 1870, John Baker (1854) was buried at Grand Ronde.[2] This was probably the same boy mentioned as in "constant attendance" at the manual labor school. In school records for 1863 his name was given as "Shik-shik Baker."[3]

Baker, William (1866c–1906), Modoc[4]	Native Name: None known by author
Alias: Billy Bateman, Spoon	Allotment: None known by author
Mother: Susan, Modoc (slave)	Father: Unknown by author

Billy Baker was the son of a native slave woman named Susan. His mother was one of five slaves who belonged to a Columbia River chief. When the tribes were removed to Grand Ronde, his former wife, **Mary Ann Keosnose** (Kiyasmu) brought all five of them with her to the reservation.

---

1   Munnick and Beckham, *Catholic Church Records—Grand Ronde*, Register I, p. 73, M-1, p. 80, B-8.
2   Ibid., Register I, p. 66, B-82, S-25
3   Annual Report Commissioner of Indian Affairs, 1863, 84–85.
4   Oliver Applegate, 1905: Testimony of William Baker and Captain Frank Quenelle.

Over the years, the slaves were bought and sold several times. Finally, **Jim Shiliqua** (Shilikwa) bought Billy Baker's mother, Susan, from a nephew of **Chief Daniel Wacheno** (Wachinu) for four horses and many other things. Shilikwa said it was at his house that Billy was born and Susan died shortly after his birth. He also said that people wanted to buy Billy, but he "did not sell him because he knew the white people had abolished slavery and he was afraid of getting in trouble."[5]

When Billy was very young, his grandmother came to get him. They lived in Washington State until he was older, but Billy was back living at Grand Ronde when the Thompson allotments were made in 1872.[6] Both Billy and a French Canadian-Tualatin man named **Edward Tebeau** received allotments at that time. However, when the regular allotments were made some years later by a Colonel Collins, both men were working on the Columbia River. **John Wacheno** (Tsinwalh) went personally to tell Billy Baker to come back and see about his land, but both men returned too late. Colonel Collins had finished allotting and had left.[7]

According to Billy Baker, before she died in 1904, **Alsea Bill**'s Modoc wife, **Mary Ann Kellogg** told him she was his aunt.[8]

It does not appear as though an allotment was ever issued to Billy Baker, but he eventually married Peter and Grace Wheeler's daughter, Sophia Wheeler-Short and lived out his life on the reservation.[9]

Barlow, Billy (1807c–1903), Mary's River band of Kalapuya	Native Name: Yemantku /YE-mant-gu/ (yéemantgu?)*
Alias: Marysville William, William Barlow	Allotment 11
Mother: Unknown to author	Father: Unknown to author

Billy Barlow had a number of children. In addition to having Marc (1864) by his wife, Mary, he had Adela (1857c), Jenny (1857c–73), Adrian (1861–61), and James (1864c–74). He also had a number of wives: Mary (1812c–92c), Hildegarde (1832c–62), Susan (1828c–78), and Annie.[10]

However, by 1872, apparently, all his wives were dead. Billy Barlow was living at **Calapooia Billy Williamson** (Hosanunda)'s place with one child, his son James. Eventually, Marysville William made a home for himself that the Indian

---

5   O. Applegate, Testimony of John Wacheno, James Shilikwa, James Winslow, William Baker, Edward Tebeau, and Captain Frank Quenel.

6   Ibid.

7   O. Applegate, Testimony of John Wacheno, Edward Tebeau, and William Baker.

8   O. Applegate, Testimony of William Baker. While Baker does not give identify Alsea Bill's wife by name in this testimony, census records identify his wife at that time as a woman named Mary Ann Kellogg.

9   Whitlow, Grand Ronde Family Register, 1901.

10 Munnick and Beckham, Catholic *Church Records — Grand Ronde*, Register I, p. 89, S-16, p. 94, M-6, p. 110, S-26, p. 82, S-10, p. 13, B-172 & 173, p. 14, S-26.

agent described as a hut with twenty fenced acres and a garden. By 1888, his sister, Jennie, was living with him and he had acquired another unnamed wife.

Forty acres of Billy Barlow's sixty-acre allotment were located between **Eliza Johnson** and **Martha Jane Sands** on the north and **Richard Cook (**Shay Shoaska) on the south.[11] **William Hartless** (Futi) was his heir.

Bass, John (1836c)	Native Name: None known by author
Alias: None known by author	Allotment: None known by author
Mother: Unknown to author	Father: Unknown to author

In 1885, John was living at Grand Ronde with his wife, Susan and the following children: Sam (1867c), Jimmie (1868c), Henry (1876c), John (1878c), and Betsy (1880c). John Bass does not appear on any GRIC after this year.

Battise, Batiste, Tumwater band of Chinook	Native Name: None known by author
Alias: None known by author	Allotment: None known by author
Mother: Unknown to author	Father: Unknown to author

In 1872, Battise was listed under the Oregon City band with his wife, Susan and his sister, Nancy.

Baxter, Nestucka (1852c–92c), Nestucca/Nehalem band of Tillamook	Native Name: None known by author
Alias: None known by author	Allotment: None known by author
Mother: Unknown to author	Father: Unknown to author

In 1885, Nestucka Baxter and his wife, Julie (1856c), were listed with their children: Bettie (1878c), Baxter (1880c), Sallie (1882c), and an unnamed baby daughter.

While the family does not appear on any GRIC after 1885, Nestucka Baxter's widow, Julie Baxter, married **Calipooia Jack** in 1892.

Beagle, Martha (1830c–1903), Yoncalla band of Kalapuya[12]	Native Name: Shkinda /SHKIN-da/ (shkínda)*[13]
Alias: None known by author	Allotment 13
Mother: Unknown to author	Father: Unknown to author

---

11 Original Blueprint of Grand Ronde Allotments, Cultural Resource Department Archives, CTGR.

12 Michelle, *Just a Memorandum*, 7. Gatschet, *Texts, Sentences and Vocables*, 367.

13 1887 GRIC listed her Indian name as "Skanda." Michelle, *Just a Memorandum*, 7, gave her name as "Scanda." Gatschet, *Texts, Sentences and Vocables*, 367, listed her as "Shcinda."

Martha Beagle (Shkinda) was **Chief Halo** (Hilu)'s niece.[14] The Tualatin, **Dr. John Smith** (Dushdaq) was married to Martha's sister, **Mary Smith** (Niudiya).[15]

In 1872, Martha was listed as the wife of **Tualatin George Beagle.** Their fifteen-year-old unnamed daughter had just recently died, but their daughters Catherine (1860c) and Susan were still living.

After Tualatin George died in 1874, Martha lived alone, but her daughter, **Susan Beagle,** made her a grandmother around 1879. By **Alexander Toto,** Susan had a daughter named Mary. By **French Prairie Frank Marc,** son of **French Prairie Marc Mickmut,** Susan had two more grandchildren: Louvenia (1882c) and a baby (1885c).[16]

After Susan died in July of 1885, Martha Beagle was left to raise the children.[17] While there is no record of her grandchildren dying, they were only listed with Martha for a couple of years. Another widow, **Jack Nancy** (Shimkhin), lived with her for a while, but ultimately, after 1887, Martha lived alone in a hut with a half acre garden and a few hogs.

When Martha Beagle died, her estate was valued at $400. Her heirs were listed as a cousin residing at Drain, Oregon, named **Jacob Fern,** and three children of **Be-el Fern:** Lucinda Jackson (1874), Laura Fern-Bond (1883) and Malinda Cunningham (1872).[18] Jacob Fern inherited Martha's hundred-acre allotment.

Beagle, Susan (1862c–85), Tualatin band of Kalapuya, Yoncalla band of Kalapuya[19]	Native Name: None known by author
Alias: Susan Toto, Susan Marc	Allotment: None known by author
Mother: Martha Beagle, Yoncalla band of Kalapuya	Father: George Beagle, Tualatin band of Kalapuya

Beagle, Tualatin George (1829c–74), Tualatin band of Kalapuya	Native Name: None known by author
Alias: Tualatin George, Old Man George	Allotment: None known by author
Mother: Unknown to author	Father: Unknown to author

Tualatin George had a number of children. By his wife, Sarah, George had Mary (1854c–71), Julienne (1869–71), Catherine (1856c–64), David (1861–64), and Louise (1856c–72). By an unidentified woman, George had Agatha (1856c–72) and

14 Oregon State Archives, Salem, Oregon, 1904, Yamhill County, Estate File 1295.

15 Michelle, *Just a Memorandum,* 7.

16 Munnick and Beckham, *Catholic Church Records—Grand Ronde,* Register I, p. 111, M-3, p. 113, B-24, p. 125, M-3.

17 Ibid., Register I, p. 131, S-10.

18 Oregon State Archives, Salem, Oregon, 1904, Yamhill County, Estate File 1295.

19 Michelle, *Just a Memorandum,* 7. Gatschet, *Texts, Sentences and Vocables,* 367.

Catherine (1859c–74).[20]

Tualatin George's daughter, Agatha (1856c–72) was probably the seven-year-old girl listed as "Aearte George" who was in "constant attendance" at the Grand Ronde manual labor school in 1863.[21]

By his wife, Catherine (1830c–70), George had Joseph (1861–64), Marcus (1864–64), and Philomene (1858c). When his wife, Catherine, died on May 17, 1872, not only was the Tualatin sub-chief, **Dave Yachkawa,** present, but the Molalla chief, **Quaiquaty** (Gwayakiti), also attended her funeral.

By a Kalapuya woman named Matilda, George had Cecile (1862). In 1872, he, and his wife, Martha were living together with their daughter's: Catherine (1859c–74) and **Susan Beagle.**

All of George's children died before maturity accept his daughter Susan. She married **Alexander Toto** on March 10, 1879. After Alexander died in 1880, Susan married **French Prairie Frank Marc** on August 12, 1883. The fact that the Tualatin sub-chief, **Dave Yachkawa**'s son, Daniel, and **Chief Kiakuts** (Kayakach)'s daughter, Emma Kiakuts was present for the ceremony would indicate the Beagle family held a position of prominence among the Tualatin people.[22]

Beaver Trapper, Sam (1796c), Molalla	Native Name: Shayum /SHA-yum/ (sháyum) [meaning grizzly]*[23]
Alias: Old Man Shiam	Allotment: None known by author
Mother: Unknown to author	Father: Unknown to author

After the signing of the treaties, Sam (Shayum) and Lisa Beaver Trapper spent time both on and off the reservation. In 1886, they were living at Grand Ronde with two of their children. However, they preferred their house on the Molalla River. They were living there when Sam died in 1893.[24]

Sam and Lisa had at least three daughters: Ida, Christine, and Nellie. Little is known about Ida and Christine, but Nellie Beaver Trapper's first husband was **Chief Yelkas**'s son, Henry. Unable to have children, Nellie and **Henry Yelkas** adopted a little boy they named Fred Yelkas (Dush-wil-gushik).[25]

After several years, Nellie abandoned Henry in favor of an Afro-American

---

20 Munnick and Beckham, *Catholic Church Records—Grand Ronde,* Register I, p. 7, B-42, p. 11, B-52, p. 11, B-53, p. 11, B-54, p. 11, B-55, p. 12, B-164, p. 33, S18, p. 34, S-25, p. 61, B-5, p. 69, S-11, p. 69, S-17, p. 77, S-30, p. 86, S-2, p. 89, B-18, p. 90, S-27, p. 23, B-91, p. 16, B-221, p. 16, B-223, p. 31, S-6, p. 74, S-14.

21 *Annual Report Commissioner of Indian Affairs,* 84-85.

22 Munnick and Beckham, *Catholic Church Records —Grand Ronde,* Register I, p. 111, M-3, p. 125, M-3.

23 Jacobs, Field Notebook 82, *Texts and Ethnology Santiam,* 122. Gatschet, *Texts, Sentences and Vocables,* 366: listed under the Umpqua as "Old Man Shiam or; Samuel."

24 "Molalla Indians," *Oregon Trail Pioneer,* 5.

25 Ibid.

Lisa Clackamas (Beaver Trapper) with Henry Yelkas. Photo courtesy of Oregon Historical Society (OHS 022578).

named Harry Clark, but Fred stayed with his father.[26] By Harry Clark, Nellie had a daughter, Bessie and numerous grandchildren.

After Sam died, Lisa Beaver Trapper went to live on her former son-in-law's land claim. She was staying at Henry Yelkas's place when she was hurt in a fall from a wagon in 1905. From Henry's place, she moved to Warm Springs. She lived there for the remainder of her life.[27]

Sam and Lisa's daughter, Nellie died July 27, 1927. She was buried in the Mountain View Cemetery at Oregon City.

---

26   Jacobs, Field Notebook 82, *Texts and Ethnology Santiam*, 122.
27   Ibid.

Beaver, Jack (1810c)	Native Name: None known by author
Alias: None known by author	Allotment: None known by author
Mother: Unknown to author	Father: Unknown to author

In 1885, Jack (1810c) was with a wife, Callie (1825c) and Brother, Canim (1835c). He was not listed on any GRIC after that year.

Belknap, Rachael, Mary's River band of Kalapuya	Native Name: None known by author
Alias: None known by author	Allotment: None known by author
Mother: Unknown to author	Father: Unknown to author

In 1872, Rachael was listed as a widow. Another woman named Lucy and her daughter, Louisa (1862c) were living with Rachael.

Bellique, John Baptiste (1845c–99c), French Canadian	Native Name: None known by author
Alias: Belleque	Allotment: None known by author
Mother: Genevieve St. Martin, French Canadian	Father: Pierre Belleque (1793–1849), French Canadian

In 1818, John Baptiste's father joined the Northwest Fur Company in New Caledonia. He became an employee of the Hudson Bay Company in 1821. After he retired around 1831 he took up a claim on French Prairie. John Baptiste Bellique was raised there.

Although John Baptiste did not appear on any GRIC until 1894, he and his wife **Victoria Vasselle** were recorded as the godparents of **Amanda Jeffries** when she was baptized on March 8, 1891 at the Grand Ronde mission.[28]

After 1894, the Bellique family was listed on every GRIC through 1898. During this time, John Baptiste worked for the agency as a "disciplinarian farmer" until he was discharged on August 2, 1895, "by order of the Department."[29]

In 1899, his wife, Victoria Vasselle-Bellique was listed as a widow. Although John Baptiste Bellique was recorded in agency records as an "Indian," no tribal affiliation could be found and no land allotment was issued to Victoria or any of her children.

Bennett, Frank, (1866c), Columbia River Chinook	Native Name: Khalawilha /ha-LA-wi-hla/ (x̣aláwiⱡa)*[30]
Alias: None known by author	Allotment: None known by author

---

28   Munnick and Beckham, *Catholic Church Records—Grand Ronde*, Register II, p. 66, B-2.
29   Records of Employee at Grand Ronde 1884–1907, Cultural Resource Department Archives, Confederated Tribes of the Grand Ronde Community of Oregon.
30   Jacobs, Field Notebook 67, *Texts and Ethnology Clackamas & Jargon*, n.p.

Mother: Unknown to author	Father: Peter Bennett, Columbia River Chinook

Frank Bennett (Khalawilha) could speak English, Wasco Chinook, and Clackamas.[31] In 1886, he was living with his wife and brother, John Bennett (Gista).[32] They were reportedly very poor. By 1888, Frank's wife had died and his father's widow, Yum-zillis (1831c) was living with him and his brother.

Frank inherited an interest in the eighty-acre allotment of **Sallie Martin,** a Clackamas widow.[33]

By 1929, he was blind, and said to have been "formerly a medicine man, but now a Shaker living on the Warm Springs Reservation."[34]

Bennett, Peter (1820c–88c), Columbia River Chinook	Name: Diyalakh /di-ya-LAH/ (diyaláx)*[35]
Alias: Columbia Peter[36]	Allotment: None known by author
Mother: Unknown to author	Father: Unknown to author

Peter Bennett (Diyalakh) spoke the language of the Gigwalat tribe like **Henry Wallace** and Henry's mother, **Lillie Wallace** (Kalloka).[37]

In 1872, Peter was with his sons, Peter (1865c) and Michal (1868c). He was also the father of two other sons called **Frank Bennett** (Khalawilha) and **John Bennett** (Gista).[38] In 1877, the family had a little place about a half mile from the Tualatin sub-chief, **Dave Yachkawa.** By 1886, Peter and his wife, Yum-zillis, were living alone and reportedly "very poor." Two years later, Yum-zillis was listed as a widow.

Big Silley (1842c)	Native Name: None known by author
Alias: None known by author	Allotment: None known by author
Mother: Unknown to author	Father: Unknown to author

In 1885, Silley was a widow with son, John (1866c), daughter, Eliza (1868c), and mother, Mariah (1825c). The family does not appear to be listed on any GRIC after this year.

---

31 Jacobs, Field Notebook 60, *Texts and Ethnology*, 144.
32 1887 GRIC: John Bennett's Indian name as "Gista."
33 *Heirs of Deceased Indians*, Allotment Record 114.
34 Jacobs, Field Notebook 60, *Texts and Ethnology*, 144.
35 Ibid., 124.
36 1872 GRIC: "Peter Bennett" aka "Columbia Peter" under the Clackamas. Albert S. Gatschet, *Texts, Sentences and Vocables*, 371: "Columbia Pete, Tialax, ½ miles from Dave."
37 Jacobs, Notebooks 67, *Texts Ethnology Clackamas & Jargon*, 134.
38 Jacobs, Field Notebook 60, *Texts and Ethnology*, 124.

Bill, Alsea (1826c–1905), Mary's River band of Kalapuya, Alsea	Native Name: Kama /KAma/ (ka'ma)*[39]
Alias: None known by author	Allotment 14
Mother: Unknown to author	Father: Unknown to author

Alsea Bill (Kama) was married to Sarah (1845c–92). They had at least six children: Mary "Mollie" (1974c), James (1876c), Marianne "Jane" (1880), Henry (1882c), Dan (1884c), and **Frederick Bill**. When Frederick was baptized, his god-parents were listed as **William Hartless** (Futi) and **Christine Petite**.[40]

In 1886, Alsea Bill was with his wife, Sarah, his daughter Mary and his son Dan. The family home was described by the agent as a hut and barn on twenty fenced acres with a garden, two horses, and some chickens.

After Sarah died, Alsea Bill married **Callo Bonaparte** (Kalukh)'s widow, **Mary Ann Kellogg** (Wilalakiya), on August 11, 1896.[41]

Alsea Bill received a forty-acre allotment and inherited his deceased son Frederick's forty acres on November 19, 1903. Mary Ann died in 1904. Alsea Bill died a year later on January 4, 1905, leaving personal assets valued at a little over two hundred dollars.

Several people filed claims on his estate and still more people filed affidavits on their behalf. Four Mary's River Kalapuya descendants—**William Hartless** (Futi), **Mary Ann Voutrin, Eliza George** (Tmulhu), and **Joseph Corner Mitch-elle**—claimed Alsea Bill was their uncle.[42] Charles and James Blacketer said they were sons of his sister, Sally Ann, and as such, also related.

Sarah Jackson and Mary Wilbur of Siletz both supported the Blacketer broth-er's claim. Sarah Jackson said she had known Alsea Bill since he was a child. He and his sister, Sally Ann Blacketer, were first moved from the Alsea valley to the Siletz Reservation where they remained a few years and then went to Grand Ronde Reservation to live.[43]

Mary Wilbur, being duly sworn, testified that she was raised with Alsea Bill and knew him as the brother of Sally Ann Blacketer. Further, she said she had known Sally's two sons, Charles and James Blacketer, for the past ten years. During that time, she understood through the family that they were the only living heirs of their mother, Sally Ann Blacketer, and their uncle, Alsea Bill.[44]

39 1887 GRIC: listed Alsea Bill's Indian name as "Ca-maw." Jacobs, Field Notebook 36, *Santiam Kalapuya Text*, 192: "kama, name of pinefu man (possibly Alsea though since he was half Alsea)."

40 Munnick and Beckham, Catholic *Church Records—Grand Ronde*, Register I, p. 117, B-32, Register II, p. 31, B-23, p. 57, S-16.

41 Ibid., Reg. II, p. 107, M-1.

42 O. Applegate, Testimony of Joe Corner-Michelle, Dave Leno, Frank Quinel, and Mary Ann Voutrin.

43 Oregon State Archives, Salem, Oregon, 1905, Polk County, Estate File 0925, Alsea Bill.

44 Ibid.

Louise Selkeah, wife of the Yamhill Kalapuya sub-chief, **Peter Selkya,** being duly sworn, said that she knew Sally Ann Blacketer "before she was married to a white man" and had known Charles and James Blacketer since they were small children. She said she had heard Alsea Bill say that Charles and James Blacketer were his nephews. Louise Selkeah insisted that William Hartless (Futi) was of an entirely different tribe and of a different family, and not related to Alsea Bill in any manner.[45]

The court found, "from due proofs presented, and by agreement of all claimants," that the heirs-at-law were: William Hartless (Futi), Eliza George (Tmulhu), James Blacketer, and Charles Blacketer. All four parties in open court consented to the findings of the court and agreed to accept equal shares of the remaining $176.75 from Alsea Bill (Kama)'s personal estate.[46] As far as his real property, only Charles and James Blacketer inherited equal shares of Alsea Bill's land allotment. The government, through Andrew Kershaw, did not acknowledge any other heirs.[47]

Bill, Frederick (1890c–92c), Mary's River band of Kalapuya, Alsea	Native Name: None known by author
Alias: None known by author	Allotment 15
Mother: Unknown to author	Father: Alsea Bill, Mary's River, Alsea

Little Frederick Bill received a forty-acre allotment. His heir was his father, **Alsea Bill** (Kama), who sold it to John Eborall on November 19, 1903.

Black, Mary, Molalla	Native Name: None known by author
Alias: None known by author	Allotment: None known by author
Mother: Unknown to author	Father: Unknown to author

In 1872, Mary was living with **Wallen Kilmonie** (Kílmanukh)'s family.

Bob, Joseph (1820c–61), Rogue River/Shasta[48]	Native Name: None known by author
Alias: None known by author	Allotment: None known by author
Mother: Unknown to author	Father: Unknown to author

Joseph Bob became "grievously ill" in December 1860. He died March 11, 1861.[49]

---

45 Ibid.
46 Ibid.
47 *Heirs of Deceased Indians*, Allotment Record 14.
48 Munnick and Beckham, Catholic *Church Records—Grand Ronde*, Register I, p. 7, B-39, p. 9, S-15.
49 Ibid.

Bob, Leslie (1886c–1913), Nestucca/Nehalem Band of Tillamook	Native Name: None known by author
Alias: Leslie Bobb	Allotment 17
Mother: Rosalia	Father: Levi Bob, Tillamook

Bob, Levi (1859–89), Nestucca/Nehalem Band of Tillamook	Native Name: None known by author
Alias: Levi Nestucka, Levi Nestuc, Levi Bobb, Levy Bob	Allotment 16
Mother: Sallie	Father: Tillamook Bob aka Nestucka Bob

Levi Bob was the son of Tillamook Bob (1806c–56c), who had at least three wives: Mary (1823c), Mollie (1804), and Sallie (1826c–1908). With these women, Tillamook Bob had a number of sons including Charlie, Carl, Dick, Peter, and Levi.[50]

In 1875, the Nestucca were removed from their original home country to the south side of the Salmon River. The Salmon River people who had always made their home on the north side of the river were also removed to the south side of the river. In 1878, Nestucca Bob's family became famous through an event that occurred on the new Salmon River Reserve.

During this time, Levi Bob and his brothers were ranching cattle. They had been hired by other farmers to pasture their cattle as well. Business was good and they were in charge of a large herd when two of their steers were driven off by the Dodson brothers, two neighboring white ranchers. The Dodsons claimed a tract of grazing land just north of the newly established Salmon River Reserve. For a number of months, the Indians had been filing complains against them for encroaching upon their land, but the agent had failed to investigate. On this particular occasion, a party of Salmon River men including Levi Bob caught up with the Dodson brothers and demanded the steers back. A quarrel followed, and one of the white men shot and killed one of Levi Bob's brothers. After Levi shot and killed the white shooter in retaliation, the other white rancher raised his weapon, but several men in Levi's party seized both him and Levi. They told the white rancher to go, sent Levi home, and sent a messenger to let the agent know that two men had been killed and that one of them was a white man.[51]

---

50 National Archive, Seattle, 1914, Annuity Payment Roll of the Tillamook band of Tillamook Indians. McChesney, *The Rolls of Certain Indian Tribes,* 18: NRIA-S-11-276, PAC-08, bx 47, Tillamook Bobb: wife Sallie, mother of Levi.

51 Clara Foster and Justine Jones, 1878 Itemizer Newspaper Extracts, Polk County, Oregon, Fatal Affray, A White Man and an Indian Killed on Salmon River, and Homicide on Salmon River, A Correct Statement of the Affair. Cawley, Indian Journal, 18 and 105: gave the Indian shooters name as Ish-la-osh or Salmon River Charlie and the dead brother's name as Twe-ko-la. Newspaper accounts at the time

For quite some time, the Grand Ronde and Siletz Indian agents had been quarreling over who had authority on the Salmon River Reserve. Although, the question had been brought to the Commissioner of Indian Affairs, it had not been addressed. As a result, when this shooting occurred, authorities were unsure which agency should take charge of the situation and a great deal of confusion followed. Eventually the case against Levi Bob was dismissed by a grand jury in Tillamook County, but the jurisdictional issue between Siletz and Grand Ronde would continue for some time.

From Salmon River, Levi Bob moved to Grand Ronde. He had a daughter, Jennie (1882c) and a son, Leslie (1886c–1913), by his wife, Rosalie. By 1886, they had a good house and barn on the reservation.

Two years later, in 1888, Levi Bob's mother and his brother **Nestucca Peter Bob** were also living with Levi and his wife, Rosalie.

After Rosalie died, Levi married **Lucinda Metzkar** in 1891. By Lucinda, he had at least four more children: Wilson (1892c), Louis Daly (1894c–1902), Francis Wilbur (1896c), and Benedict (1898). Louis Daly's godparents were Augustin and Marianne Russie. Francis Wilbur's godparents were **Frank Quenel** and his wife, LaRose Nipissing. Benedict's godparents were Elizabeth and **Peter Menard**.[52]

Levi received a 201.27 acre allotment. His son Leslie inherited an eighty-acre allotment. Levi Bob died June 7, 1898.[53] In 1928, Levi's property was sold by his heirs, Wilson Bob, **Lucinda Metzkar, Norris Apperson,** Florence Wacheno, and Adam Wacheno.

Bob, Paul (1825c–66), Rogue River[54]	Native Name: None known by author
Alias: Paul Bobb	Allotment: None known by author
Mother: Unknown to author	Father: Unknown to author

Paul Bob became ill in December 1865. He died at Grand Ronde March 24, 1866.

Bob, Peter (1846c), Nestucca/Nehalem Band of Tillamook[55]	Native Name: None known by author
Alias: Nestucka Peter, Peter Nestuc	Allotment: None known by author

---

of the incident gave the Indian charged with the death of the white man as "Levy." Rialto Bensell, letter to the editor, June 28, 1878, *Weekly Corvallis Gazette*, Corvallis, OR, NSDP Document D177.

52 Munnick and Beckham, *Catholic Church Records —Grand Ronde*, Register II, p. 92, B-5, p. 104, B-4, p. 117, B-6. McChesney, *The Rolls of Certain Indian Tribes*, 18.

53 Munnick and Beckham, *Catholic Church Records —Grand Ronde*, Register II, p. 117, S-6.

54 Ibid., Register I, p. 42, B-118, p. 43, S-11.

55 National Archives, Seattle, Annuity Payment Roll of the Tillamook band of Tillamook Indians, 1914. There were two men with the name "Nestucka Peter" aka "Peter Bob" with the same year of birth listed on the GRIC.

| Mother: Unknown to author | Father: Nestucca Bob |
| | aka Tillamook Bob |

Peter was the son of Tillamook Bob (1806c–56c).[56] He lived with his brother, **Levi Bob,** at Grand Ronde from 1885 through 1888. It was probably this "Nestucka Peter" whose wife, Mary (1856c), was baptized in "danger of death" September 1, 1881, at Grand Ronde. **Joseph Michelle** was his sponsor at that time.[57]

Bob, Peter (1846c), Nestucca/Nehalem Band of Tillamook	Native Name: None known by author
Alias: Peter Bobb	Allotment: None known by author
Mother: Sallie	Father: Nestucka Bob aka Tillamook Bob

Peter was the son of Tillamook Bob and Sallie (1824c–1908).[58] In 1885, he was with his wife, Molly (1847c) and his children—Henry (1868c), Jones (1870c), Ellen (1874c), John (1880c), and an unnamed baby son. Peter's father was also living with his family at that time.

Boggs, Charles (1832c–95) Umpqua	Native Name: None known by author
Alias: Charley Box, Old Man Charley	Allotment 18
Mother: Old Amanda	Father: Unknown to author

In 1872, Charley Boggs and his wife, Nancy (1841c–1903) were living with **General Louis Cass** and the General's two wives, Orpha and Kentuck.

Although "very poor," Charley and Nancy Boggs had a place of their own by 1886. Besides their son, **Jimmie Boggs,** Charley's mother, Old Amanda (1806c–86c) was also living with them. Their place was described as a house and poor barn on one fenced acre with a small garden and one hog.

Over the next couple of years living conditions for Charley and Nancy slowly improved. By 1888, they had increased the number of fenced acres to twenty, expanded their small garden to a half-acre plot, and acquired several horses.

Their allotment was located just south of Nancy, widow of **Klickitat Dick Hall,** and north of **Coquille Charlie** (Nagashta), **Chief Peter McCoy** (Inchaishi), and **Dan Robinson.**[59] During this time, Dan Robinson's daughter, Clara (1892-1983) would occasionally "go down to the creek to that old lady's place," to visit her. They spoke Chinook Jargon together as Nancy Boggs could not speak English.[60]

---

56 Annuity Payment Roll of the Tillamook Band of Tillamook Indians Prepared in 1914 Under the Provision of the Act of August 24, 1912 (37 Stat. L., 519-535).
57 Munnick and Beckham, *Catholic Church Records—Grand Ronde,* Register I, p. 119, B-13.
58 Ibid.
59 Original Blueprint of Reservation Allotments.
60 Zenk, *Chinook Jargon,* 267.

Clara, daughter of Dan Robinson and Felicite Menard.

After Charley became seriously ill in early February 1895, Father Croquet baptized him at home. Charley died a month later.[61] Nancy Boggs spent the remainder of her life on the old place. When she died, **Solomon Riggs** (Gunconnacli) was her closest living heir.

Boggs, James (1871c–99c), Umpqua	Native Name: None known by author
Alias: Jimmie Box	Allotment 20
Mother: Nancy	Father: Charley Boggs

Solomon Riggs (Gunconnacli) inherited James Boggs's eighty-acre allotment. He sold it to W. N. Jones in 1906.

Boggs, Nancy (1841c–1903c), Umpqua	Native Name: None known by author
Alias: Charley Box, Old Man Charley	Allotment 19
Mother: Unknown to author	Father: Unknown to author

---

61 Munnick and Beckham, Catholic *Church Records—Grand Ronde*, Register II, p. 100, S-4.

After Nancy died, **Solomon Riggs** (Gunconnacli) sold all 120 acres of her allotment property to W. N. Jones in 1906.

Bogus, Chief Charley (1823c–63), Umpqua	Native Name: None known by author
Alias: None known by author	Allotment: None known by author
Mother: Unknown to author	Father: Unknown to author

Along with his brother, **Winchester Jo,** Chief Charley Bogus was one of the headmen of the Confederated Bands of the Umpqua.[62] He was the fourth signer on the Umpqua Treaty of November 11, 1854, after **Chief Louis Napesa, Chief Peter McCoy** (Inchaishi), and **General Jackson.**[63]

Charley Bogus had five children by his wife, Mary: William (1855c–1919), John (1859c), Callixte (1860c), Michel (1861c–63), and Norbert (1862c).[64]

On August 9, 1863, Charley Bogus died and was buried at Grand Ronde.[65] By 1872, his widow, Mary, and sons **William Warren** and **John Warren** were living with Chief Jo's son, **Winchester Jo.**[66] William and John were listed as Winchester Jo's cousins. Their mother, Mary Bogus, was listed as Winchester Jo's aunt.

Bonaparte, Callo (1829c–94), Tualatin band of Kalapuya[67]	Native Name: Kalukh /KA-luh/ (qálux)*[68]
Alias: Bonaparte Kellogg	Allotment 21
Mother: Unknown to author	Father: Unknown to author

Bonaparte (Kalukh) and his sister, Nancy, were related to **James Shiliqua** (Shilikwa), **John Pratt** (Gwaimit), **William Wishikin, Antoine Metzgar** (Tamulch), and **Henry Wallace**'s mother, **Lillie Wallace** (Kalloka).[69]

---

62 Affidavit from Martha Johnson taken in Lincoln County, Oregon, dated March 1, 1952: Martha Johnson was a full blood Indian over ninety years of age who had lived on the Oregon coast all her life. She said, "…John Warren's father was Bogus, a Chief of the Confederated Bands of the Umpqua Tribes of Indians" and that she was acquainted with a man named Jo, "also known as Winchester Jo who was an uncle of John Warren's and who was also a chief of the Confederated Bands of the Umpqua Tribe of Indians."

63 Kappler, Treaty with the Umpqua and Kalapuya, 1854.

64 Munnick and Beckham, *Catholic Church Records—Grand Ronde,* Register I, p. 7, B-7, B-8, p. 18, B-30, B-31, p. 19, B-32, p. 23, B-88, p. 29, S-35.

65 Ibid., Register I, p. 27, B-29, S-30.

66 Ibid., Register I, p. 26, S-23: Winchester Jo's father was probably the "Umpqua Chief Tyee Jo" that died May 27, 1863 and was buried in the presence of the Umpqua Chiefs, Louis Napesa and Peter McCoy.

67 Jacobs, Field Notebook 55, *Texts and Ethnology,* 192: his tribe was given as Tualatin.

68 Ibid., 120.

69 Oregon State Archive, Salem Oregon, 1909, Yamhill County, Estate File 1327.

Bonaparte had a number of wives. One of his wives, Susanne of the Rogue River nation, was baptized February 17, 1862. At that time, Susanne was very ill.[70] On October 23, 1881, Martha, another wife of Bonaparte, died and was buried at Grand Ronde.[71] On November 15, 1884, Bonaparte married a woman named **Mary Ann Kellogg** (Wilalakiya) in the presence of **Jacob Taylor** and Melanie Winslow.[72]

In 1885, in addition to his new wife, Bonaparte's sister, "Old Nancy (1833c)" was living with him. They had two huts on twenty fenced acres with two small gardens and three and a half acres in cultivation.

From 1888 through 1893, both Bonaparte and Mary Ann were listed under the surname of Kellogg. In 1894, Mary Ann was listed as a widow. Father Croquet documented the specific date in church records. January 6, 1894, he wrote, "Bonaparte, of this place, died aged more than 70 years; his body was buried here the next day."[73]

Bonaparte received a trust patent on a 280-acre allotment in 1891. Allotment records show that Bonaparte's heir, **Alsea Bill** (Kama), sold forty acres of it in 1904. Charles and James Blacketer inherited the remaining acreage in 1916.

Bond, Frank (1857c–1922), Yamhill band of Kalapuya	Native Name: None known by author
Alias: Frank Barnes	Allotment 12
Mother: Margaret Lapan	Father: Unknown to author

Frank Bond was married to Pauline Shadden in 1876. After she died on June 23, 1878, he married Jenny White on March 22, 1879. Frank had at least three children: Betty (1876c), Henry (1878c), and Louise (1881c–85). Betty and Henry were with him in 1885, but by 1886, he and his mother, **Margaret Lapan** (Chalwina), were living alone in a hut on twenty fenced acres with a small garden and six cultivated acres. In addition, they were cultivating five acres on a second twenty-acre plot of land and had accumulated three horses, six hogs, a wagon, and several harnesses.

A short time later, he married Angelica Wheeler. After Angelica, he married **Adeline Ann Hutchins** in 1888.[74] Some people said that his wife Adeline Ann behaved badly because she had she-dog power. "She would rather go with men than eat."[75] She was killed on November 21, 1907; eight days later, on November 29, Frank married **Chief Halo** (Hilu)'s granddaughter, Laura Fern.[76]

---

70 Munnick and Beckham, *Catholic Church Records—Grand Ronde,* Register I, p. 17, B-9.

71 Ibid., Register I, p. 119, S-10.

72 Ibid., Register I, p. 128, M-3.

73 Ibid., Register II, p. 91, S-1.

74 Ibid., Register I, p. 96, M-2, p. 111, M-6, Register II, p. 49, M-7.

75 Jacobs, Field Notebook 62, *Texts and Ethnology,* n.p.

76 National Archives, Salem, Oregon, Polk County, November 29, 1907, Marriage Laura Fern to Frank Bond. Whitlow, Grand Ronde Family Register, 1901.

Frank Bond with his wife, Laura Fern. Photo courtesy of Oregon Historical Society (OHS 0054 G-015)

After receiving a 236.49 acre allotment, Frank did not sign the Surplus Land Agreement in 1901. In 1911, as the husband of the deceased Adeline Ann Hutchins and heir to Captain Santiam's estate, Frank also refused to agree to the sale of **Captain Santiam's** allotment despite protests from **Abraham Hudson.**[77]

Bope, Adrian (1833c–63), Rogue River	Native Name: None known by author
Alias: None known by author	Allotment: None known by author
Mother: Unknown to author	Father: Unknown to author

Bope was baptized September 9, 1863. He died ten days later.[78]

Bope, Peter (1843c–62), Rogue River	Native Name: None known by author
Alias: None known by author	Allotment: None known by author
Mother: Unknown to author	Father: Unknown to author

Peter was baptized December 30, 1861. He died in early January.[79]

Bourgeau, Helen (1839c–69), Chinook, French Canadian	Native Name: None known by author

---

77 Letter to Knott C. Egbert, Superintendent & S. D. A., Siletz, Oregon from #811 Yeon Bldg, Portland, Oregon, December 30, 1911.

78 Munnick and Beckham, Catholic *Church Records — Grand Ronde,* Register I, p. 29, S-34

79 Ibid., Register I, p. 16, S-1.

Alias: Helen Lacourse	Allotment: None known by author
Mother: Josette Chinook	Father: Sylvain Bourgeau, French Canadian

Helen Bourgeau married Pierre Lacourse, a former boat builder for the Hudson Bay Company, on December 29, 1856, in the Catholic Church at St. Paul. Theodore Gervais and Jean Baptiste Bourgeau, Helen's half brother, witnessed the ceremony.[80]

Helen and Pierre Lacourse had several children including Moise, baptized November 30, 1857, Domitille, baptized July 22, 1860, and a son, Dolphisse, baptized June 7, 1863.

Moise's godparents were Louis Bergevin and his wife, Magdeline Servant. It is said that Bergevin was a prosperous man, generous with his neighbors and kindly disposed.[81]

Domitille's godparents were Jean Baptiste Bourgeau and his wife, Genevieve Martineau. Dolphisse's godparents were Helen's half sister, Madeleine Bourgeau, and **Pierre Menard.**[82]

Pierre Menard, **Charlie Petite,** and others were present when Helen was buried at Grand Ronde on May 10, 1869.

Bozarris, Marco (1861c–69)	Native Name: None known by author
Alias: None known by author	Allotment: None known by author
Mother: Unknown to author	Father: Unknown to author

Marco was a student at the manual labor school on the Grand Ronde Indian Reservation. July 30, 1869, in his annual report, Marco's teacher, W. R. Dunbar wrote:

There have been two deaths among the scholars since I took charge (1st of June last), Marco Bozarris, age eight years, died July 11, of the brain fever. **Catherine Campbell,** aged eleven years, died July 28, of continued fever. They were both good and smart children and were esteemed very highly by all the agency people.[83]

Brous, James (1832c), Shasta[84]	Native Name: None known by author
Alias: None known by author	Allotment: None known by author

---

80 Ibid., Register I, p. 57, S-8. Munnick and Warner, *Catholic Church Records—St. Paul*, 82, A-12.

81 Ibid.

82 Munnick and Warner, *Catholic Church Records—St. Paul*, 90, 108, 137.

83 *Annual Report Commissioner of Indian Affairs*, 169.

84 Gatschet, *Texts, Sentences and Vocables*, 364: under Shasta at Grand Ronde, "Jim Brous, abt. 45 y."

Mother: Unknown to author	Father: Unknown to author

In 1875, Father Croquet baptized three of James's children by his wife, Emeline: Abraham (1870c), John (1873c), and Elisa, who was only a few weeks old. On December 4 of that year, James and Emeline buried their daughter, Elisa. July 8, 1877, they buried their son Abraham.[85] No further information for the family can be found.

Brown, Charles, Santiam band of Kalapuya	Native Name: None known by author
Alias: None known by author	Allotment: None known by author
Mother: Unknown to author	Father: Unknown to author

In 1872, Charles Brown was living with French Prairie **Joe Howard** (Waimish) and his wife, **Mary Hutchins.**

Brown, Louis (1861c)	Native Name: None known by author
Alias: None known by author	Allotment: None known by author
Mother: Unknown to author	Father: Unknown to author

In 1886, Louis Brown was with his wife, Minnie (1858c), and daughter, Pollie (1872c). The Indian agent noted that the family was "poor." They were not listed on any GRIC after this year.

Brown, John (1815c–88), Umpqua	Native Name: None known by author
Alias: None known by author	Allotment: None known by author
Mother: Unknown to author	Father: Unknown to author

In 1878, the Grand Ronde Indian Legislature passed a provision of law that made John Brown and a few other aging men exempt from working on the reservation road system. However, they were still required to pay the road tax.[86]

In 1888, John and his wife, **Mary Brown,** were living in a hut on twenty fenced acres next to **Winchester Jo.** John Brown died on August 6 that same year.[87]

Brown, Mary (1814c–90), Umpqua	Native Name: None known by author
Alias: None known by author	Allotment 22

85   Munnick and Beckham, *Catholic Church Records—Grand Ronde,* Register I, p. 95, S-27, p. 102, S-16.

86   National Archives, Seattle, Grand Ronde/Siletz, Land and Enrollment Program records, Field Notes and Land Survey 1875–1898, Land Description Book 1878, Box 115; Grand Ronde Justice Court.

87   Munnick and Beckham, Catholic *Church Records—Grand Ronde,* Register II, p. 45, B-36, p. 46, S-17.

Mother: Unknown to author	Father: Unknown to author

Mary was the wife of **John Brown** of Umpqua. She received a 120-acre allotment. Mary's heirs were **John** and **William Warren.** In 1905, the Warren brothers sold eighty acres of Mary Brown's property to W. J. Jones.

Brown, William, Calapooia band of Kalapuya	Native Name: None known by author
Alias: None known by author	Allotment: None known by author
Mother: Unknown to author	Father: Unknown to author

In 1872, William Brown was with his wife and daughter, Mary.

Bruce, James, Shasta	Native Name: None known by author
Alias: Jim Bruce	Allotment: None known by author
Mother: Unknown to author	Father: Unknown to author

In 1872, James Bruce and his wife Emily were listed under the Rogue River/Shasta with their two sons, Bernard (1869c) and Ben Butler (1854c).

On January 4, 1876, when the Fifth Annual Session of the Grand Ronde Indian Legislature convened, James Bruce was elected along with **Jack Long** to represent the Shasta. James was also appointed Court Administrator for that year along with **Chief Louis Napesa.**[88]

Buck, Charles, Molalla	Native Name: None known by author
Alias: None known by author	Allotment: None known by author
Mother: Unknown to author	Father: Unknown to author

In 1872, Charles Buck was living alone. He was not listed in any GRIC after that year.

---

88 National Archives, Seattle, Grand Ronde/Siletz, Land and Enrollment Program records, Field Notes and Land Survey 1875–1898, Land Description Book 1878, Box 115; Grand Ronde Justice Court.

C

Cambers, Ann, Rogue River/Shasta	Native Name: None known by author
Alias: None known by author	Allotment: None known by author
Mother: Unknown to author	Father: Unknown to author

In 1872, Ann Cambers was living with the widow **Kitty Chikate** and Kitty's aunt.

Campbell, Catherine (1858c–69)	Native Name: None known by author
Alias: None known by author	Allotment: None known by author
Mother: Unknown to author	Father: Unknown to author

Catherine was a student at the manual labor school. She died July 28, 1869, of a "continued fever." On July 30, the teacher, W. R. Dunbar, acknowledged her death in his annual report. He wrote that Catherine was a good and smart child who was held in high esteem by all the agency people.[1]

Campbell, William (1869c–84), Santiam band of Kalapuya	Native Name: None known by author
Alias: Santiam Bill	Allotment: None known by author
Mother: Unknown to author	Father: Unknown to author

In 1872, Bill Campbell was living with **Captain Santiam.** He was still alive in 1877 when the Swiss ethnologist Albert Gatschet visited Grand Ronde. Father Croquet wrote in church records that "William Cammel," twenty-five years old, died April 2, 1884, and was buried at Grand Ronde the next day.

Carey, Ellen (1858c–78), Santiam band of Kalapuya	Native Name: None known by author
Alias: None known by author	Allotment: None known by author
Mother: Unknown to author	Father: Unknown to author

Ellen Carey was the niece of **Peter Carey.**[2] **She married John Davis** of the Rogue River Tribe on September 1, 1875. Witnessing the ceremony were Joseph Tole and **Elizabeth Petite.** After John Davis died, Ellen married **James Matheney**

---

1 *Annual Report Commissioner of Indian Affairs*, 169.
2 1872 GRIC.

on January 22, 1878. Ellen died in September of 1878 at age twenty.[3]

Carey, Peter (d. before 1877), Santiam band of Kalapuya	Native Name: None known by author
Alias: Cultus Peter, Peter Kerry[4]	Allotment: None known by author
Mother: Unknown to author	Father: Unknown to author

In 1872, Peter Carey and his wife, Lucy, were listed with their children: Susan (1857c), Monroe (1867c–73c), and Joseph (1864c–78). A nephew, Frank Henry (1857c–83), and a niece, **Ellen Carey** (1858c–78), were also living with the family at that time.

Carpenter, Mary, Rogue River/Shasta	Native Name: None known by author
Alias: None known by author	Allotment: None known by author
Mother: Unknown to author	Father: Unknown to author

In 1872, Mary and her son, Chas were with the Rogue River/Shasta. The Indian agent also noted that Mary was a relative of **Old Ben Riley.**

Cass, Louis (1815c–86c), Umpqua	Native Name: None known by author
Alias: General Cass	Allotment: None known by author
Mother: Unknown to author	Father: Unknown to author

In 1872, Louis Cass was living with his hayash wife, Orpha, and his second wife, Kentuck. **Charley Boggs** and his wife, Nancy, were also living with them at that time.

In 1885, Louis Cass (1815c) was living with his wife, Judith (1825c), and "his sister," the Widow Cass (1845c). Neither wife, Orpha or Kentuck was mentioned.

Chagwinim, Clackamas	Native Name: Chagwinim /CHAG-we- nem/ (cháġwnəm) ["wart, growth"]*[5]
Alias: None known by author	Allotment: None known by author
Mother: Unknown to author	Father: Unknown to author

No information has been found to identify Chagwinim by her English name, but **Victoria Wishikin** (Kinishi), who was born at Grand Ronde around 1865,

---

3 Munnick and Beckham, *Catholic Church Records—Grand Ronde*, Register I, p. 80, B-9, p. 94, M-8, p. 106, M-2.

4 1872 GRIC: "Peter Carey" aka "Cultus Peter" under the Santiam. Gatschet, *Texts, Sentences and Vocables*, 368: under the Santiam as "Peter Kerry, perhaps dead now." Johnson and Zenk, *Chinuk Wawa*, 196: Kultas, a word meaning "worthless."

5 Jacobs, Field Notebook 59, *Texts and Ethnology*, 116: Clackamas meaning.

described her as a powerful woman doctor with some sort of growth on her face.

Prior to relocating to the reservation, Chagwinim was the doctor who almost killed **Chief Daniel Wacheno** (Wachinu) by sending her poison spirit arrow into him.[6]

In those days, women doctors were not like ordinary women. Then, if a woman doctor wanted a man, they would just buy him. Chagwinim would take a boy to be her husband and invariably he would die or leave her. Even knowing that a union with her was bad, parents could not prevent her from buying their sons because they were afraid of her. Even if they already had marriage plans for their son, if Chagwinim wanted the boy, she got him. That was how much the people feared her.

Chamberlain, Modoc slave	Native Name: Tchimbelon /tchim-be-lon/[7]
Alias: None known by author	Allotment: None known by author
Mother: Unknown to author	Father: Unknown to author

Chamberlain was a slave owned by the Tualatin **Chief Kiakuts** (Kayakach) at the time of Kayakach's death.[8]

Chantelle, Charles (1884–1919), Luckiamute band of Kalapaya, Iroquois, French Canadian	Native Name: None known by author
Alias: None known by author	Allotment 31
Mother: Anna Amos, daughter of Bertha Wheeler, Luckiamute band of Kalapuya	Father: Sam Chantelle, French Canadian, Iroquois

Charles Chantelle received another eighty-acre allotment.[9]

Chantelle, Sam (1842c–1915), French Canadian, Iroquois[10]	Native Name: None known by author
Alias: Sam Chantel, Toussaint Chantel	Allotment 29
Mother: Marie Ann Nepissank, Iroquois	Father: Laurent Quintal aka Larou Chantelle, French Canadian

6 Jacobs, Field Notebook 52, *Texts and Ethnology*, 60. Jacobs, *Clackamas Text*, Part II, 511-512.

7 Gatschet, *Texts, Sentences and Vocables*, 94: "Tchimbelon," a Modoc, a slave to Kayakach at one time.

8 Gatschet, Frachtenberg & Jacobs, *Kalapuya Texts*, Part 3, 160–73.

9 *Heirs of Deceased Indians*, Allotment Records 31.

10 Munnick and Beckham, Catholic *Church Records—Grand Ronde*, Register I, 127, M-2: Father Croquet gave Sam's name as "Toussaint Chantel."

Sam Chantelle's father, Laurent Quental, entered the fur trade in 1817 on the English River. From 1823 to 1836, he held the position of middleman for the Hudson's Bay Company in Snake Country. Then his status changed from an employee of the Hudson's Bay Company to that of an independent trader in the Columbia District.[11]

When Laurent married Chief Napesa's sister, Marie Ann in 1839, he was described in Catholic Church records as a "free man of the prairies."[12] His neighbor wrote many years later that Laurent Quintal was a French Canadian who had a native wife and lived in the early days on Calapooia Creek with his very large family. He told how Laurent had a premonition that he was going to die and was bitten by a rattlesnake that same day. According to this report, Laurent died within a few hours.[13]

Sam Chantelle was **Chief Louis Napesa**'s nephew. Although Napesa was the adopted Chief of the Umpqua, his sister, Sam's mother, was never adopted and never lived on the reservation. **James Winslow** recalled when Sam first came to Grand Ronde, how Chief Napesa went to the Indian agent on Sam's behalf and it was agreed Sam would stay as one of the Umpqua people.[14]

Sam Chantelle married Anna Amos, daughter of **Bertha Wheeler** (Tewimme), at Grand Ronde, June 23, 1884, in the presence of **Peter Lafferty** and Mary Quenel.[15] The following year, he and Anna were listed with their children, Henrietta (1878c), Mary (1880c), Paul (1884c), and new baby son.

In 1886, Sam Chantelle owned two horses, a harness, and a wagon, but by 1888, his assets had increased substantially. He had built a house and barn, fenced fifteen acres, and put in two acres of oats and a family garden.

Sam received a fee patent on a 270-acre allotment in 1907.[16] On December 18, 1914, Sam wrote his last will and testament acknowledging both his stepdaughter, Filinese LaChance, and his son, **Charles Chantelle,** as his heirs. With John T. Houck and **Fabian Quenel** acting as witnesses, Sam made Charles executor of the will.

When Sam died April 8, 1915, his total estate, including one horse, one mower, one wagon, and sixty acres of land, was valued at $1,400.[17]

---

11 Hudson's Bay Company Archives, Provincial Archives of Manitoba, Winnipeg, Biography of Larou Chantelle or Laurent Quintal.

12 Harriet D. Munnick, *Catholic Church Records of the Pacific Northwest — Vancouver and Stellamaris Mission,* St Paul.

13 Samuel Handsaker, *Pioneer Life,* Eugene, OR, 1908.

14 O. Applegate, Testimony of Captain Frank Quenelle, James Winslow, David Leno, and John Wacheno.

15 Munnick and Beckham, Catholic *Church Records — Grand Ronde,* Register I, p. 127, M-2.

16 *Heirs of Deceased Indians,* Allotment Records 29.

17 National Archives, Salem, Oregon, 1915, Yamhill County, Estate File 1789.

Charley, Charles (1823c–63) Kalapuya[18]	Native Name: None known by author
Alias: None known by author	Allotment: None known by author
Mother: Unknown to author	Father: Unknown to author

Being dangerously ill, Charles was baptized April 24, 1863. He died and was buried May 4, 1863.[19]

Charley, Coquille (1836c–91), Cow Creek band of Umpqua	Native Name: Nagashta /Na-gash-ta/[20]
Alias: Socrates, Sarcully Dummy, Charles Coquille	Allotment 33
Mother: Widow Kate	Father: Unknown to author

Coquille Charley (Nagashta) was born without ears. As a result of this deformity, he was unable to hear and could not speak. To communicate, he was forced to rely on sign language, which he learned to combine with his talent for dramatic storytelling.

Rev. Summers called him Socrates and described him as "the most perfect natural pantomimist he had ever seen." The Indian agent at Grand Ronde entered Charley on the census as "Sarcully Dummy."

Given his hearing impairment, Charley's presence off the reservation did not threaten the town citizens. Indeed, he was able to earn his living by giving mock speeches, some humorous and some solemn, wherever there was a small group of idle people.[21]

Rev. Summers described one of his enactments of a fight this way:

[…] Here there were many warriors, running to hide behind the trees; then bows were drawn and arrows flew, as one warrior after another cautiously peered out from cover. Now he would present a warrior wounded in the side and would writhe with frightful contortion of features and fall to the ground. Then, with terrible grimaces, he would pull the arrow from his side and picture either the death or the recovery of the unfortunate brave.[22]

In 1885, Charley's mother, the Widow Kate (1825c), was living with him and his wife, Rosalie. However, the following year, Charley was no longer with Ro-

---

18   Munnick and Beckham, Catholic *Church Records — Grand Ronde*, Register I, p. 25, B-24, S-18.

19   Ibid.

20   1887 GRIC listed "Sarcully Dummy" with his Indian name of "Nagashta."

21   Cawley, *Indian Journal*, 46.

22   Ibid.

salie, but had a wife named Susan (Intaternatta), who was listed as a cousin to
James Pierce (Clamarchnet).[23]

Coquille Charley and Susan lived with James Pierce and his family from time
to time over the next few years. After Charley's death, James Pierce inherited
Charley's eighty-acre allotment. James sold the property in 1904.[24]

Charley, Wasco (1839c–97c), Wasco band of Chinook	Native Name: Wataneklah /Wa-ta-ne-klah/
Alias: Wasko Charley	Allotment 24
Mother: Unknown to author	Father: Unknown to author

Wasco Charley (Wataneklah) married **Mary Holmes** (Pusak), the half sister
of **David Holmes.** He received a 240-acre allotment. A trust patent was issued to
Abram Charlie, his son by Mary Holmes. Mary Holmes sold the property to J. T.
Lady on May 17, 1904.

Checkaon, Peter (1831c–1907), Yamhill band of Kalapuya, Tualatin band of Kalapuya25	Native Name(s): Chikhyan /CHIH-yan/ (chíxyan]),* Shapnana /SHAP-na-na/ (shápnana),* Sepina /SE-pi-na/ (sépina)*26
Alias: Tualatin Peter, Wapato Peter, Chickeau, Cheekee, Chekean, Chickee, Chickeen, Peter Chikeet	Allotment 25
Mother: Unknown to author	Father: Unknown to author

Peter Checkaon (Chikhyan) was a brother or half brother of **Margaret Lapan**
(Chalwina), who was the widow of **Charley Lapan, Tom Hutchins** (Liham), and
William Miller (Quilinick) consecutively. Margaret called Peter *naika au* in Chi-
nook Jargon meaning "my brother."[27]

Chikhyan was elected three times to serve on the Grand Ronde Indian Legislature. In 1876, he and **John Pratt** (Gwaimit) were elected by the Wapato Lake
band to represent their interests. In 1878 and again in 1880, he was elected by
popular vote to represent the interest of the people living in the west precinct of

23 1872 GRIC: Susan was listed as a cousin to Jim Pearce and living with his family.
    Coquille Charlie was listed separately. 1887 GRIC: "Susan Dummy" with the Indian
    name "Inta-ter-natta."

24 *Heirs of Deceased Indians*, Allotment Record 33: "Sarcully Dummy" aka "Coquille
    Charlie."

25 Jacobs, Field Notebook 36, *Santiam Kalapuya Text*, 192.

26 Gatschet, *Texts, Sentences and Vocables*, 77, gives name as "tchexian, mase. tcixyan."
    Jacobs, Field Notebook 51, *Music and Ethnology*, 49, gives another name as capnana.
    Jacobs, Field Notebook 36, *Santiam Kalapuya Text*, 192: sepina listed as a third native
    name.

27 Jacobs, Field Notebook 51, *Music and Ethnology*, 49.

the reservation. In 1878, he paid the Grand Ronde Indian Court six dollars for a license to also practice law.[28] Albert Gatschet described Chikhyan as "a justice in a skin coat."[29]

Chikhyan was married at least three times. Around 1867, he had a son, Enos, by his first wife, **Susan Cheekee** (Pukhwani).[30] After Susan's death, he married Marianne (Bochean), the widow of **Sugar Monroe,** on May 27, 1874. Father Croquet noted in church records that the parties had been "dispensed from the impediment of Disparitatis Cultus by a special faculty received from the Archbishop."[31]

About two years after Chikhyan married Marianne, Rev. Summers visited them at Grand Ronde. In his journal, Rev. Summers described the interior of Chikhyan's home:

> ... a deep fire-place filled a third of one end of the one room. Along one side and across the opposite end stood a row of kegs, sacks and flour-barrels, filled with roots and seeds of savage diet and with meal and flour such as we use. A boy of a year old tumbled about the floor with infant unconsciousness whether he was black, white or copper colored. His proud young mother hastened to offer chairs for us to sit down on: one was an armchair with one arm broken and one rocker absent; the others were sections of tree-trunks.[32]

Determined to acquire an ancient bowl that he saw hanging from the wall, Rev. Summers visited with Marianne (Bochean) while waiting for Chikhyan to return home.[33] After Chikhyan arrived, Summers called his attention to the bowl and explained his reason for wanting to buy it. Summers reminded Chikhyan that Indian people kept no records. Very soon, he said, all the original work of native people would be scattered or destroyed. He told Chikhyan it was his intention to set the bowl upon a shelf with all his other Indian relics so that long after the two of them were in the land of the spirits students might come and read the story of his people.

Chikhyan said:

> I see what you mean. I have not intended to part with it but to keep it as

---

28 National Archives, Seattle, Grand Ronde/Siletz, Land and Enrollment Program records, Field Notes and Land Survey 1875–1898, Land Description Book 1878, Box 115; Grand Ronde Justice Court.

29 Gatshet, *Texts, Sentences, & Vocables*, 29.

30 Jacobs, Field Notebook 51, *Music and Ethnology*, 49: Chikhyan married wife number one, Pukhwani, maybe Yamhill name; Eustace Howard's mother's aunt was named Sarah.

31 Munnick and Beckham, Catholic *Church Records—Grand Ronde*, Register I, p. 87, M-6.

32 Cawley, *Indian Journal*, 22.

33 Ibid., 33.

a curious thing while I lived. I meant to show it to younger Indians as an example of what we once used, and then leave it to my little boy. But more people will see it if you have it than if I give it to him, so you may have it. Tell me what you will pay and then I will tell you what I gave for it.[34]

Peter and Marianne's son, Augustin, was born April 25, 1875. He died July 4, 1883.[35]

After his mother Marianne died, Chikhyan married the Hutchins brothers' sister, Sarah Hutchins, on January 19, 1892, in the presence of Edward Lamson, William Miller, and Margaret Lapan. Sarah died January 15, 1895.[36]

Chikhyan received a 238.40-acre allotment at Grand Ronde and exchanged eighty acres of it with **John B. Hutchins** for 160 acres. Consequently, Chikhyan received a fee patent on 318.40 acres in 1901. He was one of the men who did not sign the Surplus Land Agreement made that same year.

Peter Chikhyan had dead people power. **Victoria Wishikin** (Kinishi) sang several of his power songs for Melville Jacobs. They were recorded in 1929.[37]

Cheekee, Susan (d. 1874c)	Native Name: Pukhwani /PUH-wa-ni/ (púx̣wani)*[38]
Alias: None known by author	Allotment: None known by author
Mother: Sarah[39]	Father: Unknown to author

Susan (Pukhwani) was married to **Peter Chikhyan.** Around 1867, Susan and Peter had a son, Enos. They were listed with him on the 1872 GRIC.

Chikate, Kitty, Rogue River/Shasta	Native Name: None known by author
Alias: None known by author	Allotment: None known by author
Mother: Unknown to author	Father: Unknown to author

In 1872, Kitty was a widow with her aunt, Lucy, and a woman named **Ann Cambers.** Kitty was probably the wife of Rogue River James Chikate, who died March 27, 1872.[40]

---

34 Ibid., 33. Chikhyan's bowl is currently in a warehouse owned by the British Museum; it has been there for over a hundred years.

35 Munnick and Beckham, Catholic *Church Records—Grand Ronde*, Register I, p. 93, B-15, p. 124, S-8.

36 Ibid., Register II, p. 75, M-1, p. 98, S-1.

37 Ibid.

38 Jacobs, Field Notebook 51, *Music and Ethnology*, 49: Chikhyan married wife number one, Pukhwani (maybe Yamhill name).

39 1872 GRIC.

40 Munnick and Beckham, Catholic *Church Records—Grand Ronde*, Register I, p. 73, B-14, S-7.

Chilivis, James (1812–82), Molalla, Klamath	Native Name: None known by author
Alias: Klamath Jim	Allotment: None known by author
Mother: Unknown to author	Father: Unknown to author

In 1872, James Chilivis, also known as "Klamath Jim," was listed under the Molalla with his wife, Dolly, and an old woman named Sarah. He was listed as "Chilvis, Molala" when he surrendered "one fort gun" to the Indian agent at Grand Ronde in 1856.[41]

Mary Ann Michelle wrote, "Jim Chilws, his wife all tattooed up to her eyes."[42] On June 7, 1880, Father Croquet recorded that "Klamat James' wife," had been buried.[43]

Rev. Summers, a frequent visitor at Grand Ronde between 1873 and 1881, recalled meeting a Klamath man named "Chilivis" who had a stone pipe that Rev. Summers thought was a good example of Klamath work.[44]

Chilowish, Ben (1835c)	Native Name: None known by author
Alias: None known by author	Allotment: None known by author
Mother: Old Edna	Father: Unknown to author

In 1885, Ben was listed with wife, Judie (1838c), and two sons, Eddie (1868c) and Ben (1870c). His mother, "Old Ena (1825c)," was also living with the family.

Chokote, Yamhill band of Kalapuya	Native Name: None known by author
Alias: Doctor Chokote	Allotment: None known by author
Mother: Unknown to author	Father: Unknown to author

Chokote had a son, Charles (1853c), who, being sick, was baptized on January 17, 1861. Father Croquet wrote that the boy was the son of a man the people commonly called a "vulgo doctor."[45]

In 1872, Chokote was listed alone. However, on one of Rev. Summers's visits to Grand Ronde between 1873 and 1881, Summers mentioned meeting "a Yamhill Indian" who was "the son of Chokote the witch doctor." This Yamhill man was very likely Chokote's son, Charles.

Summers wrote that the young man showed him how to use a large black pestle with a knob at the pointed end that corresponded to the handle. This kind, the young man said, "was often hung from a supple tree limb in the way that the white man hangs his water bucket and used as a pounder." He explained further

41　*List of Guns Turned in by Indians 6th April, 1856,* National Archives, Washington, DC.
42　Michelle, *Just a Memorandum,* 4.
43　Munnick and Beckham, Catholic *Church Records—Grand Ronde,* Register I, p. 115, S-7.
44　Cawley, *Indian Journal,* 22, 102.
45　Munnick and Beckham, Catholic *Church Records—Grand Ronde,* Register I, p. 7, B-5.

how his mother used it to crush a variety of things in her baskets. Once in a while, he said she used it for finer grinding by setting it in a mortar and grinding seeds by hand using a circular motion.[46]

Churchill, Tom (1809–1900c), Yoncalla band of Kalapuya, Mary's River band of Kalapuya[47]	Native Name: Kaltas Lipom /KAL-tasli-POM/ (kəltəs–lipóm) ["bad apple"].* [48] Chacheclue /Cha-che-clue/
Alias: Muddy Tom, Muddy Fern	Allotment 23
Mother: Unknown to author	Father: Unknown to author

Muddy Tom (Kaltas Lipom) belonged to the Fern family. **Chief Halo** (Hilu) was his brother or half brother. Halo's son **Jake Fern** testified that his Uncle Tom went to the signing of the Treaty at Calapooia Creek with his father and the medicine man, **Polk Scott** (Puk). It was his Uncle Tom who signed for the Yoncalla.[49] The treaty itself supports Jake Fern's testimony because the last name on the Yoncalla Treaty signed November 29, 1854, was that of "Tom (Chacheclue)." Neither Chief Halo nor Polk Scott (Puk)'s name appears there.[50] The fact that Tom signed the treaty in place of his brother, the official Yoncalla chief, may have earned him the name "Kaltas Lipom" or bad apple.

In 1872, Muddy Tom, his wife, Betsy (1814c–1900c), and their fourteen-year-old son, Alexander, were listed with the Mary's River band of Kalapuya. Thirteen years later, in 1885, Muddy Tom Churchill was listed with his wife, Betsy, his sister, Sallie (1825c), and his brother, "Old Blind Ben" (1820c). Ben's daughter, Mary Pete (1864c), and his son, Henry Pete (1868c), were also listed with the family.

In 1886, only Muddy Tom's brother, **Blind Ben Pete** (Lamptumpif), was still living with him and his wife, Betsy. They lived in a hut with a poor shed on forty fenced acres, of which about twenty acres were in cultivation, and a small garden, two horses, and some chickens. Blind Ben was not listed with them after 1886.

Muddy Tom and Betsy were together through 1900. Apparently Muddy Tom and Betsy died around the same time as she is not listed as an heir to his personal

---

46 Cawley, *Indian Journal*, 102.
47 Jacobs, Field Notebook 46, *Santiam Kalapuya Text*, n.p., Tom Churchill was part "Pinefu" and perhaps part "Pe-ena." The Pe-ena was a tribe of the Yoncalla originally located just south of where the town of Yoncalla is now. Gatschet, *Texts, Sentences and Vocables*, 368: he was listed as "Kalapuya *now with the Marysville.*" 1872 GRIC: "Thomas Churchill" aka "Muddy Tom" and tribe as Mary's River band of Kalapuya. *Heirs of Deceased Indians*, Allotment Record 23: "Thomas Churchill" aka "Mudy Fern."
48 Gatschet, *Texts, Sentences and Vocables*, 368, listed him as "Old Lipom, across this [?] bridge, Old Tom, Kaltas Lepom." Johnson and Zenk, *Chinuk Wawa Dictionary*, 161: lipum meaning apple.
49 O. Applegate, Testimony of Jacob Fearn.
50 Kappler, *Treaty with the Umpqua & Kalapuya, 1854*.

estate, which was estimated as being worth somewhere between $150 and $300.

In 1901, when **Muddy Jim Stewart** placed a claim on Muddy Tom Churchill's estate, **Joseph Shanagaretta**'s daughters, Elizabeth Shangaretta-Menard and Mary Shangaretta-Michelle, contested his claim, stating they were nieces of said Thomas Churchill deceased and his only legal heirs. Further, they pointed out that Muddy James Stewart had died since putting in his claim. In addition to their own testimony, they produced **Peter Menard** and **Nancy Kenoyer** (Tunishni) as witnesses on their behalf.

The witnesses testified that Muddy Thomas Churchill, Joseph Shangaretta, Mary Shangaretta-Michelle, and Elizabeth Shangaretta-Menard "all belonged to a tribe of Indians anciently located on lands at and about the city of Corvallis in Benton County Oregon." They said that James Stewart belonged to a tribe of Willamette Valley Indians originally from the region in Oregon known as Washington County.[51]

Perhaps antagonized by the opposition, James Stewart's stepson, **Abraham Hudson,** told the court that neither Elizabeth Menard nor Mary Mitchell were related to Muddy Thomas Churchill and were not entitled to any share of his property. He also said that he had four or five witnesses including **John Warren** who would testify to this fact in court.

Andrew Kershaw, the Indian Superintendent, wrote a letter to the court, dated May 1, 1907, that settled the matter. Kershaw wrote:

> I have lived here for eighteen years, and knew Thomas Churchill and Joseph Shangaretta personally. During the time preceding the death of Churchill, I understood from both parties that Shangaretta was the only living heir of Churchill, the name of James Stewart not being mentioned in connection with Churchill until after the death of Churchill. Both Shangaretta and Churchill died during the same fiscal year, but no exact dates of either death are on file at this office. Churchill died at the house of Shangaretta.[52]

Further, Kershaw brought to the attention of the probate judges the Supreme Court decision in *McKay et al vs. Kalyton* that placed outside state jurisdiction any controversy regarding title to lands held in trust. With this in mind, Kershaw wrote that any decision the state might make in regard to allotted land would be null and void and would not be observed by the Indian Office.

In the end, the court held that Elizabeth Shanagaretta-Menard and Mary Shangaretta-Michelle were the only heirs of the deceased, Muddy Tom Churchill.

---

51 Jacobs, Notebook 46, *Santiam Kalapuya Text,* 85: J. B. Hudson said, "Jim Stewart or Muddy Jim; he was a Yoncalla but of what village he did not know. His people maybe sold him for a slave and he got up to the Yamhill-Grand Ronde country, even as far as Vancouver."

52 Oregon State Archives, Salem, Oregon, 1901, Polk County, Estate File 0938.

The claim of James Stewart's widow, **Mary Hutchins** (Duniwi), was rejected and disallowed.[53]

In 1912, Muddy Tom Churchill's forty-acre allotment was sold to H. Heine by unspecified heirs, presumably Elizabeth Shangaretta-Menard and Mary Shangaretta-Michelle.

Churchill, Tom (1846c)	Native Name: None known by author
Alias: None known by author	Allotment: None known by author
Mother: Unknown to author	Father: Unknown to author

In 1885, this younger Tom Churchill (1846c) appeared with his wife, Lillie (1854c), and his mother, Bettie (1824c). He does not appear on any GRIC after 1885.

Condon, Bill (1849c–87c), Umpqua	Native Name: None known by author
Alias: Umpqua Bill	Allotment: None known by author
Mother: Anna Condon-Mapple	Father: Unknown to author

In 1872, Umpqua Bill Condon was living at **Coquille Charlie** (Nagashta)'s place. He married Sarah Umpqua a couple of years later. After Sarah, Umpqua Bill married **Jennie Sansousee** in 1876.[54]

In 1885, Umpqua Bill and Jennie Sansousee were listed with their daughter, Josephine Lillie ("Josie"), and son, Henry.[55] Umpqua Bill's mother, the Widow Mapple, and his Aunt Milley were also living with the family.

At that time, Umpqua Bill's livestock included three horses, four head of cattle, and approximately thirty hogs. In addition, he had a good house and barn on twenty fenced acres with nine acres in cultivation and a good garden.

When Umpqua Bill died less than two years later, the agent's list of family assets had substantially changed. On one side of the equation, the Condon livestock had dwindled to a horse and cow, but Jennie now had two houses rather than one. Perhaps, without Umpqua Bill, Jennie decided she needed to scale down the size of the farm and traded or sold the livestock in exchange for the second house.

Condon, Josephine Lillie (1877c), Umpqua	Native Name: None known by author
Alias: Josephine Tipton	Allotment: 28
Mother: Jennie Sansousee, Umpqua	Father: Umpqua Bill Condon

---

53 Ibid.

54 Munnick and Beckham, *Catholic Church Records—Grand Ronde*, Register I, p. 89, M-8, p. 97, M-3. Oregon State Archives, Salem, Oregon, 1903, Polk County, Estate File 1034, Jenny Condon: DOD was listed as April 30, 1903.

55 Munnick and Beckham, Catholic *Church Records—Grand Ronde*, Register I, p. 101, B-2.

(L to R) Umpqua Bill Condon's daughter, Josephine Lillie Tipton, and Victoria Wishikin-Howard. Photo Courtesy Barbara Danforth Private Collection

Josephine Lillie Condon received a twenty-acre allotment. She also inherited twenty acres of Umpqua **Richard "Dick" Cook** (Shay Shoaska)'s allotment in 1926.

Cook, Frank (1861c)	Native Name: None known by author
Alias: Frank Clark	Allotment: None known by author
Mother: Unknown to author	Father: Unknown to author

Frank Cook appears to have had at least four wives: Mary Ellen, **Clinnie Williams, Mary Holmes** (Pusak), and Mary Williamson-Allen (Skampup).

He divorced his wife Mary Ellen in Yamhill County, Oregon, on September

25, 1892.[56] In 1896, he was listed on the GRIC as "Frank Clark" with his wife, Clinnie Williams, and a "stepson, Cephas Tipton." His name changes sporadically from "Frank Clark" to "Frank Cook" through 1914. From 1896 through 1905, Clinnie was listed as Frank's wife.

On the 1906 GRIC, Frank was living with **David Holmes**'s sister, Mary, former wife of **Wasco Charlie**. Later, after **Robert Allen** died in 1918, Frank Cook married Robert's widow, Mary Williamson-Allen.[57]

Cook, Richard (1827c–1916), Umpqua	Native Name: Shay Shoaska /shay-sho-a-ska/[58]
Alias: Dick Cook	Allotment 32
Mother: Unknown to author	Father: Unknown to author

In 1872, Dick Cook (Shay Shoaska) was single and staying with **Abe Mapple** and Abe's wife, Carrie.

His earliest recorded marriage was to a woman named Mary, whom Father Croquet baptized at their home on October 8, 1883.[59] At that time, Mary was gravely ill. She died sometime before the agent took the annual census in 1885. The following year, Dick married the widow Charlotte but, once again, in 1887, he was listed as a widower living alone. In 1888, Dick took another wife, Martha, whom Father Croquet baptized on July 22.[60] After Martha died, Dick married a woman named Jane around 1892. On June 29, 1898, Father Croquet baptized "Jane, wife of Richard Cook, gravely ill, age about 50 years." Although Jane survived her illness, she divorced Dick in April of 1905.[61] Then Mary "Mollie" Taylor was married to Dick for a short time between 1912 and 1914.

Dick Cook received a 240-acre allotment. In determining heirship, he claimed he was a cousin to **Chief Peter McCoy (Inchaishi), Susan Pony, Eliza Day,** and a woman he called "Mrs. Tacumtia."[62] After Dick's death, **Umpqua Bill Condon**'s daughter, **Josephine Lilly Condon,** inherited twenty acres of his allotment. On May 8, 1926, she paid the fifteen-dollar heirship fee. On September 9, 1926, **John Warren** placed a claim against the estate in the amount of four hundred dollars.

---

56 Oregon State Archives, Salem, Oregon, 1892 Yamhill County Divorce.

57 Oregon State Archives, Salem, Oregon, 1916, Polk County Estate, File 1594.

58 *Heirs of Deceased Indians*, Allotment Record 32, gave Indian name as "Clas-ja-ah-sha." A photo of him is signed "Shay Shoaska."

59 Munnick and Beckham, Catholic *Church Records—Grand Ronde*, Register I, p. 125, B-22.

60 Ibid., Register I, p. 43, B-35.

61 National Archives, Salem, Oregon, Polk County Circuit Court Case Files, Index to Divorce Cases 1859–1909, File 3539, Richard Cook vs. Jennie Cook.

62 National Archives, Salem, Oregon, 1907, Polk County, Liza Day, Estate File 1276. On November 9, 1886, Father Croquet baptized an elderly woman at Siletz named "Anna Tecumsa." This may be the woman Dick was claiming as a cousin.

Dick Cook (Shay Shoaska). Photo courtesy of the late Jackie Whisler

Cooks, Gay (1820c–95c), Tualatin band of Kalapuya, Yamhill band of Kalapuya	Native Name: Kuksh /*kuksh*/ (kuksh)*[63]
Alias: James Box, James Cook, Cooks Gay	Allotment 55
Mother: Unknown to author	Father: Unknown to author

In 1872, Gay Cooks (Kuksh) was listed as "James Box" on the GRIC with his wife, Eliza, and "Lily, a daughter of a former wife." Lily (1861c–76) married **Luckiamute Dave Davis** (Wudsnaqueet).

In 1885, Cooks was listed with his wife Sarah (1832c). The following year, he was listed with a wife named Julia (1833c). Their assets were described as a good

---

63 Gatschet, *Texts, Sentences and Vocables*, 371: Cooks was listed under Tualatin with a wife but no children. Gatschet, *Texts, Sentences and Vocables*, 77: "kuksh, mase. near Kinai."

house, barn, wagon, hack, sixty fenced acres with fourteen in cultivation, a garden, six cattle, three horses, and chickens, among other things.

Cooks was also listed in government records as James Cook and as Cooks Gay. He appears on the 1887 GRIC as Cooks Gay with an unnamed wife. By 1889, this wife had apparently died and he was listed on the census as an old widower.

A year later, he was living with **Eliza Johnson** (Khakhshni). Eliza was a Yamhill *tamanawas* woman and a good old-time doctor.[64] They were together until 1895 when Eliza was listed as a widow.

While the GRIC listed Eliza Johnson as Gay Cooks' wife, a letter from the acting commissioner to the Grand Ronde Indian agent, Edward Lamson, dated March 28, 1893, identified her as Gayo's sister. The commissioner wrote,

> Inspector Miller calls attention to the claim of one Cook Gayo that the Post Office at Grande Ronde and most of the buildings therewith connected, are upon the lands of Gayo's sister, Eliza Johnson, who would like to have this property removed.

On October 3, 1894, the Post Office was moved about three miles northwest to Grand Ronde Agency.

Gay Cooks received a 60.04-acre allotment described in estate records as "land rough and unimproved."[65] His sole heir was Eliza Johnson, who sold twenty acres of the allotment to Joel Flannery in 1903. A fee patent was issued to her for the remaining acreage in 1907.[66]

Cow Creek Liza (1836c), Cow Creek band of Umpqua	Native Name: None known by author
Alias: None known by author	Allotment: None known by author
Mother: Unknown to author	Father: Unknown to author

In 1886, Cow Creek Liza was married, but living alone. The Indian agent noted on the report that she was "poor."

Cowell, Dwawaya, Clackamas	Native Name: Dwawaya /dwa-WA-ya/ (dwawáya)*[67]
Alias: None known by author	Allotment: None known by author
Mother: Sigawali, wife of Chief Wacheno, Clackamas	Father: Unknown to author

---

64 Berreman, Interview with Mose Hudson, 1934. Johnson and Zenk, *Chinuk Wawa*, 188: term meaning "spirit."

65 National Archives, Salem, Oregon, 1907, Yamhill County, Estate File 1231.

66 *Heirs of Deceased Indians*, Allotment Record 55.

67 Jacobs, Notebook 59, *Texts and Ethnology*, 52.

Dwawaya was **Victoria Wishikin (Kinishi)**'s cousin on her Clackamas grand-mother's side. Some of her songs were recorded.[68]

Cowell, Sigawali, Clackamas, Tualatin band of Kalapuya	Native Name: Sigawali /si-ga-WA-li/ (sigawáli)*[69]
Alias: None known by author	Allotment: None known by author
Mother: Dwawaya, Clackamas	Father: Stephen Cowl, Tualatin band of Kalapuya

Cowell, Stephen (d.1890c), Tualatin band of Kalapuya	Native Name: Kawalh /KA-wahl/ (káwał)*[70]
Alias: None known by author	Allotment: None known by author
Mother: Unknown to author	Father: Unknown to author

Stephen Cowell (Kawalh) was a Tualatin man with a Clackamas wife named Dwawaya. They had a daughter, Sigawali, who was named after her mother's mother. This elder Sigawali was one of **Chief Daniel Wacheno** (Wachinu)'s wives.

Stephen may not have had a spirit power as he never sang.[71]

Cowl, John (1825c)	Native Name: None known by author
Alias: None known by author	Allotment: None known by author
Mother: Unknown to author	Father: Unknown to author

In 1885, John was with his wife, Sallie (1835c), and daughter, Emmie (1863c).

Cowl, Samuel, Tualatin band of Kalapuya	Native Name: None known by author
Alias: None known by author	Allotment: None known by author
Mother: Unknown to author	Father: Wankhpa

In 1872, Samuel Cowl was with his wife, Adelia, and their five children: Charley (1861c), an unnamed daughter (1867c), George (1868c), Francis (1870c), and an infant daughter. Adelia's mother, Mariah, was also living with them.

Cowl, Widower (1845c)	Native Name: None known by author
Alias: None known by author	Allotment: None known by author
Mother: Unknown to author	Father: Unknown to author

In 1885, he was with his son, Henry (1868c), and daughter, Lucy (1872c).

---

68   Jacobs, Field Notebook 54, *Texts and Ethnology*, 60.
69   Jacobs, Notebook 59, *Texts and Ethnology*, 52.
70   Ibid.
71   Ibid.

Coyle, Tom, Santiam band of Kalapuya	Native Name: None known by author
Alias: None known by author	Allotment: None known by author
Mother: Unknown to author	Father: Unknown to author

In 1872, Tom and his wife, Eliza, were with their four daughters: Jane (1865c), Louise (1868c), Margaret (1869c), and Ann (1871c).

Crawford, Henry James (1857c–79c), Tualatin band of Kalapuya[72]	Native Name: None known by author
Alias: Heiny Crawford	Allotment: None known by author
Mother: Unknown to author	Father: Lame Jim Shiliqua, Tualatin band of Kalapuya[73]

Henry Crawford was one of three children singled out for special mention by W. R. Dunbar, the teacher of the manual labor school at Grand Ronde, in his annual report. In addition to Henry Crawford, two other children, **John Harris** and **George Moffit,** were recognized. On August 6, 1870, Dunbar wrote that they were "quite intelligent and studious; are good readers and spellers, write a good hand, and have stored their minds with a large amount of practical knowledge."

Henry married Henriette in the Catholic Church at Grand Ronde December 8, 1872. Their witnesses were **James Allen** and **Peter Kenoyer** (Kinai).

After Henriette died, Henry married Anna Kidno December 27, 1875. Witnessing their ceremony were Napoleon Arquette and **Sophie Petite.** By Anna, Henry had Tais Claia Melicie (1877c–86c), Harriet Emerence (1880c–88c), and Philomissa (1883c). Philomissa's godparents were **William Hartless** (Futi) and Marianne Gengra. A few months later, Anna Crawford became godmother to Nancy and **Peter Wheeler** (Kutskait)'s little boy, Stephan, who had been born in July that same year.[74]

Henry Crawford was elected sergeant of arms at the seventh annual session of the Grand Ronde Indian legislature in 1878. According to Grand Ronde court records, Anna was widowed in 1879, but Father Croquet recorded Henry's death in church records much later. Croquet wrote that "Henry Crawfort" died February 26, 1882.[75]

---

72 Munnick and Beckham, *Catholic Church Records—Grand Ronde*, Register I, p. 78, M-6.

73 Gatschet, *Texts, Sentences and Vocables*, 370.

74 Munnick and Beckham, *Catholic Church Records—Grand Ronde*, Register I, M-13, p. 96, B-33, p. 104, B-1, p. 114.

75 Ibid., Register I, p. 120, S-3. National Archives, Seattle, Grand Ronde/Siletz, Land and Enrollment Program records, Field Notes and Land Survey 1875–1898, Land Description Book 1878, Box 115; Grand Ronde Justice Court: listed Ana Crawford as one of the "widows" required to pay taxes to the Indian Legislature in 1879.

Curl, Henry (1858c–1930), Santiam band of Kalapuya	Native Name: Chuck[76]
Alias: None known by author	Allotment: None known by author
Mother: Unknown to author	Father: Unknown to author

Henry Curl (l) and John Silas (r). Photo courtesy of Barbara Danforth Collection.

Father Croquet wrote December 11, 1881, that he had married Henry Curl and Polly, "both of this place," in the presence of **William Warren** and Mary Shangaretta, wife of **David Holmes.**[77]

Four years later, Henry was listed with his wife, Polly, his son, Jimmie (1883c), and an infant. In 1888, the young couple was living alone. Their children were not listed.

---

76 1887 GRIC.

77 Munnick and Beckham, Catholic *Church Records — Grand Ronde*, Register I, p. 120, M-4.

Apparently, Henry was somewhat of a ladies' man. In 1893, **Thomas Norwest** told him repeatedly to stay away from his wife, **Olive Voutrin,** but Henry ignored him. Finally, Thomas caught Henry outside his house and fired a shot at him.

During the official investigation of the incident, **Frank Quenel** testified that some eighteen years earlier, around 1875, he had experienced a very similar incident involving Henry Curl. Frank claimed Henry started leaving letters at his house for his wife. When Henry ignored his warning, Frank said, he met up with Henry and would have killed him had his gun not jammed. Frank said, Henry "was a man of bad reputation then and it has not improved since."[78]

A short time later, Henry married a Tillamook woman named Agnes Dick. They had a son, Marion (1894c).[79]

Agnes died of tuberculosis December 17, 1924. Henry died six years later of myocarditis.[80]

Cyprian, Old Man (1798c–78), Rogue River[81]	Native Name: None known by author
Alias: None known by author	Allotment: None known by author
Mother: Unknown to author	Father: Unknown to author

Old Man Cyprian had a son named Marcus who was baptized November 13, 1863. Cyprian died and was buried February 20, 1878.[82]

78 National Archives, Washington, DC, affidavit taken from Frank Quenel by Benj Miller, Indian agent, 1893.

79 U. S. Indian Census Rolls, 1885–1940, Grand Ronde Reservation, 1934. Jacobs, Notebook 52, *Texts and Ethnology*, 150: "Henry Curl's (Kalapuya—is married to a Tillamook woman who talks Tillamook) wife is Agnes Dick."

80 U.S. Indian Census Rolls, 1885–1940, Siletz Reservation, 1930.

81 Gatschet, *Texts, Sentences and Vocables*, 366: listed under Rogue River.

82 Munnick and Beckham, *Catholic Church Records—Grand Ronde*, Register I, p. 29, B-58, p. 106, S-5.

D

Dave, Gregoire (1831c–62), Molalla	Native Name: None known by author
Alias: None known by author	Allotment: None known by author
Mother: Unknown to author	Father: Unknown to author

Gregoire Dave was baptized March 14, 1861. He died in August of 1862.[1]

Davis, Dave (1841c–1908), Luckiamute band of Kalapuya[2]	Native Name: Wudsnaqueet /wuds-na-queet/[3]
Alias: David Davies, Peter Davis, Luckiamute Dave	Allotment 37
Mother: Unknown to author	Father: Unknown to author

Luckiamute Dave Davis (Wudsnaqueet) was married to a woman named Mary. She died June 7, 1866.[4] After her death, Dave married Sarah Jane. They were still together in 1872. Mary Judson, her daughter, **Sarah Judson,** and a man named Judge Wilson were also living with Dave and his wife, Sarah Jane at that time.

On May 27, 1876, Dave married the fifteen-year-old Lily Mary Cooks. Lily Mary died in October of that same year. Dave married Sophia Wheeler on January 16, 1883.[5]

He had a number of children: Rose (1868c–85), Julia (1876c), Philomene (1876–84), Johnnie (1880c), Henry (1882c), Lawrence (1883c), Charley (1885c), Herbert (1885c–93), and Howard Davis (1887c–89).[6]

In 1886, Dave and Sophia had a good house and barn on eighty fenced acres with a small garden. In addition, they had three horses and five hogs, and were cultivating sixty acres.

Dave received a fee patent on a 240-acre allotment in 1907. In addition, his sons **Herbert** and **Howard Davis** each received an eighty-acre allotment that

---

1 Munnick and Beckham, *Catholic Church Records—Grand Ronde*, Register I, p. 9, B-25, p. 22, S-25.
2 Gatschet, *Texts, Sentences and Vocables*, 369: under the "Lakmayuk" as "Davis, a ½ breed."
3 1887 GRIC gives his Indian name as "Wuds-na-queet."
4 Munnick and Beckham, *Catholic Church Records—Grand Ronde*, Register I, p. 44, S-22.
5 Ibid., Register I, p. 98, M-5, p. 100, S-18, p. 123, M-1.
6 Ibid., Register I, p. 125, B-8, p. 127, S-1, p. 130, B-4, S-4, Register II, p. 38, B-6, p. 49, B-49, p. 70, B-14, p. 101, B-10.

Dave inherited.[7] Sophia died December 4, 1907. Luckiamute Dave died the following year.[8]

Davis, David (1869c), Tualatin band of Kalapuya	Native Name: None known by author
Alias: None known by author	Allotment: None known by author
Mother: Unknown to author	Father: Unknown to author

David Davis was an orphan. In 1888, he was living on sixty fenced acres with no improvements.

Davis, Herbert (1885c–93), Luckiamute band of Kalapuya	Native Name: None known by author
Alias: None known by author	Allotment 38
Mother: Sophie Wheeler	Father: David Davis, Luckiamute band of Kalapuya

Herbert Davis received an eighty-acre allotment. His father, **David Davis,** inherited it in 1907.

Davis, Howard (1887c–89), Luckiamute band of Kalapuya	Native Name: None known by author
Alias: None known by author	Allotment 39
Mother: Sophie Wheeler	Father: David Davis, Luckiamute band of Kalapuya

Howard Davis received an eighty-acre allotment. His father, **David Davis,** inherited it in 1907.

Davis, John (1850c–77c), Rogue River/Shasta	Native Name: None known by author
Alias: Couchon John, Rogue River John	Allotment: None known by author
Mother: Unknown to author	Father: Unknown to author

In 1872, John was with his wife, Kitty, and a relative of Kitty's called Girty. He married **Ellen Carey** in 1875. Their witnesses were Joseph Tole and **Elizabeth Petite.**[9]

---

7   *Heirs of Deceased Indians*, Allotment Records, 37, 38, 39.
8   Oregon State Archives, Salem, Oregon, 1908 Polk County, Estate File 1624.
9   Munnick and Beckham, *Catholic Church Records—Grand Ronde*, Register I, p. 95, M-8.

Davison, Old (1809c–86c), Santiam band of Kalapuya	Native Name: None known by author
Alias: None known by author	Allotment: None known by author
Mother: Unknown to author	Father: Unknown to author

In 1885, Old Davison (1809c) was listed as the "father of **Santiam George Hauxhurst.**"

Day, Alexander (1833c–93) Umpqua, Mexican	Native Name: None known by author
Alias: Alex Day, Alick Dai, Alack Day	Allotment 35
Mother: Unknown to author	Father: Unknown to author

Born in Los Angeles, California, Alexander Day came to Oregon when he was a young man. By 1873, he testified he had been "a citizen of Oregon for about twenty years" and "a resident of Grand Rounde"; he gave his occupation as "laborer."[10]

Alex had one daughter, Josephine (1863–63), by a native woman named Pauline (1838c–63). After Pauline died, he married **Chief Louis Napesa**'s oldest daughter, Mary Ann Nippising, on January 30, 1864.[11] However, by 1867, Alex was determined to get the marriage annulled and submitted his case first to the Indian agent at Grand Ronde and then to the Commissioner of Indian Affairs.

On September 9, 1867, the Commissioner of Indian Affairs wrote Indian Agent Harvey at Grand Ronde:

> I have to acknowledge the receipt of your letter of the 5th instant concerning the exploits of Alex Day, the Mexican half breed. I gave Day no advice whatever, and entirely refused to entertain his case, but told him that if you wished me to consider it, you would doubtless write me about it, and until you did so, I should pay no attention to it. Squire Lovelady's decision that the Catholic Priest had no right to marry is too absurd for comment. The attention of the Grand Jury should be called to the matter, and in the meantime the Mexican ought not to be permitted to come upon the Reservation.[12]

No further information could be found to indicate whether Alex was actually

---

10 National Archive, Salem, Oregon, Polk County Circuit Court Case Files, Index to Divorce Cases 1859-1909, File 831, Alexander Day vs. Sarah.

11 Munnick and Beckham, *Catholic Church Records —Grand Ronde*, Register I, p. 29, B-56, S-40, S-40, p. 30, M-1.

12 Amos Harvey to J. W. P. Huntington, September 5, 1867, BIA Microfilm M-2, Roll 24, National Archives, Washington DC. J. W. P. Huntington to Agent Harvey, September 9, 1867, BIA, RG 75, National Archives—Pacific NW Region, Seattle, WA.

banned from the reservation, but four years later, on September 29, 1871, Father Croquet wrote in the church records that "Marianne Nepucing" had been forced to contract her previous marriage against her will and therefore her marriage to Alexander Day was null. After this declaration, the Archbishop Francis Norbert Blanchet himself joined in marriage Alexander's former wife, Mary Ann Nipissing and **David Leno**.[13]

As for Alexander Day, he did not wait for the annulment. He married **Sarah Laurence** in November of 1867. They were still together in 1872, but Alex Day filed a case for divorce against Sarah in District Court for the State of Oregon, Polk County, in November 1873.

As grounds for his complaint, Alexander accused Sarah of committing adultery with a Klickitat Indian named Joe. He claimed that after he caught them sleeping together, Sarah left him to continue her relationship with Joe. To support herself, she was cooking for a white man at the government mills on the reservation.[14]

The Umpqua chief, **Peter McCoy** (Inchaishi), testified in court on Alexander's behalf. After stating that he had known Sarah since she was a little girl and Alexander Day for the past eighteen years, Peter described an incident that happened one morning in January or February 1873. On this specific occasion, Peter caught Sarah and Klickitat Joe together in his barn when he went to feed his horses. According to Peter, "They were abashed, but tried to laugh away their shame."[15]

After his divorce from Sarah was granted, Alexander married a woman named Jenny in the Catholic Church December 11, 1873. **Peter Checkaon** (Chikhyan) and his wife were their witnesses.[16]

November 4, 1879, when the Eighth Annual Session of the Grand Ronde Legislature convened, the Assembly was organized with the election of Alexander Day as sergeant of arms.[17]

From April through June 1880, Alex worked as an assistant sawyer at the agency mill. He also hauled lumber from the Indian mill to the agency headquarters for $1.50 per day.[18]

By 1885, Alexander had married yet again. This time, he married **Eliza Day,** an Umpqua woman, who was one of the Indian doctors at Grand Ronde.[19]

---

13 Munnick and Beckham, *Catholic Church Records—Grand Ronde*, Register I, p. 70, M-2.

14 National Archive, Salem Oregon, Polk County Circuit Court Case Files, Index to Divorce Cases 1859–1909, File 831, Alexander Day vs. Sarah.

15 Ibid.

16 Munnick and Beckham, Catholic *Church Records—Grand Ronde*, Register I, p. 85, M-9.

17 National Archives, Seattle, Grand Ronde/Siletz, Land and Enrollment Program records, Field Notes and Land Survey 1875–1898, Land Description Book 1878, Box 115; Grand Ronde Justice Court.

18 National Archives, Seattle, Cash Book, 1875–1907, RG75, BIA, Grand Ronde, Box. 190, Book 10819.

19 Berreman, interview with John Warren, 24: John gave Liza Day's tribe as Cow Creek and supported J. B. Hudson's statement that she was a doctor.

For a long time, Indian doctors had been trying to kill white people by casting their power at them, but the poison would always pass straight through their bodies. Once in a while, depending upon where the person was hit, the power might injure the person, but only temporarily. The doctors reasoned that this might be happening because the body of a white person was not like that of an Indian. Since their tamanawas power always went through the white person, they thought perhaps white blood was thinner than red blood.[20]

This popular native belief and the power of the Indian doctors irritated the Indian agent at Grand Ronde. Soon he arranged a public confrontation that was intended to humiliate Alexander Day and any Indian doctors present. In reporting the incident to the commissioner of Indian affairs, Agent McClane wrote:

> When I first came here there were very few of the Indians or half-breeds but what believed in the power of Indian doctors. … There were a number in my office one day, and among them some of those would-be doctors. One, a part Spanish and part Indian, a quite intelligent man, with considerable property, stated that his wife had the power of doing that thing. I told him I would give him $100 if he would bring her and all the rest of the doctors that possess that power to practice on me, and if they succeeded in killing me they should have the $100 and not be prosecuted for the killing. Oh no, says he, we can't do that; we can't kill a white man, but can kill an Indian or a horse.[21]

As McClane so shrewdly observed, Alexander Day was one of the more successful farmers at Grand Ronde. In 1886, he reportedly had a good house and barn on eighty fenced acres with forty-five acres in cultivation. In addition, he had eight horses, a large herd of cattle, twenty-four hogs, chickens, two plows, a harrow, a wagon, a hack, a large garden, and a reaper.

At this time, Alexander also had an adopted son, **Joseph Jeff Day,** and an older woman relative named **Susan Pony** living with them.

Alexander received a 160-acre allotment with forty acres in trust status. His wife, Eliza, sold eighty acres of his property to W. N. Jones in 1906. A year later, she sold forty more acres of his allotment to W. S. Bentley.

Day, Eliza (1834c–1907), Umpqua[22]	Native Name: None known by author
Alias: Liza Day	Allotment: None known by author
Mother: Unknown to author	Father: Unknown to author

Eliza was widely known at Grand Ronde as one of the "old time Indian

---

20 Jacobs, Field Notebook 36, *Texts and Ethnology*, 173.
21 *Annual Report Commission of Indian Affairs*, 1886, 209–11.
22 National Archives, Salem, Oregon, 1907, Polk County, Estate File 1276. Berreman, interview with John Warren, 24: John gave Liza Day's tribe as Cow Creek.

doctors."[23] When she died on May 19, 1907, she left a personal estate valued at $641.50. While **Rosa Tim-Tim** (Elmermach) and Clara Chapman (1863c) both testified that they were Eliza's only heirs, **Richard "Dick" Cook** (Shay Shoaska) firmly denied their claims. He testified that he was related to Eliza along with **Chief Peter McCoy** (Inchaishi) and **Susan Pony,** a woman called "Mrs. Tacumtia." He said they all lived at Grand Ronde and were cousins.[24]

Supporting Dick Cook (Shay Shoaska)'s testimony regarding Susan Pony's relationship to Eliza is the fact that Susan lived with Eliza and Alexander Day from 1885 to 1892. After Alex died, Susan lived with Eliza and Alexander Day's adopted son, **Joseph Jeff Day,** from 1894 to1896. During that time Susan Pony was listed on the census for the first few years as an aunt, but more often she was listed as a "cousin."

No further information could be found to help determine Eliza's legal heirs and the final judgment of the court could not be located.[25]

Day, Joseph Jeff (1878-1921),[26] Yoncalla band of Kalapuya, Umpqua, Chinook, Iroquois	Native Name: None known by author
Alias: Joseph Lashman	Allotment 36
Mother: Clara Laurence, Chinook, Iroquois	Father: William Laishmin, Umpqua, Yoncalla band of Kalapuya

Alexander Day adopted Joseph Jeff when he was a baby.[27] Joseph Jeff's mother, **Clara Laurence** and Alexander's former wife, **Sarah Laurence,** were sisters.

Joe Day married **Salome Wacheno.** They had a number of children: Alexander (1909c), Golda (1913c), Clifford (1919), Marcus (1915c–25c), Ace (1907c–31), and Floyd (1920c).[28]

Joe Day received a forty-acre allotment in 1907. His children inherited additional allotment land from **Nancy Yocum** (Tohokuhsah) of the Rogue River nation.[29]

In the last few weeks of Joe's life, **Mary Ann Hoffer, Frances Gilbert,** and **Victoria Wishikin** (Kinishi) took turns providing around-the-clock nursing care for both him and his wife, Salome Wacheno.[30]

---

23 Berreman, interview with John Warren, 24: John stated Liza Day was an Indian doctor.

24 Ibid.

25 National Archives, Salem, Oregon, 1907, Polk County, Estate File 1276.

26 National Archives, Central Plains Region, Leavenworth Prison, Inmate File 5333, Louie Savage: gave Joe Day as a mix of Cow Creek Umpqua, Umpqua and Cherokee.

27 Michelle, *Just a Memorandum,* 4.

28 Oregon State Archives, Salem, Oregon, 1921, Polk County, Estate File 1886.

29 *Heirs of Deceased Indians,* Allotment Records: 36, 269.

30 Oregon State Archives, Salem, Oregon, 1921, Polk County, Estate File 1886.

Left to right: Joe Day, Andrew Riggs, and Jack Lawler. Photo courtesy of Barbara Danforth Private Collection.

Joe had enough money to pay for nursing expenses and funeral costs, but after he died on July 15, 1921, it was necessary for his personal property to be sold in order to help pay for the support of his minor children. From Joe's personal property, probate court ordered the sale of an eight-year-old black mare, a nine-year-old iron gray horse, and an old farm wagon. The court ordered that the proceeds from the sale were to be used for the support of Joe's children. All other claims had to be paid out of later funds.[31]

The children's maternal grandfather, **John Wacheno** (Tsinwalh), took the children to live with him, but given his age he could not care for them permanently. Since the children's paternal grandmother, **Clara Laurence,** was also unable to care for the children, she and John Wacheno arranged for a man named Glen Ebineth to administer the proceeds of Joe's estate on the children's behalf.[32] There is no record to indicate who was assigned guardianship.

Day, Nancy (1800c–80), Umpqua	Native Name: None known by author
Alias: None known by author	Allotment: None known by author
Mother: Unknown to author	Father: Unknown to author

---

31 Ibid.
32 Ibid.

The only information about Nancy Day was found in a Catholic Church record that listed her as Umpqua and gave her death date as February 21, 1880.[33] She may have been the mother of **Alexander Day.**

Dick, Frederick (1830c–70), Yamhill band of Kalapuya[34]	Native name: None known by author
Alias: None known by author	Allotment: None known by author
Mother: Unknown to author	Father: Unknown to author

Dick, John (1851c), Klickitat husband of Clackamas wife[35]	Native Name: None known by author
Alias: None known by author	Allotment: None known by author
Mother: Unknown to author	Father: Unknown to author

The story of the marriage of **Chief Daniel Wacheno** (Wachinu's) daughter to John Dick had been told many times. It is one of those stories that deserve being repeated as it is a happy tale, filled with descriptions of ancient customs, romance, and family.

It begins prior to the removal of Indian people to reservations when John Dick, a Klickitat, was visiting the Clackamas people. In their village he saw and liked a young girl who was the daughter of Chief Wacheno and the younger of two sisters.[36]

Determined to make her his wife, John Dick sent two messengers, his aunt and a Klickitat woman doctor, to arrange the marriage with the family. When the women returned, the aunt told John that the chief's older daughter was to be his bride and listed the terms of the marriage.[37]

After accepting the arrangement, Wacheno invited John Dick's family to stay with the Clackamas while preparation was made for the marriage. In the days that followed, many presents were brought to Wacheno's lodge and fastened to a horizontal pole, perhaps fifteen to twenty feet long, that ran down the center of the house. Among the gifts were all sorts of beautiful things including beads, blankets, clothing, and yards of calico.[38]

The last night before the official ceremony, relatives of the bride sang several specific marriage songs over and over again and danced until around midnight. Their singing and dancing called upon a "happy spirit" and made everything connected with the marriage "bright."[39]

---

33 Munnick, and Beckham, *Catholic Church Records—Grand Ronde*, Register I, p. 113, S-2.
34 Ibid., Register I, p. 66, B-81, S-24.
35 Jacobs, Notebook 53, *Texts and Ethnology*, 40.
36 Ibid.
37 Ibid., 40–44.
38 Ibid.
39 Ibid.

The next morning an old man who understood how to handle the spirit within the gifts and an elderly woman were tied together with strings of beads. The woman held buckets that were also lashed together. The man held a pan full of money. After the bride was wrapped in a beaded shawl with only enough of her face exposed to permit her to see, a woman from among her relatives was found to carry her.[40]

With an elderly woman leading the way, breaking strands of beads and scattering them beneath their feet, the bridal party marched in a group toward the groom's relatives, who were sitting at a sort of middle ground.

The old man with the pan of money advanced ahead of the bride. When he reached his destination and cried out, the bride's party stopped. Then the groom's family was stripped of various items of clothing, which the bride's mother replaced.

Although John Dick's family did not sing or dance during the ceremony, one elderly Klickitat women performed a feather ceremony to drive away the evil spirits and leave the young couple in peace.[41]

Finally, Nancy was placed on a small hammock underneath the famous Pow-Wow tree. Then one of the men carrying John Dick on his back placed him beside his bride. The blanket was thrown over them and they were pronounced man and wife.[42]

A short time after the wedding, John Dick took Nancy to live at Yakama. Before they left, Wacheno invited John's family to return for the winter dance and gambling game later that year.[43]

At Grand Ronde, John and Nancy Dick were listed on the 1886 GRIC with their two sons, Eddie (1880c), and John (1883c). At that time, they were living with Chief Wacheno and his wife, Maria. A niece, Julia (1868c), was also living with the family.

After Nancy died, John Dick married her younger sister.[44]

Dick, Midden (1860c), Tillamook	Native Name: None known by author
Alias: None known by author	Allotment: None known by author
Mother: Unknown to author	Father: Unknown to author

In 1885, Midden Dick and his wife, Milly (1865c), were living with their children, Fred (1881c), Ellen, and an infant son.[45]

---

40 Ibid.
41 Jacobs, Notebook 53, *Texts and Ethnology*, 40-44. Lynch, *Free Land for Free Men*, 50.
42 Lynch, *Free Land for Free Men*, 50.
43 Jacobs, Notebook 53, *Texts and Ethnology*, 44.
44 Ibid.
45 Jacobs, Notebook 52, *Texts and Ethnology*, 150: Victoria Howard gave the location of two Tillamook men, Fred and Joe Dick, as at Delake. The Fred Dick listed here at age four may be the same man living at Delake in 1929.

Old Dick (1820c)	Native Name: None known by author
Alias: None known by author	Allotment: None known by author
Mother: Unknown to author	Father: Unknown to author

In 1885, Old Dick was listed with his wife and sister, Lou (1835c).

Dick, Rose (1868c) Nehalem band of Tillamook	Native Name: None known by author
Alias: None known by author	Allotment: None known by author
Mother: Unknown to author	Father: Unknown to author

In 1886, Rose Dick was listed as a married woman with a daughter, Polly (1883c). A widow, Mollie, was living with them. Both women were without assets and considered very poor. Clara Pearson, from Siletz, remembered Rose as having three children, a girl and two boys. One of the boys lived only a few weeks. The other son died when he was between seven and eight years old. Rose's little girl grew up, but Pearson could not remember her name.[46]

Didacus, Dick (1825c–65), Umpqua[47]	Native Name: None known by author
Alias: None known by author	Allotment: None known by author
Mother: Unknown to author	Father: Unknown to author

Didacus, Dick (1850c–66), Luckiamute band of Kalapuya[48]	Native Name: None known by author
Alias: None known by author	Allotment: None known by author
Mother: Unknown to author	Father: Unknown to author

Dowd, Elizabeth (1876c), Wasco band of Chinook, French Canadian, Irish	Native Name: None known by author
Alias: Lizzie Dowd	Allotment 42
Mother: Julie LaChance, Wasco band of Chinook, French Canadian	Father: John Patrick Dowd, Irish

Elizabeth was issued an eighty-acre allotment.

Dowd, George (1886c), Wasco band of Chinook, French Canadian, Irish	Native Name: None known by author
Alias: None known by author	Allotment 47

---

46   Jacobs, Elizabeth, field notebook 106, *Misc Ethnographic Notes*, 79.
47   Munnick and Beckham, *Catholic Church Records—Grand Ronde*, Register I, p. 41, B-116, p. 42.
48   Ibid., Register I, p. 44, B-19.

Mother: Julie LaChance, Wasco Chinook, French Canadian	Father: John Patrick Dowd, Irish

George received an eighty-acre allotment.

Dowd, John Jr. (1880–1928), Wasco band of Chinook, French Canadian, Irish	Native Name: None known by author
Alias: None known by author	Allotment 44
Mother: Julie LaChance, Wasco Chinook, French Canadian	Father: John Patrick Dowd, Irish

John Dowd Jr. exchanged eighty acres of his allotment for forty acres of his mother, **Julia LaChance**'s, allotment.

Dowd, Joseph (1871c), Wasco band of Chinook, French Canadian, Irish	Native Name: None known by author
Alias: None known by author	Allotment 41
Mother: Julie LaChance, Wasco Chinook, French Canadian	Father: John Patrick Dowd, Irish

Around 1903, Joseph Dowd married Mary Emily Logsden. They had a number of children. In 1904, Joseph Dowd exchanged his eighty-acre allotment for forty acres of **John Warren**'s land.

Dowd, Patrick (1882–1921), Wasco band of Chinook, French Canadian, Irish	Native Name: None known by author
Alias: None known by author	Allotment 45
Mother: Julie LaChance, Wasco Chinook, French Canadian	Father: John Patrick Dowd, Irish

Patrick Dowd exchanged eighty acres of his allotment for forty acres of his mother, **Julia LaChance**'s, allotment.

Dowd, Rosa (1878c–1904), Wasco band of Chinook, French Canadian, Irish	Native Name: None known by author
Alias: Rosa Taylor, Mary Rosa Dowd	Allotment: 43
Mother: Julie LaChance, Wasco Chinook, French Canadian	Father: John Patrick Dowd, Irish

Rosa married **Levi Taylor** on October 10, 1894. They had a number of children, but only Mabel Rosaline Taylor (1900–1905) lived beyond the first year.

Rosa Dowd received an eighty-acre allotment that **John Dowd Sr.** inherited in 1914.

Dowd, Thomas (1884-1901), Wasco band of Chinook, French Canadian, Irish	Native Name: None known by author
Alias: None known by author	Allotment 46
Mother: Julie LaChance, Wasco Chinook, French Canadian	Father: John Patrick Dowd, Irish

Thomas Dowd received an eighty-acre allotment that **John Dowd Sr.** inherited. John Dowd Sr. sold the entire allotment in 1907.

Dumyawakh, Clackamas	Native Name: Dumyawakh /DUM-ya-wah/ dúmyawax̣*[49]
Alias: None known by author	Allotment: None known by author
Mother: Unknown to author	Father: Unknown to author

In the old days, when an elder sang a strong power sang, people would tell their children to listen carefully because maybe, after that aging person's death, their power would come to one of them.[50]

Dumyawakh, a Clackamas woman, was **Mary Smith** (Niudiya)'s sister. Her tamanawas song suggested she had a hunter power. Through the song she spoke of throwing a bow over her shoulder and going over the big mountain.[51]

When **Victoria Wishikin** was a child, Dumyawakh was the lady who pieced her ears. In 1929, Victoria recorded one of Dumyawakh's songs.[52]

Durbin, James (1827c–88c), Luckiamute band of Kalapuya	Native Name: Quella[53]
Alias: Luckiamute Jim	Allotment: None known by author
Mother: Unknown to author	Father: Unknown to author

In 1872, Jim Durbin (Quella) and his wife, Sally (1835c–85) were listed under the Luckiamute band of Kalapuya. In 1877, the Grand Ronde Legislature appointed him sheriff. In 1881, he served as administrator of the Grand Ronde Indian Court.[54]

---

49 Jacobs, Field Notebook 51, *Texts and Ethnology*, 26.
50 Ibid.
51 Ibid.
52 Ibid.
53 1887 GRIC.

His wife, Sally, being gravely ill, was baptized as Sara Mary Durbin on March 17, 1885. She died two days later.[55] After her death, James lived alone on their farm. At that time, he had a house and barn on forty fenced acres with ten acres in cultivation, three horses, four hogs, and some chickens.

In later years, James lived with his relative, a Tualatin man named **Gay Cooks,** and his family.[56]

---

54 Gatschet, *Texts, Sentences and Vocables,* 369: listed under the "Lakmayuk" as "Jim Durbin; once sheriff." National Archives, Seattle, Grand Ronde/Siletz, Land and Enrollment Program records, Field Notes and Land Survey 1875–1898, Land Description Book 1878, Box 115; Grand Ronde Justice Court.

55 Munnick and Beckham, *Catholic Church Records—Grand Ronde,* Register I, p. 130, S-3.

56 Michelle, *Just a Memorandum,* 5.

E

Edemchoey, Jacob (1840c–95), Cow Creek band of Umpqua	Native Name: Edmonshi /Ed-mon-shi/[1]
Alias: Cow Creek Jake	Allotment 48
Mother: Unknown to author	Father: Unknown to author

Edemchoey (Edmonshi) became chief at a very young age. The first official record of him serving in this capacity was the 1862 GRIC where he was listed as chief of the Cow Creek band of Umpqua with thirty-six men, women, and children under his leadership.[2] He was perhaps twenty-two years old.

As was the custom during this time period, Edemchoey had multiple wives. Records show that he had at least two in the late 1860s: **Sallie Jake** and Cecile Sims. By 1872, Sallie Jake and their children were no longer living with him. Perhaps in keeping with the new ban on plural marriages, only his wife Cecile Sims, her mother, Susie Sims, Cecile's grandmother, Aloisa, and an old woman called Niki were living with him at that time.

In 1876, the people elected Edemchoey and **Bob Spores** to represent the interest of the Cow Creek at the fifth annual session of the Grand Ronde Indian Legislature.[3]

By 1885, Cecile's brothers, Dan and **William Simmons,** were staying with the family. Cecile's brother Dan is not mentioned on any GRIC after 1885, but her brother William took up farming on his own around 1886.

Edemchoey received a 180-acre allotment. His wife, Cecile, inherited the property.

Elijah, Chief (d. 1856c), Rogue River	Native Name: Tewahait /Te-wah-hait/ [4]
Alias: None known by author	Allotment: None known by author
Mother: Unknown to author	Father: Unknown to author

Elijah (Tewahait) was a Rogue River chief. He was the fifth signer on the treaty with the Rogue River, made November 15, 1854. Most of his band of approximately a hundred Rogue River women and children joined **Chief Sam Wilder**

---

1 Cawley, *Indian Journal*, 22: listed his Indian name as "Ed-mon-shi."
2 National Archive, Washington DC Condon, 1862 GRIC of the Indians Belonging/ Located upon the Grand Ronde Indian Agency.
3 National Archives, Seattle, Grand Ronde/Siletz, Land and Enrollment Program records, Field Notes and Land Survey 1875–1898, Land Description Book 1878, Box 115; Grand Ronde Justice Court.
4 Kappler, *Treaty with the Rogue River, 1854.*

(Toquahear)'s band on the Grand Ronde Reservation prior to the final Rogue River engagements with the military in June of 1856.

However, some of his family still remained in the Rogue River area. Joel Palmer used two of his nieces as messengers to the war chiefs, Limpy and **George** (Chocultah), when requesting their surrender.[5]

At Grand Ronde, in late November 1856, a son of Chief Elijah who had been sick for some time reportedly asked his father to kill Chief Sam (Toquahear)'s sister, a woman doctor. Elijah's son believed she was responsible for his illness.

In response to his son's request, Old Chief Elijah took his bow and arrow went to where the doctor was dancing and killed her. In keeping with the native custom, Chief Sam (Toquahear)'s brother and the brother of the murdered woman went after Chief Elijah in retaliation. As a result, the old chief was killed and one or two others were wounded in the process.[6]

A few months later, the total number of this band was counted as twenty-seven people.[7]

Eliza, Calapooia (1836c), Santiam band of Kalapuya	Native Name: Chaishna /CHAISH-na/ (cháicna)*[8]
Alias: Eliza Young, Eliza Kirk, Calapooia Lisa, Brownsville Lisa	Allotment: None known by author
Mother: Unknown to author	Father: Unknown to author

Calapooia Eliza (Chaishna) worked for a number of years as a house servant for the Spores family, who lived at Spores Ferry. She married **Jim Young** from the Santiam band of Kalapuya. They were listed on the Brownsville census for 1880 as Jim and Eliza Kirk.

In 1886, Eliza was listed on the GRIC with her husband and their son, Albert (1870c). At that time, they had two horses, harness, hack, and a small garden. However, Eliza lived most of her life in Brownsville, Oregon.

Elkin, Luther (1803c–93c), Yamhill band of Kalapuya	Native Name: Ilkin /IL-kin/ (ilkin)*[9]
Alias: Old Elkin, Louis Elkin	Allotment 50
Mother: Unknown to author	Father: Unknown to author

Elkin (Ilkin) was an "old time doctor."[10] In 1872, he was living with his wife,

---

5   *Annual Report Commissioner of Indian Affairs, 1856,* 215.
6   Letter to the Editor, *Oregon Statesman,* December 2, 1856.
7   1857 GRIC.
8   Jacobs, personal papers, accession 1693-71-13, bx 90, file 4.
9   Jacobs, Notebook 36, *Santiam Kalapuya Text,* 192. Gatschet, *Texts, Sentences and Vocable,* 360.
10   Gatschet, Frachtenberg, and Jacobs, *Kalapuya Texts,* Part 3, 184.

Nancy Elkin (Kizad). Their home was described by Rev. Summers as "a little farm amid the forest" with "two dwelling houses set end to end and looking very dilapidated."[11]

Despite the pressure placed on Indian people to take up farming, Ilkin and his family continued to depend largely on traditional gathering practices at least through the early 1880s. During one of Rev. Summers's visits, he found on the walls and benches inside their home various baskets, trays, and fans used for collecting camas and other roots. On a low shelf, he saw perhaps a dozen bags of small bulbs, dried berries, and dried meat set back for the winter.[12]

William Shufon's nieces and nephews, Esther M. Brammer, Mary L. Day, Sarah J. Elliott, Joseph Hauxhurst, and John Albert Biggs, inherited equal shares of Ilkin's 280-acre allotment in 1914.[13]

Elkin, Nancy (1811c–96c), wife of Yamhill Kalapuya husband	Native Name: Kizad /Ki-zad/[14]
Alias: Anna Elken	Allotment: None known by author
Mother: Unknown to author	Father: Unknown to author

Nancy Elkin (Kizad) was from the Yamhill band of Kalapuya. Her brother, Hou-mo was Louise Selkeah's grandfather and William Shufon said she was his aunt.[15] Nancy was also the *hayash* wife of **Luther Elkin**.[16] She tried to teach Rev. Summers how to correctly pronounce Ilkin's name on one of his visits to their home. Summers said Kizad pronounced the name *"Che-ah-ill Il-kill,"* but prolonged the second syllable of the tribal name every time, as she repeated it. He described their interchange in this way:

Seeing that I said the words after her as often as she sounded them, she would shake her head and, approaching her face to mine, raise her voice and repeat the "language lesson," then wait for me to try again. After many attempts I got the sounds nearly like hers, and her pleasure in my success seemed to give her confidence also; for she led us to her camas oven in the yard, where we had seen her yesterday.[17]

By 1894, Kizad was a widow. She died on January 13, 1896.[18]

---

11 Cawley, *Indian Journal*, 33.
12 Ibid., 36, 38.
13 Oregon State Archives, Salem, Oregon, 1908, Yamhill County, File 1312. National Archives, Seattle, PAO-10, bx 1614, Mary Hauthurst, Pincess Watlistai.
14 Cawley, *Indian Journal*, 23: Indian name Ki-zad.
15 National Archives, Seattle, PAO-10, bx 1614, Mary Hauthurst, Pincess Watlistai.
16 Johnson and Zenk, *Chinuk Wawa*, 35: *hayash*, meaning important.
17 Cawley, *Indian Journal*, 32–33.
18 Munnick and Beckham, *Catholic Church Records—Grand Ronde*, Register II, p. 104, S-2.

F

Fellet, Felix (1867c), Rogue River	Native Name: None known by author
Alias: None known by author	Allotment: None known by author
Mother: Unknown to author	Father: Unknown to author

In 1887, Felix was listed as an orphan living alone. He was still alone and without assets the following year. He was not listed on any GRIC after 1888.

Fern, Be-el (1844c), Yoncalla band of Kalapuya[1]	Native Name: None known by author
Alias: None known by author	Allotment: Donation Land Claim
Mother: Dunifo	Father: Chief Halo, Yoncalla Kalapuya

Be-el was the second son of **Chief Halo** (Hilu). He was removed to Grand Ronde with his mother and brother, Jake, when he was just a boy. Due to extremely poor living conditions on the reservation, they moved back and forth between their original home in the Yoncalla Valley and Grand Ronde for a number of years.

Be-el married an Indian woman named Salista.[2] They had John (1859c–61c), Garfield (1881c–87c), Lizzie (1861c–63c), and Edwin (1883c–30). They also had a son, Stafford (1868c), and three daughters: Laura (1886c–1971), Lucinda (1876c–1932), and Melinda Fern (1885c–1909).[3] Laura Fern married **Frank Bond**, Lucinda Fern married Tom Jackson, and Melinda Fern married William Cunningham.[4]

Be-el and Salista were domestic servants for the Applegates. Be-el helped with farm work. Salista came to the house several times a week to wash and iron, bringing the younger children, Edwin and Garfield, with her.

Both Be-el and his brother, Jake, settled land claims in Douglas County, Oregon. In 1880, at the age of thirty-six, Be-el was farming at Pass Creek.[5]

---

1 Kruse, *The Halo Trail*, 21.
2 Ibid., 36.
3 O. Applegate, Testimony of Jake Fern and Polk Scott.
4 Munnick and Beckham, *Catholic Church Records—Grand Ronde*, Register II, p. 115, M-4. St. Michael's Catholic Church Burial Records, 1909. National Archives, Salem, Oregon, Polk County, November 29, 1907, Marriage Laura Fern.
5 http://ftp.us-census.org/pub/usgenweb/census/or/douglas/1880, 1880 Mt. Scott Census

Salista died first and Be-el not long afterwards. Both Be-el and Salista were buried in Yoncalla Valley.[6]

As time went by, the remaining members of the family did not fare well. Be-el's son Edwin developed a sore leg that was painful and slow to heal. When none of the family's remedies would work, Be-el's oldest brother, John, took Edwin to the reservation where he could receive better care. Eventually, Edwin recovered, but John never returned to Yoncalla.[7]

In 1905, all that remained of Halo's family was Be-el's children: Stafford, Melinda, Lucinda, Laura, and a second cousin named Enoch Spores, who was at Chemawa Indian School.[8]

Fern, Jake (1850c–18), Yoncalla band of Kalapuya[9]	Native Name: None known by author
Alias: Jefferies Halo	Allotment: Donation Land Claim
Mother: Unknown to author	Father: Chief Halo, Yoncalla Kalapuya

Jake was **Chief Halo**'s third and youngest son. He married Mary, the daughter of Billy Umpqua.[10] In 1880, Jake was homesteading at Pass Creek in Douglas County where he had built a comfortable house.[11]

Jake and Mary had at least thirteen children: Mack (1871–1930), Alex (1870–97), Samler (1874–1919), Ben Harrison (1890–1996) , Ronny (1888–97), Lennen or Lenan (1891–96), David (1878–97), Hamilton (1876), Omega (1881–87), Franklin (1879), Bertha (1889–97), Alma (1892–96) and Gertrude (1880–96).[12]

Their son Alex was killed accidentally by **Be-el Fern**'s son Stafford in 1890. Over the next twenty-four months, all Jake's children but Mack, Samler, and Gertrude also died.[13]

Jake Fern died in 1918, two years after his wife, Mary. They were both buried in the Yoncalla Valley.[14]

---

6   Kruse, *The Halo Trail*, 38, 41: *Salista* was also known as Sallyanne or Ann.
7   Ibid., 57.
8   O. Applegate, Testimony of Jake Fern.
9   Kruse, *The Halo Trail*, 70, gives death date as 1918.
10   Ibid., 51.
11   http://ftp.us-census.org/pub/usgenweb/census/or/douglas/1880, 1880 Mt Scott Census.
12   O. Applegate, Testimony of Jake Fern and Polk Scott.
13   Kruse, *The Halo Trail*, 60.
14   Ibid., 71–72.

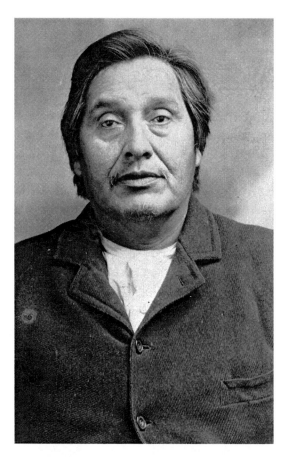

Jake Fern, son of Chief Halo and Dunifo.
Photo Courtesy Douglas County Museum
of Natural & Cultural History.

Foster, Addie (1888c–94c), Clackamas, kānaka	Native Name: None known by author
Alias: None known by author	Allotment 53
Mother: Annie, Clackamas	Father: James Foster, Clackamas, kānaka or Polynesian from the Hawaiian Islands

Addie received a forty-acre allotment. **James Foster** sold the property on November 15, 1903.

Foster, Frank (1868c–92c), Clackamas, Klamath	Native Name: Slige /sli-ge/[15]
Alias: None known by author	Allotment 54
Mother: Unknown to author	Father: Clackamas Tom Foster

Frank Foster (Slige) married Clarissa Quenel in 1886. According to the GRIC of that year, the young couple was considered poor with only a cow and calf, but by 1888, they were doing somewhat better. They had built a barn and acquired two horses and a dozen chickens.

Four years later, on May 27, 1892, Frank accidentally drowned. His body was recovered several weeks later and buried at Grand Ronde.[16]

After his death, Frank's widow, Clarissa, married John Langley. John Langley sold twenty acres of Frank Foster's 259.96-acre allotment in 1903.

Foster, James (1847c–1914), Clackamas, kānaka or Polynesian from the Hawaiian Islands[17]	Native Name: None known by author
Alias: None known by author	Allotment 51
Mother: Full Clackamas	Father: Clackamas, kānaka or Polynesian from the Hawaiian Islands

Ana, James's wife, was Clackamas. By her, he had Josephine (1882c–98) and Addie (1888c–94c).[18]

In 1888, James Foster and his family had two houses and a barn on twenty fenced acres with six acres in cultivation. The second house was probably the one **Homer Hoffer** (Tamaguin) left for him when Homer moved to the Yakama Reservation in 1874. At this time, the Foster family also had two horses, a cow, twenty hogs, and a dozen chickens.

James Foster served for a brief period on the Grand Ronde Indian Police Force in 1894.[19]

He received a fee patent for 153.36 acres of allotment land in 1907. Ana Foster inherited an interest in the allotment of **Margaret Martin,** who was her aunt on her mother's side of the family.[20]

---

15 1887 GRIC gave Frank's Indian name as "Sli-ge."

16 Munnick and Beckham, Catholic *Church Records—Grand Ronde,* Register II, p. 78, S-4.

17 Michelle, *Just a Memorandum,* 4: his mother was full Clackamas; his father was Clackamas and kānaka.

18 Munnick and Beckham, Catholic *Church Records—Grand Ronde,* Register I, p. 119, B-14.

19 National Archives, Seattle, Grand Ronde/Siletz Tribal Program Records Box 162, Agency & Tribal Council Records 1876-1951.

20 Oregon State Archives, Salem, Oregon, 1908, Yamhill County, Estate 1272: Ann Foster and Julia Gendron's mothers were Margaret Martin's sisters.

James died at home on July 2, 1914. The will that disposed of his six hundred dollar estate was signed with his right thumbprint. Dolly Teabo was the administrator of the estate. James Foster's nephew, Joseph M. Teabo, was his sole heir.[21]

Foster, Josephine (1882c–98c), Clackamas, kānaka	Native Name: None known by author
Alias: None known by author	Allotment 52
Mother: Annie, Clackamas	Father: James Foster, Clackamas, kānaka or Polynesian from the Hawaiian Islands

Josephine received a forty-acre allotment. **James Foster** sold the property on November 15, 1903.

Foster, Thomas (1844c–87), Clackamas, Klamath[22]	Native Name: None known by author
Alias: Clackamas Tom	Allotment: None known by author
Mother: Clackamas	Father: Klamath

"Clackamas Tom" Foster was married at least three times. In 1872, he was with his wife, Rachel. Also with him was his son, **Frank Foster** (Slige), and daughter, Pauline (1870c).

He was elected with **Foster Wacheno** (Inawalh) to represent the Clackamas during the fifth annual session of the Grand Ronde Indian Legislature on January 4, 1876. He later served as administrator of the Grand Ronde Indian Court in 1881.[23]

Clackamas Tom died April 18, 1887. He was buried at Grand Ronde the following day.[24]

Fowock, James, Umpqua	Native Name: None known by author
Alias: None known by author	Allotment: None known by author
Mother: Unknown to author	Father: Unknown to author

In 1872, James Fowock was living alone.

---

21 Oregon State Archives, Salem, Oregon, 1914, Polk County, Estate, File 1732.
22 Michelle, *Just a Memorandum*, 6: Tom's father was Klamath and his mother Clackamas.
23 National Archives, Seattle, Grand Ronde/Siletz Tribal Program Records Box 162, Agency & Tribal Council Records 1876–1951.
24 Munnick and Beckham, *Catholic Church Records—Grand Ronde*, Register I, p. 27, S-6.

Frank, Nellie (1868c), Clackamas, Umpqua	Native Name: None known by author
Alias: Nelly Silas, Nellie Williams, Nellie Kenoyer, Nellie Knighton	Allotment 89
Mother: Lucy Umpqua	Father: Cascade Frank Johnson, Clackamas

Nellie Frank was Lucy Umpqua's daughter by **Cascade Frank Johnson.**[25] After, Nellie's father died, her mother married **La Coque Sam Newby.** In 1887, Nellie Frank was living with **John Kelly** (Palaikhi) and his wife, Susan. Nellie was listed as John's "granddaughter."

Around 1890, Nellie Frank (1868c) married **Johnny Williams** (Matiyas) in the presence of **John Voutrin** and **Josephine Hubbard;** however, the union was short lived.

By 1893, Nellie and **Louis Kenoyer** (Pakhawatas) were married by civil ceremony. Their son, Frederic, was baptized on April 9 of that year. On the 1894 GRIC, Nellie was listed as "Nellie Williams (1868c)" and described as a widow with an infant son, but the following year, she and Louis had reunited. Their second son was born March 4, 1896.

In 1902, both of Nellie and Louis Kenoyer's boys died from typhoid. A few months later, she and Louis separated again.

Nellie was listed alone on the GRIC for 1903. On November 11, 1906, she received an allotment of 119.94 acre under the name of "Nellie Frank."

Frank, Nelly, Umpqua	Native Name: None known by author
Alias: None known by author	Allotment: None known by author
Mother: Unknown to author	Father: Unknown to author

In 1872, the widow Nellie Frank was living with **Chief Peter McCoy** (Inchaishi). She was listed as his grandmother.[26]

Frank, Shasta (1817c), Shasta[27]	Native Name: None known by author
Alias: None known by author	Allotment: None known by author
Mother: Unknown to author	Father: Unknown to author

---

25 Ibid., Register I, p. 98, B-15. Michelle, *Just a Memorandum*, 3-4.

26 Cultural Resource Department Archives, Confederated Tribes of Grand Ronde Community of Oregon, *The Elder's Scroll of 1984* listed Nellie Frank as Peter McCoy's sister rather than his grandmother.

27 Gatschet, *Texts, Sentences and Vocables*, 364: under Shastas on Grand Ronde, "Shasta Frank, abt. 60 y."

French, Charles, Rogue River/Shasta	Native Name: None known by author
Alias: French Prairie Charley	Allotment: None known by author
Mother: Unknown to author	Father: Unknown to author

In 1872, French Prairie Charley lived alone.

Frigginger, John, Mary's River band of Kalapuya	Native Name: None known by author
Alias: None known by author	Allotment: None known by author
Mother: Unknown to author	Father: Unknown to author

In 1872, John Frigginger lived alone.

Fuller, Dick (1865c), Tillamook	Native Name: None known by author
Alias: None known by author	Allotment: None known by author
Mother: Unknown to author	Father: Unknown to author

In 1885, Dick Fuller was living with his widowed sister, Susan, and her daughter, Jennie (1866c). He was not listed on the GRIC after 1885.

Fuller, John (1835c), Tillamook	Native Name: None known by author
Alias: None known by author	Allotment: None known by author
Mother: Unknown to author	Father: Unknown to author

In 1885, John Fuller was listed with his wife, Sallie (1844c), and their two sons, Louie (1866c) and Marshell (1868c).

The following year, on April 28, 1886, John married Susanne in the presence of **William Miller** (Quilinick) and Marianne Gingra. At that time, Father Croquet noted in church records that they were "Indians living on the sea coast."[28] John Fuller was not listed on the GRIC after 1885.

Fuller, Louis (1866c), Tillamook	Native Name: None known by author
Alias: None known by author	Allotment: None known by author
Mother: Unknown to author	Father: John Fuller

---

28   Munnick and Beckham, Catholic *Church Records — Grand Ronde*, Register I, p. 3, M-2.

Louis Fuller was probably the same man listed as "Louie (1866c)," the son of **John Fuller,** on the GRIC for 1885.

Louis Fuller was not listed on any GRIC after 1885, but he had a son by Agnes Dowd, Edward (1888–1916), who was baptized "at the sea coast" by Father Croquet on November 28, 1888. The child's godfather was **Andrew Jeffries.**[29]

In 1889, Louis married Lulu Winslow in Benton County.[30] By 1929, he was living at Siletz and considered "an excellent interpreter.[31]

Fuller, Susan (1813c), Tillamook	Native Name: None known by author
Alias: None known by author	Allotment: None known by author
Mother: Unknown to author	Father: Unknown to author

In 1885, Susan was listed as a widow with her daughter, Jennie (1866c), and her brother, **Dick Fuller** (1865c). She was not listed on the GRIC after 1885.

29 Ibid., p. 49, B-50.
30 Oregon State Archives, Salem, Oregon, Marriages, 1889, Benton County, File 6-115.
31 Jacobs, Notebooks 52, *Texts and Ethnology*, 150 (damaged pages).

G

Gendron, Agnes (1886–1918), Clackamas, French Canadian	Native Name: None known by author
Alias: Agnes Jondran	Allotment 85
Mother: Julia Agnes, Clackamas	Father: Jean Baptiste Gendron, French Canadian, Clackamas

January 30, 1907, Agnes Gendron received a fee patent for an eighty-acre allotment.

Gendron, Edward (1840c–69c), Clackamas, French Canadian[1]	Native Name: None known by author
Alias: Edward Jondro, Jondreau, Jeaudoin	Allotment: None known by author
Mother: Polly, Wakanasisi band of Clackamas	Father: Joseph Gendron, French Canadian

Edward's father, Joseph Gendron, was a free trapper well known in fur trade history for the prank he played on the Protestant missionaries at The Dalles in 1840, reciting passages from *The Arabian Nights* in French in the guise of prayers.

While church records list Louise Chinook as Edward's mother, native people state his mother was "Pauly of the nation of The Dalles." Besides Edward, Joseph Gendron and Polly had Catherine (1839c), Catherine (1844c), Jean Baptiste (1846c), LaRose (1847c), and **Sophie Gendron.**[2]

The first Catherine Gendron's godparents were Pierre Belleque and Catherine Lonetain. The second Catherine's godparents were Augustin Rochon and Catherine Russie. Catherine Russie was the daughter of Augustin Russie I. She accompanied her husband, Andre Chalifoux I, to the west in 1838 on the same brigade that brought Father Blanchet and Demers.[3]

Both Edward and **Jean Baptiste Gendron's** godparents were Augustin Rochon and Celeste Jeaudoin. Augustin Rochin and Celeste were married in 1842. Fond of children, Augustin and Celeste had none of their own, but raised various

1 Michelle, *Just a Memorandum*, 7–8: Polly of the "Whaconeseese band of Clackamas" had Edward, Sophie, Bacheth, and Larosa Jondro. O. Applegate, Testimony of Frank Quenel.

2 Munnick and Warner, *Catholic Church Records—St. Paul*, 26b. Michelle, *Just a Memorandum*, 7–8: Mary Ann wrote that Edward, Sophie, Bacheth, and Larosa were all full siblings.

3 Munnick and Warner, *Catholic Church Records—St. Paul*, 26b.

nieces and nephews and at their death left their money to the local orphanage.[4]

LaRose Gendron's godparents were Amable Arquette and his wife, Marguerite Chinook. Amable Arquette entered the service of the Hudson's Bay Company in 1823. He was one of the settlers from French Prairie who went to California for cattle in 1837. He took a claim near Donald and had a large family. While helping to blast a mill channel around Oregon City, he was permanently blinded. Both he and Marguerite are buried at St. Paul.[5]

After his father died, Edward's mother married **James Winslow.**[6]

On September 29, 1861, Edward Gendron, at the age of twenty, married Victoria Vasselle. Thomas Pisk and a woman identified only as Mary were their witnesses.[7]

Edward and **Victoria Vasselle** had at least four children, but they all died young.[8]

Gendron, Jean Baptiste (1846c–88c), Clackamas, French Canadian [9]	Native Name: None known by author
Alias: Jean Baptiste Jondro, Jondreau, Jeandoin, Jean Winslow	Allotment: None known by author
Mother: Polly, Wakanasisi band of Clackamas	Father: Joseph Gendron, French Canadian

Jean Baptiste was a full brother to **Edward, LaRose,** and **Sophie Gendron.**[10] He married a woman named Lucy in 1875. By her, he had Charles (1867c), Jonas (1867c–86c), Joseph (1868c–70c), and Henry (1869c–86c). In 1878, he married a Clackamas woman, **Julia Agnes.** By her he had Mary and **Agnes Gendron.**[11]

In 1885, Jean Baptiste left Julia Agnes to live with **Mary Winchester,** former wife of **Winchester Jo.** He and Julia Agnes were listed separately on the census from that year until his death in 1888.

Gendron, Julia Agnes (1859c–1919), Clackamas	Native Name: None known by author
Alias: Julia Agnes Jondro, Julia Agnes Lafferty, Julia Laferte, Julia Jondron	Allotment 83

4   Ibid.
5   Ibid., A-2.
6   O. Applegate, Testimony of Victoria Vasselle-Jeffries.
7   Munnick and Beckham, *Catholic Church Record — Grand Ronde*, Register I, p. 14, M-4.
8   O. Applegate, Testimony of Victoria Vasselle-Jeffries.
9   Michelle, *Just a Memorandum,* 7.
10   Ibid.
11   Munnick and Beckham, Catholic *Church Records — Grand Ronde*, Register I, p. 50, B-29, p. 55, B-53, p. 66, S-22, p. 93, M-5, p. 104, S-21, p. 108, M-8, p. 111, B-7, p. 112, S-9, p. 118, B-10, p. 122, B-10, p. 127, B-1, Register II, p. 45, S-16, p. 29, B-16.

Mother: Clackamas	Father: Unknown to author

Julia Agnes married **Jean Baptiste Gendron** on May 21, 1878.[12] They were separated by 1885 and listed separately on the GRIC.

By 1886, Julia Agnes was living with **Peter Lafferty.** They had four children: Clara, Agnes Julia (1887c), Oliver (1891c) and Francis (1894c).[13] On the 1888 GRIC Julia was listed as a widow with two young daughters. Her mother was also living with her.

In 1906, Julia Agnes Gendron-Lafferty received a fee patent on her entire 290-acre allotment. She also inherited an interest in the allotment of **Margaret Martin,** who was her aunt on her mother's side of the family.[14]

Gendron, LaRose (1850c), Clackamas, French Canadian	Native Name: None known by author
Alias: LaRose Jondro, LaRose Jandreau	Allotment: None known by author
Mother: Polly, Wakanasisi band of Clackamas	Father: Joseph Gendron, French Canadian

By 1872, **Chief John Kawache** only had a handful of families from the Oregon City bands listed under his leadership. Besides his sons, **Joe Apperson** (Washamsh) and **Homer Hoffer** (Tamaguin), there were the families of **John Kelly** (Palaikhi), **Henry Winslow, Mark Winslow,** and **Charles Petite.** LaRose Gendron was also listed on this census with her sister, Sophie Gendron. Next to LaRose's name was a notation that she was a "sister to John." This might suggest that Chief John Kawache and the Gendron children shared the same mother but had different fathers. Catholic Church records give "Pauly of The Dalles" as LaRose's mother. Louise Chinook was listed as the mother of **Edward, Sophie,** and **Jean Baptiste Gendron,** but several other Indian sources claim all four children were full siblings and Polly of The Dalles was their mother.[15]

Gendron, Louie (1847c)	Native Name: None known by author
Alias: Louie Jonro, Louis Gangron	Allotment: None known by author
Mother: Unknown to author	Father: Unknown to author

In 1885, Louie was listed with his sons Joseph (1878c) and Louie (1879c). The following year, he was listed with his sons Joseph (1878c) and William (1883c). Apparently, the family's only assets were three horses. They do not seem to be listed on any GRIC after 1886.

---

12 Ibid., Register I, p. 107, M-8.
13 Ibid., Register II, p. 70, B-22, p. 94, B-20, p. 27, B-16.
14 Oregon State Archives, Salem, Oregon, 1908, Yamhill County, Estate 1272.
15 Michelle, *Just a Memorandum,* 7. O. Applegate, Testimony of Frank Quenel.

Gendron, Mary (1882c), Clackamas, French Canadian	Native Name: None known by author
Alias: Agnes Jondran	Allotment 84
Mother: Julia Agnes, Clackamas	Father: Jean Baptiste Gendron, French Canadian, Clackamas

On January 30, 1907, Mary Gendron received a fee patent for an eighty-acre allotment.

Gendron, Sophie (1848c–77), Clackamas, French Canadian[16]	Native Name: None known by author
Alias: Sophie Jondro, Sophie Jandreau, Sophie Petite, Sophie Winslow	Allotment: None known by author
Mother: Polly, Wakanasisi band of Clackamas	Father: Joseph Gendron, French Canadian

Six months after a Protestant minister married Sophie Gendron and **Charlie Petite,** they had Father Malo marry them for the second time in the Catholic Church at St. Paul. The ceremony was held on July 25, 1860, and was witnessed by Charlie's father, Amable Petite. Some thirty years earlier, Amable Petite had married Charlie's mother, Susanne Tawakon, in much the same way. Amable and Susanne were first married at Fort Vancouver by the Anglican chaplain Herbert Beaver on March 27, 1837. They were remarried by the Catholic priests in December the following year.[17]

By 1872, Sophie and Charlie Petite had a number of children including **Henry, Christine, Mary,** and **Elizabeth Petite.**

After Charlie died, Sophie married **Henry Winslow.** After Sophie died, **Mark Winslow's** half brother, **James Winslow,** finished raising Sophie and Charlie Petite's children.[18]

George, Chief, Umpqua	Native Name: Cheenlenten /Cheen-len-ten/[19]
Alias: None known by author	Allotment: None known by author
Mother: Unknown to author	Father: Unknown to author

George (Cheenlenten) was one of the signers on the treaty at Calapooia Creek in Douglas County on November 29, 1854. At Grand Ronde, on May 4, 1861, the priest Adrian Croquet wrote: "… have baptized Henriette about one year old,

---

16 Ibid.
17 Munnick and Warner, *Catholic Church Records — St. Paul,* A-77.
18 Michelle, *Just a Memorandum,* 8.
19 Kappler, *Treaty with the Umpqua and Kalapuya, 1854.*

born of Georges, an Umpqua chief, and of Mary of this mission."[20]

George, Chief, Rogue River	Native Name: Chocultah /Cho-cul-tah/[21]
Alias: Joquah Trader	Allotment: None known by author
Mother: Unknown to author	Father: Unknown to author

Chief George (Chocultah) was chief of a band of Rogue River people from the country below Evans Creek in southern Oregon and the sixth signer on the treaty of November 15, 1854.

During times of trouble with the Americans, Chief George (Chocultah)'s band united on occasion with Chief Limpy's band. It was said that together they made up an active and dangerous force.

His people from the Rogue River—twenty men, forty-three women, and thirty-seven children—were brought to Grand Ronde by military escort.[22] The main band of Rogue River people came to Grand Ronde by wagon, but Chief George (Chocultah)'s band came by steamship.[23]

George, Eliza (1841c–1911c), Mary's River band of Kalapuya[24]	Native Name: Tmulhu /TMU-hlu/ (tmúɬuʔ)*[25]
Alias: Eliza Sappenfield, Eliza Scott	Allotment: None known by author
Mother: Unknown to author	Father: Marysville George, Mary's River Kalapuya

Eliza George (Tmulhu) was related to **William Hartless** (Futi) and **Mary Ann Monada**. They were first cousins, but Eliza called William Hartless her brother. Like William, Eliza spoke the Mary's River Kalapuya dialect.[26]

At Grand Ronde, she became a well-known medicine doctor. When at her dance, Eliza sang and jumped high. **Victoria Wishikin** (Kinishi) recorded two of her power songs for Melville Jacobs in 1929.[27]

---

20 Munnick and Beckham, *Catholic Church Records—Grand Ronde*, Register I, p. 9, B-31.

21 Kappler, *Treaty with the Rogue River, 1854*. Douthit, *Joseph Lane and the Rogue River Indians*, 483: Chief George (Cholcultah) as "Joquah Trader."

22 1856 GRIC.

23 O. Applegate, Testimony of Kitty Tom and Applegate Jack.

24 Michelle, *Just a Memorandum*, 9: "Sambo Sabinfield and his wife, Liza both Calapooia." O. Applegate, Testimony of James Winslow: "My mother, not now alive, told me that Marysville Tom and George were brothers to Mary Voutrin's mother. They were the fathers of Bill Hartless and Polk Scott's wife [Eliza]."

25 1887 GRIC gives her Indian name as "Ta-moo-sun." Jacobs, Notebook 51, *Music and Ethnology*, 50: Indian name "Tmulu."

26 O. Applegate, Testimony of Mary Ann Voutrin. Jacobs, Notebook 51, *Music and Ethnology*, 50.

27 Jacobs, Notebook 51, *Music and Ethnology*, 50.

On the 1885 GRIC, Eliza was listed as the wife of **Sambo Sappenfield** (Chawatkha) with their children, Frank, Susan, and Henry. She and Sambo were listed together as husband and wife until 1899 when Eliza was listed as a sixty-five-year-old widow.

After Sambo died, Eliza was listed alone until she became the wife of **Polk Scott** (Puk) in 1902. In 1909, Eliza was living once again as a widow. She does not appear on any GRIC after 1910.

There does not seem to be any record of Eliza receiving an allotment at Grand Ronde in her own name, but she did inherit Sambo Sappenfield's two hundred acres.[28]

George, Lebanon (1846c)	Native Name: None known by author
Alias: None known by author	Allotment: None known by author
Mother: Unknown to author	Father: Unknown to author

In 1886, Lebanon George was listed as a poor forty-year-old widower.

George, Marysville (d. 1872c), Mary's River band of Kalapuya	Native Name: None known by author
Alias: None known by author	Allotment: None known by author
Mother: Unknown to author	Father: Unknown to author

Marysville George was a prominent man among his people. "**Chief Louis Napesa** knew him well."[29] He was the brother of **Marysville Tom** and **Louise Monada.** His daughter, **Eliza George** (Tmulhu), was an important medicine doctor at Grand Ronde.[30]

According to the GRIC, Marysville George died prior to 1872 leaving two widows (his hayash wife, Nancy Hartless, and an unnamed second wife) and his son, Andre (1857c).

George, Santiam (1837c), Santiam band of Kalapuya[31]	Native Name: None known by author
Alias: None known by author	Allotment: None known by author
Mother: Unknown to author	Father: Unknown to author

In 1885, he was listed with his wife, Polly (1844c), and his children: Molly (1873c), Manda (1875c), and Sam (1877c).

---

28 *Heirs of Deceased Indian*, Allotment Record 186.
29 O. Applegate, Testimony of David Leno.
30 Ibid.
31 Gatschet, *Texts, Sentences and Vocables*, 368: "Old George" under Santiam.

Gidina, Tualatin band of Kalapuya, Yamhill band of Kalapuya	Native Name: Gidina /gi-DI-na/ (gidína)*[32]
Alias: None known by author	Allotment: None known by author
Mother: Unknown to author	Father: Unknown to author

Gidina was married to Big Susan long before she was the wife of **Jacob Wheeler** (Shwa).[33]

Gilbert, Anetta, Cow Creek band of Umpqua	Native Name: None known by author
Alias: None known by author	Allotment: None known by author
Mother: Unknown to author	Father: Unknown to author

In 1872, Anetta Gilbert and her son, William (1867c), were listed with the **Isaac Stephen** family, but the agent also noted a woman named "Annetta Gilbert" living with the Cow Creek chief, **Jacob Edemchoey**.

Gilbert, Frances (1868c–1934c), Molalla, Tillamook, Watlala (Cascade) band of Chinook	Native Name: None known by author
Alias: Josephine Frances Kelly, Josephine Shirley	Allotment: None known by author
Mother: Cinthy, Cascade Chinook[34]	Father: Tom Gilbert, Molalla, Tillamook

When Frances was growing up, her parents wanted her to take up white ways and would not allow anything but English to be spoken in their home. As a result, Frances did not learn Chinook Jargon until much later in life.[35]

Frances married **John Kelly** on July 27, 1885. After living on their own for a few years, Frances and John moved in with Frances's parents. The family home was described by the Indian agent as a house and barn on twenty fenced acres. Tom Gilbert reportedly owned two horses and a wagon. Frances and John had a third horse and a buckboard.

Frances and John Kelly had two sons: John (1889) and Ernest (1887). Her husband, John, and son Ernest both died in 1896. Sometime later Frances remarried and moved to Portland, Oregon.

---

32 Jacobs, Notebook 51, *Music and Ethnology*, 51. Gatschet, *Texts, Sentences and Vocable*, 77.

33 Melville Jacobs, Notebook 51, *Music and Ethnology*, 51.

34 Munnick and Beckham, *Catholic Church Records—Grand Ronde*, Register I: while the mother of "Josephine Gilbert" is not listed in the Catholic Church record of her birth. Cinthy appears to have been the only wife of Tom Gilbert.

35 Zenk, *Chinook Jargon*, 268.

Frances Gilbert-Kelly with a daughter of her second cousin, who was visiting in 1935. Joel V. Berreman Collection. Photo courtesy of the Confederated Tribes of the Grand Ronde Community of Oregon.

Frances did not return to Grand Ronde until her mother became seriously ill. She took care of her mother until Cinthy (Chewlyish) died around 1921. A few months later, Frances also had to bury her son, John.[36] Grieving over her loss, Frances chose not to return to her second husband, but to remain at Grand Ronde.

In her elder years, although her health prevented her from working very hard, Frances went with other Grand Ronde people to pick hops. She tended her garden, caught crawfish and trout in a little spring nearby, and gathered blackberries and "chittum" bark to sell. A man took her picture and it was in the newsreel at the movies. Apparently, this pleased her very much.[37]

She received "dower rights" to John T. Kelly's 199.58-acre allotment. She and her son, John D. Kelly, sold it to P. R. Fendall in 1911. Frances also inherited her father's allotment, the allotment of her uncle, **Steven Savage** (Palhilh), and a one-fifth interest in the Enoch and Mary Fisherman land allotment. She lived out her

---

36 Berreman, interview with Frances Gilbert-Shirley.
37 Ibid.

life alone in an old house, poorly but comfortably furnished, on approximately thirty acres of the inherited allotment land.[38]

Gilbert, Thomas (1840c–1908), Molalla, Tillamook	Native Name: Kiyukiyush /gi-yu-GI-yush/ (kiyukíyush)*[39]
Alias: Molalla Tom, Wawa Tom[40]	Allotment 57
Mother: Tillamook Mary	Father: Paul Toto, Molalla

"Molalla Tom" Gilbert (Kiyukiyush) came to Grand Ronde when the Molalla were first removed to the reservation. He and **Steven Savage** (Palhilh) were half brothers.[41] **Margaret Toto** (Chamala) was his half sister.[42] While they shared the same father, they had different mothers. Molalla Tom's mother was Tillamook Mary.[43] She was living with him and his family in 1885.

Described as five feet five inches tall and weighing 190 pounds, Molalla Tom had a Clackamas wife, Cinthy.[44] They were married November 21, 1881, in the presence of his daughters, Cecelia (1872c–88) and **Frances Gilbert**.[45]

In many ways Molalla Tom was a responsible citizen. In 1880, he was elected to serve on the Grand Ronde Indian Legislature representing the west precinct with **John Wacheno** (Tsinwalh) and **Peter Kenoyer** (Kinai).[46] However, he also supported his family by illegally selling whiskey to Indian people.

Molalla Tom's bootlegging caused **Dave Yachkawa**, a Tualatin sub-chief, to file a number of complaints against him, including one in September 1871. J. C.

38 Ibid.

39 Jacobs, Notebooks 58, *Texts and Ethnology*, 12. Jacobs, Santiam Kalapuya Ethnologic Texts, 81.

40 Cawley, *Indian Journal*, 20: "Molalla Tom" nickname "Wawa Tom due to his talkative nature." Johnson and Zenk, Chinuk Wawa, 120: wawa word meaning to talk, say, tell.

41 Gatschet, Frachtenberg, and Jacobs, *Kalapuya Texts*, Part 3, 189.

42 Affidavit State of Oregon, County of Yamhill, taken from Josephine (Frances) Shirley January 25, 1917 and Macasca Sutton, February 3, 1917.

43 1885 GRIC: living with Tom Gilbert, Tillamook Mary, age 63, his mother. Michelle, *Just a Memorandum*, 6: Tom Gilbert's mother, Yoncalla, and father, Molalla.

44 Oregon State Archive, Salem, Oregon, Polk County, Inmate File 1467. Michelle, *Just a Memorandum*, 6: Mary Ann wrote that Tom's wife, Chewlyish, father, Klamath and mother, Clackamas. Berreman, interview with Frances Gilbert-Shirley: her mother was a Cascade Indian who became paralyzed before her death. Frances took care of her.

45 1872 GRIC listed Tom and his wife Cinthy with Babtiste, age five, Etly, age three, and Cecilia, age three months. Also living with the family was Tom's grandmother, Mary. Munnick and Beckham, *Catholic Church Records—Grand Ronde*, Register I, p. 74, B-18, B-19.

46 National Archives, Seattle, Grand Ronde/Siletz, Land and Enrollment Program records, Field Notes and Land Survey 1875–1898, Land Description Book 1878, Box 115; Grand Ronde Justice Court.

Cartwright responded to A. B. Meacham's inquiry about the incident in a letter dated September 11, 1871. Cartwright wrote that the charge against Tom Gilbert would need more evidence as Yachkawa's "testimony had been disregarded in more than one case."[47]

The continuous conflict between Molalla Tom and Yachkawa was destined to end violently. The final drama was brought about when Yachkawa once again turned Molalla Tom in for bootlegging. In response, on November 28, 1882, Molalla Tom picked up an axe and started out for the home of Yachkawa. Once there, he killed Yachkawa and his aging wife, **Sarah Kiakuts** (Washkayak).[48]

Among the Molallas, it was an old custom for a murderer to paint half his face black and the other half white to let people know that children might die if they ate or drank from the utensils he used.[49] Now perhaps this custom had been set aside, but almost certainly Molalla Tom thought about it. In any case, everyone knew he had committed the murders.

After he was arrested, his case was heard in Polk County Circuit Court where he was convicted and sentenced to death in December 1882. Upon appeal, the transcript of the judgment showed two separate indictments against Molalla Tom for two distinct crimes, but only one verdict and one judgment. Not being able to determine by the records whether Molalla Tom was convicted of killing Dave Yachkawa or Sarah (Washkayak), the Supreme Court of Oregon reversed the court decision and ordered a retrial.[50]

Molalla Tom was rearrested and convicted of one reduced charge of manslaughter on December 6, 1883. He was released July 5, 1884, having served six months of a one-year sentence.[51]

According to the GRIC, by 1888, Molalla Tom was living once again at Grand Ronde with his wife, Cinthy, his son-in-law, **John Kelly,** his daughter, Frances, and his two-year-old grandson.

Gwayakiti, Sarah (1841c–91), Molalla, Clackamas[52]	Native Name: None known by author
Alias: Sara, Sarah Wishikin	Allotment: None known by author
Mother: Wagayuhlen, Clackamas	Father: Chief Quaiguaty (Gwayakiti), Molalla

Sarah was the daughter of **Chief Quaiquaty** (Gwayakiti), the principal chief

47 J. C. Cartwright to A. B. Meacham, September 11, 1871, Letters Received by the Bureau of Indian Affairs, Washington, DC, RG 75, Microcopy M-234, Roll 609, National Archives, Washington, DC.
48 Jacobs, Notebook 58, *Texts and Ethnology*, 12.
49 Leo J. Frachtenberg, *Molala Ethnology*.
50 *The Pacific Reporter*, Vol. 112, 436–37.
51 Oregon State Archive, Salem, Oregon, Polk County, Inmate File 1467
52 Jacobs, Field Notebook 51, *Music and Ethnology*, 10.

of the Molalla band of Molalla and his wife, **Wagayuhlen Gwayakiti**. She could speak a number of languages, including Clackamas, Molalla, and Chinook Jargon.[53]

Sarah received her tamanawas in a dream. If she had not, she would have died. She used no words in her song, but by the way she danced and sang people could tell it was a type of grizzly power or more specifically that of a half dead or wounded grizzly. She also received the tamanawas of the morning light through a dream. This power would have brought her all sorts of riches and fine things if she had lived longer.[54]

Sarah married **William Wishikin.** They had a number of children: Aik, Antoinette (1869c–75), Moses (1872–73), Henriette (1874c–75c), and **Victoria Wishikin** (Kinishi).[55]

Once when Sarah left her husband , her mother forced her to return. Wishikin paid Wagayuhlen Gwayakiti for sending Sarah back, as was the practice in those days.[56]

After Wishikin died in 1875c, Sarah married **Foster Wacheno** (Inawalh).

In the end, the illness that killed Sarah caused her legs and feet to swell. She could neither stand nor walk around. Her daughter Victoria Wishikin was taking care of her when Sarah's brother, **Moses Allen** (Shkayinch), stopped by her house. He asked Sarah if he could get their mother's brother, **Polk Scott** (Puk), to examine her and explain the extent of her illness.[57]

After gaining her consent, Moses returned about noon the following day. He said he had located Polk , who would be coming presently. When Polk arrived, he sat by Sarah and began to sing his curing songs. After a time, he told Moses that he could not save Sarah as she had been dying too long before he reached her. He said the sickness resembled a little fish or salmon. He tried to catch it, but it slipped through his fingers. Polk told him he would come again the next evening to doctor her, but if she did not improve they would just have to wait for her to die.[58]

The next evening, Polk Scott doctored her again. This time, he used the fullest strength of his spirit power, but at last, he said, "my doctoring is of no avail. She is leaving us now."[59]

Moses told Polk that he had said nothing bad. That was why he had wanted

---

53 Jacobs, Notebooks 67, *Texts Ethnology Clackamas & Jargon*, 138.
54 Jacobs, Field Notebook 51, *Music and Ethnology*, 10: Victoria recorded both of these power songs.
55 McChesney, *The Rolls of Certain Indian Tribes*, Testimony of Edward Franklin Teabo, 79.
56 Jacobs, Field Notebook 53, *Texts and Ethnology*, 48.
57 Jacobs, *Clackamas Text*, Part II, 512–14. Jacobs, Field Notebook 51, *Music and Ethnology*, 10: Jacobs wrote that Victoria Howard's mother "died prematurely of TB."
58 Jacobs, *Clackamas Text*, Part II, 512–14. Jacobs, Field Notebook 51, *Music and Ethnology*, 10.
59 Ibid.

**Photo passed down to descendants of Victoria
Howard unidentified but very likely Victoria's mother,
Sarah Gwayakiti. Notice flattened head customary
for prominent families of this generation. Courtesy of
Barbara Danforth Private Collection.**

him to doctor Sarah because he knew Polk would be frank and honest.[60]

On November 6, 1891, Sarah Gwayakiti died after receiving the sacraments of the church.[61]

Gwayakiti, Sophie (1818c–98), Molalla	Native Name: None known by author
Alias: Sophie Hubbard, Sophie Hobart, Sophie Wacheno	Allotment: None known by author
Mother: Unknown to author	Father: Unknown to author

Sophie was **Chief Quaiquaty (**Gwayakiti**)'s** sister. She was once married to

---

60 Jacobs, *Clackamas Text*, Part II, 512–14.
61 Munnick and Beckham, *Catholic Church Records—Grand Ronde*, Register II, p. 72, S-14.

Chief Daniel Wacheno (Wachinu), but left him.[62] She had a half Clackamas son named **Dan Wacheno Hubbard** (Shkukaush). Catholic Church records recorded her death as on May 4, 1898, under the name "Sophie Hobart."[63]

Gwayakiti, Wagayuhlen (1818c–89c), Clackamas[64]	Native Name: Wagayuhlen /wa-GA-yu-hlen/ (waġáyu+ən)*[65]
Alias: None known by author	Allotment: None known by author
Mother: Unknown to author	Father: Unknown to author

Wagayuhlen was the hayash wife of **Chief Quaiquaty** (Gwayakiti), **Polk Scott** (Puk)'s sister, and the mother of **Moses Allen** (Shkayinch) and **Sarah Gwayakiti.**[66] **Mary Ann Kilmonie** (Kilipashta), a much younger Clackamas-speaking woman with a Molalla husband, was Wagayuhlen's cousin.[67]

Wagayuhlen's power told her that in her tamanamas dance a certain person who understood should cut her arm with a sharp arrowhead knife. A piece of her hair was to be cut and scorched; after the burned hair was soaked in the blood from her arm, she needed to eat it. Her power allowed her to do that. She also had the power necessary to pierce ears. People would bring their children to her in winter. They would sing and dance all night. After the fifth night, at the moment of dawn, beads and other gifts would be spread out on the ground and Wagayuhlen would pierce the ears of children.[68] She had other powers, but perhaps the strongest was her power to cure people by taking away their disease.[69]

A busy medicine doctor, she treated men, women, and children.[70] Her work kept her so busy that she purchased a second wife for her husband from the Klamath people at Oregon City. It was her intention that the young girl would relieve her of her household duties.[71]

Wagayuhlen's daughter **Sarah Gwayakiti** was widowed in 1875 and Sarah's daughter Antoinette Wishikin also died. Shortly thereafter, Sarah and her daughter Victoria went to live with Wagayuhlen. Later, **Victoria Wishikin** (Kinishi) re-

62 Jacobs, Field Notebooks 61, *Texts and Ethnology,* 4

63 Munnick and Beckham, *Catholic Church Records—Grand Ronde,* Register II, p. 115, S-4.

64 Michelle, *Just a Memorandum,* 6: Skhins was Molala; his wife was Clackamas.

65 Jacobs, Field Notebook 52, *Texts and Ethnology,* 42: "(Clack,) Wagayulen, name of Mrs. H's mother's mother."

66 Jacobs, Notebook 51, *Music and Ethnology,* 10. Jacobs, Notebooks 52, *Texts and Ethnology,* 41: Wagayulhin was the name of Mrs. H's mother's mother. Jacobs, *Clackamas Chinook Text,* Part II, 492–93, 647, Note 426, stated Sarah and Moses Allen had the same mother. Michelle, *Just a Memorandum,* 6.

67 Jacobs, Notebooks 69, *Texts Ethnology Clackamas & Jargon,* 101. Jacobs, Field Notebooks 59, *Texts and Ethnology,* 60.

68 Jacob, Field Notebook 51, *Music and Ethnology,* 20.

69 Jacobs, Field Notebook 52, *Texts and Ethnology,* 52.

70 Jacobs, Notebooks 69, *Texts Ethnology Clackamas & Jargon,* 113.

71 Jacobs, Field Notebooks 52, *Texts and Ethnology,* 19.

called an occasion during this time when she and her grandmother went to pick gooseberries. Not long after they arrived at the berry patch, Victoria heard her grandmother weeping. Confused by her tears, Victoria learned later that this was a place where her sister Antoinette had once played standing sticks upright in the ground. Although some time had passed since her death, the sticks were still there standing as her sister had left them. Victoria said that the next morning her grandmother went outside and wept. When she came inside, she did not wash her face nor did she eat until the sun was far to one side.[72]

Wagayuhlen spent her time from early morning until late at night visiting the sick at Grand Ronde. When she returned from doctoring, she would ask her granddaughter, Victoria Wishikin, to make a fire and get some water. Then she cooked their meal. After dinner they would talk about her day, but Wagayuhlen would never criticize or speak disparagingly about anyone. She believed all the Indian people on the reservation were her family, not just those from her tribe.[73]

After becoming crippled from a fall, Wagayuhlen tapped her cane as she sang and danced. Her granddaughter, Victoria Wishikin, recorded Wagayuhlen's song for Melville Jacobs in 1929.[74]

Gwayakiti, Yainex (1833c–1902c), Klamath slave[75]	Native Name: None known by author
Alias: Gainex Quackerty	Allotment 167
Mother: Unknown to author	Father: Unknown to author

Yainex was probably named for a place on the eastern border of the Klamath Reservation. Long ago, it was the location of a great slave market and a convenient place for all the tribes within a hundred miles in all directions to meet in the fall of each year.

At Oregon City, **Wagayuhlen Gwayakiti** purchased a woman from the Klamath as a second wife for her husband. Yainex Quacherty was this second wife. Wagayuhlen said that by the time the second wife married **Chief Quaiquaty** (Gwayakiti), the woman already had two children who had died.[76]

Yainex Gwayakiti received an allotment of a hundred acres that was sold by her heirs, Caroline Orton and Short Bob on October 18, 1907.[77]

---

72 Jacobs, *Clackamas Text*, Part II, 502.
73 Ibid., 534–36.
74 Jacobs, Field Notebook 51, *Music and Ethnology*, 7.
75 *Heirs of Deceased Indians*, Allotment Record 167, gave her name as "Gainex" and her lifespan as 1833–January 31, 1902. 1872 GRIC gave name as "Yiamox."
76 Jacobs, Notebooks 52, *Texts and Ethnology*, 10, 19.
77 *Heirs to Deceased Indians*, Allotment Record 167.

H

Hall, Dick (1824c–1913), Umpqua	Native Name: None known by author
Alias: Klickitat Dick	Allotment 63
Mother: Unknown to author	Father: Unknown to author

Rev. Summers wrote that when he stopped at the home of Klickitat Dick in search of Indian artifacts, Klickitat Dick's wife, whom he described as "large, strong, and very wrinkled," met him at the gate with her dog. She told him not to come in, but Rev. Summers, seeing that she was not going to physically stop him, opened the gate and entered the house anyway. He wrote:

> Seeing we would come in anyhow, she put herself in front and led the way to the kitchen door. This opened from a well-filled woodshed; a padlock attached to three yards of chain fastened it ... She had only a rather good frame house, somewhat base looking, with long strips of coarse native matting around one of the rooms, rising about four feet above the floor.[1]

After Rev. Summers left Klickitat Dick's place to search a neighboring home for artifacts, Klickitat Dick's wife gathered her friends and followed him there. Summers wrote:

> ...[S]he now made herself and her friends merry at our expense. It was ridiculous in their eyes to be wandering about, picking up the worthless old things, which even they did not use any more, when we could get so much better ones at the stores all bright and new.[2]

For short periods of time, any number of relatives lived with Klickitat Dick. **Jenny Mackey** said she lived at Klickitat Dick's house after her mother died until she married **Solomon Riggs** (Gunconnacli) around 1867.[3] In 1872, Solomon's aunt, Lelivess, was staying with Klickitat Dick and his wife, Mollie. At that time, Klickitat Dick's son, Charles Oscar (1856c), was also staying with him.

After his wife Mollie drown in 1887, Klickitat Dick married Douglas Sampson Jones's aunt, Nancy Palouse.[4] After they were married, the medicine woman, **Su-**

---

1   Cawley, *Indian Journal*, 29.
2   Ibid.
3   Berreman, interview with Jenny Riggs.
4   GRIC 1887: Klickitat Dick's new wife Nancy was listed as Roll #81, "Nancy Santiam," widow, age fifty. Michelle, *Just a Memorandum*, 4: "Nancy Chcatte" [Klickitat]. National Archives, Seattle, NRIA-S-11, PAC-08, Nancy Hall: Nancy Palouse aka Nancy

san Hollingsworth, and Esther Jones lived with Klickitat Dick and Nancy.[5]

Klickitat Dick's allotment was in the heart of the Umpqua section of the reservation. **Nancy Boggs** lived just south of them. **Richard Cook** (Shay Shoaska) lived to the north.[6] Klickitat Dick sold a hundred acres of his allotment to L. Weiss. After he died on October 3, 1913, a fee patent for eighty acres of his allotment was issued to his heirs Jasper Palouse, **Douglas Sampson Jones,** and George Demour with provisions for his widow, Nancy Palouse-Hall, who was unallotted.[7]

A short time later, a fire took several houses including Nancy's home with everything in it.[8] However, Nancy did not die in the fire. She was killed December 31, 1914, by **Mary Jones** (Sana), Douglas Sampson's second wife, who stabbed her to death in an intoxicated rage.[9]

Halo, Chief (1800c–78c), Yoncalla band of Kalapuya	Native Name: Hilu /HI-lu/ (hílu)[*10]
Alias: Halo Fearn	Allotment: None known by author
Mother: Unknown to author	Father: Cheomeshun[11]

Halo (Hilu) was chief of the Yoncalla band of Kalapuya. When legal papers for his family's land claim required a surname, Chief Halo picked out the name *Kamafimi*, meaning fern.[12] Since the word was difficult for some Americans to pronounce, his name was recorded on the deed as "Fearn." Later, the spelling was corrected to "Fern."

According to an old story, Halo's father was killed in a raid on his village when Halo was a very young man. Returning from hunting, he found his father dead and his people greatly outnumbered and fighting furiously. In that moment, Halo suddenly was gifted with a great power and insight. He could see that the force attacking his people was one of great evil. He held up his hands and called out to God to join the Yoncalla in their fight. Then, singlehandedly, Halo

---

Hall was the first wife of Santiago.

5   Zenk, interview with Esther LaBonte, 1982, transcript 1, 2009, (23:34). National Archives, Seattle, NRIA-S-11, PAC-08, Nancy Hall: Nancy Palouse aka Nancy Hall was the first wife of Santiago.

6   Original Blueprint of Reservation Allotments.

7   *Heirs of Deceased Indians*, Allotment Records, 63.

8   Zenk, interview with Esther LaBonte, 1982, transcript 1, 2009 (23:34).

9   Ibid.

10 Gatschet, *Texts, Sentences and Vocables*, 367:listed under the Yoncalla as "old man Helo." Johnson and Zenk, *Chinook Wawa*, 40: *hilu*, meaning lacking, without; be absent, gone, expired.

11 Private Conversation with traditional storyteller Esther Stutzman, Coos and Kalapuya woman, 2002, Confederated Tribes of Grand Ronde Community of Oregon.

12 Baker, *The Last of the Yangolers*, 4: Baker gave *Cam-aphee-ma* as a Chinook Jargon term. Jacobs, Field Notebook 45, *Yoncalla Texts*, 109: *kamafima* (fern), Mrs. Albertson's Indian name; maiden name: Laura Fearn (later Blackerty, now Albertson).

Chief Halo. Photo Courtesy Douglas County Museum of Natural and Cultural History.

killed seven of the warring raiders at the head of the valley and eleven more in the hills back of Shoestring.[13]

Chief Halo had a brother or half brother named **Muddy Tom Churchill** (Kaltas Lipom).[14] He also had several wives and a number of children: John, Beel, Jake, Molliette, and Lalouise.[15]

While he was present during the signing of the Treaty at Calapooia Creek in 1854, Halo refused to sign.[16] Furthermore, he resisted removal from the home-

---

13   Kruse, *The Halo Trail,* 3.
14   O. Applegate, Testimony of Jake Fern aka Jefferies Halo. *Heirs of Deceased Indians,* Allotment Record 23: "Tom Churchill" aka "Mudy Fern."
15   Kruse, *The Halo Trail,* 9.
16   O. Applegate, Testimony of Jake Fern.

land of the Yoncalla even up until the day Subagent Metcalf came for him and his people. In the end, he was allowed to stay in the Yoncalla Valley, but his family was removed.

Halo's wife, Dunifo, sons **Jake** and **Be-el Fern,** and other relatives were first taken to a temporary reservation on the Umpqua River. After about a year, they were moved from the Umpqua to the Grand Ronde Reservation. The old chief followed them to Grand Ronde a year or two later.[17]

The family did not stay continuously but moved back and forth between their old home in the Umpqua valley and the reservation until about 1870.[18]

Chief Halo died during the spring of 1878. His body was buried at Yoncalla.

Hardin, Ben (1825c), Rogue River/Shasta	Native Name: None known by author
Alias: None known by author	Allotment: None known by author
Mother: Unknown to author	Father: Unknown to author

In 1885, Ben Hardin, a bachelor, was living with his sister, **Mary Neal.** who had been at Grand Ronde for some time. She was listed with the Rogue River/ Shasta in 1872.

Harding, Ben (1851c–96c), Santiam band of Kalapuya[19]	Native Name: Kwana /KWA-na/ (kwá?na)*[20]
Alias: Ben Hayde	Allotment: None known by author
Mother: Unknown to author	Father: Unknown to author

Ben Harding (Kwana) was **Louis Kenoyer's** uncle and a cousin to **Sambo Sappenfield** (Chawatkha).[21]

In 1890, Ben (Kwana) was listed with his wife, Julia. In 1891, he was listed as single. He remained single through 1895. He was not listed on any GRIC after that year and there is no record of his receiving an allotment.

Harney, Fred (1852c–98c)	Native Name: None known by author
Alias: None known by author	Allotment: None known by author
Mother: Unknown to author	Father: Unknown to author

Fred Harney was from the Siletz Reservation. He married **Jenny Sansousee**

---

17 O. Applegate, Testimony of Jake Fern and Polk Scott.

18 Ibid.

19 1872 GRIC: "Ben Hayden" under Santiam tribe.

20 Jacobs, Field Notebooks 36, *Santiam Kalapuya Text*, 192.

21 Jacobs, Field Notebooks 46, *Santiam Kalapuya Text*, 5.

on March 20, 1894. Their witnesses were **Cephas Tipton** and **Josephine Lillie Condon.**[22]

Jenny was listed alone on the 1894 and 1895 GRIC. Fred Harney was not listed at Grand Ronde until 1896. Jennie was listed as his widow in 1898.

Harrigood, Charles, Kalapuya[23]	Native Name: None known by author
Alias: Charles Haregood	Allotment: None known by author
Mother: Unknown to author	Father: Unknown to author

In 1872, Charles was listed with his wife, Mary, under the Santiam Kalapuya. According to Albert Gatschet, he was still alive in 1877.

Harris, John (1857c), Santiam band of Kalapuya	Native Name: Captain Santiam
Alias: Coyote John	Allotment: None known by author
Mother: Unknown to author	Father: Captain Santiam

In his annual report, dated August 6, 1870, W. R. Dunbar, the teacher of the manual labor school at Grand Ronde, made special mention of John Harris along with two other students. Dunbar wrote they were quite intelligent and studious. In addition to praising their reading, writing, and spelling, he wrote that these three children had stored in their minds a large amount of very practical knowledge.[24]

In 1872, Coyote John Harris was listed on the GRIC under the Santiam band of Kalapuya. John Harris was listed on the 1885 GRIC as a son of Captain Santiam.

Hartless, William (1855c–1920), Mary's River band of Kalapuya, Alsea[26]	Native Name: Futi /FU-ti/ (fút'i),* Skamayu /SKA-ma-yu/ (sḳámayu?)* [25]
Alias: William Heartless	Allotment 64
Mother: Paula, /PAU-la/ (páu?la?),*[27] Alsea	Father: Marysville Tom, Mary's River band of Kalapuya

22 Munnick and Beckham, *Catholic Church Records—Grand Ronde*, Register II, p. 92, M-2.
23 1872 GRIC listed his tribe as Santiam band of Kalapuya. Gatschet, *Texts, Sentences and Vocable*, 368: "Charley Haregood" as "Kalapuya now with the Marysville."
24 *Annual Report the Commissioner of Indian Affairs*, 1870, 65.
25 Jacobs, Notebook 36, *Santiam Kalapuya Text*, 192. Gatschet, *Texts, Sentences and Vocable*, 370. Jacobs, Notebooks 81, *Texts and Ethnology Santiam*, 76: William got into some mischief which earned him the name Skamayu from "some old lady." The name is derived from the word *skama* meaning grandson.
26 1888 GRIC gave his tribe as Mary's River Kalapuya. Jacobs, Notebook 36, *Santiam Kalapuya Text*, 192: Hudson said Hartless was half Alsea and half Pinefu or Mary's River Kalapuya.
27 Jacobs, Notebooks 46, *Santiam Kalapuya Text*, n.p.

The William Hartless family. Seated left to right: William Hartless (Futi), Charley Hartless and wife, Christine Petite-Hartless. Photo courtesy of Oregon Historical Society (OrHi 56429).

William Hartless (Futi) was the son of **Marysville Tom** and an Alsea woman called Paula.[28] His mother had a few little spots tattooed on each cheek.[29]

After William married **Christine Petite** in 1884, they had twelve children but all were born dead and nameless except for Martin (1888-1918), Benedict (1894c–1943), Michel (1896–96), and Charley (1902–22).[30]

In addition to farming, William was employed at the Grand Ronde Agency.

---

28 Oregon State Archives, Salem, Oregon, 1905, Polk County, Estate File 0925, Alsea Bill. Jacobs, Notebooks 46, *Santiam Kalapuya Text*, n.p. Henry Zenk, *Chinook Jargon*, 269.

29 Jacobs, Notebooks 46, *Santiam Kalapuya Text*, n.p.

30 Munnick and Beckham, *Catholic Church Records—Grand Ronde*, Register II, p. 48, B-46, p. 85, B-7, p. 104, B-1, p. 105, S-4.

He worked as an assistant blacksmith from 1883 to 1885.[31] By 1888, he and his wife, Christine, had a house and barn with a garden, three horses, a dozen chickens, four hogs, and a small herd of cattle, among other assets. From 1894 to 1896, he worked for the agency as an apprentice blacksmith and assistant carpenter.[32]

After William received a trust patent on a 280-acre allotment, he exchanged forty acres with his uncle, **Alsea Bill** (Kama). In 1903, the old trust patent was canceled, but another trust patent was issued in 1904.[33]

Shortly after William dictated Mary's River Language texts for Leo Frachtenberg, his son Martin enlisted in the Navy. Martin was fighting in France when he was killed on his birthday, October 9, 1918. His body was returned to the reservation and buried in the Grand Ronde cemetery.[34]

Prior to his death, Martin had taken out a war risk insurance policy with a face value of ten thousand dollars naming his sixteen-year-old brother, Charles, as beneficiary. His father used the insurance money to send Charles, who was in poor health, to live at Lapwai in Nez Perce country. Even though it was doubtful that Charles would ever recover, William wanted him educated.[35] A little over a year later, in January of 1920, William wrote his last will and testament with Philip Warren and **Abraham Hudson** acting as witnesses. In his will, William left all his real and personal property, valued at around a thousand dollars, to his son, Benedict. To his son Charles, he left nothing. William believed Charley was "amply provided for by the government." While William named **Henry Petite** administrator for his estate, Henry declined the appointment after William's death. In his place, a man named Paul Fundman was approved by the court to control Charles's money until Charley became of legal age.[36]

William's long illness had taken all of his liquid assets. Without funds to pay for his father's casket, Charles wrote Fundman asking him to pay the cost of the funeral from his trust fund. While there is no record indicating whether or not the request was granted, Charles expressed concern sometime later about his rapidly depleting account. Unhappy with the way his funds were being handled, Charley unsuccessfully petitioned the court for control of his trust fund. March 20, 1922, Charlie's body was found in a gulch in Idaho.[37] There was $1,071 remaining in his account. He left the money to his brother, Benedict.[38]

---

31 Grand Ronde Agency Ledger Book, Records of Employees at Grand Ronde July 1883–September 1907 (Cultural Resource Department Archives, Confederated Tribes of the Grand Ronde Community of Oregon).

32 Ibid.

33 *Heirs of Deceased Indians*, Allotment Records, 64.

34 National Archive, Seattle, NRIA-S-11-276, PAC-08, bx 47, Charles Hartless.

35 Oregon State Archives, Salem, Oregon, 1920, Polk County, Estate 1911. National Archive, Seattle, NRIA-S-11-276, PAC-08, bx 47, Charles Hartless.

36 Ibid.

37 Ibid

38 Ibid.

Hauxhurst, George (1843c), Santiam band of Kalapuya	Native Name: None known by author
Alias: Santiam George	Allotment: None known by author
Mother: Jane	Father: John

In 1872, Santiam George was living with his wife, Sarah, and fifteen-year-old daughter, Lucy. In 1885, he was with a wife named, Lucinda (1845c), and his children, Louiza (1868c) and Ben (1870c). Also living with Santiam George was his father "Old John (1822c)" and his mother "Old Jane (1825c)."

Hauxhurst, Widow (1836c)	Native Name: None known by author
Alias: None known by author	Allotment: None known by author
Mother: Unknown to author	Father: Unknown to author

In 1885, the Widow Haurhurst was with her son, Gustus (1868c).

Henry, Chief, Shasta	Native Name: None known by author
Alias: None known by author	Allotment: None known by author
Mother: Unknown to author	Father: Unknown to author

Chief Henry was sketched by Émile de Girardin (1802–1881), a French journalist and politician on the Grand Ronde Reserve in 1856. Girardin signed the sketch "Henry, Shasta chief and warrior."[39] At that time there were a total of 124 people in Henry's band. By 1857, that number had declined to thirty-six.

Henry, William (1822c)	Native Name: None known by author
Alias: None known by author	Allotment: None known by author
Mother: Unknown to author	Father: Unknown to author

In 1885, William Henry was with his wife, Judith (1836c), and children Mary Jane (1866c) and Henry (1868c). Also living with William Henry and his family was his brother, "Old John (1825c)."

Hines, Jim (1822c–1901), Santiam band of Kalapuya	Native Name: Huyiduwa /HU-yi-du-wa/ (húiṭuʔwa)*[40]
Alias: James Hines	Allotment 65
Mother: Unknown to author	Father: Unknown to author

---

39 His sketch, C114442, is available through the National Archive of Canada and can be viewed in *Ntsayka Ikanum (Our Story)* on the website of the Confederated Tribes of the Grand Ronde Community of Oregon.

40 1887 GRIC gives his Indian name as Hat-wa. Jacobs, Field Notebook 82, *Texts and Ethnology Santiam*, 114.

Raised near Mt. Jefferson, Jim Hines (Huyiduwa) was part Santiam and spoke that language.[41] One of his relatives was a young man called Huchish, the same name given to the Santiam myth panther. Huchish was also raised at Jefferson, but died before he turned twenty. **Frank Michelle**'s wife was Jim Hines' niece.[42]

Jim and his wife, Lucy, had at least one child, a daughter named Julia (1873c). They were listed together on the GRIC from 1885 through 1887. Jim's farm was described as a small house with one barn on twenty fenced acres. Among other things, he had three horses, a hack, and a garden. From 1888 through 1899, Jim lived with his last wife, **Mary Santiam** (Chantwa).

Jim Hines received a trust patent for an 80.34-acre allotment. He exchanged the entire allotment for 120 acres of land from Frank Michelle's son, Joseph Michelle. After Jim Hines died, his heir, **Joseph Michelle,** sold Jim's allotment to Paul Fundman.[43]

Hoffer, Andrew (1874c–1922), Clackamas, Tumwater band of Chinook, Watlala (Cascade) band of Chinook, Yakama	Native Name: None known by author
Alias: Andre Hopper	Allotment: Yakama Reservation
Mother: Louisa Johnson, Clackamas, Watlala (Cascade) band of Chinook	Father: Homer Hoffer, Yakama, Tumwater band of Chinook

Andrew was born in Grand Ronde, but raised in Yakama. Later, he returned to Grand Ronde and married Lottie Holmes. Together, he and Lottie had a number of children including Joseph, Alvin (1893–1988), Henry (1899–1976), Clara (1904c–1928), Rena (1904c–1996) (see photo, next page), Andrew (1906–45), Mary (1908–30), Adelbert (1910–40), Homer (1912c–1933c), and Ernest (1917c–1996).[44] In 1901, their son Henry was one of the active Indian Shakers at Grand Ronde.[45]

Although Andrew's wife and children maintained their treaty rights on the Grand Ronde Reservation, Andrew chose to hold his allotment at Yakama and claim his treaty rights there.[46]

After drinking some homemade liquor Leonard Armstrong and Sam Countryman had given him, Andrew died from alcohol poisoning on June 30, 1922.[47] He was buried in St. Mary's Cemetery at White Swan, Washington.

---

41 Jacobs, Notebooks 46, *Santiam Kalapuya Text*, n.p.
42 Jacobs, Notebook 82, *Texts and Ethnology Santiam*, 122. Michelle, *Just a Memorandum*, 7: Mary Ann wrote that Frank Michelle's wife was Jim Hines' niece.
43 *Heirs of Deceased Indians*, Allotment Records, 65.
44 Confederated Tribes of Grand Ronde Family Tree Records.
45 Zenk, 1988, Grand Ronde Notebook 9, p. 12.
46 O. Applegate, Testimony of Andrew Hoffer.
47 Oregon State Archives, Salem, Oregon, 1922 Coroner's Report Yamhill County

Andrew Hoffer and Lottie Holmes's daughter, Rena Irene Hoffer. Photo courtesy of Barbara Danforth Private Collection.

Hoffer, Homer (1854c–96), Tumwater band of Chinook, Yakama[49]	Native Name: Tamaguin[48]
Alias: Homer Hopper	Allotment: None known by author
Mother: Yakama woman	Father: Chief John Kawache, Tumwater band of Chinook

48 Michelle, *Just a Memorandum*, 10–11.
49 Michelle, *Just a Memorandum*, 10–11. Oregon State Archives, Salem, Oregon, 1907, Yamhill County, Estate File 1349, Joseph Apperson: gave Homer's DOD as October 18, 1896.

When the manual labor school was organized at Grand Ronde on October 1, 1862, Homer Hoffer (Tamaguin) was in constant attendance. His teacher, C. M. Sawtelle, wrote in his annual report dated August 1, 1863:

> During the first two months we received twenty-three children, the most of whom we boarded and clothed through the winter. All but two were as wild as quails when we commenced with them, having had no previous instruction; and all were worse than naked, being clad in filthy cast-off garments.
>
> Among the boys, the most extraordinary is Homer, son of Tumwater, chief. He is truthful, honest, energetic, ambitious, and well-disposed. Surely, nature had some aim in producing such a little prodigy. He is the only flat-head among the boys.[50]

Homer married Louise Johnson. They had three children: Andrew, Mary Ann, and Edward.[51] Although Louise tried to follow the traditional practice of head-flattening, the agent stopped her.[52] Louise died in childbirth with Edward.

After her death, Homer decided to move to the Yakama Reservation to be with his mother's people. His father, **Chief John Kawache,** allowed him to take Andrew, but forced him to leave Edward and Mary Ann behind to "represent him" at Grand Ronde.

In preparing to leave, Homer took Edward to **Eliza Johnson** (Khakhshni), who had asked to raise him. Since Homer had a nice house and barn on his allotment, he told **James Foster** to ask the agent if he could have it.

Chief John instructed his son, **Joe Apperson** (Washamsh), to take Homer's daughter, Mary Ann, to the agent until Homer was gone. After Homer left, Mary Ann lived with her uncle, Joseph Apperson, and her grandfather, Chief John. The years were unhappy ones for her.[53]

Homer returned briefly to Grand Ronde in 1885 with his wife, Julia Ann, and his children, Jimmie, John, Sarah, and a baby.

His daughter, **Mary Ann Hoffer,** married **Joseph Michelle,** the agency farmer, in 1886 and raised a large family.[54] Edward Hoffer died at about age five. **Andrew Hoffer** married **Lottie Holmes** and died at Grand Ronde in 1922.

---

50 *Annual Report Commissioner of Indian Affairs,* 1863, 84–85.
51 Michelle, *Just a Memorandum,* 10–11.
52 Zenk, Interview with Vincent Mercier, 1989, Grand Ronde Notebook 8, 55.
53 Michelle, *Just a Memorandum,* 10–11.
54 Munnick and Beckham, *Catholic Church Records—Grand Ronde,* Register I, p. 43, M-2, p. 64, B-23, p. 72, B-26, p. 97, B-28, p. 110, B-8.

Hoffer, Mary Ann (1871–1958c), Clackamas, Tumwater band of Chinook, Watlala (Cascade) band of Chinook, Yakama	Native Name: None known by author
Alias: Mary Ann Michel, Mary Ann Michelle	Allotment: None known by author
Mother: Louise Johnson, Clackamas, Watlala (Cascade) band of Chinook	Father: Homer Hoffer, Yakama, Tumwater band of Chinook

Joseph Michelle family. Left to right: Ethel, Joseph Michelle, Joe Ezra, Adela, Mary Ann Hoffer-Michelle and Frances Clarence. Photo courtesy of Oregon Historical Society (CN 022565).

Mary Ann was the daughter of **Chief John Kawache**'s second to oldest son, **Homer Hoffer** (Tamaguin), and Louise Johnson. She was born and raised at Grand Ronde by her uncle **Joe Apperson** (Washamsh).

In 1886, she married **Frank Michelle**'s son, **Joseph Michelle**, the agency farmer. She and Joseph had a number of children, including Florence, Edith (1890–90), Joe Ezra (1891), Adelia (1894), Francis Clarence (1897), Ethel (1900), and Loyd (1903).

A caregiver all of her life, Mary Ann wrote a letter to **Eustace Howard** and **Victoria Wishikin** (Kinishi)'s daughter, Agatha, in February 1953 after returning home from a month's stay in the hospital. She wanted to let Agatha know about some new tribal business and to help her with information Agatha would need to fill out a tribal enrollment application for her children and grandchildren. After the business part of the letter was out of the way, Mary Ann wrote in a shaky hand and without punctuation:

> I live here in Grand Ronde Maybe you remember where the old Catholic Church use to stand little ways from the agency store first house here at the corner a big school house on the other side of the road from me I just got home last Sunday the 8th of February I was in the hospital almost a month I am pretty bad off with the enlarging of the heart and the pneumonia with it I didn't think I was going to get home again My doctor put me in a home I didn't like it so Clarence went to see me and I told him to go and talk to my doctor I gave him the reason so he let me out I am awful weak but I am able to sit around the house Clarence and his wife live with me I am just helpless I am glad I can do this for you [55]

By May of 1956, Mary Ann was confined to a wheelchair and staying in a nursing home in Grand Ronde, but she never stopped caring about others. In July of 1958, she wrote to console Agatha Bloom during the time when Agatha's husband, Joe Howe, was critically ill. Mary Ann wrote:

> Your letter was on hand last Thursday but I was surprised because Priscilla told me he had the cancer of the throat That was a mean disease No cure That's what got Joe He had the cancer of the stomach It was no cure just suffer It was nice they let you keep him at home with you till the last I sure grieve with you I know what it is to give up a mate but the good lord take them away from suffering but we are left behind to take it as it comes of it and try and lead a happy life I am sure they pray for us I came out of the hospital last Monday My doctor revived me again I don't see why I can't die I am so helpless and hardly get around and got to live I guess I got to live till the lord is ready to take me[56]

A short time later, the Lord was ready and Mary Ann left this world, but not before leaving a wealth of historical information in her many letters to friends and family. *Just a Memorandum*, a document that contains genealogical information for most of the families living at Grand Ronde during Mary Ann's lifetime, is perhaps her most famous work.

---

55 Barbara Danforth Private Collection, letter #2 dated February 12, 1953, to Agatha Bloom from Mary Ann Michelle.
56 Barbara Danforth Private Collection, letter #13 dated July 23, 1958, to Agatha Bloom from Mary Ann Michelle.

Mary Ann Michelle, granddaughter of Chief John Kawache of Tumwater Chinook. Photo courtesy of Barbara Danforth Private Collection.

Hollingsworth, Susan (1827c–1913c), Klickitat wife of Molalla[57]	Native Name: Khimshtani /HIM-shta-ni/ (xímshtani)*[58]

---

57   Jacobs, Field Notebook 53, *Texts and Ethnology*, 72.

58   Jacobs, Field Notebooks 52, *Texts and Ethnology*, 90. Jacobs, Field Notebook 52, *Texts and Ethnology*, 102: "Mrs. H. heard that Klickitat get crawfish power (Susan's power was crawfish—for doctoring perhaps)."

Alias: Susan Sampson	Allotment: None known by author
Mother: Unknown to author	Father: Unknown to author

Susan (Khimshtani) was a powerful medicine woman. She also had a tremor that caused her body to shake constantly. After a few people accused her of intentionally killing many of the children at the Grand Ronde government boarding school by coming in just at lunch and watching them closely as they ate, she developed a reputation for being a mean medicine woman.[59] In those days, Susan's appearance, as well as the stories told about her, so frightened children they would often hide themselves when she rode by on her horse.[60]

Susan was the wife of Joe Hollingsworth.[61] Later in life, she was the wife of **Molalla Sampson** (Chawatkha) and inherited his allotment. After Molalla Sampson died, she lived with **Klickitat Dick Hall** where **Douglas Sampson Jones**'s daughter, Esther Jones-LaBonte, remembered her as "a harmless old woman who would do nothing; not even the dishes."[62]

Holman, James, Luckiamute band of Kalapuya	Native Name: None known by author
Alias: None known by author	Allotment: None known by author
Mother: Unknown to author	Father: Unknown to author

James Holman was Luckiamute **Jacob Wheeler** (Shwa)'s uncle. In 1872, he was living with Luckiamute Jake's family.

Holmes, David (1847c–98), Luckiamute band of Kalapuya	Native Name: Faliper /Fal-i-per/[63]
Alias: None known by author	Allotment 66
Mother: Unknown to author	Father: Unknown to author

David Holmes (Faliper) and David Davis were stepbrothers. David Holmes's mother and David Davis's father were once married. David Holmes's mother had a daughter, Mary (Pusak), by a third husband.[64]

In 1872, David Holmes was a young bachelor. He married Susan Jassley (1846c–76), the widow of **Albert Jassley** of the Rogue River tribe, on

---

59 Jacobs, Notebooks 53, *Texts and Ethnology*, 72.
60 Zenk, *Chinook Jargon*, 283.
61 Jacobs, *Autobiography of a Tualatin*, n.p. (paragraph 21).
62 Zenk, *Chinook Jargon*, 283. Susan Samson is listed on the GRIC for 1913, but not on 1914 GRIC.
63 1887 GRIC: Indian name Fal-i-per.
64 National Archive, Seattle, NRIA-S-11-276, PAC-08, bx 44, David Davis, Testimony of Frank Quenel: David Holmes' half sister, Mary aka Mary Charley Cook.

Left to right: David Holmes, Jasper Holmes, and his younger brother.

February 11, 1873.[65]

After Susan's death, David married Mary Shangaretta on January 14, 1878. David and Mary had a number of children: Marvin, Lottie (1879–1920), Hattie (1880–1965), Louanna (1882–1902), Jasper (1883–1941), Abraham Joseph (1886–1975), Paul (1887–1916), Theresa (1891–1975), Catherine (1892–1965), David (1894–1971), and Henry (1896–98).[66]

David was appointed road supervisor by the Grand Ronde Indian Legislature in 1876. In 1879, he was appointed justice of the peace. After he resigned Decem-

65 Munnick and Beckham, *Catholic Church Records—Grand Ronde,* Register I, p. 81, S-9, p. 86.

66 Ibid., Register I, p. 86, M-3, p. 98, S-7, p. 105, B-44, p. 106, M-1, p. 118, B-6, p. 123, B-1, p. 129, B-15. Register II, p. 26, B-6, p. 50, B-55, p. 65, B-24, p. 78, B-12, p. 93, B-6, p. 106, B-12.

Grandchildren of David Holmes and Mary Shangaretta through son, David, and Veta Smith. Left to right: Artheliz, Paul, and son David's stepdaughter, Vivian. Photo from Joel V. Berreman Collection. Courtesy of the Confederated Tribes of the Grand Ronde Community of Oregon.

ber 27, **James Pierce** (Clamarchnet) took over as the judge for the Grand Ronde Indian Court on January 3, 1880. In 1880, David's appointment as road supervisor was renewed along with that of **John Smith.** David Holmes remained serving in this capacity through 1882.[67] He also worked as an interpreter for Indian Agent P.B. Sinnott, receiving $75 quarterly for his services.[68]

In addition to working for the agency and serving on the Indian Legislature, David was working hard on his farm. By 1888, he had a very successful ranching operation that included a nice house and barn on ninety-five acres with a herd of approximately sixty head of cattle besides the typical hogs and chickens kept by farmers at that time.

67 National Archives, Seattle, Grand Ronde/Siletz, Land and Enrollment Program records, Field Notes and Land Survey 1875–1898, Land Description Book 1878, Box 115; Grand Ronde Justice Court.

68 Confederated Tribes of the Grand Ronde Community of Oregon Archives, Grand Ronde Agency Ledger Book, Records of Employees at Grand Ronde July 1883–September 1907.

Around 1891, David and Mary's five-year-old son, Abraham Joseph, became very ill. When the agency doctor could not cure him, David sent for one of the old time Indian doctors. According to the family, the Indian doctor saved the boy's life.[69]

David Holmes received a 200-acre allotment. After his death, his property was divided between his heirs as follows: his wife, Mary Shangaretta, received eighty acres, their children, Lottie, Hattie, Jasper, Abraham Joseph, Theresa, Catherine, David, fifteen acres each, and his granddaughter, Pauline Sutton, fifteen acres.

All the Holmes children grew up speaking Chinook Jargon. **Jasper Holmes** "spoke it so well it got mixed up in his English."[70] **Paul Holmes** married a woman named Carolyn. David Holmes and Mary's daughter, **Lottie Holmes,** married **Andrew Hoffer.** Their daughter, **Hattie Holmes,** married **Joseph Leno. Louann Holmes** married **Moses Sitton.**

For most of his life, their son, **David Holmes,** made his living as a blacksmith, carpenter, and a logger, but he had a shop in Bay City before he married Veta Smith at the age of thirty-five. He also did some work as a lawyer, working with child custody and child family placement problems. His first case was with the Hoffer children, Henry, Delbert, Glen, Elvina, Nora, Rena, Homer, and Ernest after they lost their parents, Lottie Holmes and **Andrew Hoffer.**[71]

In 1900, the elder David Holmes's widow, Mary Shangaretta-Holmes married **Joseph Corner Michelle.** Active in the Indian Shaker religion, she traveled with her new missionary husband to Pendleton, Warm Springs, Siletz, and Hoquiam.[72]

Holmes, Hattie (1880–1965), Mary's River band of Kalapuya, Luckiamute band of Kalapuya, Iroquois	Native Name: None known by author
Alias: Adelaide Holmes, Hattie Leno	Allotment 68
Mother: Mary Shangaretta, Mary's River Kalapuya, Iroquois	Father: David Holmes, Luckiamute band of Kalapuya

Hattie Holmes married **Joseph Leno.** On June 28, 1907, she received a fee patent on an eighty-acre allotment. She and Joseph had at least eight children by 1914.

Holmes, Jasper (1883-1941) Mary's River band of Kalapuya, Luckiamute band of Kalapuya, Iroquois	Native Name: None known by author

---

69 Berreman, interview with David Holmes.
70 Zenk, *Chinook Jargon*, 269–70.
71 Information taken from David Clark (1952), son of Arthelia Holmes and Elton Clark., CTGR.
72 Zenk, 1982, Field Notes, Nathan Leno, p. 1. Zenk, 1988, Grand Ronde Field Notebook 9, p. 12.

Alias: None known by author	Allotment 70
Mother: Mary Shangaretta, Mary's River Kalapuya, Iroquois	Father: David Holmes, Luckiamute band of Kalapuya

Jasper Holmes received an eighty-acre allotment. He married a woman named Sophie. They had at least three children.

Holmes, Lottie (1878c–1920), Mary's River band of Kalapuya, Luckiamute band of Kalapuya, Iroquois	Native Name: None known by author
Alias: Lottie Hoffer	Allotment 67
Mother: Mary Shangaretta, Mary's River Kalapuya, Iroquois	Father: David Holmes, Luckiamute band of Kalapuya

In 1898, Lottie Holmes married **Andrew Hoffer.** They had at least ten children. On August 5, 1907, Lottie received a fee patent for eighty acres of land at Grand Ronde.[73]

Holmes, Louana "Lulu" (1882c–1902) Mary's River band of Kalapuya, Luckiamute band of Kalapuya, Iroquois	Native Name: None known by author
Alias: Louana Sutton, Louana Sitton	Allotment 69
Mother: Mary Shangaretta, Mary's River band of Kalapuya, Iroquois	Father: David Holmes, Luckiamute band of Kalapuya

Louana Holmes married **Moses Sitton.** In 1902, they had one daughter, Pauline Sutton. On January 19, 1933, a woman named Zelda Catherine Pope (Dick), Louana's heir through her daughter Pauline, sold Louana's entire eighty-acre allotment to Weymouth Crowell.

Holmes, Mary, (1841c), Luckiamute band of Kalapuya	Native Name: Pusak /pu-sak/[74]
Alias: Mary Charley, Mary Wasko	Allotment: None known by author
Mother: Unknown to author	Father: Unknown to author

---

73 *Heirs to Deceased Indians*, Allotment Record 67.

74 1887 GRIC gave her Indian name as Po-soe. Written communication with Henry Zenk, August 21, 2010: Henry wrote that Ida Dowd told him that "old lady Bob Allen later married Frank Cook who had earlier been married to Pusak (a sister of Davis Holmes, Mary Shangaretta's husband)." National Archive, Seattle, NRIA-S-11-276, PAC-08, bx 44, David Davis, Testimony of Frank Quenel.

Mary (Pusak) was the elder **David Holmes's** half sister. She married **Wasco Charley** (Wataneklah).[75] On March 2, 1884, Father Croquet noted in church records that Charley was from the Warm Springs Reservation.

In 1888, Wasco Charley and Mary's farm included a barn, two horses, four hogs, and a dozen chickens.

Wasco Charley received an allotment of 240 acres. After his death, Mary Holmes-Charley sold twenty acres of his allotment to J. T. Lady. Their son, Abram Charlie, inherited the remaining acreage.

On the 1906 GRIC, Mary Holmes was living with **Frank Cook.**

Holmes, Paul (1887–1916), Mary's River band of Kalapuya, Luckiamute band of Kalapuya, Iroquois	Native Name: None known by author
Alias: None known by author	Allotment 71
Mother: Mary Shangaretta, Mary's River band of Kalapuya, Iroquois	Father: David Holmes, Luckiamute band of Kalapuya

Paul Holmes married a woman named Caroline. He also received an eighty-acre allotment.

Hooker, Jim (1854c)	Native Name: None known by author
Alias: None known by author	Allotment: None known by author
Mother: Unknown to author	Father: Unknown to author

Jim Hooker was one of twenty-three children who attended the manual labor school at Grand Ronde during 1863. His teacher, C. M. Sawtelle, wrote in his annual report dated August 1, 1863, that "all but two were as wild as quails" when they started school, "having had no previous instruction."[76]

Howard, Eustace (1872c–1938), Pudding River band of Kalapuya, Santiam band of Kalapuya, French Canadian	Native Name: None known by author
Alias: Eustace Philip Tipton, Auguste Tipton[77]	Allotment 221

75 *Heirs of Deceased Indians*, Allotment Record 24: "Wasco Charley" aka "Wa-ta-ne-klah."
76 *Annual Report Commissioner of Indian Affairs*, 1863, 84-85.
77 *Heirs of Deceased Indians*, Allotment Record 221: "Auguste Tipton" aka "Eustace Howard." Oregon State Archives, Salem, Oregon, 1938, Polk County, Death Certicate Clackamas County, File 304.

Mother: Mary Hutchins, Santiam Kalapuya[78]	Father: Joe Howard (Waimish), Pudding River band of Kalapuya (Ahantchuyuk), French Canadian[79]

Eustace Howard. Photo courtesy of Barbara Danforth Private Collection.

78 Jacobs, Field Notebook 78, *Texts and Ethnology Santiam*, 8. Jacobs, Field Notebook 57, *Texts and Ethnology*, 128: "Joe Hudson, E's [Eustace Howard's] grandfather bought a Molale wife. E's mother was Santiam and bought by a Wasco husband, latter she has a Molale husband. E's own father was part French." Michelle, *Just a Memorandum, 9:* Mary Ann wrote that Dick Tipton's wife, Mary, was Kalapuya and she had a son, Eustace Howard, by a previous relationship. Jacobs, Field Notebook 76, *Texts and Ethnology Santiam,* 6: J.B. Hudson gave Eustace's father's Tualatin name as Joe Waimic (Howard).

79 Jacobs, Field Notebooks 46, *Santiam Kalapuya Text*, 5: JB Hudson remembered Eustace Howard's father, Joe Waimish or Joe Howard as a member of the Ahantchuyuk people around Woodburn and Champoeg. Gatschet, *Texts, Sentences and Vocable*, 368: listed him under the French Prairie or Ahanthuyuk as "Joe Wimyss, Wimis?"

Eustace's mother was the daughter of **Chief Joseph Hutchin** (Yalkama). His father, **Joe Howard** (Waimish), died when he was seven years old.[80] December 22, 1888, **Jacob Levi Taylor** became his godfather.[81]

When Eustace was a child, an elderly woman relative came just before sunrise several times a week to visit. Before returning home, to prevent Eustace from becoming "mischievous or a lazy bum," she would spend fifteen to twenty minutes with him. As his older relative it was her role to warn him against doing a multitude of bad things such as "breaking white people's laws, stealing, and going to jail."[82]

Eustace was an adolescent when his mother, **Mary Hutchins**, married **Dick Tipton** on May 18, 1886. Dick left Mary in 1892 in favor of **Joseph Apperson** (Washamsh)'s widow, **Nancy Kenoyer** (Tunishni).

Eustace lived with his mother until 1903, working as a laborer and as an apprentice miller for the agency.[83] He was only married once and that was to **Victoria Wishikin** (Kinishi).[84] They had one child together, a daughter, Agatha (1904).[85]

Even though Eustace received a 42.80-acre allotment at Grand Ronde in 1908, he chose to live his elder years in his home at West Linn. Melville Jacobs collected Santiam Kalapuya language texts from him there in 1928.

In one of his sessions with Jacobs, Eustace fondly recalled a childhood of shinny, baseball, and playing the clarinet in the Grand Ronde Indian Band.[86] He also described how hard it was for him to recall the old stories and his reason for struggling with it. On one particular occasion, he interrupted a panther myth to explain how he felt about his work. In part, he said,

> I thought to myself that not ever anything like this would I ever be doing. Like this I am relating about myself, my language. Long ago now I quit my language when all my people died. There is no one any more for me to talk my language to. That's why I never thought I could do it. It is very hard for me to tell a story.
>
> That's the way it is. That's why it's hard for me to say even little bits. I told this to this writer (Jacobs) but even so he said never mind. Even

---

80 Jacobs, Field Notebook 78, *Texts and Ethnology Santiam*, 8.

81 Munnick and Beckham, *Catholic Church Records—Grand Ronde*, Registry I, p. 50, B-53.

82 Jacobs, Field Notebook 83, *Texts and Ethnology*, n.p.

83 *Record of Employees at Grand Ronde, 1884–1907*

84 Jacobs, Field Notebooks 57, *Texts and Ethnology*, 32.

85 Oregon State Archives, Salem, Oregon, 1938, Polk County, Clackamas County Death Certificates, File 304: informant on death certificate was listed as Mrs. John Bloom, who is believed to be his daughter, Agatha.

86 Jacobs, Field Notebooks 57, *Texts and Ethnology*, 32. Jacobs, Field Notebooks 59, *Texts and Ethnology*, 2. Jacobs, Field Notebook 54, *Texts and Ethnology*, 86: "ikalkaluma, (shinny) club; made of young oak or vine maple; one of vine maple is crooked —; the other of an oak limb, burnt, then bent like a spoon at the end; *antákwi*, oak club for shinny." Drucker, *Clackamas Notes*, n.p. (38 in transcript), shinny called *wagalgal*.

the little you know is good. Then I think to myself it is hard for me to say anything even a story. So that's all the little I know.

Whoever talks (reads) what I say maybe he will want to see what kind of person told this. If I live a little longer, if my life is longer, if I live long enough, they will see how my words are. That's all that I want to tell now. Well now I'll go on with my storytelling, just a little bit of it is left.[87]

Plate 20—Eustace Howard. Photo courtesy of William R. Seaburg.

The stories Eustace shared, he first heard when he was about nine or ten years old from some "fine old ladies."[88]

---

87 Jacobs, Field Notebook 79, *Santiam Kalapuya*, 39-47.
88 Jacobs, Field Notebook 46, Santiam Kalapuya, 5. Jacobs, Field Notebook 78, Texts and

In his elder years, Eustace suffered from cerebral thrombosis, chronic myocarditis, and generalized arteriosclerosis. He died on December 14, 1938, in Clackamas County, Oregon.[89]

Howard, Joseph (d. 1884c), Pudding River Kalapuya, French Canadian	Native Name: Waimish /WAY-mish/ (wáymish)*[90]
Alias: Jo Wymas, French Prairie Jo	Allotment: None known by author
Mother: Unknown to author	Father: Unknown to author

In 1872, French Prairie Joe Howard (Waimish) was living at Grand Ronde with his wife, **Mary Hutchins**. At that time, a Santiam man named **Charles Brown** was staying with them.

Joe Howard was probably the same Joe Howard whom the Indian Legislature ordered in 1876 to allow the widening of a road "from Jo Howard's place to **Jack Babcock's** place, and then, through to Santiam Mac's place."[91]

Joe Howard and Mary Hutchin had two sons. One of them was **Eustace Howard.**

When Albert Gatschet visited Grand Ronde in 1877, French Prairie Joe (Waimish) was still alive. However, he was not listed on the 1885 GRIC.

Howard, Joe	Native Name: None known by author
Alias: None known by author	Allotment: None known by author
Mother: Unknown to author	Father: Unknown to author

A man by the name of Joseph Howard married Agnes of the Siletz Reservation at Grand Ronde July 17, 1880. Their witnesses were Frank Mercier and Mary.[92]

This may have been the same Joseph Howard who was "put off" the Siletz Reservation in 1882. The agent wrote:

> In the removal of Joseph Howard, a quarter breed, and his wife, an Indian woman, as per instructions from your office, I may say that Howard left the reserve when ordered; his wife refusing to go was taken off by the

Ethnology Santiam, 8.

89 Oregon State Archives, Salem, Oregon, 1938, Clackamas County, Death Certificates, Case 304.

90 Jacobs, Field Notebooks 46, *Santiam Kalapuya Text*, 6. Jacobs, Field Notebooks 76, *Texts and Ethnology Santiam*, 61. Jacobs, Field Notebooks 78, *Texts and Ethnology Santiam*, n.p.

91 National Archives, Seattle, WA, Grand Ronde/Siletz, Land and Enrollment Program records, Field Notes and Land Survey 1875–1898, Land Description Book 1878, Box 115; Grand Ronde Justice Court.

92 Munnick and Beckham, *Catholic Church Records—Grand Ronde*, Registry I, p. 116, M-13.

police. The cause of removal of Howard was his persistency in gambling and drinking when outside.[93]

Agnes Howard died at Siletz April 29, 1884. "She was buried there in the place of the Indians."[94]

Howard, Stephanie (1867c–96), Clackamas, Tualatin band of Kalapuya, Klamath	Native Name: Lhimiki /HLI-mi-ki/ (ɬímiki)*[95]
Alias: Stephanie Allen, Stephanie Wheeler[96]	Allotment 2
Mother: Sarah Silas, Clackamas, Klamath	Father: Tualatin band of Kalapuya

Stephanie Howard (Lhimiki) married **Frank Wheeler** (Aiwai) on November 3, 1890. They had two children, Abraham Wheeler (1893–1909) and Ida Wheeler (1891–1920). Ida was just five and Abraham three when their mother died.

The incident that led to Stephanie's death occurred on the way home from a trip she had made with her husband in the spring of 1896. A man named **Jim Young** had returned with them. After stopping at Sheridan a town a few miles from the reservation to rest, Frank and Jim left Stephanie in the wagon to look for whiskey.

Jim Young returned to the wagon ahead of Frank and wanted Stephanie to have sex with him. When she refused, he offered her a drink of whiskey. At first she refused the whiskey, but he said he would go away if she would have one drink. True to his word, after Stephanie took the bottle and had one drink from it, Jim went away.

A short time later, Frank returned to the wagon with some other people and they all returned to Grand Ronde, however, Jim Young was known for his strong spirit power and soon Stephanie fell ill. Her legs, feet, and abdomen swelled. She lay ill for some time before her mother, **Sarah Silas,** took her home. Still, even under Sarah's care, Stephanie's condition continued to decline.

---

93 E. A. Swan, Report to Commissioner, August 28, 1882, *Indian Police,* in *United States, Interior Department, Report of the Secretary of the Interior,* Vol. 2 (Washington, DC: Government Printing Office, 1882, 199–202, NADP Document D54).

94 Munnick and Beckham, *Catholic Church Records — Grand Ronde,* Registry I, p. 127, S-6.

95 Jacobs, Notebooks 53, *Texts and Ethnology,* 73: "Mrs. H. tells of a part Clackamas-part Twalate woman named limiki (Frank Wheeler's first wife) who while waiting in a wagon for some of her relatives was approached by a bad and powerful medicine man (Jim Young)."

96 *Heirs of Deceased Indians,* Allotment Record 2: "Stephanie Allen" received a fee patent that was issued to her heir, "Ida (Wheeler) Riggs." Munnick and Beckham, *Catholic Church Records — Grand Ronde,* Registry 1, p. 64, M-3: Francis Wheeler and Stephanie Howard were married November 3, 1890.

One day a couple of Stephanie's relatives went to check on her. Even before they entered the house, they could hear her screams.

Once inside, they found Sarah holding Stephanie's head while a Klickitat doctor, **Mary Ann Kilmonie** (Katamkhin), tried to help her.[97] In her delirium, Stephanie imagined Mary Ann was Jim Young. In reliving the attempted rape, she fought her with all her might.

Mary Ann believed that if she could just get Stephanie to reveal the identity of her attacker, Stephanie might be saved. Shaking Stephanie, she would ask over and over, "Who am I?" In response, Stephanie finally said, "It is you, Jim Young."

Then Stephanie grew quiet, and that evening, she died. Those that prepared her body said that sometime during the night, after they removed her from her bed and laid her out on raised planks, an odor came out of her mouth and anus. It was the smell of whiskey.[98]

Stephanie was buried March 28, 1896, at the age of twenty.[99] She received a forty-acre allotment that her daughter, Ida Wheeler-Riggs, inherited. **Samuel Riggs** paid the heirship fee of fifteen dollars for her.

Howe, Ben (1851c)	Native Name: None known by author
Alias: None known by author	Allotment: None known by author
Mother: Unknown to author	Father: Unknown to author

In 1886, Ben was living with his wife, Allie (1868c), and a daughter. Nancy, his widowed mother-in-law, was also living with the family. They were poor.

Howe, Dick (1841c)	Native Name: None known by author
Alias: None known by author	Allotment: None known by author
Mother: Unknown to author	Father: Unknown to author

In 1886, Dick Howe was living with his wife, Mary (1856c), and their two sons, Solomon (1870c), and Ben (1873c). His assets for that year were listed as two cows.

Hubbard, Daniel Wacheno (1848c–80), Clackamas, Molalla[100]	Native Name: Shkukaush /SHKU-kaush/ (shkúk'awsh)* [101]

---

97 Jacobs, Field Notebooks 59, *Texts and Ethnology*, 60.

98 Jacobs, Field Notebook 67, *Texts and Ethnology*, n.p. Jacobs, *Clackamas Text*, Part 2, 520–22.

99 Munnick and Beckham, *Catholic Church Records—Grand Ronde*, Registry II, p. 70, B-15, p. 88, B-17, p. 104, S-5.

100 Jacobs, Field Notebooks 55, *Texts and Ethnology*, 10: "Mrs. H's great uncle, half Molala, half Clackamas, made up that his name was Igaksdak (Flint) boasting. Family responded, "Oh well, then we will call you *labutai* meaning bottle in Chinook Jargon. Johnson and Zenk, Chinuk Wawa, 163: *labutai (lapotay)* is the word for bottle.

101 Jacobs, Field Notebooks 61, *Texts and Ethnology*, 4

Alias: None known by author	Allotment: None known by author
Mother: Sophia Gwayakiti-Wacheno, Molalla	Father: Clackamas

Daniel Wacheno Hubbard (Shkukaush) was the son of **Sophie Gwayakiti**. She married **Chief Daniel Wacheno** (Wachinu), but did not stay with him.

In 1872, Daniel Wacheno Hubbard was living alone. Church records listed his death on August 15, 1880, under the name "Daniel Hobart."[102]

Hubbard, Jane (1813c–93c), Clackamas, Watlala (Cascade) band of Chinook	Native Name: None known by author
Alias: None known by author	Allotment 72
Mother: Eliza Johnson, Cascade Chinook, Clackamas[103]	Father: Unknown to author

Jane lived with **Moses Allen** (Shkayinch)'s family from 1886 through 1889. She was listed on the GRIC as Moses's sister, but was more likely a cousin through his aunt, **Sophia Gwayakiti,** and her son, **Dan Wacheno Hubbard** (Shkukaush).

Jane received a 120-acre allotment. Heirs to her allotment were **John Wacheno** (Tsinwalh), **Daniel Wacheno** (Wadams), and **Charles Wacheno.**

Hubbard, Chief, Mary's River Kalapuya	Native Name: Hinephor /hine-phor/[104]
Alias: None known by author	Allotment: None known by author
Mother: Unknown to author	Father: Unknown to author

Chief Hubbard (Hinephor) signed the Treaty with the Kalapuya, Etc., 1855, as second chief. He made his mark along with George (Ah-mo), who was First Chief of the Chepenapho band of Kalapuya.

Hubbard, Jo (Mrs.) (1830c)	Native Name: None known by author
Alias: None known by author	Allotment: None known by author
Mother: Unknown to author	Father: Unknown to author

A man by the name of Joel Hobbart died at Buena Vista and was buried at Grand Ronde on September 17, 1882.[105] He was very probably the husband of the woman listed as "Mrs. Jo Hubbard" on the 1885 GRIC. At that time, Mrs. Jo Hub-

---

102 Munnick and Beckham, *Catholic Church Records—Grand Ronde*, Register I, p. 116, S-13.

103 Michelle, *Just a Memorandum*, 6: Mary Ann wrote that Liza Johnson's father was Cascade and mother was Clackamas.

104 Kappler, Treaty with the Kalapuya, Etc., 1855, 665, 668: spelled both as Himpher and Hine-pher.

105 Munnick and Beckham, *Catholic Church Records—Grand Ronde*, Register I, S-12, p. 122.

bard was listed as a widow living with her sister, "Old Blind Mary (1835c)," and **Ann Martin.**

Hubbard, Joel (1835c), Clackamas, Molalla[106]	Native Name: None known by author
Alias: None known by author	Allotment: None known by author
Mother: Molalla	Father: Clackamas

In 1872, Joel was living with his wife, Caroline (1840c), his son, Abraham, and his daughter, Clara. Joel's brother-in-law, James, and father-in-law, Wallace, were also with the family.

Joel Hubbard and **Steve Savage** (Palhilh) represented the Molalla at the fifth annual session of the Grand Ronde Legislature on January 4, 1876.[107]

By 1885, Joel and Caroline's family had grown substantially. They had a number of children, including Abraham (1863c), James (1865c), Wallace (1867c), Clara (1868c), William (1870c), and Daniel (1872c).

Hubbard, Josephine (1876c–1904), Clackamas, Molalla, Watlala (Cascade) band of Chinook	Native Name: None known by author
Alias: Josephine Michelle, Josephine Corner	Allotment 73
Mother: Jane Hubbard, Cascade Chinook, Clackamas	Father: Molalla

A Molalla and Clackamas woman, Josephine was **Moses Allen** (Shkayinch)'s cousin. She was also related to **Lucy Sampson,** a Tillamook and Lower Chinook.[108]

Josephine is supposed to have had *tcu'yuclumdix*, the power of the setting sun. This is a dark power. Toward night, it causes you to think mean and quarrelsome things. No one can do anything with such people. Their children die.[109]

Josephine Hubbard married **Joseph Corner Michelle** at McMinnville, Oregon, in September 1890. She was listed as his wife from 1891 through 1899. Then on the GRIC for 1900, she was listed as a "widow." However, in fact, Joseph Corner Michelle had divorced her.[110] If she had children by Joseph, none of them

---

106 Michelle, *Just a Memorandum,* 6: Mary Ann listed his father as Clackamas and his mother as Molalla.

107 National Archives, Seattle, WA, Grand Ronde/Siletz, Land and Enrollment Program records, Field Notes and Land Survey 1875–1898, Land Description Book 1878, Box 115; Grand Ronde Justice Court.

108 1890 GRIC. O. Applegate, Testimony of Mose Lane.

109 Jacobs, Field Notebook 53, *Texts and Ethnology,* 106.

110 National Archives, Salem, Oregon, Polk County Circuit Court Case Files, Index to Divorce Cases 1859–1909, File 3086, Joseph Corner vs. Josephine Corner.

This 1898c photograph pictures Josephine Hubbard and her husband, Joseph Corner Michelle, with a group of people from the Cascade. Left to right: Mary Bradford-Warcormac, Margaret Warcormac-McLaughlin, Georgia Miller-Jackson, Alice Warcormac-Williams, Georgia Forman, Josephine "Josie" Hubbard, Henry Thomas, Joe Corner Michelle, Warcormac, Virginia Miller, Ed Thomas, unidentified elderly women in front. Photo courtesy of Oregon Historical Society (OrHi 38169).

survived.

After 1899, Josephine was listed alone on each GRIC through 1904. Apparently, she remarried. Certainly, she had other relationships as reportedly she lost so many children the elders came to believe she was trying to hide her power song. "In an attempt to save her last three children, they made her dance and sing."[111]

While the last three of Josephine's children may have lived for a time, certainly by 1904, all of her children had died, as Charles, John (Tsinwalh), and **Daniel Wacheno** (Wadams) were listed as her only heirs and inherited her allotment. In 1905, Daniel and **John Wacheno** (Tsinwalh) sold twenty acres of her allotment to T. S. Mann. The following year they sold another forty-acre parcel to W. N. Jones.

---

111 Jacobs, Field Notebook 51, *Music and Ethnology*, 21. Jacobs, Field Notebook 53, *Texts and Ethnology*, 106.

In 1912, John (Tsinwalh) and **Charles Wacheno** sold the remaining twenty acres to Joel Flannery.

Victoria Wishikin (Kinishi) recorded one of Josephine Hubbard's songs for Melville Jacobs in 1929.[112]

Hubbard, William (1843c–78), Molalla[113]	Native Name: None known by author,
Alias: Molale Bill	Allotment: None known by author
Mother: Amy	Father: Unknown to author

In 1872, William Hubbard was listed under the Molalla. He died February 5, 1878.[114]

Hudson, Abraham Joseph (1879), Santiam band of Kalapuya	Native Name: None known by author
Alias: Abe Hudson	Allotment 62
Mother: Mary (Duniwi)	Father: John Hutchins, Santiam Kalapuya

Abraham Hudson and **John "Mose" Hudson** were full brothers. Mose Hudson once recalled how his brother, Abe's little boy, Floyd (1917c–1928c), fell from a foot log bridge into the Yamhill River on his way to school. After searching the river for perhaps two days, the rescue party gave up, but Mose and his brother refused to quit. They called in the Indian Shakers from Siletz. After the Shakers began searching, Mose said, "the one with the best dream power was the first to find the boy's body."[115]

Abraham added more to the story. He said that one old woman told him the morning of the last search where the boy's body would be found that day. She described the boy's clothes as she had seen them in her dream and said he would be found by a certain young man on an island below the bridge. She even described the position of the body. The body was found in the exact position and place where she predicted.[116]

The first night of the search **John Wacheno** (Tsinwalh) was there. After the Shaker leader told them there was someone present whose power was keeping them from finding the body, Wacheno did not return. The next night, in his absence, the Shakers found the boy's body.[117]

---

112 Jacobs, Field Notebook 51, *Music and Ethnology*, 27.
113 Gatschet, *Texts, Sentences and Vocable*, 373: listed him with the Molalla as "Molale Bill."
114 Munnick and Beckham, *Catholic Church Records—Grand Ronde*, Register I, p. 106, S-3.
115 Jacobs, *Santiam Kalapuya Ethnology Texts*, Part 1, 52.
116 Berreman, interview with Abe Hudson.
117 Jacobs, Field Notebook 59, *Texts and Ethnology*, 34.

Hudson, John Basile (1868–1954), Santiam band of Kalapuya	Native Name: None known by author
Alias: Mose Hudson, Hutchins	Allotment 62
Mother: Mary (Duniwi)	Father: John Hutchins, Santiam Kalapuya

John "Mose" Hudson married Magdelen Henrietta "Hattie" Sand, the daughter of the Rogue River woman, **Martha Jane Sands**. Mose and Hattie had seven daughters: Marion (1892), Pearl (1894), Gertrude (1896), Velma (1907), Ila (1908), Martha (1910), and Eula (1911). Their daughter Gertrude married **Julius Mercier.** Velma married Harold Dean Mercier. Ila married **Joseph Dowd Jr.** Martha married Hubert Mercier. Eula married **Edward Petite.**

Mose and Hattie Hudson's daughters, Velma (left) and Ila Hudson (right). Photo courtesy of Barbara Danforth Private Collection.

From time to time, for over twenty-five years, Mose worked tirelessly with

189

a number of linguists interested in indigenous languages. Besides his work with Melville Jacobs in 1928, Mose provided Santiam words and phrases for Morris Swadesh and Robert Morris in July 1953.[118]

In November 1953, a few months after his consultation with Swadesh and Morris, Mose became ill.[119] By September 1954, his daughter Velma Mercier wrote **Eustace Howard** and **Victoria Wishikin** (Kinishi)'s daughter, Agatha Bloom:

> The folks aren't well, especially papa. We just about lost him this spring and he hasn't been well since. He was practically dying, but God spared him for us a little longer. [?] Emanuel and I were with him during the crisis at the hospital. He has a very bad heart and failing fast. Do if you can come up and see him as I doubt whether he'll be here long. Gertrude lives with them now. I told them I heard from you and papa said, Oh that's right she is one of the last Molallas.[120]

On December 17, 1954, another letter arrived at the Bloom residence from Velma Hudson-Mercier. She wrote:

> [...] mother is holding up pretty good in her loss of papa, of course she's trying to be brave. He died at the Manor (old New G R Hotel) here at new town. It has been changed into a convalescent home or hospital. He was there almost three weeks. He got so bad nothing could be done at home so they took him to the Manor. He had no white corpuscles and was dehydrated. He got better for a few days. Then his heart gave way. We saw him everyday sometimes two times. Was with him when he died also the priest, Arvella and Stella also Emma Leno. He died so pitifully told us all goodbye and Wednesday we took mama to see him. He kept saying "God bless you, take care of your children" etc. He knew he was going to leave us. He prayed all the time. Oh, he was a wonderful man, but I wouldn't ask for him back now as he suffered so long and ones heart just ached for him. I wish you could have seen him. He looked asleep.[121]

Mose's wife, Hattie died a little over a year later, Velma wrote on May 3, 1856:

---

118 Indiana University Archives of Traditional Music, accession #85-555-F, Oregon, Grand Ronde, Kalapuya, Morris Swadesh and Robert Milton, *Santiam Words and Phrases* spoken by John "Mose" Hudson July 5, 1953, OT-7049 and OT-7049.

119 Barbara Danforth Private Collection, letter #5 dated November 5, 1953, to Agatha Bloom from Velma Mercier.

120 Barbara Danforth Private Collection, letter #8 dated September 9, 1954, to Agatha Bloom from Velma Mercier.

121 Barbara Danforth Collection, letter #9 dated December 17, 1954, to Agatha Bloom from Velma Mercier.

[...] Yes, mother had a light stroke, but came out of it fine and was joking to Eula and Martha, so Eula told her she had better rest and save her strength and talk later as they were going for medicine for her. She said alright and closed her eyes and died. They thought she had just gone to sleep.[122]

Hutchins, Adeline Ann ((1867c–1907c), Santiam band of Kalapuya, Molalla	Native Name: None known by author
Alias: Adeline Hudson, Adeline Bond, Adeline Barnes	Allotment: None known by author
Mother: Margaret (Sanyef), Molalla	Father: Joseph Hutchins, Santiam

In 1888, Adeline Ann Hutchins married **Margaret Lapan** (Chalwina)'s son, **Frank Bond.** After they separated in 1904, she lived with **Louis Savage** until he was arrested for the shooting death of **Foster Wacheno** (Inawalh). She was living with Enoch Spores when he killed her.[123]

Hutchins, Chief Joseph (1817c–91c), Santiam band of Kalapuya[124]	Native Name: Yalkama /YAL-ka-ma/ (yálkama)*[125]
Alias: Jo Hudson	Allotment: None known by author
Mother: Unknown to author	Father: Unknown to author

Chief Joseph Hutchins (Yalkama) was a brother of **John** (Lalafu) and **Tom Hutchins** (Liham) and one of the men who negotiated the terms of the Santiam treaty with the United States at Champoeg in 1851. Opposing the offer made to the Santiam, he said:

We have been willing to throw away the rest of our country and reserve the land lying between the forks of the Santiam! You thought it was too much. Then we agreed to take only half of it and take in the people south of us if they were willing. You thought it was too much! Then we agreed to take a small piece between the Creek and the North Branch. You want us still to take less. We can not do it. It is too small. It is tying us up in too

---

122 Barbara Danforth Collection, letter #11dated May 3, 1956, to Agatha Bloom from Velma Mercier.

123 Letter to Knott C. Egbert, & S.D.A., Siletz, Oregon, from 811 Yeon Bldg, Portland, Oregon, dated December 30, 1911.

124 Gatschet, *Texts, Sentences and Vocable*, 368: under the Santiam as "Joe Hudson" with his brothers, "John and Tom Hudson."

125 1887 GRIC: lists his Indian name as "Yalcaman." On the unratified treaty with the Santiam band of Kalapuya negotiated by John Gains, Yelkma's name was written as "Alquema aka Joseph." Kappler, Treaty with the Kalapuya, Ect., 1855: his Indian name was spelled "Yelk'ma." Jacobs, Field Notebook 86, *Texts and Ethnology*, 38.

small a space.[126]

To the American argument that the Santiam would be better off giving up the land, he replied:

> We understand fully what you mean and that it may be better for us, but our minds are made up. Placing his finger on the place on the map which designated the fork in the Santiam River, he said, We wish to reserve this piece of land. We do not wish to leave this. We would rather be shot on it than be removed.[127]

While he was listed as second chief of the Santiam band, only the principal chief, a man called Louis (Towyecolla), and the third chief signed the January 10, 1854, treaty. Yalkama's name does not appear on this document. Apparently, Joel Palmer could not get his signature until March 1, 1854.[128]

Yalkama became principal chief of the Santiam around 1857 and was listed on the census that year with eighty-five people in his band.

All the records indicate Yalkama represented the Santiam people well. When the superintendent of Indian Affairs, A. B. Meacham, arrived for the first time at Grand Ronde in 1869 asserting that he wanted to make things better for the people, Yalkama responded this way:

> I have heard tyees talk like you do now. Then they go back home and send us something a white man doesn't want. We are not dogs. We have hearts. We may be blind. We do not see the things the treaty promised.[129]

He told Meacham the Santiam people wanted a schoolhouse, a blacksmith shop, harnesses, plows, and a working sawmill. Some of the people wanted a church and most importantly they wanted the land divided and land patents issued on each parcel. Throughout Yalkama's speech, Meacham could not help but notice how the people supported his words with frequent applause.[130]

On the reservation, Yalkama was a regular speaker in councils with the Americans. Although he knew English well, he always used Chinook Jargon so that the people might better understand what was being said.

In 1871, described as a fine-looking, well-dressed man wearing a white shirt and buck gauntlets, he summed up the problems of the people. He said,

When we first made the treaty it was not said whether a priest would

---

126 Mackey, *The Kalapuyans*, 98–112.
127 Ibid.
128 Joel Palmer to George Manypenny, January 23, 1855, Microcopy T-494, Roll 5, Frs. 239–43, RG 75, BIA, National Archives, Washington, DC.
129 Meacham, *Wigwam and War-Path*, 101–38.
130 Ibid.

teach us or somebody else. I know what was promised us. I was promised eighty acres of land, others less. If we had a good agent, we would have been better off. The agents wanted only the money. They did not want to help the Indian. The blankets and shoes and goods for Indians---the house was full of them. I do not know who got them. Perhaps a rat tyee got them. But I am an Indian and I think it all right. Outside belongs to the whites. Indians sold it, but I never saw the money.[131]

Two daughters of Joseph Hutchins (Yalkama) and Sanyef: Sallie Hutchins-Jones (l) and Mary Hutchins-Howard (r). Photo courtesy of Barbara Danforth Private Collection.

131 *Annual Report Commissioner of Indian Affairs,* 1871, Minutes of a Council with Grand Ronde Indians at their Reservation, Oregon, by Commissioner Felix R. Brunot, September 14, 1871, 149–53.

Yalkama had *mitaluk,* the power to foresee trouble and detect crime or other wrong doing.[132] He mixed clay that he could only get from one place on a wet bank with hummingbird eggs to make red paint for good luck in gambling and other things. When he was playing the bone game, he stayed away from his wife and painted his wrists and shirt with the same red paint for luck.[133]

Yalkama's wife, Sanyef, was also known by the English name Marguerite Molalla or **Margaret Hutchins.**[134] Yalkama and Sanyef had a number of children: Mary (1847c), Davis (1854c–75), Elsie (1859c– 66), Francis (1862-1863), Bernard (1865c), Adrienne or Adeline Ann (1867c), Andrew (1869c)[135], and Sarah "Sallie" (1872c).[136]

In 1872, with their oldest daughter, Mary, married to Joe Howard, Yalkama and Sanyef only had four children living at home: Davis, who was eighteen, Adeline "Ada Ann," five, Andrew "Henry," three, and Sarah "Sallie," four months. By 1886, only Adeline Ann and **Sarah Hutchins** were still living with them.

When **Adeline Ann Hutchins** married **Frank Bond** in 1888, the family was living on a ninety-acre parcel of land in a house the agent noted was in poor condition. In addition to the house, they had a barn, a small orchard, and two granaries. By way of assets, they owned a wagon, a hack, four horses, ten hogs and had planted a fifteen-acre crop.

Yalkama died around 1891 and was buried in an unmarked grave on the old homestead.[137]

Hutchins, John (1814c–95), Santiam band of Kalapuya	Native Name: Lalafu /LA-la-fu/ (lálafuʔ)*[138]
Alias: John Hudson, Sr.	Allotment 58
Mother: Unknown to author	Father: Unknown to author

John Hutchins (Lalafu), **Chief Joe Hutchins** (Yalkama)'s brother, married

---

132 Jacobs, Field Notebook 84, *Texts and Ethnology,* 100–02.

133 Ibid.

134 Jacobs, Field Notebooks 76, *Texts and Ethnology Santiam,* 18: gave "Sanyef" as the Indian name of a Molalla woman named Margaret married to Joe Hudson. Michelle, *Just a Memorandum,* 9: gave "Jenavive" as the name of his Molalla wife.

135 Munnick and Beckham, *Catholic Church Records, - Grand Ronde,* Register I, p. 27, B-29, B-30, p. 29, S-41, p. 38, B-32, p. 42, S-1, p. 52, B-90, p. 61, B-60, p. 74, S-13.

136 Affidavit State of Washington, County of Pierce, taken from Sarah Jones on January 25, 1917: Sarah states she is the daughter of Joseph and Margaret Hutchins, she had no brothers, but had a half sister who died without issue [perhaps Adeline Ann]. On the above photo, Sarah and Mary Hutchins were identified as half sisters.

137 Berreman, interview with J. B. Hudson.

138 Jacobs, Field Notebooks 78, *Texts and Ethnology Santiam,* 123: Lalafu, John Hudson (father of Mose and Abe Hudson). Jacobs, Field Notebook 84, *Texts and Ethnology,* 10. State of Oregon, County of Lincoln, Affidavit from Hoxie Simmons dated March 19, 1951: Hoxie Simmons knew John Hutchins and gave John's Indian name as "Lalafo."

Mary (Duniwi).[139] John and Mary had three sons: Ephreham, **John Basile "Mose,"** and **Abraham Joseph "Abe" Hudson.**

By 1888, the family had a house and barn on twenty fenced acres with a nice garden where they were pasturing five horses of their own and two that belonged to **Jimmie John,** the adopted son of **Dr. John Smith** (Dushdaq). Ephreham had died, but Mose and Abe were still living at home. After marrying Hattie Sands, Mose also brought her to live with his parents.

John Hutchins ran the Warm House dance lodge on the south Yamhill River along with his brother, Chief Joseph Hutchins, and **Calapooia Billy Williamson** (Hosanunda).[140] John believed in the ancient Dream Power religion and even though both his sons were confirmed Catholics, they also believed in much of the old religious teachings.[141]

John Hutchins received an allotment which his sons, Abraham and Mose Hudson, inherited.[142] A fee patent for the entire 96.07 acres was issued to them on January 28, 1924.

Hutchins, Margaret (1830c–90), Molalla[143]	Native Name: Sanyef /san-YEF/ (sanyéef)*[144]
Alias: Mary Hudson, Marguerite Molalla, Mary, Genevieve[145]	Allotment 60
Mother: Unknown to author	Father: Unknown to author

Margaret (Sanyef) was the wife of **Chief Joseph Hutchins** (Yalkama). **Wallen Kilmonie** (Kilmanukh) was her half brother; they had the same father but different mothers. **Mary Ann Kilmonie** (Kilipashta) was her stepmother and **Margaret Toto** (Chaimala), her stepsister.[146]

Margaret was received 228.24 acres of allotment land that included the old place. Her heirs were **Adeline Ann Hutchins** and **Sarah "Sallie" Hutchins.**[147]

---

139 State of Oregon, County of Lincoln, Affidavit dated March 19, 1951, Statement from Hoxie Simmons.

140 Du Bois, *The Ghost Dance*, 30.

141 Jacobs, Field Notebooks 36, *Santiam Kalapuya Text*, 148: "It is interesting to me that Hudson himself was not completely skeptical of all this. He believes, I am convinced, in spite of his Catholic allegiances, that there is such an acquisition as a power, and that it can be taken by another…"

142 *Heirs of Deceased Indians*, Allotment Records, 58.

143 Affidavit, State of Washington, County of Pierce, taken from Sarah Jones January 25, 1917: mother died June 5, 1890.

144 Jacobs, Field Notebooks 76, *Texts and Ethnology Santiam*, n.p. (18).

145 Michelle, *Just a Memorandum*, 9: gave "Jenavive" as the name of his Molalla wife.

146 Affidavit, State of Oregon, County of Yamhill, taken from Josephine (Frances) Shirley January 25, 1917 and Macasca Sutton, February 3, 1917.

147 *Heirs of Deceased Indians*, Allotment Records, 60.

Hutchins, Mary (1847c–96c), Santiam band of Kalapuya	Native Name: None known by author
Alias: Mary Tipton, May Howard, Mary Hudson	Allotment: None known by author
Mother: Unknown to author	Father: Joseph Hutchins, Santiam Kalapuya

Mary Hutchins was married a number of times. She was first bought by a Wasco man. Her second husband was Molalla. By 1872, she was married to **Joe Howard** (Waimish) who was part Ahantchuyck and part French.[148] By Joe, she had two sons. Her youngest son died around 1882, but her older son, **Eustace Howard,** was with her when she married **Dick Tipton** on May 18, 1886. Witnessing the ceremony were **Thomas Norwest** and Rosa, **Peter Petite's** wife.

After they were married, Mary and Eustace lived with Dick Tipton and Dick's son, **Cephas Tipton**. In 1889, Dick left Mary. After their separation, she and Eustace lived alone until Eustace married **Victoria Wishikin** (Kinishi).

Hutchins, Mary (1832c), Umpqua, Yoncalla band of Kalapuya[149]	Native Name: Duniwi /DU-ni-wi/ (t̪úuniʔwiʔ)* [150]
Alias: Mary Hudson, Mary Stewart	Allotment: None known by author
Mother: Duniwi, Som-oh-shon band of Umpqua[151]	Father: Donewah band of Yoncalla

Mary (Duniwi) married **John Hutchins** (Lalafu) around 1868. She was the mother of **John "Mose" Hudson** and **Abraham Hudson**.

After Lalafu died, Mary married **Muddy Jim Stewart** (Tkintkinu). Muddy Jim died September 16, 1904.[152]

Hutchins, Sarah (1832c–97c), Santiam band of Kalapuya	Native Name: None known by author

---

148 Jacobs, Field Notebook 78, *Texts and Ethnology Santiam*, 8. Jacobs, Field Notebook 57, *Texts and Ethnology*, 128.

149 State of Oregon, County of Lincoln, Affidavit dated March 19, 1951, Hoxie Simmons knew Mary Hudson Stewart. She was a member of the Yoncalla and Umpqua tribes who lived in the Umpqua river basin of western Oregon. He testified that Mary Hudson's mother was a member of the Som-oh-shon band of Umpqua. Mary Hudson's father was of the Donewah band of Yoncalla.

150 Jacobs, Field Notebooks 36, *Santiam Kalapuya Text*, 192: "tuniwi, Yoncalla woman's name (JB Hudson's mother)."

151 State of Oregon, County of Lincoln, Affidavit dated March 19, 1951: Hoxie Simmons said Duniwi was the Indian name of Mary Hudson's mother.

152 Oregon State Archives, Salem, Oregon, 1904, Polk County, Estate Files 0899.

Alias: Sarah Hudson, Sarah Cheekee, Sarah George[153]	Allotment 56
Mother: Unknown to author	Father: Unknown to author

Sarah was a sister of **Tom** (Liham), **John** (Lalafu), and **Chief Joseph Hutchins** (Yalkama). She was a widow living with John and his family from 1885 through 1886 and living with Joseph from 1887 through 1888. On January 19, 1892, she married **Peter Checkaon** (Chikhyan).[154]

She received an allotment under the name "Sarah Cheekee." After her death, her heir, Peter Checkaon exchanged forty acres of her property with **John "Mose" Hudson.**

Hutchins, Sarah E. (1872c), Santiam band of Kalapuya, Molalla	Native Name: None known by author
Alias: Sallie Hudson, Sarah E. Jones	Allotment 61
Mother: Margaret (Sanyef), Molalla	Father: Joseph Hutchins (Yalkama), Santiam band of Kalapuya

Sarah E. Hutchins married William Jones (1879c), a Clallam Indian of the Mitchell Bay Tribe, and moved to Washington State. Over the years, she and William had a number of children. The oldest child was a little girl named Grace.

By 1896, both Sarah's parents, her step-grandmother, **Mary Ann Kilmonie** (Kilipashta), and her half sister, **Mary Hutchins-Howard,** had died. Out of her immediate family, only Adeline Ann, was still living.[155]

Sarah Hutchins-Jones was living in Kalama, Washington, when she received the patent for her sixty-acre allotment at Grand Ronde on January 30, 1907.[156] The following year, she also inherited the family estate valued at five hundred dollars.[157]

After her step-cousin **Louis Savage** was sent to Leavenworth for the murder of **Foster Wacheno,** Sarah corresponded with him from 1906 through 1913. Another woman, probably Sarah's oldest daughter, also wrote to Louis from Kalama

---

153 *Heirs of Deceased Indians,* Allotment Record 56: "Sarah George" aka "Sarah Cheekee."

154 Jacobs, Field Notebooks 51, *Texts and Ethnology,* 49.

155 Affidavit State of Washington, County of Pierce, dated January 25, 1917, signed Sarah Jones from the allotment folder of Isadore Kilmoni, Grand Ronde: Sarah testified that she was the daughter of Joseph and Margaret Hutchins and she "had no brothers but had a half sister who dies without issue." No mention of her half sister, Mary Hutchins-Howard who was the mother of Eustace Howard.

156 *Heirs of Deceased Indians,* Allotment Records, 61.

157 Oregon State Archives, Salem, Oregon, 1908 Yamhill County Estate 1292.

Sallie Hutchins-Jones and Louie Savage, 1886c. Photo courtesy of Barbara Danforth Private Collection.

during his prison stay. Her name was simply listed as "Grace" and her relationship was given as "niece." Sarah Jones wrote to Louis Savage regularly at first, but as the years went by her letters eventually stopped.[158]

Hutchins, Tom (1822c–86c), Santiam band of Kalapuya	Native Name(s): Liham /LI-ham/ (líham),* Yuwi /YU-wi/ (yúwi?)*[159]
Alias: Tom Hudson	Allotment: None known by author
Mother: Unknown to author	Father: Unknown to author

---

158 National Archives, Central Plains Region, Louie Savage Inmate File 5333.

159 Jacobs, Field Notebooks 83, *Texts and Ethnology Santiam*, n.p: "liham was the name of this Indian man, he went blind late in life, his wife killed him in a fight." Jacobs, Field Notebooks 78, *Texts and Ethnology Santiam*, 123: "yuwi, Tom Hudson."

Tom Hutchins (Liham) was a brother to **Chief Joseph Hutchins** (Yalkama) and **John Hutchins** (Lalafu).[160] He signed the treaty of 1855 with the United States as third chief of the Santiam band of Kalapuya[161] He and **French Prairie Mack Mickmut** represented the Santiam band of Kalapuya when the fifth annual session of the Grand Ronde Indian Legislature, convened on January 4, 1876.[162]

In 1872, he was married to a woman named Margaret. He married Julienne (1847c–77) on November 23, 1875. Although he was not a Catholic and had not been baptized, the priest married him and the recently widowed **Margaret Lapan** (Chalwina) on September 27, 1878. In 1885, he and Margaret were living together with two children: Ellen (1865c), and Johnny (1867c).

Tom Hutchins had a very powerful spirit power. It was that of a three-legged coyote who had come to him in a dream. Men with coyote as a spirit power are rascals. They are smart, but mean, and feared by everyone. They travel around a lot and can even get by with taking another man's wife on occasion.

Eventually, in later years, Tom went blind. In 1886, his wife, Margaret (Chalwina), killed him in a fight. After he was buried, a professor from Willamette University got his body.[163]

---

160 Gatschet, *Texts, Sentences and Vocables*, 368: listed under the Santiam as "Tom Hudson" with his brothers, "Joe and John Hudson."
161 Kappler, *Treaty with the Kalapuya, Etc., 1855.*
162 National Archives, Seattle, WA, Grand Ronde/Siletz, Land and Enrollment Program records, Field Notes and Land Survey 1875–1898, Land Description Book 1878, Box 115; Grand Ronde Justice Court.
163 Jacobs. Field Notebooks 83, *Texts and Ethnology Santiam*, 34.

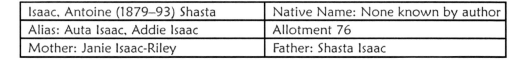

Isaac, Antoine (1879–93) Shasta	Native Name: None known by author
Alias: Auta Isaac, Addie Isaac	Allotment 76
Mother: Janie Isaac-Riley	Father: Shasta Isaac

Antoine received a forty-acre allotment. His heirs were Janie, Julia, and Frank Olaman Isaac. They sold the property to Wallace McCamant on January 15, 1907.

Isaac, Frank (1866c–1934), Shasta	Native Name: Tichihsi /ti–chih–si/ [1]
Alias: Olaman Isaac	Allotment 77
Mother: Janie Isaac-Riley	Father: Shasta Isaac

Mary Ann Tom, Shasta Tom's second wife, was Frank Isaac (Tichihsi)'s aunt.[2]

On December 13, 1893, Frank married Hattie Riggs. **Joseph Jeff Day** and **Isabel Petite** witnessed the ceremony.[3]

Isaac, Janie (1852c–1916), Shasta	Native Name: None known by author
Alias: Janie Riley	Allotment 74
Mother: Unknown to author	Father: Unknown to author

After Shasta Isaac died, Janie had to provide for their three remaining children, Frank, Antoine, and Julia. Even though her large farm included two houses and two barns, putting food on the table must have been difficult.

Throughout this time, the Isaacs had a strong friendship with the Norwest family. When Janie Isaac's daughter, Julia, was baptized April 8, 1888, her godmother was **Frank Norwest** and **Alice Wilder's** daughter, Josette Norwest. When Janie's son **Frank Olaman Isaac** was baptized December 13, 1893, Frank Norwest and his wife Mary were listed as his godparents.

Around 1891, Janie married **Bob Riley.** She and her children were listed with him on the GRIC for that year. Antoine, Janie's youngest child by **Shasta Isaac,** was baptized April 17, 1892. His godparents were his sister, **Julia Isaac,** and **Cephas Tipton. Antoine Isaac** died the following year at the age of fourteen.

Janie Isaac-Riley received a 148.05-acre allotment. On October 29, 1906, she received a fee patent for 110 acres of her allotment. Her heirs Frank Oleman Isaac and Julia Isaac received a fee patent November 22, 1920 for the remaining 38.05 acres.

---

1   1887 GRIC: listed Frank's Indian name as "Ti-chih-si."
2   Whitlow II, Grand Ronde Agency Deaths (1901–1938).
3   Munnick and Beckham, *Catholic Church Records—Grand Ronde*, Register II, p. 90, M-4.

Isaac, Julia (1871c–1931) Shasta	Native Name: None known by author
Alias: None known by author	Allotment 75
Mother: Janie Isaac-Riley	Father: Shasta Isaac

Julia Isaac received a forty-acre allotment.

Isaac, Shasta (1833c–87c), Shasta	Native Name: None known by author
Alias: Isaac Shasta	Allotment: None known by author
Mother: Unknown to author	Father: Unknown to author

In 1872, Shasta Isaac was living with his wife, **Janie Isaac** (1852c–1916), and three children: Albert, Edward, and an infant daughter, **Julia** (1871c–1931). Also living with the family that year were Shasta Isaac's brother, **Applegate Jack** (Itchkadowa) and a man named **Gilbert Smith.** Besides their children, Albert, Edward, and Julia, the Isaacs had two sons: **Frank Oleman Isaac** and **Antoine Isaac.** On April 17, 1892, Father Croquet baptized their son, Antoine. **Cephas Tipton** and **Julia Isaac** were Antoine's godparents.[4]

---

4   Ibid., Register II, p. 38, B-13, p. 76, B-9, p. 86, B-9.

Jack, Applegate (1832c–1918), Shasta band from Applegate Creek[1]	Native Name: Itchkadowa /etch-kak-taw-wah/[2]
Alias: Applegate Jackson, Applegate John	Allotment 10
Mother: Unknown to author	Father: Unknown to author

Applegate Jack (Itchkadowa) came overland to the reservation with the main band from Table Rock about two years after the signing of the peace treaty.[3]

At Grand Ronde, he appears to have lived off and on with his brother, **Shasta Isaac,** but by 1888, he had his own place, a hut with twenty fenced acres. A widower, he lived alone. He received a fee patent for 95.60 acres in 1906.

Jack, Calapooia (1837c–1901c), Luckiamute band of Kalapuya[4]	Native Name: None known by author
Alias: Tuck Calipona, Jack Calipona, Calipona Jack	Allotment 34
Mother: Unknown to author	Father: Unknown to author

Calapooia Jack was well known among the people by the nickname Tuck. In agency records his name was often written as Jack Calipona or Calipona Jack.

In 1888, Calapooia Jack and his wife, Anna, had a house and barn on twenty fenced acres with three horses, a wagon, harness, and eight tons of hay. Shortly after Anna died, Calapooia Jack married Julia (1841c–1902c), the widow of **Nestucka Baxter.**

On the 1898 GRIC he was listed as "Calipona Jack" with his wife, Julia, and a daughter, Mary Jack (1890c). Calipooia Jack died before Julia. They had no chil-

---

1   O. Applegate, Testimony of Applegate Jack: he belonged to the Itchkadowa or Applegate Creek band of Rogue River under Toquahear or Chief Sam. Annual Report Commissioner of Indian Affairs, 1854, 464: Joel Palmer: "I next visited the Etch-kah-taw-wah, or Applegate Creek and the Haw-quo-e-hov-took, or Illinois Creek bands, usually called the Chasta band of Rogue Rivers." Gatschet, *Texts, Sentences and Vocables,* 364: listed under the Shasta as "Jack, abt 50 yrs."

2   1887 GRIC listed his Indian name as "Ie-cow-towa." In personal communication with Dr. Henry Zenk, August 21, 2010, he observed that this name might be the same as Applegate Jack's band, which is given elsewhere as Itchkadowa or Etch-kah-taw-wah.

3   O. Applegate, Testimony of Applegate Jack.

4   1888 GRIC listed "Calipooia Jack" as Luckimute. *Heirs of Deceased Indians,* Allotment Record 34: "John Calipona" aka "Tuck," and his life span as 1837c–1901.

dren together.[5] Mary Jack (1890c), identified sometimes as a daughter and other times as a granddaughter, lived with Jack and Julia from 1897 through 1899. After 1899, Mary was no longer listed on the GRIC.

Julia Jack was **Lucy Sampson's** aunt. After Lucy's husband, **Jack Amos** (Shaklu), died around 1893, Lucy Sampson lived at Calipooia Jack's house until she married Moses Lane.[6]

Calapooia Jack received a 76.35-acre allotment under the name "John Calipona." Eventually Moses Lane inherited the property. In 1921, Moses Lane's heirs, Perry Battise, Harriet Klamath, and L. D. Klamath, all from the Siletz Agency, sold Calapooia Jack's allotment to T. J. Werth.[7]

Jack, Nancy, Tumwater band of Chinook	Native Name: Whahmenne[8]
Alias: None known by author	Allotment: None known by author
Mother: Unknown to author	Father: Unknown to author

In 1872, Nancy Jack (Whahmenne) was listed as the wife of **Chief John Kawache** of Oregon City. Nancy Jack had no children by John.

Jackson, Adrian (1760c–1861), Umpqua[9]	Native Name: None known by author
Alias: None known by author	Allotment: None known by author
Mother: Unknown to author	Father: Unknown to author

Adrian was baptized November 18, 1860 at about a hundred years old. He died on March 3, 1861 and was buried at Grand Ronde.[10]

Jackson, General, Umpqua	Native Name: Tasyah /Tas-yah/[11]
Alias: None known by author	Allotment: None known by author
Mother: Unknown to author	Father: Unknown to author

General Jackson (Tasyah) was the fourth signer on the Treaty made at Calapooia Creek between the Americans and the Umpqua and Yoncalla band of Kalapuyan people.[12] Émile de Girardin (b.1802–81) sketched a likeness of him in April

---

5   McChesney, *The Rolls of Certain Indian Tribes*, Testimony of Moses Lane, 57.
6   O. Applegate, Testimony of Old Amos Kilya.
7   *Heirs of Deceased Indians*, Allotment Records, 34.
8   Michelle, *Just a Memorandum*, 4, gave Nancy Jack's Indian name as Whahmenne.
9   Munnick and Beckham, *Catholic Church Records—Grand Ronde*, Register I, p. 9, S-10.
10   Ibid.
11   Kappler, *Treaty with the Umpqua and Kalapuya, 1855*.
12   Ibid.

1856 on the Grand Ronde Reservation.[13]

Jacques, Kalapuya (1802c–72), Kalapuya[14]	Native Name: None known by author
Alias: None known by author	Allotment: None known by author
Mother: Unknown to author	Father: Unknown to author

Jacques died and was buried at Grand Ronde August 10, 1872. Present at his funeral were **Chief Louis Napesa, James Winslow,** and others.[15]

Jake, Sallie (1841c–99c), Cow Creek band of Umpqua	Native Name: None known by author
Alias: Susie Jake	Allotment 49
Mother: Unknown to author	Father: Unknown to author

Sallie Jake was one of **Chief Jacob Edemchoey**'s wives. She was listed as married but living without her husband in 1886. However, she had her children: John (1868c), Cow Creek Jo (1869c), Susie (1875c), Mary (1876c), and May Jake, all living with her. They had no assets and were listed as "poor."

James, Amelie (1821c–61)	Native Name: None known by author
Alias: None known by author	Allotment: None known by author
Mother: Unknown to author	Father: Unknown to author

Amelie was the wife of Rogue River James. She was baptized on October 3, 1861, and died a few weeks later. Father Croquet wrote in the church records for October 22, 1861, that he had "buried Amelie, James's wife, of Rogueriver nation, of this mission."[16]

James, Marysville, Mary's River band of Kalapuya	Native Name: None known by author
Alias: Kalapooia James	Allotment: None known by author
Mother: Unknown to author	Father: Unknown to author

Marysville James and his wife, Mary, had at least three children: Alphonse (1857c), Elizabeth (1860c–63), and Victoria (1862).[17]

---

13 General Jackson's sketch, C114442, is available through the National Archive of Canada and can be viewed in Ntsayka Ikanum (Our Story) on the website of the Confederated Tribes of the Grand Ronde.
14 Munnick and Beckham, *Catholic Church Records—Grand Ronde*, Register I, p. 76, S-21.
15 Ibid.
16 Ibid., Register I, p. 14, S-29.
17 Ibid., Register I, p. 8, B-18, p. 19, B-35, p. 24, S-2.

Jassley, Albert (d. 1873c), Rogue River/Shasta	Native Name: None known by author
Alias: Albert Jesley, Albert Gesley	Allotment: None known by author
Mother: Unknown to author	Father: Unknown to author

In 1872, Albert and his wife, Susan were listed with the Rogue River/Shasta. After Albert died, Susan married **David Holmes** (Faliper) in 1873.[18]

Jeff, Joseph (1853c–72), Molalla	Native Name: None known by author
Alias: None known by author	Allotment: None known by author
Mother: Unknown to author	Father: Unknown to author

After a long illness, Joseph died March 25, 1872, at Grand Ronde.[19]

Jefferies, Joseph (1842c–1909), Yamhill band of Kalapuya[20]	Native Name: Tukshin /TUK-shin/ (túkshin)*[21]
Alias: Yamhill Jo	Allotment 268
Mother: Yamhill	Father: Yamhill

Short in stature, Yamhill Jo (Tukshin) was a good hunter, but considered an old man by the late 1870s. In 1878, the Indian Legislature passed a provision of law that made him and some of the other old men exempt from working on the reservation roads. They were still required, however, to pay the annual road tax.[22]

His wife, Mary, was a Modoc slave woman called Breasts or Itgatumakh in Clackamas and Big Breasts or hayash tutush in Chinook Jargon.[23]

After Mary (Itgatumakh) died, he married **Wallen Kilmonie** (Kilmanukh)'s widow, **Mary Kilmonie** (Katamkhin), around 1905.[24]

While Yamhill Joe received a 240-acre allotment, a sale for noncompetence was approved August 11, 1908, and a patent was issued October 29, 1908, to Wallace McCamant for 160 acres of Yamhill Jo's allotment.

In 1909, Yamhill Joe was killed by an unknown assailant, who stabbed him to

---

18 Ibid., Register I, p. 82, S-9, p. 86, M-3, p. 98, S-7.
19 Ibid., Register I, p. 72, S-6.
20 1872 GRIC: "Joseph Jeffries" aka "Yamhill Joe."
21 Michelle, *Just a Memorandum*, 6. Jacobs, *Clackamas Text*, Part 2, 557. Jacobs, Field Notebooks 36, *Santiam Kalapuya Text*, 192: "tuksin, Old Yamhill Joe, pure Yamhill." Jacobs, Field Notebook 51, *Music and Ethnology*, 44.
22 National Archives, Seattle, Grand Ronde/Siletz, Land and Enrollment Program records, Field Notes and Land Survey 1875–1898, Land Description Book 1878, Box 115; Grand Ronde Justice Court.
23 Jacobs, Field Notebook 51, *Music and Ethnology*, 44. Jacobs, *Clackamas Text*, Part II, 556–57, 660 and 564–65, and Notes, 660.
24 Affidavit, State of Oregon, County of Yamhill, taken from Josephine (Frances) Shirley January 25, 1917, and Macasca Sitton, February 3, 1917.

death in his home. **Douglas Sampson Jones** prepared his body for burial after it was found. In addition to the stab wound, he discovered the body had been severely mauled and partially eaten by the eleven dogs that Yamhill Joe kept in his house and was in the habit of feeding at the dinner table.[25]

On October 9, 1924, Yamhill Joe's heirs, Smiscon and Frank So-Happy, sold the remaining eighty acres of his 240-acre allotment to Weymouth Crowell.

Jefferies, Mary (1855c–1903), Modoc slave	Native Name: Itgatumakh /it-GA-tu-mah/ (itgát'umax) ["breasts"],* Hayash-tutush /HA-yash tu-TUSH/ (háyash–tutúsh) ["big breasts"]*[26]
Alias: Yamhill Mary	Allotment: None known by author
Mother: Unknown to author	Father: Unknown to author

Yamhill Mary (Itgatumakh) was stolen from her own people when she was just a child and raised among the Clackamas. She became a strong woman doctor with coyote as one of her spirit powers.

She and her husband, **Yamhill Jo Jefferies** (Tukshin), lived in a very remote area of the Grand Ronde Reservation where they continued to secretly hold religious dances long after such ceremonies were banned.[27] They never had any children.

Yamhill Mary lived a long life and died an old woman on May 16, 1903.[28]

Jeffries, Amanda (1889–1969), Spokane, Chehalis, Chinook, French Canadian[29]	Native Name: None known by author
Alias: Amanda Jeffrey	Allotment: None known by author
Mother: Eleanor of Champoeg, French Canadian, Spokane	Father: John E. Jeffries, Chehalis, Chinook, English, French Canadian

Amanda was the daughter of **Frank Quenel's** nephew, **John E. Jeffries,** and

25 Zenk, Interview with Esther LaBonte, 1982, transcript 4, 2009 (20:48).
26 Jacobs, Field Notebook 51, *Music and Ethnology*, 44. Jacobs, Field Notebook 67, *Texts and Ethnology*, n.p: "about hayactutuc, Big Breasts—a Modoc woman brought here as a slave child to the Clackamas." Johnson and Zenk, Chinuk Wawa, 162. Michelle, *Just a Memorandum*, 6. Jacobs, Notebooks 67, *Texts Ethnology Clackamas & Jargon*, 38.
27 Jacobs, Notebooks 67, *Texts Ethnology Clackamas & Jargon*, 36.
28 Jacobs, *Clackamas Text*, Part II, 556–57, 660, 564–65, and Notes 660, Endnote 537: Shaman Mary had a coyote spirit-power that was expressed in a song recorded by Jacobs. It was not a doctoring song. Endnote 538: "Mary was a Modoc who had been taken as a child to become a slave among the Clackamas. She died before her husband, Yamhill Joe." Whitlow, Grand Ronde Family Register, 1901.
29 St. Michaels Catholic Church records, Burial 1969, 422.

John's second wife, Eleanor of Champoeg. Eleanor's father was French Canadian and Spokane. Her mother was also part native.[30] Amanda's mother never lived at Grand Ronde and was never adopted there.[31]

Amanda, moved to Grand Ronde and was baptized March 15, 1891, at St. Michael's Catholic Parish. Her godparents were **John Baptiste Belleque** and his wife, **Victoria Vasselle.**[32]

In 1894, Amanda was listed on the GRIC as a six-year-old orphan along with her half brothers, **Andrew** and **Edmund Jeffries.**

Although she was never adopted into any tribe at Grand Ronde, eventually Amanda married into the Umpqua tribe. She and Solomon Riggs's son **Andrew** had a large family. By 1958, Amanda wrote she had twenty-two grandchildren and ten great-grandchildren. She also wrote that she was related to **Eustace Howard,** presumably through their French Canadian ancestry.[33]

Amanda Jeffries and Andrew Riggs. Courtesy of Joann White-Colton and Bud White, grandchildren of Clara Robinson-Riggs.

---

30 O. Applegate, Testimony of Captain Frank Quenel.

31 Ibid.

32 Munnick and Beckham, *Catholic Church Records—Grand Ronde*, Register II, p. 66, B-2.

33 Danforth, private letter collection, Letter 15.

Jeffries, Andrew (1875c–1937), Chelalis, Chinook, Coos, French Canadian, English	Native Name: None known by author
Alias: Andrew Jeff, Andrew Jeffrey	Allotment 165
Mother: Josephine Gauthier, French Canadian, Coos	Father: John E. Jeffries, English, Chehalis, Chinook, French Canadian

Andrew's father was Frank Quenel's nephew, **John E. Jeffries.** John was at least half Chinook and Chehalis. Andrew's mother was either one half or one quarter Coos. In 1905, **Frank Quenel,** who had never met Andrew's mother, testified he had heard her father was a white man, possibly Scotch, and her mother was a French Indian. John Jeffries said Edmund and Andrew's mother was half French Canadian and half Coos.[34]

Andrew was listed on the GRIC for 1887 as "Andrew Jeff," a nephew of Frank Quenel. In 1888, the agent listed Andrew's tribe as Umpqua. After living with the Quenel family for a number of years, in 1890, Andrew and his brother **Edmund Jeffries**'s status was changed by the agent to "orphans " and they appear to be living on their own.

On October 29, 1906, Andrew Jeffries was issued a fee patent for eighty acres of allotment land.

Jeffries, Edmund (1874c–1914) Chelalis, Chinook, Coos, French Canadian, English	Native Name: None known by author
Alias: Edmund Jeff, Edmund Jeffrey	Allotment 166
Mother: Josephine Gauthier, French Canadian, Coos	Father: John E. Jeffries, English, Chehalis, Chinook, French Canadian

Edmund and Andrew were full brothers. Edmund arrived at Grand Ronde about a year after his brother, **Andrew Jeffries. Frank Foster** (Slige) was Edmund's godfather, when he was baptized April 8, 1888.[35] At that time, Edmund was living with **Frank Quenel** and listed as Umpqua.

At the age of twenty, Edmund was hired as an assistant teacher for the agency.[36] Despite a significant age difference, he married **Clementine LaBonte,** a widow with numerous children, in 1899.

On August 5, 1907, Edmund received a fee patent for eighty acres of allotment land. He died October 7, 1914.[37]

---

34 O. Applegate, Testimony of Frank Quenel and John E. Jeffries.
35 Ibid., Register II, p. 38, B-10.
36 *Records of Employees at Grand Ronde, 1884–1907.*
37 *St. Michael's Catholic Church Burial Records, 1914.*

Jeffries, John E., Chinook, Chehalis, French Canadian, English	Native Name: None known by author
Alias: Edward John Jeffrey	Allotment: None known by author
Mother: Josette Quenel, French Canadian, Chinook, Chehalis[38]	Father: Edward J. Jeffries, English

John Jeffries was not of treaty blood and was never adopted at Grand Ronde. He came to the reservation the first time in 1892. When he returned in 1895, he took a job at the agency where he worked as the sawyer until he resigned in 1907.[39]

John Jeffries had two sons, **Andrew** and **Edmund Jeffries,** by a woman with some Coos blood. He had a daughter, **Amanda Jeffries,** by a Spokane Indian woman. [40] The boys arrived at Grand Ronde about five years before their father, staying with **Frank Quenel** and his family.

From 1903 through 1906, John, his third wife, **Victoria Versalle,** and daughter, Amanda, were all listed on the annual census under John's son, Andrew Jeffries. While Victoria inherited her father, **Louis Vasselle's,** allotment, she did not receive any treaty benefits at Grand Ronde and neither did John or Amanda.

Jerry, Applegate, Kalapuya	Native Name: None known by author
Alias: Calapooia Jerry	Allotment: None known by author
Mother: Unknown to author	Father: Unknown to author

In 1872, Jerry Applegate was living with his ten-year-old son.

Jim, Luckiamute, Luckiamute band of Kalapuya	Native Name: None known by author
Alias: None known by author	Allotment: None known by author
Mother: Unknown to author	Father: Unknown to author

Old Jim was **Jacob Wheeler** (Shwa)'s uncle.[41]

Jo, Chief (1823c–63), Umpqua	Native Name: None known by author
Alias: Tayi Jo	Allotment: None known by author
Mother: Unknown to author	Father: Unknown to author

---

38 Munnick, *Catholic Church Records — St. Louis and Brooks*: Josette's father was a French Canadian named Abraham Quinelle and her mother was a Chinook and Chehalis woman named Angelique Tsihelis or Saucso.

39 *Records of Employees at Grand Ronde, 1884–1907.*

40 O. Applegate, Testimony John E. Jefferies and Frank Quenel.

41 Gatschet, *Texts, Sentences and Vocables*, 369.

Jo was one of the Umpqua chiefs. His brother, **Charley Bogus,** signed the treaty made at Calapooia Creek November 29, 1854.[42] His son, Joseph, was buried at Grand Ronde in March of 1861. Chief Jo died about two years later, on May 27, 1863. The Umpqua chiefs, **Louis Napesa** and **Peter McCoy** (Inchaishi), among others, attended his funeral. His widow, Anna, died in early November that same year.[43]

Jo, Winchester (1834c–80), Umpqua[44]	Native Name: None known by author
Alias: None known by author	Allotment: None known by author
Mother: Unknown to author	Father: Umpqua Chief Jo

Winchester Jo had the following children by his wife, **Mary Winchester:** Eugene (1858c), Thomas (1861c), Victor (1862c–63), Stephen (1865c–80), Ebba (1867c–70), and Simon (1870c–78).[45]

Out of all their children, only Stephen and Simon were still living with the family in 1872. During that time, Mary Winchester's Aunt Orpha, Sally Nichols, and Sally's mother, Molly, were also living with Winchester Jo, along with **Chief Charley Bogus**'s widow, Mary Bogus, and her children, **William Warren** and **John Warren.** Mary Bogus was listed as Winchester Jo's aunt and William and John Warren were listed as his cousins.

The fifth annual session of the Grand Ronde Indian Legislature convened January 4, 1876. Along with other representatives, Winchester Jo and **Chief Solomon Riggs** (Gunconnacli) were there to represent the Umpqua. In a joint effort to preserve his native language, he and **Chief Peter McCoy** (Inchaishi) provided Umpqua language vocabulary to Albert Gatschet in December of the following year.[46]

November 4, 1878, the seventh annual Indian Legislature resumed with the election of Winchester Jo, Peter McCoy, and Solomon Riggs as representative for the south precinct of the reservation. The Legislature appointed Winchester Jo prosecuting attorney for the coming year.[47]

---

42 State of Oregon, County of Lincoln, affidavit dated March 1, 1954: Martha Johnson stated an Umpqua chief named Jo was an uncle to John Warren, son of Chief Charley Bogus.

43 Munnick and Beckham, *Catholic Church Records—Grand Ronde*, Register I, p. 9, S-12, p. 26, S-23, p. 29, B-57, S-45.

44 Gatschet, *Texts, Sentences and Vocables,* 366. An affidavit taken from Martha Johnson in Lincoln County, Oregon, June 27, 1954.

45 Munnick and Beckham, *Catholic Church Records—Grand Ronde,* Register I, p. 7, B-1, B-2, p. 21, B-71, p. 29, S-36, p. 37, B-11, p. 51, B-79, p. 61, S-2, p. 63, B-24, p. 88, B-14, p. 106, S-8, p. 115, S-8.

46 Gatschet, *Umpqua,* 76.

47 National Archives, Seattle, Grand Ronde/Siletz, Land and Enrollment Program records, Field Notes and Land Survey 1875–1898, Land Description Book 1878, Box 115; Grand Ronde Justice Court.

A year later, on November 4, 1880, Winchester Joe died and was buried at Grand Ronde.[48]

John, Alsea (1836c)	Native Name: None known by author
Alias: None known by author	Allotment: None known by author
Mother: Unknown to author	Father: Unknown to author

In 1885, Alsea John was living with his wife, Helen (1850c), and two sons, Allen (1872c) and John (1874c). His mother, identified only as "Old Woman," was also living with the family.

John, Chief (d.1864), Itchkadowa or Applegate band of Rogue River[50]	Native Name: Tecumtum [Elk Killer][49]
Alias: None known by author	Allotment: None known by author
Mother: Unknown to author	Father: Unknown to author

Chief John (Tecumtum) was one of the most famous Pacific Northwest Indian leaders. The last to surrender after the Rogue River wars, he was taken to the Yaquina Reserve on July 19, 1856. There he held a revolt that resulted in both him and his son, Adam, being taken to Vancouver as prisoners of war. From Vancouver, they were transferred to Alcatraz in July 1858. On this trip, Tecumtum, armed with a wooden club, made another desperate attempt to escape. The skirmish ended when Adam was shot in the leg and Tecumtum through the face. One of the soldiers then proceeded to pound Tecumstum with a rifle until the stock broke.

After being imprisoned at Alcatraz for a number of years, Tecumtum was finally released in 1862. William H. Rector, Superintendent of Indian Affairs in Oregon, wrote about him:

> This chief was a brave and daring leader, and although of better principles than most of his race, he exerted such a powerful influence over his people that Agent Metcalf deemed it advisable to cause him and his son Adam to be arrested and placed in confinement. In order that they should be securely confined, they were placed in charge of the military authorities, and by them sent to California, where they have remained prisoners for five years. During my visit to the agency his daughters made a very strong appeal for their release and return to their families. They desired

48 Munnick and Beckham, *Catholic Church Records—Grand Ronde*, Register I, p. 117, S-17.
49 Kappler, *Treaty with the Rogue River, 1854*.
50 Douthit, *Joseph Lane and the Rogue River*, 483. *Annual Report Commissioner of Indian Affairs*, 1854, 464, Joel Palmer: "I next visited the Etch-kah-taw-wah, or Applegate Creek and the Haw-quo-e-hov-took, or Illinois Creek bands, usually called the Chasta band of Rogue Rivers."

Tecumtum's daughter in dentalia necklace and nose ornament. Photo courtesy of Oregon Historical Society (OrHi 4315).

Tecumtum's daughter, Mary. Photo courtesy of Oregon Historical Society (OrHi 57081).

that the remnant of his days might be spent with them. I made application to General Wright, commanding this military department, for their release, which was granted. They returned in due time, and were at once sent to Grand Ronde agency. I have seen them but once since their return, but learned from Agent Condon that their conduct is acceptable, and that they exert a very salutary influence over other Indians in inducing them to remain at home and live like white people. The old man is now far advanced in years, but his son is in the prime of life, and, although he has lost a leg in battling for life and liberty, he is of great service to the agent. Thus far my act has resulted in good, and I have but little fear that any harm will result from restoring them to liberty.[51]

Tecumtum died on the Grand Ronde Reservation June 6, 1864.

---

51 Annual Report of the Commissioner of Indian Affairs, 1862, William H. Rector, 255. T. McF. Patton to J. B. Condon, May 22, 1862, BIA, Microfilm M-2, Roll 30, National Archives, Washington, DC.

John, Jimmie (1864c)	Native Name: None known by author
Alias: Jimmie Smith, Richard Smith	Allotment 205
Mother: Unknown to author	Father: Unknown to author

In 1872, Jimmie John was listed on the GRIC as "Richard," the "son" of **Dr. John Smith** (Dushdaq). In 1877, a slave named Jimmie John was living with **Lame Jim Shiliqua** (Shilikwa) and his family.[52] On the 1885 GRIC, Jimmie John was listed as the "adopted son" of Dr. John Smith (Dushdaq).[53]

Jimmie John received a 60.28-acre allotment. His former wife, **Mary Jones** (Sana), was issued a fee patent on the property in 1906.[54]

John, Umpqua	Native Name: None known by author
Alias: Old John	Allotment: None known by author
Mother: Unknown to author	Father: Unknown to author

In 1872, Umpqua John was listed with his wife, Pattie.

John, Salmon River (1826c–76), Salmon River band of Tillamook	Native Name: None known by author
Alias: Captain John, Hyas John	Allotment: None known by author
Mother: Unknown to author	Father: Unknown to author

"Captain John" was listed on 1862 GRIC as Chief of the Salmon River band of Chinook. There were forty-four people under his leadership.[55] He stayed around the Salmon River most of the time.

According to church records, John had a number of children. He had Lewis (1868c), Julienne (1869c), and David (1870c) by a woman named Mary. By his wife Susanne he had Stephen (1869c). He also had a son, Joseph Victor (1873c).[56] Clara Pearson said "Hyas John" had three wives. He had one surviving son named Baxter by his first wife. His second wife was a Tillamook woman, but they had no children. He had another son Stephen, with his third wife.[57]

Captain John's son Baxter married Jennie Alsea. They had children, but it is unclear as to whether their children lived long enough to have children of their

---

52 Gatschet, *Texts, Sentences and Vocables,* 370: "shillukua; his son, Henry Crawford, his slave Jimmy John, stays him; wife; no ch."
53 Michelle, *Just a Memorandum,* 9: Mary Ann wrote that Jimmie John lived mostly with Dr. Smith.
54 National Archives, Seattle, NRIA-S-11-276, PAC-08, bx 50, Mary John [Jones].
55 National Archives, Washington, DC., Condon, 1862, GRIC of the Indians Belonging/ Located upon the Grand Ronde Indian Agency, Oregon.
56 Munnick and Beckham, *Catholic Church Records—Grand Ronde,* Register I, p. 57, B-82, p. 59, B-20, p. 62, B-15, p. 63, B-22, p. 83, B-32, p. 100, B-32.
57 Jacobs, *(Nehalem) Misc Ethnographic Notes,* Field Notebook 106, 111.

own. Baxter ended up going blind from the bad power of a medicine doctor.[58]

Like Captain John, Stephen chose to live on the Salmon River. After his brother died, he wanted to marry Baxter's widow, Jennie Alsea, but she would not live with him.[59]

John, Tyee, Umpqua	Native Name: None known by author
Alias: None known by author	Allotment: None known by author
Mother: Unknown to author	Father: Unknown to author

In a journal entry dated April 5, 1862, Corporal Royal Bensell wrote that Umpqua Tyee John had caused some excitement with the soldiers stationed at Ft. Yamhill by confronting one of them within the restricted area. Although the soldiers had been warned by their superior officers not to mingle with the people without special permission, many of them ignored the order.[60]

After Tyee John told the soldier he had military orders to throw in the river any soldier who could not show him a pass, the soldier made a point of crossing the boundary. While Corporal Bensell did not say what specifically transpired, he did say that the following day the soldiers received a lecture from their captain and Tyee John's orders to arrest any soldier over the boundary was confirmed. Hearing this, Bensell made note that not very many soldiers believed an Indian had any right to arrest them and "Such orders, if persisted in, will result in a row."[61]

On December 6, 1863, Lt. Davison accused his detachment of "having gone and disturbed the domestic quiet of Tyee John's family." Bensell claimed the accusation was false.[62]

Johnson, Ben (1802c–89c), Pudding River Kalapuya[64]	Native Name: Qiantato /Qian-ta-to/[63]
Alias: Old Ben, French Prairie Ben	Allotment: None known by author
Mother: Unknown to author	Father: Unknown to author

In 1885, French Prairie Ben (Qiantato) was described as an eighty-three-year-old widower. He was listed in the same manner and location on each GRIC from

---

58 Ibid, 103.
59 Ibid, 104.
60 Barth, *All Quiet on the Yamhill,* 11.
61 Ibid.
62 Ibid., 11, 21, 24, 47, 52, 84, 113.
63 1887 GRIC gave his Indian name as Qiantato.
64 Gatschet, *Texts, Sentences and Vocables,* 368-369: "French Prairie Ben" under the French Prairie or Ahantchuyuk people along with Sambo, French Prairie Mac, French Prairie Mac's son, Frank, and French Prairie Ben and Joe Wymas. 1888 GRIC: listed with Santiam Band of Kalapuya.

1889 through 1891. Then on the 1892 GRIC his name appears as "Benjamin Johnson." He does not appear on any GRIC after this year.

Johnson, Eliza (1840c–1909), Umpqua	Native Name: Syilsha /Si-il-sha/[65]
Alias: Eliza Orton, Eliza Allen, Elizabeth Frances Pickett	Allotment 150
Mother: Unknown to author	Father: Unknown to author

Eliza (Syilsha) was the wife of **Rogue River Frank Pickett**. Frank died in August 1884 leaving her a widow. In 1885, she was living with her sister, **Mary Johnson,** and her brother, **Levi Taylor.**

"Elizabeth Frances Pickett, widow of this place, age 50" was baptized May 1, 1886.[66] She was listed on the GRIC for that year as living alone in a shanty with a small barn. She had twenty-five fenced acres with five acres cultivated, a wagon, plow, harrow, cradle, scythe, hogs, four horses, and harness.

Eliza married **Tom Orton** in February 1888. **William Warren** and Josette Norwest were their witnesses.[67] On the GRIC, she was listed as much older than Tom. Her age was given as sixty-six and Tom was listed as thirty-six. At that time, they had a barn on six acres with a garden and one horse.

By 1900, Eliza and her sister Mary were living together . The agent listed them as full Umpqua. After Mary died in 1902, Eliza inherited her 140-acre allotment.

July 30, 1904, Eliza married **Robert Allen.** Immediately following the ceremony, Robert moved in with her.[68] From the start, Robert refused to work or contribute anything toward their support. In March of 1905, he abandoned Eliza completely.

April 9, 1907, Eliza received a forty-acre allotment. When she sued Robert for divorce, she asked the court to allow her to legally retain the 180 acres of land she currently held in her own name. Her decree was granted.[69]

Johnson, Eliza (1845c–1919c), Clackamas, Watlala (Cascade) band of Chinook[70]	Native Name: Khakhshni /HAH-shni/ (x̣áx̣shni),* Gwichachkham /GWI-cha-cham/ (gwíchachx̣am)*[71]

---

65   1887 GRIC gave her Indian name as "Si-il-sha."

66   Munnick and Beckham, *Catholic Church Records—Grand Ronde*, Register I, p. 3, B-12.

67   Ibid., Register II, p. 38, M-1.

68   Berreman, interview with Abe Holmes.

69   National Archive, Salem, Oregon, Polk County Circuit Court Case Files, Index to Divorce Cases 1859-1909, File 3409, Eliza vs. Robert Allen.

70   *Heirs of Deceased Indians*, Allotment Record 82: "Eliza Johnson" aka "Eliza Cooks." Michelle, *Just a Memorandum*, 4: Mary Ann wrote that Liza Johnson's father was Cascade, her mother was Clackamas. Jacobs, Field Notebooks 59, *Texts and Ethnology*, 42: "xaxni died in 1919 of flu."

71   Jacobs, Field Notebook 56, *Texts and Ethnology*, 70: "Xaxcni, a Clackamas, Cascade

Alias: Eliza Gay, Eliza Cooks, Eliza Wheeler	Allotment 82
Mother: Tuscan, Clackamas[72]	Father: Watlala (Cascade) band

Eliza (Khakhshni) was a tamanawas woman and an old time doctor.[73] **Victoria Wishikin** (Kinishi) recalled an incident that happened once when she was picking berries with her at Grand Ronde. Victoria said she and Eliza had ridden to the mountains. While they were there, Eliza's horse died, probably from something in the water.[74]

Victoria volunteered to let Eliza take a turn riding her horse for the trip home, but Eliza told her she would walk. She asked Victoria to leave her. She wanted Victoria to take her things and to tell her daughter, Sarah Johnson (Waganwish), that she would be home that evening.

Eliza got a long thick stick to use as a cane. Victoria rode ahead but waited for Eliza some distance down the mountain. With each step, Victoria watched Eliza hit the ground with her cane and exhale vigorously the single word, "ha." Then, to Victoria, Eliza's appearance began to change.

Once again, Eliza told Victoria not to keep stopping and waiting for her to catch up, but to just go tell her daughter she would be home presently. Victoria rode ahead, but again stopped some distance down the mountain to wait for Eliza. As Eliza came toward her, Victoria thought again that something in her appearance was changing. Again, Eliza told Victoria not to keep stopping and waiting for her to catch up, but to just go tell her daughter she would be home soon.

Victoria finally did what Eliza told her, but later, when Victoria thought about the ride down the mountain, she could not help wondering whether it was grizzly power that helped Eliza on the mountain that day.[75]

Eliza's sister, Louisa Johnson-Hoffer, was the wife of **Chief John Kawache**'s son, **Homer Hoffer** (Tamaguin).[76] Eliza's husband died around 1871, leaving her with five children, Louisa, Sarah, Minnie, Solomon, and Cecelia; within months only three of the children were still with her.[77] In 1872, she was living with Sarah (1865c), Minnie (1867c), and Solomon (1871c).

---

woman's name, (Mrs. Michelle's grandmother)." 1887 GRIC: gave her Indian name as "Hars-net." Jacob, Field Notebook 51, *Music and Ethnology*, 19: Jacobs noted "Gwitcatcxam was probably also another name of hers."

72 1872 GRIC gives her mother's Indian name as "Tuscan."

73 Berreman, Interview with Moses Hudson. Jacob, Field Notebook 51, *Music and Ethnology*, 19: Victoria Howard said she started to doctor, but was not very strong.

74 Jacobs, *Clackamas Text*, Part II, 536: Victoria Howard first called Khakhshni her "sister." Then she corrected her relationship to Khakhshni as actually being that of older cousin.

75 Jacobs, *Clackamas Text*, Part II, 536, and 657. Jacobs, Field Notebooks 59, *Texts and Ethnology*, 47.

76 Eliza Johnson was listed on the 1887 GRIC as the aunt of Mary Ann Homer Hoffer.

77 Michelle, *Just a Memorandum*, 4.

In 1887, Eliza was living with her niece, **Mary Ann Hoffer.** The following year, she was listed as a widow living at Henry Winslow's place. Eliza's daughter, **Sarah Johnson** (Waganwish), was married to **Henry Winslow** at that time. Eliza lived with them until she married **Jacob Wheeler** (Shwa). Eliza was with Jacob only a short time. Around 1890, she left him in favor of **Gay Cooks** (Kuksh).[78]

While several sources list Eliza as Cooks' wife, a letter from the acting commissioner to the Grand Ronde Indian agent, Edward Lamson, dated March 28, 1893, identifies her as "Gayo's sister, Eliza Johnson." The acting commissioner wrote,

> Inspector Miller calls attention to the claim of one Cook Gayo that the Post Office at Grande Ronde and most of the buildings therewith connected, are upon the lands of Gayo's sister, Eliza Johnson, who would like to have this property removed.

Fourteen years later, in 1907, Eliza finally received a fee patent for her 96.69-acre allotment.[79] She died of the flu in 1919.[80]

In 1929, Victoria Wishikin recorded several of Eliza's tamanawas songs for Melville Jacobs. While the exact nature of this power song could not be determined from the words, Jacobs thought perhaps it was connected with fire.[81]

Johnson, Frank (1850c–80), Clackamas[82]	Native Name: None known by author
Alias: Frank Yahton, Cascade Frank	Allotment: None known by author
Mother: Unknown to author	Father: Unknown to author

Cascade Frank Johnson married Lucy Umpqua September 22, 1872. In 1873, he and Lucy had a daughter Father Croquet baptized as "Isadore Sango." The child's godmother was **Anne McCoy** (Ashtamme). Isadore died when she was about six months old. Another daughter, Catherine, was born in August 1874, but also died as an infant.

In June 1876, Cascade Frank and Lucy Umpqua had a little girl they named Nelly Frank. Her sponsors were **Louis McCoy** and **Christine Petite.**

After Frank's death, his widow, Lucy Umpqua, married **Sam Newby.**[83] In

---

78 Jacob, Field Notebook 51, *Music and Ethnology,* 51: Jacobs noted that she was a wife of Jake Wheeler for a time. Then she left him and was Kuksh's wife."
79 *Heirs of Deceased Indians,* Allotment Records, 82, gives her name as Eliza Johnson (Cooks)
80 Ibid.
81 Jacob, Field Notebook 51, *Music and Ethnology,* 19.
82 1872 GRIC: "Frank Yahton aka Cascade Frank" under the Clackamas. Munnick and Beckham, *Catholic Church Records—Grand Ronde,* Register I, p. 116, S-14: buried August 22, 1880, at Grand Ronde.
83 Michelle, *Just a Memorandum,* 3-4.

1887, Cascade Frank and Lucy Umpqua's daughter, Nellie Frank, was living with Lucy Umpqua's mother, Susan (Pshkaidi) and **John Kelly** (Palaikhi).[84]

Johnson, Jenny (1832c), Umpqua	Native Name: None known by author
Alias: Jenny Arquette	Allotment: None known by author
Mother: Mary Bogus[85]	Father: Unknown to author

Jenny married **Yoncalla Tom Johnson** (Gunsuntjonie). By 1872, they had Francis (1868c–85), Joseph (1870c), and Catherine (1872c). Charley (1876c–92) was born a few years later.[86]

After Yoncalla Tom died, Jenny married **Peter Arquette** around 1894. She and Peter did not have children. Jenny claimed her rights at Grand Ronde under the treaty with the Umpqua. Peter claimed his treaty rights at the Umatilla Indian Reservation.[87]

Johnson, John (1854c–67), Rogue River	Native Name: None known by author
Alias: None known by author	Allotment: None known by author
Mother: Unknown to author	Father: Unknown to author

John Johnson (1854c) died and was buried at Grand Ronde.[88]

Johnson, Julia Ann (1813c–1902), Cow Creek band of Umpqua[89]	Native Name: Sawanatta /Sa-wa-natta/[90]
Alias: Julia Ann Pierce	Allotment 154
Mother: Unknown to author	Father: Unknown to author

Julia Ann Johnson (Sawanatta) was **James Pierce** (Clamarchnet)'s aunt.[91] She was listed as a widow as early as 1885. She lived with James Pierce and his wife until 1895.

Julia Ann received an eighty-acre allotment. Her sole heir was the woman doctor, **Anne McCoy** (Ashtamme).[92]

---

84 Jacobs, Field Notebook 51, *Music and Ethnology*, 21.
85 An unrecorded source gave Jenny as an older daughter of Mary Bogus from a relationship prior to her marriage to Charley Bogus.
86 Munnick and Beckham, *Catholic Church Records—Grand Ronde*, Register II, p. 81, S-7.
87 O. Applegate, Testimony of Peter Arquette.
88 Munnick and Beckham, *Catholic Church Records—Grand Ronde*, Register I, p. 30, B-3, S-1.
89 Whitlow, Grand Ronde Family Register, 1901.
90 1887 GRIC listed her Indian name of "Sa-wa-natta" and reported her as living with her nephew, Jim Pierce.
91 1892 GRIC listed Julia Ann Johnson as an eighty-year-old aunt to Jim Pearce.
92 Berreman, Interview with Moses Hudson.

Johnson, Lucy (1849c–1927), Rogue River	Native Name: None known by author
Alias: Lucy Neal, Lucy Lawney, Lucy Tom	Allotment 105
Mother: Unknown to author	Father: Johnson, Applegate band of Rogue River[93]

Lucy Johnson married Lawney, the son of the Shasta chief, Tyee Tom, in 1882. They had a son named Martin Tom (1886–92). **Lawney Tom** (Pootpam) and Lucy separated around 1890.

Lucy's cousin, Cilly, was the wife of the Cow Creek chief, **Jacob "Jake" Edemchoey.** After Lawney left, Lucy lived with Jake's family until his death in 1895.[94]

While living with Jake and Cilly, Lucy had at least one relationship, giving birth to a daughter named Lucia who was baptized at two weeks and four days on August 29, 1891. The name of the baby's father was not recorded, but the child's godparents were listed as **Jesse Smith** and **Allie Metcalf.**[95]

On the 1892 GRIC, "Lucy Lawney" was listed as a widow with an infant daughter, Lucia (1891). While there was no further record of this baby, the GRIC for 1894 lists Lucy with a daughter named Ellen (1892c). Ellen was listed with her through 1897. At that time they were living with **Mary Ann,** second wife of Tyee Tom.

Later, Lucy married the former husband of **Mary Winchester,** a white man named William Neal. However, William continued to live on Mary Winchester-Gendron's allotment, probably to preserve any inherited rights to it, while Lucy lived on hers. Lucy and her daughter, Ellen, were listed together on the 1898 and 1899 GRIC. In 1890, Lucy was listed alone. Neither of her natural daughters appeared on any census after this year.

The GRIC for 1903 was the first to list William Neal's half Paiute daughter, Flora, as a "stepdaughter" residing with Lucy Johnson-Neal. Earlier, Flora had been listed alone. Flora died in 1911, leaving two orphan daughters, Adeline and Bertha Menard. Their grandfather, William Neal, became their guardian and Lucy, their primary caregiver.

After William Neal's death, Lucy sold all their livestock. In order to make a living, she kept only the chickens and turned her attention to making and selling baskets.[96]

Lucy made beautiful hazel baskets in different sizes. She buried hazel switch-

---

93 O. Applegate, Testimony of Lucy Neal.
94 Michelle, *Just a Memorandum,* 3.
95 Munnick and Beckham, *Catholic Church Records—Grand Ronde,* Register II, p. 69, B-11.
96 The 1920 U.S. Federal Census listed Lucy Neal as a widow, age seventy-three, living as head of household with "adopted daughters," Adeline Menard and Bertha Menard. Their ages are given as fourteen and thirteen years of age.

Lucy Johnson-Tom-Neal.

es in a particular type of black mud for four to five days. After the mud dyed them black, she dug them up and used them as beautiful trim for the baskets.

Adeline recalled their annual trip to Dallas during the week of the fair when many Grand Ronde people would camp on the outskirts of town next to an old barn and join in the festivities. During this time, Lucy would take a wagonload of her baskets into the town of Dallas and trade them for various things including school clothes for Adeline and Bertha.

Although Lucy gave up farming after William's death, she continued to harvest the things God placed naturally on the earth for Indian people. Each season, she and the girls would go to "certain places" around Grand Ronde to pick berries, hazelnuts, and other things to store for the winter.[97]

Lucy received a twenty-acre allotment at Grand Ronde. Her son, Martin Lawney (1886–92c), also received twenty acres, which she inherited.[98] After **Cilly Sims** died on October 17, 1913, Lucy inherited not only her allotment, but the allotments of the Cow Creek chief, Jacob Edemchoey, and Cilly's mother, **Susan Sims,** on May 13, 1914.[99]

Lucy died in the Oregon State Hospital on February 22, 1927, of cerebral arteriosclerosis at the age of seventy-five.[100] After her death, her body was returned to the reservation where she was buried in the Grand Ronde cemetery.

Johnson, Mary (1836c–1902), Umpqua	Native Name: None known by author
Alias: Mary Riley, Mary George	Allotment 179
Mother: Umpqua	Father: Umpqua

In 1885, Mary Johnson was listed as the sister of **Eliza Johnson** (Syilsha) and **Levi Taylor.**

She married **Bob Riley** in 1886. By 1888, they had a small farm with a house and barn on twenty fenced acres with a good garden. Around 1891, Bob Riley left Mary. In 1900, she was listed as full Umpqua under the name "Mary George" with her sister, "Eliza Picket."[101]

Mary Johnson-Riley received 140 acres of allotment land. After she died, her sister, Eliza Johnson was listed as her sole heir. On October 29, 1903, Eliza sold twenty acres of Mary's allotment to D. S. Bentley. Eliza was issued a fee patent April 9, 1907, for the remaining 120 acres.[102]

Johnson, Sarah (1865c), Clackamas, Watlala (Cascade) band of Chinook, Klamath	Native Name: Waganwish /wa-GAN-wesh/ (waġánwəsh)*[103]
Alias: Sara, Sarah Monroe, Sarah Winslow, Sarah Wheeler	Allotment: None known by author
Mother: Eliza Johnson, Clackamas and Watlala (Cascade) Chinook	Father: Klamath

---

97 Interview with Adeline Menard, 1981, Cultural Resource Department Archives, CTGR.

98 Oregon State Archives, Salem, Oregon, Polk County, Estate File 1030: May 1, 1908.

99 *Heirs of Deceased Indians*, Allotment Record 105, 48.

100 Oregon State Archives, Salem, Oregon, State Hospital, Vol. 2G, File 3817.

101 1900 Federal Census for District 812 Grand Ronde Reservation.

102 *Heirs of Deceased Indians*, Allotment Record 179.

103 Jacobs, Field Notebooks 59, *Texts and Ethnology*, 50: "waganwec, name of xaxcni's daughter (Frank Wheeler's last wife); her mother, xaxcni was by birth part Clack., part Cascades; her husband who was father of waganwec, was part Klamath by birth though he spoke perfect Clackamas."

Frank Wheeler (right) with his wife, Sarah Johnson-Wheeler (standing). Photo courtesy of Barbara Danforth Private Collection.

Sarah (Waganwish) was the daughter of **Eliza Johnson** (Khakhshni). Louise Johnson-Hoffer, **Chief John Kawache**'s daughter-in-law, was her aunt.

Sarah married Patrick Monroe April 14, 1879. After Patrick's death, Sarah married **Henry Winslow** on February 28, 1881. By Henry, Sarah had at least four children: Andrew (1884–85), Jose (1885c), **Matilda Clara "Tillie,"** and **LaRose Winslow.** After Henry died September 6, 1897, Sarah married **Frank Wheeler** (Aiwai).[104]

---

104 Munnick and Beckham, *Catholic Church Records—Grand Ronde*, Register I, p. 111, M-6, Register II, p. 6, B-17, p. 51, B-2, p. 112, S-8, p. 113, M-2.

Johnson, Yoncalla Tom (1826c–91c) Yoncalla band of Kalapuya	Native Name: Gunsuntjonie /Gun-sunt-jonie/[105]
Alias: Thomas Johnson	Allotment 80
Mother: Unknown to author	Father: Unknown to author

Yoncalla Tom Johnson (Gunsuntjonie) married a woman named Jenny (1832c). By 1872, they had Francis (1868c–85), Joseph (1870c), and Catherine (1872c). **Charles Johnson** (1873c–96c) was born later.[106]

In 1886, the family was listed as living in a small house with two barns on forty fenced acres with nine acres in cultivation, a good garden, three horses, and seven hogs.

Yoncalla Tom received a 220-acre allotment that Jenny inherited.[107]

Johnson, Charles (1873c–96c), Yoncalla band of Kalapuya	Native Name: None known to author
Alias: Charley Johnson	Allotment 81
Mother: Jenny	Father: Yoncalla Tom Johnson, Yoncalla band of Kalapuya

Charles Johnson received a forty-acre allotment. His mother and heir, Jenny Johnson, was issued the fee patent for the allotment on March 13, 1907.[108]

Jones, Billy (1857c–92c), Molalla	Native Name: Skewints /SGE-wints/ (sgéwints) ["thick eyebrows"],* Khalilwai /Ha-lil-wai/ (x̱álɪlwai)*[109]
Alias: William Jones	Allotment 79
Mother: Unknown to author	Father: Unknown to author

On May 1, 1882, Billy Jones (Skewints) married **John Kelly**'s daughter Philomene in the presence of **Thomas Norwest** and Sophie Wheeler.[110] Philomene was a member of the Pudding River (Ahantchuyuk) people, who were originally from around the Woodburn and Champoeg region and closely related to the

---

105 1887 GRIC listed Yoncalla Tom Johnson's Indian name as "Gun-sunt-jonie."
106 Munnick and Beckham, *Catholic Church Records—Grand Ronde*, Register II, p. 81, S-7.
107 *Heirs of Deceased Indians*, Allotment Record 80.
108 Ibid., Allotment Record 81.
109 1887 GRIC listed his Indian name as "Skiwinch." Field Notebook 62, *Texts and Ethnology*, n.p., gave his Indian name as Skewints for his thick eyebrows and Khalilwai as another name of Billy Jones, "probably a Wasco name." Jacobs, Field Notebook 46, *Santiam Kalapuya Text*, 5: John B. Hudson called him a "Molale man" and also gave his name as Skewints.
110 Munnick and Beckham, *Catholic Church Records—Grand Ronde*, Register I, p. 121, M-9, p. 129, B-2.

Santiam people.[111]

In 1885, Billy and Philomene had the following children: Mollie (1876c), Jennie (1880c), and Ben (1882c). However, these children were not listed with the family in 1886. That year, Billy and Philomene only had their son, Nazaire (1885c–86c), living with them.

Two years later, Billy and Philomene's place was described by the agent as a small forty-acre farm with a house. Their son Nazaire had died, but they had another son, Andrew (1886c–88c), living with them.

Around 1892, Billy died, leaving Philomene with three surviving children, Walter (1889c), Harry (1891c–1934), and Ella (1892c). On July 30, 1893, when John Herald "Harry" Jones was baptized, his godparents were listed as **John Wacheno** (Tsinwalh) and **Victoria Wishikin** (Kinishi).

Student picture of Billy Jones's son, Harry W. Jones. Photo courtesy of Harry Jones's daughter, Kathryn Harrison.

---

111 Jacobs, Field Notebook 46, *Santiam Kalapuya Text*, 6.

All three children were listed with Philomene through 1895. After that year, Ella Jones does not appear on any GRIC. Philomene died on May 23, 1898. Her son Walter did not appear on any GRIC after 1904.[112]

Billy Jones received an allotment of 238.44 acres at Grand Ronde. His only heir was his son, Harry W. Jones. Industrious and well educated, Harry W. Jones graduated valedictorian from Chemawa Indian School in 1910 and was still "talking Indian" as late as 1928.[113] On August 14, 1914, Harry Jones was issued a fee patent for 160 acres of his father's allotment. He did not receive a fee patent for the remaining 78.44 acres until August 7, 1918.

Jones, Douglas Sampson (1857c–1929) Klamath, Umpqua[114]	Native Name: None known by author
Alias: Jonas Sampson, Douglas Jones, Henry Jones	Allotment 86
Mother: Unknown to author	Father: Unknown to author

Henry Petite and his wife **Jane Leno** were present when Douglas Sampson married Philomene Nellie Kelly (Fernwewa), a Klickitat and Clackamas woman, on October 26, 1885.[115] Douglas Sampson and Philomene had a number of children, including Scott Genute (1887–1960), Rosette (1889c–1904), Stephen (1891c), Martha Sandy (1893c), Esther Mary (1895–1987), and Eli (1897c–1904). Philomene died shortly after Eli was born on September 8, 1897.

At Grand Ronde, Douglas Sampson and his family lived in a house on twenty fenced acres with four horses and one set of harness. Douglas Sampson's aunt, **Nancy Palouse-Santiago,** married **Klickitat Dick Hall** around 1888.[116] Nancy and

---

112 Munnick and Beckham, *Catholic Church Records—Grand Ronde*, Register II, p. 117, B-7, S-5.

113 Jacobs, Field Notebook 46, *Santiam Kalapuya Text*, 6: JB Hudson remembered "filamin, name of girl, sister of Ufaf; her son is Harry Jones; filamin married sqewints, Billy Jones, a Molale man, and their only surviving child is Harry Jones, who talked Indian yet, at 10–12 and is still living."

114 *Heirs of Deceased Indians*, Allotment Record 86: "Jones, Sampson Douglas" was listed with a life span of 1849 to November 13, 1929. *Heirs of Deceased Indians*, Allotment Record 63, lists his name as "Douglas Sampson (Jones)." Jacobs, Field Notebook 51, *Music and Ethnology*, 21, gave his name as Douglas Jones. Munnick and Beckham, *Catholic Church Records—Grand Ronde*, Register I, p. 132, B-41, M-8: listed as "Henry Jones."

115 Munnick and Beckham, *Catholic Church Records—Grand Ronde*, Register I, p. 132, B-41, M-8. Jacobs, Field Notebook 51, *Music and Ethnology*, 21, 23.

116 1900 Federal Census for District 182, Grand Ronde Indian Reservation: Both families were identified as Umpqua until 1900 when Douglas Sampson was listed on the GRIC as the son of a Klamath father and a Molalla mother. National Archives, Seattle, NRIA-S-11-276, box 47, Nancy Hall: Nancy was a half sister to Nellie Palouse. Douglas Sampson Jones was her nephew. Nancy Hall's brother-in-law, Meshach Tipton, testified that Nancy was half Modoc and half Klamath.

Douglas Sampson Jones. Photo courtesy of Douglas Sampson Jones's great-granddaughter, Dolores Parmenter.

Douglas Sampson Jones's daughter, Esther Jones-LaBonte, with little girl. Photo courtesy of the Douglas County Museum of Natural and Cultural History.

Klickitat Dick acted as grandparents to Douglas Sampson's children.[117] In 1893, Douglas Sampson married Jimmie John's former wife, Mary (Sana).

Douglas Sampson had the reputation of being an Indian "you did not want to bother." To his daughter, Esther Mary Jones, he was "a good old man," but she had to admit that sometimes he enjoyed doing "mean things." Foremost in her mind was the time he put her brother, **Scott Genute Jones,** on a wild horse with his feet tied underneath. Then Douglas let the horse go and watched it buck.[118]

Douglas Sampson received a 180-acre allotment on the Grand Ronde Indian Reservation. He did not sign the Surplus Land Agreement in 1901.[119]

Esther Jones-LaBonte recalled a time when Douglas Sampson acquired a white spot on his body that slowly grew. At the same time a white man in Dixonville developed a dark spot on his body. According to Esther, by the time her father died in 1929 he had turned completely white and the guy in Dixonville had turned black.[120]

---

117 Zenk, interview with Esther LaBonte, 1982, transcript 1, 2009 (23:34).
118 Ibid., transcript 4, 2009, 17:40.
119 *Heirs of Deceased Indians*, Allotment Record 86.
120 Zenk, 1982, interview with Esther LaBonte, transcript 4, 2009 (18:01).

Jones, Mary, Molalla, (1830c–1916), Yoncalla band of Kalapuya	Native Name: Sana /SA-na/ (sána)*[121]
Alias: None known by author	Allotment: None known by author
Mother: Unknown to author	Father: Unknown to author

Mary (Sana) was **Victoria Wishikin** (Kinishi)'s aunt and the last wife of **Douglas Sampson Jones**. Mary was Molalla and Yoncalla Kalapuya. When she sang her power song, she used the Molalla language.[122]

Mary's first husband, Jimmie John, slit her open with a knife and left her to die, but she regained consciousness. Pushing her entrails back and binding her wound with her clothes, she started home to her Molalla people. Just as she got home, a great storm came up, producing hailstones as big as bullets. Mary took this as a sign that Jimmie thought she was dead. Later, in October 1908, she married **Douglas Sampson Jones**.[123]

Mary's tamanawas could bring bad weather. When people went off to pick blackberries, she would sometimes warn them that it might rain, and so it would. She made it rain so they would come back home.

Sometime after killing Nancy Hall in 1914, Mary predicted the day of her own death. Knowing the time was near, she sent Douglas Sampson to the store with a description of the clothes she wanted as her burial garments. He bought her two embroidered dresses. On the way back home, he stopped at **Victoria Wishikin** (Kinishi)'s house to ask her and **Eustace Howard** to stay with them until Mary died.[124]

Jones, Mary Ann, Molalla	Native Name: None known by author
Alias: None known by author	Allotment: None known by author
Mother: Unknown to author	Father: Unknown to author

In 1872, Mary Ann and her daughter, Leni Baker, were living with **Moses Allen** (Shkayinch)'s family.

Jones, Molel (1855c), Molalla	Native Name: None known by author
Alias: None known by author	Allotment: None known by author
Mother: Unknown to author	Father: Unknown to author

In 1885, he was married to Molel Mary. They had a son named Johnny (1883c) and an infant daughter.

---

121 Jacobs, Field Notebook 51, *Music and Ethnology*, 23.
122 Jacobs, Field Notebook 51, *Music and Ethnology*, 23. Zenk, *Chinook Jargon*, 272.
    National Archives, Seattle, NRIA-S-11-276, box 50, Mary John.
123 Jacobs, Field Notebook 51, *Music and Ethnology*, 8.
124 Zenk, interview with Esther LaBonte, 1982, transcript 1, 2009 (15:00).

Jones, Scott (1886–1960), Umpqua, Clackamas, Klickitat	Native Name: None known by author
Alias: Scott Genute Jones, Eugene Genute Scott Jones[125]	Allotment 86
Mother: Philomene Nellie Kelly, Klickitat, Clackamas	Father: Douglas Sampson Jones, Klamath, Umpqua[126]

Scott Jones and his daughter, Lenora "Marian" Jones. Photo courtesy of Barbara Danforth Private Collection.

---

125 Personal communication with Esther Jones-LaBonte's daughter, Rosette "Fritzi" Manangan: Scott Jones's middle name was General. His nickname was Scotty.

126 The Thirteenth Census of the U.S: 1910 Indian Population, Oregon, Polk County, Grand Ronde Indian Reservation: Scott's father of the Klamath tribe; mother of the Klickitat tribe.

In 1910, Scott was working as a laborer, cutting wood and selling it. Josephine LaBonte, the daughter of **Clementine LaChance** and Alexander LaBonte, and Josephine's son, Ralph Easter (1906–1937), were living with him. Scott had a daughter by Josephine LaBonte named Lenora (1906–1937).

On September 15, 1919, Scott received a fee patent for a sixty-acre allotment.[127] As **John Kelly** (Palaikhi)'s heirs, on February 11, 1921, he and his sister, Esther Jones-LaBonte, were issued a fee patent for the remaining sixty acres of John's allotment.

Joshua (1820c), Rogue River/Shasta	Native Name: None known by author
Alias: None known by author	Allotment: None known by author
Mother: Unknown to author	Father: Unknown to author

In 1885, Joshua (1820c) was listed as a bachelor living with **Ben Hardin** and Ben's sister, **Mary Neal.** The next year, he was listed simply as Joshua, a widower. At that time, he had only a poor barn on twenty fenced acres. The Indian agent classified his condition as very poor. Joshua was not listed on any GRIC after 1886.

Judson, Charlie (d. 1872c), Modoc slave	Native Name: None known by author
Alias: Charlie Judas[128]	Allotment: None known by author
Mother: Unknown to author	Father: Unknown to author

Charlie Judson was a Modoc slave living with the Clackamas. He made flint points and wooden vessels. Charlie's first wife was the daughter of a rich Molalla man from Oregon City. His second wife was a Modoc woman.[129]

Charlie had a son by his Oregon City wife. When the son married, Charlie gave ten or more horses to the bride's parents. **Washkeya** contributed a couple of racehorses. Three or four slaves were contributed by the boy's mother's people. Eventually, the young couple had three children, but they all died young.[130]

Charlie Judson's son was mentioned in a letter from W. C. Johnson to E. R. Geary on June 7, 1861. Johnson wrote that an Indian, son of Judus of the Yamhill Reservation, had drowned while fishing at the Willamette Falls in Oregon City.[131]

Charlie Judson died just prior to the GRIC being taken in 1872. His second wife, Susan, and third wife, Mary, were listed that year under the Luckiamute

---

127 *Heirs of Deceased Indians*, Allotment Record 87.
128 1872 GRIC gave his name as "Chs. Judson." Philip Drucker, *Clackamas Notes*, n. p: gave his name as "Judas." Drucker, *Clackamas Notes*, n.p., gave his name as "dcudus."
129 Drucker, *Clackamas Notes*, n.p.
130 Ibid.
131 W. C. Johnson to E.R. Geary, June 7, 1861, Microfilm M-2, Roll 19, letters 3 January–27 December, 1861, letter 108#, BIA, National Archives, Washington, DC.

band of Kalapuya. Charlie's widow Susan was living alone. His widow Mary and their daughter, Sally, were living with **Luckiamute Dave Davis**'s family.

Judson, Emily (1806c–97c), Clackamas	Native Name: None known by author
Alias: Emily Kilmoni, Emily Judas	Allotment: 98
Mother: Unknown to author	Father: Unknown to author

Emily Judson was the widow of Charlie Judson's only son, who drowned at Willamette Falls in 1861. In 1872, she was listed with the Clackamas under **James Wacheno** and his wife, Annie, but the agent noted Emily was "by herself."

John Wacheno (Tsinwalh) said **Charlie Judson's** son gave ten or more horses and three or four slaves for a rich man's Molalla daughter. This woman, possibly Emily, lived in **Chief Daniel Wacheno** (Wachinu)'s house with the old folks after her husband died. Then she picked up an Oregon City man who was poor and did not pay for her.[132]

In 1889, Emily Judson was listed as an eighty-two-year-old widow living with **Wallen Kilmonie** (Kilmanukh) and his family. She does not appear on the GRIC again until 1895, when she is listed with Wallen and his wife, Mary (Katamkhin).

Emily Judson received a 120-acre allotment as "Emily Kilmoni." Her heirs were **Margaret Toto** (Chaimala) and **Mary Kilmonie** (Katamkhin).[133]

Judson, Sarah (1861c–77), Luckiamute band of Kalapuya	Native Name: None known by author
Alias: Sallie Judson	Allotment: None known by author
Mother: Mary Judson	Father: Unknown to author

In 1872, Sarah Judson and her mother, Mary Judson, were under the Luckiamute band of Kalapuya with **Luckiamute Dave Davis** and his wife. A man named Judge Wilson was also living with them. Sarah Judson died on the reservation at about age sixteen.[134]

---

132 Drucker, *Clackamas Notes*, n.p.
133 *Heirs to Deceased Indians*, Allotment Record 98.
134 Munnick and Beckham, *Catholic Church Records — Grand Ronde*, Register I, p. 105, S-27.

K

Kate, Molalla (1841c–1938c), Molalla	Native Name: Muswi /MUS-wi/ (múswi) ["short, fast"],* Shumnatks /SHUM-natksh/ (Shúmnatks)*[1]
Alias: Catherine Smith, Kate Chantel, Kate Chantal, Kate Williams, Kate Matches	Allotment: None known by author
Mother: Chief Yelkas's sister, Molalla	Father: Natilkai[2]

Molalla Kate (Muswi) was the daughter of **Chief Yelkas'** sister.[3] She came to Grand Ronde with the Molalla band of Molalla. When she arrived, she was about fourteen years old.

Around 1860, Molalla Kate and her family escaped the reservation in the dark of night. They made their way back to Molalla Prairie. From there they went to Oregon City to look for work. For a time, Kate worked in Dr. John McLoughlin's house. She was an excellent weaver and glovemaker.[4]

At one time, she was married to Renaldo Matches. By Renaldo, she had her son, **Johnny Williams** (Matiyas). Johnny had a son named Matthew Williams (1897) who was living at Siletz in 1957.

In 1888, Molalla Kate was married to James Smith. They were living in Salem near Chemawa Indian School. By James, she had her daughter, Lizzie (1879c–1952c).[5] Lizzie married Hoxie Simmons of the Siletz Reservation on April 16, 1896. They had Frederick (1898), Lester (1903), Pearl (1910), and Edwin (1910).[6]

Kate's last husband was Louis Chantel. They were married at Grand Ronde July 29, 1894. **Frank Norwest** and his wife, Mary, were present and acted as witnesses to the ceremony.[7]

---

1   Drucker, *Molalla Field Notes,* interview with Kate Shantell: the name Shumnatks was used "in address." Muswi was given to her at puberty. Jacobs, Field Notebooks 52, *Texts and Ethnology,* 34: V.H. "Muswi name of Molale Kate (prob. a Molale name)."
2   Drucker, *Molalla Field Notes,* n.p.
3   Jacobs, Field Notebooks 39, *Santiam Kalapuya,* 196.
4   Personal communication with Billy Jones's granddaughter, Kathryn Jones-Harrison, August 27, 2010, at Grand Ronde, Oregon.
5   State of Oregon, Lincoln County, Affidavit from Hoxie Simmons dated September 9, 1957. Jacobs, Field Notebook 51, *Music and Ethnology,* 41: gives Johnny William's Indian name as Matiyas.
6   Hoxie Simmons, Affidavit, State of Oregon, County of Lincoln, dated September 18, 1957.
7   Munnick and Beckham, *Catholic Church Records — Grand Ronde,* Register II, p. 96, M-4.

**Louis Chantel in mail carrier uniform with Molalla
Kate (Muswi). Photo Courtesy of Kathryn Harrison.**

Louis Chantel carried the mail between Siletz and Grand Ronde.[8] Through his spirit song, he told how he and earth could talk to one another.[9]

Steve Savage (Palhilh) boarded with Molalla Kate and Louis at their home in Logston for a few weeks in 1910. At that time, Steve and Molalla Kate were two of the last known Molalla speakers. During this visit, they were able to speak together, probably using their native Molalla language for the last time.[10]

Another visitor to the Chantel home was **Billy Jones**'s son, Harry, and his family. Although she was just a little girl at the time, Harry Jones' daughter, Kath-

---

8   *Molalla Indians*, 5.

9   Jacobs, Field Notebooks 53, *Texts and Ethnology*, 107.

10   Jacobs, Field Notebook 33, *Chasta Costa etc., Santiam*, n.p.

ryn Harrison, can still remember the family trips to see Molalla Kate and Louis in the late 1920s.[11]

Around this same time, in 1928, Molalla Kate worked with Melville Jacobs providing Molalla language texts. Jacobs wrote that Molalla Kate obviously spoke the Molalla language fluently at one time, but his not knowing Chinook Jargon hindered their work.[12] Philip Drucker tried again to get Molalla language texts from her in 1934.

Molalla Kate died September 12, 1938. Louis Chantel, described as an, "exceedingly intelligent, alive, and nice old man," died October 30 of that year.

Kawache, John (1814c–85), Tumwater band of Chinook[13]	Native Name: Kawache /KAU-che/ (káwchə),*[14] Quilalla /Quil-al-la/
Alias: Chief John, Oregon City John	Allotment: None known by author
Mother: Unknown to author	Father: Unknown to author

Chief John Kawache had the spirit power of a bug commonly called a water-skipper that allowed him to walk on top of water.[15] Like his father before him, Chief John was a very wealthy man. He was the chosen chief of the people and as such could not be deposed. On the one hand, he could exact obedience; on the other, he was obliged to help the people.

Although government representatives claimed to make every attempt to recover the property Chief John lost when his band was removed to Grand Ronde, most of it was stolen by the white citizens and never found.[16]

He was listed on the 1855 treaty with the Willamette Valley tribes as Quil-al-la or John, second chief of the Willamette Tumwater band. His band was originally located on the west side of the Willamette River.[17] On the 1856 and 1857 GRIC, the

---

11 Personal communication with Billy Jones's granddaughter, Kathryn Jones-Harrison, August 27, 2010, at Grand Ronde, Oregon.

12 Jacobs, Field Notebook 33, *Chasta Costa etc., Santiam*, n.p.

13 1872 GRIC: "John Kawache" aka "Oregon City John." Kappler, 1902: The Willamette Tumwater band of Chinook was the name given for his band on the Treaty with the Kalapuya, Etc. They were also called Cascade Indians by Father Croquet and others. In later years, they were simply "the Oregon City Band of Clackamas."

14 Drucker, Clackamas Notes, n.p. Jacobs, Field Notebooks 53, *Texts and Ethnology*, 20. Jacobs, Field Notebook 63, *Texts and Ethnology* 44. Clackamas: "Mrs. Michell's father's father had a water fly power."

15 Jacobs, Field Notebook 63, *Texts and Ethnology* 44.

16 B. Jennings to Joel Palmer, June 21 1856, *Correspondence and Papers of Joel Palmer*, Superintendent of Indian Affairs in Oregon Territory, 1853–1857, and Indian Agent at Siletz 1870–1876 (Special Collection, Knight Library, University of Oregon, Eugene, OR).

17 1856 GRIC

Willamette Tumwater band was one of three "Oregon City bands."[18]

In 1872, Chief John was living with his wife, **Nancy Jack** (Whahmenne).[19] Although he had no children by Nancy Jack, Chief John had three sons by two other wives. **Homer Hoffer** (Tamaguin) and **Moses Apperson** (Wannexke) were his sons by his Yakama wife. **Joe Apperson** (Washamsh) was his oldest son and a half brother to Homer and Moses.

In 1885, Chief John was living with the family of his son, Joe Apperson. He died September 13, 1885.[20]

Kelches, Jack (1842c), Tillamook	Native Name: Unknown to author
Alias: None known by author	Allotment: None known by author
Mother: Unknown to author	Father: Unknown to author

In 1885, Kelches was living with his wife, Hester Ann (1847c), and his children, Milley (1868c), John (1870c), Henry (1875c), Susan (1878c), Sarah (1880c), and Mary (1883c).

Kellogg, Emma (1856c–82), Umpqua	Native Name: Unknown to author
Alias: None known by author	Allotment: None known by author
Mother Unknown to author	Father: Unknown to author

Emma married **Jack Babcock** in April 1872 and **John Sailas** in 1874.[21]

Kellogg, John (1836c), Umpqua	Native Name: Unknown to author
Alias: None known by author	Allotment: None known by author
Mother Unknown to author	Father: Unknown to author

In 1872, John Kellogg was living with the medicine doctor, **Sam Patch,** and Sam's sister, **Mary Patch,** along with **Thomas Kellogg.** Any relationship between John and Thomas Kellogg was not listed. One or both of them may have been related to **Emma Kellogg** (1856c–82), who married **Jack Babcock** in April 1872, or to the Mrs. Kellogg who was listed as a widow living with **Thomas Orton** in 1872.

John Kellogg was not listed on any census after 1886.

---

18 1857 GRIC

19 Michelle, *Just a Memorandum,* 4: Mary Ann gave her Indian name as "Whahmenne."

20 Munnick and Beckham, *Catholic Church Records—Grand Ronde,* Register I, p. 7, B-6, p. 132, S-13.

21 Ibid., Register I, p. 74, M-1, p. 87, M-5.

Kellogg, Mary Anna (1822c–1904c), Modoc, widow of Wapato Lake/ Tualatin husband[22]	Native Name: Klhwashatunch /KHLWA-sha-TUNCH/ (qɬwáshaṭúnch) ["jaybird eyes"]*, Wilalakiya /wi-la-la-ki-ya/ (wilalak'íya)*[23]
Alias: Marion Kellogg	Allotment: None known by author
Mother: Unknown to author	Father: Unknown to author

Father Croquet christened her with the name Mary Anna, but many white people called her Marion. The Clackamas called her Wilalakiya, which does not seem to have any translation. Although she was Modoc, she was raised among the Molalla, who called her Klhwashatunch, which in English means jaybird eyes. The name was given in tribute to her very poor eyesight. One of her tamanawas powers was mole.

Mary Ann Kellogg married **Callo Bonaparte** (Kalukh) on November 15, 1884. **Levi Taylor** and Melanie Winslow were their witnesses. After Bonaparte died in 1894, Mary Ann Kellogg married **Alsea Bill** (Kama) on August 11, 1896, in the presence of **William Warren** and Caroline LaBonte.[24]

Mary Ann died in a house fire around 1904. Twenty-five years later, **Victoria Wishikin** (Kinishi) recorded several of her power songs for Melville Jacobs. In one of the songs, her power told her that he was coming to her "an arrow on both sides."

Kellogg, Old, Umpqua[25]	Native Name: Unknown to author
Alias: None known by author	Allotment: None known by author
Mother Unknown to author	Father: Unknown to author

Old Kellogg was married to Marianne (1800c–70). He had Martha (1852c–70) and Cecile (1861–62). His daughter Martha attended the funeral of her sister, Cecile, along with others.[26]

Kellogg, Thomas, Umpqua[27]	Native Name: Unknown to author
Alias: None known by author	Allotment: None known by author
Mother Unknown to author	Father: Unknown to author

22 Jacobs, Field Notebook 51, *Music and Ethnology*, 16, listed her as a Modoc raised among the Molalla people and noted she was burned to death.

23 Jacobs, Field Notebook 51, *Music and Ethnology*, 16. Jacobs, Notebooks 69, *Texts Ethnology Clackamas & Jargon*, 7.

24 Munnick and Beckham, *Catholic Church Records—Grand Ronde*, Register I, p. 129, M-3, p. 107, M-1.

25 Gatschet, *Texts, Sentences and Vocables*, 366: "Old Man (Clock) Kellogg" under the Umpqua tribe.

26 Munnick and Beckham, *Catholic Church Records—Grand Ronde*, Register I, p. 14, B-192, p. 22, S-24, p. 62, B-16, p. 63, S-11, p. 66, B-85, S-26.

27 1872 GRIC listed his tribe as Umpqua.

In 1872, Thomas Kellogg was living with **Calapooia Sam Patch** and his sister, **Mary Patch,** along with **John Kellogg.** Any relationship between John and Thomas Kellogg was not recorded.

Kellogg, Widow (1812c–88c)	Native Name: Unknown to author
Alias: None known by author	Allotment: None known by author
Mother Unknown to author	Father: Unknown to author

In 1885, she was listed as Mrs. Kellogg, a widow and the mother of **Thomas Orton** (1845c–87c). The Widow Kellogg was still living with Thomas Orton's family in 1886, but the following year, she was with **Peter McCoy** (Inchaishi)'s family.

Since the Widow Kellogg cannot be located on the GRIC after 1888, she may have been the woman Father Croquet baptized April 8, 1889, as "Lucy, the widow of John Kellogg, aged about eighty years and gravely ill." If so, she died the next day.[28]

Kelly, Charlotte (1844c–74)	Native Name: Unknown to author
Alias: None known by author	Allotment: None known by author
Mother Unknown to author	Father: Unknown to author

Charlotte was married to **Thomas Kelly** of the Clackamas nation. They had a son whom Father Croquet baptized as John Baptist on Christmas evening in 1861. The baby died less than a month later.

In 1872, Charlotte was listed with **Chief Daniel Wacheno** (Wachinu)'s band of Clackamas. At that time, she had two children: John Baptist (1859c) and Elizabeth (1865c). Charlotte died May 28, 1874, at age thirty.

Kelly, Ernest (1887c–1902c), Molalla	Native Name: Unknown to author
Alias: None known by author	Allotment 91
Mother: Josephine Francis Gilbert	Father: John T. Kelly

On October 19, 1911, Ernest Kelly's heirs, **Frances Gilbert** and John D. Kelly, sold his entire 79.64 acres of allotment land to P. R. Fendall.

Kelly, John T. (1865c–96c)	Native Name: Unknown to author
Alias: John Kelley	Allotment: Allotment 90
Mother Unknown to author	Father: Unknown to author

John Kelly and **Frances Gilbert** were married by Father Croquet on July 27,

---

28 Munnick and Beckham, *Catholic Church Records — Grand Ronde,* Register I, p. 52, B-8, S-10.

1885, in the presence of **William Simmons** and Cecelia Gilbert.[29]

They had Ernest Joseph on February 3, 1887. His godparents were **Daniel Robinson** and his wife, Felicite Menard.[30] The GRIC for 1888 listed John Kelly, Frances, and Ernest living with Frances's parents, **Tom Gilbert** (Kiyukiyush) and Lucinda "Cinthy".

In addition to Ernest, John and Frances had a son, John Dean Kelly, on August 7, 1889. John D. Kelly's godparents were Frank Mercier and his wife, **Mary Petite.**[31]

Like his father-in-law, John was in the bootleg whiskey business. In July 1890 he was arrested for selling liquor to Indians and sentenced to a hundred-dollar fine and a year in the State Penitentiary.[32]

John T. Kelly received a 199.58-acre allotment at Grand Ronde. His heirs were his wife, Frances, and his son, John D. Kelly. Eva Simmons-Knighton paid the fifteen-dollar heirship fee.

Kelly, John (1801c–81), Pudding River band of Kalapuya[33]	Native Name: Unknown to author
Alias: None known by author	Allotment: None known by author
Mother: Unknown to author	Father: Unknown to author

John Kelly had a daughter named Nelly Philomene (1864c–98), who was baptized April 13, 1879, at age twelve. Mary, Michelle's wife, was her godmother.[34] Her brother, **Ufaf Kelly,** died in his early twenties.[35]

John was probably the same John Kelly who married Lucy Lussenda of Siletz (1856c) on July 28, 1876, with **Frank Bond** and Mary Wacheno acting as witnesses. Later, John Kelly married "Mary, Moses' widow," with Peter LaChance and Nelly Philomene Kelly acting as their witnesses. On this last occasion, Father Croquet noted that the bride and groom were "both Indians of the Reservation (un-baptized.)"

John's wife Mary (1831c–81) died in May 1881. John died a few months later.[36]

John Kelly's daughter, Nelly Philomene, married **Billy Jones** (Skewints).

29 Ibid., Register I, p. 131, M-5.
30 Ibid., Register II, p. 27, B-9
31 Ibid., Register II, p. 54, B-15
32 Oregon State Archives, Salem, Oregon, July 5, 1890, Inmate Penitentiary, File 2385
33 Jacobs, Field Notebooks 46, *Santiam Kalapuya Text*, 5.
34 Jacobs, Field Notebooks 46, *Santiam Kalapuya Text*, 5: JB Hudson remembered "filamin" as being from Ahantchuyuk people around Woodburn and Champoeg. *Catholic Church Records—Grand Ronde*, Register I, p. 111, B-8 and Register II, p. 117, S-5: Philomene Jones died May 23, 1898.
35 Jacobs, Field Notebooks 46, *Santiam Kalapuya Text*, 6: listed Indian name of Philomene Nellie's brother as "Ufaf."
36 Munnick and Beckham, *Catholic Church Records—Grand Ronde*, Register I, p. 111, B-8, p. 133, M-8, p. 99, M-7, p. 118, B-8, S-3, S-4.

Kelly, John (1822c–1911), Clackamas, Klickitat	Native Name: Palaikhi /PA-lai-hi/ (pálayx̱i)*[37]
Alias: Stuttering John	Allotment 88
Mother: Chagikhlit /CHA-gih-lit/ (Chágix̱lit)*[38]	Father: Unknown to author

John Kelly (Palaikhi) was a part Clackamas man who had the spirit power of fire. With fire as a spirit power, he could make bad weather like hail, lightning, and thunder. His fire power, if it hit a person, would make them ill. Although his tamanawas was strong enough, John never doctored himself, but his mother was a strong Clackamas doctor and his wife, Susan (Pshkaidi), was a powerful Klickitat doctor.[39]

Aroused, this man would fight furiously and could not be held. There was a time, however, when he was beaten unconscious and not expected to live. When he came to, he started singing his power song. Since his power came from the sky, a bad hailstorm came bringing thunder, lightning, and darkness.[40]

In 1872, John and his wife, Jane, were listed under the Oregon City bands with their daughter, Fernwewa (1869c). Fernwewa was the same daughter known as Philomena Nellie, who later married **Douglas Sampson Jones**.[41]

In 1885, John was listed with his wife, Jennie, and a daughter, Louvenia (1867c). Two years later, in 1887, Susan, a full Umpqua woman, was listed as his wife.[42] John and Susan had a ten-year-old granddaughter named **Nellie Frank** living with them.[43] In 1888, their farm was described as a house, two horses, one wagon, and a harness.

By 1890, John and Susan were alone. Nellie Frank, the daughter of **Cascade Frank Johnson** and Lucy Umpqua and granddaughter of Susan had married **Johnny Williams** (Matiyas), but she and Johnny were only together a short time. Nellie Frank was back living with John and Susan in 1894.[44]

John's granddaughter, Esther Jones-LaBonte, remembered him from her childhood as short in statue and blind in one eye; she recalled how he worked as

---

37   1887 GRIC listed his Indian name as "Paw-li-he." Jacobs, Field Notebook 51, *Music and Ethnology*, 21, 23 noted a song of a part-Clackamas man named Palaikhi. "His mother was a very strong doctor; this man married a Klickitat woman Pshkaidi; a surviving granddaughter is Mrs. Esther LaBonte, now of Grand Ronde."

38   Ibid.

39   Jacobs, Field Notebook 51, *Music and Ethnology*, 21, 23.

40   Ibid.

41   Zenk, Interview with Esther LaBonte, 1982, transcript 1, 2009 (26:17).

42   1887 GRIC gave Indian name as Pawcheet-na. Jacobs, Field Notebook 51, *Music and Ethnology*, 21 gave Indian name as pcqaidi.

43   Zenk, interview with Esther LaBonte, 1982, transcript 1, 2009 (26:16): Esther further identified her grandfather John Kelly's step-granddaughter as "Nellie Knighton." She said, "He had married her grandmother long ago."

44   Zenk, 1887, Grand Ronde Field Notebook 8, p. 10.

Esther Jones-LaBonte with Meshach Tipton, Umpqua elder (seated). Meshach Tipton was Nancy Santiago-Hall's brother-in-law. He was once married to her half sister, Mary Palouse, whose first husband was Limpy. Photo courtesy of Doloris Parmenter.

a dishwasher in Portland where he was given $9 to cut his hair.[45]

John received a 220-acre allotment at Grand Ronde. He sold 160 acres to Wallace McCamant with a non-competent deed on January 30, 1908. After his death on December 14, 1911, his grandchildren, Esther Jones-Demont (1895c–1987) and

45 Gatschet, *Texts, Sentences and Vocables*, 374: listed under the Klickitat as "John Kelly." Zenk, interview with Esther LaBonte, 1982, transcript 1, 2009 (26:17)

John Kelly's grandson, Scott Jones. Photo courtesy of Barbara Danforth Private Collection.

Scott Jones (1887c–1960), inherited his property.[46] Esther married Silas John La-Bonte in 1917. Scott Jones married Josephine Sara LaBonte around 1906.

Kelly, Ufaf, Pudding River band of Kalapuya	Native Name: Ufaf /U-faf/ (úfaaf)*[47]
Alias: None known by author	Allotment: None known by author
Mother Unknown to author	Father: John Kelly, French Prairie Ahantchuyuk (Pudding River)

---

46 *Heirs of Deceased Indians*, Allotment Record 88.
47 Jacobs, Field Notebooks 46, *Santiam Kalapuya Text*, 6.

Ufaf was the son of John Kelly. Philomene Nelly Kelly was his sister. Ufaf died in his early twenties.[48]

Kenoyer, Caroline (1882), Pudding River of Kalapuya, Tualatin band of Kalapuya	Native Name: None known by author
Alias: Caroline, Catherine Kernoyer, Caroline Robinson	Allotment 9
Mother: Nancy (Tunishni), Pudding River band of Kalapuya (Ahantchuyuk)	Father: Peter Kenoyer, Tualatin band of Kalapuya

Caroline was about ten days old when Father Croquet baptized her on January 1, 1882. Her godparents were **Thomas Norwest** and **Elizabeth Petite.** She was confirmed in the Catholic Church November 26, 1893.

In 1906, Caroline married **Dan Robinson.** On February 22, 1907, she received a fee patent for her forty-acre allotment.[49]

Kenoyer, Louis (1867–1937), Pudding River band of Kalapuya, Tualatin band of Kalapuya	Native Name: Pakhawatas /ba-ha-WA-tas/ (p̣axawát'as)*[50]
Alias: None known by author	Allotment 92
Mother: Nancy (Tunishni), Pudding River band of Kalapuya (Ahantchuyuk)	Father: Peter Kenoyer (Kinai), Tualatin band of Kalapuya

Louis Kenoyer (Pakhawatas) worked as a school teacher for the agency.[51] His father died when he was at Chemawa.[52] He never heard his native language after he was seventeen.

Around 1892, Louis and **Nellie Frank,** former wife of **Johnny Williams** (Matiyas), were married by civil ceremony. They had two sons. Their first son, Frederic Kenoyer, was baptized in April 1893. The baby's godparents were Frank Mercier and **Elizabeth Petite.** Their second son, Joseph August Kenoyer, was born March 4, 1896, and baptized a few weeks later. Joseph's godmother was Louis's sister,

---

48   Ibid.
49   *Heirs of Deceased Indians*, Allotment Records 9, 92.
50   Gatschet, *Texts, Sentences and Vocables*, 77: "Pakauatash masc. (Louis) of Kinai."
     Jacobs, *Autobiography of a Tualatin*, par. 1: "My name is Daxawadas."
51   *Record of Employees at Grand Ronde, 1884–1907.*
52   Leo Frachtenberg, *Kalapuya Ethnology* (found among papers in J. P. Harrington's Office, American Philosophical Society Library, 1959).

Caroline Kenoyer.[53] In 1902, both his sons died of typhoid.[54] In 1903, Louis left Nellie and married Rosa Taylor. Rosa and her two small children were living with Louis that year. Nellie was living alone.

On March 23, 1908, Louis received a fee patent for a 79.47-acre allotment at Grand Ronde; however, by 1915, he was living in Toppenish. After locating him there, Leo Frachtenberg asked for his help in reviewing Gatschet's earlier work on the Tualatin Language. Louis later provided Tualatin language vocabulary and text to DeAngulo and Freeland in 1928–29 and Melville Jacobs in 1936.

Kenoyer, Nancy (1847c–1907c) Pudding River band of Kalapuya[55]	Native Name: Tunishni /TU-nish-ni/ (túnishni),* Kupan /KU-pan/ (k'úpan)*[56]
Alias: Nancy Apperson, Nancy Tipton, Nancy Pratt	Allotment: None known by author
Mother: Unknown to author	Father: Unknown to author

Nancy (Tunishni) was related to **Ben Harding** (Kwana) and **Sambo Sappenfield** (Chawatkha).[57] After she married **Peter Kenoyer** (Kinai), they had a number of children, including Peter (1861–61), Charley (1862c–74), an unnamed daughter, Louis (1867–1937), Margaret (1871–86), Philomene (1873–74), Rosa (1877–79), Lucy (1880), and Caroline.[58]

After Peter died, Nancy married **Joe Apperson** (Washamsh) on August 16, 1887. The following year the Apperson family included Nancy, Joe Apperson, his son, **Mathew Apperson,** her son, **Louis Kenoyer** (Pakhawatas), and her daughter, **Caroline Kenoyer.**

Joe Apperson died around 1890. By 1892, Nancy was listed as the wife of **Dick Tipton;** her daughter, Caroline Kenoyer, was listed as Tipton's stepdaughter. Dick Tipton's former wife, **Mary Hutchins,** was listed as a widow.

---

53 Munnick and Beckham, *Catholic Church Records — Grand Ronde*, Register II, p. 84, B-2, p. 105, B-7.

54 Zenk, Interview with Clara Riggs, 1982, Grand Ronde Community — 2, CR 3/21/82 (II-66).

55 Jacobs, Field Notebooks 46, *Santiam Kalapuya Text*, 161: J. B. Hudson said, "Nancy — she was hantcyuk 'Half Prairie' woman." Gatschet, *Texts, Sentences and Vocables*, 6: Kenoyer's wife is a Kalapuya from French Prairie near Sheridan.

56 Jacobs, Field Notebooks 59, *Texts and Ethnology*, 26: "Louis Kenoyer's mother was of some near-Santiam tribe; tunicni was her name; qinaya was his father's name." 1887 GRIC gave her Indian name as "Go-pen." Gatschet, *Texts, Sentences and Vocables*, 6 listed Nancy's Indian name as "Gopan."

57 Gatschet, *Texts, Sentences and Vocables*, 94. Jacobs, Field Notebooks 46, *Santiam Kalapuya Text*, 5: Ben Harding was uncle of Louis Kenoyer.

58 Munnick and Beckham, *Catholic Church Records — Grand Ronde*, Register I, p. 25, B-17, p. 55, B-58, p. 68, B-21, p. 84, B-38, p. 89, S-19, p. 90, S-30, p. 104, B-34, p. 112, S-7, p. 120, B-1.

In 1906, Nancy was the wife of **John Pratt** (Gwaimit). Neither Nancy nor John appear on any GRIC after that year. John's death was recorded as June 10, 1909. Although Nancy is known to have died before John, the exact date of her death is not known.[59]

Kenoyer, Peter (1840c–86), Tualatin band of Kalapuya	Native Name: Kinai /KI-nay/ (q'ínay)*[60]
Alias: Peter Conoyer, Peter Marc Cornoyer	Allotment: None known by author
Mother: Unknown to author	Father: Kamach, Tualatin band of Kalapuya[61]

Peter Kenoyer (Kinai)'s father, Kamach, was the younger brother of **Chief Kiakuts** (Kayakach) and a prominent man in his own right.[62]

Peter married a Molalla woman named Catherine who died February 17, 1863.[63] On May 24, 1863, he married a Kalapuya woman from French Prairie, called Tunishni by her own people but also known by the English name, **Nancy Kenoyer**. Together they had nine children, including twins.[64]

During a council meeting with Felix Bruncot, a clerk, T. K. Cree, Superintendent Meacham, and Rev. Parrish in 1871, Peter spoke in English, telling them,

I have not much to say. For four or five years now I have wanted my land surveyed. It is now being done, and I want to settle down on it and live and die on it.

In regard to gambling, Peter said,

I am getting old, but I am easily led astray; I may go to a race, bet a little, but I don't want my children to learn it. It is bad. I ought not to do it myself. We get off the side of the road, where no good man can see us, and we gamble, but when a good man comes along, we are ashamed of it. So it is with the white man when he does what he knows is wrong.[65]

59   Oregon State Archives, Salem, Oregon, 1909, Yamhill County, Estate File 1327.
60   Gatschet, *Texts, Sentences and Vocables*, 1: "Kinai, called Peter Conoyer, about 40 years old." Gatschet, *Texts, Sentences and Vocables*, 77. Jacobs, Field Notebooks 59, *Texts and Ethnology*, 26.
61   Jacobs, *Santiam Kalapuya Ethnologic Texts*, Part 1, 160: given as kámatc.
62   Ibid.
63   Munnick and Beckham, *Catholic Church Records—Grand Ronde*, Register I, p. 25, S-8.
64   Ibid., Register I, p. 25, B-17, p. 55, B-58, p. 68, B-21, p. 84, B-38, p. 89, S-19, p. 90, S-30, p. 104, B-34, p. 112, S-7, p. 120, B-1
65   *Annual Report Commissioner of Indian Affairs*, 1871, Minutes of a Council with Grande Ronde Indians at their Reservation, Oregon, by Commissioner Felix R. Brunot, September 14, 1871, 149–153.

Men stick gambling on the Grand Ronde Reservation. Photo courtesy of Oregon Historical Society (CN022573).

A few months later, Peter sent three of their children—Charley, Charlotte, and Louis (Pakhawatas)—to the "language school" at the agency.[66] **Louis Kenoyer** remembered how on the morning of the first day of school, the sky looked like a storm might be coming.

Frightened of storms, Louis told his father he did not want to go to school, but his father told him it made no difference whether it rained or thundered. It made no difference that he was afraid. He had to go to school. It seemed to Louis that they had scarcely left their house before the first roar of thunder sent him running for home. Peter allowed him to stay, but "for this day only."[67]

Several years later, on August 26, 1877, a new boarding school was dedicated.[68] Indian agent Sinnott sent two messengers to tell the people that they had to take their children to the boarding school the following morning. If they did not, they would be arrested by the Indian police and put in jail.

---

66 Jacobs, Collection 40, *Autobiography of a Tualatin,* par. 2 and 4. Cawley, *Father Croquet of the Grand Ronde,* Story 23, gave daughter's name as Charlotte.

67 Ibid.

68 *Annual Report Commissioner of Indian Affairs,* 1876, Sinnott: "The school was dedicated August 26, 1877." Annual Report Commissioner of Indian Affairs, 1886, McClane: "There is but one school, but we use two houses; one is called the carpenter's house; why it should be so, I cannot tell."

Children in school uniforms posing in front of old blockhouse at Grand Ronde. Photo courtesy of Oregon Historical Society (OrHi 85526).

At the boarding school, there were five nuns who took care of the children. If they became ill, they were treated by the white doctor. At the end of each month, the children were allowed three days of vacation with their families.[69]

That spring Louis did not return to school, but was allowed to stay at home to help his father plow and plant the fields. While Peter sowed the wheat, Louis followed behind him with a three-horse team harrowing the ground. After they had planted thirty acres, the nine-year-old Louis worked on fences.[70]

After the planting season, Peter was able to get a pass from the Indian agent for his family to live in Salem for a few months. In town, Nancy washed clothes for the Americans and picked berries for market while Peter cut wood for a white man who was paying $3 a cord.[71]

When the Shasta chief, **Tyee Shasta Tom,** was caught holding a dream dance, Peter Kenoyer (Kinai) was a judge on the Indian court. Since there were laws at Grand Ronde against the new dream doctrine and against bringing news of it on the reservation, the agent had the Indian police break up the new dream dance, On this occasion, two Rogue River people were fined fifteen dollars each and a third man was fined $7.50. Everyone who had entered the dance lodge was forced to stay there until morning and fined fifty cents each.[72]

In 1879, Peter was elected to serve on the Grand Ronde Indian legislature and

69   Jacobs, *Autobiography of a Tualatin,* par. 4 and 5.
70   Ibid., par. 7.
71   Ibid., par. 10.
72   Gatschet, *Texts, Sentences and Vocables,* 188–89.

re-elected the following year. On November 13, 1879, he paid six dollars for his license to practice law along with the Tualatin sub-chief, **Dave Kachkawa,** and **James Winslow.**[73]

After the Grand Ronde Indian Legislature appointed Peter court attorney, one of the complaints he brought to court was a charge made December 30, 1882, of "trading a horse and then trading back again without sufficient satisfaction" against **William "Billy" Warren.**[74]

Witnesses in the case were **Frank Norwest,** Peter Kenoyer, and Peter's wife, Nancy. The three defense attorneys were **Bill Shufon** (Sanik), **Alexander Day,** and **Frank Norwest.** The sheriff at the time was **Henry Winslow.** Court clerk was Frank Norwest. The defendant, Billy Warren, elected to plead guilty.

James Pierce (Clamarchnet), the justice of the peace, fined Billy $2.50 plus $13.50 in court costs and gave him two weeks to pay. Billy put up one rifle as security. Records indicate the gun had to be sold at auction by **Frank Quenel** to pay court costs.[75]

Peter Kenoyer died September 4, 1886.

Keosnose, Mary Ann, Clackamas, Wakanasisi band of Chinook[76]	Native Name: Kiyasnu /ki-Ya-snu/ (k'iyásnu)*[77]
Alias: Mary Ann Kesno, Kensano, Cassino	Allotment: None known by author
Mother: Unknown to author	Father: Unknown to author

Mary Ann was the wife of the Columbia River chief, Cassino (Kiyasnu). Kiyasnu was an important man on the Columbia in the early 1800s. He had great influence not only among his own people but among neighboring tribes as well.

After the European fur traders set up a post on the north side of the Columbia, many tribes were against fur company men being in the country without paying tribute. One dark night in 1829, war canoes floated noiselessly down upon Fort Vancouver. According to an undocumented source, Chief Kiyasnu of the Multnomah rallied his tribe in support of the Hudson's Bay men and the guns at the fort were set. Throughout the night the sound of war drums could be heard on both sides of the river.

By morning, John McLoughlin, chief factor of the Hudson's Bay Company, knew that to acquire authority in the Oregon Country, he would have to gain the

---

73   National Archives, Seattle, WA, Grand Ronde/Siletz, Land and Enrollment Program records, Field Notes and Land Survey 1875–1898, Land Description Book 1878, Box 115; Grand Ronde Justice Court.

74   Ibid.

75   Ibid.

76   Oliver Applegate, Testimony of Captain Frank Quenelle, James Shilikwa and John Wacheno.

77   Frachtenberg, *Molalla Ethnology,* n.p.

Indians' respect. To this end, legend has it that McLoughlin sent out Indian runners calling for a council at Fort Vancouver.

At the appointed time, men representing all the various tribal nations in Oregon Territory entered the gates of the fort. After everyone had arrived, they formed a semicircle, indicating they were ready to talk.

Suddenly, Colin Fraser, a six-foot-tall Highlander, appeared before them wearing a Scottish kilt and carrying bagpipes. For one hour he strode up and down the fort yard playing the pipes. According to the Indian way, any man who commanded another man with such a gift as this was a man of great power, and to have that man offer such a gift to them was an honor and sign of respect. While the music kept playing, McLoughlin presented them with a ready-made treaty that promised Ft. Vancouver would never be molested. After such a performance, all the chiefs were more than happy to sign.

As it turned out, the question of peace or war with the Hudson's Bay men was not the most critical issue Chief Kiyasnu and the rest of the Indian people would have to face. Between 1829 and 1833 epidemics struck the tribes of Oregon Country, decreasing their numbers at an alarming rate. At the village of Wakanasisi, six miles from Fort Vancouver, the dead were heaped in open tombs six feet deep and 160 feet long. Within three weeks of the first outbreak the tribe, once five hundred warriors strong, was reduced to Chief Kiyasnu and six others.

In 1856, Kiyasnu's widow, Mary Ann, was brought to the Grand Ronde Reservation with several of her slaves.[78]

Kiakuts, Chief (1804–64c), Tualatin band of Kalapuya	Native Name: Kayakach /KA-ya-kach/ (q'áyaq'ach)*[79]
Alias: Kayakach, Kiakutz	Allotment: None known by author
Mother: Unknown to author	Father: Unknown to author

Chief Kiakuts (Kayakach) was the principal chief of the Tualatin people. Prior to removal, his band lived at Wapato Lake.[80]

In 1856, the GRIC listed seventy-five people under Kayakach's leadership. The next year, the number had increased to eighty-one members. About this time, Joel Palmer came to ask the various bands of Kalapuya people to get together and elect one chief. The results of that election were reflected in the 1862 GRIC. It listed all the Willamette Valley bands, 686 people, all under the leadership of

---

78 O. Applegate, Oliver, Testimony of Captain Frank Quenelle, James Shilikwa and John Wacheno.

79 Jacobs, *Santiam Kalapuya Ethnologic Texts*, Part 1, 163, 165. Gatschet, *Texts, Sentences and Vocables*, 77: "Kayakatch mase. A chief, Emmie's father." Munnick and Beckham, *Catholic Church Records—Grand Ronde*, Register I, p. 15, B-214: Father Croquet spelled his name "Kaiakatz."

80 Jacobs, *Santiam Kalapuya Ethnologic Texts*, Part 1, 160–73.

Chief Kayakach.[81] Clearly Kayakach had earned the reputation of being a formidable leader.

Not surprising, Kayakach's spirit power was the eagle. It was a strong power that brought him great wealth. When he died, he left an estate that included a yoke of oxen, two cows, two mares, one colt, one calf, ten hogs, about a hundred bushels of wheat, and two Modoc slaves.[82] In addition, he left his American-made house on approximately sixty acres of unsurveyed land with 150 apple trees which were still standing in 1877. All of this he left to his wife and children, along with a hundred dollars in cash.[83]

Tualatin Chief Kayakach had three children with his wife, Susanne or Sarah: Francis (1852–62), Mary Emma (1857c), and a son, John Baptist (1861–63). He had a son, Joseph (1864–1864) with another wife, Marianne.[84] His oldest son lived to be ten years old. His second son lived until he was about two. The youngest son died around the same time as Chief Kayakach, leaving only his daughter Emma Kiakuts out of all his children.

Kiakuts, Sarah (1804c–82), Tualatin band of Kalapuya	Native Name: Washkayak /wash-GA-yak/ (washgáyaq) ["she-jaybird"],* Pononapa[85]
Alias: Sarah Kayakach, Sarah Shlawin, Susanne Kayakach, Sarah Yachkawa	Allotment: None known by author
Mother: Unknown to author	Father: Unknown to author

Sarah (Washkayak) was **Chief Kiakuts** (Kayakach)'s hayash wife and the mother of Francis, Mary Emma and John Baptist.[86] However, both her sons died before their father.[87]

After Kayakach died, Sarah married **Chief Shlawin,** who then adopted her daughter, Emma Kiakuts. After Shlawin died in October of 1875, Sarah mar-

---

81 1856 GRIC. 1857 GRIC. Condon, James B., 1862 GRIC of the Indians Belonging/ Located upon the Grand Ronde Indian Agency, Oregon.

82 Gatschet, *Texts, Sentences and Vocables,* 94: At one time Kayakach owned four slaves; "one was a Modoc; Tchimbelon, another a [?] or Modoc, Lukue; the 3rd a Apinefu (a lukamiute); Lankmat; the 4th Galak a tchayankelt (Santiam, Eugene)."

83 Jacobs, *Santiam Kalapuya Ethnologic Texts,* Part 1, 160–73.

84 Munnick and Beckham, *Catholic Church Records—Grand Ronde,* Register I, p. 20,B-50, S-19, p. 15, B-214, p. 16, B-238, p. 11, B-59

85 Jacobs, Field Notebooks 58, *Texts and Ethnology,* 12: gave her name as "Wacgayaq, or she-jay-bird." Munnick and Beckham, *Catholic Church Records—Grand Ronde,* Register I, p. 96, M-12: Father Croquet recorded her name as "Sarah Sloan." 1872 GRIC: listed her name as "Sarah Slowan." The Pacific Reporter, 436–37, listed her by the Indian name "Pononapa."

86 Johnson and Zenk, *Chinuk Wawa,* 134: *hayash* meaning big.

87 Munnick and Beckham, *Catholic Church Records—Grand Ronde,* Register I, p. 20,B-50, S-19, p. 15, B-214, p. 16, B-238, p. 11, B-59

ried the Tualatin sub-chief, **Dave Yachkawa,** on December 25 of that year. **Peter Checkaon** (Chikhyan)'s wife, Marianne (Bochean), and **Chief John Kawache's** son, **Moses Apperson** (Wannexke) acted as their witnesses.[88]

In 1877, Yachkawa told Albert Gatschet about an old woman that lived with him who could draw blood by singing from the chest to the head of a patient. Most certainly Sarah was this old woman as she was Yachkawa's wife and widely known as a big doctor at Grand Ronde.[89]

Sarah and Dave Yachkawa were murdered November 28, 1882, by **Tom Gilbert** (Kiyukiyush). Apparently, Tom committed the double homicide because Yachkawa had turned him in for illegally selling liquor.[90]

Kidnos, John (1808c–78c), Tualatin band of Kalapuya[91]	Native Name: Kidnu /KID-nu/ (kídnu)*[92]
Alias: None known by author	Allotment: None known by author
Mother: Unknown to author	Father: Unknown to author

John Kidnos (Kidnu) had at least nine children: Julienne (1854c), William (1856c), Joseph (1857c), Michael (1859c–74), Elisha (1866c), Rosalie (1867c), Charlotte (1868c), Cecile (1872c), and Adrienne (1877c). On February 24, 1871, his wife, Mary (1831c) died at Grand Ronde.[93]

In 1872, he was listed with his Kalapuya wife, Susan, and four of his children: William, Michael, Rosalie, and Cecile.[94] In 1877, John and his wife only had their two daughters still living at home.[95]

Kiki, Henry (1824c–89c), Molalla, Clackamas, Klamath[96]	Native Name: Lhkailhkai /HLKAI-hlkai/ (ɬqáyɬqay)*[97]

---

88 Ibid., Register I, p. 96, M-12.

89 Gatschet, *Texts, Sentences and Vocables,* 401.

90 Jacobs, Field Notebooks 58, *Texts and Ethnology,* 12.

91 Gatschet, *Texts, Sentences and Vocables,* 30.

92 Gatschet, *Texts, Sentences and Vocables,* 370: under the Tualatin as "Kidnu, old; wife; 2 girls single." Gatschet, *Texts, Sentences and Vocables,* 77: "Kidnu."

93 Munnick and Beckham, *Catholic Church Records—Grand Ronde,* Register I, p. 67, B-9.

94 Ibid.,Register I, p. 19, B-37, B-38, p. 31, B-16, S-5, p. 44, B-16, p. 44, B-16, p. 52, B-1, p. 74, B-16, p. 88, S-12, S-11, p. 102, B-12, p. 108, S-15, p. 107, S-10.

95 Gatschet, *Texts, Sentences and Vocables,* 370. Michelle, *Just a Memorandum,* 5: Mary Ann wrote that Kidnos was Tualatin and his wife, Susan, was Calapooia. They had one daughter, Rosella.

96 Michelle, *Just a Memorandum,* 6: Henry Kiki's father was Klamath and his mother was half Klamath and half Clackamas. Drucker, Molalla Field Notes, Interview with Kate Shantell: Henry Kiki and the Molalla Chief Yelkas were cousins.

97 Jacobs, Field Notebook 51, *Music and Ethnology,* 14. Gatschet, *Texts, Sentences and Vocables,* 373: "under Klamath as 'kaikai, tlailhkei, Molale.'" Drucker, *Molalla Field Notes,* interview with Kate Chantelle, gave his name as LkaiLkai. Munnick and Beckham, *Catholic Church Records—Grand Ronde,* Register I, p. 19, B-40: Father

Alias: None known by author	Allotment 93
Mother: Clackamas, Klamath	Father: Molalla, Klamath

Henry Kiki (Lhkailhkai) spoke in the 1871 council with the Americans. He said,

> Long ago the chief [white representative] said we would buy your lands. The calico and other things, they said, we give you [were gifts]. We want to know about our lands. I have a wagon; I bought it. My house I got the same way. My clothes I bought; the government never gave me any of them. I got harness, and oxen, and a plow, some time ago. I guess that was all I got for my lands. Now we want to know what we get for our lands. We need a grist-mill, harness and horses, and plows, and wagons, and that is all we want. [98]

Henry had two wives: hayash wife, Mary Ann, and second wife, Sarah, who was also Klamath. They had a number of children: Lucy (1858c), Louise (1860c), Catherine (1864), Sophie (1866), Gery Eugene (1868c–77c), Elizabeth (1869), Julia Ann (1871c–76c), Jane or Joanna (1873c–86c), David (1873c), George (1881c–85c), Stephen, and **Rose Kiki** (Ilhikhsha).[99] His daughter Catherine married Joe Thompson (1857c).

Sometime late in 1888, Henry's wife Mary Ann died. Henry died the following year. His widow, Sarah, married **Moses Allen.** During probate, Henry's real property was appraised at $540. In 1907, a fee patent for 226.24 acres of allotment land was issued to his heirs: Madeline Wallace, Maurine Thompson, Anne Sitton, and his son, **Stephen Kiki.** Having already received a 39.94-acre allotment in his own name, Stephen sold his interest in Henry's allotment property for fifty dollars in 1908.[100]

Kiki, Stephen (1879c–1910), Molalla, Clackamas, Klamath	Native Name: Unknown to author
Alias: None known by author	Allotment 94
Mother: Sarah, Klamath	Father: Henry Kiki (Lhkailhkai), Molalla, Clackamas, Klamath

---

Croquet spelled his name "Kaiekaie."

98 *Annual Report Commissioner of Indian Affairs,* 1871, Minutes of a Council with Grand Ronde Indians at their Reservation, Oregon, by Commissioner Felix R. Brunot, September 14, 1871, 149–53.

99 Munnick and Beckham, *Catholic Church Records—Grand Ronde,* Register I, p. 19, B-40, B-41, p. 31, B-23, p. 43, B-4, p. 50, S-22, p. 55, B-62, p. 102, S-7, p. 58, B-10, p. 68, B-15, p. 100, S-22, p. 84, B-37, p. 109, B-21.

100 Heirs to Deceased Indians, Allotment Record 93. Oregon State Archives, Salem, Oregon, 1908, Polk County, Estate File 1288.

When he was a boy, Stephen Kiki was often appreciated by the elders for his humor. Even though he knew he was too young and ignorant to tell a story, night after night, he would announce he was going to tell one. Then holding his mouth, he would hem and haw until he made everyone laugh.[101]

Stephen's mother, Sarah, was full Klamath, but she never spoke Klamath to Stephen and did not sing. Even though his father, **Henry Kiki** (Lhkailhkai), spoke both Molalla and Clackamas perfectly, Stephen was not fluent in either language. He spoke Chinook Jargon and English. The words in his power songs may have been Molalla or, less likely, Clackamas.[102]

One of Stephen's power songs was sung by **Victoria Wishikin** (Kinishi) and recorded for Melville Jacobs in 1929. While the exact nature of Stephen's power is unknown, it was said that when he danced and sang, he held a knife in his hand.[103]

A person with knife as a spirit power could kill a person with just a single blow. A doctor with this power could quickly heal people who had been stabbed.[104] In the end, Stephen died from a stab wound. **John Wacheno** (Tsinwalh) delivered the fatal blow after finding Stephen in bed with his wife. Wacheno was arrested but quickly released.[105]

Kiki, Rose (1837c), Clackamas, Molalla, Klamath[106]	Native Name: Ilhikhsha /i-hlih-sha/ (íɬixsha)*[107]
Alias: Rose Wallace	Allotment: None known by author
Mother: Unknown to author	Father: Henry Kiki, Klamath, Clackamas, Molalla

Rose (Ilhikhsha) was Stephen Kiki's half sister. She had dead person spirit power. With this power, a person cannot hold on to things. Rose wore just a few old rags and always had dirt on her.[108]

She married **Henry Wallace.** Once when Henry was sick, the Indian doctor, **Polk Scott** (Puk), attributed Henry's illness to his having had sexual intercourse when he was already ill. Rose was not happy with the diagnosis as apparently they had not had sex for a very long time.[109] By Henry Wallace, Rose only had one

---

101 Jacobs, Field Notebook 56, *Texts and Ethnology*, 18.

102 Jacobs, Field Notebook 51, *Music and Ethnology*, 32–33

103 Ibid.

104 Jacobs, Field Notebooks 78, *Texts and Ethnology Santiam*, 54.

105 Jacobs, Field Notebook 51, *Texts and Ethnology*, 32.

106 Michelle, *Just a Memorandum*, 5: Mary Ann wrote Louysa's mother, Rose, was Klamath. Jacobs, Notebooks 67, *Texts Ethnology Clackamas & Jargon*, 106, gave Ilhikhsha as part Molalla and part Clackamas. 1887 GRIC gave her Indian name as Ic-lac-shill.

107 Jacobs, *Clackamas Texts*, Part 2, 514 –15, gave her name as itixca.

108 Jacobs, Field Notebook 51, *Music and Ethnology*, 23.

109 Jacobs, *Clackamas Texts*, Part 2, 514 –15. Jacobs, Field Notebook 67, Texts, *Ethnology*

child, Louisa (1873c–1913).[110]

In 1929, **Victoria Wishikin** (Kinishi) recorded one of Rose's power songs for Melville Jacobs.[111]

Kilear, Amos (1803c–1913), Yamhill band of Kalapuya	Native Name: Kilya /KIL-ya/ (ḳílya)*[112]
Alias: Amos Gilear, Old Gilya, Old Amos, Blind Amos	Allotment 6
Mother: Unknown to author	Father: Unknown to author

Amos (Kilya) had dead person spirit power. With this gift, in Kilya's dreams, he could communicate with people living in the land of the dead.

Once Kilya used his power to help a Yamhill woman named **Margaret "Maggie" Lapan** (Chalwina). She feared her son, **Frank Bond,** had died as he was late returning home from the coast. Kilya told the old woman to give him the coat Frank always wore. With the coat as a pillow, he would be able to see what had become of her son during the night through his spirit powers. She gave him the coat and the two parted.

The following morning, Kilya came to her and told her he had seen her son in a dream; he was at Garibaldi, Oregon. He was all right. Later, as Kilya had assured her he would, the missing Frank Bond returned home.[113]

Kilya was a big man, but perhaps it was his power as much as his appearance that caused the Americans to fear him. Rev. Summers wrote that when he first came to Grand Ronde he was warned about Kilya. He had been told that Kilya had "killed three or four wives in his lifetime and any number of white men and was at one time incarcerated in a United States prison."[114]

Nevertheless, Rev. Summers borrowed a horse at the agency and rode out to Kilya's place to try to buy an antique Klickitat article Kilya owned. Kilya was not at the house when he arrived, but his wife called him in from the field. Rev. Summers later wrote that as he approached, Kilya had "the most villainous countenance he ever looked upon." While he immediately made up his mind not to go in the house with Kilya, Rev. Summers did not give up on the artifact he hoped

---

Clackamas & Jargon, n. p: "itixca insisted that she never copulated since the conception of her daughter. Wallace recovered."

110 Ibid.

111 Jacobs, Field Notebook 51, *Music and Ethnology*, 23–24

112 1887 GRIC gave his Indian name as Kilya. Jacobs, Field Notebooks 36, *Santiam Kalapuya Text*, 192: "kilya, (Amos) Yamhill man." Jacobs, Field Notebooks 46, *Santiam Kalapuya Text*, 70: J. B. Hudson described him as "an old Yamhill medicine doctor, Kilya, called Amos by the whites." Jacobs, Field Notebook 51, *Music and Ethnology*, 45.

113 Jacobs, *Santiam Kalapuya Ethnologic Texts*, Part 1, 70–71. Jacobs, Field Notebook 46, 61: E. Howard tells Frank Bond and Kilya story. It is translated by J. B. Hudson.

114 Cawley, *Indian Journal*, 35.

to purchase.[115]

Kilya was married at least twice. By Harriet, he had Julia (1865c), Joseph (1867c), Pauline (1870c), Jack (Shaklu) (1868), Merose (1871c), and Jane (1872c).[116]

He then married a Luckiamute woman called **Bertha Wheeler** (Tewimme), the former wife of **Steve Morufi**. Bertha was **Jacob "Jake" Wheeler** (Shwa)'s sister.[117] When Kilya married her, she had a daughter, Anna, who was "just old enough to run about."[118]

Kilya had only been married to Bertha a short time when Rev. Summers made his visit to their home in 1875. The road to his place was probably little more than a trail at that time, but in 1880 the Indian Road Department opened a new road to his place that cut through **Peter Menard** and **David Holmes** (Faliper)'s land.[119]

In 1885, Kilya and Bertha had three of Kilya's children from his previous marriage—Jack, Jane, and Merose—as well as Bertha's daughter, Anna, all living at home, but the following year, only Kilya's son **Jack Amos** (Shaklu) was still living with them. Their home was described as a poor house and shed on ten fenced acres with a small garden and orchard.

By 1887, Kilya was a widower and completely blind. People said his power made him steal. He did it because he had no other choice. Amos's son Jack lived with him until 1889.[120] Then Jack married **Lucy Sampson** and began making his own place.

Eventually, Kilya received a forty-acre allotment at Grand Ronde. He lived a very long life and prized himself on being able to remember the land before the "Bostons" first came to his country. He claimed to remember John McLoughlin and many of the early missionaries including Jason Lee.[121]

After Kilya's death, Frank Bond and Louise Selkeah inherited his allotment. The property was sold March 20, 1914. **Victoria Wishikin** (Kinishi) sang several of his power songs and they were recorded by Melville Jacobs in 1930.[122]

Killum (1815c), Tillamook	Native Name: Unknown to author
Alias: None known by author	Allotment: None known by author
Mother: Unknown to author	Father: Unknown to author

---

115 Ibid.

116 Jacobs, Field Notebook 51, *Music and Ethnology*, 45, gave Jack Amos's Indian name as Cakla.

117 Oregon State Archives, Salem, Oregon, 1904, Yamhill County, Estate File 1176.

118 O. Applegate, Testimony of Amos Kilya.

119 National Archives, Seattle, Grand Ronde/Siletz, Land and Enrollment Program records, Field Notes and Land Survey 1875–1898, Land Description Book 1878, Box 115; Grand Ronde Justice Court.

120 Jacobs, Field Notebook 51, *Music and Ethnology*, 45.

121 O. Applegate, Testimony of Amos Kilya. Oregon State Archives, 1909, Polk County, Estate File 1327, John Pratt.

122 Jacobs, Field Notebook 51, *Music and Ethnology*, 45–47.

In 1885, Killum was living with his wife, Minnie, and his children, May (1874c), Bob (1880c), and Henry (1882c). Killum's brother, **Ketchum** (1835c), was also living with the family at that time.

Kilmonie, Isadore (1879c–93) Clackamas, Tumwater band Chinook	Native Name: Unknown to author
Alias: None known by author	Allotment 96
Mother: Stephanie Apperson, Clackamas, Tumwater band of Chinook	Father: Unknown to author

Isadore Kilmonie was the son of **Stephanie Apperson.** After his mother died of tuberculosis, **Mary Ann Kilmonie** (Katamkhin) and **Wallen Kilmonie** (Kílma-nukh) raised him.

He received a 120-acre allotment. In April of 1907, a fee patent for forty acres of his allotment was issued to his heirs. The fifteen-dollar heirship fee was paid by Smiscon and Frank So-Happy from Yakama, **Mascasca Sitton,** and Pauline Sutton.[123] The remaining eighty acres were held in trust. In probate court, the sole heir to his personal estate was "a cousin," **Margaret Toto** (Chaimala).[124]

Kilmonie, Mary Ann (1816c–90c), Clackamas[125]	Native Name: Kilipashta /Kl-li-pash-ta/ (kílipashṭa)*[126]
Alias: None known by author	Allotment 97
Mother: Unknown to author	Father: Unknown to author

Mary Ann Kilmonie (Kilipashta) had several husbands including **Paul Toto. Margaret Toto** (Chaimala) and **Wallen Kilmonie** (Kilmanukh) were her natural children by two different fathers. **Tom Gilbert** (Kiyukiyush), **Mary Hutchins** (Sanyef), **Steve Savage** (Palhilh), and **Alexander Toto** were her stepchildren.[127]

Once at a spirit power dance, Doctor Smith's wife, **Mary Smith** (Niudiya), and Mary Ann (Kilipashta) were gossiping. They made a comment about some of the people attending the dance who did not have their heads flattened. The custom of flattening a baby's head at birth was an indication of the child's social status. An unflattened head was a sign that the person was of a lower status and their children were called "mauls."

Overhearing their remarks, **James Winslow** became offended. He told them

---

123 *Heirs to Deceased Indians*, Allotment Record 96.
124 Oregon State Archives, 1907, Yamhill County, Estate File 1204.
125 Jacobs, *Clackamas Text*, Part II, 561.
126 Jacobs, Field Notebook 59, *Texts and Ethnology*, 60. Jacobs, Field Notebook 69, *Texts and Ethnology*, 109.
127 Affidavit State of Oregon, County of Yamhill, taken from Josephine (Frances) Shirley January 25, 1917 and Macasca Sutton, February 3, 1917.

to go ahead and laugh, and said that if they (**Sophie Gendron** and **Charlie Petite's** children) had heads like yours, "they would be like cattle." To this the women also laughed until someone finally hushed them.[128]

Kilmonie, Mary Ann (1852c–1912c), Klickitat wife of part Clackamas and part Molalla husband	Native Name: Katamkhin /ka-TAM-hen/ (ḵaṭámxən),*[129] Twilhapam /TWI-hla-pam/ (twíiɫapam)*[130]
Alias: Marion Kilmoni, Yamhill Mary	Allotment: None known by author
Mother: Unknown to author	Father: Unknown to author

Mary Ann (Katamkhin) was married to Skylix in Yakama where she was raised, but ran away from her own people to be with **Wallen Kilmonie** (Kilmanukh). When she left, she took with her a number of old things, including a buffalo hide satchel, which she sold to Rev. Summers. She had other things but would not sell them all.[131]

Although she and Wallen were never married legally or by Indian custom, Wallen Kilmanukh never lived with any other woman.[132] Together, they had a number of children, but none of them lived very long.

Katamkhin was a strong doctor. **Stephanie Howard** (Lhimiki) was her patient when she fell ill after her encounter with the shaman, **Jim Young**.[133]

Traditionally, a female doctor would wear a buckskin gown and a beaded cape with a headband like those of the men when working on her patient.[134] Perhaps Katamkhin dressed this way also, but unlike others, when she started to sing she put a dog on her shoulders and walked around with it. Sometimes people got tired of her because once she started to sing she would not stop. She had lots of songs.[135]

Katamkhin had the power to understand dogs and could repeat what they said to her. She once told Rev. Summers that a nearby white farmer had shot one of her little dogs, about the size of a cat, for stealing sheep. He shot it between the

---

128 Jacobs, *Clackamas Text*, Part II, 561. Jacobs, Field Notebook, *Texts and Ethnology*, 54: an oak block a foot long was used for a maul, after whites came; round-headed (unflattened) people were called "mauls." Victoria Howard guided Jacobs in drawing a sketch of a maul on this page to illustrate the Clackamas attitude and humor.

129 Jacobs, Field Notebook 62, *Texts and Ethnology*, 102.

130 Ibid., 101: twilhapam was another name of hers. Cawley, Summers Indian Journal, 23, lists her as a Klikitat woman with English name, Mary Ann, and Indian name, Tat-wa-ni.

131 Cawley, *Summers Indian Jourrnal*, 44.

132 Affidavit State of Oregon, County of Yamhill, taken from Josephine (Frances) Shirley January 25, 1917 and Macasca Sutton, February 3, 1917. Michelle, *Just a Memorandum*. 11.

133 Jacobs, *Clackamas Text*, Part 2, 520–22.

134 Drucker, *Clackamas Field Notes*, n.p. (26 in transcript).

135 Jacobs, Field Notebook 62, *Texts and Ethnology*, 101.

legs of her horse while she was riding with her little child behind the saddle. At the time, she just quieted her pony and rode on, but afterwards she rode by the farmer's house occasionally. When she did, she noticed he had large dogs and asked if they ever stole his sheep. Although the farmer insisted his dogs were innocent of such deeds, sometime later, he paid her five dollars for the dog he had killed.[136]

In addition to understanding dogs, Katamkhin could handle the dead. With this power, she could not only prepare dead bodies for burial, but she could hear the dead talk and understand what they said.[137]

After all this, she had yet another power that made a successful hunter of her husband.[138] Rev. Summers recalled meeting her husband after one of his hunting trips. Wallen Kilmanukh told Rev. Summers how he had killed several deer a few days earlier and wounded others. Now he was preparing to go back to the mountain for more.[139]

After Kilmanukh died in 1905, Katamkhin married **Yamhill Jo Jefferies** (Tukshin). She does not appear on the GRIC after 1912.

Kilmonie, Wallen (1841c–1905) Molalla, Clackamas[140]	Native Name: Kílmanukh /KIL-ma-nuh/ (kílmanux)*[141]
Alias: William Kilmonie, Walling Kilmoni, Molel Wallen	Allotment 95
Mother: Mary Ann Kilmonie (Kilipashta), Clackamas[143]	Father: Molalla[142]

Wallen Kilmonie (Kílmanukh) not only raised his half brother, **Alexander Toto,** but in 1872, Wallen's mother and a woman named Mary Black were also living with him and his wife, **Mary Ann Kilmonie** (Katamkhin).

Kílmanukh and Katamkhin had three children: Peter (1861c–72), Stephan (1866c–75), and Eliza (1869c–77). They had at least three more children by 1885: Esa Dar (1876c), Julia (1880c), and William (1882c). However, all of them died.[144]

After Alexander Toto and his wife, **Stephanie Apperson,** died of tuberculo-

---

136 Cawley, *Summers Indian Jourrnal*, 40.
137 Jacobs, Field Notebook 62, *Texts and Ethnology*, 101. Jacobs, Field Notebook 53, *Texts and Ethnology*, 73.
138 Jacobs, Field Notebook 62, *Texts and Ethnology*, 101.
139 Cawley, *Summers Indian Jourrnal*, 40.
140 Oregon State Archives, 1906, Yamhill County, Estate File 1110: gave his DOD as January 22, 1905.
141 Jacobs, Field Notebook 62, *Texts and Ethnology*, 102
142 Ibid.
143 Michelle, *Just a Memorandum*, 6, gave mother as Clackmas and father as Molalla. Cawley, Summers Indian Journal, 22, gave a man with English name of Warren [Walling] and Indian name Poyu-say as Klamath with a Wapato Lake mother.
144 Ibid.

sis, Kilmanukh and Katamkhin raised Stephanie's son, Isadore. In 1886, Isadore was the only child living in Kílmanukh's house. He was listed as their grandson on the GRIC for that year.

Kílmanukh's mother, **Mary Ann Kilmonie** (Kilipashta), lived with the family from 1872 until her death in 1890. A woman named **Emily Judson** also lived with Kilmanukh's family off and on over the years.

Mary Ann Kilmonie (Kilipashta) and Emily Judson each received a 120-acre allotment at Grand Ronde. Their heirs were Kilipashta's daughter, **Margaret Toto** (Chaimala), and Wallen Kilmanukh's widow, Mary Ann Kilmonie (Katamkhin).[145]

Wallen Kílmanukh received a 260-acre allotment at Grand Ronde. After he died on January 22, 1905, his real property was valued at $275 and personal property at $121.50. His wife was his sole heir. Besides his wife, Mary Ann Kilmonie (Katamkhin), Wallen Kílmanukh's heirs were listed as "distant relatives" Smiscon and Frank So-Happy in Yakima and **Macasca Sitton** and Pauline Sutton at Grand Ronde.[146]

King, Robert (1837c), Rogue River[147]	Native Name: Unknown to author
Alias: Kings Valley Bob	Allotment: None known by author
Mother: Unknown to author	Father: Unknown to author

In 1872, Kings Valley Bob was living with his wife, Mary. Also living with the family was Mary's grandmother, Loti, and a relative of Mary's named Lolci.

On November 4, 1879, he was elected to serve with **Semoll McCoy** and **Isaac Stevens** on the Grand Ronde legislature as a representative for the south precinct of the reservation.[148]

In 1885, he was living with his wife, Kate (1857c). He had several children: Maniah (1873c), Judith (1878c), and Reubin (1880c).

Kiny, George (1854c–72) Tualatin band of Kalapuya	Native Name: Unknown to author
Alias: George Kimsey, George King	Allotment: None known by author
Mother: Unknown to author	Father: Unknown to author

George was baptized December 5, 1872, when in danger of death and died

---

145 *Heirs of Deceased Indians,* Allotment Record 97, 98. Oregon State Archives, 1906, Yamhill County, Estate File 1110, gives Wallen Kilmone's sole heir as his wife "Mary Yamhill, formerly Mary Kilmone."

146 *Heirs of Deceased Indians*, Allotment Record 95.

147 Gatschet, *Texts, Sentences and Vocables,* 366: under the Rogue River as "Bob, of Kings Valley, abt 40."

148 National Archives, Seattle, WA, Grand Ronde/Siletz, Land and Enrollment Program records, Field Notes and Land Survey 1875 –1898, Land Description Book 1878, Box #115; Grand Ronde Justice Court.

December 9 at the age of 18.[149] In 1872, the agent listed George Kimsey as the "adopted son" of **Chief Shlawin** and noted that he had only recently died.

Kiny, Tualatin, Tualatin band of Kalapuya	Native Name: Unknown to author
Alias: Green Kiny, Kinny	Allotment: None known by author
Mother: Unknown to author	Father: Unknown to author

On May 19, 1861, Father Croquet baptized Peter, a three-month-old infant born to Kiny and Nancy of the "Twalatay Nation." The child died in July of that year.[150] In 1872, Green Kiny was with his wife, Mary.

Kiwandi, Chief, Nestucca/Nehalem band of Tillamook	Native Name: Unknown to author
Alias: None known by author	Allotment: None known by author
Mother: Unknown to author	Father: Unknown to author

On the 1857 GRIC, Chief Kiwandi was listed as a Nestucca chief with forty-seven people under his leadership.

Kiwandi, George (1842c) Nestucca/ Nehalem band of Tillamook	Native Name: Unknown to author
Alias: George Cowanty	Allotment: None known by author
Mother: Unknown to author	Father: Unknown to author

On October 4, 1882, charges were filed against George in the Grand Ronde Indian Court for adultery. Jack Wheeler and James Wheeler were witnesses. The sheriff, **Isaac Stevens,** arrested George; **James Pierce** (Clamarchnet) heard the case.

After Judge Pierce found George guilty and sentenced him to pay a fine of thirty dollars plus court costs, Tualatin sub-chief **Lame James Shiliqua** (Shilikwa) offered to put up a horse as security to get George out of jail. Judge Pierce accepted the horse as security, but stipulated that the horse was to be sold at the courthouse door by Sheriff Isaac Stevens at the end of three weeks if the fine was not paid.

At the time stipulated, **David Leno** paid $11.75 for the horse. Apparently, George did not make good and Shilikwa lost his horse. Records show that all court costs were paid with the exception of the $1.50 owed to Judge Pierce.[151]

149 Munnick and Beckham, *Catholic Church Records—Grand Ronde*, Register I, p. 79, B-68, S-36.

150 Ibid., Register I, p. 10, B-35, p.10, S-22.

151 National Archives, Seattle, Grand Ronde/Siletz Tribal Program Records Box 162, Agency & Tribal Council Records 1876–1951.

In 1885, George was listed on the GRIC with his wife, Nancy and a number of children: Henry (1865c), Louis (1868c), Marion (1880c), and John (1881c).

Kooch, James, Umpqua	Native Name: Unknown to author
Alias: Lazy Jim	Allotment: None known by author
Mother: Unknown to author	Father: Unknown to author

In 1872, James Kooch was listed as living alone.

Kowkama, Molalla	Native Name: Unknown to author
Alias: Long Hair	Allotment: None known by author
Mother: Unknown to author	Father: Unknown to author

He signed the treaty as Third Chief of the Molalla band of Molalla.[152]

Kwalichadakh	Native Name: Kwalichadakl /kwa-LI-cha-tah/ (Kwalitchacaq)*[153]
Alias: None known by author	Allotment: None known by author
Mother: Unknown to author	Father: Unknown to author

Dave Yachkawa mentioned Kwalichadakh as one of the doctors at Grand Ronde in 1877 who could swallow fire and bring it back mixed with blood.[154]

Kwinnam, Catherine (1853c–65) Santiam band of Kalapuya	Native Name: Unknown to author
Alias: None known by author	Allotment: None known by author
Mother: Unknown to author	Father: Unknown to author

Catherine Kwinnam was twelve when she died at Grand Ronde.[155]

Klickitat, Lizette (1826c–1902), Klickitat	Native Name: None known by author
Alias: Lissette Nepissank, Lizette Nippising	Allotment 140
Mother: Unknown to author	Father: Unknown to author

Lizette Klickitat was the hayash wife of **Chief Louis Napesa.** She and Napesa

---

152 Kappler, *The Treaty with the Kalapuya, Etc., 1855.*
153 Gatschet, *Texts, Sentences, and Vocables,* 401.
154 Ibid.
155 Munnick and Beckham, *Catholic Church Records — Grand Ronde,* Register I, p. 41, B-117.

had two surviving daughters, Mary Ann and LaRose Nipissing. Mary Ann Nippising married **David Leno.** LaRose Nippising married **Frank Quenel.**

When Lizette received her allotment, she exchanged 80.27 acres with Frank Quenel. After she died, a fee patent was issued for the entire 80.27 acres to her daughter, LaRose Nipissing-Quesnel, and her granddaughters, Jane Leno-Petite and Cecelia Leno-Warren.[156]

---

156 *Heirs of Deceased Indians,* Allotment Record 140.

L

LaChance, Adolphine (1852c–98c), Wasco band of Chinook, French Canadian	Native Name: None known by author
Alias: Delphine Davis, Delphine Brothers	Allotment: None known by author
Mother: Susanne Goodriche, Wasco, French Canadian	Father: Pierre Pepin dit LaChance, French Canadian

On September 9, 1872, Adolphine LaChance married Samuel T. Brothers of Yamhill County in the presence of her father, Peter Papin (LaChance), and Peter Parizeau (Parazoo). Born in France, Peter Parizeau came to the Oregon Country with the Hudson's Bay Company. He was employed at Fort Umpqua in Douglas County until he retired to farm on a claim south of Champoeg. In later years, he moved to a backwoods claim in Douglas County where he lived mainly by the hunt.[1]

In 1894, Adolphine was listed as "Delphine Davis," the mother of May Brothers (1878c), Daisy Brothers (1879c), Ernest Brothers (1885c), Willard Brothers (1887c), Edward Davis Jr. (1891c), Matilda Davis (1893c), and an unnamed infant.[2] In 1898, Willard Brothers was listed as an orphan.

LaChance, Clementine (1856–1951), Wasco band of Chinook, French Canadian	Native Name: None known by author
Alias: None known by author	Allotment: None known by author
Mother: Susanne Goodriche, Wasco, French Canadian	Father: Pierre Pepin dit LaChance, French Canadian

On January 28, 1878, Clementine LaChance of Yamhill County, and Alexander LaBonte, who the priest thought "was near the point of death," were married at St. Paul in the presence of Julianna LaBonte-Vivet.[3] Although Alexander was

1 Munnick and Warner, *Catholic Church Record—St. Paul*, A-75.
2 Munnick and Beckham, *Catholic Church Records—Grand Ronde*, Register II, 81.
3 Munnick, *Catholic Church Records—Vancouver and Stellamaris*: Alexander LaBonte's grandfather was Louis LaBonte I, longtime servant of the fur companies, who settled at French Prairie. His grandmother was Margaret Cobaway or Kilakotah, daughter of a minor Clatsop chief, Coboway. His grandparents, Louis and Margaret LaBonte, had a farm across the river from French Prairie that was said to be one of the best in the country.

very sick, he survived, and for many years he and Clementine lived at St. Paul.

Clementine and Alexander first appeared on the GRIC with their children in 1894.[4] At that time, they had eight children still living at home: Susan, Caroline, Josephine, Margaret, Peter, John B., Joseph, Bart, and Louis.

After Alexander LaBonte died in 1896, Clementine married **Edmund Jeffries** in 1899. On the 1900 GRIC, she was listed as Edmund's wife with the following children: Josephine, Margaret, Peter, John, Joseph, Bart, Louis, and three unnamed sons ages five, three, and one. Only her last son was listed as the natural child of Edmund Jeffries. The rest of the children were listed as his stepchildren.

Clementine's brother, **Narcisse LaChance**, said he never knew of Clementine being adopted by any of the treaty tribes at Grand Ronde and to his knowledge she never applied for an allotment.[5]

LaChance, Josephine (1873c), Wasco band of Chinook, French Canadian[6]	Native Name: None known by author
Alias: None known by author	Allotment 103
Mother: Amanda Grimm	Father: Pierre Pepin dit LaChance Jr.

Josephine received an eighty-acre allotment at Grand Ronde.

LaChance, Julia (1846c–1903c), Wasco band of Chinook, French Canadian	Native Name: None known by author
Alias: Julie, Julia Dowd	Allotment 40
Mother: Susanne Goodriche, Wasco, French Canadian	Father: Pierre Pepin dit LaChance, French Canadian

On February 13, 1865, Julia LaChance married a man from Ireland named John Patrick Dowd (1827c–1921) in the presence of Peter Cleary, Thomas O'Connor, John O'Connor, and her father, Peter Pepin dit LaChance. Julia and her new husband settled on a farm near Champoeg and later moved to the reservation.

They arrived at Grand Ronde around 1887. At that time, they had a number of children: Joseph (1871c), Anna (1874c), Patrick (1882c–1921), Elizabeth (1876c), Rosa (1879c–1904), John (1880c–1928), Thomas (1885c–1900c), and George (1886c).

Since they had no place to live, the Indian agent placed their eight children in the agency school and listed the family on the 1888 GRIC under the Umpqua.[7]

---

4   Michelle, *Just a Memorandum*, 1: Alex LaBonte, breed, wife, the daughter of La-Chance, children: Caroline, Susie, Josephine, Kate, Ed, Jack, Joe, Louie, Bart, and Gus. All these children went to school at Grand Ronde. Munnick and Beckham, *Catholic Church Records—Grand Ronde*, Register I, p. 109, B-22, p. 126, B-17, p. 130, B-11.

5   O. Applegate, Testimony of Narcisse LaChance.

6   Munnick and Warner, *Catholic Church Records—St. Paul*, 77.

7   Michelle, *Just a Memorandum*, 1.

They were very poor. All they owned was one horse, and eventually, a small garden. By 1896, John Jr., and Patrick were working as school assistants. Joseph was the agency school teacher.[8]

Julia LaChance-Dowd received a 200-acre allotment at Grand Ronde. Her children, **John Jr., Joseph, George, Patrick, Thomas, Elizabeth,** and **Rosa Dowd,** each received eighty acres. After Rosa and Thomas died, their father inherited their allotment property.

Julia LaChance-Dowd died in 1903. John Dowd died in 1921, at the age of ninety-four. Both were buried at Grand Ronde.[9]

LaChance, Mary (1851c–1902c), Wasco band of Chinook, French Canadian	Native Name: None known by author
Alias: Mary Langley, Mollie Barker, Maria, Marie Pepin	Allotment 270
Mother: Susan Goodriche, Wasco, French Canadian	Father: Pierre Pepin dit LaChance, French Canadian

On August 8, 1867, Mary LaChance married Israel Langley, the son of Jean Langlois and Margaret Bissonnet. By Israel, Mary had nine children. After she left him, she married a white man named Carey Barker in Tacoma, Washington. They came to Grand Ronde together around 1889.[10]

Besides her children by Barker, her children by Israel Langley—Bill, Jack, and Agnes—all went to school at Grand Ronde.[11] Her son, John Langley, worked as an Indian blacksmith for the agency.[12]

In 1891, Mary was listed as "Mollie Barker" with her children, John Langley (1870c), Willard Langley (1874c), Susie Langley (1876c), Allen Langley (1880c), Hugh Langley (1882c), Hattie Langley (1886c), and Clinton Barker (1890c).

Mary died around Thanksgiving in 1902. After her death, Carey Barker left Grand Ronde with their two children, Clinton and a little girl. Their daughter died on the road to Salem, but their son, Clinton, survived. He was living with one of his half-sisters on French Prairie in 1905.[13]

In response to how Mary LaChance-Langley happened to receive a 167.48-acre allotment at Grand Ronde, Mary's brother, **Narcisse LaChance** testified:

When Inspector Armstrong came here I think Mr. Barker came and took

---

8   *Records of Employees at Grand Ronde, 1884–1907.*

9   St. Michael's Catholic Church Burial Records, 1903 and 1921.

10 O. Applegate, Testimony of Narcisse D. LaChance: while this report gives the place of Mary LaChance and Barker's marriage as "Sonoma, Washington," other records place them in Tacoma, Washington during this time period.

11 Michelle, *Just a Memorandum,* 1.

12 *Records of Employees at Grand Ronde, 1884–1907.*

13 O. Applegate, Testimony of Narcisse LaChance, David Leno, Willard Langley.

the matter up with him and my understanding is that it was through his work that it was done.[14]

Mary's son, Willard Langley said:

I think either my mother or my stepfather, Mr. Barker, applied to the agent for an allotment. My understanding is that Mr. Simpson, who was the agent, told her that if she would select a place he would try to get it for her. So she selected a place and moved on it, made improvements and lived there. It did not seem that the agent accomplished anything toward getting their allotment through and finally when Inspector Armstrong came here over four or five years ago Mr. Barker went to him about the matter and I think it was through his action that the land was allotted to my mother. This was a year or two before she died.[15]

Mary's heirs were listed as Clinton Barker, Carry Barker, John Langley, William Langley, Hugh Langley, Hattie Langley, Susan Langley, and Allen Langley.[16]

LaChance, Narcisse (1875c–1967c), Wasco band of Chinook, French Canadian	Native Name: None known by author
Alias: Narcisse David Pepin	Allotment 102
Mother: Susan Goodriche, Wasco, Franch Canadian	Father: Pierre Pepin dit LaChance, French Canadian

Narcisse was the youngest son of Pierre and **Susan LaChance.** When he was baptized on September 7, 1875, at the St. Paul Mission, his sponsors were Dr. T. F. J. Brentano and Mrs. Brentano.

After the family moved to Grand Ronde, Narcisse attended the agency school. Then he either worked at the agency as an apprentice or worked for local farmers. Over the next eighteen years he never spent more than six away from the Grand Ronde Reservation.

Originally, it was **David Leno** who asked Colonel Collins about allotting land "to the boy" (meaning Narcisse) and the allotting agent did not hesitate even though Narcisse had not applied to the agent or Indian chiefs for adoption into any of the tribes on the reservation. Apparently, neither the Indian agent nor the allotting agent advised Narcisse and his family of the process and they simply did not know they needed to get tribal approval.[17]

Being only a boy at the time of allotment, Narcisse did nothing with his eighty

14 O. Applegate, Testimony of Narcisse D. LaChance.
15 O. Applegate, Testimony of Willard Langley.
16 *Heirs to Deceased Indians,* Allotment Record 270.
17 O. Applegate, Testimony of Narcisse D. LaChance.

acres.[18] The property lay in wait until he married Felineze Norwest, the daughter of a Luckiamute woman named Anna Amos, on July 21, 1898. Then he cleared and fenced the land, slashed some timber, and built a pretty good barn and other outbuildings.

By Felineze (1883–1917c), Narcisse had Joseph David (1898–98), Elizabeth Susan (1900), Lizzie (1902–1931), Mary Rosalyn (1903–1971), Anne (1906), Ava Caroline (1906c), Dottie Hattie (1909–1971), and Nora Tilmer (1913–1991).[19]

After Felineze's death in 1917, Narcisse married Mary Agnes, the daughter of Abraham Guibeau and Eleanor Dumont, on October 19, 1918, in Raymond, Washington. By Mary Agnes, Narcisse also had a number of children: Agnes, Amarillas, Narcisse, Jane, Eldon, Jack, John, Maxine Leona, Catherine, and Mary Alice Jane.

LaChance, Susan (1830c–1912), Wasco band of Chinook, French	Native Name: None known by author
Alias: Susan Goodriche, Susanne Pepin	Allotment 101
Mother: Nancy Twinishe of Winakske, Nancy of The Dalles, Wasco Chinook, Warm Springs	Father: John Goodriche

On the return from a Snake Country expedition, Peter Skene Ogden's brigade met up with a wounded French Canadian and a native woman carrying a small baby, all near starvation. This woman was Susan Goodriche's mother, Nancy Twinishe.[20]

Nancy and her French husband had been trapping along the headwaters of the Missouri when a party of Blackfoot came to their camp. Professing to be friendly, the Blackfoot stacked their guns in the center of the camp, but holding knives concealed under their arms and beneath their shirts they slowly began to position themselves for an attack. Suspicious, Nancy pretended to attend to her work, but as soon as no one was watching, she slipped into the woods with her baby.

From her hiding place she could hear all the sounds of the slaughter. The next morning she found the naked bodies of her companions left slashed, stabbed and scattered upon the ground. The Blackfoot had taken everything including the clothes they were wearing.

Alone and without food, Nancy started out for a cache that she remembered

---

18   Ibid.
19   Confederated Tribes of Grand Ronde Family Tree.
20   Munnick, *Catholic Church Records—Vancouver and Stellamaris Mission*, 83, B-57: chief's name given as Wanakske. Notice similarity between the name Wanakske and the native name of Chief Kawache's youngest son, Wannexke (Moses Apperson). Perhaps another inherited name.

keeping far down the river. Fearing another encounter with the Blackfoot, she traveled only by night. After ten days of traveling with very little to eat, her milk dried up and she could not feed her baby.

Her *mukluks* (moccasins) had worn out and she was soaking her feet in the river when a Frenchman from her trapping party staggered out of the brush. Although he was severely cut up, he had survived the attack by pretending to be dead. Together they made it to the cache where they found dried meat and other supplies. Nancy sewed some clothes for the trapper and a tent for temporary shelter.

They had just decided to start out for Fort Vancouver or any other Hudson's Bay post when they met up with Peter Skene Ogden's brigade. With Ogden was a man named Goodrich who was on his way to The Dalles to open a store for McLoughlin. He wanted Nancy to marry him. After some encouragement from Ogden, Nancy finally accepted his proposal. They were married by Indian ceremony during the return trip. Once they reached Fort Vancouver, they were married again according to civil law.[21]

A few years later, in the summer of 1830, Goodriche drowned at The Dalles after volunteering to take another man's place in running the rapids. Nancy was not with him on this occasion as she was pregnant.

Susan Goodriche had a half brother named Casnut who was also Wasco and an uncle on her mother's side of the family named Halela.[22] In addition, she had two cousins, Marquerite St. Martin and Abraham Arquette, at Yakama.[23]

Raised at Fort Vancouver, Susan once took a fall off the porch of Dr. John McLoughlin's house while playing with some other children and was left permanently lame. Although she walked with a cane the rest of her life, the impairment did not seem to hamper her ability to perform all the chores required in raising a large family.[24]

On January 8, 1844, she married Pierre Pepin dit LaChance. Pierre had served as a middleman and blacksmith for the Hudson's Bay Company from 1838 to 1843.[25] After he retired, he and Susan lived at St. Paul. They had at least fifteen children together. When Pierre became an American citizen, they took a land claim in Marion County.[26]

---

21 Munnick and Warner, *Catholic Church Records — St. Paul*, A-38. Munnick, *Grandma was an Indian*, 6-9.

22 This may have been the same man who signed the Treaty with the Kalapuya, Etc., 1855 as Hal-la-le, doctor of the Tekopa band of Kalapuya.

23 Letter to the Indian Agent, Superintendent and S.D.A., Fort Simco, State of Washington, dated May 23, 1912, notarized statement taken from Susan Lachance to certify her relationship to the Wasco tribe, witnessed by Thom Countryman and John E. Jeffries.

24 Munnick, *Grandma was an Indian*, 8.

25 Hudson's Bay Company Archives, Provincial Archives of Manitoba, Winnipeg, Biog. Pierre Pepin dit LaChance.

26 Munnick and Warner, *Catholic Church Records — St. Paul*, A-38.

Pierre and Susan followed their daughter, Tilmer, to the Grand Ronde Reservation after she married **David Leno** and they lost their home in Gopher Valley.[27] Their son **Narcisse LaChance** testified that the family came to the reservation two years before his father died (about 1886). He said they lived the first year or so with David Leno. Then, about 1887, Peter LaChance rented a place belonging to the Wapato Lake sub-chief, Lame James Shiliqua (Shilikwa).[28] In 1887, Peter and Susan LaChance also appear for the first time on the GRIC with their children, Prosper and Narcisse, and their granddaughter, Josephine.[29]

Susan received a 241.12-acre allotment at Grand Ronde. She left the property to her son, Thomas P. LaChance, and her daughter, **Clementine LaChance.**

Perhaps through some agreement made between the sub-chief **James Shiliqua** and the Indian agent, Susan LaChance was listed as belonging under the Wapato Lake band of Kalapuya in 1905 for the Surplus Land Payment and on a Report of Heirship in 1912.[30]

LaChance, Widow	Native Name: None known by author
Alias: None known by author	Allotment: None known by author
Mother: Unknown to author	Father: Unknown to author

In 1885, she is listed as a single mother with a son, Parris (1870c), and daughter, LaRose (1877c).

Laderoute, John Baptiste (1831c–61), Kalapuya	Native Name: None known by author
Alias: None known by author	Allotment: None known by author
Mother: Unknown to author	Father: Unknown to author

John had a wife named Mary. After John Baptiste's death on January 16, 1861, his son, Marcel, was born six months later on August 30, 1861.[31]

Laferte, Marshell (1831c–89c), Nez Perce[32]	Native Name: None known by author

---

27 O. Applegate, Testimony of James Winslow. Michelle, *Just a Memorandum*, 2.

28 O. Applegate, Testimony of Narcisse D. LaChance.

29 1888 GRIC: Susan LaChance, her son, Prosper, age twenty-three, Narcisse, age sixteen, and her granddaughter, Josephine, age fifteen, were listed with the Wapato Lake band of Kalapuya.

30 National Archives—Pacific NW Region, Seattle, BIA records 75, Box 293, Fo. 101, Grand Ronde LaChance Deed & Purchase & Fee Patent.

31 Munnick and Beckham, *Catholic Church Records—Grand Ronde*, Register I, p. 7, S-1, p. 12, B-163.

32 1888 GRIC listed his tribe as "Pendenille."

Alias: Marshall Laforte, Michel dit Plasee, Placie, Plasse	Allotment: None known by author
Mother: Josephte Nez Perce	Father: Michel Laferte, French Canadian

Marshell Laferte's father, Michel Laferte dit Placide, Placie, Plasse (1790c–61), was a Pacific Fur Company employee who arrived in the Oregon Country on the *Tonquin*. He was a boatman with the Northwest Company in 1813–14. Then for several years he was with Peter Ogden in the Snake River country. He was with John Work in the same region from 1831 to 1832. Besides his son, Marshell (1831c), he and Josephte Nez Perce had a number of children: Antoine (1825), Olivier (1827), Marie (1834), Catherine (1838), Madeleine, and Pierre.[33]

Marshell Laferte arrived at Grand Ronde in 1874 where he met Angelique Desrivieries. After both of them were confirmed at St. Michael's Church, they were married. Angelique was the daughter of Pierre Desrivieries, a native hunter and middleman with the Hudson's Bay Company, and a woman named Marie Manon.[34]

Marshell earned at least part of his living working for the agency. In 1885, he was working for two dollars a day as an assistant carpenter on agency buildings with **Frank Norwest** and **John Menard**.[35] In 1888, Marshell and Angelique's daughter, Nellie Angelia, their grandson, Willie, their son, Peter Lafferty, and Peter's wife and baby were all living with them.

By the time allotments were formally made, most of the Indian people at Grand Ronde were willing to give an allotment to the Laferte family because they had lived within the community for such a long time.[36]

Lafferty, Paul (1889c), Clackamas, Molalla, Nez Perce, French Canadian	Native Name: None known by author
Alias: None known by author	Allotment 100
Mother: Anastasie Winslow, Clackamas, Molalla	Father: Peter Lafferty, Nez Perce, French Canadian

On January 20, 1908, Paul Lafferty married LaRose "Rosie" Winslow. They had a number of children including Eleanor Florence (see photo, next page). After Rosie died in 1919, Paul married Elizabeth "Lizzie" Leno on July 6, 1924.[37]

---

33 Munnick and Warner, *Catholic Church Records—St. Paul*, A-52.

34 Hudson's Bay Company Archives, Provincial Archives of Manitoba, Winnipeg, Biog. Marshell Laforte and Biog. Pierre Desrivieries.

35 Grand Ronde Agency Ledger Book, Records of Employees at Grand Ronde July 1883–September 1907, Confederated Tribes of the Grand Ronde Community of Oregon Archive.

36 Michelle, *Just a Memorandum*, 8.

37 Zenk, *Chinook Jargon*, 274.

Paul Lafferty received an eighty-acre allotment.[38] February 10, 1906, he exchanged his eighty acres with James Winslow for forty acres. On July 21, 1913, he was issued the fee patent for the entire forty acres.

Paul Lafferty and LaRose Winslow's daughter, Eleanor Florence (1914–18). Taken at William Hartless's place. Photo courtesy of Barbara Danforth Private Collection.

Lafferty, Peter (1867c–1922), Nez Perce, French Canadian	Native Name: None known by author
Alias: Peter Laferty, Peter Laferte	Allotment: None known by author
Mother: Angelique Deriviere	Father: Marshell Laferte, Nez Perce, French Canadian

Peter was raised at Grand Ronde but left on or around 1885. He returned in 1887 and married **Anastasie Winslow** (1871c–1913), the daughter of **Mark Win-**

---

38 *Heirs of Deceased Indians*, Allotment Record 100.

slow and **Pauline Montour.** They had two children, Harvey and Paul (1889c–1949c).[39] In 1891, Peter married another Clackamas woman named Julia Agnes. **Julia Agnes** was the former wife of **Jean Baptiste Gendron.** Peter and Julia Agnes had four children: Clara, Agnes (1887–1956), Oliver (1891–1902), and Francis (1894–1902).[40]

Julia Agnes Lafferty testified in 1905 that Peter was never adopted at Grand Ronde and did not claim any treaty rights on the Grand Ronde Reservation.[41]

Peter and Julia Agnes Lafferty's daughter, Agnes Lafferty-O'Conner. Photo courtesy of Barbara Danforth Private Collection.

39   Munnick and Beckham, *Catholic Church Records — Grand Ronde,* Register II, p. 28, M-1, p. 38, B-5, p. 71, B-22, p. 95, B-20.
40   O. Applegate, Testimony of Julia Ann Lafferty.
41   Ibid.

Lamson, John (1840c), Umpqua	Native Name: None known by author
Alias: None known by author	Allotment: None known by author
Mother: Unknown to author	Father: Unknown to author

In 1872, John was listed under the Umpqua with the **Jack Smith** family. He married Susan of the Umpqua nation January 11, 1875, in the presence of **Co-quille Charley** (Nagashta) and Mary, his wife.[42] He was listed on the 1885 GRIC as "Jack" Lamson, along with his wife, Judith (1845c), and his children, Henry, James, Bob, and Janet. He does not appear on any GRIC after 1885.

Lane, Chief Jo, Takelma band of Rogue River[43]	Native Name: Apserkahar ["Horse-rider"]
Alias: None known by author	Allotment: None known by author
Mother: Unknown to author	Father: Unknown to author

Chief Jo Lane (Apserkahar) was a Rogue River war chief and one of **Chief Sam Wilder** (Toquahear)'s brothers.[44]

In 1850, Oregon territorial governor Joseph Lane traveled into southern Oregon hoping to conclude a treaty of peace with the Takelma band of Rogue River. With a company of fifteen white men and a party of Klickitat led by a *tayi* called **Quatley**, he found Apserkahar and his people at Graves Creek.[45] Apserkahar agreed to a peace council with them, but at some point became alarmed and signaled his men to attack. They quickly came to his defense, but too late. Quatley seized Apserkahar and held him while Lane took him from the village at gunpoint. With Apserkahar as a hostage, his band was forced to sign Lane's peace compact.

Over the next three years, a relationship grew between Joseph Lane and Apserkahar, leading Apserkahar to adopt the name of this American politician. At the same time, the pledge made between them was tenuous and in August 1853, it was broken after a Jacksonville card player insulted a native family.

The card player was killed after refusing to pay the traditional bride's price for a native woman that a Shasta native in Tipsey's band from Bear Creek had brought to him. The settlers retaliated by hanging the first two Rogue River men they could find.

Returning to Tipsey's camp where Apserkahar's people and the Shastas were trading skins and horses, the Shasta man persuaded his chief to join Tipsey's

---

42 Munnick and Beckham, *Catholic Church Records—Grand Ronde,* Register I, p. 91, M-1.

43 Douthit, *Joseph Lane and the Rogue River,* 478, 485, gave his Indian name as Apserkahar or Apssokahah meaning "Horse-rider" and his relationship as "co-leader" with "his brother," Chief Sam.

44 Ibid., 482–85. *Oregon Statesman,* letter to the editor, December 2, 1856, gives the name of a third brother as Tom and mentions one of their sisters.

45 Johnson and Zenk, *Chinuk Wawa,* 165: tayi defined as "chief."

band in an attack on the men at Jacksonville and encouraged Apserkahar to join forces also. While Apserkahar wanted to wait until his story could be verified, Tipsey's urges and the wishes of his own young men persuaded him to prepare for battle.

Meanwhile, the settlers in the Rogue River valley had rounded up about two hundred men. They joined forces with another eighty residents from the Shasta Valley, and together they sent out a call for additional support. Major Alden, then at Ft. Jones in California, joined the group, taking charge until Joseph Lane, brigadier-general of the American volunteers, could get to the scene.

At this point, Apserkahar led a coalition with a fighting force estimated at about seven hundred men. A battle between the two forces ensued August 24, 1853. It ended with an armistice and the setting of a date to negotiate a treaty for early September.[46]

At the arranged time, Superintendent of Indian Affairs Joel Palmer, who had the authority to represent the United States government in treaty making, joined Lane, who was camped with his men about two and a half miles from Apserkahar's forces at the base of Table Rock. Lane had already talked with Apserkahar and his brothers, **Chief Sam Wilder** (Toquahear) and Jim. The chiefs had agreed to talk peace if Lane would come to their encampment with a small party of about ten unarmed men.

On September 8, 1853, the small unarmed group rode into the council area. Both Lane and Palmer made long speeches to the chiefs that were translated twice: first into Chinook Jargon by a white man and then into the native language of the Rogue River by an Indian interpreter. The replies of the Rogue River chiefs were also twice translated in reverse order. Then, with the approval of Joel Palmer, Joseph Lane began to negotiate peace terms.

Just as treaty negotiations were nearing a conclusion, an Indian runner rode into camp with the message that a group of Americans under the command of a man named Owens had captured Tayi Jim Taylor, tied him to a tree, and shot him to death at Applegate Creek.[47] The news threw the council into turmoil, but somehow calm was restored.

At the end of the day, it was agreed to cease hostilities. Further, the Rogue River chiefs agreed to sell their land to the Americans and move to some reserved location that would be selected at a later date.

The following morning, September 9, 1853, the treaty council resumed. Joseph Lane told the Rogue River people that he was glad to see so many of them had stayed. Acknowledging the absence of others, he reminded them that Chief Apserkahar had told them that he and the other white men in his party were the "chiefs to talk with them" and that their "great chief, your father, who lives a

---

46 Nesmith, James W. "A Reminiscence of the Indian War, 1853." *Quarterly of the Oregon Historical Society* 7 (1906), 216–17.

47 Carey, *The Mission Record Book*, 230–66.

long, long way over the mountain, has sent us to see you and to talk with you."[48]

Then at the end of a long speech, the Americans proposed that if the Rogue River people would agree to sell their country as it was described in the treaty of peace made and concluded the day before, they would be paid $55,000 on the first of the month. The Takelma band of Rogue River signed the agreement.

After the signing, Governor Lane named Apserkahar's wife Sally and their two children Ben and Mary. In return, Apserkahar gave Lane a Modoc slave whom Lane named John "and kept as a personal servant."[49]

After the War of 1855, Apserkahar was only at Grand Ronde a short time before the Rogue River people were divided into two groups. One group under Apserkahar went to the Siletz Reservation. The remaining group, under his brother, Chief Sam (Toquahear), stayed at Grand Ronde.[50]

Lane, Joe (1849c)	Native Name: None known by author
Alias: None known by author	Allotment: None known by author
Mother: Unknown to author	Father: Unknown to author

When the manual labor school was organized at Grand Ronde on October 1, 1862, Joe Lane, age fourteen, was in attendance and missed only a few weeks of school that year.[51]

Lapan, Catherine, Umpqua	Native Name: None known by author
Alias: None known by author	Allotment: None known by author
Mother: Unknown to author	Father: Unknown to author

In 1872, Catherine was listed under the Umpqua with son, James (1870c), and daughter, Minnie (1869c). They were not living with Catherine's husband, **Charley Lapan,** but rather with **Bob Tucker** and his family.

Lapan, Charley (d. 1878), Umpqua	Native Name: None known by author
Alias: Cross eyed Charley, Charley Lapointe, Charley Lapone	Allotment: None known by author
Mother: Unknown to author	Father: Unknown to author

In 1872, Charley Lapan was living with his wife Mary and their children Frank and Lucy. Probably due to the ban on multiple wives, Charley's other wife Catherine and her children were living with **Bob Tucker** and his family.[52]

---

48 Tipsey's band did not participate in the council and did not sign the treaty.

49 Douthit, *Joseph Lane and the Rogue River*, 479.

50 *Oregon Statesman* (1857) and Lt. Philip Sheridan in his memoirs stated that Chief Sam's brother, Chief Joe, was alive and living at Grand Ronde in 1856–57.

51 *Annual Report Commissioner of Indian Affairs*, 84–85.

52 The 1872 GRIC: "Charley Lapan" aka "Cross-eyed Charley" and listed him with the

Charley was elected to the Grand Ronde Indian Legislature in 1877 at the same time as **Chief Louis Napesa, Frank Quenel, Foster Wacheno** (Inawalh), **Joseph Apperson** (Washamsh), **Dave Yachkawa, Winchester Jo, Jim Bruce, Jim Price, Jake Wheeler** (Shwa), and **Solomon Riggs** (Gunconnacli).

This was the group of legislators that passed the law directed specifically at **John Baptiste Menard, Frank Norwest,** and **Marshell Laferte,** who "did not belong on the reservation."[53] Although the three young men were part native, they were not from any of the treaty tribes assigned to the Grand Ronde Reservation. This law forbade them from causing further "trouble or disturbances."[54]

Charley Lapan's name was spelled "Charley Lapointe" when he married Margaret "Maggie" (Chalwina) on February 5, 1878, in the presence of Jacques and **Peter Wheeler** (Kutskait)'s wife. Father Croquet noted that Charley and Maggie had not been baptized and "both were Indians of this reservation."[55]

Charley died later that same year. **Margaret**, his widow, married **Thomas Hutchins** (Liham) in September 1878.

Lapan, Margaret (1837c), Yamhill band of Kalapuya	Native Name: Chalwina /CHAL-wi-na/ (chalwína)*[56]
Alias: Margaret Hudson, Margaret Miller, Margaret Lapointe	Allotment: None known by author
Mother: Unknown to author	Father: Unknown to author

Margaret (Chalwina) married **Charley Lapan,** an Umpqua man, February 5, 1878. She married **Tom Hutchins** (Liham) September 27, 1878.[57] She killed Tom in a fight in 1886. For several years after his death, Margaret remained single, living with her son, **Frank Bond.** In 1888, they were living on sixty fenced acres with a house, a barn, and a small garden. In addition, they owned a plow, four horses and a wagon.

Margaret married **William Miller** (Quilinick) on August 26, 1888. Their witnesses were **Frank Michelle** and his wife, **Mary.**[58]

Victoria Wishikin (Kinishi) sang several of Margaret's power songs for Melville Jacob in 1929.[59]

Umpqua. Munnick and Beckham, *Catholic Church Records — Grand Ronde*, Register I, p. 106, M-4: listed as "Charley Lapointe." Gatschet, *Texts, Sentences and Vocables*, 366: listed with the Umpqua as "Charley Lepone."

53 National Archives, Seattle, Grand Ronde/Siletz Tribal Program Records Box 162, Agency & Tribal Council Records 1876–1951.
54 Ibid.
55 Munnick and Beckham, *Catholic Church Records — Grand Ronde*, Register I, p. 106, M-4.
56 Jacobs, Field Notebook 51, *Music and Ethnology*, 47.
57 Munnick and Beckham, *Catholic Church Records — Grand Ronde*, Register I, p. 108, M-12.
58 Ibid., Register II, p. 45, M-4.
59 Jacobs, Field Notebook 51, *Music and Ethnology*, 47.

Larney, Peter (1847)	Native Name: None known by author
Alias: None known by author	Allotment: None known by author
Mother: Unknown to author	Father: Unknown to author

In 1885, Peter was living with his wife, Ellen (1853c), and children Allen, Johnny, and an infant daughter who was unnamed.

Lashman, William (1859c–1907), Yoncalla band of Kalapuya, Umpqua[60]	Native Name: Laishmin /LAISH-men/ (láyshmən).* Shweki /SHWE-ki/ (shwéki)*[61]
Alias: Billy Lashman, William Williams, Elisha Laishmin, Lashman Williamson, Elias Williams	Allotment 254
Mother: Unknown to author	Father: Calapooia Billy Williams, Yoncalla, Umpqua

William Lashman (Laishmin) was a fine singer and knew both Yoncalla and the Umpqua language.[62]

In 1872, he had a wife named Sarah. Next, he married **Clara Laurence,** but left her before their baby was born. Clara stayed with the **Isaac Stevens'** family but one night, after the baby was born she just left. Clara's sister, **Sarah** and her husband, **Alexander Day** adopted the baby, whom they named **Joseph Jeff Day.**[63]

On August 19, 1883, William Lashman married Margaret Alsea, with **William Warren** and Mary Shangaretta-Holmes acting as witnesses.[64]

By 1885, William and **Nancy Newby** were living together with two children, Susan (1875c) and Henry (1878c). Three years later, he and Nancy had apparently separated. William was listed that year with a considerably older woman named Sarah. Their arrangement was short lived. The following year, he was living alone.

William Lashman received a 220-acre allotment under the name of Elias Williams. He did not sign the Surplus Land Agreement in 1901. He was issued a fee patent for his entire 220-acre allotment on October 29, 1906.[65]

---

60 1872 GRIC listed his tribe as "Calapuya." The 1888 GRIC gave his tribe as Yoncalla.
61 1887 GRIC: Indian name as Sa-ma-ca. Gatschet, *Texts, Sentences and Vocables,* 367. Jacobs, Field Notebooks 46, *Santiam Kalapuya Text,* 52. Jacobs, Field Notebooks 46, *Santiam Kalapuya Text,* 44: J.B. Hudson gave "Bill Williamson as (a Yoncalla-Umpqua)."
62 Jacobs, Field Notebook 46, 52.
63 Michelle, *Just a Memorandum,* 4.
64 Munnick and Beckham, *Catholic Church Records—Grand Ronde,* Register I, p. 125, M-4.
65 *Heirs to Deceased Indians,* Allotment Record 254.

La Tete, Hias, Cow Creek band of Umpqua	Native Name: Hayash-Latet /HA-yash la-TET/ (háyash latét) ["big-head"],* Quintioosan /Quin-ti-oo-san/
Alias: None known by author	Allotment: None known by author
Mother: Unknown to author	Father: Unknown to author

On September 19, 1853, a treaty with the Cow Creek was signed on Cow Creek in the Umpqua Valley, Oregon Territory. Joel Palmer negotiated the terms with Principal Chief Bighead (Quintioosan), Jackson (Myweletta), Tom (son of Quintioosan), and Tom (Talsapeer).

Shortly after the Cow Creek Treaty was signed, their chief, Myweletta, died. After the war, the Cow Creek were brought to Grand Ronde as prisoners of war. On the GRIC in 1856, their chief was listed under the Chinook jargon name, "Hayash Latet" with eighty people under his leadership.[66] By the following year, this band had dwindled to a total of thirty-seven people.

Laurence, Clara (1859c), Chinook, Iroquois	Native Name: None known by author
Alias: Clara Jordon	Allotment: None known by author
Mother: Theresa Wakaikam, Chinook	Father: Laurent Karokitchego, Iroquois

Clara was **William** and **Sarah Laurence's** sister or half sister. She married **William "Billy" Lashman** July 28, 1876, in the presence of **Solomon Riggs** (Gunconnacli) and **Jenny Mackey.** By William Lashman, she had Joseph Jeff on April 20, 1878. **Joseph Jeff Day** was adopted by **Alexander Day.**[67]

Although Clara does not appear on any later GRIC, she must have been in the area or in communication with people at Grand Ronde as she was present during the settling of Joseph Jeff's estate in 1921. At that time, she was using the name Clara Jordon.[68]

Laurence, Sarah (1839c), Chinook, Iroquois	Native Name: None known by author
Alias: Sarah Day	Allotment: None known by author
Mother: Theresa Wakaikam, Chinook	Father: Laurent Karokitchego, Iroquois

Sarah was William and **Clara Laurence's** sister or half-sister. In 1885, she was living with her brother, **William Laurence's,** family. She married **Alexander Day**

---

66 Johnson and Zenk, *Chinuk Wawa*, 162.

67 Munnick and Beckham, *Catholic Church Records—Grand Ronde*, Register I, p. 106, B-5.

68 Oregon State Archives, Salem, Oregon, Polk County Probate 1921, File 1886. Jacobs, Elizabeth, Field Notebook 104, Coos-U. Coquille, 1: lists "Mrs. Jordan" under idako Cow Creek Umpqua.

in November 1867.

According to Clara Pearson, Sarah, (Mrs. Jordan's sister) spoke Rogue River. Sarah's mother was from Camas Prairie.[69]

Laurence, William (1847c), Chinook, Iroquois, husband of Santiam Kalapuya wife	Native Name: None known by author
Alias: William Lawrence	Allotment: None known by author
Mother: Theresa Wakaikam, Chinook	Father: Laurent Karokitchego, Iroquois

William Laurence's father served as a boatman with the Hudson Bay's Company starting in 1815 and assisted the priests by taking the role of godfather to numerous children both at the Cascades and Willamette Falls.

According to Catholic Church records, William was born at St. Louis, Oregon, in 1847. He married a Rogue River woman called Nancy at Grand Ronde June 15, 1861. Their witnesses were Thomas Pisk and Louise.[70]

By 1872, William was married to a woman named Molly and listed on the GRIC with the Santiam band of Kalapuya. Rose, Molly's half sister, Annie, a half cousin to Molly, and William's adopted son, Andrew, were also living with William and his wife, Molly.

Leno, David Ambroise (1840c–1908), Rogue River, Hispanic	Native Name: None known by author
Alias: Ambroise Leno, Abraham Leno, Lino	Allotment 107
Mother: Marie Sassete (Shasta)	Father: Joseph Leno, Hispanic[71]

David Ambroise Leno was the son of Joseph Leno and Marie Sassete (Shasta). He was born in September 1840 and raised on French Prairie. He had a brother, Joseph, who was born in April 1842.[72]

After his father died in the California gold mines, Dave's mother, a full Rogue River woman, married a Yamhill Kalapuya named Amos. She and Dave came to Grand Ronde with her new husband under the 1855 treaty with the Kalapuya.[73]

On November 4, 1860, Dave Leno married **Harriet Lindsey**, a Rogue River woman. Thomas Pisk and **Mark Winslow** witnessed the ceremony.[74] Both Har-

69 Jacobs, Elizabeth, Field Notebook 104, Coos-U. Coquille, 173.

70 Munnick and Beckham, *Catholic Church Records—Grand Ronde,* Register I, p. 10, M-2.

71 Michelle, *Just a Memorandum,* 2.

72 O. Applegate, Testimony of David Ambroise Leno. Munnick and Warner, *Catholic Church Records— St. Paul,* 14, 21, A-59. Martinus Cawley, *Father Crockett of the Grand Ronde,* Story 13.

73 O. Applegate, Testimony of David Ambroise Leno, 1905.

74 Munnick and Beckham, *Catholic Church Records—Grand Ronde,* Register I, p. 6, M-1.

riet and Dave's mother had the customary face tattooing of Rogue River women referred to as one-eleven markings.[75]

After Harriet left him, Dave married **Chief Louis Napesa**'s oldest daughter, Marianne Nipissing, in 1871. By Marianne, David had Cecile (1866), Jane (1868–1922c), Dennis Joseph (1870–74), and Priscilla (1873–1973c).[76]

After Marianne's death, David took charge of the blacksmith shop and began living at the Grand Ronde agency. He met Delma "Tilmer" LaChance when the La-Chances started attending church there.[77] After Dave married Tilmer in 1879, they had Joseph Peter, Benjamin (1882), Louis (1882–83), Josephine "Dollie," Henry (1884), George, Edwin, Mary Agnes (1889–1982), Francis (1890), David Andrew (1894–1971), Elizabeth (1895–1962), Julia Mirtle (1897), and Augustine Edward (1900–89).[78]

In 1886, Dave Leno was listed as owning assets that included a large new house, good barn, a wagon, two sets of harness, outbuildings, two horses, four head of cattle, chickens, turkeys, geese, ducks, sixty fenced acres, thirty-five acres in cultivation, a garden, good orchard, a blacksmith's shop on the road to the coast, a reaper, a cradle, two scythes, two plows, a harrow, and a large assortment of crafting tools.

In addition to earning $152 every three months working as a blacksmith for the agency, Dave served on the Grand Ronde Police Force from 1890 to 1894.[79]

Together, David Leno and his children, Joseph, George, Edwin and Dolly Leno, received over 342 acres of allotment land at Grand Ronde.[80]

His daughter, Cecile Leno, married **John Warren.** Jane Leno married **Henry Petite. Joseph Leno** married **Hattie Holmes, George Leno** married Adeline Robinson, **Edwin Leno** married Ruby Dean, and **Josephine "Dolly" Leno** married John Pichette.

After a lifetime of hard work and building an impressive estate, when David died August 7, 1908, his property had three mortgages against it. A portion of his allotment land had to be sold to satisfy debt and expenses in administration of the estate.[81] Still there was enough money left for his family to buy him an oak casket worth $50.50. Father Felix Bucher preformed the funeral service, estimating Dave's age for church records at seventy-nine years.[82]

---

75   Michelle, *Just a Memorandum*, 2.

76   Munnick and Beckham, *Catholic Church Records—Grand Ronde*, Register I, p. 6, M-1, p. 47, B-94, p. 66, B-83, p. 70, M-2, p. 80, B-7, p. 86, S-1, p. 90, S-6, p. 110, M-1, p. 117, B-31, p. 122, B-12, p. 125, S-6, p. 126, B-16, p. 130, B-10

77   Michelle, *Just a Memorandum*, 2–3.

78   Munnick and Beckham, *Catholic Church Records—Grand Ronde*, Register I, p. 27, B-7, p. 53, B-6, p. 66, B-26, p. 83, B-37, p. 100, B-5, p. 111, B-12.

79   Confederated Tribes of the Grand Ronde Community of Oregon Archive, Grand Ronde Agency Ledger Book, Records of Employees at Grand Ronde July 1883–September 1907.

80   *Heirs of Deceased Indians*, Allotment Record 107, 108, 109, 110, 111.

81   Oregon State Archives, Salem, Oregon, 1908, Yamhill County, Estate File 1421.

82   St. Michael's Catholic Church Burial Records, 1908.

Long after David Leno died, Esther Jones-LaBonte recalled a curious incident described by a white man. According to Esther, the white man saw another man standing early one morning at the gate to the Grand Ronde cemetery. After the white man greeted him, the man identified himself as Dave Leno. When the white man told the people around Grand Ronde, they were puzzled. What, they wondered, was Dave Leno, who had been dead for so many years, doing standing by the cemetery gate?[83]

Leno, Edwin Buchanan (1888c–1917), Rogue River, Wasco band of Chinook, French Canadian, Hispanic	Native Name: None known by author
Alias: Edwin Lano	Allotment 111
Mother: Tilmer LaChance, Wasco Chinook, French Canadian	Father: David Leno, Rogue River, Hispanic

In 1904, Edwin married Arcino Mary Pichette (1875c–1958c), the daughter of **Roc Pichette** and Victoria Despard. On October 29, 1906, he was issued a fee patent on a forty-acre allotment.[84]

Leno, George (1885c–1975), Rogue River, Wasco band of Chinook, French Canadian, Hispanic	Native Name: None known by author
Alias: George Lano, Abraham George Leno	Allotment 110
Mother: Tilmer LaChance, Wasco Chinook, French Canadian	Father: David Leno, Rogue River, Hispanic

George married Adeline Robinson (1888–1960), daughter of **Dan Robinson** and Felicite Menard. On October 29, 1906, he was issued a fee patent for 41.16 acres of allotment land.[85]

Leno, Joseph (1880c–1914c), Rogue River, Wasco band of Chinook, French Canadian, Hispanic	Native Name: None known by author
Alias: Joseph Peter Lano	Allotment 108
Mother: Tilmer LaChance, Wasco Chinook, French Canadian	Father: David Leno, Rogue River, Hispanic

Joseph Leno married **Adelaide "Hattie" Holmes** (1880–1965), daughter of

---

83 Zenk, interview with Esther LaBonte, 1982, transcript 1, 2009 (4:44).
84 *Heirs to Deceased Indians*, Allotment Record 111.
85 Ibid., Allotment Record 110.

David Holmes and Mary Shangaretta. He was issued a fee patent on June 28, 1907, for forty acres of allotment land.[86]

Leno, Josephine Catherine (1883c), Rogue River, Wasco band of Chinook, French Canadian, Hispanic	Native Name: None known by author
Alias: Dolly Pichette, Dolly Lano	Allotment 109
Mother: Tilmer LaChance, Wasco Chinook, French Canadian	Father: David Leno, Rogue River, Hispanic

Josephine "Dolly" Leno married John Baptiste Pichette, son of **Roc Pichette** and Victoria Despard. On August 9, 1917, Dolly Leno-Pichette was issued a fee patent for forty acres of allotment land.[87]

Lewis, John (1846c–67), Shasta	Native Name: None known by author
Alias: None known by author	Allotment: None known by author
Mother: Unknown to author	Father: Unknown to author

In 1872, John was married to a woman named Guildy. They had a daughter named Louisa (1867).

Lewis, Joseph (1855c)	Native Name: None known by author
Alias: None known by author	Allotment: None known by author
Mother: Unknown to author	Father: Unknown to author

When the manual labor school was organized at Grand Ronde on October 1, 1862, Joseph Lewis, age eight, was in attendance for a few weeks.

His teacher, C. M. Sawtelle, wrote in his annual report dated August 1, 1863:

During the first two months we received twenty-three children, the most of whom we boarded and clothed through the winter. All but two were as wild as quails when we commenced with them, having had no previous instruction; and all were worse than naked, being clad in filthy cast-off garments.[88]

Lindsey, Harriet (1842c–1942), Rogue River	Native Name: None known by author
Alias: Harriet Leno, Harriet Corton	Allotment: None known by author
Mother: Unknown to author	Father: Unknown to author

86 Ibid., Allotment Record 108.

87 Ibid., Allotment Record 109.

88 *Annual Report Commissioner of Indian Affairs*, 1863, 84–85.

Harriet belonged to **Chief George** (Chocultah)'s band. Her country was below Evans Creek in southern Oregon. Harriet and her cousin, **Martha Jane Sands,** had been visiting friends and Tututni relatives at the mouth of the Rogue River when the war broke out. Soldiers attacked the village they were staying in, but they escaped.[89]

Later, they were discovered hiding in a beaver dam and were brought along with a group of Umpqua people to the Grand Ronde Reservation under **Chief Louis Napesa** and **Chief Peter McCoy** (Inchaishi).[90] A young girl of about fourteen, Harriet waited for months before her family finally arrived later that same year.[91]

Harriet was the wife of **Jim Rose** when she was first invited with several other young women to Fort Yamhill by Lt. Sheridan's Indian wife, Molly. They were escorted into a large room where Sheridan came and looked them over. Later, Sheridan bought Harriet from Jim and gave her a pony that she rode when she accompanied him on trips.[92]

As an adolescent, Harriet had one-eleven tattooed on her chin. Traditionally it would be made wider after she was married, but Phil Sheridan did not like it, so rather than enhancing the lines, for the rest of her life she tried to cover them up.[93]

They had been together about three years when threat of a civil war became apparent and Sheridan got news that his assignment would probably change. In anticipation of his departure, Sheridan made arrangements for Harriet to marry **David Leno,** the Indian blacksmith at the fort.[94] They were married in the Catholic Church November 4, 1860.

Harriet lived with David and worked as a domestic in Salem for three or four years. Then she left David and moved to The Dalles, where she met and married Ben Corton. By Ben, she had three children.[95] The first two died, but the third, Marian Corton (1871c), became a professional actress.

Harriet's third marriage, to a man named Lindsey, was a happy one. They traveled in Europe for a time. After her husband and daughter died, Harriet returned to Grand Ronde in 1939 to stay with Hattie Sands-Hutchins. While living with Hattie, Harriet made her promise never to talk about Phil Sheridan as long as she was still alive as she was very ashamed of that period of her life. Harriet died at Grand Ronde in 1942.[96]

---

89 Zenk, Grand Ronde Field Notebook 9, 1988, 65. O. Testimony of Harriet Lindsey.
90 Ibid.
91 Oliver Applegate, Testimony of Harriet Lindsey, 1905.
92 Zenk, Grand Ronde Field Notebook 9, 1988, 65–66.
93 Lampson, *Some Visitors from the Grand Ronde,* 26.
94 O. Applegate, Testimony of Harriet Lindsey.
95 Ibid.
96 Lampson, *Some Visitors from the Grand Ronde,* 26. Zenk, Grand Ronde Field Notebook 9, 1988, 70.

Little, Billie (1845c)	Native Name: None known by author
Alias: None known by author	Allotment: None known by author
Mother: Unknown to author	Father: Unknown to author

In 1885, Billy Little was living with his wife, Matilda, and his children, Oscar, Sallie, and Paul.

Logan, Jane (1843c–89c), Salmon River band of Tillamook	Native Name: None known by author
Alias: None known by author	Allotment: None known by author
Mother: Jane	Father: John Logan

"Mrs. Logan" was listed on the 1888 GRIC with her daughter, Daisy (1881c). They had one horse.[97]

Daisy was baptized by Father Croquet on January 30, 1887, as Mary Daisy, daughter of John Logan and Jane.[98] Her godparents were **Joseph Corner Michelle** and Louisa Tole. Daisy's sister, Josepha (1883c), was also baptized. Josepha's godparents were Joseph Corner Michelle and Melanie Winslow.

In 1889, Daisy was listed as an orphan.

Logsden, John (1865c–1908), Rogue River[99]	Native Name: None known by author
Alias: None known by author	Allotment: None known by author
Mother: Unknown to author	Father: Unknown to author

Although John Logsden was never listed on any GRIC, his daughter, Emily Logsden, married **Joseph Dowd** after Joe's first wife, **Louise Menard,** died. Joe and Emily moved back and forth between Siletz and Grand Ronde from 1903 to 1918. John Logsden was present for the *t'isay* game at the Wacheno house in 1904 when **Foster Wacheno** (Inawalh) was shot by **Louis Savage.**

When John Logsden died on March 5, 1908, he left forty acres of property in Yamhill County. His estate was valued at two hundred dollars and his personal property, including three horses, one cow with a calf, one yearling, a wagon, two stoves, and four chairs, was valued at $150. His family bought his burial garments and coffin from Harry Kershaw at the Willamina store for $48.24 and charged the cost to his estate.[100]

---

97 1888 GRIC listed her tribe as Salmon River.

98 Munnick and Beckham, *Catholic Church Records—Grand Ronde*, Register II, p. 25, B-3, B-4.

99 National Archives, Central Plains Region, Louie Savage Inmate File 5333: tribe given as Rogue River.

100 National Archives, Salem, Oregon, 1908, Yamhill County Estate, File 1447.

Long, Jack (1852c), Shasta	Native Name: Potinic /Po-ti-nic/[101]
Alias: John Long	Allotment: None known by author
Mother: Unknown to author	Father: Unknown to author

Jack (Potinic) was **Reuben Long**'s brother. When the manual labor school was organized at Grand Ronde October 1, 1862, "John" Long (1852c) was in attendance about half the time.[102]

By 1872, Jack was married to a woman called Lucy. In 1876, he was elected to represent the Shasta along with **Jim Bruce** at the fifth annual session of the Indian legislature.[103]

Long, Reuben (1849c–1901), Shasta	Native Name: Sahapa /Sa-ha-pa/[104]
Alias: None known by author	Allotment 112
Mother: Unknown to author	Father: Unknown to author

In 1886, Reuben (Sahapa) was listed as a bachelor with a small garden, twenty acres fenced, and six acres cultivated. In 1888, he was listed as a widow without any notable assets. The following year, he was living with his wife, Polly Speer (1854c–1913).[105] When Polly's nephew, John Brown, visited, he stayed with her and Reuben. Polly said he was her sister's child and besides John Kelsey, he was her nearest relative.[106]

Reuben Long received 75.95 acres of allotment land. His wife, Polly, inherited the property. Polly sold it to William F. Schaad on November 20, 1911.[107]

Long, Sallie (1843c)	Native Name: None known by author
Alias: None known by author	Allotment: None known by author
Mother: Unknown to author	Father: Unknown to author

In 1885, Sallie (1843c) was living with her daughter, Jennie (1866c), and son, Bennie (1868c), at Grand Ronde.

---

101 1887 GRIC: "Jack Long" was listed just after Reuben Long with the Indian name of "Potinic."

102 *Annual Report of the Commissioner of Indian Affairs*, 1863, 84–85.

103 National Archives, Seattle, WA, Grand Ronde/Siletz, Land and Enrollment Program records, Field Notes and Land Survey 1875–1898, Land Description Book 1878, Box 115; Grand Ronde Justice Court.

104 1887 GRIC listed his Indian name as Sa-ha-pa.

105 National Archives, Seattle, NRIA-S-11-276, PAC-08, box 63, Polly Speer, Testimony of William Simmons: Polly took her name from Jack Speer, a California Indian Hoop or Round Valley, with whom she had been consorting for a few years. After Jack died, Chetco Ben came to Grand Ronde and took her to Siletz.

106 Ibid.

107 *Heirs to Deceased Indians*, Allotment Record 112.

Louis, Santiam band of Kalapuya	Native Name: Towyecolla /Tow-ye-colla/[108]
Alias: None known by author	Allotment: None known by author
Mother: Unknown to author	Father: Unknown to author

During treaty negotiations at Champoeg in 1851, Louis (Towyecolla) was the first chief of the Santiam Band of Kalapuya. He told the American agents the Santiams were willing to part with all their lands except a small portion, which they wished to reserve to live upon, graze their herds on, and cultivate.

When Towyecolla signed the Treaty of 1855, the band was composed of sixty-five men, eighty women, and ten boys. The Santiam had no slaves. By the time **Joseph Hutchins** (Yalkama) replaced him as chief in 1857, the Santiam Band of Kalapuya had dwindled to a total of eighty-five people.

Lowery, Tom (1848c)	Native Name: None known by author
Alias: None known by author	Allotment: None known by author
Mother: Unknown to author	Father: Unknown to author

In 1885, Tom was living with his wife, Lucy Ann (1854c), and his children, Henry, Jane, and an infant child.

Luckiamute, Jack (1843c), Luckiamute band of Kalapuya	Native Name: None known by author
Alias: None known by author	Allotment: None known by author
Mother: Unknown to author	Father: Unknown to author

In 1885, Luckiamute Jack was living with his wife, Lucinda (1851c), his son, Willie (1873c), and an infant son.

Lukwa, Modoc slave	Native Name: Lukwa
Alias: None known by author	Allotment: None known by author
Mother: Unknown to author	Father: Unknown to author

He was one of four slaves known to have been once owned by the Tualatin **Chief Kiakuts** (Kayakach).[109]

---

108 Kappler, *Treaty with the Kalapuya, Etc.*, 1855: given as "Louis or Tow-ye-colla."
109 Jacobs, *Santiam Kalapuya Ethnologic Texts*, Part 1, 160–73. Gatschet, *Texts, Sentences and Vocables*, 94.

M

Mack, Benjamin (1852c), Clackamas	Native Name: None known by author
Alias: None known by author	Allotment: None known by author
Mother: Widow Wacheno	Father: Unknown to author

In 1885, Benjamin was with his son, Markie (1875c), his mother, the Widow Wacheno (1830c), and his grandmother, Old Mollie (1804c).

Mackey, Jennie (1847c–1938), Clackamas, Lower Chinook	Native Name: None known by author
Alias: Jennie McKay, Jane Mackey, Jennie Riggs	Allotment: None known by author
Mother: Clackamas	Father: Billy Chinook, Lower Chinook

On the day the American military picked up the Clackamas people, Jennie and her mother had gone to Oregon City for fish. Since Jennie's mother was very ill, they were assigned to the group being transported to Dayton by boat. From Dayton they were marched across country to Grand Ronde.

On the reservation, they found some little cabins that had been constructed for them along Agency Creek behind the present day Catholic Church. The door of each cabin faced the creek. Inside, bunk beds had been built for their comfort, but neither Jennie nor her mother had ever slept in a bed of this sort. After just a few days, Jennie's mother died.[1]

Jenny always insisted she was a full Klickitat, but given the testimony of other Grand Ronde people, it would appear that she was at least part Lower Chinook.

In regard to Jenny's ancestry, **Amos Kilya** said that she was related to **Lucy Sampson,** a known Lower River Chinook and Kalapuya woman.[2] Jenny's daughter-in-law, Clara Riggs, claimed that Billy McKay, Chief Comcomly's grandson, once came to Grand Ronde looking for Jenny. At that time, Billy McKay identified himself as Jenny's father.[3] Added to this information is Frank Norwest's claim that he and Jenny Mackey were cousins.[4]

In order to determine how all these people could be correct, it is necessary to

---

1 Zenk, #19 interview with Clara Riggs, June 25, 1982.
2 O. Applegate, Testimony of Old Amos Kilya.
3 Zenk, interview with Clara Riggs, 1984: Jenny's father was Billy McKay and her mother was Chinook. Jacobs, Elizabeth, Field Notebook 104, Coos-U. Coquille, 173: Clara Pearson from Siletz said Jenny was Klickitat.
4 Berreman, interview with Frank Norwest, 1934: Frank Norwest said Jennie Riggs was his cousin.

Jenny Mackey-Riggs. Courtesy of Joann White-Colton and Bud White, grandchildren of Clara Robinson-Riggs.

carefully examine the family tree of both Billy McKay and **Frank Norwest.** While Billy McKay was Lower Chinook, one of his stepmothers was a Umatilla woman. Accepting that Billy McKay was Jenny's father, and if Jenny and Frank Norwest were cousins, this Umatilla woman and Frank Norwest's mother, Judith Walla Walla may have been sisters.

Billy McKay was brought up in Dr. John McLoughlin's household and afterwards sent east to be educated. He served as a clerk in the Hudson's Bay store at Oregon City from 1843 to July 1849. During this time, he is known to have had a wife named Catherine who died in 1848.[5] After Catherine's death, Billy must

5   Linda Kracke, 2009, www.museum.bmi.net, descendant of Alexander McKay.

have had a brief relationship with Jenny's mother. Jenny was probably born just prior to his leaving for California to pan for gold in 1850. When he returned a few months later, Billy settled on the Umatilla River. After the Umatilla people drove him off the land in 1855, Billy returned to the Hudson's Bay Company to serve as a guide and interpreter, and married a woman named Margaret Campbell in 1856. He remained with the Company until it was forced to shut down in 1861. Then, after serving two years with the American military, he pursued a long medical career, serving as a licensed physician at a number of Indian agencies including Warm Springs, Umatilla, and Yakama.[6]

As for Jenny, she was only at Grand Ronde a short time before an older man named **Solomon Riggs** (Gunconnacli) offered a bride's payment of many horses, beads, and yellowhammer feathers for her. They were married around 1867 by traditional ceremony.[7] After traditional marriages were forbidden by the American government, Solomon married Jennie again by Catholic ceremony in 1871.[8]

Between 1868 and 1892, Jennie and Solomon had fourteen children.[9] In addition to raising children, Jenny took care of **Klickitat Dick Hall** in his last years between 1909 and 1913. After Klickitat Dick died, Jennie took care of his wife, Nancy Santiago-Hall, who by this time was suffering from extreme mental health problems and was very combative. Just a few months before Nancy died on December 31, 1914, Nancy's nephew, **Douglas Sampson Jones** came to get her.[10]

After Solomon died in 1920, Jenny lived with her son Samuel and his family. In 1934, she still had in her possession a large string of small dentalia, a stone elbow pipe inlaid with lead around the base of the stem, some pictures of her people in tribal dress, and a Klickitat coiled bucket.[11]

Jennie went blind about a year before she died, but she was never seriously ill. She just died naturally from old age. When the end came, she asked her daughter-in-law, Clara to send someone to get her son, **Samuel Riggs,** who was logging. Predicting the date and time of her death, Jenny instructed them to strip her bedroom of all her possessions, burn them on the hillside, and smudge the room with fir after she was dead. If they did not do this, the family believed that Jennie would take three others with her in a short period of time; however, since they

---

6   Clarke, *Pioneer Days of Oregon,* 453.
7   Berreman, interview with Jenny Riggs.
8   Munnick and Beckham, *Catholic Church Records — Grand Ronde,* Register I, p. 70, M-1,: Father Croquet recorded her name as "Anne Jenny Mackey." St. Michael's Catholic Church Burial Records, 1938, 394, listed Jane Riggs as about 106 years old, and accredited her with being the "last woman to be sold or traded for." Jenny died Jan. 19 and was buried January 22 at Grand Ronde.
9   Munnick & Beckham, Catholic *Church Records — Grand Ronde,* Register I, p. 69, B-28, p. 88, B-10, p. 98, B-13, p. 110, B-1, p. 117, B-35, p. 124, B-5, Register II, p. 1, B-1, p. 50, B-52, p. 52, S-7, p. 57, B-19, p. 58, S-1, p. 77, B-8.
10 National Archives, Seattle, NRIA-S-11-276, PAC-08, bx 47, Nancy Hall.
11 Berreman, interview with Jenny Riggs.

followed her instructions, no one else from the family died.[12]

Mackey, Louis Samuel (1855c–85)	Native Name: None known by author
Alias: None known by author	Allotment: None known by author
Mother: Unknown to author	Father: Unknown to author

Louis Samuel Mackey married Martha Jane October 18, 1877. Witnessing the ceremony were **Cascade Frank Johnson** and **Nelly Frank.** On July 1, 1878, they had Father Croquet baptize their three-month-old son, Albert. **Stephanie Apperson** was recorded as the child's godmother.

May 9, 1880, they had Father Croquet baptize their baby daughter, Estella, but she died after only three months and was buried July 3. Their son Gilbert was born November 5, 1881. He died April 2, 1882.

Louis Samuel died and was buried at Grand Ronde on February 24, 1885. His sixteen-month-old daughter, Ida Mackey, died a few months later.[13]

Mackey, Samuel (1820c–80)	Native Name: None known by author
Alias: None known by author	Allotment: None known by author
Mother: Unknown to author	Father: Unknown to author

Samuel became very ill in July of 1880. After lingering for several weeks, he died and was buried July 27 on the Grand Ronde Reservation.[14]

Manning, Dick (1847c)	Native Name: None known by author
Alias: None known by author	Allotment: None known by author
Mother: Unknown to author	Father: Unknown to author

In 1885, Dick Manning was listed with his wife, Jane (1850c) and children, Tom, Henry, Bettie, and an infant son.

Mapple, Abe, Umpqua[15]	Native Name: Hohunkuk /Ho-hunk-uk/[16]
Alias: Abe Mauple, Old Man Mabel	Allotment: None known by author
Mother: Unknown to author	Father: Unknown to author

---

12 Zenk, #19, interview with Clara Riggs, June 25, 1982.

13 Munnick and Beckham, *Catholic Church Records—Grand Ronde,* Register I, p. 105, M-7, p. 115, B-7, S-10, S-11, p. 119, B-20, p. 120, S-5, p. 129, S-3, S-5.

14 Ibid., Register I, p. 116, B-21, S-11.

15 Gatschet, *Texts, Sentences and Vocables,* 366: under the Umpqua as "Old man Mabel."

16 National Archives, Seattle, NRIA-S-11-276, PAC-08, Mary Taylor-Cook, testimony of Josephine Lillie Condon-Tipton: gave Ho-hunk-uk as Richard Cook's father's name and Bill Condon's father as Oh-zoohs-neh. They were half brothers having the same mother but different fathers.

Abe Mapple (Hohunkuk) was the father of Richard Cook. In 1872, Abe was listed as an Umpqua married to a woman named Carrie. At that time, **Richard Cook** (Shay Shoaska) was living with them.

Mapple, Anna (1805c–87), Umpqua	Native Name: None known by author
Alias: Anna Mauple, Mary Ann Mauple	Allotment: None known by author
Mother: Unknown to author	Father: Unknown to author

Anna was the widow of **Matthew Mapple** (Ohzoohsneh). Richard Cook's father, **Abe Mapple** (Hohunkuk), and her husband, Matthew Mapple, were half brothers. **Richard Cook**'s mother raised Anna's son, **Bill Condon.**[17]

When Anna was baptized July 24, 1885, at more than eighty years of age, her godparents were **Peter Petite** and his wife, **Rose Tim-Tim.**[18] Having been widowed since 1879, Anna was now living with her son, Bill Condon, and his family.

Anna Mapple died February 14, 1887.[19]

Mapple, Matthew (1814c–79), Umpqua[20]	Native Name: Ohzoohsneh /Oh-zoohs-neh/[21]
Alias: None known by author	Allotment: None known by author
Mother: Unknown to author	Father: Unknown to author

According to Matthew Mapple (Ohzoohsneh)'s granddaughter, Josephine Lillie Tipton, both her grandfather and her father, **Bill Condon,** were killed at Grand Ronde by whites.[22]

When Matthew died on July 21, 1879, the priest estimated his age as sixty-five.[23]

Marc, French Prairie Frank (1863c–84c), Pudding River band of Kalapuya	Native Name: None known by author
Alias: None known by author	Allotment: None known by author
Mother: Catherine	Father: Marc Mickmut, Pudding River (Ahanthuyuk)

17 National Archives, Seattle, NRIA-S-11-276, PAC-08, Mary Taylor-Cook, testimony of Josephine Lillie Tipton.

18 Munnick and Beckham, *Catholic Church Records—Grand Ronde,* Register I, p. 111, S-11, p. 131, B-14.

19 Ibid., Register II, p. 25, S-2.

20 Gatschet, *Texts, Sentences and Vocables,* 366: under the Umpqua as "Old man Mabel."

21 National Archives, Seattle, NRIA-S-11-276, PAC-08, Mary Taylor-Cook.

22 Ibid.

23 Munnick and Beckham, *Catholic Church Records - Grand Ronde,* Register I, p. 111, S-11. Gatschet, *Texts, Sentences and Vocables,* 366: under the Umpqua as "Old man Mabel."

Frank was baptized at two months old on January 29, 1864. In 1872, he was listed on the GRIC with his parents, **French Prairie Marc Mickmut** and Catherine. When Gatschet visited Grand Ronde in 1877, he listed Frank under the Pudding River band of Kalapuya and made a note that French Prairie Frank was still single.[24]

Francis Marc married **Susan Beagle** on August 12, 1883, in the presence of **Daniel Yachkawa**, son of **Dave Yachkawa**, and **Emma Kiakuts**, daughter of **Chief Kiakuts** (Kayakach). Frank and Susan had at least two children. Their children were orphans living with their grandmother, **Martha Beagle** (Shkinda), in 1885.

Marshell, Joseph (1835c)	Native Name: None known by author
Alias: None known by author	Allotment: None known by author
Mother: Unknown to author	Father: Unknown to author

In1885, Joseph was listed with wife, Julia Ann (1840c), and son, Joseph.

Martin, Ann (1817c–89c), Yamhill band of Kalapuya	Native Name: Tuckali /Tuck-a-li/[25]
Alias: None known by author	Allotment: None known by author
Mother: Unknown to author	Father: Unknown to author

Ann Martin (Tuckali) was the mother of Peter Selkya's wife, Louise (Comadeer).[26] **Callo Bonaparte** (Kalukh) and **Jack Nancy** (Shimkhin) were first cousins to Louise's father.[27] Official agency records show Ann living with **Peter Selkya** and Louise in 1872. While there are no GRIC for 1873 through 1884, Ann is known to have been living with the Selkya family in 1885 and continued to live with them until she died around 1888. From this information, it seems likely she was also living with her son-in-law when Rev. Summers stopped at Peter's house in 1876. In describing this visit, Summers wrote that "several women living in the household" showed him a long string of deer toes, a seed tray, and the usual cooking and water buckets. Summers was attracted in particular to a pretty satchel hanging on the wall. The bag was ornamented with rows of deer on one side and geometric figures on the other. He found a second sack hanging near the first which was also nice, but much plainer. "They were unlike anything Rev. Summers had seen."[28] At that time, Peter told Rev. Summers that the mother of one of the women living with him had made the satchel when she was young and was famous among her people for the beauty of her basketry.[29]

---

24 Gatschet, *Texts, Sentences and Vocables*, 368.
25 1887 GRIC: gave Indian name as "Tuck-a-li."
26 1887 GRIC: gave Indian name as "Com-a-deer."
27 National Archives, Seattle, RG 75, Allotte Case Files, 1894-1956, #21 Callo Bonaparte.
28 Cawley, *Indian Journal*, 40.
29 Ibid.

Ann Martin, the mother of Louise, was very likely the weaver of the satchel and the artist Peter praised to Rev. Summers. Her satchel of deer figures ended up in Rev. Summers' collection and is now one of those stored in a museum warehouse in London, England.

Martin, John (1843c–88c), Clackamas	Native Name: None known by author
Alias: None known by author	Allotment: None known by author
Mother: Retty	Father: Unknown to author

In 1872, John and his wife, Sallie (1831c–89c), were listed under **Chief Daniel Wacheno** (Wachinu)'s band of Clackamas. At that time, John's mother, Retty, his cousin, Eliza, and his niece, Rachel, were also living with him.

John had at least two children: Ellen (1868c) and Henry (1870c). In 1885, he was living with a wife named Mary (1850c), his two children, his grandmother, Old Susan, and his aunt, Old Jane.

In 1888, John's wife, **Sallie Martin,** was listed as an Oregon City Clackamas widow.

Martin, Margaret (1822c–89), Clackamas	Native Name: None known by author
Alias: None known by author	Allotment 113
Mother: Unknown to author	Father: Unknown to author

Margaret may have been the same woman listed as "Mary Martin," the wife of **John Martin** on the 1885 GRIC. Margaret Martin received a 138.05 acre allotment. She died in July 1889.[30]

On June 24, 1908, Andrew Kershaw petitioned to be appointed administrator of her estate, which consisted only of her allotment property valued at three hundred dollars. Since none of her heirs had applied for administration of the estate, Andrew Kershaw was appointed to act as administrator. **Frank Quenel, Fabian Quenel,** and **Daniel Robinson** were appointed estate appraisers.

Upon review, the court found that Margaret's heirs were **Ann Foster,** age fifty, living at Grand Ronde, and **Julia Ann Gendron,** now the wife of **Peter Lafferty** and living at Salem. The two women were "daughters of sisters to Margaret Martin."[31]

Martin, Sallie (1819c–89), Clackamas	Native Name: None known by author
Alias: None known by author	Allotment 114
Mother: Unknown to author	Father: Unknown to author

---

30 Munnick and Beckham, *Catholic Church Records — Grand Ronde*, Register I, p. 57, S-14.
31 Oregon State Archives, Salem, Oregon, 1908 Yamhill County Estate File 1272.

In 1872, Sallie was listed with her husband, **John Martin,** under **Chief Daniel Wacheno** (Wachinu)'s band of Clackamas; however, by 1885, she and John had separated.

In 1886, a "Mrs. Martin," probably Sallie Martin, was listed as "a widow" with twenty fenced acres. Two years later, Sallie had added a small house to her property.

Sallie received allotment of 120 acres. She exchanged forty acres with **John Wacheno** (Tsinwalh) for an eighty-acre parcel, giving her a total of 160 acres of land. She died September 25, 1889.[32] On April 13, 1908, her heirs, **Frank Bennett** (Khalawilha) and Eliza Gerand were issued a fee patent for the entire 160 acres.[33]

Mary, California	Native Name: None known by author
Alias: None known by author	Allotment: None known by author
Mother: Unknown to author	Father: Unknown to author

In 1872, California Mary was an old woman living with **Thomas Wacheno's** family.

Mary, Spanish (1858c), wife of Shasta husband	Native Name: None known by author
Alias: Mary Smith, Mary Norwest	Allotment: None known by author
Mother: Unknown to author	Father: Unknown to author

Spanish Mary came to Grand Ronde as a small child from the Rogue River Valley.[34] She married **Willie Smith** (1845c–85c) who was a brother of **Leander Smith.**[35] She and Willie had a number of children: Castine (1867c), Sallie (1869c), Jane (1872c), Mary (1876c), John (1878c), David (1880c–1925), Cecelia (1881c–86c), Henry (1881c), Mary Isabelle (1882c–1904c), and Anna Lotta "Lulu" (1885c–1909).[36]

In 1886, Mary Smith was listed as a widow with her children: Jessie, David, Belle, and an infant. A widow named Kate (1821c) was also living with her. Kate was listed as having a horse and a small garden. Mary Smith had six acres fenced with three acres in grain, a small garden, a small house with a barn, and a horse.

Mary Smith married **Frank Norwest** on September 5, 1887, in the presence of

---

32 Munnick and Beckham, *Catholic Church Records—Grand Ronde,* Register II, S-6, p. 55.

33 *Heirs to Deceased Indians,* Allotment Record 114

34 Zenk, *Chinook Jargon,* 279.

35 Gatschet, *Texts, Sentences and Vocables,* 364, under the Shasta as "Willie Smith, brother of Lelander Smith." Note: Gatschet listed both Lelander and Willie Smith as Shasta. Elsewhere Joel Palmer gives Lelander as Klamath.

36 Munnick and Beckham, *Catholic Church Records—Grand Ronde,* Register II, p. 2, B-4, B-6, S-6, p. 3, S-7, p. 23, B-39, B-40, p. 28, B-14.

Alexander Day and Josette Norwest.[37]

Three of Mary's children by Willie received allotments. **David** and **Isabel Smith** received sixty acres each. **Anna Lotta Smith** received eighty acres.

Matheney, James (1830c–80), Yamhill band of Kalapuya	Native Name: None known by author
Alias: Yamhill Jim, James Mattini, Yamhill James Matting, Yamhill James Mattine, Mafeena	Allotment: None known by author
Mother: Amanda	Father: Unknown to author

In 1872, James's mother was listed as a woman named Amanda.[38] She was living with James and his wife, Mary, at that time. James and Mary also had a son, William (1871c). William died in 1875. His mother died in December of that year.[39]

The Grand Ronde Indian Legislature appointed him justice of the peace shortly after he married **Ellen Carey** (1858c–78), the niece of **Peter Carey.** They were married January 22, 1878. Ellen died in September of that same year.[40]

McCoy, Anne (1822c), Umpqua	Native Name: Ashtamme /Ash-tam-me/[41]
Alias: Ann Mackey, Ann McKye	Allotment: None known by author
Mother: Unknown to author	Father: Unknown to author

Anne (Ashtamme) was the wife of the Umpqua **Chief Peter McCoy** (Inchaishi) and an important woman doctor at Grand Ronde. She is known to have doctored **William Warren** when he became ill. After she treated him, William recovered, but only for a short time.[42]

McCoy, Lincoln (1853c–1908), Umpqua	Native Name: None known by author
Alias: Lincoln McKye, Lincoln McKay	Allotment 137
Mother: Unknown to author	Father: Chief Peter McCoy, Umpqua

37 Ibid., p. 33, M-4.
38 Ibid., Register I, p. 98, S-11: Amanda was probably the same woman Father Croquet called "Ann Matting" when he recorded her death on June 12, 1876.
39 Ibid., p. 96, S-29, p. 94, S-18.
40 National Archives, Seattle, WA, Grand Ronde/Siletz, Land and Enrollment Program records, Field Notes and Land Survey 1875–1898, Land Description Book 1878, Box 115; Grand Ronde Justice Court. Munnick and Beckham, *Catholic Church Records— Grand Ronde,* Register I, p. 106, B-1, M-2, p. 106, S-22, p. 114, S-5.
41 1887 GRIC gave her Indian name as "Ash-tam-me."
42 Zenk, Grand Ronde Field Notebook 9, 1988, 78.

Lincoln was the son of **Chief Peter McCoy** (Inchaishi). Like other chiefs, Peter wanted his son to be educated. Therefore, when the Grand Ronde Manual Labor School was organized on October 1, 1862, Lincoln was one of the children who attended.[43]

November 1, 1880, he served on the ninth annual session of the Grand Ronde Indian Legislature with **Isaac Stevens** and **John Warren.** They were elected to represent the southern district of the reservation in the new Indian government.[44]

In 1885, Lincoln was living with his wife, Judith, his sister, Manda, and aunt, **Martha Jane Sands.**

He was listed on the 1887 and 1888 GRIC with his wife, **Elizabeth Petite** (1864c–1908), and his brother, **Spencer McCoy.** By Elizabeth, Lincoln had Evelyn (1889c–1950), Sophie (1890c–1906), Abraham Peter (1891c–1912), and Stella (1893c–1908), Rachel (1896c), Gertrude (1897c), Joseph (1901c), Margaret (1906c–1920), and Vernon (1908–1908).[45]

By 1888, the family had twenty fenced acres, a horse, three head of cattle, a hog, a plow, harrow, and eleven tons of hay. In 1906, Lincoln received a fee patent on 212.16 acres.[46]

Elizabeth died before Lincoln, leaving him with seven children ranging from Evelyn, age nineteen, to Marguerite, age two. After Lincoln died on March 8, 1908, a number of relatives helped in caring for his orphan children, including **Mary Petite, Henry Petite,** and their aunt, **Christine Petite.** In addition, the children were left a large estate valued at over $1,000.[47]

When Lincoln's son, Abraham Peter McKye, died on April 8, 1912, he in turn left the property to his siblings with the exception of a tract of allotment land that he had given to his aunt, Christine Petite-Hartless, with the provision that she care for him until he died. **William Hartless** (Futi) and **Mary Ann Hoffer** witnessed the signing of his will.

By this time, Abraham Peter McKye's sister Evelyn was married to Philip Warren. His sisters Rachel and Gertrude were attending Chemawa Indian School in Salem. Rachel would eventually marry Carl Logsdon and Gertrude would marry Lawrence Smith. His brother Joe was only eleven and his sister Marguerite was two.[48]

---

43 *Annual Report Commissioner of Indian Affairs*, 1863, 84-85.

44 National Archives, Seattle, WA, Grand Ronde/Siletz, Land and Enrollment Program records, Field Notes and Land Survey 1875–1898, Land Description Book 1878, Box 115; Grand Ronde Justice Court.

45 Munnick and Beckham, *Catholic Church Records—Grand Ronde*, Register II, p. 72, M-8, p. 53, B-7, p. 59, B-7, p. 70, B-18, p. 86, B-9, p. 101, B-9, p. 109, B-2, p. 126, B-11. Oregon State Archives, Salem, Oregon, 1912, Polk County, Estate File 1767. Oregon State Archives, Salem, Oregon, 1908, Polk County, Estate File 1252.

46 *Heirs to Deceased Indians*, Allotment Record 137.

47 Oregon State Archives, Salem, Oregon, 1908, Polk County, Estate File 1252.

48 Oregon State Archives, Salem, Oregon, 1912, Polk County, Estate File 1767.

McCoy, Louis (1855c–85) Umpqua	Native Name: None known by author
Alias: Louis Samuel Mackey	Allotment: None known by author
Mother: Unknown to author	Father: Unknown to author

In 1872, Louis McCoy was seventeen and living with **James Semoll**'s family. Louis died February 22, 1885 and was buried the following day.

McCoy, Peter (1812c–1911), Umpqua[49]	Native Name: Injice, Inchaishi /in-CHAI-shi/ (incháysi)*[50]
Alias: Peter McKye, Peter McKay, Peter Mackey, Peter Makai, Umpqua Peter, Chief Peter McCoy	Allotment 136
Mother: Unknown to author	Father: Unknown to author

Peter McCoy (Inchaishi) was the second signer for the Umpqua on the treaty made at Calapooia Creek with the United States on November 29, 1854. His name was recorded as "Peter or Injice." After the treaty was signed, he and **Chief Louis Napesa** brought the Umpqua people to the Grand Ronde Reservation.[51]

Peter had at least four children: Manda (1853c), **Lincoln**, William (1858–70), and **Spencer McCoy.** In 1872, he was living with his wife, **Anne McCoy** (Ashtamme). Anne's aunt Ellen was also living with them, as well as Peter's grandmother, the widow **Nelly Frank.**[52]

Peter followed the ancient Dream Power religion of the people. He was a Dreamer before the new "Ghost Dance" ideas were brought to Grand Ronde around 1872. He was also one of people who incorporated the new dance beliefs into the old Dream Power religion.[53]

In December 1877, Peter and **Winchester Jo** dictated Umpqua language texts for Albert Gatschet. When the seventh annual session of the Grand Ronde Indian Legislature resumed on November 4, 1878, Peter was elected to represent the people of the south precinct along with Winchester Jo and **Solomon Riggs** (Gunconnacli) . He was also appointed road supervisor along with **John Wacheno** (Tsinwalh) that year.[54]

---

49 1872 GRIC: listed as "Peter McKye (Umpqua Peter). Gatschet, *Texts, Sentences and Vocables,* 366: under the Umpqua as "Peter McKay, formerly chief" with "Samoll McKay, his boy."

50 1887 GRIC lists his Indian name as "Inzalasa." Gatschet, *Umpqua Texts,* .n.p. (handwritten before introduction): "Peter McKay's Indian "name is Intchaishi; he is Cow Creek, but speaks good Umpqua, or so Winchester Jo says. Others say he is an Umpqua."

51 O. Applegate, Testimony of Harriet Lindsay and Martha Jane Sands.

52 *The Elder's Scroll* listed Nellie Frank as Peter McCoy's sister.

53 Du Bois, *The Ghost Dance,* 30.

54 National Archives, Seattle, WA, Grand Ronde/Siletz, Land and Enrollment Program records, Field Notes and Land Survey 1875–1898, Land Description Book 1878, Box

Peter received a 140-acre allotment. His heirs were Lincoln's children: Rachel Logsden, Gertrude Smith, Evelyn Warren, and Joseph McCoy.

McCoy, Semoll (d.1885c), Umpqua	Native Name: None known by author
Alias: Spencer Samall, Semoll McKye, Samall McCoy	Allotment: None known by author
Mother: Maria	Father: James Semoll

Semoll McCoy was the son of **James Semoll** and Maria. Maria was dead by 1872. After James Semoll died, **Chief Peter McCoy** (Inchaishi) finished raising Semoll.

November 4, 1879, the eighth annual session of the Grand Ronde Legislature convened with the election of **Semoll McCoy, Isaac Stevens,** and **Kings Valley Bob King** as representatives to the Indian Legislature for the south precinct of the reservation.[55]

Semoll McCoy married a widow named **Martha Jane Sands.** Before he died, he was helping her raise her children, Hattie and **Nicholas Sands,** but by 1885, Martha Jane was once again a widow.[56]

McCoy, Spencer (1867c–91), Umpqua	Native Name: None known by author
Alias: Spencer McKye	Allotment 138
Mother: Unknown to author	Father: Chief Peter McCoy

Spencer was another son of **Chief Peter McCoy** (Inchaishi). In 1888, at twenty-one years of age, he was living with his brother **Lincoln McCoy** and Lincoln's wife **Elizabeth Petite.** Spencer received an eighty-acre allotment at Grand Ronde. His heir was Lincoln McCoy. On December 8, 1903, Lincoln sold forty acres of the property to D. S. Bentley; he sold the remaining acreage to John Eborall on August 8, 1904.[57]

Menard, Amanda (1886–1906), Mary's River band of Kalapuya, Lower Chinook, Paiute, Iroquois, French Canadian	Native Name: None known by author
Alias: None known by author	Allotment 119

115; Grand Ronde Justice Court.

55 Ibid.

56 Michelle, *Just a Memorandum,* 4: Mary Ann wrote, "Semoll McCoy wife Martha Jane, Rogue River;" and "Nicholas sons and Hatty sons stepchildren to McCoy."

57 *Heirs to Deceased Indians,* Allotment Record 138. Munnick and Beckham, *Catholic Church Records—Grand Ronde,* Register I, p. 129, S-2.

Mother: Elizabeth Shangaretta, Mary's River band of Kalapuya, Lower Chinook, Iroquois	Father: Peter Menard, adopted Mary's River band of Kalapuya, Paiute, French Canadian

Amanda Menard was planning her wedding when came down with the measles after a picnic. She died on the day she had planned to be married. Father Felix Bucher performed the burial service a few days later.[58]

On October 19, 1907, her father, **Peter Menard** received a fee patent for her entire eighty-acre allotment.[59]

Menard, Frank (1881–1911), Mary's River band of Kalapuya, Lower Chinook, Paiute, Iroquois, French Canadian	Native Name: None known by author
Alias: Francis Menard	Allotment 117
Mother: Elizabeth Shangaretta, Mary's River band of Kalapuya, Lower Chinook, Iroquois	Father: Peter Menard, adopted Mary's River band of Kalapuya, Paiute, French Canadian

In 1904, Frank Menard married **Flora Neal.** They had two daughters, Adeline (1905–1990) and Bertha (1908–1969).

Oddly, Frank's younger brother, **Peter Menard** and his little sister, **Amanda Menard** each received twice as much land as Frank. In contrast to their eighty acres, Frank was issued a fee patent for a forty-acre allotment on June 28, 1907.

Menard, John Baptiste (1843c–97), adopted Mary's River band of Kalapuya, Paiute, French Canadian[60]	Native Name: None known by author
Alias: None known by author	Allotment 115
Mother: Josephte Youte, Paiute	Father: Pierre Menard, French Canadian

John Menard was the son of the old French Prairie homesteader **Pierre Menard** and a Paiute woman named Josephte.[61] John followed his brother, **Peter Menard,** to Grand Ronde sometime after 1863.[62]

Their father, who the priest at St. Paul called an ancient citizen of that parish,

---

58 Personal communication with Lavern Bean, wife of Freeman Bean at Grand Ronde, 1997. St. Michael's Catholic Church Records, 1906 Burials

59 *Heirs to Deceased Indians*, Allotment Record 119.

60 1888 GRIC listed John's tribe as Mary's River band of Kalapuya.

61 Munnick and Beckham, *Catholic Church Records—St. Paul,* 47, 70, 114. 1850 Marion County Census.

62 O. Applegate, Testimony of Peter Menard.

died at Grand Ronde in 1877. John remained a bachelor until December 11, 1882, when he married **Elizabeth Petite,** the teenage daughter of **Charles Petite** and **Sophie Gendron.** During this time, John had also been seeing Anna Amos, **Amos Kilya's** stepdaughter, and she was pregnant.

Anna's baby daughter, Felineze, was born April 2, 1883. Anna said at first that the child was John Menard's but then claimed that **Frank Norwest** was the father. The case was taken to Indian court where it was decided that Frank Norwest rather than John was the baby's father and Frank Norwest was required to pay support for the child.[63]

Sam Chantelle, who had acted as a witness at John Menard's wedding to Elizabeth, married Anna Amos in June of 1884. Shortly afterwards, Elizabeth divorced John.

John worked with Frank Norwest and **Marshell Laferte** on a project for about a month during the summer of 1885 repairing some of the agency buildings.[64] At the same time, he worked his farm, a small homestead that included a house and barn on twenty fenced acres with seven acres in cultivation. Then he married **Catherine Voutrin,** a descendent of the Mary's River band of Kalapuya, on July 12, 1886.

For the remainder of his years, John was ill a great deal of the time. He suffered from acute rheumatism, intermittent fever, heart disease, and inflammation of the liver.[65]

He only had one child, a son, whom he and Catherine named Adolphe. Adolphe died a few months after he was born in March 1889.

During the years following Adophe's death, perhaps John pondered the situation with Anna Amos because before he died on May 22, 1897, he provided for "his daughter," Felineze Norwest-LaChance, leaving her his 280-acre allotment at Grand Ronde. His wife, Catherine, died five months after John, on October 23 that year.[66]

Menard, Louise (1872–1900), Mary's River band of Kalapuya, Lower Chinook, Paiute, Iroquois, French Canadian	Native Name: None known by author
Alias: Louisa Menard, Louise Dowd	Allotment 120

---

63 O. Applegate, Testimony of Captain Frank Quenel.
64 Confederated Tribes of the Grand Ronde Community of Oregon Archives, Grand Ronde Agency Ledger Book, Records of Employees at Grand Ronde July 1883–September 1907.
65 National Archives, Seattle, Grand Ronde/Siletz Agency, Medical Records.
66 Munnick and Beckham, *Catholic Church Records — Grand Ronde*, Register II, p. 109, S-4, p. 113, S-10.

Mother: Elizabeth Shangaretta, Mary's River band of Kalapuya, Lower Chinook, Iroquois	Father: Peter Menard, adopted Mary's River band of Kalapuya, Paiute, French Canadian

Louise Menard married **Joseph Richard Dowd** on November 25, 1893, and moved to Siletz. They had two daughters, Elizabeth Irene and Mary Earl Dowd.

After Louise died in 1900, her oldest daughter, Elizabeth, eventually inherited her allotment at Grand Ronde "subject to Joseph Dowd having tenancy as he desired until his death." On February 11, 1921, Elizabeth Irene Dowd was issued a fee patent for Louise's entire 160 acres.[67]

Menard, Peter (1840c–1908), adopted Mary's River band of Kalapuya, Paiute, French Canadian	Native Name: None known by author
Alias: None known by author	Allotment 116
Mother: Josephte Youte, Paiute	Father: Pierre Menard, French Canadian

Peter was **John Baptiste Menard**'s full brother. The boys were raised on French Prairie and very likely spoke a number of languages including French, English, and Chinook Jargon.[68]

In the early 1860s, after "stealing" a Clackamas wife, Peter arrived at Grand Ronde when the military still occupied Fort Yamhill.[69] At that time, a man could not stay on the reservation longer than ten days unless he was accepted by the tribes.

Peter contacted the Tualatin sub-chief, **Dave Yachkawa,** the Umpqua chief, **Louis Napesa,** and the Mary's River Kalapuya chief, **Joseph Shangaretta,** who agreed that he could remain at Grand Ronde as one of the people. After Peter also got approval from the Indian agent, the agency farmer informally assigned him a piece of land and he began to farm.

By his Clackamas wife, Peter had a daughter, Jane (1863c).[70] After Jane's mother died, Peter married Elizabeth Shangaretta in 1869.

By Elizabeth, Peter had Felicite (1870–1902c), Louise, Adlin (1874), Josephine (1874–83), Joseph (1876–86), Magdelin (1879–83), Frank, Peter, Charlie (1885), Paul (1887), Edward (1888–90), Margaret (1891–1976), Lindsay (1893–1963), and

---

67 *Heirs to Deceased Indians,* Allotment Record 120.

68 Zenk, *Chinook Jargon,* 276.

69 O. Applegate, Testimony of Peter Menard and Captain Frank Quenel. According to native matrimonial law, if a man took a woman without paying the bride's price or if he took another man's wife, it was considered stealing and a very serious offense.

70 Michelle, *Just a Memorandum,*.6: Mary Ann wrote that living at Grand Ronde were Peter Menard, his grown daughter named Jane, a brother, John, and his father, "Old Menard."

Amanda Menard.[71]

In 1880, Peter Menard was elected by popular vote to represent the people living in the west precinct for the ninth annual session of the Indian legislature, and then elected president of the assembly by the delegates once it convened.[72]

By 1886, the agent described his farm as a good house with two barns, a large garden, an orchard, and sixty additional acres cultivated on rented land. In addition to the crops, Peter had five horses and was raising about twenty-three hogs and a number of chickens.

When Peter died on July 3, 1910, his estate was valued at $2,000. After a portion of the real property was sold to pay his debts and cover the cost of administrating the estate, his children, **Francis Menard,** Jane Smith, Margaret Menard, **Peter Menard,** and Lindsey Menard each received a seventh of the estate or the sum of $46.46. Peter's daughters, **Louise Menard** and Felicite had died before their father, but each had children who were still alive; Louise's daughter, Elizabeth Irene Dowd, received a thirty-fifth interest in the estate or $9.29. Felicite's children by **Dan Robinson**—Clara, James, and Adeline Robinson—and Felicite's children by **Charlie Russie,** Archie and Guy Russie, each received the same amount.[73]

Menard, Peter Jr. (1883c–1930), Mary's River band of Kalapuya, Lower Chinook, Paiute, Iroquois, French Canadian	Native Name: None known by author
Alias: None known by author	Allotment 118
Mother: Elizabeth Shangaretta, Mary's River band of Kalapuya, Lower Chinook, Iroquois	Father: Peter Menard, adopted Mary's River band of Kalapuya Paiute, French Canadian,

October 7, 1883, Peter Menard Jr. was baptized at the St. Michael's Church. **Marshell Laferte** and Michael's wife, Angelica, were his godparents.

Peter married Adella Payne. They had a number of children, including Marjorie, Serena (1909), Jane (1910), Elizabeth (1912–1939), Ruth (1914–1936), Mary (1916), Elray (1925–1926, Marvin (1927–1930), and Geraldine.

On June 28, 1907, Peter Menard was issued a fee patent for his entire eighty-acre allotment.

---

71 Munnick and Beckham, *Catholic Church Records—Grand Ronde*, Register I, p. 58, M-1, p. 62, B-12, p. 75, B-23, p. 88, B-11, p. 97, B-7, p. 111, B-9, p. 118, B-11, p. 123, S-2, p. 126, S-12, p. 126, B-21, Register II, p. 3, B-10, p. 48, B-45, p. 65, S-13, p. 66, B-3, p. 87, B-16.

72 National Archives, Seattle, WA, Grand Ronde/Siletz, Land and Enrollment Program records, Field Notes and Land Survey 1875—1898, Land Description Book 1878, Box 115; Grand Ronde Justice Court.

73 National Archives, Salem, Oregon, 1908, Yamhill County Estate, File 1412.

Peter Menard Jr. (1883–1930).

Peter Menard Jr.'s daughters, Geraldine and Mary, with his widow, Adella Payne-Menard. Photo courtesy of Mary Loy.

He died June 12, 1930, of tuberculosis. His widow, a full Rogue River woman named Adella Payne-Menard, was said to be one of only a few women still making baskets at Grand Ronde in 1934.[74] His daughter, Mary Menard, married Donald Paul Voutrin, son of **John Baptiste "Bob" Voutrin** and Caroline Agnes LaBonte, in 1935.

Menard, Pierre (1799–1877), French Canadian	Native Name: None known by author
Alias: Pierre Minard, Pierre Mennard	Donation Land Claim at French Prairie
Mother: Theresa LaBonte dit Vegiard, French Canadian	Father: Louis Menard, French Canadian

Pierre Menard, a French Canadian fur trapper from Berthier, Canada, first arrived in Oregon Territory around 1842 with his Paiute wife, Josephte, and their two sons. Almost immediately upon arriving, Pierre contacted Father Blanchet

---

74   Berreman, interview with Adella Menard.

to have his family baptized and to marry Josephte in the Catholic Church at St. Paul.[75]

Another French Canadian named Louis Pichette was named Josephte's godfather for this occasion. Louis Pichette was on the hunting brigade that was led south toward the sources of the Willamette River by Thomas McKay in the winter of 1818–19 and joined John Work's Snake Expedition in 1831.

Josephte's godmother was Susanne Tawakon, daughter of the Iroquois hunter Thomas Tawakon. Thomas was one of many Iroquois who ignored Governor Simpson's 1825 order expelling the Iroquois from the Columbia District. Instead, Thomas took a land claim on the north side of the Yamhill River next to Joseph McLoughlin and several other Iroquois families.

On the same day Josephte Menard was baptized, Father Blanchet baptized her two sons by Pierre: Joseph (1840c) and Peter (1839c). Louis Pichett was named as Joseph's godfather. A man named Jean Baptiste Dubreuil was named godfather for Peter.[76] Jean Baptiste Dubreuil was a French Canadian boatman. He was a member of the Hunt Expedition in 1810.

The day after baptizing Josephte and the children, on April 11, Father Blanchet performed Pierre Menard and Josephte's wedding ceremony at St. Paul.[77] One of their witnesses was a boatman for the fur traders named Jacques Servant who was interested in homesteading at St. Paul. The other witness was a man named Mahumuhumu, who was listed as a middleman for the Hudson's Bay Company in 1843.[78]

Father Blanchet noted that Josephte was of the "Nation of Youtes" in reference to the Paiute nation, which consists of many different bands distributed across a region that today encompasses many states, including Oregon, California, Nevada, Idaho, and Arizona.

The Paiute, like most of the other tribes who had come in contact with the early American explorers, trappers, and settlers, experienced epidemics of smallpox, measles, and other diseases that devastated their communities.

By the time Josephte married Pierre Menard, the Paiute were engaged in an ever increasing conflict with the Americans over Paiute land. The conflict would continue throughout the Civil War era.

On May 18, 1845, Father Blanchet baptized Paul, Pierre Menard's third son by Josephte, at the St. Paul Catholic Mission.[79] Paul's godfather was Joseph Barnabe.

---

75 Munnick and Warner, *Catholic Church Records — St. Paul.* p. 46, B-3.
76 Ibid., p. 47, B-4.
77 Ibid,, p. 47, B-5.
78 Ibid., p. 47, M-2.
79 Oregon Territorial Census for Champoeg County, 24 Reel 77, Documents 12188–12277b, date enumerated: March, 1845, National Archives, 800 Summer Street NE, Salem, Oregon: "Pierre Minard" was head of household with three male children under the age of twelve years.

Barnabe's wife, Elizabeth Boucher, was his godmother.[80] Joseph Barnabe was one of the delegates from Champoeg who in 1846 prepared the pre-territorial memorial to Congress.

In 1847, Pierre Menard was farming a land claim at the big bend of the Willamette River about a mile north of St. Paul between the claims of Charles Plante and George Aplin. By this time, he had five sons by Josephte: Paul, Francois Xavier, Andre, **John Baptiste,** and **Peter Menard.**[81]

After nine years of marriage, Josephte Menard died in September 1851. Estimating her age at twice her actual years, Father Cenas recorded the event.[82]

At the age of thirteen, Joseph Menard, her oldest son, followed her in death on March 17, 1852. His father does not appear to have been present for either funeral.

Several months later, Pierre married Mary Blackfoot. Their ceremony was performed in the presence of Amable Petit and Ambroise Jean on June 21, 1852, at the St. Paul parish.[83]

Shortly after they were married, Pierre filed his land claim in Clackamas County District Court, Oregon Territory, with accompanying affidavits from neighboring landholders Etiene Lucier, Jacque Servant, and George Aplin, who stated Pierre had been living and working his land continuously since September 30, 1847. With this formality out of the way, Pierre's attention once again returned to improving his land claims.[84]

On January 6, 1857, Mary Blackfoot died.[85] A little over two years later, on May 23, 1859, Pierre was officially awarded his land claim, but within just a few months, on April 18, 1860, the Willamette River flooded, washing out much of the area.[86]

More rains in November 1861 washed away more houses, barns, bridges, storehouses, and mills. If the Menards were not evacuated in April, they certainly were by November.

Severe cold weather followed. Champoeg and Linn City were swept clean. Much of Oregon City and Portland were ruined. The water was more than fifty feet above the low water mark and boats were said to have sailed over the fields of Champoeg where houses had once stood.

With his claim washed out, Pierre decided to take another wife. On September 6, 1861, he and Theresa Sastee (Shasta) were married in the Catholic Church at St. Paul.[87]

---

80 Munnick and Warner, *Catholic Church Records — St. Paul*, 114.

81 1850 Marion County Census: Josette, Pierre b. 1793, Canada, and five sons: Pierre, ten, Baptiste, nine, Paul, eight, F.X., six, and Andre, nine months.

82 Munnick and Warner, *Catholic Church Records — St. Paul*, p. 41, S-23.

83 Ibid.

84 Genealogical Material in Oregon Donation Land Claims Vol. I, Abstracted from applications by Genealogical Forum of Portland, Oregon, 1957, File 1908.

85 Munnick and Warner, *Catholic Church Records — St. Paul*, p. 84, S-1.

86 McKay, *St. Paul, Oregon*, 47.

87 Munnick and Warner, *Catholic Church Records — St. Paul*, 120, p. 119, S-5.

Exactly when Pierre Menard arrived at Grand Ronde is not known, but the old mountain man died there on June 11, 1877. Father Croquet estimated his age as about eighty years before burying him in the mission cemetery on the Grand Ronde Indian Reservation.[88]

Mercier, Arthur (1884–1967), Clackamas, Chinook, Iroquois, French Canadian, Belgian	Native Name: None known by author
Alias: None known by author	Allotment 129
Mother: Mary Petite, Clackamas, Chinook, Iroquois, French Canadian	Father: Francis Mercier, Belgian

Arthur Mercier married Mary Agnes Leno (1889–1982), daughter of **David Leno** and Tilmer LaChance.

After he received his eighty-acre allotment, he exchanged it for eighty acres from **Narcisse LaChance.** He received a fee patent March 13, 1907, for the entire allotment.[89]

Mercier, Joseph C. (1869), Clackamas, Chinook, Iroquois, French Canadian, Belgian	Native Name: None known by author
Alias: None known by author	Allotment 131
Mother: Mary Petite, Clackamas, Chinook, Iroquois, French Canadian	Father: Francis Mercier, Belgian

On January 30, 1907, Joseph Mercier was issued a fee patent on a 203-acre allotment.

Mercier, Josephine (1886–1949), Clackamas, Chinook, Iroquois, French Canadian, Belgian	Native Name: None known by author
Alias: Josephine Boydson	Allotment 130
Mother: Mary Petite, Clackamas, Chinook, Iroquois, French Canadian	Father: Francis Mercier, Belgian

Josephine Mercier married Jasper Boydson (1876–1949). On October 29, 1906, Josephine was issued a fee patent for an eighty-acre allotment.[90]

---

88 Munnick and Beckham, *Catholic Church Records—Grand Ronde,* Register I, p. 102, S-10.
89 *Heirs of Deceased Indians,* Allotment Records 129.
90 Ibid., Allotment Records 130.

Mercier, Julius (1883–1953), Clackamas, Chinook, Iroquois, French Canadian, Belgian	Native Name: None known by author
Alias: None known by author	Allotment 128
Mother: Mary Petite, Clackamas, Chinook, Iroquois, French Canadian	Father: Francis Mercier, Belgian

Julius Mercier married Gertrude Hudson (1896–1982), daughter of **John "Mose" Hudson** and Magdelen "Hattie" Sands.

Metcalf, Edwin (1873), Shasta	Native Name: None known by author
Alias: None known by author	Allotment 125
Mother: Unknown to author	Father: Robert Metcalf, Shasta

Edward received a forty-acre allotment. On October 25, 1907, a fee patent was issued for the entire allotment.[91]

Metcalf, Mary C. (1877), Shasta	Native Name: None known by author
Alias: Allie Metcalf, Allie Riggs	Allotment 126
Mother: Mary	Father: Robert Metcalf, Shasta

Mary "Allie" Metcalf married **Solomon Riggs** (Gunconnacli) and **Jenny Mackey**'s oldest son, Eddie Riggs.

After receiving an allotment in her own name, she was issued a fee patent on October 19, 1907, for the entire forty acres.[92]

Metcalf, Robert (1843c–1904), Shasta	Native Name: None known by author
Alias: None known by author	Allotment 124
Mother: Unknown to author	Father: Unknown to author

Robert was born in California and removed to Grand Ronde as a child with the rest of the Shasta people.[93] At Grand Ronde, he married a woman called Mary or Molly. They had: James (1867c), Frankie (1870c), Ellen (1871c), Edwin (1873c), and Mary Christine Josephine, who was better known as "Allie" (1875c).[94]

By 1888, Robert and Mary had two houses and two barns on sixty fenced acres with a half acre garden, a herd of three cattle, three horses, twenty hogs, and a few chickens. Their children, Edward and Allie, were attending school.[95]

---

91 Ibid., Allotment Records 125.
92 Ibid., Allotment Records 126.
93 *Records of Employees at Grand Ronde, 1884-1907.*
94 Munnick and Beckham, *Catholic Church Records—Grand Ronde*, Register I, p. 106, M-3, p. 82, B-25, p. 130, B-6.
95 Michelle, *Just a Memorandum*, 3: Edward and Allie were stepchildren to Mary Metcalf.

At the Grand Ronde Agency, Robert Metcalf served on the Grand Ronde Police Force from 1889 to 1894.[96] By 1890, his daughter, Allie, was working as an assistant teacher at the agency school.[97]

Robert received a 180-acre allotment. When he died September 17, 1904, his estate was valued at $902. His heirs were his widow, Mary, his son, **Edwin Metcalf,** and his daughter, Allie.[98]

Allie Metcalf (center) posing with friends. Photo courtesy of Oregon Historical Society (CN022581)

---

96 National Archives, Seattle, WA, Grand Ronde/Siletz, Land and Enrollment Program records, Field Notes and Land Survey 1875–1898, Land Description Book 1878, Box 115; Grand Ronde Justice Court.
97 *Records of Employees at Grand Ronde, 1884–1907.*
98 Oregon State Archives, Salem, Oregon, Polk County, Estate File 0911.

Metzkar, Antoine (1838c–98), Tualatin band of Kalapuya[99]	Native Names: Tamulch /TA-mulch/ (t'ámulch) ["tubby barrel" or "wash tub"],* Atwin /a-TWIN/ (at'wín)*[100]
Alias: Metzcar, Metzgar, Mesker	Allotment 121
Mother: Unknown to author	Father: Unknown to author

Antoine Metzkar (Tamulch) was related to **William Wishikin, James Shiliqua** (Shilikwa), **John Pratt** (Gwaimit), **Callo Bonaparte** (Kalukh), **Jack Nancy** (Shimkhin), and **Henry Wallace**'s mother, **Lillie Wallace** (Kallola).[101] He had a cold wind spirit power.[102]

Antoine married a Klickitat woman named Eliza. They had two daughters, Cecile (1865c) and Lucinda. In 1885, Antoine was living with his wife, Millie, and their children, Jane and Daniel. Two years later, Antoine was living with a woman named **Mary Sansousee.**

When he died on January 19, 1898, the only surviving heir to his 219.91-acre allotment and personal estate was his daughter Lucinda.[103]

In 1909, Lucinda also inherited a share of John Pratt's estate after being declared a second cousin "through a common ancestor on their fathers' part, claimed entirely through a male line of ancestors…"[104]

Metzkar, Lucinda (1863c–1927), Tualatin band of Kalapuya, Klickitat[105]	Native Name: None known by author
Alias: Lucinda Apperson, Lucinda Allen, Lucinda Bob, Lucinda Wacheno	Allotment: None known by author
Mother: Eliza, Klickitat	Father: Antoine Metskar, Tualatin band of Kalapuya

Lucinda married **Moses Apperson** (Wannexke). After Moses's death in 1886, she and her two children, Melinda and Norris, were listed on the GRIC as "very poor." In 1887, she married **Nelson Allen**. After his death, she married **Levi Bob** around 1890. After Levi died, she had a brief relationship with **Peter Arquette.**

---

99 Michelle, *Just a Memorandum,* 5: Mary Ann wrote that "Entwan Medgeca" was Tualatin and his wife was Klickitat.

100 Jacobs, Field Notebooks 46, *Santiam Kalapuya Text,* n.p. Jacobs, Field Notebook 59, *Texts and Ethnology,* 118: Clackamas nickname. Oregon State Archives, Salem, Oregon, 1909, Yamhill County, Estate File 1327, gave his name as "Antoine Matchen."

101 Oregon State Archives, Salem, Oregon, 1909, Yamhill County, Estate File 1327, John Pratt.

102 Jacobs, Field Notebooks 59, *Texts and Ethnology,* 118.

103 Munnick and Beckham, *Catholic Church Records—Grand Ronde,* Register II, p. 117, S-1.

104 Oregon State Archives, Salem, Oregon, 1909, Yamhill County, Estate File 1327, John Pratt.

105 Michelle, *Just a Memorandum,* 5.

Their son, Stephen Wilson, was born January 2, 1892.[106] In February 1898, Lucinda married **John Wacheno** (Tsinwalh) at Sheridan, Oregon.[107]

Lucinda Metzkar-Wacheno with "Bessie," her daughter by John Wacheno. Photo courtesy of Barbara Danforth Private Collection.

Before Lucinda married John Wacheno, he had taken another wife without observing the custom for widowers. It was expected that the deceased wife's relatives would decide when the husband had mourned long enough. They would either give him a new wife or let him select one for himself. The relatives of his dead wife, Philomene Mary Sutton, made John abandon this woman and marry Lucinda.[108]

Eventually, John and Lucinda's marriage ended after John filed for divorce in Polk County Circuit Court on July 25, 1907. A vicious court battle for custody of their three minor children, Florence, Adam, and Simon, followed and lasted late into the fall of that year. Lucinda was the owner in her own right of 270 acres of land free from any liens and encumbrances and valued at $4,000, but in the end, John was awarded care and custody of the children.[109]

---

106 Munnick and Beckham, *Catholic Church Records— Grand Ronde*, Register II, p. 74, B-1.
107 National Archives, Oregon, Polk County, Circuit Court Case Files, Index to Divorce Cases 1859-1909, File 3566, *John Wacheno vs. Lucinda.*
108 Berreman, interview with John Wacheno.
109 National Archives, Salem, Oregon, Polk County Circuit Court Case Files, Index to Divorce Cases 1859–1909, File 3566, *John Wacheno vs. Lucinda.*

Michel, Jennie (1870c–1905), Mary's River band of Kalapuya, Iroquois	Native Name: None known by author
Alias: Jennie Michelle, Jennie Parr, Jennie Russie	Allotment 132
Mother: Susan, Mary's River Kalapuya	Father: Louis Michel Monada, Iroquois

Jennie and **Joseph Corner Michelle** were full brother and sister. In 1888, she was listed as an orphan living on twenty fenced acres with her brother, Joseph. Later, she married Eli Parr, Sr. and had a son by him. In 1892, she married **Charlie Russie.** She and Charlie were divorced in 1898.

Jennie received a 160-acre allotment that her son, Eli Parr inherited.

Michelle, Frank (1811c–92), Lower Chinook, Iroquois	Native Name: None known by author
Alias: Frank Michel, Francis Michel, Hair Lipped Frank, Blind Michelle[110]	Allotment 133
Mother: Lower Chinook	Father: Iroquois

Frank Michelle was Iroquois and Lower Chinook.[111] He was related to **Lucy Sampson** who was also part Lower Chinook.[112] His wife, **Mary Michelle** (Skitap), was full Kalapuya.[113]

Both Frank and Mary sang and danced five nights in winter, but neither of them doctored.[114] They had one son named **Joseph Michelle.**

In 1879, Frank served on the Grand Ronde Legislature, representing the west precinct along with **Peter Selkya** and **Frank Norwest.**[115] A few years after Frank went blind, his son, Joseph married **Mary Ann Hoffer** and brought her to live

---

110 1872 GRIC: "Hair Lipped Frank."

111 1888 GRIC listed Frank as Santiam Kalapuya. Michelle, *Just a Memorandum*, 7: Frank's father was Yaraqua Canadian and his mother was full blooded Lower Chinook. Jacobs, Field Notebooks 54, *Texts and Ethnology*, 28: V. H. said "Jos Michelle's father was Iroquois probably and had a hair lip." Jacobs, Field Notebooks 46, *Santiam Kalapuya Text*, n. p: J. B. Hudson said, "Frank Michelle was part French Canadian and his mother was possibly Chinook or Cowlitz."

112 Oliver Applegate, Testimony of Old Amos Kilya.

113 Michelle, *Just a Memorandum*, 7: Mary was full Kalapuya. Jacobs, Field Notebooks 46, *Santiam Kalapuya Text*, n.p., J. B. Hudson said Mary's name was skitap and this was also the name of her band who were one of the Kalapuya speaking bands located originally on "the east side of the Willamette across from Independence."

114 Jacobs, Field Notebooks 46, *Santiam Kalapuya Text*, 74.

115 National Archives, Seattle, WA, Grand Ronde/Siletz, Land and Enrollment Program records, Field Notes and Land Survey 1875–1898, Land Description Book 1878, Box 115; Grand Ronde Justice Court.

Joseph A. Michelle. Photo courtesy of Barbara Danforth Collection.

with the family. Mary, Frank's wife, died January 6, 1890.[116]

Frank received a 260.40-acre allotment. His son, Joseph Michelle, sold the property June 16, 1905.

Michelle, Joseph A. (1868c–1945), Kalapuya, Lower Chinook, and Iroquois	Native Name: None known by author
Alias: Joe Michel, Joseph Abraham Michelle	Allotment 134
Mother: Mary (Skitap), Kalapuya	Father: Frank Michelle, Iroquois and Lower Chinook[117]

---

116 Munnick and Beckham, *Catholic Church Record—Grand Ronde*, Register II, p. 57, S-2.

117 1888 GRIC listed Frank as Santiam Kalapuya. Michelle, *Just a Memorandum*, 7: Frank's father was Yaraqua Canadian and his mother was full blooded Lower Chinook. Jacobs, Field Notebooks 54, *Texts and Ethnology*, 28: V. H. said "Jos Michelle's father was probably Iroquois." Jacobs, Field Notebooks 46, *Santiam Kalapuya Text*, n.p., J. B. Hudson said, "Frank Michelle was part French Canadian and his mother was possibly Chinook or Cowlitz."

After working as the agency farmer for a number of years, Joseph Michelle married **Mary Ann Hoffer** and raised a large family.

When Joseph received his allotment, he exchanged 120 acres of it with **Jim Hines** (Huyiduwa) for 80.34 acres. After receiving a fee patent for Hine's former land on March 9, 1901, Joseph Michelle exchanged it with **Jacob Wheeler** (Shwa). On June 22, 1904, a trust patent was issued to Joseph Michelle for the eighty acres previously held by Jacob Wheeler. On January 6, 1908, Joseph Michelle was issued a fee patent for a second parcel of eighty acres, bringing his total allotment to 160 acres.[118]

Michelle, Joseph Corner (1868–1945), Mary's River band of Kalapuya, Iroquois[119]	Native Name: None known by author
Alias: Joseph Corner, Joseph Conner, Joseph Michel, Abraham Michelle	Allotment 131
Mother: Susanne, Mary's River band of Kalapuya	Father: Louis Michel Monada, Iroquois

Joseph Corner Michelle was the son of **Louis Michel Monada** and a Mary's River woman called Susanne. At age three, he was listed on the 1872 GRIC under the Mary's River Kalapuya with his father, mother, and grandmother, **Louise Monada.**

In 1888, he was listed as single and living on twenty fenced acres with his sister **Jennie Michel.** To support the two of them, he worked as an assistant carpenter and later as a temporary industrial teacher for the agency.[120]

Joseph was married several times. He married Anne Dowd in 1889. Next, he married **Josephine Hubbard** at McMinnville in September 1890.[121] After their divorce in 1900, he married Mary Shangaretta-Holmes. In 1904, he was involved in the **Foster Wacheno** (Inawalh) tragedy with **Louis Savage.** The following year, he and his wife Mary Shangaretta had a little girl they named Susanne.

Some said Joseph acquired a tamanawas power that brought him bad luck. To make matters worse, he never sang or danced with his power. This was partially why so many of his children died.[122]

Both Joseph Corner Michelle and Mary became active in the Indian Shaker

---

118 *Heirs to Deceased Indians*, Allotment Record 134.

119 O. Applegate, Testimony of Mary Ann Voutrin: her full brother had a son, "Abraham Mitchelle" and a daughter, Jennie Parr. The 1872 GRIC: Joseph was listed as Mary's River. The 1888 GRIC listed Joseph's tribe as Clackamas.

120 *Records of Employees at Grand Ronde, 1884–1907.*

121 National Archives, Salem, Oregon, Polk County Circuit Court Case Files, Index to Divorce Cases 1859–1909, File 3086, *Joseph Corner vs. Josephine Corner.*

122 Jacobs, Field Notebooks 53, *Texts and Ethnology*, 106.

Left to right: Mary Shangaretta-Michelle, Joseph Corner Michelle, and daughter, Susanne.

religion.[123] A missionary of the church, Joseph brought the religion to Otis where a small group of Indian families, including the Logans and **Henry Curl,** were living in 1927.[124]

Since the Shakers did not have a church at Grand Ronde, they held services in various houses. While waiting for the service to start, people would sit clapping softly, rubbing their faces, or brushing evil off them. The minister usually started with, "My friends, my brothers and sisters, the Lord in his mercy has called us together here to praise his name," followed by a sentence or two in an Indian

123 Gunther, *The Shaker Religion,* 37–76. Zenk, Grand Ronde Field Notebook 9, 1988, interview with Eula Petite, 12.

124 Jacobs, Field Notebook 45, Yoncalla Text, 108. Zenk, Grand Ronde Field Notebook 9, 1988, interview with Eula Petite, 12.

language. Like in the ancient Dream Power religion, the Indian Shakers dreamed songs.[125]

Joseph Corner Michelle received 203 acres of allotment land at Grand Ronde. By 1930, his daughter, Susanne Dick, had moved out and was raising her own family. To help them in their retirement years, Joseph's wife, Mary, sold her portion of the original **David Holmes**'s allotment.[126]

Michelle, Mary (1841c), Kalapuya	Native Name: *Skitap* /*SKI-tap*/ (sq'íiṭap)*[127]
Alias: Mary Michel	Allotment: None known by author
Mother: Unknown to author	Father: Unknown to author

Mary (Skitap) was a full Kalapuya woman and the wife of **Frank Michelle.**[128] Both Frank and Mary sang and danced five nights in winter, but neither of them doctored.[129]

Mary's people originally lived on the east side of the Willamette across from Independence. Her uncle was **Jim Hines** (Huyiduwa).[130]

Mickmut, Marc (1839c–79), Pudding River band of Kalapuya[131]	Native Name: Minkmut ["limber, pliant"][132]
Alias: French Prairie Marc, Mark Mickmut	Allotment: None known by author
Mother: Unknown to author	Father: Unknown to author

In 1869, French Prairie Marc Mickmut and his wife, Catherine (1837c–77), had a daughter, Lizzette, who died in 1870.[133] In 1872, he was listed with Catherine and their children, Lucy (1859c), Philomene (1866c), and **French Prairie Frank Marc.**[134]

On January 4, 1876, the fifth annual session of the Grand Ronde Indian legis-

---

125 Gunther, *The Shaker Religion*, 37–76. Zenk, Field Notes, 1982, interview with Nathan Leno, 1: "grandmother [Mary Shangaretta-Holmes-Michelle] spoke English; some Washington language (others?)."

126 National Archives, Seattle, NRIA-S-11-276, PAC-08, Mrs. Mary Corner.

127 Jacobs, Field Notebooks 46, *Santiam Kalapuya Text*, n.p.

128 Michelle, *Just a Memorandum*, 7.

129 Ibid.

130 Michelle, *Just a Memorandum*, 7.

131 1872 GRIC listed French Prairie Mac under the Santiam. Gatschet, *Texts, Sentences and Vocables*, 368: listed under the French Prairie or Ahanthuyuk as "French Prairie Mac" with son, "Frank," who was still single.

132 Gatschet, *Texts, Sentences and Vocables*, 78.

133 Munnick and Beckham, *Catholic Church Records—Grand Ronde*, Register I, p. 66, S-28.

134 Ibid., p. 105, S-30, p. 112, B-15, S-13.

lature convened with two representatives from each tribe on the reservation attending. French Prairie Mac and **Tom Hutchins** (Liham) represented the Santiam band of Kalapuya.[135]

Catherine died a few days after their son, John Baptiste, in 1877. French Prairie Marc was buried August 26, 1879.

Miller, Jacob (1833c–87), Coquille[136]	Native Name: None known by author
Alias: Jack Miller	Allotment: None known by author
Mother: Unknown to author	Father: Unknown to author

In 1885, Jacob "Jack" Miller was listed with his wife Mary (1842c), and son, Henry (1866c). He and his wife Mary (1846c) had an ordinary house with a barn on eighty fenced acres, five and a half acres cultivated, a small garden, two wagons, a plow, three head of cattle, three horses, two sets of harnesses, a cradle, and a scythe.

On April 4, 1887, Jacob Miller, gravely ill, was baptized by Father Croquet. He died and was buried April 11, the same year.[137]

Miller, Mrs. Captain Lilly (1830c)	Native Name: None known by author
Alias: None known by author	Allotment: None known by author
Mother: Unknown to author	Father: Unknown to author

In 1885, Mrs. Captain Lilly was listed as a widow. She had a son, **William Miller** (Quilinick).

Miller, Mary (1842c) Rogue River	Native Name: None known by author
Alias: None known by author	Allotment: None known by author
Mother: Unknown to author	Father: Unknown to author

Mary was the former wife of **Jacob "Jack" Miller.** She was listed on the GRIC in 1887 as a widow.

Miller, William (1836c–97), Yamhill band of Kalapuya	Native Name: Quilinick /Quil-i-nick/[138]
Alias: Yamhill William, Billy Miller	Allotment 135
Mother: Mrs. Captain Lilly	Father: Unknown to author

135 National Archives, Seattle, Grand Ronde/Siletz Tribal Program Records Box 162, Agency and Tribal Council Records 1876–1951.

136 Gatschet, *Texts, Sentences and Vocables,* 367: "Jack Miller" under "Coquille or Salt Chuck."

137 Munnick and Beckham, *Catholic Church Records—Grand Ronde*, Register II, p. 27, B-10, p. 28, S-5.

138 The 1887 GRIC: gave his Indian name as "Quil-i-nick."

Yamhill William Miller (Quilinick) was probably related to Webley Haux-hurst's native wife, Mary (Wat-tiat), as not only were they both from the Yamhill band, but once when Yamhill William's wife was working in Salem she turned to the Hauxhurst family for help.[139] Following her arrival, on July 24, 1856, Webley Hauxhurst wrote to Joel Palmer from Salem that an Indian woman, wife of Yam-hill William, had come to his residence. She was "unwell and not able to support herself." Hauxhurst asked Palmer "to let her companion know of her arrival so he may come over and take her away."[140]

Yamhill William had several wives: Louise (1822–82) in 1872, Mary Ann in 1885, and **Margaret "Maggie" Lapan** (Chalwina) in 1888.[141] **Frank Michelle** and his wife, **Mary Michelle** (Skitap), witnessed his marriage to Margaret (Chalwina).

Before he died on June 28, 1897, Yamhill William received a 279.13-acre allot-ment at Grand Ronde.[142] His wife, Margaret was his only heir.

Moffit, George (1860c)	Native Name: None known by author
Alias: None known by author	Allotment: None known by author
Mother: Unknown to author	Father: Unknown to author

George Moffit was one of three students singled out for special mention by the teacher of the manual labor school at Grand Ronde. On August 6, 1870, Dun-bar wrote that George Moffit, **Henry Crawford,** and **John Harris** were "quite in-telligent and studious; are good readers and spellers, write a good hand, and have stored their minds with a large amount of practical knowledge."

Monada, Louis Michel (1839c–79), Mary's River band of Kalapuya, Iroquois	Native Name: None known by author
Alias: Louis Machell, Louis Michel, Louis Michelle	Allotment: None known by author
Mother: Louise, Mary's River band of Kalapuya	Father: Louis Shaegoskatsta, Tete Frize, Le Frise, Marchelle, Michelle, Monada, Louis Maranda, Iroquois[143]

---

139 Death Certificate, Tillamook County, dated November 21, 1907 for 87 year old Indian daughter of Stawin (Stay-win), chief of Yamhill Indian tribe.

140 Webley Hauxhurst to Joel Palmer, July 24, 1856, *Correspondence and Papers of Joel Palmer,* Superintendent of Indian Affairs in Oregon Territory, 1853–1857, and Indian Agent at Siletz 1870–1876 (Special Collection, Knight Library, University of Oregon, Eugene, OR).

141 Munnick and Beckham, *Catholic Church Records—Grand Ronde,* Register II, p. 47, M-4.

142 Ibid., p. 110, S-6.

143 O. Applegate, Testimony of Joseph Corner, David Leno, Mary Ann Voutrin, James Winslow, John B. Voutrin, and Captain Frank Quenelle.

Louis Michel Monada was a full brother to **Mary Ann Monada. William Hartless** (Futi) and **Elisa George** (Tmulhu) were his first cousins on his mother's side. **Marysville George** and **Marysville Tom** were his uncles.[144]

Louis Michel Monada was probably the same "Louis Michael" whom Agent J.B. Condon in September 1861 authorized to "round up any Marysville Indians residing anywhere within the Willamette Valley.[145]

Using the name Michel Monada, Louis and **Joseph Shangaretta** witnessed the marriage between Thomas Pisk and Martha Jane of the Rogue River nation on May 21, 1862. Then, on July 19, 1863, Louis Monada was named godfather to Aloise, the daughter of Joseph Shangaretta and **Nancy Pisk**.[146]

Father Croquet married "Michel Monada" and a woman named Susanne on January 9, 1865, with **David Ambroise Leno** and **Victoria Vasselle** witnessing the ceremony.[147] On April 16, 1869, they had a son, **Joseph Corner Michelle**. In 1872, Louis' mother, **Louise Monada** was living with Louis, Susanne and their baby Joseph. Besides Joseph, Louis Michel Monada and Susanne had a daughter named **Jennie Michel.**

Father Croquet buried "Louis Michel Monada" at Grand Ronde on September 22, 1879. He estimated his age as around forty years.[148]

Monada, Louise (1800c–79) Mary's River Kalapuya	Native Name: None known by author
Alias: None known by author	Allotment: None known by author
Mother: Unknown to author	Father: Unknown to author

Louise was married to an Iroquois fur trapper and mountain man from Sault St. Louis, Canada, named Louis Shaegoskatsta on July 12, 1839 with Michel LaFramboise and J.B. Jeaudoin acting as witnesses.[149]

She and Louis had two children: **Mary Ann Monada** and **Louis Monada.** In 1872, she was staying with her son, Louis, and his family at Grand Ronde.

On August 26, 1879, the priests at Grand Ronde buried "Louise Monada" in the mission cemetery. After her death, her friends and relatives sent word to her daughter, Mary Ann Monada, that Louise had died and asked Mary Ann to come live on the Grand Ronde Reservation.[150]

144 O. Applegate, Testimony of Joseph Corner Michelle, David Leno, Mary Ann Voutrin, James Winslow, John B. Voutrin, and Captain Frank Quenelle.

145 J. B. Condon, Letter of Authority for Louis Michael, September 30, 1861 (BIA, Microfilm M-2, Roll 30, National Archives, Washington, DC).

146 Munnick and Beckham, *Catholic Church Records—Grand Ronde*, Register I, p. 20, M-1, p. 27, B-36.

147 Ibid., Register I, p. 37, M-2.

148 Munnick and Beckham, *Catholic Church Records—Grand Ronde*, Register I, p. 112, S-15.

149 Harriet Munnick, *Catholic Church Records—Vancouver.*

150 O. Applegate, Testimony of Joseph Corner Michelle, David Leno, Mary Ann Voutrin, James Winslow, John B. Voutrin, and Captain Frank Quenelle. Munnick & Beckham,

Monada, Mary Ann (1834c–1929), Mary's River band of Kalapuya, Iroquois	Native Name: None known by author
Alias: Mary Ann Brule, Mary Ann Voutrin, Vautrin, Voutrant, Mary Ann Shaegoskatsta	Allotment 229
Mother: Louise, Mary's River Kalapuya	Father: Louis Shaegoskatsta, Tete Frize, Le Frise, Marchelle, Michelle, Monada, Louis Maranda, Iroquois

Mary Ann's father was Louis Shaegoskatsta. Louis was known to have been with David Thompson in the employment of the North West Fur Company as early as 1808. He was a frequent member of the hunting party on brigades and called "Tete Frize" or "Le Frise" because of his curly hair.

Mission St Paul at Wallamet, a lithograph by Vander Schedlen based on a sketch by Nicholas Point. This image shows the Catholic Mission in the 1850s featuring a family residence, a presbytery, and education facilities for both girls and boys. Photo courtesy of Oregon Historical Society (Ba019299).

Catholic Church Records—Grand Ronde, Register I, p. 112, S-14.

He married a Mary's River Kalapuya woman named Louise on July 12, 1839. Mary Ann was born in 1834 at present-day Corvallis. Her full brother, **Louis Michel Monada,** was born in 1836.

When Mary Ann was small, she was taken to French Prairie where she went to the "Sister's school" at St. Paul until she was fifteen.[151]

In 1848, Mary Ann married Joseph Brule, the son of a native woman called Marguerite Sok and Iroquois Jacques, in the St. Paul Catholic Church. The father of the bride, "Louis Maranda, dit Le Frize," was still alive and present for the ceremony.[152] Mary Ann had six children by Brule. Two years after Brule died, she married John Baptiste Vautrin, a French Canadian.

Vautrin was a middleman employed by the Hudson's Bay Company from 1833 to 1867. They were married in Oregon, but moved to the Company's post at Victoria. By Vautrin, Mary Ann had nine children. Seven of the children were living in 1885, but only five—**Peter, Catherine, John Baptiste "Bob," Francis,** and **Olive Voutrin**—went with their parents to the Grand Ronde Reservation after they learned from Bishop Saghers that Mary Ann's mother, **Louise Monada,** had died there in August of 1879.

Mary Ann said she had quite a few relatives at Grand Ronde "who belonged under the treaty" and they were glad to have her living on the reservation with them.[153]

Her full brother, Louis Michel Monada, was dead, but he had a son named **Joseph Corner Michelle** and a daughter, **Jennie Michel,** living at Grand Ronde. Also alive were her first cousins, **William Hartless** (Futi) and **Elisa George** (Tmulhu).[154]

Joseph Shangaretta and several other chiefs talked to the agent about her rights and he agreed that it was all right for Mary Ann and her family to stay. At that time, the only chief to object was **Chief Peter McCoy** (Inchaishi). His objection was due to the French blood of Mary Ann's children.[155]

Mary Ann received a 250-acre allotment at Grand Ronde. A fee patent was issued to her on April 9, 1907.[156]

Monroe, Marianne (1835c–91), Yamhill band of Kalapuya	Native Name: Bochean /Bo-chean/[157]
Alias: Marianne Sugar, Marianne Checkean	Allotment: None known by author
Mother: Unknown to author	Father: Unknown to author

---

151 O. Applegate, Testimony of Mary Ann Voutrin.

152 Munnick, *Catholic Church Records—Vancouver and Stellamaris Mission.*

153 O. Applegate, Testimony Mary Ann Voutrin.

154 Ibid.

155 O. Applegate, Testimony of Captain Frank Quenel and Mary Ann Vautrin.

156 *Heirs of Deceased Indians,* Allotment Records 229.

157 Cawley, *Indian Journal,* 22: gave Marianne Checkaon's Indian name as Bochean.

After her husband **Soka Monroe** died, Marianne (Bochean) married **Peter Checkaon** (Chikhyan) on May 27, 1874. Her seven-year-old daughter, Julienne Monroe, died a few months later. Her son, Peter Monroe, lived until he was twelve; he died in 1879.

On April 14, 1879, Marianne's son Patrick Monroe married **Sarah Johnson** (Waganwish). Their witnesses were **Peter Kenoyer** (Kinai) and **Susan Beagle.**

Marianne's daughter, Estella married **Steve Savage** (Palhilh) on January 3, 1877, with Joseph Selkeah and Susan Beagle witnessing the ceremony.

Monroe, Soka (1833c–73), Yamhill band of Kalapuya	Native Name: None known by author
Alias: Sugar Monroe, William Monroe	Allotment: None known by author
Mother: Unknown to author	Father: Unknown to author

Soka "Sugar" Monroe had a son named Alexander who died in 1864 at the age of ten. By his wife, **Marianne Monroe** (Bochean), Soka had even more children: Patrick (1859c–80), Estella (1862c–84), Julienne (1864c–74), Peter (1867c–79), Anne (1869–73), and Henriette (1872). [158]

In 1864, when their daughter Julienne was baptized, her godparents were Peter Marc and **David Leno**'s wife, **Harriet Lindsey.** In 1867, **Peter Petite** and **Martha Jane Sands** were named godparents to Soka's son, Peter Monroe. In 1869, when Soka's daughter, Anne, was baptized, her godparents were **Peter Menard** and his wife, Elizabeth Shangaretta.

On Christmas Day 1871, Soka and Marianne (Bochean) were married in the Catholic Church. Their witnesses were **William Miller** (Quilinick) and his wife, Louise. A few days later, their infant daughter, Henriette was baptized. Her godmother was **Nancy Kenoyer** (Tunishni).

Soka died in March 1873.

Montour, Anne (1811c), Molalla[159]	Native Name: None known by author
Alias: Anne of Molalla	Allotment: None known by author
Mother: Unknown to author	Father: Unknown to author

On July 13, 1861, Anne of the Molalla married Louis Montour (1821c–71).[160] Louis was the son of a French and Cree Métis named Nicholas Montour, who had worked for the fur companies off and on. For a time, Nicholas held a land claim where the town of Gervais now stands, but Father Croquet noted in his records

---

158 Munnick and Beckham, *Catholic Church Records—Grand Ronde*, Rgister I, p. 5, B-16, p. 21, B-65, p. 35, B-216, p. 110, S-1, p. 80, B-74, S-1, p. 66, M-6.

159 Ibid., Register I, p. 11, M-3.

160 Ibid.

that his son, Louis Montour, was from St. Louis, a small community in present-day Marion County, Oregon.[161]

Chief Louis Napesa and **Louis Vasselle,** among others, were at Louis Montour's funeral in 1871.[162] He was buried at Grand Ronde.

In 1872, Louis Montour's widow, Anne Montour, was living at Grand Ronde with her sister, Ella, and another woman, identified on the GRIC only as Mary.

Montour, Pauline (1853c–73), wife of part Clackamas, part Molalla husband	Native Name: None known by author
Alias: None known by author	Allotment: None known by author
Mother: Unknown to author	Father: Unknown to author

Pauline Montour was **Mark Winslow's** wife. She died and was buried May 28, 1873, in the presence of **Frank Quenel,** Frank's wife, LaRose Nipissing, and others.

Morris, Kiuwantah, Cow Creek of Umpqua	Native Name: Kiuwantah /Ki-u-wan-tah/[163]
Alias: Nestucca Morris	Allotment: None known by author
Mother: Unknown to author	Father: Unknown to author

In 1872, "Ki-wonth-ta Morris" was listed under the Cow Creek band of Umpqua with his wife, Susan. He was the same man Rev. Summers called "Nestucca Morris."[164] Rev. Summers described a lecture Morris gave to three women who "had come up from Siletz Bay for two months work" and were living in "a camp of wood cutters east of town."[165]

Apparently, the women and Morris "were from the same family" and Morris explained in their native language the differences between some of the shells and fossils Summers had in his collection. The women who were "tattooed with three broad perpendicular stripes" on their chins listened attentively.[166]

Summers wrote:

> And ignorant though I am of the Siletz tongue, his gestures told his meaning perfectly. It was a most interesting surprise to me, first to learn that the speaker had so much knowledge; secondly

---

161 Ibid.
162 Ibid., Register I, p. 70, S-18.
163 Cawley, *Indian Journal,* 45.
164 Ibid.
165 Ibid.
166 Jacobs, Field Notebooks 36, *Santiam Kalapuya Text,* 182: "not the Santiam, but the Mary's River through southern Oregon region had slight face tattoos."

that he could and would so eloquently instruct the squaws; and lastly, that they clearly understood every word of it.[167]

Morufi, Steve, Yamhill band of Kalapuya	Native Name: None known by author
Alias: None known by author	Allotment: None known by author
Mother: Unknown to author	Father: Unknown to author

Old Steve's original home was on the Yamhill River near where the town of Ballston is now. He was the first husband of **Bertha Wheeler** (Tewimme).[168]

Moss, Joshua, Clackamas	Native Name: None known by author
Alias: None known by author	Allotment: None known by author
Mother: Unknown to author	Father: Unknown to author

In 1872, Joshua was living alone.

---

167 Ibid.
168 O. Applegate, Testimony of Narcisse Lachance.

N

Nachan, Polly (1806c–93), wife of adopted Umpqua husband	Native Name: Nachem /NA-chem/ (nácham)*¹
Alias: Polly Nachion	Allotment 139
Mother: Unknown to author	Father: Unknown to author

Polly (Nachem) came to Grand Ronde with **Chief Louis Napesa** and his wife, **Lizette Klickitat.** When Napesa died, Polly and Lizette continued to live together. After Lizette Klickitat died, Polly lived with Lizette's daughter, LaRose Nipissing, for the remainder of her life.

Over the years, the GRIC usually listed her simply as an old woman living with Napesa, but Albert Gatschet, noted Polly's presence at Grand Ronde in 1877 as "Na-uka'xanilksh, tribe of Natchem, woman staying with old Louis [...]"²

In 1888, she was listed as Napesa's widow along with Lizette. Polly's widow status was further confirmed by Rev. Summers, who wrote that Napesa had several wives.

In a court battle over the estate of Polly Nachan, several women claimed to be her long lost relatives. A woman named Adlin Lobre testified that Polly was born in a village near present day Astoria, Oregon. Adlin said Polly's father was Big Foot Charley and her mother a Chinook woman called Rosie (Colloust). As a little child, Adlin Lobre said, Polly was stolen from her family by a white hunter who kept her for many years before selling her for two hundred dollars to a Frenchman named Peter Nachan. According to Adlin's testimony, Polly never saw her mother again and eventually her mother gave up hope she would ever find her.³

Another woman named Mary Jette said Polly Nachan was the oldest of three sisters. Her younger half-sister, Ellen (Gullallcin) received reports of Polly, but she was never able to contact her after Polly was taken from their home as a child. Polly did eventually locate her other half-sister, who had married Adolph Jette. Mary Jette testified Polly visited them at the Jette farm between Butterville and

---

1   Gatschet, *Texts, Sentences and Vocables,* 316: listed "under former captives."
2   Ibid.
3   State of Washington, Pierce County, Affidavit from Adlin Lobre in regard to heirship to estate of Polly Nachen Grand Ronde Allotee 139, February 10, 1917. State of Washington, Grays Harbor County, Affidavit from Mary J. Jette and James Weston regarding heirship to estate of Polly Nachen, Grand Ronde Allottee No. 139. State of Oregon, Yamhill County, Grand Ronde Indian Reservation, Affidavit taken from Mary [Shangaretta] Michel in regard to estate of Polly Nachen Grand Ronde Allottee 139 dated February 1, 1917 and witnessed by A.J. Hudson and Joe R. Wild, and stamped W.W. Sheppard, Examiner of Inheritance.

Champoeg, but always "refused gratuities stating she had enough for her own use." After her sister died, Polly did not make the trip to Champoeg again.[4]

Mary Jette also testified she and her family visited **Joseph Shangaretta** in 1873 and found Polly Nachan residing with his family at the time. Both Mary Jette and Adlin Lobre said their mothers were Polly's sisters. They claimed Joseph Shangaretta's wife, **Nancy Pisk,** was also related to Polly Nachan.[5]

Nancy Pisk's daughter, Mary Holmes-Michelle, testified that she knew Polly, but Polly and her mother came from different tribes and spoke different languages.

Mary reaffirmed what the GRIC indicated, that Polly lived with Chief Louis Napesa first and that when he died she lived with LaRose Nipissing-Quenel until she died. She denied that Polly had ever lived with the Shangaretta family and denied any family relationship to Polly.[6]

Polly Nachan received an allotment of 120.93 acres, forty acres more than Lizette Klickitat. Petitioning for heirship were the following people: Mary Jette, Inez Brawdy, **James Weston,** Louis Weston, Archie Pellard, Lucy Fitzpatrick, Amelia Alden Anderson, Rose Cricks, Alinda Boldt, Mable White, and the heirs of Adlin Lobre. In addition, LaRose Nipissing-Quenel had a claim against the estate for $466.66.[7] No record was found as to the final disposition of the case.

Nancy, Jack (1821–1904c), Tualatin band of Kalapuya	Native Name: Shimkhin /SHIM-hen/ (shímxin),* Kanatamakh /KA-na-ta-m ah/ (qánat'amax)*[8]
Alias: Uncle Nancy, Nancy Jack, Nancy Sterwin	Allotment 211
Mother: Unknown to author	Father: Unknown to author

When Shimkhin first went to the mountain, he came back with the power of *sgiyub.* Skiyup only came to a very few, but to those she did come to, she told them to put on a woman's dress and transform themselves into a woman.

---

4 Ibid.

5 Ibid.

6 Ibid.

7 Oregon State Archives, Salem, Oregon, Yamhill County, Estate Polly Nachan, File 133-1913.

8 1872 GRIC: "Nancy Soomkeah" aka "Uncle Nancy." Berreman, Interview with J. B. Hudson: J. B. Hudson gave her name as "Sinkin or Shimkin. 1887 GRIC gave her name as "Shim-gun." Michelle, *Just a Memorandum,* 6: Mary Ann wrote her name as Jack Nancy or "Shymken." Jacobs, Collection 40, *Autobiography of a Tualatin:* Louis Kenoyer gave her name as "Cumxi." Jacobs, Field Notebook 59, *Texts and Ethnology,* 116: qanatamax, camxin, names of an old widow Tualatin doctor lady. Jacobs, Field Notebook 51, *Music and Ethnology,* 9, 46. Jacobs, Field Notebook 67, *Texts Ethnology Clackamas & Jargon,* n.p., (V. Howard) "my father, his father's sister, her name was cimxim." Gatschet, *Texts, Sentences and Vocables,* 77: "shimxin, fem."

To not follow the directions of skiyup was to risk possible death, but with skiyup as a spirit power, if you danced five consecutive nights each year for five years, it was possible to become a doctor.[9]

Shimkhin, a big man with coarse features and large hands, chose to put on the cedar bark dress of a woman, ride sidesaddle, and work along side the women. She preferred the English name Nancy. When people called her Jack, it made her very angry.[10] At the same time, her appearance upset some of the Americans. They would "get after her, beat her, strip her and make her wear pants." After such encounters, Shimkhin would simply go home and put back on her own clothes. Soon they grew bored and left her alone.[11]

Shimkhin also returned from the mountain with the power of coyote, which gave her clairvoyance. In addition, she had dead person power. It showed her how to use a pitch-wood torch to drive the spirit of a recently deceased person away. Working from evening to almost sunrise, she smudged the house of the deceased with smoke from her torch and stood to her dance.[12]

When she doctored, Shimkhin had two or three dogs that always accompanied her. They sat beside her. Before beginning the treatment, she shared with them the food the family had been asked to prepare for her. Shimkhin ate virtually everything and gave anything that was left to her dogs.[13]

She sang and used her torch to brush away any dead person's shadow that had been placed on the patient at night. Dancing and singing, Shimkhin rapidly swung the flaming torch back and forth across the patient who lay before her. If a patient started perspiring, she believed her treatment was working and would continue. If the patient did not perspire, she might stop treatment for that night, but would try again the following night.[14]

The time of doctoring was usually determined by when the illness began. If the patient took sick in the daytime, treatment was given during daytime hours. If the illness began in the evening, the doctor would treat the patient at night. Dead person shadow was a common cause of illness and was treated at night since that was when dead people usually came around.[15]

John "Moses" Hudson thought he remembered Shimkhin as having a husband for a while. **John Wacheno** (Tsinwalh) said she was married many times.[16]

---

9   Jacobs, *Santiam Kalapuya Ethnologic Texts,* Part 1, 179.
10 Jacobs, Elizabeth, Field Notebook 105, Coos–U. Coquille, 91. Berreman, interview with John Basile "Mose" Hudson, 14.
11 Jacobs, Elizabeth, Field Notebook 105, Coos–U. Coquille, 92.
12 Jacobs, Collection 40, *Autobiography of a Tualatin.* Jacobs, Field Notebook 53, *Texts and Ethnology,* 107, gave "water" as one of her powers. Nancy Jack had it named in one of her power songs.
13 Jacobs, Notebooks 67, *Texts Ethnology Clackamas & Jargon,* 32.
14 Ibid., 31: Shimkhin was the only doctor Victoria Howard knew who used the pitch brand treatment in curing patients.
15 Ibid., 31–32.
16 Drucker, *Clackamas Notes,* 24.

Clara Pearson, at Siletz, remembered Shimkhin as periodically buying a young boy or girl. She said, gender did not seem to be an issue, but Shimkhin wanted them to be very good looking. To seal the arrangement, Nancy bought her young lovers nice clothes and a horse. When they ran away, she would buy another.[17]

In 1877, when Albert Gatschet visited Grand Ronde, Shimkhin was living with **Old Yamhill Sambo Sappingfield** (Chawatkha). In 1886, she was listed as "Uncle Nancy," "a single female," with a hut and shed on forty fenced acres and one acre in cultivation. At that time, Shimkhin also owned four horses, a harness, wagon, a plow, and a harrow.

In 1887, she was listed as a widow living with another widow named **Martha Beagle** (Shkinda), but the following year she was once again living alone.

Shimkhin received a hundred-acre allotment. Like the other women, she could not vote when the Surplus Land was sold in 1901. Shortly after her death, Shimkhin's heir, **Lame James Shiliqua** (Shilikwa), sold sixty acres of her allotment to Paul Fundman. On May 18, 1907, he sold the remaining forty acres to A. J. Bewley.[18]

In 1929, **Victoria Wishikin** (Kinishi) recorded one of Shimkhin's songs for Melville Jacobs.

Napesa, Chief Louis (1809c–88), Canadian Native, Adopted Umpqua	Native Name: Napesa /Na-pe-sa/, Settesin /Set-te-sin/
Alias: Louis Nepissank, Nipissing, Nippusing, Nepucin	Allotment: None known to author
Mother: Unknown to author	Father: Louis Nipissing, Canadian Native

Napesa was the son of Louis Nipissing, a Canadian Indian also known as Tom-a-Pierre, who brought him to Oregon during the fur trading era.

One of Nepesa's wives was a woman called Louise Nez Perce. A few days after she died, Napesa buried their eighteen-month-old son in the St. Paul Cemetery on August 5, 1847. **Charlie Petite** and his father, Amable Petit, attended the funeral.[19]

A short time later, Napesa left St. Paul and began ranching in the Umpqua valley. By the time the Rogue River War broke out, he had built a nice home and was operating a ranch with over sixty head of cattle.[20]

Since he could speak English, Napesa was adopted by the Umpqua people.[21] Under his leadership, the Umpqua agreed to the terms of the treaty at Calapooia

---

17 Jacobs, Elizabeth, Field Notebook 105, Coos–U. Coquille, 91.

18 *Heirs of Deceased Indians*, Allotment Record 211.

19 Munnick and Warner, *Catholic Church Records—St. Paul*, 157

20 *Annual Report Commissioner of Indian Affairs*, 1871, 149–53. Cawley, Father Crockett of the Grand Ronde, story 20.

21 Michelle, *Just a Memorandum*, 9.

Creek on November 29, 1854, which Napesa signed as their First Chief.[22]

After the people were relocated, Napesa was listed on the GRIC for 1856 as chief of the Umpqua band of Umpqua with a total of 228 people depending upon his leadership. On the 1857 GRIC, Napesa was listed as chief of 206 Umpqua.

In June 1860, when Father Croquet and the Rev. Mesplie visited Grand Ronde for the first time, they found only a small number of Indians as most of them had gone fishing, but Father Croquet wrote that Louis Nepesa was totally devoted to them and opened his home to regroup those who were still around.

By **Lizette Klickitat**, Napesa had at least eight children of whom only two daughters, Mary Ann Nipissing and LaRose Nipissing, survived. When the manual labor school was organized at Grand Ronde, both Mary Ann and LaRose attended for a few weeks in 1863.[23]

In 1871, Napesa spoke in a council meeting with Commissioner Brunot, Superintendent Meacham, and others. All of his words were good, but this part of his speech in particular deserves quoting:

> Some time ago the Indians had flat heads. The whites said it was bad, and they quit. The superintendent before, got here at night and left in the morning; never said anything to us. We understand what Mr. Meacham tells us. You hear what has been said. You may take these words, or may be not. We sent our words east before, but they never went.
>
> Mr. Meacham promised us a mill. We have it. He said our land should be surveyed, and it has been done. We need a grist-mill. Everyone has not enough horses to plow deep. Some men have good horses, plow deep, and get good crops. You may think what we say is not true, but I think it is true. If we had a good superintendent we would be all right.[24]

On the reservation, Napesa was known as one of the best trackers around. In fact, he was so good that some people said he talked with the wild animals and they helped him.[25] Napesa sang his power songs in Clackamas, but rarely used Clackamas in routine communication. His power was earth or something to do with earth. **Victoria Wishikin** (Kinishi) recorded one of his songs for Melville

---

22 Kappler, *Treaty with the Umpqua and Kalapuya, 1855*. State of Oregon, County of Lincoln, Affidavit, March 1, 1952: Indian name was given as "Napesa" by Martha Johnson who knew him. Cawley, Indian Journal, 22: gives his Indian name as Settesin. Jacobs, Elizabeth, Field Notebook 105, Coos–U. Coquille, 1, 127: Cetsən was an Umpqua term for a rich man who was considered particularly brave and had a strong spirit power.

23 *Annual Report Commissioner of Indian Affairs*, 1863, 84–85.

24 *Annual Report Commissioner of Indian Affairs*, 1871, Minutes of a Council with Grand Ronde Indians at their Reservation, Oregon, by Commissioner Felix R. Brunot, September 14, 1871, 149–53.

25 Cawley, *Indian Journal*, 20.

Jacobs in 1929.[26]

Rev. Summers had to call upon Napesa's tracking abilities on one occasion in August 1874. Summers and a party of several people including two ladies were out for a drive. While eating lunch, they turned out their horses but when they went to get them, the horses were nowhere to be found. After much effort, the party eventually ran into the Indian agent who escorted them back to Grand Ronde where they met with Napesa.[27]

Napesa set his fee at six dollars, but the missionaries said they were glad to get him as Napesa was getting old and did not go into the woods as he had before. He found their horses deep in the mountains several miles from the road. The moment the horses saw him, they came straight to his side.[28]

In 1877, after the sixth annual session of the Grand Ronde Indian Legislature was convened, the assembly was organized with the election of Chief Napesa as president and his son-in-law, **Frank Quenel,** as court clerk.

Chief Napesa's Indian court passed a number of noteworthy provisions of law on the reservation. They set up a form of credit through a reservation treasury, gave the United States Circuit Court jurisdiction over murder cases, established an appeal process, and added a provision for the court to hear divorce cases. Finally, the court divided the reservation into three districts, with each district or precinct having three elected representatives.

On November 4, 1878, the seventh annual Indian legislature resumed with the election of Napesa, **Peter Checkaon** (Chikhyan), and **Jacob Wheeler** (Shwa) as the tribal representatives for the west precinct. Napesa and **Dave Yachkawa** were appointed court administrators for that year.[29]

Rev. Summers wrote in his *Indian Journal* that Napesa had two wives at Grand Ronde. While this relationship is not mentioned elsewhere, a woman named Polly Nachan was listed on each GRIC from 1872 through 1888 as living with Napesa and Lizette. After Napesa's death in 1888, Lizette and **Polly Nachan** (Nachem) were listed as widows living together.

Napoleon, Paul (1841c–66), Umpqua[30]	Native Name: Unknown to author
Alias: None known to author	Allotment: None known to author
Mother: Unknown to author	Father: Unknown to author

---

26 Jacobs, Field Notebook 51, *Music and Ethnology*, 27: V. H. sang a song that belonged to "Mrs. Quenelle's father" in reference to Napesa's daughter, LaRose who married Frank Quenel. Victoria Wishikin-Howard did not know his tribe, but said his wife was Klickitat.

27 Ibid.

28 Ibid.

29 National Archives, Seattle, Grand Ronde/Siletz, Land and Enrollment Program records, Field Notes and Land Survey 1875–1898, Land Description Book 1878, Box 115; Grand Ronde Justice Court.

30 Munnick and Beckham, *Catholic Church Records—Grand Ronde*, Register I, p. 45, B-26.

Neal, Flora (1888–1911), Paiute wife of Mary's River Kalapuya husband[31]	Native Name: Unknown to author
Alias: None known to author	Allotment: None known to author
Mother: Polly Dufur, Paiute	Father: William Neal

Flora's mother was Polly Dufur, a Paiute from the Warm Springs Agency. Her uncle, Edmund Dufur (To-na) and her first cousin, Theresa Dufur (Pus-la), lived on that reservation[32]

Flora's father was William Neal, an American from Missouri with red curly hair and a beard.[33] He married her mother according to Indian custom when her mother's family was camped near Albany, Oregon. For the first nine years of their marriage, her parents were apparently childless, but finally, on June 30, 1888, Flora was born. A second daughter arrived a few years later, but their mother's health declined with the birth of the new baby and William found himself caring for an ailing wife, a toddler, and a baby who was also seriously ill.

After Polly's death, William rode not to Polly's relatives at Warm Springs but to the Indian Reservation at Grand Ronde. If he had originally planned to take an Indian wife back to his Albany home, that plan must have changed as he talked marriage terms with **Mary Winchester,** widow of the Umpqua Chief, **Winchester Jo.**

When William met Mary, she was living on the allotment that had been issued to her and Winchester Jo and expecting to receive the long promised patent on it at any time.

She may have been pushing forty, but by all accounts, she was still operating the family farm quite successfully. She not only had sixty acres of the farm cultivated in wheat, oats, and potatoes, but owned a herd of over 220 sheep, thirty-one head of cattle, seventeen hogs, and three horses.

If William did ask her to live with him in Albany, Mary would not leave the home she had built at Grand Ronde and the graves of her family. William agreed to live with her at Grand Ronde and on July 2, 1890, they were married at Dallas, Oregon.[34]

After their wedding, William went to Albany to get his children. He returned to the Grand Ronde Reservation with the children ten days later, July 12. Critically ill, the baby only lived a short time, but Flora survived.[35]

By this time, there were 361 Indian people living at Grand Ronde. Of these,

31 O. Applegate, Testimony of William Neal.
32 National Archives, Washington, DC, 1900 Warm Springs Indian Census gave roll 86, Edmund Dufer, a forty-one-year-old widower, with To-na as his Indian name. Roll 87, Theresa, his five-year-old daughter, was listed with the Indian name of Pus-la.
33 CTGR, Interview with Adeline Menard, 1989.
34 Oregon State Archives, Salem, Oregon, 1909, Polk County, Estate File Mary Neal.
35 O. Applegate, Testimony of William Neal and Lucy Tom-Neal. July 1895, GRIC listed Mary Neal, wife, with daughter Flora, age ten.

the agent estimated 300 could use English well enough for ordinary communication, and felt that all of them more or less understood the English language. The agent wrote his superiors that the people were expressing concerns because there was no word regarding their patents and a great number of the surrounding whites were taking pleasure in telling them that they would never be given land.

The fact that the language in the treaties had reserved Grand Ronde as a "temporary" reserve had plagued the Indian people since the 1870s.[36] For seventeen years they lived in fear that the government would take from them the last place they could call home. Finally on April 29, 1891, a number of allotments were approved among them a forty-acre allotment for Mary Winchester-Neal.

Some nine years earlier, the Secretary of the Interior had published Indian Office Regulations mandating the Christian-only/English-only education of Indian children on reservations. Following this mandate, William and Mary placed Flora in the reservation boarding school just before her fifth birthday in 1893. At that time, parents were only allowed to take their children home once a month, from Friday evening until Monday morning.

When Mary died on April 30, 1897, William contacted Father Croquet, who performed the sacraments. After the funeral, she was buried next to Winchester Jo in the Grand Ronde Cemetery.[37]

Despite the fact that her father was still alive, Flora Neal was listed as an orphan on the GRIC that year. Mary's death no doubt also changed William's status on the reservation and created concerns regarding his inheritance of Mary's allotment.

Even though he had worked the farm for years, the patent was in her name. The legality of some of the Indian marriages was being questioned and he was a white man without ties to the Grand Ronde Indian community. For this reason alone, he may have decided to marry another woman from one of the Grand Ronde treaty tribes.[38]

Nine months after Mary's death, on December 18, 1897, William Neal entered into another marriage agreement. This time, he married a Rogue River woman, **Lucy Johnson,** former wife of **Lawney Tom** (Pootpam). The marriage was performed in Sheridan, Oregon.

Lucy's first marriage to Lawney Tom had not fared well. Some of their unhappiness may have had something to do with the death of their son, Martin.[39]

---

36 Cawley, *Indian Journal*, 89: Rev. Summers documents the Indians' concern about the possibility of being moved from their homes during the 1877 Fourth of July celebration held at Grand Ronde.

37 Munnick and Beckham, *Catholic Church Records—Grand Ronde*, Register II, p. 109, S-3 gives DOD as April 30, 1897. Oregon State Archives, Salem, Oregon, 1909, Polk County, Estate File, Mary Neal lists her DOD as May 1, 1896.

38 Oregon State Archives, Salem, Oregon, 1909, Polk County, Estate File, Mary Neal: William did not legally acquire Mary's allotment until 1909.

39 Michelle, *Just a Memorandum*, 3: Mary Ann said they also had a daughter, Ivey, and

Whatever their problems, Lawney's relationship with the recently widowed Marcelline Sulkey certainly did not help the situation. After moving in with Lawney's father, **Shasta Tom** and his wives, **Kitty** (Acattycon) and **Mary Ann Tom,** for about a year, Lawney abandoned Lucy completely in favor of **Marcelline Riggs.**

It is easier to understand William Neal's reasons for marrying Lucy than it is to understand any benefit Lucy may have received from the arrangement; by all accounts, they never lived together. William continued to live on Mary Winchester's allotment probably to preserve any inherited rights to it, and Lucy lived on hers.

A few months after William and Lucy were married, Superintendent and Special Disbursing Agent Andrew Kershaw decided to allow the children at the boarding school to visit their homes only one day a month, going home in the morning and returning that same evening. For the next few years William saw even less of Flora.

Since the Catholic Church had assumed a fulltime parenting role in her life, Flora did not experience the puberty ceremony that in former days had been customary for young Indian girls. Rather, shortly after her twelfth birthday on July 1, 1900, she received the essential rite of Confirmation where the forehead of the baptized is anointed with sacred chrism, together with the laying on of the minister's hand and the words *Accipe signaculum doni Spiritus Sancti,* or in English, Be sealed with the Gift of the Holy Spirit.

On the GRIC for 1903, the eighteen-year-old Flora Neal was listed as a step-daughter residing with Lucy Neal, a married woman.

A few months later, Flora married **Frank Menard,** who was one of fourteen children born to **Peter Menard** and Elizabeth Shangaretta.[40] His family lived just north of the agency.

Flora and Frank had their first child, a little girl, on October 4, 1905. They named her Adeline Elvina. Their second daughter, Bertha, was born January 20, 1908.

Like Flora, Frank was Catholic and the church was a central part of their lives.[41] After Father Croquet's retirement in 1898, a new priest, Father Felix Bucher, transferred from Saint Mary's Parish in Siletz to Saint Michael's Parish in Grand Ronde early in 1907. Father Felix became Flora and Frank's family priest at that time.

---

that Martin died.

40 O. Applegate, Testimony of William Neal.

41 Munnick and Beckham, *Catholic Church Records — Grand Ronde,* Register II, p. 103, C-14: November 3, 1895, Francis Menard received Confirmation from the Most Reverend Archbishop William Gross.

Frank Menard (1881–1911). **Flora Neal-Menard (1888–1911).**

It is difficult to say exactly when Flora learned that Frank had contacted tuberculosis or how long he had it before he became incapacitated. Records show he was still working for the Grand Ronde agency on December 31, 1908.

The only known treatment for the disease at that time was to attempt a natural cure and prevent its spread by moving the patient into a quiet environment, isolated from the community, where the air was pure and freely circulating.

Their daughter, Adeline, only six years old at the time, remembers the hospital tent outside the door of their house where her mother nursed her father until his death on July 12, 1911, and later stayed after contracting the disease while caring for her husband.

One night, the need to see her mother overwhelmed little Adeline, who slipped out of bed and sneaked into the tent. Flora let Adeline lay beside her for a while before sending her back to her own bed. Running from the tent to the house that night, Adeline recalled seeing "saints marching crossing the sky" and "all the people following them."[42]

Years later, Adeline felt that her mother, grieving over the death of her husband, simply died of "a broken heart," but Father Felix remembered Flora's death

---

42 Personal communication between Adeline Menard's son, Kenneth Haller and her grandson, Wilbur West, August 21, 2010.

in vivid detail.[43]

Having been called to Flora's bedside to perform the last rites, he later wrote in his journal how in the last hours she had asked her father, William Neal, to set three plates; one for himself, one for Father Felix, one for her. However, when Flora tried to eat, the priest wrote that she was so weak she could hardly hold the teaspoon and had to go back to bed.[44]

It was at this point that Father Felix witnessed what he later called her "holy death."

He described how Flora sat up "appearing strong and agile" and "was transformed at once in body and dress." He said her face, "before so thin and emaciated, appeared round and expressing beauty," a beauty that made Father Felix think how "vain the efforts of human beings to enhance appearance by rouge and otherwise." As he watched, "her breasts were encased in elegant chamois with a row of white buttons" and her dark eyes turned a sky blue.[45]

Although Father Felix went to her side, she did not notice him. When Father Felix asked Flora's father if he saw what was happening to her, William Neal nodded.[46]

The whole scene only lasted about five minutes, then changed to normal with Flora regaining consciousness. Perhaps thirty minutes later, she died.[47]

Father Felix wrote that throughout it all, Flora's stepmother, Lucy Johnson, "did not conduce for peace of mind, but continued to stir up antagonism against her."[48] Still, it was Lucy who adopted Flora and Frank's daughters, Adeline and Bertha, and it was she who raised them after their grandfather died on February 6, 1917.

Neal, Mary (1840c) Rogue River/ Shasta	Native Name: Unknown to author
Alias: None known to author	Allotment: None known to author
Mother: Unknown to author	Father: Unknown to author

In 1872, Mary was listed as **James Scroggins**'s niece. In 1885, she was listed as a sister to **Ben Hardin.**

---

43 Personal communication with Adeline Menard's daughter, Marion Haller-Davidson, June 14, 1993.

44 Cletus Edward La Mere, *Father Felix Bucher, S.D.S., Missionary and Mystic of Grand Ronde, Oregon.* (Lafayette, OR, 1996): 80.

45 Ibid.

46 Ibid.

47 Ibid.

48 Ibid.

Newby, Nancy (1831c–1915c), Umpqua	Native Name: Unknown to author
Alias: Nancy of the Umpqua	Allotment 149
Mother: Unknown to author	Father: Unknown to author

Nancy was married to **Sam Newby** in 1875, but they were separated sometime before 1885. She received a twenty-acre allotment. **Joseph Jeff Day** had a ten-dollar claim against her estate in 1919.

Newby, Samuel (1845c–86c), Umpqua[49]	Native Name: Unknown to author
Alias: La Coque, Lecoq Sam Newby, William Sam Newby	Allotment: None known to author
Mother: Unknown to author	Father: Unknown to author

In 1872, La Coque Sam Newby was living with his wife, Molly. After Molly died in September 1874, he married Nancy of the Umpqua on March 28, 1875. **William Warren** and **Clara Lawrence** witnessed the ceremony.[50]

He was baptized as William Sam Newby on May 30, 1875.[51] By 1885, he was living with his wife, Susan, an aunt, Mollie Ann, and sister, Susan King. His former Umpqua wife, Nancy, was no longer living with him.

In 1886, "Mrs. Nuby," a widow, was listed with her daughter, Nellie. Sam had just died March 2, 1886. His widow was the same woman known as Lucy, former wife of **Cascade Frank Johnson. Nellie Frank** was Sam's stepdaughter.[52]

Nichols, Sally, Umpqua	Native Name: Unknown to author
Alias: None known to author	Allotment: None known to author
Mother: Unknown to author	Father: Unknown to author

In 1872, Sally Nichols was living with **Winchester Jo**'s family.

Norwest, Alexander (1875–1971), Rogue River, Iroquois, Walla Walla	Native Name: Unknown to author
Alias: None known to author	Allotment 142
Mother: Alice Wilder, Rogue River[53]	Father: Frank Norwest, Iroquois, Walla Walla, adopted Santiam band of Kalapuya

---

49 1872 GRIC: "La Coque." Gatschet, 1877c, p. 366: under Umpqua as "Lecoq Sam Newby."

50 Munnick and Beckham, *Catholic Church Records—Grand Ronde*, Register I, p. 92, M-3.

51 Ibid., Register I, p. 93, M-3, p. 94, B-18.

52 Michelle, *Just a Memorandum*, 3-4.

53 *Annual Report Commissioner of Indian Affairs*, 1863, 84–85.

Norwest, Frank (1847c–1940), adopted Santiam band of Kalapuya, Iroquois, Walla Walla[54]	Native Name: Unknown to author
Alias: None known to author	Allotment 141
Mother: Judith Walla Walla	Father: Jean Baptiste Tyikwarhi /Tyik-war-hi/, Iroquois[55]

Frank Norwest in 1935 with his favorite horse. Photo from Joel V. Berreman Collection. Courtesy of the Confederated Tribes of the Grand Ronde Community of Oregon.

54 1888 GRIC: listed his tribe as the Santiam band of Kalapuya. Michelle, *Just a Memorandum,* 1: Mary Ann wrote "the Norwest family" was adopted by the Grand Ronde Tribes.
55 Hudson's Bay Company Archives, Provincial Archives of Manitoba, Winnipeg, Biography, Jean Baptiste Tyequariche.

Frank Norwest was the youngest son of Jean Baptiste Tyikwarhi and Judith Walla Walla. Years earlier, his father took the name "Northwesterner" in tribute to his long association with the North West Fur Company; the name was gradually anglicized to Norwest.

Frank Norwest came to Grand Ronde as a very young man in his teens. He probably spoke a number of native languages, but is known to have used French, English, and Chinook Jargon.[56] There was no boarding school at Grand Ronde when he arrived, but the agent made Frank attend the Grand Ronde day school.[57]

At school, he met **Alice Wilder.** After her father gave his consent, Frank and Alice were married January 22, 1868 by Father Croquet in the Catholic Church.[58] By Alice, Frank had a number of children: Mary (1868–71c), Odeale (1869), Josephette (1872), Susette (1872), Charles (1874), Alexander (1877), Clarissa (1879), Marianne or Melvanie (1881), and Catherine (1884).[59]

Lena Norwest (center), daughter of Frank Norwest and Spanish Mary. Courtesy of Joann White-Colton and Bud White, grandchildren of Clara Robinson-Riggs.

---

56 Zenk, *Chinook Jargon*, 279.
57 Michelle, *Just a Memorandum*, 9.
58 Ibid.
59 Munnick and Beckham, *Catholic Church Records—Grand Ronde*, Register I, p. 52, M-1, p. 56, B-67, S-4, p. 77, B-50, p. 80, S-4, p. 91, B-36, p. 100, B-31, p. 112, B-10, p. 120, B-2, p. 126, S-13, p. 127, B-2, p. 130, S-6.

Frank was a representative of the west precinct at the eighth annual session of the Grand Ronde Legislature on November 4, 1879. After the assembly convened, he was elected court clerk under the president, **Peter Selkya.**[60]

Four years later, in 1883, the Grand Ronde Indian Court heard a paternity suit against Frank. The court found him to be the father of Anna Amos' child, Felineze, and required him to pay child support.[61] In 1885, Frank Norwest was listed with his wife, Rachel, and his minor children: Minnie, Jennie, Jolannie, Louis, and Henry. On September 5, 1887, Frank married Spanish Mary Smith. By **Spanish Mary,** he had Clara (1888), Lena (1892), Leo (1894), and Alphas (1900).[62]

In 1888, they had a house and barn on forty fenced acres. In addition to producing 200 bushels of wheat, sixty bushels of potatoes, and eight tons of hay that year, Frank had five head of cattle, five horses, ten hogs, and a dozen chickens in addition to his plow, harrow, wagon, and a hack.

Frank received a 220-acre allotment. Frank and Alice's son, Alexander and their daughter, Melvanie (1881–1902), also received eighty acres each.[63]

Norwest, Mary (1832c), adopted Santiam band of Kalapuya, Iroquois, Walla Walla[64]	Native Name: Unknown to author
Alias: Marie Anne Tahikwarihi, Mary Andrew, Mary Ann Arquette, Arcouet	Allotment: None known to author
Mother: Judith Walla Walla	Father: Jean Baptiste Tyikwarhi Norwest[65]

Mary was a full sister to **Frank** and **Thomas Norwest.** She married Amable Abraham Arquette, the son of Amable Arquette and Marguerite Chinook, on July 17, 1848. Their ceremony was held in the presence of many friends and relatives including such noteworthy Hudson's Bay men as Alexis Aubichion and Michel Laframboise.[66]

Like her father, Mary's father-in-law, Amable Arquette, was an employee of the Hudson's Bay Company. He entered service April 23, 1825, as a mason and continued in this capacity for a number of years. After 1833, he appears in the

---

60 National Archives, Seattle, Grand Ronde/Siletz, Land and Enrollment Program records, Field Notes and Land Survey 1875–1898, Land Description Book 1878, Box #115; Grand Ronde Justice Court.

61 O. Applegate, Testimony of Captain Frank Quenel.

62 Munnick and Beckham, *Catholic Church Records—Grand Ronde,* Register II, p. 33, M-4, p. 43, B-30, p. 50, S-24, p. 52, S-8, p. 59, B-4, p. 82, B-32, p. 96, B-25, p. 122, B-5.

63 *Heirs of Deceased Indians,* Allotment Records 141, 142, 143.

64 Michelle, *Just a Memorandum,* 1: Mary Ann wrote "the Norwest family" was adopted by the Grand Ronde Tribes.

65 Hudson's Bay Company Archives, Provincial Archives of Manitoba, Winnipeg, Biography, Jean Baptiste Tyequariche.

66 Munnick and Warner, *Catholic Church Records—St. Paul,* 10.

records as a trapper selling furs to the Company. In 1834, it was noted that he "re-built [the] powder magazine" at Fort Vancouver. From 1835 through 1842, he was listed as one of the Willamette River Valley settlers and as a farmer at St. Paul.[67]

By 1872, Mary Norwest was listed under the Santiam band of Kalapuya as "Mary Andrew" with her son, Hyacinthe Wallace Arquette (1862c). She had at least four other children: Francois Napoleon (1855c), Amable (1857c–60), John Ar-quette, and **Peter Arquette.**

Genevieve St. Martin-Belleque was godmother to Mary's oldest son, Pierre. Her son, Francois Napoleon, was born in Butterville. Francois' godparents were Baptiste and Louise Goyet. Mary's son, Amable, was also born when the family lived at Butterville. His godparents were **Charlie Petite** and Anne Russie. Mary's sons, John and Hyacinthe Arquette, were baptisted at St. Louis.[68]

Although not listed on the 1872 GRIC, her son, Francois Napoleon, was at Grand Ronde in 1876 and died there in 1883.[69]

Norwest, Melvanie (1882–1901), Rogue River, Iroquois, Walla Walla	Native Name: Unknown to author
Alias: Marianne Malvina Norwest	Allotment 143
Mother: Alice Wilder, Rogue River[70]	Father: Frank Norwest, Iroquois, Walla Walla, adopted Santiam band of Kalapuya

A fee patent was issued on April 4, 1921, to Melvanie Norwest's heir, **Frank B. Norwest,** for an eighty-acre allotment.

Norwest, Thomas (1831c–88), adopted Luckiamute band of Kalapuya, Iroquois, Walla Walla	Native Name: Unknown to author
Alias: Thomas Baptiste Tahekwarihi, Tyequariche, Ottawa, Tommy Norwest[71]	Allotment: None known to author
Mother: Judith Walla Walla	Father: Jean Baptiste Tyikwarhi, Iroquois[72]

In 1839, Thomas Norwest was about eight when his family camped with a

---

67 Hudson's Bay Company Archives, Provincial Archives of Manitoba, Winnipeg, Biography, Jean Baptiste Tyequariche.

68 Munnick and Warner, *Catholic Church Records—St. Paul*, A-2.

69 Gatschet, *Texts, Sentences and Vocables*, 374: under halfbreeds as "Napoleon Arcouet."

70 *Annual Report Commissioner of Indian Affairs*, 1863, 84–85.

71 Application made by Thomas Norwest for Indian War Pension, in 1897. Munnick and Warner, *Catholic Church Records—St. Paul*, A-72.

72 Hudson's Bay Company Archives, Provincial Archives of Manitoba, Winnipeg, Biography, Jean Baptiste Tyequariche.

Hudson's Bay Company caravan near the newly built Catholic Church at St. Paul. Preparing for a great wedding celebration, the scene was a panorama of gaiety as each man of the party, from James Douglas, acting as Fort Vancouver's chief factor, down to the last trapper, rode in with their Indian wives and children.

Riding with Dr. John McLoughlin's Ojibway wife, Margaret Wadin, was her stepson, Joseph McLoughlin, her son, Thomas McKay, and her son-in-law, William Glen Rae.

Joseph McLoughlin was the natural son of an Iroquois woman from eastern Canada and Dr. John McLoughlin. After he came to Oregon County to join his father, Joseph became employed with the Hudson Bay's Company and was famous for his horsemanship. He died shortly after this celebration from a fall over a cliff in the Umpqua region.

The dark and powerfully built Thomas McKay walked with a limp as a result of a childhood accident, but some said he could shoot off a duck's head at 120 yards. At a hundred paces, he could drive a dozen balls through a Spanish dollar. He often bragged that he always shoot a bear in the mouth to save the skin. A favorite storyteller among the fur traders, Thomas McKay began all the tales of his adventures with "It rained and rained and it blew and blew... and my God how it did snow."

By this time, William Glen Rae had been married to Joseph McLoughlin's half sister, Eloise, almost a year. He would become Chief Factor at Yerba Buena in 1842 and commit suicide in 1844.

Also accompanying the royal party was Company officers John McLeod, Dr. Tolmie, and George T. Allen. Behind them rode the well known brigade leader, Michel LaFramboise, now in his fifties, with his bride-to-be, Emelie Picard, his soon to be father-in-law, Andre Picard, and Josephte, his ten-year-old daughter by Emelie.

Further along in the caravan, riding with their wives and children, was a group of Iroquois: Louis Shaegoskatsta, Thomas Tawakon, **Louis Napesa**'s sister, Mary Ann Nipissing, and Jean Baptiste Tyikwarhi.

Young Thomas Norwest rode beside his parents with his siblings: Catherine, Agnes, Lazare, Marie Anne and Cecile. Four out of the five Tyikwarhi children were ill and baptized "under conditions of death." The godmother of all five children was "Dame the widow LeBlanc."[73]

Dame LeBlanc was the widow of the Iroquois Louis LaBlanc, who was an apprentice of the Columbia District. Dr. John McLoughlin wrote that Louis LaBlanc was a good man with the axe and understood fishing.[74] After LaBlanc's epilepsy became problematic, John McLoughlin wrote John Rowand at Saskatchewan:

---

73 Munnick, *Catholic Church Records—Vancouver and Stellamaris Mission.*
74 Rich, *The Letters of John McLoughlin, 1825–1838*, Letter 33.

This will be handed to you by Louis LaBlanc who is sent across the mountains on account of his subject to fall into fits. I request you would have the goodness not to send him on any winter voyages in case of accident as he has been known to fall twice on the same day.[75]

In 1856, Thomas Norwest married Louise Assiniboine and took a claim near the Tsetes and Tawakons on the north side of the Yamhill River, one mile north of Dayton in a grove of brush. Thomas and Louise had a number of children including a son, **Thomas Norwest**.[76]

By 1885, Thomas Norwest was a widower living with his son, Thomas, and **Samson Wilder** on the Grand Ronde Reservation. He died of pneumonia January 2, 1888.[77]

Norwest, Thomas (1860c–1900), adopted Luckiamute band of Kalapuya Iroquois, Walla Walla, Assiniboine[78]	Native Name: Unknown to author
Alias: Tom Norwest, Jr.	Allotment 148
Mother: Louise Assiniboine, Assiniboine	Father: Thomas Norwest, Iroquois, Walla Walla

After his father died in 1888, Thomas Norwest was listed at Grand Ronde as thirty-five, single, and without assets. In October 1888, he married **Olive Voutrin**, who was Mary's River Kalapuya.[79]

Thomas Norwest received a 166.36-acre allotment. After his death, **Frank Norwest** petitioned for the sale of Thomas' real property as it had not been improved and was not cultivated. In listing Thomas Norwest's heirs, Frank wrote that Thomas Norwest's wife, Olive, was a "reputed wife whose place of residence was unknown." He listed Charlie Norwest on the Umatilla Reservation and Cecile Chantelle at Elk Creek in southern Oregon as Thomas Norwest's only heirs.[80]

Apparently, Olive had left the reservation to find work in Seattle, Washington. If she did not return, her mother, **Mary Ann Monada**, said she hoped to inherit the property.[81] The final court judgment on the estate was not found.

---

75 Ibid.

76 Munnick and Warner, *Catholic Church Records—St. Paul*, A-72.

77 Munnick and Beckham, *Catholic Church Records—Grand Ronde*, Register II, p. 48, M-6, p. 121, S-1.

78 1888 GRIC listed his tribe as Luckiamute band of Kalapuya. Michelle, *Just a Memorandum*, 1: "the Norwest family" was adopted by the Grand Ronde Tribes.

79 Munnick and Beckham, *Catholic Church Records—Grand Ronde*, Register II, p. 48, M-6, p. 121, S-1.

80 National Archives, Salem, Oregon, 1905, Polk County Estate, File 1362.

81 O. Applegate, Testimony of Mary Ann Voutrin.

Odall, Marysville Chief, Mary's River Kalapuya	Native Name: None known by author
Alias: None known by author	Allotment: None known by author
Mother: Unknown to author	Father: Unknown to author

In 1856, Chief Odall was sketched by Émile de Girardin (1802–81), a French journalist and politician visiting at Grand Ronde.[1]

Oneal, Alexander, Cow Creek band of Umpqua	Native Name: None known by author
Alias: None known by author	Allotment: None known by author
Mother: Unknown to author	Father: Unknown to author

In 1872, Alexander was living alone.

Oregon, Baptiste, Clackamas	Native Name: None known by author
Alias: None known by author	Allotment: None known by author
Mother: Unknown to author	Father: Unknown to author

In 1872, he was listed with his wife, Susan, and their adopted daughter, Nancy.

Orton, Jake (1868c–92c)	Native Name: Meka-Tseltsa /ME-ka tsel-tsa/*[2]
Alias: Coquille Jake Orten	Allotment: None known by author
Mother: Unknown to author	Father: John Orten, Shghastalas /SHGAS-ta-las/*[3]

---

1 The sketch, C114442, is available at the National Archive of Canada and can be viewed on the website of the Confederated Tribes of the Grand Ronde.

2 Jacobs, Field Notebook 33, *Chasta Costa etc., Santiam, Kalapuya*, 14. Jacobs, Elizabeth, Field Notebook 104, Coos–U. Coquille, 174: Jake Orton was a brother to Wolverton Orton and George Orton. Bensil Orton was Wolverton Orton's nephew. National Archives, Seattle, NRIA-S-11-276, PAC-08, bx 59, Mrs. Mollie Pierce-Orton, testimony from Hoxie Simmons: Wolverton Orton and Jake Orton were first cousins.

3 Ibid.: "cyatalas, John Orten (father), Chas Orten (brother), meka tseltas, Jake Orten' name."

Coquille Jake (Meka-Tseltsa) of the Siletz reservation married **Louisa Wallace** November 19, 1890, at Grand Ronde in the presence of Frank Mercier and his wife, **Mary Petite.**[4] Jake and Louisa were listed as husband and wife in 1891. A year later, he left Louisa. From Siletz, in 1928, he provided Shasta Costa language texts to Melville Jacobs.

Orton, Nancy (1847c–1902), Umpqua	Native Name: None known by author
Alias: None known by author	Allotment 151
Mother: Unknown to author	Unknown to author

In 1885, Nancy was living with **Thomas Orton.** They must have separated around 1886 as Tom was listed as single on the GRIC for that year. In 1888, Nancy was living alone on a farm of fifteen fenced acres with a house and barn. Other than a horse, she had no livestock and nothing in cultivation. She remained single for the rest of her life.

Nancy received a twenty-acre allotment that her heir, **Lincoln McCoy,** sold to Helen M. Miller.

Orton, Thomas (1839c–93), Umpqua	Native Name: None known by author
Alias: None known by author	Allotment 152
Mother: Mrs. Kellogg	Unknown to author

Tom was married to Mary on March 23, 1882, in the presence of **Isaac Stevens** and Sarah, **Henry Winslow**'s wife. Mary died March 11, 1883.[5]

In 1885, Tom was living with his wife, Nancy, his mother, Mrs. Kellogg, and his aunt, Sansousee. The following year, Tom was listed as a single man, alone and without assets. He married **Eliza Johnson** (Syilsha) in February 1888. **William Warren** and Josette Norwest were their witnesses.[6]

In 1888, Tom and Eliza had a barn on six acres with garden and one horse. Eliza was listed on the 1892 GRIC, but Tom was not listed after 1891.

Tom Orton received a 120-acre allotment that his wife, Eliza, inherited.

---

4   Munnick and Beckham, *Catholic Church Records—Grand Ronde,* Register II, p. 64, M-3
5   Ibid., Register I, p. 120, M-6, p. 123, S-3.
6   Ibid., Register II, p. 38, M-1.

P

Patch, Elizabeth (1805c–65), wife of Molalla husband	Native Name: None known by author
Alias: None known by author	Allotment: None known by author
Mother: Unknown to author	Father: Unknown to author

Elizabeth was the wife of Molalla James. She was baptized at Grand Ronde by Father Croquet May 29, 1865.[1]

Patch, Mary (1836c–76), Umpqua	Native Name: None known by author
Alias: None known by author	Allotment: None known by author
Mother: Unknown to author	Father: Unknown to author

Mary was listed under the Umpqua with her brother, **Sam Patch** in 1872. She became critically ill February 14 and died February 19, 1876.[2]

Patch, Samuel, Umpqua	Native Name: None known by author
Alias: Calapooia Sam	Allotment: None known by author
Mother: Unknown to author	Father: Unknown to author

Sam was an old-time doctor.[3] Phil Sheridan mentioned him in his personal memoirs. Sam was listed with his sister, **Mary Patch,** on the 1872 GRIC.

When Albert Gatschet visited the Grand Ronde Reservation in 1877, Sam Patch was still living there.[4]

Paul, Samuel (1790c–1870), Yamhill band of Kalapuya[5]	Native Name: None known by author
Alias: Old Man Sambo	Allotment: None known by author
Mother: Unknown to author	Father: Unknown to author

Pawley, Appolline (1842c–62), Umpqua[6]	Native Name: None known by author

1   Munnick and Beckham, *Catholic Church Records — Grand Ronde,* Register I, p. 38, B-30.
2   Ibid., Register I, p. 97, B-4, S-3.
3   Lampson, *Some Visitors from the Grand Ronde,* 20–30. Sheridan, *Personal Memoirs of P. H. Sheridan,* chapter VII.
4   Gatschet, *Texts, Sentences and Vocables,* 366: listed with the Umpqua.
5   Munnick and Beckham, Catholic *Church Records — Grand Ronde,* Register I, p. 64, B-44.
6   Ibid., Register II, p. 24, B-98, p. 25, S-5.

Alias: None known by author	Allotment: None known by author
Mother: Unknown to author	Father: Unknown to author

Being "dangerously ill," Appolline was baptized December 27, 1862. At around twenty years old, she died and was buried February 11, 1863.[7]

Penny, July (1828c–68), Rogue River/ Shasta	Native Name: None known by author
Alias: July Jacques	Allotment: None known by author
Mother: Unknown to author	Father: Unknown to author

July Penny was Rogue River Jacques' wife. She died at Grand Ronde in September of 1868.[8]

Pereau, Mother, Clackamas	Native Name: None known by author
Alias: Perrault	Allotment: None known by author
Mother: Unknown to author	Father: Unknown to author

In 1872, "Mother Pereau" or Perrault was listed under the Clackamas as Louis Tole's aunt. Pereau is another spelling for "Perrault."

Jean Baptiste Perrault came from Riviere du Loup as a boatman for the Hudson's Bay Company. He settled on French Prairie with a Chinook wife. His widow, a woman called Angele Chehelis, married Sylvain Bourgeau in 1857.[9] Very likely, "Mother Pereau" was related not only to Louis Tole but to one of Perrault's wives.

Pete, Ben (1820c), Mary's River band of Kalapuya	Native Name: Lamptumpif /LAMP-tum-bif/ (lámptumpif) ["spanks-his-ass"]*[10]
Alias: Old Ben, Blind Ben	Allotment: None known by author
Mother: Unknown to author	Father: Unknown to author

At one time, Ben Pete (Lamptumpif) encountered a great grizzly that apparently left scars on a certain part of Ben's anatomy. From that day forward, the people called him Lamptumpif.[11] In 1885, Ben was listed with his children,

---

7   Ibid., Register I, p. 23, B-98, p. 24, S-5.
8   Ibid., p. 55, B-60, S-12.
9   Munnick and Warner, *Catholic Church Records — St Paul*, A-76.
10 Gatschet, *Texts, Sentences and Vocables*, 368, 370.
11 Personal communication with Henry Zenk, August 9, 2000, information copied by Henry Zenk from Santiam slip files, Jacobs (1928-36): Lamptumpif— spank-his-ass (i.e., buttocks)—was the name of Blind Ben, who was raised near Marysville. He was torn by a grizzly.

Henry and Mary Pete. They were living with Ben's brother, **Muddy Tom Churchill** (Kaltas Lipom), and Muddy Tom's wife, Betty.

In 1886, Ben was listed as blind and still living with his brother. His children, Henry and Mary Pete, were not listed on any GRIC after 1885. Ben was not listed after 1888.

Peter, Santiam	Native Name: None known by author
Alias: None known by author	Allotment: None known by author
Mother: Unknown to author	Father: Unknown to author

On January 29, 1864, it was snowing when three soldiers, including Corporal Royal Bensell, started out to arrest Santiam Pete for some unspecified offense. It was just getting light when they aroused him from his sleep. According to Bensell, Santiam Pete was very indignant that they arrested him. He pointed out several others who he called equally guilty of the crime, but Bensell felt Santiam Pete just wanted company in jail.[12]

Santiam Peter's wife, Lucy (1832c), was baptized in danger of death on January 15, 1872. Later that year, on August 18, Frank Henry was baptized as Santiam Pete's adopted son.[13]

Petite, Charlie (1837c–67c), adopted Tumwater band of Chinook, Chinook, Iroquois, French Canadian[14]	Native Name: None known by author
Alias: None known by author	Allotment: None known by author
Mother: Susanne Tawakon, Iroquois, Chinook	Father: Amable Petit, French Canadian

Charlie Petite was the son of Amable Petit (1797c–1867). Amable was a middleman in the service of the Hudson Bay's Company until he retired in 1842. Rev. Beaver first married him and Charlie's mother, Susanne Tawakon, on March 27, 1837. Then Amable Petit had a Catholic priest remarry them in 1838. Charles Tsete, an Iroquois with the Hudson Bay's Company, was Charles Petite's godfather.[15]

Charlie Petite's grandfather on his mother's side was Thomas Tawakon, an Iroquois boute, trapper, and steersman, first with the Northwest Company and

---

12 Barth, *All Quiet on the Yamhill*, 121.
13 Munnick and Beckham, *Catholic Church Records — Grand Ronde*, Register I, p. 71, B-1, p. 76, B-46, p. 46, B-95.
14 O. Applegate, Testimony of Captain Frank Quenel. O. Applegate, Testimony of Mary Petite-Mercier.
15 Munnick and Warner, *Catholic Church Records — St Paul*, 4.

then with the Hudson's Bay Company from 1815 to 1845.[16] His grandmother, on his mother's side was "a woman of the country, Chinook" and distantly related to the Clackamas tribes.

Charlie and **Sophie Gendron** were married July 25, 1860. His wife was the daughter of Joseph Gendron, a free fur trapper and a Clackamas woman called Polly of The Dalles. He and Sophie had a number of children: **Christine, Elizabeth, Mary, Henry,** Josephine (1870c–81), Louisa (1872c–82), and **Edward.**[17]

Charlie Petite was adopted by the Oregon City Tumwater and drew annuities under that treaty.[18]

Petite, Christine (1862c–97), Clackamas, Chinook, French Canadian, Iroquois[19]	Native Name: None known by author
Alias: None known by author	Allotment: None known by author
Mother: Sophie Gendron, French Canadian, Clackamas[20]	Father: Charlie Petite, French Canadian, Iroquois, Chinook, adopted Willamette Valley Tumwater band of Chinook

Christine Petite had a son, Charles, at Grand Ronde on February 19, 1881. Charles's sponsors were her brother, Henry and her sister, **Elizabeth Petite.** Three years later, on November 27, 1884, Christine married **William Hartless** in the presence of Frances Johnson and **Catherine Voutrin.**

On October 9, 1888, Christine had Martin Hartless. His godparents were **Frank Wheeler** and **Jennie Michel.** On June 25, 1893, she gave birth to Benedict Hartless. His godparents were John B. Servous Williamson and **Elizabeth Dowd.** On New Years day 1896, Michael Hartless was born. His godmother was **Mary Ann Monada.** Less than two months later, Michael died. Christine and William had their youngest son, Charlie Patrick, around 1902.

Petite, Edward (1876c–1957), Clackamas, Chinook, Iroquois, French Canadian[21]	Native Name: None known by author
Alias: Edwin Petite	Allotment 266
Mother: Sophie Gendron, French Canadian, Clackamas	Father: Charlie Petite, French Canadian, Iroquois, Chinook, adopted Willamette Valley Tumwater band of Chinook

---

16 Boute: a term for the skilled position of bowsman in a canoe or boat.
17 Munnick and Beckham, *Catholic Church Records—Grand Ronde*, Register I, p. 45, B-28, p. 53, B-11, p. 62, B-7, p. 73, B-13, p. 119, S-9, p. 120, S-2.
18 O. Applegate, Testimony of Captain Frank Quenel.
19 O. Applegate, Testimony of Captain Frank Quenel. O. Applegate, Testimony of Mary Petite-Mercier.
20 Jacobs, Field Notebook 56, *Texts and Ethnology*, 122.
21 Ibid.

In 1893, Edward worked as a blacksmith for the agency.[22] He married Anna Dowd in 1901. Edward received a 120-acre allotment at Grand Ronde.

Petite, Elizabeth (1864c–1908), French Canadian, Iroquois, Chinook, Clackamas[23]	Native Name: None known by author
Alias: Elizabeth Menard, Elizabeth McCoy	Allotment: None known by author
Mother: Sophie Gendron, French Canadian, Clackamas	Father: Charlie Petite, French Canadian, Iroquois, Chinook, adopted Willamette Valley Tumwater band of Chinook

Elizabeth's first husband was **John Menard.** They were married December 11, 1882, in the presence of **Sam Chantelle** and **Christine Petite.** After John, she married **Lincoln McCoy** in 1886.

By Lincoln McCoy, Elizabeth had Evelyn (1890c–1950), Sophie (1891), Stella (1993), Mary Rachel (1895), Gertrude (1897), Joseph, Margaret, and Vernon.[24]

Elizabeth Petite-McCoy died at Chemawa on January 15, 1908. She was buried January 17, 1908, at Grand Ronde.[25] Her oldest daughter, Evelyn, married Phillip Warren that same year.[26]

Petite, Henry (1868c–1933), Clackamas, Chinook, Iroquois, French Canadian	Native Name: None known by author
Alias: None known by author	Allotment 155
Mother: Sophie Gendron, French Canadian, Clackamas	Father: Charlie Petite, French Canadian, Iroquois, Chinook, adopted Willamette Tumwater band of Chinook

Originally from French Prairie, Henry could not only read and write, but he could speak English, Chinook Jargon, and a little French.[27]

He was living with the **James Winslow** family when he married Jane Leno (1868c–1922) on October 13, 1885. After the wedding, the young couple stayed with the Winslow family until they could find a home of their own.[28]

Henry and Jane had a number of children: Charles (1886c), Caroline (1889c),

---

22 *Records of Employees at Grand Ronde, 1884–1907.*

23 Ibid.

24 Munnick and Beckham, *Catholic Church Records—Grand Ronde,* Register I, p. 123, M-13, Register II, p. 72, M-8, See Pius Lincoln McKye.

25 St. Michael's Catholic Church records, 1908 Burials.

26 Ibid.

27 Zenk, *Chinook Jargon,* 279.

28 Michelle, *Just a Memorandum,* 8.

Edwin (1892c–1903), Ernest (1893–1952), James (1896–1963), Mary (1898c), Louis (1899c–1905), Ella (1900c–07), Rex (1901c–05), Henry Jr. (1904–05), John Paul (1906c) Florence (1907–11), Peter, and Anthony.[29]

Henry received an allotment of 181.68 acres.[30] He did not sign the Surplus Land Agreement in 1901.

Petite, Isabel (1879c), Umpqua, Chinook, Iroquois, French Canadian[31]	Native Name: None known by author
Alias: Isabel Sorenson	Allotment 157
Mother: Rosie Tim-Tim, Umpqua	Father: Peter Petite, French Canadian, Iroquois, Chinook

Petite, Mary (1864c–1932), Clackamas, Chinook, Iroquois, French Canadian	Native Name: None known by author
Alias: Mary Mercier	Allotment 127
Mother: Sophie Gendron, French Canadian, Clackamas	Father: Charlie Petite, French Canadian, Iroquois, Chinook, adopted Willamette Tumwater band of Chinook

Mary was the daughter of **Charlie Petite** and **Sophie Gendron.** She married Frank Mercier, a United States citizen, in the presence of **David Ambroise Leno** and his wife, Tilmer LaChance, on March 27, 1882. Frank was the nephew of the Belgian Cardinal Francis Mercier and Father Adrian Croquet.[32]

Frank had a land claim in Yamhill County about six miles from the reservation. He and Mary lived there for about six years. When he lost his property, he and Mary heard that land allotments were being made on the reservation. After Agent McClane told him Mary and three of their children were eligible, Frank moved the family back to the reservation.[33]

Frank and Mary had a number of children. Their son **Julius Adrian Mercier** married Gertrude Hudson, son **Arthur Mercier** married Mary Agnes Leno, and son Henry (1890c) married Mary Pearl Hudson. Their daughter, Josephine, married Jasper Boydson.[34]

Mary received a 260-acre allotment. On October 29, 1906, she was issued a fee

---

29 Munnick and Beckham, *Catholic Church Records—Grand Ronde,* Register II, p. 23, B-26, p. 37, S-17, p. 39, B-14, p. 48, S-20, p. 57, B-18, p. 75, B-2, p. 87, B-13, p. 107, B-14.

30 *Heirs of Deceased Indians,* Allotment Record 155.

31 Affidavit taken from Rosie Tim-Tim, by Charles E, Coe, Superintendent, Roseburg Agency, dated February 6, 1917.

32 Zenk, interview with Gertrude Mercier, 1979, Field Notes, Indigenous French, 3.

33 O. Applegate, Testimony of Francis Mercier. O. Applegate, Testimony of Mary Petite-Mercier.

34 Munnick and Beckham, *Catholic Church Records—Grand Ronde,* Register I, p. 121, M-7, p. 125, B-10, Register II, p. 29, B-17, p. 58, B-1, p. 71, B-19, p. 86, B-8, p. 102, B-14.

patent for the entire allotment.[35]

Petite, Mary Ann (1884–92), Umpqua, Chinook, Iroquois, French Canadian[36]	Native Name: None known by author
Alias: None known by author	Allotment 158
Mother: Rosie Tim-Tim, Umpqua	Father: Peter Petite, French Canadian, Iroquois, Chinook

After Mary Ann died, an eighty-acre allotment was issued to her heirs, Maude E. Willings, **Isabel Petite,** Basil Parr, and Irene Parr.

Petite, Peter (1845c–1902), Chinook, French Canadian, Iroquois, husband of an Umpqua woman[37]	Native Name: None known by author
Alias: None known by author	Allotment 156
Mother: Susanne Tawakon, Iroquois, Chinook	Father: Amable Petit, French Canadian

Peter was born in January 1845.[38] **Charlie Petite** was his older brother. Their mother died shortly after their father in November 1878.[39]

Peter married a woman named Mary Ann. By her, he had a son, Henry (1869c–99), who was also known as Henry Parr. Parr was the surname of his stepfather.[40]

After Henry grew into a young man, he and his half brother, Joseph Parr, were in trouble with the law on several occasions. In 1892 they were arrested and convicted of rioting. Shortly after they were released on this offense, they were arrested again. This time they were arrested for stealing a gelding and assault with a deadly weapon.[41]

On June 15, 1895, they pled guilty. Their attorney asked the court to consider the circumstances under which the shooting took place in deciding punishment. The boys received four years. Henry died in prison and left one surviving child by a woman named Louisa Perry.[42]

---

35 *Heirs of Deceased Indians,* Allotment Records 127.
36 Affidavit taken from Rosie Tim-Tim by Charles E. Coe, Superintendent, Roseburg Agency, February 6, 1917.
37 Ibid.
38 Munnick and Warner, *Catholic Church Records — St Paul,* 110.
39 Ibid., 118.
40 Affidavit taken from Rosie Tim-Tim by Charles E, Coe, Superintendent, Roseburg Agency, February 6, 1917.
41 Oregon State Archives, Salem, Oregon: Joe Parr, June 27, 1892, Umatilla File 2816, Joe Parr, April 25, 1896, Mult File 3655, Henry Parr, February 14, 1887, Umatilla File 1879, Henry Parr, June 27, 1892, Umatilla File 2815, Henry Parr, June 19, 1895, Umatilla File 3439.
42 Ibid.

After Mary Ann, Peter married an Umpqua woman named **Rosa Tim-Tim** (Elmermach). They farmed at Lookingglass, Oregon, for a few years before moving to Grand Ronde in 1883.[43] Shortly after they arrived, they had their daughters, Isabel and Helen, baptized. Their daughter Mary Ann was born at Grand Ronde in March 1885.[44]

Peter received a 280-acre allotment. In 1901, Peter Petite was one of sixty men who signed the Surplus Land Agreement.

In July 1902, Peter was committed to the Oregon State Hospital. A few months later, on September 24, he died of apoplexy.[45] Later, his body was returned to Grand Ronde for burial.[46]

After Peter's death, **Isabel Petite** and **Mary Ann Petite** inherited his allotment along with Basil Parr, Peter's grandson by Henry, and Irene Parr, Peter's great granddaughter.[47]

Pichet, Roc (1838c), French Canadian[48]	Native Name: None known by author
Alias: Roch Pichet	Allotment: None known by author
Mother: Marguerite Bercier, French Canadian	Father: Louis Pichett dit Dupre, French Canadian

Around 1835, Roc Pichet's family settled on a farm three miles southeast of St. Paul on Champoeg Creek where his father built a large two-story log house that became an inn for newly arriving families and travelers passing through the area.[49]

Roc Pichet's family came to Grand Ronde after the Dowd family had settled there. In 1888, the agent listed Roc and his wife, Victoria Despard, with their nine children, ranging in age from two to thirty years old, under the Cow Creek band of Umpqua. Their sole assets were two horses, one hack, and a harness. However, they were not listed on any GRIC after this year.

---

43 http://ftp.us-census.org/pub/usgenweb/census/or/douglas/1880, 1880 Mt. Scott Census.

44 Munnick and Beckham, *Catholic Church Records—Grand Ronde,* 127.

45 Oregon State Archives, Salem, Oregon, September 24, 1902, Death, State Hospital, Vol. 1 G: gives cause of death as apoplexy. It should be noted that, historically, the word "apoplexy" was used to describe any sudden death that began with a sudden loss of consciousness, especially one where the victim died within a matter of seconds after losing consciousness.

46 Affidavit taken from Rosie Tim-Tim-Russie, by Charles E, Coe, Superintendent, Roseburg Agency, February 6, 1917.

47 *Heirs of Deceased Indians,* Allotment Records 156, 157, 158.

48 Michelle, *Just a Memorandum,* 1: Roc Pichette was a "Frenchman and his wife was a breed."

49 McKay, *St. Paul, Oregon 1830–1890.*

Picketjoe, Peter (1808c–68), Rogue River[50]	Native Name: None known by author
Alias: None known by author	Allotment: None known by author
Mother: Unknown to author	Father: Unknown to author

Pickett, Frank (1834c–84), Rogue River[51]	Native Name: None known by author
Alias: Rogue River Frank	Allotment: None known by author
Mother: Unknown to author	Father: Unknown to author

In 1872, Frank was listed with his wife, Mary, and Mary's sister, Susan.

He married Eliza on September 1, 1878. Their witnesses were Frank Mercier and an Umpqua woman named Charlotte. He died August 17, 1884, and was buried the same day.[52]

Pierce, James (1841c–1911), Cow Creek band of Umpqua	Native Name: Clamarchnet /Cla-march-net/, Tomalchow /To-mal-chow/[53]
Alias: Whiskey Jim Pierce	Allotment 153
Mother: Unknown to author	Father: Unknown to author

James Pierce (Clamarchnet) was a prominent representative of the Indian court and served as an Indian judge for a number of years. Once, Rev. Summers found James dressing a deerskin and, in regard to his skills, Summers wrote,

> He is a good hunter, though he mourns over the fact that game is far less abundant in the mountains than formerly, in consequence of which he has every year less meat and fewer skins. One of these he has very tightly stretched on the ground and pegged down around the edge. To soften and smooth it he patiently rubs it, in this position; with the brain of the animal, using either his hands, or a convenient stone. Not only Indians, but white men, hold these native-dressed skins at a much higher value than those prepared in any other way, as they are said to remain always pliable, through all sorts of ill usage.[54]

---

50 Munnick and Beckham, *Catholic Church Records — Grand Ronde*, Register I, p. 55, B-61, S-13.

51 Gatschet, *Texts, Sentences and Vocables*, 366: listed with the Rogue River as "Frank Pickett."

52 Munnick and Beckham, *Catholic Church Records — Grand Ronde*, Register I, p. 109, B-20, M-11, p. 128, S-8.

53 1887 GRIC: listed Jim Pearce with the Indian name "Cla-march-net." Cawley, *Indian Journal*, 22: Whiskey Jim aka "To-mal-chow."

54 Cawley, *Indian Journal*, 30.

Inside the house, Rev. Summers found James Pierce's wife, whom he described as "quite fair, with well-shaped features, remarkably brilliant eyes and pleasant manners." Rev. Summers wrote that although Jim's wife, like many of the others, repeatedly denied having any antique heirlooms, he still went "prowling about" reportedly "under her smiling guidance" and soon discovered some dice of beavers' teeth, a rattle of deer toes, a necklace of deer toes, a tiny work basket, a tray, and a very large covered pannier.

To his request to see more native artifacts, she said,

> Once we had many things; and made many baskets and robes of fur; we had beautiful ornaments that we made for ourselves and our little ones; we had many children then, and wide hunting grounds; and all the mountains and all the streams were ours as well. But we are numerous no more, and the few of us who are yet alive know how to do very little that our mothers did. No one makes the olden basket now— no one!

James's wife, Mary, died April 9, 1878. In July of that year, James married another woman, also called Mary (1842c–91c), with **Bill Condon** and **Jenny Sansousee** as witnesses. It was very probably this Mary whom Rev. Summers spoke with in 1881 and from whom he acquired the heirlooms.[55]

After **David Holmes** (Faliper) resigned as Justice of the Peace for the Indian court on December 27, 1879, Jim Pierce took over the position January 3, 1880. He served in this capacity through 1882.[56]

Jim's aunt was **Julia Ann Johnson.** She was staying at his house from 1886 to 1895c. Susan (Intaternatta), the wife of **Coquille Charley** (Nagashta), was James's cousin. Susan and Coquille Charley lived with Jim from time to time. In 1888, the widow **Mary Ann Sansousee** was also living with Jim's family. March 3, 1892, Jim Pierce married Rogue River Molly.[57]

Rogue River Molly was from a Jacksonville band between Rogue River and Shasta called Mah-ah-dis-tite. She was related to the **John Smith, Reuben Long,** and "Mrs. Aiken from Logsden." At one time, she was the wife of Jake Orton. Coquille Thompson's wife took care of Molly for about eight months before she

---

55 Rev. Summers gave his collection of Indian heirlooms and artifacts to a friend, the Reverend S. C. Freer, for safekeeping. On September 6, 1900, Freer passed the collection on to the British Museum. His collection, with the exception of three pieces, has been stored in a British warehouse since the collection was accessioned in 1900. A note attached to one of the baskets in the Summers Collection stated the basket was purchased at Grand Ronde from Whiskey Jim's wife in 1881.

56 National Archives, Seattle, Grand Ronde/Siletz, Land and Enrollment Program records, Field Notes and Land Survey 1875–1898, Land Description Book 1878, Box 115; Grand Ronde Justice Court.

57 Munnick and Beckham, *Catholic Church Records—Grand Ronde*, Register II, p. 75, M-3. Michelle, *Just a Memorandum*, 4.

went to the state hospital where she died.[58]

Jim Pierce received a 160-acre allotment and was one of the men who did not sign the Surplus Land Agreement in 1901.[59]

Pisk, Martha Jane, Rogue River[60]	Native Name: None known by author
Alias: None known by author	Allotment: None known by author
Mother: Unknown to author	Father: Unknown to author

Martha Jane married Thomas Pisk at Grand Ronde on May 21, 1862. **Louis Michel Monada** and **Joseph Shangaretta** acted as their witnesses.[61]

Thomas Pisk was the son of Thomas Pisk Kipling, a Métis employed with the Hudson's Bay Company and a half brother to **Nancy Pisk**.[62]

By Thomas, Martha Jane had Thomas, Abraham, and Josephine. None of their children lived more than a few months. Martha Jane buried her husband, Thomas, in December 1864 and less than three months later she buried their last child, Josephine.[63]

Pisk, Nancy (1828c–98c), Lower Chinook, Red River Métis, wife of a part Mary's River Kalapuya husband	Native Name: None known by author
Alias: Nancy Shangaretta	Allotment: None known by author
Mother: Lower Chinook	Father: Thomas Pisk Kipling, Red River Métis

Nancy Pisk was the daughter of a Métis named Thomas Pisk Kipling and a lower Chinook woman.[64] Her father was a Hudson's Bay Company employee like

58 National Archives, Seattle, NRIA-S-11-276, PAC-08, bx 59, Mrs. Mollie Pierce-Orton, testimony of Hoxie Simmons taken April 24, 1940.

59 *Heirs of Deceased Indians*, Allotment Record 199: when Nancy Scroggins died March 31, 1902, she left all her estate including her allotment to Molly Pierce.

60 Munnick and Beckham, *Catholic Church Records—Grand Ronde*, Register I, p. 20, M-1.

61 Ibid.

62 Ibid., Register I, p. 36, S-42. McChesney, *The Rolls of Certain Indian Tribes*, statement 115, from Elizabeth Shangaretta-Menard: She stated that her mother was the daughter of Thomas Pisk and his first wife. The 1860 Astoria Census listed Thomas Pisk Kipling, age fifty-nine, with Gabrella Kipling (age thirty), Thomas Kipling (age twenty-one), Jack Kipling (age twenty), Margaret (age nineteen), Charles (age nineteen), Mary (age eighteen). The younger Thomas Pisk listed with Elizabeth's grandfather, Thomas Pisk Kipling, on the 1860 Census for Astoria was probably the same man who later married the Rogue River woman called Martha Jane at Grand Ronde Reservation.

63 Ibid., Register I, p. 23, B-92, p. 25, S-6, p. 27, B-31, p. 31, B-15, S-7, p. 37, B-6, S-1.

64 Thomas Pisk Kipling was one of the Métis who lived along the Assiniboine and Red Rivers. The Métis were the Cree, Ojibwa, Salteaux, and Menominee mixed-blood

Nancy Pisk (second from right) with her three adopted daughters.

his father and his father's father.

In 1846, Thomas Pisk Kipling was living with his family at Cape Disappointment where he had taken a 640-acre land claim adjoining Peter Skene Ogden's claim.[65] He and his daughter Nancy were still living at this place, according to descendants, when the treaty with the Chinook was signed in 1851. At that time, Thomas Pisk Kipling knew the Chinook in Washington Territory better than any other Hudson's Bay Company employee.[66]

Kipling's daughter, Nancy Pisk, married **Joseph Shangaretta** and moved to the Grand Ronde Reservation after the signing of the 1855 treaty with the Kalapuya. She and Joseph had three daughters: Elizabeth (1854c), Mary (1859), and Aloise (1863–64). Aloise died on the road to Salem when she was about eighteen

children of French Canadian, Scots, and English fur traders. McChesney, *The Rolls of Certain Indian Tribes*, statement 115, from Elizabeth [Shangaretta] Menard: "My maiden name was Elizabeth Sangaretta, and I am a lower Chinook descendant. My mother's name was Nancy Sangaretta who was a Lower Chinook descendant who died about 8 years ago, age 70 years, and who was a daughter of Pisk's first wife, a Lower Chinook Indian woman, who died years ago."

65 *Oregon Provincial Government Land Claims Records*, Vol. II, p. 87.

66 Names of the Parties Acquainted with the Indians in 1846, Hudson's Bay Company Archives, Providential Archives of Manitoba, Winnipeg, B. 223/2/4.fos. 159-246.

months old.[67] They also raised three adopted daughters: Elizabeth (1869c), Jenny (1868c), and Louisa (1873c).[68]

Pony, Susan (1818c-1911), Umpqua[69]	Unknown to author
Alias: None known by author	Allotment 159
Mother: Unknown to author	Unknown to author

According to **Richard Cook,** Susan Pony was related to him, **Eliza Day, Peter McCoy** (Inchaishi), and a woman he called Mrs. Tecumsia.[70] Dick said they all lived at Grand Ronde and were cousins.[71]

Susan Pony was listed as **Alexander Day's** aunt on the earliest census, but from 1887 to 1893 she was listed as a cousin. She lived with the family until Alexander died around 1893. Then from 1894 to 1896, Susan Pony was listed as a cousin living with Alexander's widow, Eliza, and his adopted son, **Joseph Jeff Day.**

Susan Pony received eighty acres of allotment land. Her heirs were: Eva Lesina and Andrew Picard. She was not on the GRIC after 1910.

Pratt, John (1847c–1909), Yamhill band of Kalapuya, Tualatin band of Kalapuya	Native Name: Gwaimit /GWA-mit/ (gwáymit),* Tsilais /TSE-kais/ (t'sə́k'ais)*[72]
Alias: Wapato John	Allotment 160
Mother: Yamhill Kalapuya	Father: Ichamulh /i-CHE-muhl/ (ichə́muɬ),* Tualatin band of Kalapuya

John Pratt (Gwaimit) and the Tualatin sub-chief, **James Shiliqua** (Shilikwa) were half brothers. Itcamut (Ichamulh) was their father but they had different mothers. John's mother was Yamhill Kalapuya.[73]

---

67 Munnick and Beckham, *Catholic Church Records—Grand Ronde,* Register I, p. 58, M-1, p. 5, B-22, p. 27, B-36, p. 37, S-43.

68 Adopted daughters, Elizabeth (1869c) and Louisa (1873c), may have been Elizabeth Tole-Harney-Blacketer (1870-1958) and Louise Tole-Sands (1872). On September 11, 1870, Elizabeth Shangaretta-Menard was recorded as a sponsor for Elizabeth Tote. In 1886, "Elizabeth" and "Louisa" were listed as daughters living with the Shangaretta family. Elizabeth Tole married George Harney on July 13, 1886, and Louisa Tole married Nicholas Sands on July 23, 1888. "Elizabeth" was not on the GRIC with Joseph and Nancy Shangaretta in 1887 and neither girl was listed with them in 1888.

69 National Archives, Salem, Oregon, 1907, Polk County Estate, File 1276.

70 On November 9, 1886, Father Croquet baptized a woman named Anna Tecumsa at Siletz, estimating her age at about eighty years.

71 Ibid.

72 Jacobs, Notebook 46, *Santiam Kalapuya Text,* 186. 1887 GRIC gave his Indian name as "Quemit."

73 Jacobs, Notebook 67, *Texts Ethnology Clackamas & Jargon,* 22 gives Victoria Howard's father's brother as, "itcamut," who had a son "cilikwa." Jacobs, Notebook 58, *Texts and Ethnology,* 122: "gwaí mit was L. Kenoyer's stepfather." Michelle, *Just a*

In 1876, John and **Peter Checkaon** (Chikhyan) represented the Wapato Lake band of Kalapuya at the fifth annual session of the Grand Ronde Indian Legislature. In 1879, John was elected to the eighth annual session of the Grand Ronde Legislature. This year, along with **Peter Kenoyer** (Kinai) and **Moses Allen** (Shkay-inch), he represented all the people living in the east precinct[74]

John married **Mary Wallace** (1859c–79c) in 1872, but he and Mary did not have children[75] After Mary Wallace died in 1879, John married his half brother, James Shiliqua's former wife, a Wasco woman called Harriet (1847c).[76] They had at least two sons, Charles (1883c) and John (1884c).[77]

By 1888, John and his family had a house and barn on forty fenced acres. In addition, they had five acres in oats, two acres in wheat, four horses, five hogs, and six dozen chickens.

In 1900, John was listed with a wife named Eliza. After she died, he married **Louis Kenoyer** (Pakhawatas)'s mother, **Nancy** (Tunishni).[78] He was still living with Nancy in 1906 when he finally received a fee patent on his 219.66-acre allotment.[79]

John died June 10, 1909. After his death, **John Wacheno** (Tsinwalh) took his team into Willamina where he bought John a burial shirt, necktie, and a silk handkerchief. He also bought a rough box coffin and dug John's grave.[80]

On the first day of July, all of John's personal property was sold to the public. Mary J. Hewitt bought two horses described as a seven-year-old bay called Cap and a three-year-old short filly for $110. **Lucinda Metzkar** bought John's cow for $15, a mowing machine for $15, and a bedstead for $2.50. **Eliza Johnson** (Khakhshni) bought a sewing machine for $2.50. **Frank Menard** bought John's wall tent and an eight-ounce duck for $4. There were no buyers for the cook stove valued

Memorandum, 6: "Jim Shellequa" his brother was John B[Pr]att. Gatschet, *Texts, Sentences and Vocables*, 370, gave Shiliqua as John Pratt's younger brother. Oregon State Archives, Salem, Oregon, 1909, Yamhill County, Estate John Pratt, File 1327, gave James Shiliqua, John Pratt, Bonapart, Antoine Metzkar, and Bill Wishikin all as brothers with a common father. Jacobs, Field Notebook 46, n.p. (approx. 161): John Pratt and Lame Jim Cilikwa were probably first cousins; they called each other brothers. John Pratt's Tualatin name was tsoklais (Mrs V. Howard called him gwainet). Pratt was Tualatin; possibly part Yamhill; he was crosseyed; Pratt later had cilikwa's Warmsprings woman.

74 National Archives, Seattle, Grand Ronde/Siletz Tribal Program Records Box 162, Agency & Tribal Council Records 1876–1951.

75 McChesney, *The Rolls of Certain Indian Tribes,* Testimony of Henry Wallace, 79. Jacobs, Notebook 58, *Texts and Ethnology*, 122.

76 Jacobs, Notebook 46, *Santiam Kalapuya Text,* n.p.

77 Michelle, *Just a Memorandum,* 6: John Pratt was Tualatin. His wife was Wasco. "Jim Shellequa" was his brother.

78 Jacobs, Notebook 46, *Santiam Kalapuya Text,* 161.

79 *Heirs to Deceased Indians,* Allotment Record 160. Jacobs, Notebook 46, *Santiam Kalapuya Text,* 161.

80 Oregon State Archives, Salem, Oregon, 1909, Yamhill County, Estate File 1327.

at $3, an old wagon without a bed valued at $1, a hack valued at $1.50, a hay rake valued at $1.50, or three old shotguns valued at $1.50. After failing to gain any offers on these last items, the administrator declared the property worthless.[81]

On the same day, **Peter Selkya**'s widow, Louise and **Amos Kilya,** testified in probate court as to John's surviving family members. Their testimony was given through John Wacheno, who acted as an interpreter.[82]

Old Kilya said that John Pratt was born near the Yamhill River and was a man by the time of the appearance of the first white men. He remembered John from the time John was a small boy attending the mission at Wapato Lake. He also knew John's father, who died near Grand Ronde.[83]

Both Kilya and Louisa Selkeah told the court that they had known the family of John Pratt for years. They said that John's brothers and sisters were **Callo Bonaparte** (Kalukh), **Nancy** (Shimkhin), **Antoine Metzkar (**Tamulch), **Bill Wishikin,** and **James Shiliqua** (Shilikwa). They said that they knew the father of all the brothers and that they had a common father. Their sister Nancy never married.[84] **Lucinda Metzkar,** the daughter of Antoine Metzkar, was one of three children born to him, but only Lucinda survived. **Victoria Wishikin** (Kinishi) was the only surviving child of Bill Wishikin.[85]

The court was aware that among Indian people cousins were often referred to as brothers and sisters. At Grand Ronde, Lucinda and Victoria were commonly known as sisters. Given the differences in terminology surrounding native family relationships, a search for additional heirs was widely made, but other than "a reputed wife of James Shiliqua," no additional heirs could be found.[86]

The final court decision was that Lucinda Metzkar-Wacheno and Victoria Wishikin-Howard were cousins and second cousins to John Pratt and as such they were his only legal heirs.[87]

---

81   Ibid.
82   Ibid.
83   Ibid.
84   Bonaparte's sister, Nancy, was living with him in 1885.
85   Oregon State Archives, Salem, Oregon, 1909, Yamhill County, Estate File 1327.
86   Ibid.
87   Ibid.

Q

Quatley, Tyee, Klickitat	Native Name: None known by author
Alias: Quarterly	Allotment: None known by author
Mother: Unknown to author	Father: Unknown to author

A band of Klickitat under Quatley scouted for the Americans during the Rogue River wars. In 1850, they were with Oregon territorial governor Joseph Lane when he traveled through southern Oregon attempting to negotiate peace treaties.

At Graves Creek, they found Apserkahar with his band. Apserkahar agreed to hold a council with them, but at some point, he became alarmed and called out to his men. They came to his defense too late. Quatley and Lane quickly seized him and took him from the village at gunpoint. With Apserkahar as a hostage, the Takelma Band of Rogue River was forced to sign a peace compact.

While the Klickitat were not one of the treaty tribes at Grand Ronde, many of them were related to people who came in under one of the western Oregon treaties. Tyee Quatley is said to have had a daughter called Sadnayoh who was one of Lt. Phil Sheridan's companions during the early years at Grand Ronde.[1]

Quenel, Alice (1877c–1923), adopted Umpqua, Chinook, Chehelis, Klickitat, Canadian Native, French Canadian	Native Name: None known by author
Alias: Esther Alice Quenel, Alice Langley, Alice Smith	Allotment 162
Mother: LaRose Nippising, Klickitat, Canadian Native, adopted Umpqua	Father: Frank Quenel, Chinook, Chehelis, adopted Umpqua, French Canadian

On October 23, 1893, Esther Alice Quenel married Jesse Smith. Witnessing the ceremony were **Abraham Hudson** and **Mary Quenel.** In 1907, she married Alexander "Jack" Langley (1880–1936).

Alice was issued a fee patent on November 9, 1907, for sixty acres of allotment land.

---

1   Cooper, *William Babcock Hazen: The Best Hated Man,* 32.

Quenel, Fabian (1880–1959), adopted Umpqua, Chinook, Chehelis, Klickitat, Canadian Native, French Canadian	Native Name: None known by author
Alias: Frank Kennell, Fabien Quenelle,	Allotment 164
Mother: LaRose Nippising, Klickitat, Canadian Native, adopted Umpqua	Father: Frank Quenel, Chinook, Chehelis, adopted Umpqua, French Canadian

Fabian Quenel married **Matilda "Tillie" Clara Winslow**, the daughter of **Henry Winslow** and **Sarah Johnson** (Waganwish).

On February 8, 1907, he was issued a fee patent for forty acres of allotment land.

Quenel, Frank (1838c–1913), adopted Umpqua, Chinook, Chehelis, French Canadian	Native Name: None known by author
Alias: Frank Kennell, Frank Quenelle, Francis Quesnel	Allotment 161
Mother: Angelique Sauc-so Tsihelis, Chinook and Chehelis[2]	Father: Abraham Quenelle, French Canadian[3]

Frank Quenel was the son of a French Canadian and a Lower Chinook woman. He was a second cousin to Mary and **Lucy Sampson,** daughters of the Tillamook doctor, Sampson.[4]

After scouting for Joel Palmer during the Cayuse War, Frank came to Grand Ronde in 1866. At that time, he was only allowed to stay a short period of time on the reservation, but in 1869, he returned hoping to stay.

After Frank married Chief Louis Napesa's daughter, LaRose, a number of chiefs including **Louis Napesa, Dave Yachkawa, Peter McCoy** (Inchaishi), **Shasta Tom, Joseph Hutchins** (Yalkama) and **John Kawache** went to Indian agent Amos Harvey asking to have Frank adopted as a treaty Indian.[5]

Later, in recalling the occasion, Frank testified that the agent asked him what

2   Munnick and Warner, *Catholic Church Records — St Paul.*

3   Michelle, *Just a Memorandum,* 7: Mary Ann wrote that Frank's father was Canadian French and his mother a full-blooded Lower Chinook. O. Applegate, Testimony of Captain Frank Quenel: Frank testified his mother was Chinook and Chehalis. O. Applegate, Interview with Amos Kilya: Amos said that through his mother, Frank was related to a woman named Lucy Sampson, who was the daughter of a Tillamook medicine doctor and the wife of Jack Amos.

4   1900 Federal Census lists Mary Sampson as an "aunt" age fifty living with Clarissa Quenel-Langley and her husband, John. Mary Sampson could not speak English.

5   O. Applegate, Testimony of Captain Frank Quenel.

tribe he wished to join. After Frank indicated he wanted to belong to the Umpqua, the agent "explained the rules to him," especially warning him against bringing liquor onto the reservation. Frank promised he would not do this and the agent agreed to enroll him with the Umpqua band. From that day forward, Frank drew annuities, as long as there were any, with the Umpqua.[6]

Frank served as court clerk on the Grand Ronde Indian Legislature for 1877 and 1880. He served as captain of the Grand Ronde Indian Police Force from 1884 through 1907.[7] In 1894, he was described in agency employment records as "a 58 year old mixed blood measuring 5 feet four inches tall and weighing 135 pounds."[8]

By LaRose, Frank had Clarissa (1870–1901), Lizette (1873–86), Henriette (1882–84), **Alice, Mary,** and **Fabian Quenel.**[9]

When Frank received his 280.27-acre allotment, he exchanged eighty acres with Chief Louis Napesa's widow, **Klickitat Lizette.** He received a fee patent for the land October 29, 1906.[10]

When Frank died, he left an estate valued at $1,000. He also had a stallion named Sacramento that was valued at $300 but described on the inventory list as "basically worthless."[11] His only surviving heirs and next of kin were his widow, LaRose, his daughters, Alice and Mary Langley, and his son, Fabian Quenel.

In old times, Grand Ronde people believed if you split a fir sapling down from the top and it split straight, you would have good luck. In 1934 there was a tree split like this growing in the yard of Frank's old place. It had grown into a tall forked tree.[12]

Quenel, Mary (1878), adopted Umpqua, Chinook, Chehelis, Klickitat, Canadian Native, French Canadian	Native Name: None known by author
Alias: Mary Langley	Allotment 163
Mother: LaRose Nippising, Klickitat, Canadian Native, adopted Umpqua	Father: Frank Quenel, Chinook, Chehelis, adopted Umpqua, French Canadian

---

6   Ibid.
7   National Archives, Seattle, Grand Ronde/Siletz, Land and Enrollment Program records, Field Notes and Land Survey 1875–1898, Land Description Book 1878, Box 115; Grand Ronde Justice Court. Confederated Tribes of the Grand Ronde Community of Oregon Archive, Grand Ronde Agency Ledger Book, Records of Employees at Grand Ronde July 1883–September 1907.
8   *Records of Employees at Grand Ronde, 1884–1907.*
9   Munnick and Beckham, *Catholic Church Records—Grand Ronde,* Register I, p. 60, M-2, p. 64, B-43, p. 81, B-20, p. 100, B-26, p. 109, B-23, p. 115, B-5, p. 123, B-13, p. 129, S-12.
10   *Heirs of Deceased Indians,* Allotment Records 161.
11   Oregon State Archives, Salem, Oregon, 1913, Yamhill County, Estate File 3472.
12   Berreman, Field Notes, 1934.

Quiaquaty (1811c–81c), Molalla	Native Name: Gwayakiti /GWA-ya-ki-ti/ (gwáyak'iti),* Skhainch /shkainch/ (shkáynch)*[13]
Alias: Quackerty, Quackety, Quai-eck-e-te	Allotment: None known by author
Mother: Unknown to author	Father: Unknown to author

Quiaquaty (Gwayakiti) was the principal chief of the Molalla band of Molalla whose name in his language was Skhainch. In the Clackamas language his name was Gwayakiti, but on the treaty made with the Americans in 1855, it was pronounced and written "Quia-quaty."

Skhainch acquired his Clackamas name from an incident that occurred at a Clackamas dance. One of the women there had a power that was saying something about *kiti*, a covering blanket. As the woman sang, Gwayakiti began making comments in jest about the song. From then on Clackamas people always called him Gwayakiti.[14]

After the Molalla were moved to the Grand Ronde Reserve, Chief Gwayakiti had over a hundred men, women, and children under his leadership and maintained this number through 1857.

By 1867, the Molalla population on the reservation had decreased by 40 percent. Sickness and lack of food were two of the primary problems, not just for the Molalla, but for all the tribes. The Molalla were more fortunate than some as the Indian agent gave them permission to return to their home country around Willamette Falls to fish during the annual salmon run. Without this supply of fish, they would not have had meat of any kind.[15]

Gwayakiti had at least two surviving children: **Moses Allen** (Shkayinch) and **Sarah Gwayakiti.** Moses and Sarah's mother was a woman the people called **Wagayuhlen.**[16] Father Croquet spelled her name Wailagh. On November, 18, 1860, he wrote, "we the undersigned priest have baptized Agnes, 4 years old, born of

---

13 Michelle, *Just a Memorandum*, 6, gave his Indian name as "Skhins." Jacobs, Field Notebook 61, *Texts and Ethnology*, 4. Jacobs, Field Notebook 59, *Texts and Ethnology*, 30: gwayakiti, a Clackamas name of Shkainch, Mrs. H.'s Molale grandf. (mother's father).

14 Jacobs, Field Notebook 59, *Texts and Ethnology*, 30.

15 *Annual Report Commissioner of Indian Affairs*, Letter of August 1860 to Edward R. Geary, 440–41.

16 1887 GRIC gave Victoria's grandmother as "See-san-wa." Jacobs, *Clackamas Chinook Texts*, Part I, 268, gives Victoria Howard's mother's mother as "Wagayutn." Jacobs, *Clackamas Text*, Part II, 492–93, 647, Note 426, stated Sarah and Moses had the same mother. 1872 GRIC: "Jonas Quackerty" was listed with his first wife, "Kiuklin" and second wife, "Yiamox." Jacobs, Field Notebook 54, *Santiam Kalapuya Text*, 10, notes from V. Howard, "her grandfather (m.) had 2 wives—one Klamath, bought at about 12 in Oregon City." Michelle, *Just a Memorandum*, 6.

Kwaikety and Wailagh of Molalla nation, of this mission."[17]

Gwayakiti was probably the same man Father Croquet baptized as John "Kwaikety" "in danger of death" on July 6, 1881.[18]

In 1929, Gwayakiti's granddaughter, **Victoria Wishikin** (Kinishi), recorded for Melville Jacobs a love song once sang by Gwayakiti at a girl's puberty dance. It was an "insulting and very devilish song."[19]

Quinaby (1808c–78c), Santiam band of Kalapuya	Native Name: Kwinupya /KWI-nup-ya/ (k'wínupya)*[20]
Alias: General Quinaby	Allotment: None known by author
Mother: Unknown to author	Father: Unknown to author

In the days prior to removal, Quinaby (Kwinupya) was living next to the old Jason Lee Mission. In 1843, when the school was moved to Chemeketa, Kwinupya went, too.

From there he was removed to the Grand Ronde Reservation but, like most of his people, his heart longed for the home country of the Santiam people.

In 1861, a settler by the name of Dickinson wrote Agent Condon regarding "Quinaba, a good industrious Indian" and listed all the reasons why he should have the liberty to work for him, but apparently Kwinupya wanted more than a temporary pass.[21]

On May 10, 1864, a Fort Yamhill detail returned to the Grand Ronde Agency around noon from a trip collecting runaways. They had been gone twenty days and traveled a distance of 262 miles. When the great gate swung open and Corporal Bensell counted all the captives, Kwinupya was among them.[22]

After 1872, Kwinupya and his wife were no longer listed on any GRIC. They had been allowed to return permanently to their home country where many American settlers found them camping on the bank of South Mill Creek.[23]

---

17 Munnick and Beckham, *Catholic Church Records — Grand Ronde*, Register I, p. 6, B-35.

18 Ibid., Register I, p. 118, B-9.

19 Jacobs, Field Notebook 51, *Music and Ethnology*, 6.

20 Gatschet, *Texts, Sentences and Vocables*, 368: listed under the Santiam as "Old Kuinabi." Jacobs, Field Notebooks 36, *Santiam Kalapuya Text*, 190: "Kwinupya, Santiam man."

21 A. Dickinson to J. B. Condon, August 16, 1861, BIA, Microfilm M-2, Roll 30, National Archives, Washington, DC).

22 Barth, *All Quiet on the Yamhill*, 148.

23 Clarke, *Pioneer Days of Oregon History*, 131.

Quinaby (Kwinupya) standing, right. Photo courtesy of Oregon Historical Society (OHS 76207).

Wife of Quinaby (Kwinupya). Photo courtesy of Oregon Historical Society (OHS 019321).

R

Reese, Tom, Rogue River/Shasta	Native Name: None known by author
Alias: Dirty-Faced Tom	Allotment: None known by author
Mother: Unknown to author	Father: Unknown to author

In 1872, he was with his wife, Nannie, and Loti King.

Riggs, Andrew (1880–1970), Umpqua, Clackamas, Lower Chinook	Native Name: None known by author
Alias: Andy Riggs	Allotment: 174
Mother: Jenny Mackey, Clackamas, Lower Chinook	Father: Chief Solomon Riggs, Umpqua

Andrew's health was poor for many years before his death. His wife, **Amanda Jeffries,** described their situation in a letter to **Eustace Howard** and **Victoria Wishikin** (Kinishi)'s daughter, Agatha Bloom dated September 28, 1958:

Andrew has been so sick with arthritis and all crippled up so as he can't walk without crutches. He can hardly use his hands. I have to wait on him hands and feet. He never sleeps of nights. He aches and pains so hard. I have a lot of children. Some live near me anyway when Andrew suffers so much. You said I must have a lot of grandchildren. I have 22 and have ten great-grandchildren. My oldest daughter is with me now since the first part of June and she is a lot of help. One of my daughters is in the state hospital in Salem with a nervous breakdown. Poor woman came all the way by herself from Los Angles. I can't see how they ever let her come alone the way she was. I sure have a lot of worries. I got awful sick a week or more ago. I got bladder infection. I could hardly walk. I was afraid I would have to stay in the hospital. I worried how Andrew would get along.[1]

Riggs, Charlotte (1817c–1912c), Umpqua	Native Name: None known by author
Alias: Charlotte Joe	Allotment 177
Mother: Unknown to author	Father: Unknown to author

---

1   Letter #16 to Agatha Bloom from Amanda Riggs dated September 28, 1958, from Barbara Danforth Collection.

Charlotte Riggs received a fee patent on a hundred-acre allotment. After Charlotte died on August 4, 1912, records showed that K. R. Smith had bought eighty acres of land from her prior to her death. He was issued a fee patent for this part of her allotment on July 21, 1913. On April 24, 1914, Charlotte's heirs, **John** and **William Warren,** received a fee patent for the remaining twenty acres of land.[2]

Riggs, Edward (1868), Umpqua, Clackamas, Lower Chinook	Native Name: None known by author
Alias: None known by author	Allotment: 171
Mother: Jenny Mackey	Father: Chief Solomon Riggs, Umpqua

Edward married **Mary "Allie" Metcalf.** On October 19, 1907, he was issued a fee patent for the entire twenty acres of allotment land.

Andrew (l) and Edward (r) Riggs. Courtesy of Joann White-Colton and Bud White, grandchildren of Clara Robinson-Riggs.

---

2   Charlotte Riggs first appears on the GRIC in 1907, taking the place formerly held by a woman listed as "Charlotte Joe." She was listed as "Charlotte Riggs" from 1907 through 1912. In 1912 her age was given as ninety-five.

Riggs, George (1879–1917), Umpqua, Clackamas, Lower Chinook	Native Name: None known by author
Alias: None known by author	Allotment: 173
Mother: Jenny Mackey	Father: Chief Solomon Riggs, Umpqua

George Riggs married Lena Jackson. After George died, his heirs sold his twenty- acre allotment. A fee patent was issued to the purchaser on March 1, 1929.

Riggs, Hattie (1881c–1933), Umpqua, Clackamas, Lower Chinook	Native Name: None known by author
Alias: Hattie Isaac	Allotment: 172
Mother: Jenny Mackey, Lower Chinook, Clackamas	Father: Chief Solomon Riggs, Umpqua

Hattie Riggs married **Frank Oleman Isaac** (1866c-1934), son of **Shasta Isaac** and **Janie Isaac.**

October, 29, 1906, Hattie was issued a fee patent for her entire eighty-acre allotment. When she died, she left the following children: Joseph (1899–1970), Mildred (1902c), Helen, Amelia (1912c), and George.[3]

Riggs, Lelivea	Native Name: None known by author
Alias: None known by author	Allotment: None known by author
Mother: Unknown to author	Father: Unknown to author

Lelivea was Solomon Riggs's aunt. She was living with **Klickitat Dick Hall** and his wife in 1872.

Riggs, Marceline (1868–99), Umpqua, Clackamas, Lower Chinook	Native Name: None known by author
Alias: Marceline Selkeah, Marceline Lawney	Allotment 188
Mother: Jenny Mackey, Clackamas, Lower Chinook	Father: Chief Solomon Riggs, Umpqua

On February 6, 1883, Marceline Riggs married Peter Joseph Selkeah (1860–87), the son of **Peter Selkya** and Louise (Comadeer). She and Peter Joseph had at least five children including **Joseph J. Selkeah** (1887c). After Peter Joseph died, Marceline married **Lawney Tom** (Pootpam) around 1889. Marceline and Lawney had four children: Albert (1890c), Abraham (1892c), Emma (1893c), and Clinton (1895c).

Marceline's heirs sold her allotment on October 8, 1912. A fee patent was is-

---

3   *Heirs to Deceased Indians,* Allotment Record 172.

sued to the buyer, C. M. Blair, for the entire 320 acres by John J. Selkeah, Abraham Lawney, Emma Lawney, and Clinton Lawney.

Riggs, Samuel (1884–1970), Umpqua, Clackamas, Lower Chinook	Native Name: None known by author
Alias: Samuel Riggs, Sammy Riggs	Allotment: 176
Mother: Jenny Mackey, Lower Chinook, Clackamas	Father: Chief Solomon Riggs, Umpqua

Sam Riggs married Ida Estella Wheeler, daughter of **Frank Wheeler** (Aiwai) and **Stephanie Howard** (Lhimiki). On April 19, 1920, he married Clara Robinson, daughter of **Dan Robinson** and Felicite Rosa Menard.

Samuel Riggs was issued a fee patent for eighty acres of allotment land on August 5, 1907.

Samuel (l) and Johnny (r) Riggs. Courtesy of Joann White-Colton and Bud White, grandchildren of Clara Robinson-Riggs.

Riggs, Solomon, Chief (1827c–1920), Umpqua	Native Name: Gunconnacli /Gun-conna-cli/[4]

---

4   1887 GRIC gave his Indian name as "Gun-conna-cli."

Alias: None known by author	Allotment 170[5]
Mother: Unknown to author	Father: Unknown to author

In 1869, Chief Solomon Riggs (Gunconnacli) spoke in council with A. B. Meacham, the new superintendent of Indian affairs. He told him his parents had taught him to live naturally upon the land, but he had since learned to work and to live in a house. He pointed out his wife, **Jenny Mackey,** and their baby, telling Meacham that he intended for the child to be educated in the manner of the white man.[6]

On September 14, 1871, Solomon again spoke in council with the Americans. He said,

I am glad to see Mr. Brunot here. I want him to take my words to the president. I am going to speak true. It has been promised that our land should be surveyed; I am glad to see it is done. We are promised a saw-mill; I see it too; I am glad of it. When I get my land it is mine, and while I live I will stay on it.

Three or four years ago it was like as if I was asleep; now I am awake. Agents five or six years ago never said to raise anything. When Mr. Meacham came he said we must raise grain as the whites do, and all the Indians have done so. Now we want a grist-mill. There are plenty of old people about me; they are poor; I am young and can take my wheat out-side. Many old people ask me to talk about the mill for them. Some agents have made us poor. We can't help the old people. We need plows and harnesses, and when we have them we will be like white people, and will make our living the same way.[7]

Solomon married Jenny Mackey, first according to the traditional custom and then in the Catholic Church. By her, he had **Edward, Marceline,** John Johnson (1871), Nazaire (1873), **George, Hattie,** Leo (1880), **Andrew, William "Willie," Samuel Victor,** Francis (1888–89), Elizabeth "Betsy" (1889–90), and Louis (1892–1920).[8]

Solomon was elected by the people to serve on the Grand Ronde Indian Legis-lature in 1876 and again in 1878. He was also appointed court treasurer that year, along with the Tualatin sub-chief, **Lame Jim Shiliqua** (Shilikwa). On May 9, 1881, the Grand Ronde Indian Legislature elected him court attorney for the remainder

---

5   *Heirs of Deceased Indians,* Allotment Records 170.

6   Meacham, *Wigwam and War-Path.*

7   *Annual Report Commissioner of Indian Affairs,* 1871, Minutes of a Council with Grand Ronde Indians at their Reservation, Oregon, by Commissioner Felix R. Brunot, September 14, 1871, 149-153.

8   Munnick and Beckham, *Catholic Church Records—Grand Ronde,* Register I, p. 70, M-1, p. 69, B-28, p. 88, B-10, p. 98, B-13, p. 110, B-1, p. 117, B-35, p. 124, B-5, Register II, p. 1, B-1, p. 50, B-52, p. 52, S-7, p. 57, B-19, p. 58, S-1, p. 77, B-8.

Chief Solomon Riggs. Courtesy of Douglas County Museum of Natural and Cultural History.

of 1881 and 1882.[9]

When the Warm House dance came to Grand Ronde in the early 1870s, at first Solomon refused to participate; however, when he heard that **Bogus Tom** did not speak Chinook Jargon, he started preaching so everyone could understand.[10]

Solomon, **Peter McCoy** (Inchaishi), and **Shasta Tom** were chiefs of the dance house that was built at Rock Creek specifically for the Warm House religion and the Shasta, Umpqua, and Rogue River people.[11]

There were eight dance costumes for the men. Of these, Solomon owned three. They were made of ankle length feathers capes with hammerhead quill

9 National Archives, Seattle, Grand Ronde/Siletz, Land and Enrollment Program Records, Field Notes and Land Survey 1875–1898, Land Description Book 1878, Box 115; Grand Ronde Justice Court.

10 Du Bois, *The Ghost Dance*, 30–31.

11 Ibid.

headbands that came low over the dancer's eyes so the dancer could not see.[12]

By 1888, Solomon and his family had two houses and a barn on sixty fenced acres with a two-acre garden. In addition, they had 120 bushels of wheat, 300 bushels of oats, 150 bushels of potatoes, fourteen tons of hay, six horses, six head of cattle, three hogs, and 24 dozen chickens. His son Andrew was an apprentice blacksmith for the agency. His son Samuel was an assistant at the agency school.[13]

In 1907, Solomon's son George died, leaving two children: Alvetta, age five and Alice, age three. The girls lived with their grandfather Solomon Riggs from June 3, 1906, to May 1, 1908.[14]

George and Lena Jackson's daughters, Alvetta (1902c) and Alice (1904c). Both died young. Courtesy of Joann White-Colton and Bud White, grandchildren of Clara Robinson-Riggs.

Riggs, William (1882–1903), Umpqua, Clackamas, Lower Chinook	Native Name: None known by author

12 Ibid.
13 *Records of Employees at Grand Ronde, 1884–1907.*
14 Oregon State Archives, Salem, Oregon, 1906, Polk County, Estate File 989.

Alias: None known by author	Allotment: 175
Mother: Jenny Mackey, Lower Chinook, Clackamas	Father: Chief Solomon Riggs, Umpqua

William received an eighty-acre allotment. After his death, his parents sold the property to Lester Wallace. The deed was approved June 23, 1906.

Riley, Ben (d. 1885c), Rogue River/Shasta	Native Name: None known by author
Alias: None known by author	Allotment: None known by author
Mother: Unknown to author	Father: Unknown to author

In 1872, Ben Riley was listed under the Rogue River/Shasta with his wife, Lucindi. He was related to Mary Carpenter and her daughter, Leni.

In 1878, the Indian Legislature passed a provision of law that made him exempt from working on agency roads along with a number of other men who were becoming elderly.

By 1885, Ben Riley's wife was listed as the "Widow Riley" (1841) with her children, Rose and Johnnie.

Riley, Bob (1829c–94c), Rogue River	Native Name: None known by author
Alias: Robert Riley	Allotment 178
Mother: Unknown to author	Father: Unknown to author

The fifth annual session of the Grand Ronde Indian Legislature convened on January 4, 1876, with two representatives from each tribe on the reservation. Bob Riley represented the Rogue River.[15]

After **Bogus Tom** brought the Warm House dance to Grand Ronde from Yreka, Bob Riley made a trip to California or Nevada. He came back with some new ideas and had more dances.[16] John Simmons said he was one of the best preachers at the dances.[17]

In 1888, Bob was listed with his wife, **Mary Johnson.** They had a small farm with a house and barn on twenty fenced acres. Around 1891, Bob left Mary for **Janie Isaac.** He and Janie were together until he died in 1894.

Bob received an allotment of 83.22 acres. On June 21, 1907, a fee patent for the entire allotment was issued to his widow, Janie Isaac-Riley.[18]

---

15 National Archives, Seattle, Grand Ronde/Siletz Tribal Program Records Box 162, Agency & Tribal Council Records 1876–1951.
16 Berreman, Field Notes, 1934.
17 Du Bois, *The Ghost Dance*, 30.
18 National Archives, Salem, Oregon, Polk County, Box 35, Folder 317, File 1013.

Robinson, Adeline (1888-1960), Rogue River	Native Name: None known by author
Alias: None known by author	Allotment 169
Mother: Felicite Rosa Menard	Father: Dan Robinson, Rogue River

Adeline Robinson married Leon Reibach. Later, she married **George Leno**. On October 25, 1907, Adeline was issued a fee patent for her entire eighty-acre allotment.

Robinson, Dan (1868c–1918c), Rogue River	Native Name: None known by author
Alias: Daniel Robinson	Allotment 168
Mother: Unknown to author	Father: Unknown to author

As a young man Dan Robinson was listed alone on the 1886 GRIC with a horse as his only asset. In 1888, he was listed as the husband of Felicite Rosa Menard (1870c–1902), whom he had married two years earlier. He had a number of children by Felicite, but when Felicite and Dan were divorced only two of their children, Clara (1892–1983) and **Adeline Robinson,** were still living.

Felicite moved in with her grandparents, Nancy and **Joseph Shangaretta,** after her marriage dissolved. They took care of the girls while she worked. A few years later, Felicite married **Charlie Russie.**

After Felicite died in 1902, her daughter Clara went to live with her father. Dan Robinson placed Clara in the Catholic boarding school at Grand Ronde. Felicite's daughter Adeline Robinson went to live with Felicite's parents, Elizabeth and **Peter Menard.**[19]

In 1896, Dan married **Louise Wallace** (Washtali), former wife of **Felix Wacheno.** Louise was the daughter of **Henry Wallace** and **Stephen Kiki**'s half sister, **Rose Kiki** (Ilhikhsha).[20] By Rose's daughter, Louise, Dan had Lizzie (1902).[21] After Louise, Dan married **Caroline Kenoyer.**[22] Dan and Caroline had a daughter, Carry Robinson.[23]

In addition to his native Rogue River language, Dan Robinson could speak English and Chinook Jargon.[24] In 1906, he served as an Indian police officer on the reservation.[25]

---

19 Zenk, Field Notes, interview with Clara Robinson Riggs, 1982 (3:23).
20 Jacobs, Notebook 51, *Music and Ethnology,* 33.
21 Ibid., 23, 24, 33.
22 1906 GRIC.
23 Personal communication with Joann White-Colton on June 6, 2011.
24 Zenk, *Chinook Jargon,* 282.
25 Confederated Tribes of the Grand Ronde Community of Oregon Archive, Grand Ronde Agency Ledger Book, Records of Employees at Grand Ronde July 1883–

Carry, daughter of Dan Robinson and Caroline Kenoyer. Courtesy of Joann White-Colton and Bud White, grandchildren of Clara Robinson-Riggs.

His daughter Adeline married an Austrian named Leon Reibach.[26] Later, she married **George Leno.** After marrying Orville White, his daughter Clara Robinson married **Samuel Riggs.** In 1929, after marrying several times, Dan's daughter Lizzie was living in Seattle. That year, **Victoria Wishikin** (Kinishi) recorded one of Lizzie's power songs for Melville Jacob.[27]

Dan Robinson received an allotment of 160 acres. He was one of the men who did not sign the Surplus Land Agreement in 1901.

September 1907.
26   *Heirs of Deceased Indians,* Allotment Records 168, 169.
27   Jacobs, Field Notebook 51, *Music and Ethnology,* 33

Robinson, Jacob (1869c–83)	Native Name: None known by author
Alias: None known by author	Allotment: None known by author
Mother: Unknown to author	Father: Unknown to author

Jacob was baptized at Grand Ronde July 2, 1883. He died July 27 and was buried the following day.

Rose, James (1840c–75), Umpqua	Native Name: None known by author
Alias: Cultas Jim	Allotment: None known by author
Mother: Unknown to author	Father: Unknown to author

The American military officer and war hero Phil Sheridan bought James Rose's wife **Harriet Lindsey** from him just before the American Civil War broke out.[28] In 1872, James was living with a new wife named Julie Ann, his mother-in-law, Susan, and an aunt named Nancy in 1872.

James Rose died July 11, 1875.

Russie, Charlie (1870c)	Native Name: None known by author
Alias: None known by author	Allotment: None known by author
Mother: Walla Walla	Father: French Canadian[29]

Charlie Russie was probably the son of Augustin Russie, who was named godparent to **Levi Bob** and **Lucinda Metzkar**'s son, Louis Daly Bob, on April 8, 1894.

When the Cayuse War broke out, Augustin Russie rode with **Joseph Shangaretta** and others in Thomas McKay's company of Indian and Métis solders.

Charlie Russie or "Charlie of Umatilla" married at least three times. On January 20, 1892, he married **Jennie Michel,** former wife of Eli Parr Sr.[30] Six years later, he and Jennie were divorced in Tillamook County.[31]

After Jennie, Charlie married Joseph Shangaretta's granddaughter, Felicite Rosa Menard on January 23, 1899. Charlie was first listed at Grand Ronde with Felicite in 1900. By Felicite, he had two boys, Archie (1898) and Guy Russie (1901).

According to Felicite's daughter, Clara Robinson-Riggs, Charlie was "not a Grand Ronde Indian" and "not home much during this time."[32] He did work for a time as the agency farmer. He resigned June 30, 1907.[33]

---

28 Zenk, Grand Ronde Notebook 9, 1988, 65.
29 1900 Federal Census District 812 Indian Population Grand Ronde Reservation
30 Munnick and Beckham, *Catholic Church Records—Grand Ronde*, Register II, p. 74, M-2.
31 National Archives, Salem, Oregon, 1898 Divorce in Tillamook County.
32 Zenk, Field Notes, interview with Clara Riggs, 1982, (3:23).
33 *Records of Employees at Grand Ronde, 1884–1907.*

After Felicite, Charlie married **Rosa Tim-Tim** on January 7, 1907, in Yamhill County.[34]

Russie, Martha (1883c)	Native Name: None known by author
Alias: None known by author	Allotment: None known by author
Mother: Unknown to author	Father: Unknown to author

Martha (1883c) received confirmation at St. Michael's Parish on October 14, 1894. In 1895, she was listed as an orphan. She was classified in this fashion through 1898.

---

34 National Archives, Salem, Oregon, January 7, 1907, Marriage to Rosa Tim-Tim, File 130. O. Applegate, Testimony of Rosie Tim-Tim.

S

Sam, Luckiamute (1826c–66), Luckiamute band of Kalapuya[1]	Native Name: None known by author
Alias: None known by author	Allotment: None known by author
Mother: Unknown to author	Father: Unknown to author

Samall, Christine Netty (1844c–84), wife of Umpqua husband	Native Name: None known by author
Alias: Christine McKye	Allotment: None known by author
Mother: Unknown to author	Father: Unknown to author

Christine Samall was the wife of **Lincoln McCoy.** She died after receiving the sacraments from Father Croquet on December 26, 1884.[2]

Samall, James, Umpqua[3]	Native Name: None known by author
Alias: None known by author	Allotment: None known by author
Mother: Unknown to author	Father: Unknown to author

James was living with three wives in 1872: hayash wife, Betsy, second wife, Jane, and third wife, Tami. Also living with the family were his son, **Louis McCoy** (1855c–85), and **Spencer Semoll McCoy,** "son of Maria now dead."

Sampson, Lucy (1854c–1905), Nehalem band of Tillamook, Clatsop, Alsea	Native Name: None known by author
Alias: Lucy Amos, Lucy Lane	Allotment 181
Mother: Alsea	Father: Dr. Samson or Sampson, Nehalem band of Tillamook, Clatsop[4]

Lucy was the daughter of a well known Tillamook doctor named Samson. Before a longhouse dance in midwinter her father, Dr. Samson, would fast for ten days. He would dance seven or eight days; sometimes ten.[5]

---

1   Munnick and Beckham, *Catholic Church Records—Grand Ronde,* Register I, p. 44, B-22.
2   Ibid., Register I, p. 128, S-13.
3   1872 GRIC.
4   O. Applegate, Testimony from Amos Kilya. Jacobs, Elizabeth, Field Notebook 105, *Coos–U. Coquille,* 23: married an Alsea woman; he was part Nehalem, part Clatsop. Dr. Samson could speak both languages.
5   Jacobs, Elizabeth, Field Notebook 105, *Coos–U. Coquille,* 39.

Clara Pearson, from the Siletz, once witnessed Dr. Samson treating a patient with an ailment of the stomach and lungs. The patient lay on a mat positioned on the floor. Dr. Samson sat at the side drawing the sickness out and drowning it in a pan of water. Woman sang songs to help him and used special sticks to pound on the ceiling. Shorter sticks called "totem sticks" were placed around with "abalone eyes" images of people's faces that watched over the sick person.[6]

After Lucy's father died, Lucy's mother brought Lucy to the Grand Ronde Reservation. Lucy's mother lived at Grand Ronde for the rest of her life. She was buried there around 1880.

Lucy's power came from a place where water boiled out of the ground. She only sang one power song and **Victoria Wishikin** (Kinishi) recorded it for Melville Jacobs in 1930.[7]

Lucy married **Jack Amos** (Shaklu) July 1, 1889, and lived with him until he died. After his death, she lived at **Calapooia Jack**'s house. Then she married Mose Lane from the Siletz Reservation.[8]

Lucy had two sisters, Mary and Sophie Sampson.[9] She was also related to **Joe Corner Michelle**'s wife, **Josephine Hubbard,** to **Solomon Riggs (Gunconnacli)**'s wife, **Jennie Mackey,** and to **Frank Michelle**'s son, **Joseph Michelle.** Calapooia Jack's wife, Julia Jack, was also her aunt and Lucy was a second cousin to **Frank Quenel.**[10]

Lucy inherited Jack Amos's allotment at Grand Ronde and received a 160-acre allotment of her own. After her death, her heirs were listed as Perry Battise, Leora D. Klamath, and Harriet L. Klamath, all from Siletz. They sold her entire 160-acre allotment at Grand Ronde to Weymouth Crowell, who was issued a fee patent on the property April 15, 1921.

Sampson, Moses (1847c), Umpqua	Native Name: None known by author
Alias: Blind Sampson	Allotment: None known by author
Mother: Unknown to author	Father: Unknown to author

In 1872, he was listed with his wife, Nancy, and daughter, Elizabeth. By 1885, he was a bachelor living alone.

Sampson, Molalla (1847c–92c), Molalla	Native Name: Machuginskti
	/ma-chu-gins-kti/ (machuginskti)*[11]

---

6   Jacobs, Elizabeth, Field Notebook 105, *Coos–U. Coquille*, 3.
7   Jacobs, Notebook 51, *Music and Ethnology*, 48.
8   O. Applegate, Testimony from Moses Lane.
9   McChesney, *The Rolls of Certain Indian Tribes*, Testimony of Moses Lane, gives Lucy Sampson's sisters as Sophie and Mary Sampson and her aunt as Julia Jack.
10 O. Applegate, Testimony of Old Amos Kilya.
11 Gatschet, Texts, *Sentences, and Vocables*.

Alias: None known by author	Allotment 180
Mother: Unknown to author	Father: Unknown to author

In 1872, Molalla Sampson was listed under the Molalla with his wife, Pechie, and daughter, Emily. In 1885, he was listed with a wife named Jasen. After 1887, Sampson was listed with his last wife, a woman named **Susan Hollingsworth (Khimshtani)**.

In 1888, Molalla Sampson and Susan (Khimshtani) were listed as Umpqua rather than Molalla by the Indian agent, who described their farm as a house with a barn on twenty fenced acres. They had also had fifteen head of cattle, seven horses, a dozen chickens, and a garden.

Louis Kenoyer (Pakhawatas) described a hunting trip around Mt. Hebo with Molalla Sampson's wife, **Susan** (Khimshtani), **Yamhill Joe Jefferies** (Tukshin), **Yamhill Mary Jefferies** (Hayas tutush), and Louis' mother, **Nancy Kenoyer** (Tunishni). On this trip, Yamhill Joe (Tukshin) was able to shoot a number of deer in a region where Molalla Sampson was also hunting; Sampson, according to Louis (Pakhawatas), "could not even see one" deer.[12]

After Susan (Khimshtani) inherited Molalla Sampson's 180-acre allotment, she sold it to C. M. Blair. On August 26, 1912, a fee patent for the entire allotment was issued to the new buyer.

Sands, John (1856c), Clackamas	Native Name: None known by author
Alias: None known by author	Allotment: None known by author
Mother: Unknown to author	Father: Unknown to author

In 1888, John was listed with his wife, Polly, and a two-year-old son.

Sands, Martha Jane (1841c–1912), Rogue River	Native Name: None known by author
Alias: Martha McCoy, Martha Semoll	Allotment 182
Mother: Unknown to author	Father: Unknown to author

Martha Jane was removed to Grand Ronde in the spring of 1856. She and her cousin **Harriet Lindsey** had been visiting friends and relatives in Umpqua country when the Rogue River War broke out. The girls were brought along with **Chief Louis Napesa** and **Chief Peter McCoy** (Inchaishi)'s band of Umpqua, to the Grand Ronde Reservation. Martha Janes's family from Rogue River was brought to the reservation later that same year.[13]

---

12   Jacobs, Collection 40, *Autobiography of a Tualatin*, paragraph 21.

13   O. Applegate, Testimony of Martha Jane Sands: "I knew her [Harriet Leno-Corton-Lindsey] all my life. We were children together, and we were about the same age, we were playmates. I call her my sister, according to the Indian way, but she is my first cousin."

Plate 43: Martha Sands (second from right) with daughter Hattie, son-in-law John B. Hudson, and their children. Photo courtesy of Oregon Historical Society (CN22570)

In 1872, Martha and her children were living with **James Scroggins's** family. She was listed as a cousin to Scroggins's wife, Margaret. In 1885, she was listed as **Lincoln McCoy**'s aunt.

Martha Jane had four children: Harry, Milton, Magdelen Henrietta, and **Nicholas Sands**.[14] Nicholas married Louisa Tole. Hattie married **John "Mose" Hudson**.

In 1888, Martha Jane, Nicholas, and Louisa were all living together on a sixty-acre farm with three houses and a barn.

Martha Jane's second husband was **James Semoll**'s son, **Semoll McCoy**. James helped her raise her children Nicholas and Hattie.[15]

Martha Jane received a 100-acre allotment. On January 10, 1908, she received

14 Munnick and Beckham, *Catholic Church Records—Grand Ronde,*Register I, p. 53, B-13, p. 67, B-6.
15 Michelle, *Just a Memorandum,* 4: Mary Ann wrote, "Semoll McCoy wife Martha Jane, Rogue River; Nicholas sons and Hatty sons step-children to McCoy."

a fee patent for the entire allotment.[16]

Sands, Nicholas (1867c–91), Rogue River	Native Name: None known by author
Alias: None known by author	Allotment 183
Mother: Martha Jane Sands, Rogue River	Father: Loyd Sands, Rogue River

Nicholas Sands received a 180-acre allotment that his sister-in-law Elizabeth Tole-Blacketeer inherited. She sold sixty acres to David S. Bentley in 1903. She sold the remaining 120 acres to W.N. Jones in 1906.[17]

Sangashee, John, Rogue River/Shasta	Native Name: Sangashee /San-ga-see/[18]
Alias: Old Man John	Allotment: None known by author
Mother: Unknown to author	Father: Unknown to author

In 1872, Sangashee was listed under the Rogue River and Shasta with his wife, Obi, and their adopted son, Allen. Also living with the family were John's niece, Lucy, and her two children, Clara and Charles.

Rev. Summers met Sangashee sometime between 1873 and 1881. He wrote that John told him his tribe used to live "far, far up the Great River," but that it was his destiny to die far away from his former home and the grave of his father.[19]

Sansousee, Jennie (1853c–1903), wife of Umpqua husband	Native Name: None known by author
Alias: Jennie Condon, Jennie Stanton, Jennie Harney	Allotment 27
Mother: Unknown to author	Father: Unknown to author

Jennie Sansousee married **Bill Condon** in 1876.[20] They were together until 1887, when Jennie was listed as a widow. By 1888, Jennie and her daughter, **Josephine Lillie Condon,** had two houses, forty acres fenced, one horse, and a cow.

In 1889, Jenny and her daughter were listed with Frank Stanton. After Frank Stanton, she married **Fred Harney** from the Siletz reservation on March 20, 1894. **Cephas Tipton** and Josephine Lillie Condon acted as witnesses. Fred died in 1898.[21]

---

16 *Heirs of Deceased Indians,* Allotment Record 182.
17 Ibid., 183.
18 Cawley, *Indian Journal,* 22: gives "San-ga-see" as his Indian name and his tribe as the Yoncalla.
19 Ibid.
20 Munnick and Beckham, *Catholic Church Records—Grand Ronde,* Register I, p. 97, M-3, p. 101, M-2.
21 Ibid., Register II, p. 92, M-2.

Jennie received an eighty-acre allotment. Her heirs were **Robert Allen** and her daughter, Josephine Lillie Tipton. They sold forty acres of Jenny's property to D. S. Bentley in 1907.

Sansousee, Mary Ann (1837c–1905), Umpqua	Native Name: None known by author
Alias: Mary Ann Metzgar, Mary Ann Metzcar, Mary Ann Pierce	Allotment 187
Mother: Unknown to author	Father: Unknown to author

Mary Ann was the wife of **Peter Sansousee.** After Peter's death, Mary Ann lived with **Antoine Metzgar** (Tamulch). Then she lived with **James Pierce** (Clamarchnet). She was still listed as a widow in 1900. On January 30, 1908, under the Reorganization Act, a fee patent for Mary Ann's allotment was issued to her heirs, **William Warren** and **John Warren.**[22]

Sansousee, Peter (d. 1878), Umpqua	Native Name: None known by author
Alias: Sansouci, Paul	Allotment: None known by author
Mother: Unknown to author	Father: Unknown to author

Peter had a number of children by his wife Agnes: Amelia (1859), Mary (1860–61), Monica (1861–61), and Louis (1861–63). Agnes died in 1863.

In 1867, Peter had a daughter, Sophie, by his wife Mary Ann.[23] Sophie was not listed with the family in 1872. Only his daughter Amelia was listed that year with him and Mary Ann. Henry, Mary Ann's brother, was also living with the family.

Santiago, Henry (1811c–87c), Umpqua[24]	Native Name: None known by author
Alias: Doctor Santiago	Allotment: None known by author
Mother: Unknown to author	Father: Unknown to author

In 1872, Henry Santiago was living with his wife, Nancy, who was related to Nellie Palouse. According to Nellie, they were half sisters with the same mother but different fathers. George Demour was Nancy's nephew.[25]

It was Nancy who explained to Rev. Summers how to play a women's game

---

22 *Heirs of Deceased Indians,* Allotment Record 187, gave her lifespan as (1837–March 9, 1905) and recorded her name as "Mary Ann Sansouci (Metzcar)."

23 Munnick and Beckham, *Catholic Church Records—Grand Ronde,* Register I, p. 5, B-5, p. 8, B-13, p. 8, S-6, p. 9, S-14, p. 15, B-219, p. 25, B-13, p. 26, S-22, p. 31, B-19, p. 48, B-11, p. 107, B-10, p. 108, S-13.

24 1872 GRIC: "Henry Santiago" under the Umpqua. Gatschet, *Texts, Sentences and Vocables,* 374: listed under the Klickitat.

25 National Archives, Seattle, NRIA-S-11, PAC-08, Nancy Hall: Her first husband was Santiago. Nancy died December 31, 1914, at the age of seventy five.

using small beaver teeth dice. She called the game *skosus* and said she "played the game as her mother, a Klamath, taught her."[26]

During Rev. Summers's visit in Santiago home, he not only learned a new dice game, but he "found" a number of items including a beautiful ancient spoon of carved bone, a tiny white water bucket, and a quiver in the Klickitat style. Santiago told him that poisoned arrows were safe in the quiver as the points could not work through.

Summers also saw what he believed to be Santiago's sacred fire-sticks: the same sticks used to light the ancient ceremonial fire. While Rev. Summers recorded the care he took not to seem overly interested in the fire-sticks, he remained silent on how the fire-sticks found their way into his possession. He wrote:

> He showed us his fire-sticks, the sacred ones, we at once concluded, but took care not to say so… He called his fire-sticks "slick-o-wish." As we looked at his earnest face, and followed his gestures, the picture of that Stone seat on the lofty brow of Spirit Mountain stole on our mental sight, for we knew he had obtained the sacred fire there more than once, and imagination easily placed him up there now, with believing followers, devotedly looking up to the skies for their gods to give them the sign of the holy flame. In spite of prohibitions it is likely they steal away there yet, and in secrecy go through their ancient rites." [27]

Eventually, Rev. Summers donated the fire-sticks, along with many other items collected from the people living on the reservation, to the British Museum in London, where they remain stored away in a warehouse even today.

By 1885, Henry Santiago was listed with a wife named Louiza, a nephew, Jones, and a niece, Kate. The agent described Santiago's place as a good house and barn on forty fenced acres with twelve acres in cultivation. By 1886, he had thirteen horses, fifteen hogs, a number of chickens, a good garden, a plow, a harrow, seven head of cattle, a wagon, a hack, and two sets of harness. Santiago was not listed on any GRIC after that year.

Santiam, Captain (1807c–92), Santiam band of Kalapuya[28]	Native Name: Culcha /*Cul-cha/*, Lipmashell /*Lip-ma-shell/*[29]
Alias: Old Santiam	Allotment 184
Mother: Unknown to author	Father: Unknown to author

Captain Santiam (Culcha) and his wife, Sarah (Roeva) had a son, John Harris

---

26 Ibid.

27 Cawley, *Indian Journal*, 41.

28 Gatschet, *Texts, Sentences and Vocables*, 368: "Old Santiam" under the Santiam tribe.

29 1887 GRIC: Indian name as "Cul-cha." Cawley, *Indian Journal*, 22: gave Indian name as Lip-ma-shell."

(1867) who was still alive in 1885.[30] **Eustace Howard** remembered Captain Santiam with another wife named **Puyiwa**.[31]

Captain Santiam received an allotment of 70.69 acres. In 1911, a potential buyer complained to Knott C. Egbert, Superintendent at Siletz, that he was interested in buying Captain Santiam's property and all the legal heirs were willing to sell except **Frank Bond**, the former husband of **Adeline Ann Hutchins**. In his letter, the interested buyer quoted a paragraph from a letter he claimed had been written to him by **Abraham Hudson**:

> By right Mr. Bonds is not an heir as Adilene [Hutchins] and he did not live as husband and wife. She was living with **Louis Savage** as husband and wife until he [Louis] was arrested, then she lived with Enoch Spiers as husband and wife[.] [A]nd then Enoch killed her while Mr. Bonds was living with **Laura Fern** until Adilene was killed before he married Laura. That is about all I could say in a letter, but if I could see you I could tell more. He does not want to sign because he wants to spite us.[32]

On October 31, 1916, Abraham Hudson and **John "Mose" Hudson** were issued a fee patent for Captain Santiam's entire allotment of 70.69 acres.

Santiam, Mary, Santiam band of Kalapuya	Native Name: Chantwa /CHANT-wa/ (chánt'wa?)*[33]
Alias: None known by author	Allotment: None known by author
Mother: Unknown to author	Father: Unknown to author

Mary (Chantwa) was **Captain Santiam** (Culcha)'s sister and the last wife of Jim Hines.[34]

Santiam, Puyiwa	Native Name: Puyiwa /PUI-wa/ (púy?wa)*[35]
Alias: None known by author	Allotment: None known by author
Mother: Unknown to author	Father: Unknown to author

Puyiwa was **Captain Santiam** (Culcha)'s wife.[36]

---

30 1887 GRIC: Indian name as "Ro-eva."

31 Jacobs, Field Notebook 86, *Texts and Ethnology*, 68.

32 Letter to Knott C. Egbert, & S. D. A., Siletz, Oregon from 811 Yeon Bldg, Portland, Oregon, dated December 30, 1911. O. Applegate, Testimony of Jake Fern: Enoch Spores was a second cousin to Laura Fern.

33 Jacobs, Notebooks 46, *Santiam Kalapuya Text*, n.p.

34 Ibid.

35 Jacobs, Field Notebook 86, *Texts and Ethnology*, 68.

36 Ibid.

Sappenfield, Sambo (1827c–98), Pudding River band of Kalapuya[37]	Native Name: Chawatkha /cha-WAT-ha/ (chawátxa)*[38]
Alias: Old Sambo	Allotment 186
Mother: Unknown to author	Father: Unknown to author

Sambo Sappenfield (Chawatkha) was **Nancy Kenoyer** (Tunishni)'s nephew and **Ben Harding** (Kwana)'s cousin. In 1872, he was listed on the GRIC with his wife, Julia, and son, Mark. Then on August 17, 1875, he married Eliza of the Kalapuya nation. At that time, Father Croquet noted in the records that neither of them had been baptized.[39]

In 1885, Sambo was listed with his wife, **Eliza George** (Tmulhu), and children Frank, Susan, and Henry. Three years later, none of the children were living with them.

Sambo received an allotment of 247.82 acres. On November 12, 1908, his widow, Eliza George, sold two hundred acres of Sambo's allotment. A fee patent was issued for the property to the purchaser, J. M. Welch. A fee patent for the remaining 47.82 acres was issued to **Cephas Tipton** on February 11 1921.

Savage, Louis (1878c–1915), Molalla, Yamhill band of Kalapuya	Native Name: None known by author
Alias: None known by author	Allotment: 16
Mother: Estella Monroe, Yamhill band of Kalapuya[40]	Father: Steve Savage, Molalla

Louis' parents, Estella Monroe and **Steve Savage** (Palhilh), were prominent people within the Grand Ronde community. When they had Louis baptized on August 25, 1878, his sponsors were **Chief Louis Napesa** of the Umpqua and **Susan Beagle,** the daughter of **Tualatin George** and **Martha Beagle** (Shkinda).[41]

After his mother died, Louis Savage lived with his grandmother, Marianne (Bochean), and his step-grandfather, **Peter Checkaon** (Chikhyan), until his grandmother died in 1891. After he turned fourteen, Louis claimed he was more or less on his own.[42]

---

37   Gatschet, *Texts, Sentences and Vocables,* 368, listed as French Prairie or Ahanthuyuk. Michelle, *Just a Memorandum,* 9: "Sambo Sabinfield and wife, Liza both Calapooia: a cousin lived near them." Jacobs, Field Notebook 46, *Santiam Kalapuya Texts,* 6: E. Howard said Sambo Sappenfield was the cousin of Ben Harding.

38   1887 GRIC: Indian name as "Yac-i-muck." Gatschet, *Texts, Sentences and Vocables,* 114: "Tchauatxa, the nephew of Kinai's wife, Sambu is a Pudding River Indian, he lives now S. of the agency, 2 miles from them, on three acres of Prairie."

39   Munnick and Beckham, *Catholic Church Records—Grand Ronde,* Register I, p. 94, M-7.

40   Ibid., Register I, p. 21, B-65: gives tribe as Yamhill.

41   Ibid., Register I, p. 108, B-19.

42   National State Archives, Salem, Oregon, Steven Savage Inmate File 4996. National Archives, Central Plains Region, Louie Savage Inmate File 5333: Louis said he was on

By all reports, Louis was one of the best educated and most industrious young men on the reservation, but on April 24, 1904, when he was about twenty-six years old, he was arrested for murder.

On the night of the incident, a group of men were playing an Indian stick game called *t'isay* at Wacheno's house.[43] Louis Savage was team leader of the side opposing **Joseph Corner Michelle's** team. The Grand Ronde Reservation Chief of Police, **William Simmons,** was the game mediator.[44]

About midnight someone brought some whiskey to the players. After a few drinks, members of opposing teams began to quarrel over "old grudges." A few months earlier, Joseph Mitchelle had pulled a knife on Louis, cutting him deep enough to leave scars on his forehead and neck. This was probably one of the old quarrels that resurfaced that night.[45]

It was almost dawn the morning of April 24 before the game broke up. Joseph Michelle and his team left first. They were standing on the porch and in the yard when Louis Savage came outside. One thing led to another and before long Louis and Joseph Michelle began to fight. Most, if not all, of the men outside had a little to drink that night and had participated in the heated quarrel with Louis Savage during the game. Therefore, they did not try to break up the fight, but instead cheered for Joseph Michelle.

Joseph Jeff Day, one of the men on Louis Savage's team, said he was still inside the house when he first heard Louis call for help. After he got to the door, he saw Joseph Mitchelle had Louis by the back of the neck and was pulling him backward while he pounded him in the stomach with his left fist as hard as he could. Somehow Louis managed to pull his gun. He pointed it up in the air and away from the crowd, but just as he pulled the trigger **Foster Wacheno** (Inawalh) came outside and walked right in the line of fire. Most of the men at the game agreed with this description of the events that evening and believed the shooting was accidental.

Louis told Joe Day later that he thought Joseph Michelle was reaching for his knife. He drew his gun to warn Michelle he was ready for him if he pulled it; however, Joseph Michelle jerked him and the gun went off.

After Foster fell to the ground dead, Louis broke free from Michelle's grip.

his own after he turned fourteen.

43 National Archives, Central Plains Region, Louie Savage Inmate File 5333: spelled "*tushi*." Jacobs, Field Notebook 36, *Santiam Kalapuya Text*, 80: the game is mentioned and spelled "*tacai*." Johnson and Zenk, *Chinuk Wawa Dictionary*: t'isay.

44 National Archives and Records Administration, Central Plains Region, Louie Savage Inmate File 5333.

45 Subpoenaed to testify on behalf of the prosecution: Andrew Kershaw, Joseph Abraham Mitchell, William Simmons, Jesse Wheeler, Orton Wheeler, Frank Wheeler, John Wacheno, Joe Day, John Warren, Stafford Fearn, Lawney Tom, Veronica Smith, and Felix Wacheno. Subpoenaed to testify on behalf of the defense: Moses Sitton, Stephen Kiki, Frank Wacheno, Jasper Holmes, Charles Snelling and Milton Holman, and Eustace Howard.

Although he had spent the only bullet in his gun, the rest of the men did not know Louis' gun was empty. Aiming the gun at the angry group of men, and warning them to keep away, he left with **Moses Sitton.** A few hours later, he gave himself up to the Yamhill County sheriff.

About six months later, on October 19, the case was called before a federal grand jury. Most of the testimony at the Coroner's Inquest was to the effect that the shooting was accidental. Some testified that Joseph Michelle jerked Louis back by the neck causing the gun to discharge. Others claimed Louis fired the shot as a warning to Michelle, who had him in a stranglehold that made him fear for his life.

On October 21, the grand jury presented to the court an indictment charging the defendant, Louis Savage, with murder. October 28, Louis Savage's attorney, B. F. Jones, entered a plea of not guilty.[46]

John Logsden was subpoenaed by both the prosecution and the defense. Later, he told Joe Day that he would have testified that the gun went off as a result of Joseph Michelle jerking Louis back by the neck, but that Dr. Kershaw forced him to sign an affidavit against Louis.

While the actual trial transcript is not available, later testimony obtained from the witnesses indicates that between the time of the inquest and the trial, some witness testimony changed. As to why this occurred, Louis said he could guess that the witnesses were close friends of Foster Wacheno and the trial occurred at a time when emotions entered largely into their testimony. A later statement offered by Andrew Kershaw supported Louis' feelings about the situation.

The attorney for the defense argued that the facts set forth in the indictment were not sufficient to constitute a crime and that the circuit court of the United States for the district of Oregon had no jurisdiction to try or punish Louis for the offense, because before the crime had been committed, both Louis and Foster had been allotted land on the Grand Ronde Reservation in severally, and as allotted Indians, both Louis and the deceased were citizens of the United States and amenable to the laws of the state of Oregon rather than laws of the United States for the alleged offense.[47]

After hearing the arguments of council, Judge Bellenger overruled Jones' complaint and set the trial for 10 a.m. the following day.

None of the twelve good and lawful men selected to sit on the jury were Indian. They were white men from all across Oregon. In recalling the case, the jury foreman, C. A. Barrett, said there was a lot of evidence presented at trial that seemed to show that the killing was accidental, but the jury could not agree on this point. Some did not believe it was accidental and were in favor of a verdict of first degree murder with a recommendation for hanging. Others were uncertain

---

46 National Archives and Records Administration, Central Plains Region, Louie Savage Inmate File 5333.

47 Heirs to Deceased Indians, Allotment Record 16: Louis had received a fee patent for a 40 acre allotment on June 15, 1903.

as to whether or not it was accidental and for that reason favored murder in the second degree.

After the jury had deliberated one day and one night, they felt they could not agree and some of the jury wanted further instructions from the court. In response, Judge Bellenger explained certain legal points and informed the jury that he thought they should agree on some verdict and urged them to do so inasmuch as the trial had been fair and held at great expense. Although still in doubt about the justice of the verdict, at least four of the twelve men changed their position at this point in deliberation.[48]

The next day, November 16, 1904, the jury returned a verdict:

We, the jury in the above entitled cause, do find the defendant Louie Savage, guilty as charged in the indictment herein, without capital punishment. [...] Whereupon, it is considered that said defendant, Louie Savage, be imprisoned at hard labor for the term of his natural life; and it is ordered that, until otherwise provided, this sentence be executed at the Penitentiary of the State of Oregon, and that he stand committed thereto until this sentence be preferred, or until he be discharged there from according to law.[49]

November 21, Louis was committed to the custody of the warden at Oregon State Penitentiary. One year later, on November 12, 1905, the United States Attorney General ordered his transfer to McNeil Island.[50]

From McNeil Island, Louis was transferred to Leavenworth Prison, where he was received on October 10, 1906. He was at Leavenworth when he learned that District Court Judge Pollock had denied his attorney's petition for a writ of habeas corpus.[51]

For Louis, the years that followed must have been long ones filled with emotional ups and downs. In March of 1913, he signed a prison agreement that gave him the privilege of being a prison trusty. A few months later he received a letter from Professor Leo Frachtenberg.

Professor Frachtenberg was a linguist interested in documenting endangered languages of Native American people. At this time, he was working at Siletz, but had heard that Louis and his father were the last two speakers of the Molalla language and had learned of Louis' situation.[52]

---

48 National Archives and Records Administration, Central Plains Region, Louie Savage Inmate File 5333.

49 Oregon State Archive, Salem, Oregon, O.S.P. Inmate Register Vol. 5 1894–1910, #3115-6164, Louis Savage File 4996.

50 Ibid.

51 National Archives and Records Administration, Central Plains Region, Louie Savage Inmate File 5333.

52 Record Unit 45, Office of the Secretary, 1890–1929, Correspondence Series I, Box 23

Louis Savage. Photo courtesy of Oregon State Archive, Salem, Oregon (File 4996)

After communicating with Frachtenberg, Louis Savage wrote his attorney, B. J. Jones, telling Jones that Frachtenberg had managed to get Andrew Kershaw to relent. Kershaw was now willing to cooperate in getting Louis' sentence modified. Louis wrote that Frachtenberg wanted Jones to begin preparing the necessary paperwork immediately. He also wrote he was feeling good about the possibility of success.

By September 19, his mood changed and he resigned his position as trusty. Apparently, a week earlier, he tried to take his life. In prison records, the doctor

---

of 112, Folder 14-16, Smithsonian Institution, Washington D.C: Leo Frachtenberg was head of a department at the Smithsonian Institution, but discharged after being accused of being a German sympathizer during World War I.

described the injury to Louis' wrist and wrote that Louis "had been despondent for some days."

Exactly when Louis learned that he had acquired tuberculosis is impossible to determine, but two days after his attempted suicide, on September 29, 1913, he was admitted to the Isolation Ward of the prison hospital where he remained through November 16, 1913.

Although by now he was seriously ill, Louis finally received good news in regard to his pardon on May 7, 1914. The commissioner of Indian affairs acknowledged his case in a letter to James Watson, writing:

> From the facts submitted by you and information obtained from the Superintendent in charge of the reservation on which the crime was committed, I am of the opinion that the ends of justice have been met and I have therefore recommended that the sentence imposed upon Savage be commuted to the time served.

Louis died on June 18, 1915, before the pardon came through. In a telegram to his father, Warden Morgan wrote: "Your son died yesterday at six-thirty pm of Pulmonary Tuberculosis. Body will be embalmed and sent to you at Government expense if you so desire; your to receive it at the railroad station and bear local expenses. Otherwise burial will be made in the prison cemetery and a neat stone erected for identification purposes."

Twenty-four hours later, on June 19, 1915, Louis was given a Christian burial and his remains interred in grave 5333 in the U.S. Prison Cemetery. Warren Morgan did not receive Steven Savage's response to his telegram until after the burial. Steven Savage had simply written, "Bury my son's body there."[53]

Savage, Steven (1849c), Molalla band of Molalla	Native Name: Palhilh /PA-hlihl/ (p'áaɬiɬ)*[54]
Alias: Steve Savage, Stephen Savage	Allotment: None known by author
Mother: Nancy	Father: Paul Toto, Molalla

Steve Savage (Palhilh) was the son of **Paul Toto** and a woman named Nancy. In 1872, his mother was still alive and living with him. **Margaret Toto** (Chaimala) was his half sister. **Tom Gilbert** (Kiyukiyush) and **Alexander Toto** were his half brothers. They shared the same father, but had different mothers.[55]

---

53 Oregon State Archive, Salem, Oregon, O.S.P. Inmate Register Vol. 5 1894–1910, 3115-6164, Louis Savage File 4996. National Archives and Record Administration, Louie Savage Inmate File 5333.

54 1887 GRIC: Indian name as "Pa-sis." Jacobs, *Santiam Kalapuya Ethnologic Texts*, Part 1, 81.

55 Affidavit State of Oregon, County of Yamhill, taken from Josephine (Frances) Shirley January 25, 1917 and Macasca Sutton, February 3, 1917. Jacobs, *Santiam Kalapuya*

When the fifth annual session of the Grand Ronde Indian Legislature convened in 1876, the Molalla sent Steve Savage and **Joel Hubbard** to represent their interests. Steve was also appointed road supervisor that year along with **Calapooia Billy Williams** (Hosanunda) .[56]

Steve married Estella, the daughter of **Sugar Monroe** and his wife, Marianne (Bochean), on January 3, 1877. He and Estella had a number of children including Andrew (1877c–77), Harris Henry (1881c–85), Helen (1884c–84), Mollie (1882c), and Louis.

Estelle died July 6, 1884.[57] The following year, Steve Savage was listed as living alone with his son Louis and his daughter Mollie. Only Steve and Louis, age ten, were listed on the 1888 GRIC.

A few years later, Steve was arrested for theft. Leaving Louis with his mother and stepfather, he served some time in the Oregon State Penitentiary.

In 1910–11, Steve Savage provided Leo Frachtenberg about thirty Molalla myths. During that time, he boarded for a few weeks with **Molalla Kate** (Muswi) and her husband, Louis Chantelle, at their home in Logsden.[58] In poor health, Steve is known to have been living at St. Helens from 1913 to 1915.[59]

After he died, **Frances Gilbert,** the daughter of Tom Gilbert (Kiyukiyush), Steve's half-brother, inherited Steve's allotment.

Years later, during the night of March 5, 1928, **John "Mose" Hudson** said he saw Steve and Tom Gilbert (Kiyukiyush) singing in a dream. Steve's son, **Louis Savage,** was also there "throwing on the drum." In Mose Hudson's dream, as Steve sang his eyes grew big and then larger.[60] Perhaps Steve had come to know some things he could not see in this world.

Sboyse, James (1846c), Kalapuya[61]	Native Name: None known by author
Alias: Jim Spoice, Spoyse	Allotment: None known by author
Mother: Unknown to author	Father: Unknown to author

"Jim Spoyse" was a *tkupi* from the *tian tkupi* band of Kalapuya-speaking people. His wife's village was called *tc ampe-ena* and was located just south of the

Ethnologic Texts, Part 1, 189.

56 National Archives, Seattle, Grand Ronde/Siletz, Land and Enrollment Program records, Field Notes and Land Survey 1875 –1898, Land Description Book 1878, Box 115; Grand Ronde Justice Court.

57 Munnick and Beckham, *Catholic Church Records—Grand Ronde,* Register I, p. 100, M-1, p. 104, B-32, p. 105, S-24, p. 109, B-19, p. 118, B-4, p. 128, B-3, S-7, p. 129, S-9, p. 130, S-7.

58 Jacobs, Field Notebook 33, *Chasta Costa etc., Santiam,* n.p.

59 National Archives, Central Plains Region, Louie Savage Inmate File 5333

60 Jacobs, *Santiam Kalapuya Ethnologic Texts,* Part 1, 189. Jacobs, Field Notebook 36, *Santiam Kalapuya Text,* 189.

61 Jacobs, Field Notebooks 46, *Santiam Kalapuya Text,* 85: John Hudson called him "Jim Sboyse."

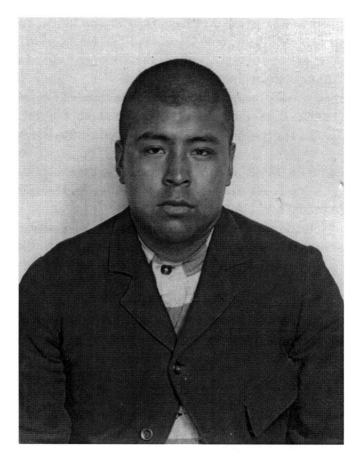

Steve Savage. Photo courtesy of Oregon State Archives (File 6132)

present town of Yoncalla. Like Cindy Jackson's mother and **Grace Wheeler,** her Indian name was Skenan. [62]

In 1886, "James Spoice" and Skenan were listed on the GRIC as "poor."

Scott, Polk (1832c–1909c), Yoncalla band of Kalapuya, Molalla[64]	Native Name: Puk /puk/ (púk)*[63]
Alias: None known by author	Donation Land Claim
Mother: Unknown to author	Father: Unknown to author

---

62 Jacobs, Field Notebooks 46, *Santiam Kalapuya Text,* 85, 125.

63 Jacobs, Field Notebook 86, *Texts and Ethnology,* 68: gave name as *puk.* Gatschet, *Texts, Sentences and Vocables,* 367: listed as "(poke) Puck Scott."

64 http://ftp.us-census.org/pub/usgenweb/census/or/douglas/1880. The 1880 Mt. Scott Census gave his age as forty-eight years. Gatschet, *Texts, Sentences and Vocables,* 367: listed under the Yoncalla. Jacobs, Field Notebook 51, *Music and Ethnology,* 48: he was part Molalla and part Yoncalla and spoke both languages.

Polk Scott (Puk) was related to the Molalla chief, **Quaiquaty** (Gwayakiti). Polk spoke both the Molalla and Yoncalla languages. He also spoke Chinook Jargon and could understand the Clackamas language.[65]

In 1854, Polk was with **Chief Halo** (Hilu) and his brother, **Muddy Tom Churchill** (Kaltas Lipom), when they went to the treaty council at Calapooia Creek near the town of Oakland in the Umpqua valley.[66]

At Grand Ronde it was said that Polk was one of the last of the good old time doctors. With his power he could swallow heated bullets and was one of those who could cure tuberulosis.[67] **Frank Norwest** called on him to cure his daughter, Susette Simmons, when the reservation doctor, Andrew Kershaw, would do nothing. Frank said he paid Polk a horse, five dollars in cash, and some blankets for the cure. After Polk Scott doctored Susette, she got well again. **William Simmons** and Susette supported Frank's account of the cure.[68]

Frances Gilbert agreed Polk could cure tuberculosis, but said she never saw him suck out pain. According to Frances, Polk used a rubbing technique much like a chiropractor does today.[69] In healing, Polk sang his doctoring songs and when he located the cause of the illness, he seized it and extracted it with his hands.[70] **Victoria Wishikin** (Kinishi) recorded one of his doctoring songs from memory for Melville Jacobs in 1930.[71]

Both **Abraham Hudson** and **John Warren** recalled a time when Polk was in a fight. They said after his stomach was ripped open by a knife, he pushed back his intestines and got well without any outside medical attention.[72]

Alexander Ross was one of the earliest voyagers to this land and described several incidents of this kind of native doctoring. He wrote:

> I once saw an Indian who had been attacked by a grizzly bear. His skull had been split open in several places and pieces of bone taken out just above the brain measuring 3/4 inch in length. He was cured so effectively by one of the shaman that in less than two months he was riding his horse in a chase. I have also seen them cut open the belly of a patient with a knife, extract a large quantity of fat from inside, and sew up the part again. The person was soon after perfectly recovered. I have witnessed

---

65 Jacobs, *Clackamas Text*, Part II, 650, Notes 459, 461.

66 O. Applegate, Testimony of Jake Fearn. Berreman, interview with John Warren, 1934: Warren gave Polk Scott's tribe as Yoncalla and accredited him as being "the last surviving Shaman."

67 Jacobs, Field Notebook 51, *Texts and Ethnology*, 23.

68 Berreman, interview with Frank Norwest and William Simmons.

69 Berreman, interview with Frances Shirley.

70 Jacobs, *Clackamas Text*, Part II, p. 650, Note 459. Jacobs, Field Notebook 51, *Music and Ethnology*, 48.

71 Jacob, Field Notebook 51, *Music and Ethnology*, 48–49.

72 Berreman, Interview with Abe Hudson and John Warren.

two or three such cases which would have baffled the skill of a regular surgeon cured by them.[73]

In 1872, Polk was listed with his wife, Fanny. By 1880, he had a new wife named Sally (1850c). They were farming at Pass Creek in Douglas County, Oregon.[74] By 1886, he was back at Grand Ronde, where he was listed as "poor."

In 1893, Polk married a woman named Mary. They were divorced May 10, 1900 after Polk Scott claimed she "deserted and abandoned him without cause."[75]

Later, Polk married **Eliza George** (Tmulhu), who was a woman doctor and the daughter of **Marysville George**. Polk and Eliza were listed together from 1902 through 1908. In 1909, Eliza was listed as a widow.

Polk Scott did not receive an allotment at Grand Ronde and did not sign the Surplus Land Agreement of 1901.

Scroggin, James (1840c–86), Rogue River[76]	Native Name: None known by author
Alias: Jim Scrogin, Scrogins, Scroggins Skrogin	Allotment: None known by author
Mother: Unknown to author	Father: Unknown to author

James was an old time doctor. He put his power in the poles of the dance house at Grand Ronde. When you entered the house you had to circle the poles without touching them. If you touched them, you would get sick and nothing could make you well. A lot of young men who did not believe died from touching them.[77]

As a result, **Chief Louis Napesa** sent for a Yakama doctor called John Bull to find out what was wrong with the poles and to overpower James Scroggins's spirit power. John Bull sang and blew on the poles, catching James' power. James jumped up and wanted it back. John Bull and Napesa wanted to kill James, but the agent stopped them. A short time later, James did die, leading many people to believe John Bull had indeed stolen his power.[78]

In 1872, James and his wife, Margaret, had a daughter, Anastasia, who does not seem to be recorded on the GRIC for that year, but Father Croquet wrote in church records January 21, 1872, that "Anastasia, born of James Skrogin and Margaret of Rogue River nation" had been baptized. The child's godmother was

73 Ross, *Adventures of the First Settlers on the Oregon or Columbia River.*
74 http://ftp.us-census.org/pub/usgenweb/census/or/douglas/1880, 1880 Mt. Scott Census.
75 Oregon State Archive, Salem, Oregon, Circuit Court Records for the State of Oregon for Polk County, Divorce Decree between Polk Scott and Mary Scott, May 10, 1900.
76 Gatschet, *Texts, Sentences and Vocables*, 366: under Rogue River as "Scrogin Jim."
77 Du Bois, *The Ghost Dance*, 30–31.
78 Ibid.

Margaret's cousin, **Martha Jane Sands.**[79]

In 1872, their son, Walter (1867c), was the only one of their children still living with them. Also living with the James Scroggin family were James's niece, **Mary Neal**, Martha Jane Sands, **Nicholas Sands,** Milton Sands, **Kate Scroggin,** and Kate's daughter, Eliza.

In 1878, James married Nannie Siletz.[80] He died March 15, 1886.[81]

Scroggin, Kate, Rogue River/Shasta	Native Name: None known by author
Alias: Scrogin, Scrogins, Scroggins	Allotment: None known by author
Mother: Unknown to author	Father: Unknown to author

On the GRIC for 1872, she and her daughter, Ann Eliza, were living with Kate's Uncle **James Scroggin.**

Scroggin, Nancy (1820–1902), wife of Umpqua husband	Native Name: None known by author
Alias: Scrogin, Scrogins, Scroggins, Nannie Siletz	Allotment 199
Mother: Unknown to author	Father: Unknown to author

Nancy Scroggin was probably the widow of **James Scroggin** called "Nannie Siletz."

She received a 98.05-acre allotment. Her heir was listed as Mollie Pierce-Orton. Mollie sold the property in 1907.

Sealy, John (1835c)	Native Name: None known by author
Alias: None known by author	Allotment: None known by author
Mother: Unknown to author	Father: Unknown to author

In 1885, John was living with his wife, Henrietta, and children, John and Henry.

Selkeah, John Joseph (1888–1921), Yamhill band of Kalapuya, Clackamas, Umpqua, Lower Chinook	Native Name: None known by author
Alias: None known by author	Allotment 190
Mother: Marceline Riggs, Clackamas, Lower Chinook, Umpqua	Father: Peter Joseph Selkeah, Yamhill band of Kalapuya

On April 16, 1913, John Joseph Selkeah married Elsie McKay, daughter of

---

79 Munnick and Beckham, *Catholic Church Records—Grand Ronde*, Register I, p. 72, B-4.

80 Ibid., Register I, p. 108, M-9.

81 Ibid., Register II, p. 2, S-5. Michelle, *Just a Memorandum*, 3: Jim Scogin and "his wife Shalot" as very old people.

Alexander McKay and Elizabeth Arquette. They had at least five children.

John Joseph Selkeah received a fee patent for his entire eighty-acre allotment on December 6, 1916.

Selkeah, Margaret (1883–99), Umpqua, Clackamas, Yamhill band of Kalapuya, Lower Chinook	Native Name: None known by author
Alias: None known by author	Allotment 189
Mother: Marceline Riggs, Umpqua, Clackamas, Lower Chinook	Father: Peter Joseph Selkeah, Yamhill

A fee patent was issued on February 11, 1921, to Margaret's heirs, John J. Selkeah, Abraham Lawney, Clinton Lawney and Eva Lawney for Margaret's entire eighty-acre allotment.

Selkeah, Mary (1820c–94)[82]	Native Name: None known by author
Alias: None known by author	Allotment 191
Mother: Unknown to author	Father: Unknown to author

Mary received a 100.23-acre allotment. Father Croquet recorded Mary Selkeah's death as occurring on January 17, 1894. Her sole heir was **Peter Selkya's** wife, Louise (Comadeer). On March 3, 1921, Louise sold Mary's allotment and a fee patent was issued to the buyer, Weymouth Crowell, for eighty acres. The remaining 20.23 acres were in trust status. After Louise died in 1924, her great granddaughter, Opal Cleo Selkeah, and her great grandson, Peter Verne Selkeah, inherited the 20.23-acre trust property.[83]

Selkya, Peter (1832c–1905), Yamhill band of Kalapuya	Native Name: Selkya /SEL-kya/ (sélk'ya)*[84]
Alias: Yamhill Peter, Chief Peter, David Shelkeah, Peter Sulkey, Sulkia, Sulkie	Allotment 192
Mother: Unknown to author	Father: Unknown to author

Selkya was a Yamhill Kalapuya sub-chief and the brother of **James Stone**, who was buried at Grand Ronde on June 5, 1861. Father Croquet noted in the

---

82 Munnick and Beckham, *Catholic Church Records—Grand Ronde*, Register II, p. 90, S-2.

83 *Heirs to deceased Indians*, Allotment Record 191.

84 Jacobs, Field Notebooks 36, *Santiam Kalapuya Text*, 192: "selkya, Peter Selky—a Yamhill man." Jacobs, Field Notebooks 47, *Santiam Kalapuya Text*, 22. Jacobs, Field Notebook 51, *Music and Ethnology*, 46. Cawley, *Indian Journal*, 23: gave his name as Peter "Sulkia." 1887 GRIC gave his Indian name as "Sulkia."

record that "James brother, Peter chief, and others" were present and witnesses to the ceremony.[85]

In looking back over his life, Selkya said:

> They now call me Peter Sulkey. I was formerly called Shelkeah or David and that was the name signed to the treaty.[86] I signed as Second Chief of the Yamhill band of Calapooia. I was often called David in French Prairie in those days.[87]

Selkya had the strong power of Thunder. When he became angry the earth shook, thunder roared, and rain poured down. When he danced the spirit dance, he did not need to hold a medicine cane or feather, but could merely stand at the dance and sing his power song.[88]

He also was a great hunter because he had the power of Deer. When people wanted to eat venison they went to Selkya's house, for they knew they would find it there. When he got old, he had to hunt by horseback, but nothing stopped him from hunting.[89]

In 1872, Peter was listed with his wife, Louise (Comadeer), his son, Peter Joseph (1859c), his daughter, Jane (1863c), and his mother-in-law, **Ann Martin** (Tuckali).[90] After her father died, Louise Selkeah was raised by **Yamhill Luther Elkin** (Ilkin) and his wife, **Nancy Elkin** (Kizad), at Ballston in Yamhill County.[91]

Rev. Summers mentioned that Peter was a relative of Ilkin.[92] He said he was present once when Selkya visited Old Ilkin bringing him venison. Summers wrote, "Sulkia does not forget to help the aged and the feeble."[93]

During the winter of 1877, Selkya provided Yamhill language vocabulary to Albert Gatschet. In 1879, he was elected to the eighth annual session of the Grand Ronde Legislature as one of the representatives of the west precinct. When the legislature convened, he was elected president of the assembly.[94]

Peter Selkya's son, Joseph, married **Marcelline Riggs** on February 6, 1883. Joseph and Marcelline gave Selkya any number of grandchildren, including Me-

---

85 Munnick and Beckham, *Catholic Church Records—Grand Ronde*, Register I, p. 10, S-21.

86 Kappler, *Treaty with the Kalapuya, Etc., 1855*, 665-669.

87 O. Applegate, Testimony of Peter Sulkey.

88 Jacobs, *Santiam Kalapuya Ethnologic Texts*, Part I, 68-69.

89 Ibid.

90 1887 GRIC: Louise's Indian name, "Com-a-deer." 1887 GRIC: Ann's Indian name, "Tuck-a-li."

91 National Archives, Seattle, PAO-10, bx 1614, Mary Hauxhurst, Princess Watlistai, testimony of Louise Selkeah.

92 Ibid.: Peter Selkya was a nephew to Old Elkin.

93 Cawley, *Indian Journal*, 39.

94 National Archives, Seattle, Grand Ronde/Siletz, Land and Enrollment Program records, Field Notes and Land Survey 1875–1898, Land Description Book 1878, Box 115; Grand Ronde Justice Court.

linda (1882), Henry (1884c), Anna (1885c) **Margaret,** and **John Joseph Selkeah.**[95]

On October 10, 1887, Joseph died and Marcelline came home with two of her children to live with Selkya, Louise, and Louise's mother, Ann Martin, who was about seventy-one years old by then.[96]

Peter received a 240-acre allotment. When he died on October 19, 1905, his grandson, John Joseph, was his sole heir. John Joseph sold 160 acres of Peter's allotment to C. M. Blair on September 27, 1912. On February 11, 1921, John Joseph received a fee patent for the remaining eighty acres of Peter's allotment land.

When John Joseph died on March 27, 1921, he left an estate that consisted solely of real property valued at two thousand dollars to his widow and children subject to the dower interest of his grandmother, Louise Selkeah.[97] Louise died May 3, 1924.

In 1929, **Victoria Wishikin** (Kinishi) recorded several of Selkya's power songs for Melville Jacobs.

Louise, wife of Peter Selkya. Photo courtesy of Smithsonian Institute (No. 01134700)

---

95 Munnick and Beckham, *Catholic Church Records—Grand Ronde*, Register I, p. 123, M-2, p. 127, B-28, p. 133, B-43.

96 Ibid., Register II, p. 34, S-14.

97 National Archives, Salem, Oregon, Yamhill County, 1921 Estate File 1447, John Sulkey. *Heirs of Deceased Indians*, Allotment Records 192, 190, 189, 188.

Semoll, James, Umpqua	Native Name: None known by author
Alias: None known by author	Allotment: None known by author
Mother: Unknown to author	Father: Unknown to author

James Semoll and Maria had a son named **Semoll McCoy.** His mother, Maria, was dead by 1872. After James Semoll died, **Peter McCoy** (Inchaishi) finished raising Semoll.

Seymour, Mohawk (d. 1872c), Kalapuya	Native Name: None known by author
Alias: None known by author	Allotment: None known by author
Mother: Unknown to author	Father: Unknown to author

In 1872, Seymour's wife, Rose, was listed as a widow.

Shadden, Edward (1842c–72), Cow Creek band of Umpqua	Native Name: None known by author
Alias: None known by author	Allotment: None known by author
Mother: Unknown to author	Father: Unknown to author

Edward had at least one child: Apolline (1860c–61). He died April 30, 1872. **James Allen, Frank Quenel,** and others attended his funeral.

Shangaretta, Joseph (1823c–1900c), Kalapuya, Iroquois[98]	Native Name: Shangaretta /shaeyng-GRE-tal/[99]
Alias: Joseph Sangaretta, Joseph Zangrata, Joe Sangaretti, Jo Sengaretta	Allotment 185
Mother: Kalapuya	Father: Louis Shangaretta, Iroquois

Joseph was the son of an Iroquois called Louis Shangaretta and **Muddy Tom**

---

98 Michelle, *Just a Memorandum*, 6: Mary Ann wrote "Joseph Shangratte, breed, can't tell you about his father, but they say his mother was a full blooded Indian, phenophs. He had an uncle living here, Muddy Tom afterwards he was Tom Churchill." Oregon State Archives, Salem, Oregon, 1901, Polk County, Estate Tom Churchill File 0938, determined Joseph Shangaretta was the nephew of Tom Churchill. Jacobs, Field Notebooks 46, *Santiam Kalapuya Text*, 85: Muddy Tom Churchill was part "Pinefu" and perhaps part "Pe-ena." The Pe-ena was a tribe of the Yoncalla originally located just south of where the town of Yoncalla is now. Gatschet, *Texts, Sentences and Vocables*, 368: list him under the "Kalapuya now with the Marysville." The Federal Census for District 812 Indian Population at Grand Ronde in 1900 gave Joseph's mother as Long Tom Kalapuya.

99 Personal Communication with Dr. Henry Zenk: Clara Riggs pronounced Shangaretta's name "shaeyng-GRE-ta" (ae for the "a" in English "as"). Older records discovered by researcher, Donald Haller show the pronounciation as "Soi-en-gah-rah-ta."

Churchill (Kaltas Lipom)'s sister or half sister. Through Muddy Tom, he was related to **Chief Halo** (Hilu) and **Old Blind Ben Pete** (Lamptumpif).

Joseph's father was originally from a village near Sault St-Louis, Canada. The first record of his association with the fur traders was made June 1, 1814, when he joined the Northwest Fur Company as a steersman at Fort William.

From Fort Williams, Shangaretta was sent to the Columbia District in 1816. He was apparently married; an entry in Company records for that year indicated his wages were paid to his wife.

After the North West and Hudson's Bay Companies merged in 1821, Shangaretta served as a hunter on Peter Ogden's Snake Expedition from 1826 to 1827 and was listed as one of the "Freemen, Engages, and Assistance" for the Hudson's Bay Company's Southern Expedition of 1828.

Between trapping and exploring, Louis Shangaretta was busy. In a letter dated April 3, 1832, John McLoughlin wrote Michel LaFramboise regarding plans for another expedition southward into California:

> I am told Louis Shanagarate [Shangaretta] wants to go with you. You can let him go if you choose. You must send word to those that have to come here to be equipt that they must send their families on after you or with you while they come here so as not to lose time. The season is advancing. No time must be lost [...][100]

Very likely Louis Shangaretta's whole family accompanied him as it was customary for the men to take their families with them. However, sometime between the birth of his youngest son in 1827 and his daughter's wedding on March 7, 1835, Shangaretta was widowed, making it impossible to say whether or not Joseph's mother was alive at the time of this expedition.[101]

Back in the Willamette Settlement in late August of 1835, Louis Shangaretta also died. His death came suddenly when "a vessel burst in his lung." McLoughlin sent for the Methodist missionary Jason Lee to perform the funeral ceremony and offered him the Shangaretta estate in exchange for taking responsibility for the Shangaretta children.[102]

On Tuesday, September 1, 1835, Louis Shangaretta's funeral was held at the Willamette Settlement. Jason Lee could not perform the ceremony, but sent the ailing Daniel Lee in his place. After he accepted the Shangaretta estate, on Tues-

---

100 Barker, *Letters of Doctor John McLoughlin Written at Fort Vancouver, 1829–1832*, Letter 229.

101 Carey, *Mission Record Book*, 230–266.

102 Morrison, *Outpost, John McLoughlin and the Far Northwest*, 309. Louis Shangaretta "burst a blood vessel in his lungs and died almost immediately." McLoughlin asked Jason Lee to attend to the orphaned children and "the little property that fell to the heirs."

day, October 13, Jason Lee went to the Campment Du Sable to collect the family.[103]

Joseph Shangaretta was educated at the Jason Lee Indian School.[104] His older sister and younger brother died there. Joseph was living in the area of the school when the Cayuse attacked the Whitman Mission in 1847.[105]

The first news of the Whitman attack reached the Willamette Valley on the evening of December 6. While the Hudson's Bay Company refused Joel Palmer's request for a war loan, Peter Skene Ogden started up the Columbia River the following day with two boats and sixteen paddlers to rescue the Whitman hostages.

Upon receiving the news, the American settlers immediately held a public meeting in Oregon City to organize a militia of volunteers. Terrified the tribes would unite against them, they wondered if they could count on the United States government for protection and which side the French Canadians would take in the event of war.

As a result of this meeting, the Provisional Government of Oregon established the first volunteer company of Oregon soldiers. On December 10, a regiment of fourteen companies of volunteers were raised. Their orders were to proceed to Walla Walla, find out who had killed the people at the Whitman Mission, and punish them. The soldiers were to confront the Cayuse before they could get other tribes to join them and stop any further Indian action.

The question of Canadian support for the Americans was answered by Thomas McKay, the part Ojibwa son of Marguerite Wadin-McLoughlin. One French Prairie resident said McKay rode along the road asking everyone he met to join him in the fight against the Cayuse. After convincing Charles McKay and Alexander McKay to ride with him, he recruited his brothers-in-law, three half brothers named Louis, Robert, and George Montour.

In all, thirty-six men including Joseph Shangaretta joined Thomas McKay in forming a company of French Canadian, native, and Métis recruits that rode through a snowstorm hauling a cannon to join the main regiment. Upon their arrival, the Americans cheered and the United States flag was raised in salute. A flag was presented to Thomas McKay bearing a lone star and a number of stripes. He in turn presented it to his company, saying, "This is the flag you are expected to defend and defend it you must." [106]

The Oregon Riflemen under Colonal Gilliam's command first confronted the

---

103 Carey, *Mission Record Book,* 230–66, September 1, 1835.

104 Carey, *Mission Record Book*: October, 13, 1835: "Jason Lee gone to Campment Du Sable to settle the affairs of the late Louis Shangareti and bring his family to this place, having been appointed thereto by Dr. McLoughlin." Then there was a second entry: "The above mentioned family, consisting of Isabel, Joseph, and Nicholas, children of said Louis. Sookta, Kartoosh, Marlooah, Solomon and… kalt, formerly slaves but free since they came here, for slaves cannot be with us. They pass over our threshold and their shackles fall. Sookta and his little son, about three years old, are both unwell."

105 Victor, *Early Indian Wars.*

106 Clark, *History of the Willamette Valley.*

Plate 48: Joseph Shangaretta. Photo courtesy of Oregon Historical Society (OrHi 85529)

Cayuse on February 24, 1848, at a place called Sand Hollow eight miles east of Wells Springs on Immigration Road. The Cayuse aligned themselves about four feet apart encircling the command. Then they would ride within gun range of the soldiers, back off, and advance again at full speed. After a time, they broke into a second circle within the first, brandishing weapons and yelling threats.

When the soldiers began to divide into north and south wings, the Cayuse moved to their right. Captain Thompson and Captain Maxon's companies, forming the left flank, were on the north side of the road. The companies of Captain English and Captain McKay were on the south or right of command when Grey Eagle and Five Crows rushed headlong toward the troops. As one of them fired, killing a dog that had run out from among the soldiers, Thomas McKay shot Chief Grey Eagle in the head, killing him instantly. At the same time, Lt. Charles McKay, using a shotgun, severely wounded Chief Five Crows in the arm and knocked him from his horse.

The wounding of their chiefs confused the Cayuse. Only after Chief Five Crows shouted for them to continue the fight were they able to regroup and re-load their rifles. Twenty minutes later, they charged again. Returning fire, the troops maneuvered to protect their supply train until they could reach a favor-able spot to form a defensive corral. The Cayuse attacked repeatedly, their rifles outdistancing those of the soldiers.

The cannon that Captain McKay's Company D had dragged around the mountain on the rear wheels of a wagon now played a crucial part in the battle. Twice in the engagement, McKay's men fired the long-barreled nine-pounder. Neither of cannon blasts were lethal, but the Cayuse momentarily fell back.

At sundown, the Cayuse retreated to shelter among the buttes of Butter Creek eight or nine miles from the spot where the battle had begun. The Battle of Sand Hollow had lasted three hours. In the safety of the buttes, the Cayuse assessed the day's fight. Eight of their warriors were dead, including Welaptulket's brother, Edward Tiloukait. They had retrieved the bodies of only six.

A second encounter between soldiers and Cayuse occurred several weeks lat-er. Gilliam, attempting to catch the hostile band by surprise, had planned a night march. The following morning about four hundred Indians, mostly Palouse, looked up to see Gilliam's command riding boldly into their camp. Although armed, the Palouse professed friendship. The soldiers were ordered to hold their fire. The Palouse succeeded in convincing the troops that the killers were north across the Snake and that all the native people on the south bank were friendly. Yet at that moment, unknown to the soldiers, the men they wanted were within gun range and others were not much farther away.

Unable to round up the killers, Gilliam ordered his men to collect over four hundred horses belonging to the Palouse. Then the troops turned and rode to-ward the Touchet River. After the soldiers had gone, the Cayuse rode in to join ranks with the Palouse and turned on their pursuers. Thus began an all-day run-ning fight in which warriors of the two tribes initiated one skirmish after another, falling back and charging time and time again.

In these encounters, the Cayuse and Palouse yelled insults at the Americans. Mungo Antoine Ansure, the regimental interpreter from Captain McKay's Com-pany D, was enlisted to help them understand what the Indians were saying. Moving through the lines, Mungo told the soldiers that they were calling them cowards. He said he responded that they would fight when they reached the Touchet River. In the course of the skirmishing, Mungo's horse was shot from under him.

Since the hostile Indians had threatened to kill Mungo, three soldiers dropped back to protect him. As the Cayuse made a run on them, attempting to kill Mun-go, one of the soldiers fell from his horse, faking an injury. The soldier then shot one of the Cayuse warriors just as he was about to kill Mungo.

That night, a few friends from other tribes joined the Cayuse and Palouse.

The following morning, the battle continued. The Cayuse and Palouse knew they must keep the soldiers from fording the swift Touchet. Within two miles of the ford, they sped ahead of them to gain the thick brush cover at the river. At this point a fierce hour-long battle ensued. Although the Indians failed at their task, they prevented the soldiers from carrying their wounded across the river until a detachment came to assist. When the long battle had ended nine or ten soldiers had been wounded including William Taylor, who had sprung up in the bushes only to be shot by an Indian a few yards away. Another soldier, Nathan Olney, saw the act and immediately retaliated, killing the man with a knife in hand to hand combat.

After carrying off their dead, the Cayuse considered making one last stand, but retired instead. War's end found great loses on both sides. Colonel Gilliam had been accidentally shot to death. Seriously ill, Thomas McKay had to retire to the Willamette Valley, where he died shortly after his return. Having lost over five hundred horses to the Americans, the Cayuse were in financial ruin, divided, and starving. Much worse, with their leaders in exile, they knew their fight was not over.

As for Joseph Shangaretta, he returned to the Salem area and aligned himself with the Santiam band of Kalapuya. Given his education, the Santiam welcomed his services.

After treaty negotiations with the Americans, Joseph Shangaretta was one of those who signed the 1855 land cession treaty on behalf of the Santiam band of Kalapuya. His signature can be found behind that of their third chief, **Tom Hutchins** (Liham).[107]

Sometime between 1863 and 1869, Joseph became chief of the Mary's River band of Kalapuya.[108] He represented the Mary's River band of Kalapuya at the fifth annual session of the Grand Ronde Indian Legislature. When the legislature convened on January 4, 1876, he was elected president of the assembly.

Joseph Shangaretta's legislative assembly adopted thirty-four provisions of law that described the Indian court system including the role, authority, and wages to be paid to each officer, established a system of taxation, a court treasury, a burial fund for the destitute, and an administrator for the estate of orphaned children. They established a road department, planned the road system, elected road supervisors, and made it mandatory for every adult male living on the reservation to build and maintain the roads without pay.

They also passed statues that established penalties for adultery, rape, juvenile delinquency, assault, testifying falsely, bribing an officer of the court, and bringing alcohol onto the reservation.[109]

---

107 Kappler, *Treaty with the Kalapuya, Ect.*, 1855.
108 O. Applegate, Testimony of Mary Ann Voutrin, Captain Frank Quinelle, and James Winslow.
109 National Archives, Seattle, Grand Ronde/Siletz, Land and Enrollment Program records, Field Notes and Land Survey 1875–1898, Land Description Book 1878, Box

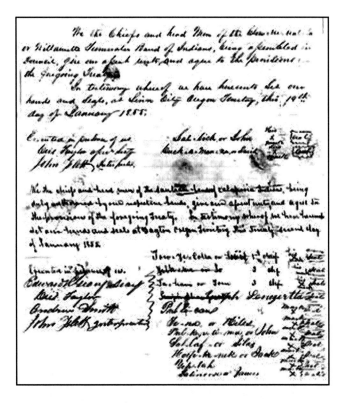

Signatures of the chiefs of the Santiam Band of Kalapuya. Shangaretta was the fourth signer. His name is written as "Sengertta." National Archives, Washington DC.

Clearly, it was Shangaretta to whom Agent J.B. McClain was referring in 1886 when he wrote:

There is one poor fellow, whom I knew when he was a boy that went to the Methodist school in 1843 and 1844 at Salem, who showed me his leg. It has been sore for the last twenty years. He is industrious; has been trying to work all these years. He says you can stick a knife or pin into his body anywhere, and he cannot feel it. He has a wife whom I knew at the same time. His own children are all married off, but he has raised three orphan girls. Two of them are married; the other goes to school. He says, looking at me and at his leg, and then showing me his hand he cut yesterday with an ax trying to make a living, "What shall I do? I had better be dead. I have got nothing but my garden; I can live on that, but when that's gone, what shall I do?"[110]

115; Grand Ronde Justice Court.

110 *Annual Report Commission of Indian Affairs*, 1886, 209–11.

Judge Joseph Shangaretta. Photo courtesy of Oregon Historical Society (OrHi CN022577)

Five years later, things had improved somewhat for Joseph Shangaretta, as he served from 1891 to 1895 as judge for the Court of Indian Offences.[111] Indian Agent John Brentano described Shangaretta's performance in this position in his annual report for 1893:

I have found the police very prompt, reliable... The Indian judge, Joseph Shangarata, deserves special mention. I must say that I have seen very few courts that try to be more just than this Indian judge. His mode of procedure is, however, somewhat primitive and will bear improving.[112]

---

111 Grand Ronde/Siletz Tribal Program Records Box 162, Agency & Tribal Council Records 1876–1951, RG 75, BIA, National Archives—Pacific NW Region, 6125 Sand Point Way, NE, Seattle, WA 98115.

112 *Annual Report Commission of Indian Affairs*, 1893, 266–67.

Joe Shangaretta (second from right) riding down street in Grand Ronde with Dan Robinson (far left), Peter Menard Jr. (center). Photo courtesy of Oregon Historical Society (CN022571)

In 1888, Joseph and his wife, **Nancy Pisk,** had a house and barn on sixty fenced acres with a one-acre garden and an acre in oats. They also had four horses, three head of cattle, four tons of hay, and sixty bushels of potatoes.

Joseph had two spirit guides, one a black man, the other an Indian, who came to him in dreams to warn him who among the people would soon die.[113] One of his granddaughters said that toward the end of his life Joseph was almost blind, but he always kept a garden and when weeding never mistakenly pulled even one carrot.

On October 5, 1894, Indian Agent John Brentano wrote the United States Commissioner of Pensions to see if either Joseph Shangaretta or **Frank Quenel** were entitled to military pensions. He wrote, "They are old and needy now and they are deserving of support. Both are imminently worthy of help." If the Commissioner responded, it was not with a check.

Joseph received a 240-acre land allotment. When he died, he was buried in **David Holmes**'s family cemetery at Grand Ronde in an unmarked grave.[114] His daughters, Mary Holmes-Mitchelle and Elizabeth Menard, inherited his real

---

113 Jacobs, *Santiam Kalapuya Ethnologic Texts,* Part 1, 67.
114 Personal communication with Merle Holmes, 1993.

property, which was valued at $450 in 1907.[115] They also inherited the estate of Joseph's uncle, Muddy Tom Churchhill .

Shepherd, Jack, Santiam band of Kalapuya	Native Name: None known by author
Alias: None known by author	Allotment: None known by author
Mother: Unknown to author	Father: Unknown to author

In 1872, he was listed with his wife, Julia.

Shiliqua, James (1830c–1908), Tualatin band of Kalapuya	Native Name: Shilikwa /SHI-li-kwa/ (shílik'wa)*[116]
Alias: Lame Jim, James Siliqua, James Selkeah, James Pratt	Allotment 193
Mother: Tualatin	Father: Itcamut /i-CHE-muhl/ ichə́muɬ,* Tualatin band of Kalapuya[117]

Lame Jim Shiliqua (Shilikwa) was a Tualatin sub-chief. He had a half brother, **John Pratt** (Gwaimit). While Gwaimit's mother was Yamhill Kalapuya, Shilikwa's mother was part or whole Tualatin.[118] Shilikwa was also related to **Antoine Metzkar** (Tamulch), **Tualatin William Wishikin,** and **Callo Bonaparte** (Kalukh).[119]

In 1855, Shilikwa was one of the men **Chief Kiakuts** (Kayakach) sent to kill **Dave Yachkawa** after the signing of the treaty.[120] He was also a Tualatin medicine doctor. One of his powers came from the vapor that rises from the mountains in

115 Oregon State Archives, Salem, Oregon, 1907, Yamhill County, Estate File 1214, Joseph Shangaretta.

116 Jacobs, *Clackamas Text,* Part II, 519-520: "My father's brother's son's name was 'silikwa,' he was a shaman." 1872 GRIC: "James Shiloguy" aka "Lame Jim." Jacobs, Field Notebooks 46, *Santiam Kalapuya Text,* n.p., gave his name as "Jim cilikwa, Lame Jim." 1887 GRIC: Indian name as "ciliqua." Jacobs, Field Notebook 52, *Texts and Ethnology,* 34: "cilikwa, atwa late name of a man."

117 Jacobs, Notebooks 67, *Texts Ethnology Clackamas & Jargon,* 22, gives Victoria Howard's father's brother, "itcamut," who had a son "cilikwa."

118 Jacobs, Field Notebooks 46, *Santiam Kalapuya Text,* n.p., "John Pratt and Lame Jim cilikwa were probably 1st cousins; they called each other brother." Jacobs, Field Notebooks 58, *Texts and Ethnology,* 122. Michelle, *Just a Memorandum,* 6, gave John Pratt and James Shiliqua as brothers. Gatschet, *Texts, Sentences and Vocables,* 370, gave Shiliqua as Pratt's younger brother. Oregon State Archives, Salem, Oregon, 1909, Yamhill County, Estate John Pratt, File 1327, gave James Shiliqua, John Pratt, Bonapart, Antoine Metzkar, and Bill Wishikin all as brothers with a common father.

119 Jacobs, Field Notebook 51, and *Music and Ethnology,* 6, 18, references this Tualatin medicine man as "Mrs. Howard's father's uncle."

120 Jacobs, *Santiam Kalapuya Ethnologic Texts,* Part 1, 169. Joel Palmer, Agreement of April 4, 1855 between LeMedicene, Dave Yatzkawa, and Chief Kayakach of the Tualatin band of Kalapuya, *Correspondence and papers of Joel Palmer.*

early morning. It was this power that caused him to smoke at certain times. On these occasions, he would take a long pull and blow puffs of smoke at the sky as he sat casually talking. Sometimes he would ask for a child to bring him water; then he would blow the water upon the child. He said this would make the child grow big.[121]

Whenever anyone came to ask him to do doctoring, he would go. Unlike other doctors, he would not eat until he had finished his preliminary examination of the patient. He said his spirit power had gone ahead of him to the house of the patient and was at full strength. To eat would only weaken his power.[122] When Shililwa did eat, he would demand absolute quiet and children were sent outside. No one could pass behind him or look at him least he choke and became sick.[123]

Shilikwa once cured **William Wishikin**'s daughter **Victoria Wishikin** (Kinishi) of deafness. Many years later, she recorded several of his doctor songs for Melville Jacobs.[124]

When Shilikwa's Wasco wife, Mary, died on May 28, 1862, he took her body back to The Dalles to be buried among her people.[125] By 1872, Shilikwa was listed with his wife Harriet and **Henry Crawford,** his son by an earlier wife. A slave named "**Jimmy John**" was also living with him.[126]

This same year the Grand Ronde Indian Legislature established a board of commissioners that controlled the Indian court treasury. James Shilikwa was elected to serve on the board with the Tualatin sub-chief Dave Yachkawa and **Henry Winslow** in 1877.

On November 4, 1878, the seventh annual session of the Grand Ronde Indian Legislature convened; Shilikwa represented the east precinct along with Dave Yachkawa and **Foster Wacheno** (Inawalh). Again that year, he was elected to serve as Court Treasurer. This time he shared the office with **Solomon Riggs** (Gunconnacli).[127]

---

121 Jacobs, Field Notebook 58, *Texts and Ethnology*, 122.

122 Jacobs, *Clackamas Text,* Part II, 519–20; p. 520, paragraph 3, line 1, "My father's brother's son's name was 'silikwa,' he was a shaman." Jacobs, Field Notebooks 46, Santiam Kalapuya Text, 161: J. B. Hudson said he was a good hand at curing burns; "little of a doctor man."

123 Jacobs, Field Notebook 54, *Texts and Ethnology*, 98.

124 Jacobs, Field Notebook 51, *Texts and Ethnology*, 31.

125 Munnick and Beckham, *Catholic Church Records — Grand Ronde,* Register I, p. 20, S-18.

126 Jacobs, Field Notebook 46, *Santiam Kalapuya Text,* n.p: JB Hudson said, a Tualatin, he was a good hand at curing burns; a little of a doctor man; his last woman was from Warm Springs perhaps, and he had a son of an earlier wife called Henry Crawford. Gatschet, *Texts, Sentences and Vocables,* 370: listed "Shillukua" under the Tualatin with his son, Henry Crawford, a slave named Jimmy John, and a wife by whom he had had no children.

127 National Archives, Seattle, Grand Ronde/Siletz, Land and Enrollment Program records, Field Notes and Land Survey 1875–1898, Land Description Book 1878, Box 115; Grand Ronde Justice Court.

Shilikwa owned two parcels of land. In 1887, he rented his property, "on the east side of the highway by the first turn west of Valley Junction," to **David Leno**, but kept for himself forty acres with a little house and barn. [128] A few months later, Shilikwa was living with a Clackamas woman named Mary.

On October 29, 1906, Shilikwa received a fee patent for 240 acres of allotment land.[129] About two years later, on July 31, 1908, the elderly Shilikwa was robbed and murdered. His body was found by his buggy in the middle of the road. His killer was never caught.[130]

Andrew Kershaw was appointed by the Yamhill County Court to administer Shilikwa's estate and **Frank Quenel, Fabien Quenel,** and **Daniel Robinson** were appointed to appraise the property. On August 27, 1908, Kershaw filed papers recording the appraised value of Shilikwa's estate at $460. On September 9 Kershaw submitted to the court an inventory of the estate that listed one promissory note, a forty-acre tract of land in Section 29, and an additional forty-acre tract in Section 32 as Shilikwa's only assets.

Between October 1906, when Shilikwa was issued his patent, and his death in July of 1908, his original allotment of 240 acres had dwindled to eighty acres. It was rumored that he had been tricked out of some of it. Reportedly, on one occasion Shilikwa had gone to Kershaw wanting to sell the back half of his allotment because it was "too hilly and brushy." "Kershaw made out the deed for the first half which was good land with his house on it. Without knowing what he was signing, Shilikwa made his mark, and before long Kershaw forced him off his place."[131]

On December 18, 1908, John Pratt petitioned the court to protect his rights as James Shilikwa's half brother and demanded an accounting of the property of Shilikwa's estate. In the petition, Pratt accused Kershaw of filing "a pretend inventory" of the estate.

According to Pratt, a great deal of personal property consisting of cattle, horses, young stock, wagon, buggy, harness, plow, hack, and "a lot of cash held by a woman pretending to be the widow of the deceased" was not mentioned in the inventory Kershaw had prepared for the court. Pratt also accused Kershaw of selling a lot of cattle belonging to the estate for $130 and failing to provide any accounting of the money. Further, he accused Kershaw of "wasting the estate in useless litigation and failing to discharge his duties properly."[132]

Pratt complained that Kershaw did not properly describe the promissory note in his inventory to the court but Kershaw had, in fact, provided the information required by law. One benefit of a promissory note is that it can be enforced in court without further evidence of the underlying reason why the money was

128 O. Applegate, Testimony of Narcisse Lachance.
129 His allotment was issued under the name James Selkeah.
130 Jacobs, Field Notebook 58, *Texts and Ethnology*, 122.
131 Berreman, interview with Abe Holmes, 52.
132 Oregon State Archives, Salem, Oregon, 1908,Yamhill County, Estate File 1310.

owed in the first place. The note held by Shilikwa was apparently unsecured. It was made in the amount of three hundred dollars by a man named Joseph Tharp and dated June 22, 1908, just five weeks before Shilikwa was murdered.

To the charge of wasting the estate in useless litigation, Kershaw testified that James Shilikwa had signed a deed of conveyance for a portion of his land through "fraud and misrepresentations made by one Joseph Murray" and that he was working to have it set aside in Yamhill County Circuit court. Kershaw finally obtained a judgment of fifty-four dollars, which was added to Shilikwa's estate in February 1909.

As far as profiting from the personal estate went, Andrew Kershaw said he had only charged the estate with routine administration fees and expenses. He did not address the charge that he had liquidated certain assets and had not accounted for the money. Nor did Kershaw address the charge that a substantial amount of Shilikwa's personal property was not mentioned on the inventory.

After all the claims (totaling $318) against the estate were paid, $134.30 was turned over to Mary Aken, the recorded widow and sole heir to James Shilikwa's estate.[133]

The court fixed November 22, 1909, as the date for hearing objections to the final settlement of the estate. John Pratt was not there. He had died some five months earlier, on June 10, 1909.

Shlawin, Chief (1805c–75c), Tualatin band of Kalapuya[134]	Native Name: Shlawin /SHLA-win/ (Shláwin)*[135]
Alias: Paul Sloan, Albert Slowan	Allotment: None known by author
Mother: Unknown to author	Father: Unknown to author

Chief Shlawin was chief of the Chalal band of Tualatin and lived on the prairie of Wapato Lake near its outlet.[136] At Grand Ronde, he lived just above **Peter Kenoyer** (Kinai)'s place.

In 1872, he was listed under the Wapato Lake band as "Albert Slowan," living with his wife, **Sarah Kiakuts** (Washkayak), and his adopted daughter, Emma, age 15.

Father Croquet recorded Shlawin's death under the name "Paul Sloan" on

---

133 Ibid.
134 Jacobs, Field Notebook 36, *Santiam Kalapuya Text,* 192: "Slawin, Yamhill man." Jacobs, Field Notebooks 46, *Santiam Kalapuya Text,* n.p., his name was given as "Clawən, a man, probably Tualatin; not a doctor, probably; he was a kind of chief or leader of the Tualatin band."
135 1872 GRIC: "Albert Slowan." Gatschet, *Texts, Sentences and Vocables,* 92: "Chief Slawin" lived on Reserve above Kinai. Gatschet, *Texts, Sentences and Vocables,* 77: listed as "Shla-win, + abt 3 yrs ago on Reserve." Jacobs, Field Notebooks 58, *Texts and Ethnology,* 12.
136 Gatschet, *Kalapuya Ethnology,* 1.

October 8, 1875.[137] Following Shlawin's death, Sarah married the Tualatin sub-chief **Dave Yachkawa**. Emma Kiakuts went to live with her uncle, Peter Kenoyer .

Short, Charley (1820c–97), Umpqua	Native Name: Tenalta /Ten-alta/[138]
Alias: Umpqua Charley, Short Charley	Allotment 195
Mother: Unknown to author	Father: Unknown to author

Charley Short (Tenalta) was probably the Umpqua Charley whose wife, Marianne (1832c), was baptized by Father Croquet on April 30, 1862. After she died May 25, Corporal Bensell witnessed Father Croquet sprinkling holy water over her body and in her grave before her relatives buried her. Then at eleven o'clock on that day Father Croquet "delivered a highly interesting discourse" to his Indian congregation, "partly in Latin, French, some English, and a good deal of Chinook."[139]

In those days, many people followed the custom of taking the body to the grave around noon on the second day. After the priest spoke "good words" over the body and "sang songs," the deceased was buried and the family returned home.[140]

There were differing beliefs regarding how to best handle any lingering spirit. Some people hired a doctor with dead person power to smudge the house and drive away the "spirit-breath."[141] Other people were in the practice of burning the home of the deceased to encourage the spirit to ascend into the next world.

After Marianne died, Charley Short had several additional wives. In 1872, he was listed with hayash wife, Nancy (Wencolla), and second wife, Louisa.[142] Also living with him were his three sons: Charley (1856c), Joseph (Chuaca), and **Jonas Short** (Summacarcas).[143]

Despite the ban against plural marriages, Charley was listed with both his wives through 1887. After that, only Nancy and his sons Joseph and Jonas were listed with him.

Charles Short received an allotment of three hundred acres. After his father's death, June 11, 1897, **Joseph Short** inherited Charles's allotment.[144] On January 15, 1907, Joseph sold twenty acres of Charles's allotment to D. S. Bentley. On the same day, he sold the remaining 280 acres of the allotment to Wallace Mc-Camont.[145]

---

137 Munnick and Beckham, *Catholic Church Records—Grand Ronde*, Register I, p. 95, S-24.
138 1887 GRIC: Charley Short's Indian name as "Ten-alta."
139 Munnick and Beckham, *Catholic Church Records—Grand Ronde*, Register I, p. 19-20, B-46, S-16. Barth, *All Quiet on the Yamhill*, 24.
140 Jacobs, Collection 40, *Autobiography of a Tualitin*, n.p.
141 Ibid.
142 1887 GRIC: Nancy Short's Indian name as "Wencolla."
143 1887 GRIC: Joseph Short's Indian name as "Chuaca."
144 Munnick and Beckham, *Catholic Church Records—Grand Ronde*, Register II, p. 109, S-5.
145 *Heirs of Deceased Indians*, Allotment Records 195.

Short, Jonas (1857c–86c), Umpqua	Native Name: Summacarcas /Summa-car-cas/
Alias: None known by author	Allotment 197
Mother: Nancy	Father: Charles Short, Umpqua

In 1885, Jonas (Summacarcas) was living with his wife, Julia (1865c), and his daughter, Belle (1883c).

On January 15, 1907, his mother, Nancy Short, and Jonas's brother, **Joseph Short** (Chuaca), sold Jonas's entire eighty-acre allotment to Wallace McCamont.[146]

Short, Joseph (1863–1927), Umpqua	Native Name: Chuaca /Chu-a-ca/
Alias: None known by author	Allotment 196
Mother: Nancy	Father: Charles Short, Umpqua

Joseph (Chuaca) married Mary Chapman (1846c–86) on November 4, 1885. **William Warren** and Felicite Rosa Menard witnessed the ceremony.

April 9, 1907, Joseph Short was issued a fee patent for his eighty-acre allotment.[147]

Shufon, William (1840c–1908), Santiam band of Kalapuya[148]	Native Name: Sanik /SA-nik/ (sániik)*[149]
Alias: None known by author	Allotment 198
Mother: Unknown to author	Father: Unknown to author

William Shufon (Sanik) had a half-sister called Mary Hauxhurst (Wat-tait).[150] They had the same mother but different fathers. Their mother was **Nancy Elkin** (Ki-zad)'s sister.

While Mary lived off the reservation with her husband, Webley Hauxhurst, William was removed to Grand Ronde where he lived his entire life.[151]

He was appointed prosecuting attorney by the Grand Ronde Indian Legislature for 1879 and defense attorney for Indian court in 1882.[152]

In 1888, William was listed as a widower with a long list of assets including

---

146 Ibid., Allotment Records 197.

147 Ibid., Allotment Records 196.

148 Jacobs, Field Notebook 36, *Santiam Kalapuya Text*, 192: Shufon was part Santiam Kalapuya.

149 1887 GRIC listed his Indian name as "Senick." Jacobs, Field Notebook 36, *Santiam Kalapuya Text*, 192: J. B. Hudson gave his Indian name as "Sanik."

150 Death Certificate, Tillamook County, dated November 21, 1907, for 87 year old Indian daughter of Stawin (Stay-win), chief of Yamhill Indian tribe.

151 National Archives, Seattle, PAO-10, bx 1614, Mary Hauxhurst, Pincess Watlistai.

152 National Archives, Seattle, Grand Ronde/Siletz, Land and Enrollment Program records, Field Notes and Land Survey 1875–1898, Land Description Book 1878, Box 115; Grand Ronde Justice Court.

a house and barn, twenty-two head of cattle, six horses, and two dozen chickens. He received a fee patent on his land on October 29, 1906.[153]

June 4, 1908, William was killed by a bull. By this time, his parents and all his siblings were also dead.[154] **Frank Wheeler** (Aiwai) prepared William's body for burial. **Charles Wacheno** and **Macasca Sitton** dug his grave.

In allocating his real and personal property, valued at $1,000, the court recognized Mary Hauxhurst's children as William's next of kin and heirs. They were nieces: Esther M. Brammer, Mary L. Day, and Sarah J. Elliott, all currently living in Tillamook, Oregon, and two nephews, Joseph Hauxhurst and John Albert Biggs, both residing at Barnegat, Oregon.[155]

All William's personal property including twenty-three head of cattle and young stock, five work horses, farming implements, and household goods were to be sold at public auction August 3, 1908. The court administer, John Albert Biggs, hired a man named Daughterty as the auctioneer. He also hired **Frank Menard** to take care of the stock before and after the sale.[156]

On the day of the sale, a number of people, both white and Indian, came to bid on various items. **Henry Petite** bought William's cart, some windows, shoes, a fork, and a spade. **Peter Arquette** bought a dog chain. **Joseph Dowd** bought a rocking chair, whip, mare, two cows, and some tools. **Sam Chantelle** bought a table, a lantern, a clock, and some tools. **John Warren** and Frank Menard bought some tools. **Charles Chantelle** bought a cow. **Frank Quenel** bought a cow, a double harness, and some chains. **William Hartless** (Futi) bought a handsaw, some tools, and four dollars' worth of flour. **Frank Bond** bought a lamp. **Lawney Tom** (Pootpam) bought a stove and tools.[157]

In the end, the sale generated $839, bringing the total value of William's personal property to $1,139. After all the claims against the estate were paid and administrative expenses subtracted, each of William's five heirs received a hundred dollars in addition to a one-fifth interest in his 79.09-acre allotment.[158]

Siblian, Lem, Rogue River/Shasta	Native Name: None known by author
Alias: Sibliau	Allotment: None known by author
Mother: Unknown to author	Father: Unknown to author

In 1872, he was living with his wife, Lolly, and his niece, Katie.

---

153 *Heirs of Deceased Indians*, Allotment Records 198.
154 National Archives, Seattle, PAO-10, bx 1614, Mary Hauxhurst, Pincess Watlistai.
   Oregon State Archives, Salem, Oregon, 1908, Yamhill County, File 1312.
155 Ibid.
156 Ibid.
157 Ibid.
158 Ibid.

Silby, Colville, Rogue River/Shasta	Native Name: None known by author
Alias: None known by author	Allotment: None known by author
Mother: Unknown to author	Father: Unknown to author

In 1872, he was living alone.

Silas, John (1857c–88c), Santiam band of Kalapuya	Native Name: None known by author
Alias: John Sailas, Kailas, Cilas	Allotment: None known by author
Mother: Sarah Santiam	Father: Santiam Sailas[159]

John "Kailas," born of Kailas and Sarah of Santiam nation, was baptized September 29, 1861 at age four. His brother, William (1856c), was baptized the same day. His sister, Sophie (Sarah) had been baptized about a week earlier. **Chief Louis Napesa** was the boy's godfather. **Sarah Silas**'s older half sister, Henriette Sailas (1844c), was his godmother.[160]

In April 1862, Henriette became godmother to several Marysville Kalapuya children. Eventually she married a Kalapuya man called Joseph. Their daughter, Catherine, was baptized on May 24, 1863. Catherine's godparents were Louis Napesa and William's wife, Louise.

In addition to Henriette, John had a half sister named Agatha. She died in August 1870 when she was nine years old. John appears to have had a half brother, also named John, who was baptized October 7, 1860.

"John Cilas" was listed on the 1872 GRIC as **Jacob Wheeler** (Shwa)'s fourteen-year-old nephew. "John Sailas" married Emma Kellogg-Babcock (1857c) April 30, 1874. Their witnesses were **Mark Winslow** and **Mary Martin.** Emma died aged twenty-five on May 6, 1882.[161]

1n 1887, John was listed on the GRIC as a thirty-four-year-old widower. He died on May 13, 1888, and was buried at Grand Ronde the following day.[162]

Silas, Santiam, Santiam band of Kalapuya	Native Name: None known by author
Alias: Santiam Sailas, Kailas	Allotment: None known by author
Mother: Unknown to author	Father: Unknown to author

Santiam Silas had at least two wives, Sarah and Louise. By Louise, he had John (1857c), Agatha (1861c–70), and Henriette (1844c). By Sarah, he had John (1857c) and William.[163]

---

159 Ibid.
160 Ibid., Register I, p. 14, B-186, p. 64, S-14, p. 86, M-5, p. 121, S-6.
161 Ibid.
162 Ibid., Register II, p. 40, S-7.
163 Munnick & Beckham, *Catholic Church Records—Grand Ronde*, Register I, p.5, B-13, p.

Silas, Sarah (1845c–99c), Clackamas, Klamath[164]	Native Name: None known by author
Alias: Sarah Howard, Sarah Allen, Sarah Wymas	Allotment: None known by author
Mother: Unknown to author	Father: Unknown to author

In 1872, Sarah was a widow, using the name "Sarah Wymas." While she was listed separately from Joseph Howard (Waimish) and his wife, Mary Hutchins, she was very likely one of Joseph Howard's former wives. All three of them were listed under the Santiam band of Kalapuya.

In 1885, Sarah was listed on the GRIC as "Sarah Howard," a widow, age forty, with her son, Joe (1870c). They were living with Sarah's brother **John Silas.**

By 1887, Sarah and her daughter, **Stephanie Howard,** were living with **Nelson Allen.** Sarah lived with Robert until she died in 1899. There is no mention of her son, Joe, after 1885.

Simmons, William (1867c–1955), Rogue River	Native Name: None known by author
Alias: Willie Simmons, Willie Sims	Allotment 194
Mother: Susie Sims, Rogue River	Father: American soldier at Ft. Yamhill[165]

William Simmons was **Cecile Sims's** brother. He served on the Grand Ronde Police Force from 1887 to April 1889.[166] When **Louis Savage** accidentally killed **Foster Wacheno** (Inawalh) in 1904, William was the Chief of Police at Grand Ronde.[167]

He married Suzette Norwest, the daughter of **Frank Norwest** and **Alice Wilder.** He and Suzette had Samuel, Eva Mary (1889), William (1895), Herbert (1900), Raymond (1902), Sylvester (1906), Walter (1903), Rufus (1905), Edger (1907), Samson (1908), Anthony (1910), Marcus (1911), and Rita (1913).[168]

Both William and Suzette spoke the old native languages. Since William spoke

14, B-186, p. 64, S-14.

164 Jacobs, Notebooks 67, *Texts Ethnology Clackamas & Jargon*, 14.

165 Berreman, interview with William Simmons.

166 Confederated Tribes of the Grand Ronde Community of Oregon Archive, Grand Ronde Agency Ledger Book, Records of Employees at Grand Ronde July 1883—September 1907.

167 National Archives and Records Administration, Central Plains Region, Louie Savage Inmate File 5333.

168 Department of the Interior, Office of the Secretary, Confederated Tribes of the Grand Ronde Community, Notice of Proposed Membership Roll, May 12, 1955. Confederated Tribes of the Grand Ronde Community of Oregon Archive, *Elders Scroll*, 1981. Munnick and Beckham, *Catholic Church Records—Grand Ronde*, Register I, p. 55, B-13, p. 67, B-5, p. 69, S-11, p. 107, B-13.

Rogue River and Suzette spoke Kalapuya, they spoke Chinook Jargon when talking together.[169]

Suzette Norwest-Simmons. Photo courtesy of Barbara Danforth Private Collection.

William worked for the agency until his health prevented him from performing the work any longer. Then he and Suzette gathered hazel shoots for baskets they made themselves to sell as their primary means of support.[170]

William Simmons received a 240-acre allotment. He did not sign the Surplus

169 Zenk, *Chinook Jargon*, 280.
170 Berreman, interview with William Simmons.

Land Agreement of 1901. On October 25, 1907, he was issued a fee patent for his entire allotment.

By 1934, out of all William and Suzette's twelve children, only four sons were still living and the elderly couple was proud of each of them. Sylvester was still living at home helping the elderly couple work their land. Edgar was a member of the Grand Ronde Tribal Council. Sampson and Mark were both in the army.[171]

Simpasse, Stephen (1835c–67), Rogue River[172]	Native Name: None known by author
Alias: None known by author	Allotment: None known by author
Mother: Unknown to author	Father: Unknown to author

Stephen had a wife named Anne (1835c–66). She became "very sick" and was baptized July 25, 1865. She died almost a year later, on July 20, 1866.

Stephen also suffered a long illness. He was baptized "being sick" April 26, 1865, and died March 3, 1867.[173]

Sims, Cecile (1849c), Rogue River	Native Name: None known by author
Alias: Cecilia, Cilly Jake	Allotment: None known by author
Mother: Susie Sims	Father: Unknown to author

Cecile was the wife of **Chief Jake Edemchoey. William Simmons** was her brother. At Grand Ronde, Cecile's mother, **Susie Sims,** lived with Cecile until she died in 1899. After her mother died, Cecile moved to Siletz. She married Dick Johnson around 1905.

When the fee patent came through on Jake's 180-acre allotment, Cecile sold sixty acres of it to Johanna Knapp. After Cecile died in 1913, her cousin, **Lucy Johnson,** inherited her property. Lucy's heirs sold the remaining 120 acres of Jacob's property to S. H. Peer in 1928.[174]

Sims, Susie (1809c–99), Rogue River	Native Name: None known by author
Alias: Susan Edemchoey, Susie Jake	Allotment: 49
Mother: Unknown to author	Father: Unknown to author

Susan received an eighty-acre allotment. In 1913, her daughter, **Cecile Sims,** sold forty acres of it to Johanna Knapp and the remaining forty acres were placed

---

171 Ibid.

172 Munnick and Beckham, *Catholic Church Records—Grand Ronde,* Register I, p. 37, B-27, p. 47, S-8.

173 Ibid.

174 Ibid.

in trust.[175]

Sitton, Macasca Sitton (1886c–1922), Molalla, Clackamas, Tualatin band of Kalapuya, Yamhill band of Kalapuya	Native Name: None known by author
Alias: Mack Sutton	Allotment 216
Mother: Margaret Toto, Molalla, Clackamas	Father: Tanus George Sutton, Tualatin band of Kalapuya, Yamhill band of Kalapuya

Macasca Sitton married Anna Thompson (1887–1923). They had at least three children: Clarinda, Alfred, and Caroline Sitton-Strong.

April 9, 1907, Macasca Sitton received a fee patent for his entire eighty-acre allotment.[176]

Sitton, Moses (1881–1907), Molalla, Clackamas, Tualatin band of Kalapuya, Yamhill band of Kalapuya	Native Name: None known by author
Alias: Moses Sutton	Allotment 214
Mother: Margaret Toto, Molalla, Clackamas	Father: Tanus George Sutton, Tualatin band of Kalapuya, Yamhill band of Kalapuya

On April 9, 1907, Moses Sitton received a fee patent for his entire eighty-acre allotment.[177]

Sixtus (1826c–66), Tualatin band of Kalapuya[178]	Native Name: None known by author
Alias: Old Six	Allotment: None known by author
Mother: Unknown to author	Father: Unknown to author

Old Six became "very sick" in May and died a few weeks later on June 6, 1866.[179]

Skinner, Charley (1828c–88), Rogue River	Native Name: None known by author
Alias: None known by author	Allotment: None known by author

---

175 *Heirs of Deceased Indians*, Allotment Records, 49.

176 Ibid., Allotment Record 216.

177 Ibid., Allotment Record 214.

178 Munnick and Beckham, *Catholic Church Records—Grand Ronde*, Register I, p. 44, S-21.

179 Ibid.

Mother: Unknown to author	Father: Unknown to author

Charley was married to Pauline. In 1888, they had a house on sixty fenced acres with fourteen acres in cultivation. They also had a couple horses and eight hogs.

"Being gravely ill," Charlie was baptized October 8 and died November 2, 1888.[180]

Skukum, Jack (1856c)[181]	Native Name: None known by author
Alias: None known by author	Allotment: None known by author
Mother: Unknown to author	Father: Unknown to author

In 1886, he was listed with an unnamed wife and three sons and two daughters. Jack had a thirty-year-old brother who was also living with the family. The family was very poor.

Skukum, John (1826c–1901c)	Native Name: None known by author
Alias: Skukum John	Allotment: None known by author
Mother: Unknown to author	Father: Unknown to author

"Skukum John" arrived at the Dayton encampment on Tuesday, April 22, 1856, from the Santiam with three men, five women, and four children.[182] He was related to **Muddy Tom Churchill** (Kaltas Lipom)'s wife, Betsy Tom.[183] In 1885, "John Skukum" was listed with his wife, Midget, and children Solomon, Lilly, and Milley. Also living with the family was "Uncle Bob."

In 1886, John was listed with an unnamed wife. The agent noted he was sixty years old and owned two horses, a wagon, and a harness. By 1895, he was listed as a widow, but the next year he had a new wife named Nannie (1820c). They were still listed together in 1898. However, in 1901, Nannie was listed as his widow.

Skukum, Peter (1851c)	Native Name: None known by author
Alias: None known by author	Allotment: None known by author
Mother: Unknown to author	Father: Unknown to author

Peter was **John Skukum**'s cousin. In 1886, he was living with an unnamed wife and three children. The family's only assets were a wagon, a harness, and two horses.

Skukum, Thomas, Kalapuya	Native Name: None known by author

---

180 Ibid., Register II, p. 47, B-44.
181 Johnson and Zenk, *Chinuk Wawa*, 189: skukum term meaning strong.
182 Palmer, *Pocket Diary*, 6.
183 National Archives, Seattle, Grand Ronde/Siletz Agency, School Records, July 1, 1895.

Alias: None known by author	Allotment: None known by author
Mother: Unknown to author	Father: Unknown to author

Thomas Skukum had a daughter, Victoria (1856c), who was baptized by Father Croquet on December 29, 1861. Croquet wrote, "… the undersigned priest has baptized Victoire Mary, 5 year old, born of (Skoukoum) Thomes of Kalapuyia nation, of this mission."[184]

Small, Grace, Santiam band of Kalapuya	Native Name: None known by author
Alias: None known by author	Allotment: None known by author
Mother: Unknown to author	Father: Unknown to author

In 1872, Grace Small was living with **Peter Carey.**

Smith, Andrew (1851c), Rogue River	Native Name: None known by author
Alias: None known by author	Allotment 200
Mother: Betsy Lily, Rogue River	Father: Andrew Smith, American captain in Indian War

Andrew was the son of Captain Andrew Smith, an American soldier stationed at the Table Rock reserve from 1854 to 1856, and a Rogue River woman. As a small boy, Andrew came to Grand Ronde under the treaty with his mother.[185]

According to Andrew, his grandfather was one of the chiefs in the Rogue River wars who bitterly opposed the Americans and never surrendered.[186] In those days, his mother had to guard Andrew carefully because he was a half-breed and her people wanted to kill him. Andrew Smith said:

> I am a Rogue River. My mother told me that I was the son of a young white man of a good family that lived on the Rogue River before the war of 1853. She said that I was born about the time of that year… When I was a little boy, the brother to the Indian Agent [John F. Miller] took me away without the permission of my mother. When I was grown, I came back, married and took care of my mother until she died.[187]

---

184 Munnick and Beckham, *Catholic Church Records—Grand Ronde,* Register I, p. 15, B-226.

185 Berreman, interview with Andrew Smith, 7.

186 Ibid.

187 O. Applegate, Testimony of Andrew Smith. Berreman, interview with Andrew Smith, 19: Andrew's father sent the Indian agent a letter asking him to find a place for Andrew off the reservation. His father was afraid some of the Rogue River people at Grand Ronde might still try to kill him. Therefore, the agent placed Andrew with

In 1888, Andrew and his wife, Jane Menard, were listed as having a baby. They were living with Andrew's aunt, a widow named **Rebecca "Becky" Smith**, and Andrew's mother, **Betsy Lily Smith.** At that time, Becky reportedly had a hut. Betsy owned a cow. Andrew had a barn, a plow, and wagon.

Jane Menard was **Peter Menard**'s oldest daughter by his Clackamas wife. Jane and Andrew Smith had at least ten children: Lillie, Andrew (1888c–1909), Ralph (1890c), Victor (1892c), Clarence (1895c), Cimanty (1897c), Samantha (1898c), Jenny (1900c), Noah (1905c), and Nettie (1908c).[188]

Andrew Smith received a 280-acre allotment. On October 29, 1906, he received a fee patent for the entire allotment. He mortgaged the property "to help his children get a good start."[189] By 1934, his house had burned down and his wife had died. A widower, Andrew was living alone in an old granary on thirty remaining acres of allotment land.[190]

Smith, Andrew Milton (1888c–1909), Rogue River, Clackamas, French Canadian	Native Name: None known by author
Alias: None known by author	Allotment 200
Mother: Jane Menard, Clackamas, French Canadian	Father: Andrew Smith, Rogue River

On October 27, 1908, Andrew Milton Smith married Margaret "Kate" Catherine LaBonte (1883–1967), daughter of Alexander LaBonte and **Clementine La-Chance.**

Kate was issued a fee patent on July 26, 1910, for his entire eighty-acre allotment.

Smith, Anna Lotta (1885c–1904c), Shasta	Native Name: None known by author
Alias: Lulu Smith, Lula Sutton	Allotment 147
Mother: Spanish Mary	Father: William Smith, Shasta

On October 25, 1907, Anna Lotta Smith was issued a fee patent for her entire eighty-acre allotment.

---

a white family where he lived for a number of years. His white foster parents never sent him to school.

188 Munnick and Beckham, *Catholic Church Records — Grand Ronde,* Register II, p. 21, M-7, p. 63, B-18, p. 83, B-38, p. 100, B-7, p. 116, B-2.

189 *Heirs of Deceased Indians,* Allotment Record 200, 201. Berreman, interview with Andrew Smith, 19.

190 Berreman, interview with Andrew Smith, 19.

Smith, Betsy Lily (1827c–97c), Rogue River[191]	Native Name: None known by author
Alias: None known by author	Allotment 202
Mother: Unknown to author	Father: Unknown to author

Betsy Lily was the mother of **Andrew Smith,** the young boy whom some of the people wanted to kill because his father was a white man. As a young woman, she lived on the Rogue River not far from Table Rock and belonged to **Chief Sam Wilder** (Toquahear)'s band.

Applegate Jack (Itchkadowa) said he knew her before the people were removed to the reservation. She was a widow and "drew annuities under the treaty with the rest of the Table Rock treaty people three times before coming to Grand Ronde."[192]

She did not go to Grand Ronde with the main band but went by steamboat with **Chief George** (Chocultah). She had two sons. Her older son died after they arrived at the reservation, but Andrew survived.

One of **Tyee Shasta Tom**'s wives, **Kitty Tom** (Acattycon), testified Betsy Smith was her aunt. She said that after the Treaty, the Rogue River people were divided. She came with the main band, in a wagon, and Betsy with her sons came by ship.[193]

Betsy received a 138-acre allotment. On April 9, 1907, her son, Andrew Smith, as her heir, received a fee patent for the entire allotment.

Smith, Cecelia (1816c–1909), mother-in-law of Rogue River	Native Name: None known by author
Alias(s): Cilly, Cecia, Secelia Smith, Ally Smith	Allotment 206
Mother: Unknown to author	Father: Unknown to author

Cecelia was the Rogue River **John Smith**'s mother-in-law. **Julia Ann Smith** was her daughter. Cecelia Smith received a 71.93-acre allotment. On November 20, 1911, her heir, Julia Anne, wife of **William Warren,** sold twenty acres to E. Julious Fraglio. A fee patent was issued to William Warren on May 9, 1914, for twenty acres of Cecilia's allotment. On March 30, 1925, a fee patent for 31.93 acres was issued to **John Warren,** "devisee of William Warren (heir)."[194]

Smith, David (1878c–1925), Shasta	Native Name: None known by author

---

191 O. Applegate, Testimony of Applegate Jack.
192 Ibid.
193 O. Applegate, Testimony of Kitty Tom.
194 *Heirs of Deceased Indians,* Allotment Record 206

Alias: David Grant Smith	Allotment 145
Mother: Spanish Mary	Father: William Smith, Shasta

When David Smith was baptized on April 24, 1887, **John "Moses" Hudson** and Hattie Sands were named his godparents.

On June 8, 1917, he was issued a fee patent for his sixty-acre allotment.

Smith, Ellen (1883–1905), Rogue River	Native Name: None known by author
Alias: None known by author	Allotment 209
Mother: Julia Ann Smith-Warren	Father: John Smith, Rogue River

Ellen Smith, **Rogue River John Smith**'s last surviving child, died four months after her father. Ellen had a 97.97-acre allotment. Eighty acres of Ellen's allotment were sold to W. N. Jones on September 11, 1906, by Ellen's heir, Louise Smith. On March 10, 1926, a fee patent was issued for the balance of Ellen's allotment to her heir, **John Warren.**[195] John was Ellen's stepfather's brother.

Smith, Gilbert, Rogue River/Shasta	Native Name: None known by author
Alias: None known by author	Allotment: None known by author
Mother: Unknown to author	Father: Unknown to author

In 1872, Gilbert Smith was living with the **Shasta Isaac** family.

Smith, Ida (1882c–91c), Rogue River	Native Name: None known by author
Alias: None known by author	Allotment 208
Mother: Julia Ann Smith-Warren	Father: John Smith, Rogue River

On May 13, 1904, eighty acres of Ida's allotment were sold to Joel Flannery. On May 29, 1904, the remaining twenty acres were sold to Flannery by Ida's father, **John Smith,** as her sole heir.[196]

Smith, Isabel (1884–1904), Shasta	Native Name: None known by author
Alias: Mary Isabel Smith, Isabel Riggs	Allotment 146
Mother: Spanish Mary	Father: William Smith, Shasta

Isabel Smith received a sixty-acre allotment. After her death, a fee patent for the property was issued to her heir, **Andrew Riggs.**

Smith, Jack, Umpqua	Native Name: None known by author
Alias: Coquille Jack	Allotment: None known by author

---

195 Ibid., Allotment Record 209.
196 Ibid., Allotment Record 208.

Mother: Unknown to author	Father: Unknown to author

In 1872, Jack was listed with his wife, Tammy, and son, James. Tammy's mother, Rachael, was also living with the family, along with a man named **John Lamson.**

Smith, Jesse (1876c), Shasta	Native Name: None known by author
Alias: John Smith	Allotment 144
Mother: Spanish Mary[197]	Father: Willie Smith, Shasta[198]

Jesse Smith was raised by his mother, **Spanish Mary,** and his stepfather, **Frank Norwest.** He married **Alice Quenel** in 1893. They had Francis (1894c), Laurence (1896c), Nicholas (1898c), Augustine (1900c), Veta (1903c), and Ralph (1905c–1973).

Jesse received a sixty-acre allotment.

Smith, John (1837c–1905), Shasta	Native Name: None known by author
Alias: None known by author	Allotment 207
Mother: Unknown to author	Father: Unknown to author

In 1864, John Smith and Mary of the Rogue River nation had a son. Father Croquet baptized the baby under the name of Ignace April 28.[199]

By his wife, Julia Anne, John Smith had a number of children: Bobe (1885c), Ed (1886c), Henrietta (1869c), Mary (1873c), John (1880c), Minnie (1885c), Ida, and Ellen. In 1872, Julia Anne's mother, Cecelia, and her brother, Budd (1858c), were also living with John Smith's family.

In 1877, John was appointed road supervisor along with **Joseph Shangaretta.** He was also appointed road supervisor from 1880 through 1882 with **David Holmes** (Faliper).[200] In addition, he served on the Grand Ronde Police Force from 1884 to 1887.[201]

By 1886, John was a very successful farmer living with Julia Anne and their three daughters, Minnie, **Ida,** and **Ellen Smith.** Also living with the family at that time was a widow named Lilly.[202]

---

197 1886 GRIC.

198 Gatschet, *Texts, Sentences and Vocables,* 364.

199 Munnick and Beckham, *Catholic Church Records—Grand Ronde,* Register I, p. 32, B-38.

200 National Archives, Seattle, Grand Ronde/Siletz Tribal Program Records Box 162, Agency & Tribal Council Records 1876–1951.

201 Confederated Tribes of the Grand Ronde Community of Oregon Archives, Grand Ronde Agency Ledger Book, Records of Employees at Grand Ronde July 1883– September 1907.

202 Michelle, *Just a Memorandum,* 3: Mary Ann wrote that besides their three daughters,

Except for **Doctor Santiago,** no one at Grand Ronde had more horses than John Smith. By 1888, he had built a large ranch with two houses and five barns that sat on 160 fenced acres; however, John only received a patent for 120 acres of it.[203]

When John died in 1905, he still spoke very little English.[204] In probate, John Smith's property was estimated at $550 and his personal property at $300. His widow, Julia Anne, was described as old in years and infirm in body, and unable to support herself by manual labor. It was also brought to the court's attention that Julia Anne could not read or write and was forced to rely upon others as she was unable to transact business on her own behalf. The court set up an account from the estate of her deceased daughter, Ellen, Smith, and her late husband from which Julia Anne could draw $20 per month for as long as she lived.[205]

On Valentine's Day 1910, Julia Anne married **William "Billy" Warren.**[206]

Smith, John (1802c–1901), Tualatin band of Kalapuya	Native Name: Dushdaq /DUSH-dak/ (dúshdaq)*[207]
Alias: Doctor Smith	Allotment 204
Mother: Unknown to author	Father: Unknown to author

Dr. John Smith (Dushdaq) was a powerful doctor. Even dancing barefoot he could outlast other dancers. His power gave him strength to doctor, but it also caused him to eat people. He was so powerful children were warned not to cross in front of him. One man that crossed his path died within a day, his body busted up from Dushdaq's power. Dushdaq could not help it. Even his own people sometimes sickened and died from it.[208]

The Indian agent believed that of all the Indians on the reservation, Dushdaq was the one man who kept the old ways alive by continuing the old practices. Determined to break up this remnant of olden times, Rev. Summers wrote:

… the agent caused John Smith and his principal supporters to appear before a court composed of their comrades, there to be tried and fined as promoters of dissatisfaction and disturbance. By the same court, any future gatherings for native dances, festivals, or ceremonials of any kind,

John's mother-in-law was living with the family. She could not remember her name.
203 *Heirs to Deceased Indians,* Allotment Record 207.
204 Gatschet, *Texts, Sentences and Vocables,* 316.
205 Oregon State Archives, Salem, Oregon, 1905, Polk County, Estate File, John Smith.
206 National Archives, Salem, Oregon, Polk County, 2003A-029 Health Division Marriage Returns, William Warren and Julie Anne Smith, 1910. GRIC for 1911 lists "Louise Smith, now Julianne Warren, wife of William Warren, widow, age 69."
207 1887 GRIC: Indian name, "Toos-ta." Michelle, *Just a Memorandum,* 6: gave his name as "Twohtuc." Jacobs, *Clackamas Text, Part II,* 523–26: Dr. John Smith's name was given as "dusdaq." Jacobs, Field Notebook 51, *Music and Ethnology,* 11.
208 Jacobs, Field Notebook 51, *Music and Ethnology,* 11.

were strictly and solemnly forbidden.[209]

Dushdaq ignored the new law and continued to cure certain types of illnesses by removing the pain from the body with his hands or sucking it out and placing it in water. People said they could only see the source of the pain on top of the water as long as he sang his power song. When he stopped, the foreign parasite became invisible.[210]

He could not cure every illness. He sometimes could see the problem, but would need to call in another doctor with that particular spirit power to cure that particular patient.

Dr. Smith could cure five different ailments. An eagle plume with five buckskin straps in different colors, representing each *wimqt* that he could cure, hung over his bed.[211] In addition, he carried a black cane carved like a snake.

John "Moses" Hudson said that he was present once when Dushdaq placed the cane on a patient who had been unable to move and then raised the patient up by its power. Dushdaq could also cause the cane to dance on the floor, keeping time with the rhythm of the dance.[212]

Frances Gilbert said she had seen him tie a handkerchief to his cane and change it into a live rattlesnake that wrapped itself around the handkerchief. Then, Frances said, he held the cane over a sick man and lifted him up with it. Afterwards, she said, the man got well and lived a long time.[213]

When Dushdaq first got his power, he went off into the wild to live for five years alone. When he returned, he was a powerful doctor. His Grizzly Woman power told him to keep away from women. When he disobeyed, he was nearly driven crazy and fled to the forest where he was eventually found.[214]

His location in the forest was discovered by a man with a strong power who dreamed about Dushdaq in the night. The next day the Doctor was found high up in the limbs of a tree. He fought so hard to escape that they had to tie him.[215]

Later, when he sang, the people learned his power was a woman with enormous breasts. She looked just like any other person, but her breasts were very long. If a person fled from her and ran uphill, she would catch him quickly because she threw her breasts over her shoulders. On the other hand, if he ran downhill, she could not catch him as she would step on her breasts. They said that Grizzly Woman always went with her breasts over her shoulders everywhere. If she learned where some wealthy man was, she would go there and marry him. Even a

---

209 Cawley, *Indian Journal*, 27–28.
210 Drucker, *Clackamas Field Notes*, 23.
211 Drucker, *Clackamas Field Notes*, 23. Jacobs, Notebooks 69, *Texts Ethnology Clackamas & Jargon*, 66: gave "*wimqt*" as the term for "a bad disease."
212 Berreman, interview with John B. Hudson.
213 Berreman, interview with Frances Shirley.
214 Jacobs, Field Notebook 51, *Music and Ethnology*, 11.
215 Ibid.

chief dare not refuse a Grizzly Woman in marriage. They were all afraid of her.[216]

It took several Indian doctors, all working together, to "straighten out" Dushdaq's power. Then for a few winters he danced. He danced until he got well. He danced until he became a powerful, mean, murderous doctor.[217]

Dushdaq healed many people, including **Victoria Wishikin** (Kinishi) when she became ill. After examining her, the Doctor told her mother, **Sarah Gwayaki-ti,** "If you do not dance for her, she may not get well." Sarah did not say anything in reply, but rather thought about his remark.[218]

It was the following day before Sarah said to the family, "If we ask and he tells us again that he can make Victoria well if we dance, then we shall do that." When they met with Dushdaq again, Sarah asked this question and he replied, yes, he did think she would get well if they danced.[219]

Once again the family discussed whether or not they should dance the forbidden dance. The following day, they went to invite people to come one and all to dance for Victoria. For several evenings in a row the people came to dance. Always it was Dushdaq who was the first to sing his power songs and the first to dance. After he was done, other people would sing and dance their songs.[220]

The first night only a few people attended and everyone went home early, but attendance increased each night until the house was crowded during the fifth and last session.[221]

Then Dushdaq's spirit power told him that another shaman was sending her spirit power out ahead to see who was attending the doctoring sessions. His power told him she was thinking about coming to the sessions uninvited.[222]

On the fourth evening, Dushdaq said that in his dreams he saw this uninvited shaman. She would attend the session that evening and she would be wearing a bird's tail.[223]

Unknown to anyone, Dushdaq had cleverly placed his power outside the entrance to the house to stand guard all through the dance. Sure enough, three Umpqua women shaman arrived that night.[224] One of the women was wearing an eagle's tail fan in her hair.[225]

After Dushdaq had sung his spirit song and his wife and Victoria's mother had sang their songs, one of the Umpqua woman shamans began to sing her power song. She sang until she was completely full of her spirit power. Her hair

---

216 Ibid.
217 Ibid.
218 Jacobs, *Clackamas Text,* Part II, 523–26, 654.
219 Ibid.
220 Ibid.
221 Ibid.
222 Ibid.
223 Ibid.
224 Jacobs, Field Notebooks 58, *Texts and Ethnology,* 124: "Ubidi, an Umpqua doctor woman, was one of the three doctor women who came in."
225 Jacobs, *Clackamas Text,* Part II, 523-526, 654.

became untied and she pulled out the eagle tail to use as a fan. All this time, Dushdaq simply kept his seat holding his grinning mouth.[226]

On the last day of the curing, Victoria was beginning to feel much better. When Dushdaq arrived, he told Victoria's family that he had dreamed that he had stolen a large pearllike shell from a woman with a strong power who had attended the last session. He laughed when he told them about it.[227]

Soon people began to gather. One woman shaman entered and looked around. Dushdaq sat in the shadows as more and more people arrived. Once again, Dushdaq was the first to sing. Then he told the people that there was no reason to continue the power dance as Victoria had been cured. After his announcement, the people celebrated all night long and ended the evening with the giving of gifts to all in attendance.[228]

Dushdaq was known to have had at least three wives: Sarah, Juliette (1825c– 86), and a Clackamas woman called **Mary Smith** (Niudiya), who was a sister to **Martha Beagle** (Shkinda).[229]

In 1872, he was listed with his wife Sarah and their "adopted son, Richard." By 1885, he was listed with his wife Juliette. The following year, he was listed with his wife Mary and **Jimmie John.**

In the late 1870s or early 1880s, Rev. Summers offered to buy from Dushdaq a carved stone pipe, a full deerskin suit consisting of a short jacket with armlets, long leggings, moccasins, and a long blouse, and various native baskets, but he could not get the doctor to part with them.[230]

Dushdaq's farm was located at the end of a road that separated the farm of **Tom Gilbert** (Kiyukiyush) from the Tualatin sub-chief **Lame Jim Shiliqua** (Shilikwa)'s place.[231] Dushdaq's home was described as a good house and barn setting on sixty acres of fenced land with twenty-six of those acres in cultivation. Near the house was a good garden for family use and an orchard. The barn provided shelter for five horses and eight cows. He had all the tools of the day for cultivating and both a wagon and a hack for transportation.

On August 4, 1914, **Julia Ann Gendron** and **James Foster** each inherited a half interest in Dushdaq's original 59.72-acre farm. Julia Ann Gendron-Lafferty, a Clackamas woman and James Foster's Clackamas wife, Anna, were cousins.[232]

---

226 Ibid.

227 Ibid.

228 Ibid.

229 Michelle, *Just a Memorandum,* 7: she was Clackamas and her Indian name was "Neowya." 1887 GRIC gave her Indian name as "Na-oat-ga." Jacobs, Field Notebook 59, *Texts and Ethnology,* 56: Niudiya had a sister whose name Victoria Howard could not remember. Michelle, *Just a Memorandum,* 7, gave her sister's name as Martha Beagle.

230 Cawley, *Indian Journal,* 26–27.

231 National Archives, Seattle, Grand Ronde/Siletz, Land and Enrollment Program records, Field Notes and Land Survey 1875–1898, Land Description Book 1878, Box #115; Grand Ronde Justice Court.

232 *Heirs of Deceased Indians,* Allotment Records 204.

Smith, Lelander (1850c), Klamath[233]	Native Name: None known by author
Alias: Lelander Smits	Allotment: None known by author
Mother: Unknown to author	Father: Unknown to author

By 1871, Meacham had forbidden the traditional marriage ceremony and the practice of taking multiple wives. In place of the traditional ceremony he introduced the Christian marriage ritual. Lelander and his bride were the first to be married under the new law.[234]

On December 23, 1871, Joel Palmer received a letter from L. S. Dyer at the Grand Ronde agency:

> Lelander Smith, who was recently married to a woman belonging to this reservation, wishes to be transferred to this agency. Mr. Meacham has given his consent provided no objection is made. The Indians here wish him to remain and there is nothing wanting but your consent. Please answer by bearer.[235]

Joel Palmer answered on January 22, 1872, giving his permission for Lelander Smith, "a Klamath Indian of this [Siletz] reservation," to reside upon and become an inhabitant of the Grand Ronde Reservation.[236]

On December 22, 1872, Father Croquet "baptized Augustine, born 5 months previous of the marriage of Leander Smits and Mary." Mary Laurence was the baby's sponsor.[237]

Smith, Mary (1813c–1904), Clackamas	Native Name: Niudiya /ni-U-di-ya/ (ni?údiya),* Gaqasuli /GAH-ka-su-li/ (gáq'asuli)*[238]
Alias: None known by author	Allotment: None known by author
Mother: Unknown to author	Father: Unknown to author

Mary (Niudiya) was one of Dr. Smith's wives. **Martha Beagle** (Shkinda) and a Clackamas woman called **Dumyawakh** were her sisters.

People said Mary possessed a power almost as strong as her husband although she never doctored. She acquired her husband's power through his sweat when they slept together.[239]

---

233 Gatschet, *Texts, Sentences and Vocables,* 364: listed under Shasta.

234 Meacham, *Wigwam and War-Path.*

235 T. S. Dyer to Joel Palmer, December 23, 1871, *Correspondence and Papers of Joel Palmer.*

236 Palmer, Affidavit of January 22, 1872. *Correspondence and Papers of Joel Palmer.*

237 Munnick and Beckham, *Catholic Church Records—Grand Ronde,* Register I, p. 78, B-73.

238 Jacobs, *Clackamas Text,* Part II, 525. Jacobs, Field Notebook 58, *Texts and Ethnology,* 128. Jacobs, Field Notebooks 59, *Texts and Ethnology,* 54.

239 Jacobs, Field Notebooks 58, *Texts and Ethnology,* 126, 128.

Smith, Rebecca (1816c–96c), Rogue River	Native Name: None known by author
Alias: Becky Smith	Allotment 203
Mother: Unknown to author	Father: Unknown to author

In 1886, Rebecca was listed as living with another widow woman named Sallie (1811c).[240] They had six acres fenced with four acres in grain. They also had a horse and a small garden.

In 1887, the widow Kate Smith (1819c) was living with Rebecca and Sallie (Dialuc). The following year, Rebecca moved in with her nephew, **Andrew Smith,** and Jane Menard, who now had a toddler. Andrew's mother, **Betsy Lily Smith,** was also living with the family. Rebecca reportedly owned a hut. Betsy owned a cow. Andrew owned a barn, a plow and wagon.

Rebecca Smith received a 76.10-acre allotment. In probate, her estate was left to her nephew, Andrew Smith.[241] On November 25, 1907, Andrew received a fee patent for her entire allotment.[242]

Smith, Simon (1852c–62), Rogue River[243]	Native Name: None known by author
Alias: None known by author	Allotment: None known by author
Mother: Unknown to author	Father: Unknown to author

Simon was ten years old when he died at Grand Ronde.[244]

Smith, Willie (1845c–85c), Shasta[245]	Native Name: None known by author
Alias: None known by author	Allotment: None known by author
Mother: Unknown to author	Father: Unknown to author

Willie was the brother of **Leander Smith.**[246] He and his wife, Spanish Mary, were listed in 1885 with their children: Castine, Sallie, Jane, Mary, John, Thomas, and an infant daughter. In 1886, Spanish Mary was listed as a widow.

Sockston, Mrs. (1855c), Rogue River	Native Name: None known by author
Alias: None known by author	Allotment: None known by author
Mother: Unknown to author	Father: Unknown to author

240 1887 GRIC: gave her Indian name as "Di-a-luc."
241 Oregon State Archives, Salem, Oregon, Polk County, Probate Court Files, File 1016.
242 *Heirs of Deceased Indians*, Allotment Records 203.
243 Munnick and Beckham, *Catholic Church Records—Grand Ronde*, Register I, p. 18, B-27, p. 19, S-7.
244 Ibid.
245 Gatschet, *Texts, Sentences and Vocables*, 364.
246 Ibid.

In 1888, Mrs. Sockston was listed with her children: Ida (1881c), Nancy (1883c), and a son (1885c). Their only asset was a horse.

Soltax, Jo (1856c)	Native Name: None known by author
Alias: None known by author	Allotment: None known by author
Mother: Unknown to author	Father: Unknown to author

In 1885, Jo was living with his wife, Katherine, and his children: Julie, Joseph, and an infant son. The following year, the only child listed with him and Katherine was a son, Maurus (1884c). They had one horse and ten hogs.

Spores, Robert (1834c), Calapooia band of Kalapuya[247]	Native Name: None known by author
Alias: Calapooia Bob	Allotment: None known by author
Mother: Judy	Father: Unknown to author

Robert Spores was married to a woman named Mary. In 1872, he and Mary were listed with his children, Zed (1869c) Lucinda, and Susan. Also with the family were Robert's mother, Judy and another woman who was identified as Bob's sister.

Robert Spores represented the Cow Creek band of Umpqua with the Cow Creek chief, **Jake Edemchoey** at the fifth annual session of the Grand Ronde Indian Legislature January 4, 1876.[248]

In 1880, he and Mary were farming at Pass Creek in Douglas County, Oregon. Robert's mother, and their son, Sanford (1875c), were also living with them at that time.[249]

In 1885, Robert and Mary were living with their children: Zed, Lucinda, Susan, and Judith. None of their children were listed with them the following year and the agent noted that they were very poor.

Spores, Jack (1851c)	Native Name: None known by author
Alias: None known by author	Allotment: None known by author
Mother: Unknown to author	Father: Unknown to author

In 1886, Jack was listed his wife and son. The family was poor.

---

247 1872 GRIC: gave his name as "Robert Spores" aka "Calapooia Bob."

248 National Archives—Pacific NW Region, 6125 Sand Point Way, NE, Seattle, WA, BIA RG 75, Grand Ronde/Siletz, Land and Enrollment Program records, Field Notes and Land Survey 1875–1898, Land Description Book 1878, Box 115; Grand Ronde Justice Court.

249 http://ftp.us-census.org/pub/usgenweb/census/or/douglas/1880,

Stevens, Frank, Cow Creek band of Umpqua[250]	Native Name: None known by author
Alias: None known by author	Allotment: None known by author
Mother: Unknown to author	Father: Unknown to author

Stevens, Isaac (1845c–1908), Cow Creek band of Umpqua	Native Name: None known by author
Alias: Isaac Stephens	Allotment 212
Mother: Unknown to author	Father: Unknown to author

In 1872, Isaac Stevens was listed under the Cow Creek band with his wife Mary and adopted sons, Louis and William. Three years later, Isaac married Julienne Harriet (1861c) on November 22, 1875.[251]

In 1879 and again in 1880, he was elected to serve as a representative for the south precinct at the annual session of the Grand Ronde Indian Legislature. In 1880, he was also appointed to serve as court treasurer for two years along with **Joseph Selkeah**.[252]

In 1888, Isaac and his wife Harriet had a house and barn on sixty fenced acres with nine acres in oats and a one-acre garden. They also had three horses, eight hogs, and six head of cattle.

Isaac served on the Grand Ronde Police Force from 1892 to 1894.[253] In 1901, he married **Tanus George Sutton** (Sakalkhida)'s widow, **Margaret Toto** (Chaimala).

On October 29, 1906, Isaac Stevens received a fee patent for 140 acres of allotment land.[254]

Sterwin, Sambo, Yamhill band of Kalapuya	Native Name: None known by author
Alias: Blind Sambo	Allotment: None known by author
Mother: Unknown to author	Father: Unknown to author

In 1872, he was living with his wife, Ellen. In 1877, the medicine doctor, **Jack Nancy** (Shimkhin), was living with him.[255]

---

250 Gatschet, *Texts, Sentences and Vocables*, 367: "Frank Stevens" under Cow Creek.

251 Munnick and Beckham, *Catholic Church Records—Grand Ronde*, Register I, p. 95, M-11.

252 National Archives, Seattle, Grand Ronde/Siletz, Land and Enrollment Program records, Field Notes and Land Survey 1875–1898, Land Description Book 1878, Box 115; Grand Ronde Justice Court.

253 Grand Ronde Agency Ledger Book, Records of Employees at Grand Ronde July 1883–September 1907, Confederated Tribes of the Grand Ronde Community of Oregon Archive.

254 *Heirs of Deceased Indians*, Allotment Record 212.

255 Gatschet, *Texts, Sentences and Vocables*, 370.

Stewart, James (1840c)	Native Name: None known by author
Alias: Muddy Jim	Allotment: None known by author
Mother: Unknown to author	Father: Unknown to author

In 1885, he was living with his wife, Mary, and sons Solomon and Jim. Also living with the family was Jim's father, "Old Ham." This family was not listed on any GRIC after 1885.

Stewart, James (1843c–1904), Kalapuya	Native Name: Tkintkinu /TKIN-tki-nu/ (tḵíntḵinu)*256
Alias: Muddy Jim	Allotment 210
Mother: Unknown to author	Father: Unknown to author

In 1872, Muddy Jim (Tkintkinu) was listed with his wife Lily and five-year-old daughter, Annie under the Mary's River band of Kalapuya.[257]

In 1885, he was living with his wife Muddy Lilly (1845c) and his son, Louie (1867c).

By 1888 Muddy Lily and the children were no longer living with Muddy Jim. He was living with a woman named Mary. They had a farm with a house with a barn on twenty fenced acres. Besides the usual farm implements, they have four horses, two hogs, and a dozen chickens.

Muddy Jim was listed as a widow in 1895. Several years later, he married **Mary Hutchins** (Duniwi). He died September 16, 1904, leaving as his sole heir his widow, Mary Hutchins. October 31, 1916, Mary received a fee patent for the entire sixty acres of Muddy Jim's allotment land.[258]

Stone, James (1826c–61), Yamhill band of Kalapuya[259]	Native Name: None known by author
Alias: None known by author	Allotment: None known by author
Mother: Unknown to author	Father: Unknown to author

James was **Chief Peter Selkya**'s brother. He was baptized on May 12, 1861. On June 5, 1861, he was buried, having died the day before. In attendance at the

---

256 Jacobs, Field Notebooks 46, *Santiam Kalapuya Text*, 102: Indian name "tkintkinu."

257 Jacobs, Field Notebooks 46, *Santiam Kalapuya Text*, 85: J. B. Hudson said, Jim Stewart or Muddy Jim was a Yoncalla. "His people maybe sold him for a slave and he got up to the Yamhill–Grand Ronde country, even as far as Vancouver." Gatschet, *Texts, Sentences and Vocables*, 368: under "Kalapuya now with Marysville." 1888 GRIC: James Stewart was listed as Mary's River.

258 *Heirs of Deceased Indians*, Allotment Record 210.

259 Munnick and Beckham, *Catholic Church Records—Grand Ronde*, Register I, p. 10, B-32, S-21.

funeral were "James' brother, Peter chief, and others."[260]

Stuart, Jack (1840c)	Native Name: None known by author
Alias: None known by author	Allotment: None known by author
Mother: Unknown to author	Father: Unknown to author

In 1885, he was listed with his wife, Mollie (1845c), and his children, Andrew, Jane, and Adam. Jack Stuart's brother, Bofus was also living with the family.

Sugar, Charley (1838c), Rogue River/ Shasta	Native Name: None known by author
Alias: Sugar Charley	Allotment: None known by author
Mother: Unknown to author	Father: Unknown to author

In 1872, Charley Sugar's horse was stolen from him in the vicinity of The Dalles by another Indian named Charley. On September 25, Sinnott, the Grand Ronde Indian agent, wrote to Joel Palmer at the Siletz Reservation to let him know that the culprit was now believed to be at Siletz. Sinnott described the horse as a roam mare with "EV" branded on her left hip and shoulder. He asked Palmer to help in recovering the animal.[261]

Charley Sugar had a son, Jack (1867c), by his wife Polly. In 1885, Jack was still alive and living with his father and Sugar Charley's wife Sarah.[262]

Sutton, George (1825c–1901), Tualatin band of Kalapuya,	Native Name: Sakalkhida /sa-KAL-hi-da/ (sak'álxida),*[263]

---

260 Ibid.
261 P. B. Sinnott to Joel Palmer, September 25, 1872. *Correspondence and Papers of Joel Palmer.*
262 Gatschet, *Texts, Sentences and Vocables,* 367: under the Coquille as "Sugar Charley." Gatschet, *Texts, Sentences and Vocables,* 366, under the Rogue River as "Sugar Charley, wife Siletz or Alsea."
263 Gatschet, *Texts, Sentences and Vocables,* 77. Jacobs, Field Notebook 54, *Texts and Ethnology,* 40. Jacobs, Field Notebook 53, *Texts and Ethnology,* 102. Jacobs, Field Notebooks 59, *Texts and Ethnology,* 60: V. Howard gave his name as "Sakalxida." She identified him further by describing him as the man with a wife named "Tcaimala" [Margaret Toto] with two brothers: Kilmanux and one other [Alexander Toto] whose name she did not remember. Victoria Howard gave "Tcaimala's" mother as a Clacka-mas woman named "Kilipacta." She also said that "Sakalxida" had seven or eight children, but all were dead. Jacobs, Field Notebooks 59, *Texts and Ethnology,* 60: the native name "Sakalxida" belonged to a man who "was [John] Watchinu's 1st wife [Mary Philomene Sutton]'s father." Jacobs, Field Notebook 53, *Texts and Ethnology,* 72–74: "Sakalxida, name of a part Yamhill—Tualatin man. He was [John] Watchinu's 1st wife's father."

Yamhill band of Kalapuya[264]	Ishilshil /i-Shil-shil/ (ishílshil)*[265]
Alias: George Sutton, Tanus George[266]	Allotment 213
Mother: Unknown to author	Father: Unknown to author

Tanus George (Sakalkhida) was raised near Carlton, just northeast of McMinnville. **John "Mose" Hudson** said he danced but he did not know if he was a medicine doctor.[267]

In 1855, Tanus George was with **James Shiliqua** (Shilikwa) and **Wankipa** when they ambushed **Dave Yatchkawa** after he threatened to kill **Chief Kiakuts** (Kayakach).[268]

After the Tualatin people were removed to Grand Ronde, Tanus George married Catherine around 1858, Matilda around 1862, Lucy around 1868, and Margaret Toto (Chaimala) in 1873.[269] Through these women, George had a number of children: Mary Philomene (1858c–91c), Marcus (1864c), Cecile (1862c–91), Moses (1868c), Jane (1872c), Louie Joseph (1877c–78c), Elizabeth (1879c–86), Jasetta (1880c), Moses (1881c–1907), Mary (1883c–90), Mascasca (1884–1922), Cecelia (1888–91), and Estelle (1890).

In 1888, Tanus George was living with his wife Margaret Toto and his children Moses, Mary, Macasca, and an infant daughter. Maria (1814c), a Clackamas widow, was also living with his family at that time. They had a house and barn on forty fenced acres with two acres in wheat and oats. They also had six horses, six hogs, and a dozen chickens.

Much later, **Mary Ann Michelle** wrote that Tanus George's only surviving children were a grown daughter, Mary Philomene Sutton, and two boys by **Margaret Toto** (Chaimala): **Moses** and **Macasca Sitton**.[270] His daughter Mary

---

264 Jacobs, Field Notebook 36, *Santiam Kalapuya Text*, 192: "isilsil, part Wapato Lake man (part Tualatin—Yamhill)." Jacobs, Field Notebook 54, *Texts and Ethnology*, 40: "Mrs. H. recounts the death of sakalxida at Grand Ronde about 1900 or 1901."

265 1887 GRIC gave his Indian name as "Ish-shill-shill." Michelle, *Just a Memorandum,* 5: Eshilshil or George Sutten, his wife, Margaret Toto, Molalla. Jacobs, Field Notebooks 46, *Santiam Kalapuya Text*, n.p: "George Sutton was a part or whole Tualatin or possibly part something else; Tualatin name, Eshilshil" and "He married, his last marriage, a Molale woman, [now known as] Mrs Steven."

266 Johnson and Zenk, *Chinuk Wawa*, 188: meaning small or little.

267 Jacobs, Field Notebooks 46, *Santiam Kalapuya Text*, 163.

268 Gatschet, *Texts, Sentences, & Vocables*, 132: Ishilshil was the third man after Wankhpa and Shilikwa. See earlier introduction of *Indian Removal* for additional description of incident.

269 Munnick and Beckham, *Catholic Church Records—Grand Ronde*, Register I, p. 81, M-3, p.105, B-41, p. 109, S-24, p. 112, B-14, p. 119, B-18, p. 126, B-23, Register II, p. 3, B-8, p. 5, S-11, p. 20, B-27, p. 39, B-8, p. 60, S-7, p. 61, B-11, p. 67, S-1, p. 68, S-6.

270 Michelle, *Just a Memorandum,* 5. National Archives, Central Plains Region, Louie Savage Inmate File 5333: Attorney's case for pardon listed Moses Sitton as mixed blood: Tualatin, Molalla and Santiam Kalapuya

Philomene married **John Wacheno** (Tsinwalh).[271]

According to **Victoria Wishikin** (Kinishi), in his early life, when Tanus George danced and sang "full power," he would make his daughter dance around him shooting arrows. Just the strength of his power would compel his daughter to dance. Victoria said it was at the girl's first winter dance that this particular daughter danced the arrow dance for her father. Then in the springtime, she fell ill. Her tongue stuck out like a snake as she gasped for air. It was her father's power that had made her sick. Several medicine women were called to make her well, but all in vain.

Even Tanus George tried to cure his daughter as it was his snake power that had wrapped themselves around the girl's neck. He sang and danced for her. He rubbed her neck and body with ashes, but she did not recover.[272]

Tanus George was also a rainmaker. Long ago, if a person wanted rain, they would go to one with such power; he would sing, perhaps alone, perhaps just with his wife and family, and he would ask his power to make it rain. Tanus George was one of the men who had this type of power.[273]

He lived to be an old man. When dying he spoke of a white muslin gown he wanted to be dressed in after he was dead. Victoria Wishikin made the gown just as he wanted it. After seeing it, he wanted a white shirt and white underwear for underneath it. The items were purchased for him from the Willamina store. Then he was happy and satisfied with his "clothes for the sky land."[274]

In probate court, Tanus George's estate was valued at $840. His heirs were his widow, Margaret Toto, his son Moses, who was residing in Polk County, and his son Marcasca, who lived in Yamhill County, Oregon. On April 9, 1907, a fee patent for his 260-acre allotment was issued to them.[275]

Moses and Mac Sitton were cousins to **Louis Savage.** Moses Sitton helped Louis escape the angry mob after the shooting death of **Foster Wacheno** (Inawalh). Mack Sitton corresponded with him when he was in Leavenworth Penitentiary.[276]

By 1982, Tanus George's family through Marcasca Sitton's daughter, Caroline Sitton-Strong, had grown significantly. Caroline wrote that her brother had been killed in action during the war and she had lost a son in a fire, but she had three boys and one girl. She also had eight grandchildren—three boys and five girls— and one great-granddaughter only a few months old.[277]

---

271 Jacobs, Field Notebooks 59, *Texts and Ethnology*, 60: the native name "Sakalxida" belonged to a man who "was [John] Watchinu's 1st wife [Mary Philomene Sutton]'s father."

272 Jacobs, Field Notebook 53, *Texts and Ethnology*, 72–74.

273 Ibid., 102.

274 Jacobs, Field Notebook 54, *Texts and Ethnology*, 40-42.

275 *Heirs of Deceased Indians*, Allotment Record 213.

276 National Archives and Records Administration, Central Plains Region, Louie Savage Inmate File 5333.

277 Danforth, Private Letter Collection, Letter 18.

Taylor, John (1810c–90), Rogue River	Native Name: Chenquenuck /Chen-que-nuck/[1]
Alias: None known by author	Allotment 218
Mother: Unknown to author	Father: Unknown to author

On June 1, 1884, Father Croquet baptized John Taylor's fourteen-year-old son, Jacob Lenai. The child's godfather was **Thomas Norwest.**

In 1885 and 1886, John Taylor (Chenquenuck) was listed with his wife, Molly, and son, James Lewis (1869c). The agent noted that John Taylor went around "in a nude state most of the time." He described their home as a "hut of the poorest quality" with a little garden on eight fenced acres. The family was "very poor."

By 1888, Taylor, Molly, and James Lewis "Levi" was still living in a hut, but they had increased the number of fenced acres to twenty. Their four hogs were listed as additional assets.[2]

John Taylor died December 4, 1890. On the GRIC for 1891, Mollie was listed as a widow living with her son, Levi.

Taylor, John (1815c–86c), Cow Creek band of Umpqua[3]	Native Name: None known by author
Alias: None known by author	Allotment: None known by author
Mother: Unknown to author	Father: Unknown to author

In 1878, the Grand Ronde Indian Legislature passed a provision of law that made a number of men exempt from working on the reservation roads due to their age. Old Taylor (1815c) was one of these men.[4]

In 1885, he was listed as Old Taylor, living with his wife, Jennie (1825c), and his brother, Old Ben (1835c). This family was not listed on any GRIC after 1885.

---

1   1887 GRIC: gave his Indian name as "Chen-que-nuck."
2   Michelle, *Just a Memorandum,* 3: "John Taylor and his wife had one son, Levi Tayr."
3   Gatschet, Gatschet, *Texts, Sentences and Vocables,* 367, listed with the Cow Creek as "John Taylor, old, wife."
4   National Archives, Seattle, Grand Ronde/Siletz, Land and Enrollment Program records, Field Notes and Land Survey 1875–1898, Land Description Book 1878, Box 115; Grand Ronde Justice Court.

Taylor, Levi (1870c–1901), Rogue River[5]	Native Name: None known by author
Alias: None known by author	Allotment 219
Mother: Unknown to author	Father: John Taylor, Rogue River

Levi Taylor married **Rosa Dowd** on October 10, 1894. Their witnesses were Mary and **Frank Norwest.** Levi and Rosa had a number of children including Myrtle (1897c), Jacob (1898), Mabel (1900–1905), and Roy (1902–1903).

Levi Taylor received a hundred-acre allotment. After he died in 1901, **Edward Petite,** an uncle of Levi Taylor's minor child, brought to the court's attention that there was a four-year-old child named Mabel Taylor currently residing at Grand Ronde who was the daughter of Levi Taylor and Mary Rosa Dowd, and petitioned the court to appoint an administrator for Levi's estate.

Rosa Dowd inherited both **John Taylor** (Chenquenuck) and Levi Taylor's allotments. After Rosa died in 1904, all three hundred acres of the allotment was sold to Ernest Heine on May 22, 1911.[6]

Taylor, Old Ben (1835c–86c)	Native Name: None known by author
Alias: None known by author	Allotment: None known by author
Mother: Unknown to author	Father: Unknown to author

In 1885, Ben was living with his brother, John, and John's wife. He was not listed on any GRIC after 1885.

Tebeau, Edward (1859c), Tualatin band of Kalapuya, Chinook, French Canadian[7]	Native Name: None known by author
Alias: Edward Franklin, Ed Teabo	Allotment: None known by author
Mother: Mary William, Chinook, Tualatin	Father: Franklin Michelle Tebeau, French Canadian

Edward's mother, **Mary William** (Duniwi), was the daughter of **Tualatin William Wishikin** and a Chinook woman.

Edward was the oldest of four children. In addition to him, Mary William-Tebeau had Joseph, William, and Agnes Tebeau. However, only Joseph and Edward were still alive in 1906.[8]

Mary William-Tebeau and her children came in with the Clackamas when they first came to Grand Ronde, but they only stayed a few years at a time. The rest of the time they stayed with Tualatin William at a place on the Columbia where he always fished for salmon.

---

5   1885 GRIC: "Lewis Taylor (1869c)" is listed as a son of John Taylor and another "Levi Taylor (1870c)" is listed as the brother of Mary Johnson.

6   *Heirs of Deceased Indians,* Allotment Records 218, 219.

7   McChesney, *The Rolls of Certain Indian,* Testimony of Edward Franklin Tebeau, 79.

8   Ibid.

**Edward Tebeau. Photo courtesy of
Oregon State Archives, File 3249.**

After Tualatin William died in 1875, Edward continued to live and fish on the Columbia. **Norris Apperson** was under promise to find him there and tell him about the allotments being issued at Grand Ronde, but never did. When Edward did return to Grand Ronde, he found the period for applying for allotments had ended. As a result, he went back to the Columbia.[9]

Edward returned to Grand Ronde around 1897. After a few years, he married **Anastasie Winslow**.[10] They were still living at Grand Ronde in 1905.

Thomas, Chief, Wishram Chinook husband of Watlala (Cascade) Chinook wife	Native Name: None known by author
Alias: None known by author	Allotment: None known by author
Mother: Unknown to author	Father: Unknown to author

Chief Thomas and **Chief John Kawache** were related on their mother's side.

9   O. Applegate, Testimony of Edward Franklin Tebeau.
10   Ibid.

Their mother's people lived on the north side of the Columbia River about eight miles below The Dalles on a small creek they called Thlate-en-cut. Thomas' father belonged to a tribe of people living at The Dalles and his wife was from the Wat-lala (Cascade) band. Since Thomas had lived as it suited him at all these places, the people recognized his right of possession.[11]

Thomas was listed on the GRIC for 1856 as a chief for a band of eighty-seven Oregon City people.

On June 21, 1856, B. Jennings wrote Joel Palmer that "The Chiefs Thomas, John, and Bill were fishing for salmon at Oregon City with the permission of the U.S. officer without objection from the white residents." He also wrote that "in searching for Indian horses, he had found some and not others," and that "white residents are charging for pasturing them."[12]

A month later, Jennings wrote Palmer that "the dried fish belonging to Chief Thomas and Chief John was too spoiled to ship to Dayton." He also wrote that he had been "looking for Indian horses, oxen and other property belonging to them, but most of it had been claimed by the whites."[13]

In 1857, Chief Thomas was listed as an Oregon City Chief of sixty-four people. He was not listed on any GRIC after that year.

Thomas, Frank (1856c)	Native Name: None known by author
Alias: None known by author	Allotment: None known by author
Mother: Unknown to author	Father: Unknown to author

In 1886, he was listed with his wife and a daughter, Winnie (1885c). They were poor.

Thomas, Isaac (1841c)	Native Name: None known by author
Alias: None known by author	Allotment: None known by author
Mother: Unknown to author	Father: Unknown to author

In 1886, he was listed with his wife, Mary (1856c), and children, Maura and Joseph. A widower named Thomas (1831c) was also living with the family. They were poor.

Thompson, Joe (1861c)	Native Name: None known by author
Alias: None known by author	Allotment: None known by author
Mother: Unknown to author	Father: Unknown to author

---

11 B. Jennings to Joel Palmer, *The Heirs of Succesion to the Willamette Valley Treaty; Treaty of the Kalapuya, Etc. January 22, 1855*, (prepared by Daniel L. Boxberger for the Tribal Council of the Confederated Tribes of Grand Ronde, January 2010), n.p.

12 B. Jennings to Joel Palmer, June 21, 1856, *Correspondence and Papers of Joel Palmer*.

13 Ibid.

Joe Thompson married **Henry Kikii** (Lhkaihkai)'s daughter, Catherine. In 1887, they were living at Grand Ronde with their two-year-old son, Morris. By 1888, Joe Thompson and Catherine had two children and had moved in with Henry.

Tim-Tim, Rosa (1858c–1923), Umpqua[14]	Native Name: Elmermach[15]
Alias: None known by author	Allotment: None known by author
Mother: Unknown to author	Father: Unknown to author

Rosa Tim-Tim (Elmermach) was a full Umpqua woman with one-eleven tattooed on her chin.[16] The daughter of one of **Eliza Day's** sisters, Rosa married **Peter Petite** around 1877 in Roseburg. In 1880, they were farming at Lookingglass, in Douglas County, Oregon.[17] Their daughter, Mary Ann, was baptized shortly after they moved to Grand Ronde in 1885.

By Peter, Rosa had seven children: Minnie Ann, Ellen, Ernest Ira, Alvin Bernard, Maud, Mary Ann and Isabel, but only **Isabel** and **Maud Petite** were still living in 1917.[18]

Rosa married **Charlie Russie** on January 7, 1907, in Yamhill County.[19]

Timeetos, Bill, Clackamas	Native Name: None known by author
Alias: None known by author	Allotment: None known by author
Mother: Unknown to author	Father: Unknown to author

Bill Timeetos was **John Wacheno** (Tsinwalh)'s cousin. At Grand Ronde, he owned a Modoc slave woman named Susan. John Wacheno, who would have been twelve at the time, said Bill sold Susan to the Tualatin sub-chief, **Lame Jim Shiliqua** (Shilikwa).[20]

Tipton, Cephas (1875c), Yoncalla band of Kalapuya, Umpqua[21]	Native Name: None known by author

---

14　Michelle, *Just a Memorandum*, 8: gave her as full Umpqua. *St. Michael's Catholic Church Burial Records*, 1923, gives her DOD as July 3, 1923.

15　McChesney, *The Rolls of Certain Indian*: gave her Indian name as "Elmermach."

16　Michelle, *Just a Memorandum*, 8: "Rosa was tattooed three marks on her chin."

17　Oregon State Archives, Salem, Oregon 1907, Polk County, Estate File, Eliza Day. http://ftp.us-census.org/pub/usgenweb/census/or/douglas/1880, 1880 Mt. Scott Census

18　Affidavit taken from Rosie Tim-Tim-Russie by Charles E, Coe, Superintendent, Roseburg Agency, February 6, 1917.

19　National Archives, Salem, Oregon, January 7, 1907 Marriage to Rosa Tim-Tim Petite, File 130. O. Applegate, Testimony of Rosie Tim-Tim.

20　O. Applegate, Testimony of James Siliqua.

21　1872 GRIC: listed as one of the "Calapooias" with such men as Polk Scott, Calapooia Billy Williams, and Robert Spores. 1888 GRIC listed as Umpqua.

Alias: None known by author	Allotment 223
Mother: Clinnie Williams, Yoncalla, Umpqua	Father: Richard "Dick" Tipton, Yoncalla band of Kalapuya

On October 16, 1919, Cephas Tipton sold 280 acres of Dick Tipton's allotment to C. M. Blair. On February 11, 1921, a fee patent was issued to Cephas Tipton for the remaining twenty acres of Dick's allotment.[22]

In 1928, Cephas was living about seven miles north of Corvallis.[23] Through Cephas, **Dick Tipton** eventually had at least one surviving grandchild, Gerald Tipton, who was in the navy and living in San Diego in 1930.[24]

Tipton, Dick (1853c–1905), Yoncalla band of Kalapuya[25]	Native Name: None known by author
Alias: Richard Tipton, Dick Tiptin	Allotment 220
Mother: Unknown to author	Father: Unknown to author

In 1872, Dick was living with wife **Clinnie Williams.** They had a son named John Baptiste on April 3, 1875. Dick also had a wife named Judith and another wife, Lucy. Lucy died on February 2, 1884.

On May 18, 1886, Dick married **Mary Hutchins. Thomas Norwest** and **Rosa Petite** witnessed the ceremony.[26] In 1888, Dick and Mary had Dick's son, **Cephas Tipton** and Mary's son, **Eustace Howard,** living with them. The next year, Cephas was back living with his mother, Clinnie Tipton.[27]

After **Joe Apperson** (Washamsh) died, Dick abandoned Mary Hutchins in favor of Joe's widow, **Nancy Kenoyer** (Tunishni). Nancy lived with him until he died August 31, 1905.[28]

His total estate was valued at six hundred dollars. His heirs were his widow, Nancy, and his son, Cephas, who had married **Josephine Lillie Condon.**[29]

---

22 *Heirs to Deceased Indians*, Allotment Record 223.

23 Jacobs, Field Notebook 45, *Yoncalla Texts*, 108.

24 Jacobs, Field Notebooks 61, *Texts and Ethnology*, n.p.

25 1872 GRIC: listed as one of the "Calapooias" with such men as Polk Scott, Calapooia Billy Williams, and Robert Spores. 1888 GRIC listed as Umpqua.

26 Munnick and Beckham, *Catholic Church Records—Grand Ronde*, Register II, p. 5, M-3.

27 Michelle, *Just a Memorandum*, 9: Dick Tipton's wife Mary had a son, Eustace Howard, by a previous relationship.

28 Oregon State Archives, Salem, Oregon, 1904, Polk County, Estate File 0894, Dick Tipton.

29 Munnick and Beckham, *Catholic Church Records—Grand Ronde*, Register II, p. 115, M-1. Oregon State Archives, Salem, Oregon, 1904, Polk County, Estate File 0894, Dick Tipton.

Tole, Elizabeth (1869c–1958), Tillamook, Lower Chinook, Clatsop[30]	Native Name: None known by author
Alias: Elizabeth Harney, Elizabeth Blacketer	Allotment: None known by author
Mother: Catherine, Tillamook	Father: Louis Tole, Lower Chinook, Clatsop

Elizabeth married George Harney on July 13, 1886. **Joseph Michelle** and Magdelen "Hattie" Sands were their witnesses. By George, Elizabeth had Adelia Harney (1891–95), Anthony Harney, and George Harney (1898–99).[31]

Next, Elizabeth married Sally Ann Blacketer's son, James. Together, they had Rena (1903c), Charles (1904c), James, Jr. (1909c), and Liola (1911c).[32] Her husband James and his brother, Charles Blacketer, inherited part of **Callo Bonaparte** (Kalukh)'s allotment in 1916. They also inherited **Alsea Bill** (Kama)'s allotment.

Tole, Louis (1831c–76c), Lower Chinook, Clatsop[33]	Native Name: None known by author
Alias: None known by author	Allotment: None known by author
Mother: Unknown to author	Father: Unknown to author

On March 8, 1863, Father Croquet referenced Louis in Catholic Church records as "Lewis Tole of the Chinooks."

In 1872, he was listed under the Clackamas with two wives: Catherine, a Tillamook woman, and Jane. By Catherine, Louis had Jude (1863c–84), Joseph (1865c), Celeste (1866–76), Genevieve (1868–89), and Elizabeth (1869c–1958). By Jane, he had Narcisse (1865–85), Louise (1872c), and Francis (1875). On July 20, 1873, Louis Tole married Jane in the Catholic Church at Grand Ronde. **Chief Louis Napesa** and his wife, **Lizette Klickitat**, witnessed the ceremony.[34]

His daughter Louise married **Nicholas Sands**. His daughter Elizabeth Tole-Harney-Blacketer testified in 1906:

My father Louis Tole, who died about thirty years ago, was a member of the Lower Chinook band of Indians; his father being a Lower Chinook and his mother a Clatsop; that at the time of the death of my father he left a wife and ten children.[35]

30 Munnick and Beckham, *Catholic Church Records—Grand Ronde,* Register I, p. 64, B-42.
31 Ibid., Register II, p. 6, M-6, p. 32, B-28, p. 41, B-18, p. 74, B-37.
32 1934 U. S. Indian Census Rolls, 1885–1940, Grand Ronde Reservation.
33 McChesney, *The Rolls of Certain Indian.*
34 Munnick and Beckham, *Catholic Church Records—Grand Ronde,* Register I, p. 25, B-12, p. 127, S-3, p. 37, B-4, p. 41, p. 45, B-34, p. 53, B-16, p. 64, B-42, p. 78, B-64, p. 83, B-35, p. 83, M-8, p. 96, B-36, p. 97, S-6.
35 McChesney, *The Rolls of Certain Indian.*

Tom, Bogus, Shasta[36]	Native Name: None known by author
Alias: None known by author	Allotment: None known by author
Mother: Unknown to author	Father: Unknown to author

Bogus Tom was removed to the reservation with the rest of the Shasta after the war in southern Oregon, but before long he went back to his original home country in northern California. Later, he returned to Grand Ronde to bring news of a dream that predicted the return of all the dead relatives of the people if Indian people would only dance in a certain way. Since there were laws at Grand Ronde against carrying this news or practicing the dance, the Indian agent had the Indian police put him off the reservation when he came back the second time.[37]

Tom, Kitty (1840c), Rogue River	Native Name: Acattycon /A-catty-con/
Alias: Mary Ann Tyee	Allotment: None known by author
Mother: Unknown to author	Father: Unknown to author

Kitty Tom (Acattycon) was the hayash wife of Tyee Shasta Tom. She was a Rogue River woman with **Chief Joe**'s band near Evans Creek in southern Oregon.[38] During removal, the Rogue River people were divided. She was with the main band that came to Grand Ronde by wagon. The other band came by ship.[39]

Tom, Lawney (1864c–1923), Rogue River and Shasta[41]	Native Name: Pootpam /Poot-pam/[40]
Alias: Loni Tom, Tom Lawney	Allotment 104
Mother: Rogue River	Father: Tyee Shasta Tom

Lawney Tom (Pootpam) married **Lucy Johnson** around 1882. By Lucy, he had one son named Martin (1886c–92c). He married **Marcelline Riggs,** the widow of **Joseph Selkeah,** around 1889. By Marcelline he had Albert (1890c), Abraham (1892), Emma (1893–1965), and Clinton (1895–1953).

After Marcelline, Lawney married Rosa, **John Wacheno** (Tsinwalh)'s daughter by Mary Philomen Sutton in 1901. He and **Rosa Wacheno** had a number of children: Marcellus (1901), Irving (1902c–1944), Elmer (1903), Matthew (1905), Ella (1907, and Orville (1910).

36 Du Bois, *The Ghost Dance*, 30–31.
37 Ibid.
38 1887 GRIC: Indian name as "A-catty-con."
39 O. Applegate, Testimony of Kitty Tom.
40 1887 GRIC: gave Indian name as "Poot-pam."
41 National Archives, Central Plains Region, Louie Savage Inmate File 5333, gave him as Rogue River and Shasta.

Lawney Tom with one of his sons. Photo courtesy of Oregon Historical Society (OHS 20157N.019).

The Wachenos had a place where they grew berries to make wine. On it was a building they called the "wine house." In the spring of 1910, Lawney owned a little white horse that **Jeffery Wacheno,** the grandson of **Chief Daniel Wacheno** (Wachinu), borrowed one day without asking. Lawney had been drinking when he learned that Jeffery had taken the horse. Grabbing a gun, he went after Jeffery. When they met, Lawney shot and killed him.[42]

After Lawney was convicted of murder in May of that year, Rosa was left to raise their children alone.[43] John Wacheno (Tsinwalh) finished raising their boys

---

42　Zenk, interview with Esther LaBonte, 1982, transcript 1, 2009 (15:00).

43　Oregon State Archives, 800 Summer Street NE, Salem, Oregon, 1910, Polk County,

after Rosa and Lawney both died.[44]

One of Lawney Tom's fun dance songs was sang by **Victoria Wishikin** (Kinishi) and recorded by Melville Jacobs in 1930.[45]

Tom, Mary Ann (1820–1914), Shasta	Native Name: None known by author
Alias: Mary Ann Tyee	Allotment 225
Mother: Unknown to author	Father: Unknown to author

Mary Ann Tom was the second wife of **Tyee Shasta Tom**. On October 29, 1906, under the name "Mary Ann Tyee," she received a fee patent for her entire hundred- acre allotment.[46]

Tom, Marysville, Mary's River band of Kalapuya	Native Name: None known by author
Alias: None known by author	Allotment: None known by author
Mother: Unknown to author	Father: Unknown to author

Marysville Tom was the brother of **Marysville George** and **Louise Monada**. He was married to an Alsea woman named Paula. **William Hartless** (Futi) was their son.

Tom, Tyee Shasta (1802c-1894), Shasta[47]	Native Name: None known by author
Alias: None known by author	Allotment: 224
Mother: Unknown to author	Father: Unknown to author

Tyee Shasta Tom was listed as the Rogue River chief at Grand Ronde on December, 1862. At that time, there were 113 people in his band.

In the September 14, 1871, council, Shasta Tom was one of those who spoke to the Americans on behalf of the people. In part, he said,

> On most of the reservation the Indians are not like whites. The whites are all over the country. They make money and plenty of it, everywhere. The Indian gets poorer every day. If you want us to be like whites, give us what we need. We have received many things, but not what we need.[48]

Tom Larney Inmate File 6131.

44 Zenk, interview with Ethel Petite Logan, 1978.
45 Jacobs, Field Notebook 51, *Music and Ethnology*, 43.
46 *Heirs to Deceased Indians*, Allotment Record 225.
47 Gatschet, *Texts, Sentences and Vocables*, 364: under the Shastas as "Old Tom; was the chief, abt 70." 1888 GRIC: gave his tribe as Shasta.
48 *Annual Report Commissioner of Indian Affairs*, 1871, Minutes of a Council with Grand Ronde Indians at their Reservation, Oregon, by Commissioner Felix R. Brunot, September 14, 1871, 149–53.

He went on to advise the Americans to act honorably in their dealings with the people because soon, Indian children would learn to write. He said the whites would be ashamed if Indian people could write the truth to Washington themselves.[49]

Shasta Tom had two wives in 1872, hayash wife **Kitty Tom** (Acattycon) and second wife **Mary Ann Tom.** He also had three sons: Nat (1856c), Louis (1863c), and **Lawney Tom** (Pootpam).

Shasta Tom, like Klamath Charlie from Siletz, believed very strongly in the new religion that came from California, which held that if Indian people danced hard enough and a certain way, their loved ones would return from the dead.

To practice the new religion, a dance house was built at Rock Creek for the Shasta, Umpqua and Rogue River tribes.[50] Chiefs of the dance house were Shasta Tom, **Solomon Riggs** (Gunconnacli), and **Peter McCoy** (Inchaishi). One of the best preachers of the religion was **Bob Riley.**[51]

There were laws at Grand Ronde against the new dream dance doctrine. Around 1877, Shasta Tom and two others were caught and fined $15 for holding a dance. Further, the agent with Indian police forced everyone caught in the dance house to stay there until morning and each participant was fined fifty cents.[52]

In 1888, Shasta Tom and his family were living on a forty-acre ranch with a house and barn. The place was nicely stocked with five horses, twenty-five hogs, two dozen chickens, two wagons, two plows, and a half acre garden.

By 1895, Shasta Tom's wives, Kitty Tom and Mary Ann Tom, were listed on the GRIC as widows. On February 11, 1921, a fee patent was issued to his son, Lawney Tom, for his entire 160-acre allotment.[53]

Totkey, Jack, Cow Creek band of Umpqua	Native Name: None known by author
Alias: None known by author	Allotment: None known by author
Mother: Unknown to author	Father: Unknown to author

In 1872, Jack was listed as alone.

Toto, Alexander (1858c–80c), Molalla	Native Name: None known by author
Alias: Alexander Wallen[54]	Allotment: None known by author
Mother: Unknown to author	Father: Paul Toto[55]

---

49 Ibid.
50 Du Bois, *The Ghost Dance*, 26, 30.
51 Ibid., 30.
52 Gatschet, *Texts, Sentences and Vocables*, 188–89.
53 *Heirs of Deceased Indians*, Allotment Records 224.
54 Munnick and Beckham, *Catholic Church Records—Grand Ronde*, Register I, p. 111, M-6.
55 Ibid., Register I, p. 14, B-197.

Alexander Toto was a half brother to **Wallen Kilmonie** (Kilmanukh), **Margaret Toto** (Chaimala), **Steve Savage** (Palhilh), and Margaret Isaac.[56] **Stephany Toto** was Alexander's full sister.

He had at least two wives, **Susan Beagle** and **Stephanie Apperson**. After he and Stephanie both died of tuberculosis, Susan Beagle married **French Prairie Frank Marc**.

Alexander left one surviving child by Stephanie Apperson named **Isadore Kilmonie**.

Toto, Margaret (1852c–1908c), Molalla, Clackamas[57]	Native Name: Chaimala /CHAI-ma-la/ (cháymala)*[58]
Alias: Margaret Sitton, Margaret Sutton, Margaret Stevens	Allotment: None known by author
Mother: Mary Ann Kilmonie, (Kilipashta), Clackamas[59]	Father: Paul Toto, Molalla

Margaret (Chaimala) was the half sister of **Wallen Kilmonie** (Kilmanukh), **Tom Gilbert** (Kiyukiyush), **Steve Savage** (Palhilh), and **Alexander Toto. Chief Joseph Hutchins** (Yalkama)'s wife, **Margaret Hutchins** (Sanyef), was her stepsister.[60]

In 1873, Margaret Toto married **Tanus George Sutton** (Sakalkhida). By George, she had two sons, **Moses** and **Macasca Sitton.**

In 1901 when George was dying, he worried about Moses and Macasca. Afraid that Margaret might desert them, he asked **Victoria Wishikin** (Kinishi), who was unmarried at that time, to take care of them should that happen.[61]

George instructed Margaret that after he was dead she was to put white fir

---

56 Affidavit State of Oregon, County of Yamhill, taken from Josephine (Frances) Shirley January 25, 1917 and Macasca Sutton, February 3, 1917.

57 Jacobs, Field Notebooks 59, *Texts and Ethnology*, 60, gave her mother as a Clackamas woman and her father as part Molalla. Jacobs, Field Notebooks 46, *Santiam Kalapuya Text*, 163: J. B. Hudson said that "George Sutton's last marriage was to a Molale woman named Mrs. Steven." Oregon State Archives, Salem, Oregon, 1907, Yamhill County, Estate 1205: gave Margaret Sutton's date of death as June 17, 1890.

58 Jacobs, Field Notebooks 59, *Texts and Ethnology*, 60: "kilipacta, a clack. woman who married a Molale man; dead some 30 years. Her daughter was tcaimala, name of a woman talked Molale, (she married sakalxida—a part Tualatin—Yamhill, her 1st husband was full Tualatin), father was part Molele; her older brother was Kilmanux (either Clack. Or Mol. Name); Mrs. H. forgets the other brother's name. Tcaimala had 7 or 8 children, all dead, one grand daughter, one great granddaughter survived."

59 Jacobs, Field Notebooks 59, *Texts and Ethnology*, 60: kilipacta, a clack. woman who married a Molale man; dead some 30 years. Jacobs, Field Notebook 69, *Texts and Ethnology*, 109.

60 Affidavit State of Oregon, County of Yamhill, taken from Josephine (Frances) Shirley January 25, 1917, and Macasca Sutton, February 3, 1917.

61 Jacobs, Field Notebook 54, *Texts and Ethnology*, 41.

**Left to right: Moses Sitton, Margaret Toto-Sutton,
Macasca Sitton, Tom Gilbert (seated). Photo courtesy
of Oregon Historical Society (OrHi 48151).**

limbs in a pan and put the pan over hot coals until the fir began to smoke, then take the pan from room to room smudging the house. He asked Margaret to smudge herself and Victoria. This was to be done each night for five nights and Margaret was not to cry because that would make his spirit "heavy."[62]

George also told Margaret never to think of him. He reassured her that even if she were to remarry, after she was dead they would be together. George believed that in the land of the dead one was always with one's first mate.[63]

After he died, Margaret took the pan and set about smudging the house. She even smudged the woodshed where George had always cut the firewood. She did this once each night for five nights, crying each time. Then, within the month, she

---

62 Ibid.
63 Ibid., 41.

left the boys and married **Isaac Stevens**.[64]

In 1907, Margaret testified she was "a cousin" of **Isadore Kilmonie**.[65] Besides Isadore's estate, Margaret inherited an interest in the allotments of **Emily Judson** and her mother, **Mary Ann Kilmonie** (Kilipashta).

When Margaret Toto died, she had one surviving son, Macasca Sitton, and one surviving granddaughter, Pauline Sutton.[66]

Toto, Paul (1831c–71), Molalla	Native Name: None known by author
Alias: None known by author	Allotment: None known by author
Mother: Unknown to author	Father: Unknown to author

Paul Toto had a number of wives including Tillamook Mary, **Mary Ann Kilmonie** (Kilipashta), and Nancy Savage. He was the natural father of **Tom Gilbert** (Kiyukiyush), **Steve Savage (**Palhilh), **Margaret Toto** (Chaimala), **Alexander Toto,** and **Stephany Toto**.[67] Paul Toto also had two stepchildren, **Wallen Kilmonie** (Kilmanukh) and Margaret Isaac.[68]

Toto, Stephany (1867), Molalla[69]	Native Name: None known by author
Alias: None known by author	Allotment: None known by author
Mother: Unknown to author	Father: Unknown to author

Stephany was **Alexander Toto**'s sister and **Wallen Kilmonie** (Kilmanukh)'s half sister.[70]

Tucker, Bob, Umpqua	Native Name: None known by author
Alias: Old Man Bob	Allotment: None known by author
Mother: Unknown to author	Father: Unknown to author

Old Man Bob was listed with his wives—first wife Libby and second wife Jane—in 1872. **Catherine Lapan**, one of **Charley Lapan's** wives, and her children, James (1870c) and Minnie (1869c), were also living with the family.

---

64 Jacobs, Field Notebooks 46, *Santiam Kalapuya Text,* 163: J. B. Hudson said that "George Sutton's last marriage was to a Molale woman named Mrs. Steven."

65 Oregon State Archives, Salem, Oregon, 1907, Yamhill County, Estate 1204.

66 Affidavit State of Oregon, County of Yamhill, taken from Josephine (Frances) Shirley January 25, 1917 and Macasca Sutton, February 3, 1917.

67 Ibid.

68 Munnick and Beckham, *Catholic Church Records—Grand Ronde,* Register I, p. 14, B-191, p. 48, B-9, p. 67, B-11, S-4.

69 Ibid.

70 Ibid.

Tucker, John, Umpqua[71]	Native Name: None known by author
Alias: Big John, Big John Umpqua	Allotment: None known by author
Mother: Unknown to author	Father: Unknown to author

Big John Tucker could make thunder talk and lightning storms. He was a rainmaker.[72]

He had a number of wives: Mary of Clackamas (1826c–76), Charlotte, and Josette. He also had a number of children: Mary (1857c–67), Louis (1862–62), Francis (1863), Augustine (1864), Rose (1865), Augustine (1865c–68), Appollonia (1861), Charlotte (1866c), Jane (1867c), and John (1864–73).[73]

In 1872, he was listed with his wife, Mary of Clackamas, and daughter, Charlotte.

Tuscan, Clackamas	Native Name: Tuscan
Alias: None known by author	Allotment: None known by author
Mother: Unknown to author	Father: Unknown to author

In 1872, Tuscan was listed under **Chief Daniel Wacheno** (Wachinu)'s band of Clackamas with her daughter, **Eliza Johnson** (Khakhshni), and Eliza's children: Sarah, Minnie, and Solomon. Homer Hoffer (Tamaguin)'s wife, Louisa Johnson, was also her daughter.

---

71 1872 GRIC: "John Tucker" aka "Big John" and listed under Umpqua. Munnick and Beckham, *Catholic Church Records—Grand Ronde*: Croquet records his name as both "Big John Umpqua" and "John Tucker." Gatschet, *Texts, Sentences and Vocables*, 4: Peter Kinai believed "Big John of the Umpqua" to have the power of a rainmaker.

72 Gatschet, *Texts, Sentences and Vocables*, 4.

73 Munnick and Beckham, *Catholic Church Records—Grand Ronde*, Register I, p. 98, S-12, p. 16, B-228, p. 21, B-69, p. 22, S-30, p. 30, B-61, p. 37, B-3, p. 41, S-25, p. 53, S-2.

Vasselle, Louis (1826c–96) Iroquois[1]	Native Name: Dr. Attallo
Alias: Louis Vassal, Lewis Vassill	Allotment 226
Mother: Unknown to author	Father: Unknown to author

By his early twenties, Louis (Dr. Attallo) was living on the "Grand Prairie" near Salem with his wife, Catherine Yiyahtol, and their two small children, Victoria and Flore. He and Catherine were married in the Catholic Church at St. Paul on July 2, 1848, in the presence of long time Hudson's Bay Company employee Amable Petit.[2] Catherine died in 1853.

Louis, like most of the Iroquois associated with the early fur trade companies, supported the Catholic priests. It was in Louis' house that Father Croquet and Rev. Mesplie gave Holy Mass for the first time to Indian people living in the Grand Ronde–Siletz area. Describing Louis Vasselle as "a mixed-blooded Iroquois," Father Croquet wrote that his "rather spacious house" was "full of Indians, who had responded to our invitation, and who, for the first time, attended the sacrifice of the Noble Victim offered for their salvation."[3]

When most of the Shasta and Rogue River people were moved from Grand Ronde Ronde to Siletz, Louis and his daughter, Victoria went with them. They lived at Siletz until about 1865. Then they moved back to Grand Ronde where Louis married a Shasta woman named Charlotte (1838c–68). **Chief Louis Napesa** and **Frank Quenel** attended Charlotte's funeral in 1868. Louis Vasselle's next wife was also a Shasta woman. She went by the English name Mary (1840c).[4]

In 1872, Louis and Mary were listed on the GRIC under **Chief John Kawache**'s Oregon City band of Tumwater. When he and Mary separated in 1886, Louis kept all the property including their farm and crop. Mary was listed on the GRIC as "very poor."

Although Louis was never adopted by any of the treaty tribes, he lived at Grand Ronde "so many years no one objected to his receiving an allotment."[5]

---

1   Fremaux, *Memoires d'un Grand Brainois*, Chapter 3, mentions "Louis Vassel" as "a mixed-blood Iroquois." Gatschet, *Text, Sentences, and Vocables*, 25: "Dr. Louis, ½ breed, Chehalis." 1872 and 1888 GRIC list his tribe as the Oregon City band.

2   Munnick and Warner, *Catholic Church Records — St Paul*, 8. McChesney, *The Rolls of Certain Indian Tribes*, 6: Victoria's mother was listed as "Catherine Kiyah" (b.1818c–53c).

3   Fremaux, *Memoires d'un Grand Brainois*, Chapter 3.

4   Munnick and Beckham, *Catholic Church Records—Grand Ronde*, Register I, p. 54, S-7. O. Applegate, Testimony of Dave Leno, Captain Frank Quenel, and Victoria Jeffries.

5   O. Applegate, Testimony of Dave Leno.

Louis died on November 26, 1896. After his death, **Victoria Vasselle** inherited his personal estate. It was valued at three hundred dollars.[6] On January 30, 1907, she also received a fee patent for Louis Vasselle's entire 100.28-acre allotment.[7]

Vasselle, Victoria (1842c), Chinook, Iroquois[8]	Native Name: None known by author
Alias: Victoria Versalle, Vassal, Victoria Belleque, Victoria Jondro, Victoria Blake, Victoria Jefferies	Allotment: None known by author
Mother: Catherine Yiyahtol	Father: Louis Vasselle

On September 29, 1861, Victoria married **Edward Gendron** at Grand Ronde. Over the next ten years, she and Edward had a number of children, but they all died as infants.

Victoria's second husband was **John Baptiste Belleque,** the son of Pierre Belleque and Genevieve St. Martin. She and John Baptiste made their home at St Paul for many years. At least two daughters, Mary and Adeline Josephine, were buried there.[9]

Around 1894, John Baptiste and Victoria moved to Grand Ronde where John Baptiste Belleque was recorded in agency records as an "Indian" but no tribal affiliation could be found for him.

After Victoria and John Baptiste were divorced in 1898, she married John Blake, a quarter Indian. When John Blake died, Victoria returned to Grand Ronde, where she married **John E. Jefferies.** She and John lived on her father, **Louis Vasselle** (Dr. Attallo)'s, allotment for a number of years.

Voutrin, Catherine (1869c–97c), Mary's River band of Kalapuya, Iroquois, French Canadian	Native Name: None known by author
Alias: Catherine Vautrin, Catherine Menard	Allotment: None known by author
Mother: Mary Ann Monada, Iroquois, Mary's River band of Kalapuya	Father: Jean Baptiste Vautrin, French Canadian

Voutrin, Francis (1884–1943c), Mary's River band of Kalapuya, Iroquois, French Canadian	Native Name: None known by author

---

6   National Archives, Salem, Oregon, 1908, Yamhill County, Estate File 1274.

7   *Heirs to Deceased Indians,* Allotment Record 226.

8   Munnick and Beckham, *Catholic Church Records—Grand Ronde,* Register I, p. 54, S-7. O. Applegate, Testimony of Dave Leno, Captain Frank Quenel, and Victoria Jeffries.

9   Munnick and Warner, *Catholic Church Records—St Paul,* 83, 138.

Alias: Francis Voutrant, Francis Vautrin	Allotment 231
Mother: Mary Ann Monada, Iroquois, Mary's River Kalapuya	Father: Jean Baptiste Vautrin, French Canadian

On October 29, 1906, Francis received a fee patent for his entire eighty-acre allotment.

Voutrin, John Baptiste Jr. (1871c–1946c), Mary's River band of Kalapuya, Iroquois, French Canadian	Native Name: None known by author
Alias: John Bob, John Baptiste Vautrin Jr., John Voutrant	Allotment 230
Mother: Mary Ann Monada, Iroquois, Mary's River Kalapuya	Father: Jean Baptiste Vautrin, French Canadian

John B. Voutrin married Caroline Agnes, daughter of Alexander LaBonte and **Clementine LaChance.** They had a number of children, including Bartholomew (1898), Mary Anne (1900c), Rosa (1902c), Coraline (1904), Katherine (1907), Robert (1908c), Everett (1910), and Donald (1916).

On April 9, 1907, he received a fee patent for an entire eighty-acre allotment.

Voutrin, Julia Ann (1886c–1907c), Mary's River band of Kalapuya, Iroquois, French Canadian	Native Name: None known by author
Alias: Julia Ann Vautrin	Allotment 228
Mother: Mary Ann Monada, Iroquois, Mary's River Kalapuya	Father: Jean Baptiste Vautrin, French Canadian

Julia Ann Voutrin was the daughter of **Peter Voutrin** and Genevieve Tole. On January 30, 1907, her father, as her sole heir, received a fee patent for her entire eighty-acre allotment.

Voutrin, Olive (1876c), Mary's River band of Kalapuya, Iroquois, French Canadian	Native Name: None known by author
Alias: Olive Vautrin, Olive Norwest	Allotment: None known to author
Mother: Mary Ann Monada, Iroquois, Mary's River Kalapuya	Father: Jean Baptiste Vautrin, French Canadian

Voutrin, Peter (1863c–1922), Mary's River band of Kalapuya, Iroquois, French Canadian	Native Name: None known by author
Alias: Peter Vautrin, Peter Voutrant	Allotment 227
Mother: Mary Ann Monada, Iroquois, Mary's River Kalapuya	Father: Jean Baptiste Vautrin, French Canadian

Peter Voutrin was the son of **Mary Ann Monada** and Jean Baptiste Vautrin. In 1888, he was listed with his wife, Genevieve Tole, and their daughter, Julia Ann (1886c). At that time, the only thing the family owned was two horses.

Peter received a 240-acre allotment. He was also one of the men who did not sign the Surplus Land Agreement in 1901. On January 30, 1907, he received a fee patent for his entire 240-acre allotment.

W

Wacheno, Charles (1886-1927), Clackamas, Molalla, Tualatin band of Kalapuya, Upper Chinook, Klickitat[1]	Native Name: None known by author
Alias: None known by author	Allotment 235
Mother: Victoria Wishikin, Molalla, Tualatin band of Kalapuya	Father: Marc Daniel Wacheno, Clackamas, Upper Chinook, Klickitat

October 19, 1907, Charles Wacheno received a fee patent for his entire eighty-acre allotment.[2]

After Charles died on September 20, 1927, at The Dalles, Oregon, his body was returned to Grand Ronde for burial. His estate was appraised at $1,000; however, he and his uncle, **John Wacheno** (Tsinwalh), owed a $700 note on one piece of property they held jointly. After Charles's debts were paid, the balance of his estate went to Charles's only surviving heir, his wife, Nettie Wacheno, who at that time was residing in Hood River.[3]

Wacheno, Charlotte (1814c–1909), Wasco Chinook, Klickitat[4]	Native Name: Wasusgani /WA-sus-ga-ni/ (wásusgani),* Washaut /WASH-aut/ (wacaut)* [5]
Alias: Watchano	Allotment 237
Mother: Wasco Chinook	Father: Klickitat

Charlotte Wacheno (Wasusgani) was one of **Chief Daniel Wacheno** (Wachinu)'s wives. Wacheno already had three wives when he bought her.[6]

Charlotte's father was a Klickitat shaman whose strongest power was a water spirit that always carried a baby on its back. When she was older, Wasusgani described occasions when one of her father's patients died. She said at first her father would hide from the patient's family, but then he would return professing

1   Munnick and Beckham, *Catholic Church Records—Grand Ronde,* Register I, p. 27, B-40.
2   *Heirs of Deceased Indians,* Allotment Record 235.
3   National Archives, Salem, Oregon, 1927, Yamhill County, Estate File 3089.
4   Jacobs, Field Notebook 54, *Texts and Ethnology,* 4: "Mrs. Howard's mother-in-law part Klickitat, part Wasco, but talked Clackamas and lived here."
5   Jacobs, Field Notebook 54, *Texts and Ethnology,* 6: "This lady (wasusgani) later married and became mother to John Watcinu and Mrs. H.'s mother-in-law. A later name, her last name, was wacant (perhaps Clackamas name)." Jacobs, Field Notebook 69, *Texts and Ethnology,* 49: name given as wacaut. 1887 GRIC: gives Indian name as "Was-as-canna."
6   Jacobs, Notebook 69, *Texts Ethnology Clackamas & Jargon,* 49.

Marc Daniel Wacheno and Victoria Wishikin's son, Charles Wacheno. Photo courtesy of Barbara Danforth Private Collection.

Charles Wacheno and family. Photo courtesy of Barbara Danforth Private Collection.

his innocence and giving them gifts to compensate for the patient's death. When Charlotte was just a little girl, he would take her upon his back with her arms around his neck, like his power. Carrying her in this fashion, he would dance and sing his spirit song to its fullest strength. Soon he would vomit blood and be perfectly well again.[7]

Wasusgani received a hundred-acre allotment. On February 11, 1921, her heirs, **John Wacheno** (Tsinwalh) and **Charles Wacheno,** were issued a fee patent for her entire allotment.[8]

Wacheno, Chief Daniel (1805c–87), Clackamas	Native Name: Wachinu /wa-CHI-nu/ (wac'hínu),* Likhanch /LI-hanch/ (líx̱anch),* Laulash /LAU-lash/ (láwlash)*[9]
Alias: Chief Watcheno	Allotment: None known by author
Mother: Unknown to author	Father: Unknown to author

Wacheno (Wachinu) was the son of a war-leader. Although the Clackamas chief at that time had two or three sons, the people thought Wacheno should be

---

7   Jacobs, *Clackamas Text,* Part II, 538. Jacobs, Notebook 69, *Texts Ethnology Clackamas & Jargon,* 50.

8   *Heirs to Deceased Indians,* Allotment Record 237.

9   Jacobs, Field Notebooks 58, *Texts and Ethnology,* 88.

the one to take his place when the time came and recommended him as chief.[10] As their new chief, Wacheno signed the treaty with the Americans in 1855.[11] At Grand Ronde, there were eighty-five people in his band in 1856 and seventy-eight the following year.

Before the Clackamas were removed from their home country there was a time when Wacheno almost died. According to Wasusgani, many doctored him, but none could discover the cause of the illness. As his illness progressed, all of his valuables were made ready to be wrapped up with his corpse. Then one of the doctors who examined Wacheno discovered that a woman doctor had sent an arrow of her poison power into him. Immediately, the family sent two slaves to get the woman. After they brought her forcibly to them, she was ordered to remove the poison she had shot into Chief Wacheno.

The woman doctor who had made him sick was named **Chagwinim**. She began doctoring Wacheno as soon as she arrived. After working over him for some time, Chagwinim suddenly stopped. The doctor who had discovered Chagwinim's wicked deed explained to the family that she had extracted her arrow. The family waited far into the night for Wacheno to get better. At last, toward morning, he moved and they knew he would recover.[12]

Chief Wacheno owned two male slaves, one from someplace in California and another from the Umpqua. He bought them when they were small and raised them to men.[13] One was a young boy named Cinkwit (Shinkwit). Wacheno raised him like a son. As a result, when Shinkwit grew up, he was able to take a "normal" or non-slave woman as his wife.[14]

Walushishi was one of the girls interested in Shinkwit, but her parents objected to the relationship. Finally, Walushishi hanged herself at Shinkwit's house. She was dying when the medicine doctor arrived. The doctor insisted she sing her power song. She was permanently deaf as a result of the hanging, but the family managed to make her understand what she needed to do to save her life. Deaf to the sound of her own voice, Walushishi struggled to sing. No one but Shinkwit could straighten up her song. He was the only one who understood how to sing it. He sang it so that the rest of the people crowding around Walushishi could also understand how to sing it.[15]

Later, after Walushishi recovered, she and Shinkwit were married. **Victoria**

---

10 Drucker, Clackamas Notes, n.p.

11 Kappler, *Treaty with the Kalapuya, Etc, 1855.*

12 Jacobs, *Clackamas Text,* Part II, 511–512. Jacobs, Field Notebook 52, *Texts and Ethnology,* 60.

13 Drucker, *Clackamas Notes,* n.p.

14 Jacobs, Field Notebook 53, *Texts and Ethnology,* 22. Jacobs, Field Notebook 59, *Texts and Ethnology,* 52.

15 Jacobs, Field Notebook 51, *Texts and Ethnology,* 24.

Wishikin (Kinishi) recorded both Walushishi's song and Shinkwit's straightened version for Melville Jacobs in 1929.[16]

Every five or six years, the Wacheno family would buy slave girls from the Klamath. Chief Wacheno bought two girls. At first, he refused to sell one of the girls. Finally, he sold her for seven or eight horses. Wachinu gave a big feast to remove her slave status. He gave her his own sister's name and gave presents to all the people.[17]

Like other men of his status, Chief Wacheno also had a number of wives including **Maria Wacheno, Charlotte Wacheno** (Wasusgani), and **Sophie Gwaya-kiti.** However, unlike other husbands, if a wife left him, Wacheno never forced her to return.[18]

Prior to the removal of the Clackamas people, Chief Wacheno was a rich man. He brought a herd of twenty-two horses with him to Grand Ronde. His horses often won the horse races held by the various Indian tribes.[19]

Once when Chief Wacheno was singing his own song at a winter spirit power dance, his granddaughter, who was also dancing, suddenly died. His power was too strong. She got warm from it and went into a faint.[20]

In their elder years, Chief Wacheno and his wife Charlotte shared a home with their sons. In 1885, they were living with their son **Marc Daniel Wacheno** (Wadams) and his family. The next year they were living with another son, **John Wacheno** (Tsinwalh), and his family.

Toward the end of Wacheno's life, it was thought that some dead people might have gotten him as he lost most of his hearing and became paralyzed as a result of an illness. Later, he recovered somewhat, but always had to use a cane and shook when he walked.[21] Father Croquet recorded his death in the Catholic Church records of St. Michael's parish on May 21, 1887.[22]

Wacheno, Felix (1877c–1906), Tualatin band of Kalapuya, Clackamas,	Native Name: None known by author

---

16 Ibid.

17 Drucker, *Clackamas Notes*, n.p.

18 Jacobs, *Clackamas Text*, Part II, 539: Charlotte Wacheno said that when one of Wacheno's wives left him, he did not go to get her back. When one left him, only a Molalla woman named Sophie and Charlotte remained. After Sophie went back to her people, only Charlotte lived with Chief Wachinu. Jacobs, Field Notebook 69, *Texts Ethnology Clackamas & Jargon*, 51: Mrs. H.'s grandfather's sister, Sophie was one of the wives of Wachinu. Jacobs, Field Notebook 59, *Texts and Ethnology*, 52: Sigawali was the Indian name of one of the elder Wachinu's wives.

19 Drucker, *Clackamas Notes*, n.p.

20 Jacobs, Field Notebook 58, *Texts and Ethnology*, 84.

21 Jacobs, *Clackamas Text*, Part II, 554. Jacobs, Notebook 69, *Texts Ethnology Clackamas & Jargon*, 105.

22 Munnick and Beckham, *Catholic Church Records—Grand Ronde*, Register I, p. 29, S-8.

Wasco band of Chinook, Klickitat [23]	
Alias: None known by author	Allotment 239
Mother: Philomene Mary Sutton, Tualatin	Father: John Wacheno, Clackamas, Wasco Chinook, Klickitat

Just prior to Felix's death, he got in trouble and was arrested. His father, John Wacheno (Tsinwalh), paid for an attorney to defend him, but Felix was seriously ill and died in Salem in October 1906. His body was returned to Grand Ronde for burial.[24]

After his death, his widow, **Louise Wallace** (Washtali), was issued a fee patent for his entire allotment on March 13, 1907.[25]

Wacheno, Foster (1843c–1904), Clackamas, Wasco band of Chinook, Klickitat	Native Name: Inawalh /i-NA-wahl/ (ináwał),* Shmaknukh /SHMAK-nuh/ (shmáq'nux)*[26]
Alias: Andre Foster Wacheno, Andrew Foster Wacheno, Foster Watchano	Allotment 232
Mother: Charlotte Wacheno, Wasco Chinook, Klickitat	Father: Chief Wacheno, Clackamas

A quiet, gentle man, Foster (Inawalh) was the oldest son of the Clackamas chief, **Daniel Wacheno** (Wachinu) and his wife, **Charlotte Wacheno** (Wasusgani).[27]

Foster served on the fifth annual session of the Grand Ronde Indian Legislature in 1876, representing the Clackamas with **Tom Foster**. He served on the legislature's seventh annual session in 1878; representing the east precinct with the Tualatin sub-chiefs, **Dave Yachkawa** and **Lame James Shiliqua** (Shilikwa). Foster was appointed justice of the peace in 1879.[28] He also served on the Grand Ronde Police Force from 1883 to 1884 and on the Court of Offenses in 1894.[29]

Foster had several wives: Anne, **Sarah Gwayakiti**, and Lucy, a Molalla woman. By Anne, he had Theresa (1874c–87) and Simon Norbert (1877c–83c).[30] His

---

23 National Archives, Salem, Oregon, 1906, Polk County, Estate File 1005.

24 Ibid.

25 *Heirs to Deceased Indians*, Allotment Record 239.

26 Jacobs, Notebook 69, *Texts Ethnology Clackamas & Jargon*, 112. Jacobs, Field Notebook 58, *Texts and Ethnology*, 86: Foster had the name inawalh when he was married to Sarah and the name shmaknukh at time of his death.

27 National Archives, Central Plains Region, Inmate File 5333, Louie Savage.

28 National Archives, Seattle, Grand Ronde/Siletz, Land and Enrollment Program records, Field Notes and Land Survey 1875–1898, Land Description Book 1878, Box 115; Grand Ronde Justice Court.

29 Grand Ronde Agency Ledger Book, Records of Employees at Grand Ronde July 1883–September 1907, Confederated Tribes of the Grand Ronde Community of Oregon Archive.

30 Jacobs, Field Notebook 58, *Texts and Ethnology*, 86: Anne's mother was named

marriage to Anne was declared null by Father Croquet on December 31, 1878, after which he and Sarah Gwayakiti were married in the Catholic Church.[31] By Sarah Gwayakiti, Foster had Lillie (1871c), George (1872c), and Henry (1876c).[32]

Foster was probably the brother whom **John Wacheno** (Tsinwalh) said saw the wolf four times on his spirit quest. According to John, Foster acquired a song and considerable power, but never danced until after he was married and his child got sick. Then he hired an Indian doctor, who told him his child would not get well unless he danced.[33]

Foster was highly respected among the Clackamas. The Clackamas men developed a special practice for certain songs and spirit powers. The leading male song helpers would swing their right arm in a wide angle arc and point toward the singer who was in the middle of the circle as they danced and sang. In this way they would specifically acknowledge the songs of certain men like Foster, **Washkeya,** and the elder Wacheno.[34]

Wacheno, Frank (1883–1920), Tualatin band of Kalapuya, Wasco band of Chinook, Clackamas, Klickitat	Native Name: None known by author
Alias: None known by author	Allotment 242
Mother: Philomene Mary Sutton, Tualatin band of Kalapuya	Father: John Wacheno, Clackamas, Wasco Chinook, Klickitat

Frank received a sixty-acre allotment. The fee patent was issued January 30, 1907.

Wacheno, James, Clackamas	Native Name: None known by author
Alias: Jim Wacheno	Allotment: None known by author
Mother: Unknown to author	Father: Unknown to author

In 1872, James was listed with his wife, Annie.

Tulambisks.

31 Munnick and Beckham, *Catholic Church Records—Grand Ronde*, Register I, p. 86, B-3, p. 101, B-5, p. 124, S-5, p. 110, M-13. Jacobs, Field Notebook 58, *Texts and Ethnology*, 86: "Foster Wachinu's 1st wife was Molale—talked nothing but it. Mrs. Foster Wachinu's [Anne's] mother was named tulambisqs."

32 Michelle, *Just a Memorandum*, 7: Foster had a wife, Lucy, a daughter Theresa, and a son Chankimnoc.

33 Drucker, *Clackamas Notes*, 25.

34 Jacobs, Field Notebook 58, *Texts and Ethnology*, 98.

Wacheno, Jeffery (1886–1910), Clackamas, Tualatin band of Kalapuya, Wasco band of Chinook, Klickitat[35]	Native Name: None known by author
Alias: John Jeff Wacheno	Allotment 243
Mother: Philomene Mary Sutton, Tualatin	Father: John Wacheno, Clackamas, Wasco Chinook, Klickitat

Jeffery received a sixty-acre allotment. The fee patent was issued October 19, 1907.

Jeffery was shot and killed by **Lawney Tom** (Pootpam) in the spring of 1910.

Wacheno, John (1853–1935), Clackamas, Wasco band of Chinook, Klickitat	Native Name: Tsinwalh /TSEN-wahl/ (tsə́nwaɬ),* Shnungiya /SHNUN-gi-ya/ (shnúngiya)*[36]
Alias: John Watchano	Allotment 238
Mother: Charlotte Wacheno, Wasco band of Chinook, Klickitat	Father: Chief Wacheno, Clackamas

Like **Chief John Kawache**'s son, **Homer Hoffer** (Tamaguin), John Wacheno (Tsinwalh)'s head was flattened at birth.[37] John had a water power similar to others, but he was the only one known to burn snails to make it rain.[38]

In 1878, John was making a living by running the agency thresher. For every hundred bushels he threshed, he got to keep five as wages. After the Grand Ronde Legislature appointed him road supervisor, he worked on the agency roads. His crew repaired the road that year from **David Leno**'s place to Litchfield's bridge and as far as **Peter Wheeler** (Kutskait)'s place from the Grand Ronde Agency.[39]

In 1880, he was elected by popular vote to represent the east precinct at the ninth annual session of the Grand Ronde Indian Legislature along with **Tom Gilbert** (Kiyukiyush) and **Peter Kenoyer** (Kinai). He also served on Grand Ronde Police Force from 1884 to 1890.[40]

John married several times. By Philomene Mary Sutton, a Yamhill and Tuala-

---

35   Munnick and Beckham, *Catholic Church Records—Grand Ronde,* Register II, p. 5, B-15, p. 49, B-48, p. 68, B-6, p. 78, S-6, p. 77, S-3.

36   1887 GRIC: gives Indian name as "Cinawa." Jacobs, Field Notebooks 58, *Texts and Ethnology,* 88: "names of Johnny Wachinu 1) cnungiya, 2) tsenwal."

37   Berreman, Interview with John Wacheno.

38   Jacobs, Notebooks 67, *Texts Ethnology Clackamas & Jargon,* 23.

39   National Archives, Seattle, Grand Ronde/Siletz, Land and Enrollment Program records, Field Notes and Land Survey 1875–1898, Land Description Book 1878, Box #115; Grand Ronde Justice Court.

40   Confederated Tribes of the Grand Ronde Community of Oregon Archives, Grand Ronde Agency Ledger Book, Records of Employees at Grand Ronde July 1883–September 1907.

Left to right: John Wacheno and William Simmons. Joel Berreman Collection. Courtesy of Confederated Tribes of the Grand Ronde Community of Oregon.

tin woman, he had **Felix, Rosa, Salome "Sallie," Frank,** and **Jeffrey Wacheno.**[41]

In 1888, John's mother, **Charlotte Wacheno** (Wasusgani), John's brother, **Marc Daniel Wacheno** (Wadams), Marc Daniel's wife, **Victoria Wishikin** (Kinishi), and their two children, **Josephine** and **Charles Wacheno,** were all living with John and his family on an eighty-acre farm with one house and barn.

When his wife, Philomene, died, John was expected to follow the custom of the Clackamas people. A widower could go nowhere. He did his chores, talked very little, and could never wash his face. He could only take a small bite of food ever once in a while until the deceased wife's elder relatives decide he had mourned long enough. Then they would either give him a woman or let him go

---

41   Munnick and Beckham, *Catholic Church Records—Grand Ronde*, Register II, p. 5, B-15, p. 49, B-48, p. 68, B-6, p. 78, S-6, p. 77, S-3. *Heirs of Deceased Indians,* Allotment Record 238.

get one for himself. If a widower chose to ignore the custom, he had to pay the relatives of his wife.[42]

John Wacheno not only took another wife without the approval of his deceased wife's relatives, but ignored other mourning practices as well. Once, he went to a Sunday baseball game even though his wife had only died the day before. On another occasion, when one of his children died, John came home from the cemetery and started to play and sing with another one of his children.[43] This was shocking behavior. Eventually, Philomene's family made John send away the woman he had chosen as his new wife and in her place marry **Lucinda Metzkar,** one of Philomene's relatives.[44]

John and Lucinda Wacheno's daughter, Florence Wacheno-McKinney and family. Photo courtesy of Barbara Danforth Private Collection.

42 Jacobs, Field Notebooks 52, *Texts and Ethnology*, 32.
43 Jacobs, Field Notebook 54, *Texts and Ethnology*, 86.
44 Drucker, *Clackamas Notes*, n.p. (17 in transcript). Berreman, Interview with John Wacheno.

Left to right: John (Tsinwalh) and Lucinda Wacheno's son, Adam Wacheno, their nephew, Charles Wacheno, and Mack Sitton. Photo courtesy of Barbara Danforth Private Collection.

John and Lucinda were married around 1898.[45] However, she was not listed on the GRIC with him until 1901. By Lucinda, John had Florence (1900c), Adam (1903–1931), and Simon (1906).[46]

Like **Jim Young** and **Moses Allen** (Shkayinch), John Wacheno also had the power of rattlesnake. With this power, it is very difficult to raise children as the rattler spirit could turn and eat your children if you did not do just what it want-

---

45   Jacobs, Field Notebook 57, *Texts and Ethnology*, 130.

46   National Archives, Salem, Oregon, Polk County Circuit Court Case Files, Index to Divorce Cases 1859–1909, Custody Case, John Wacheno vs. Lucinda, 3566.

ed. As a result, all of John's children died before he did.[47]

John received 203.50 acres of allotment land. In addition, he inherited a great many of the old allotments around Grand Ronde, but due to his heavy drinking, he lost most of the property.[48] By 1934, he still owned twenty acres but could not remember where it was located. As a result, he lived out his days in a pitifully ill-kept shack on a patch of land owned by his nephew.

In the past, a number of people had died in this house causing it to have a reputation for being an awful, bad place. Therefore, in order to sleep, two lights were left burning throughout the night. It was thought that if one light went out, the other light would prevent a dead person from grabbing anyone left alone.[49] Despite all his best efforts, maybe a dead person eventually did get John, but since he was suffering from heart trouble and crippled with rheumatism, perhaps he was ready to go.[50]

Wacheno, Josephine (1883–1907), Clackamas, Tualatin band of Kalapuya, Molalla, Upper Chinook, Klickitat	Native Name: None known by author
Alias: Veronica Wacheno, Veronica Smith	Allotment 234
Mother: Victoria Wishikin, Tualatin band of Kalpuya, Molalla	Father: Daniel Wacheno, Clackamas, Upper Chinook, Klickitat

On January 30, 1908, her heir, **Marc Daniel Wacheno** (Wadams), was issued a fee patent for her entire eighty-acre allotment.[51]

Wacheno, Marc Daniel (1862c–1908), Clackamas, Wasco band of Chinook, Klickitat[53]	Native Name: Wadams /Wad-ams/[52]
Alias: Daniel Wacheno, Dan Watchano	Allotment 233
Mother: Charlotte Wacheno, Wasco Chinook, Klickitat.	Father: Chief Wacheno, Clackamas

When Marc Daniel (Wadams) was a boy, his father sent him to the mountain for his spirit power. Afterwards, he danced for it ever year for three or four years. Daniel acquired the power to make rain, but he could never stop it.[54]

---

47 Jacobs, Field Notebook 53, *Texts and Ethnology*, 76.
48 Berreman, Field Notes, 1934.
49 Jacobs, Field Notebook 54, *Texts and Ethnology*, 94.
50 Berreman, Field Notes, 1934.
51 *Heirs to Deceased Indians*, Allotment Record 234.
52 1887 GRIC: Indian name as "Wad-ams."
53 Munnick and Beckham, *Catholic Church Records—Grand Ronde*, Register I, p. 27, B-40.
54 Drucker, *Clackamas Notes*, 25.

Marc Daniel married **Victoria Wishikin** (Kinishi) in Yamhill County in August 1875.[55] They were married again in the Catholic Church by Father Croquet on December 12, 1882. Victoria recorded one of his love songs from memory in 1929.[56]

Marc Daniel had a number of children: Dan (1880c), Henry (1882c), **Josephine "Veronica"** (Slakin), Sarah (1884), **Charles, Susanna**, Andrew (1891), Florentia (1894), and Clara Cora (1898).[57]

He received a 216.17-acre allotment, but only received a fee patent for 196.17 acres of it. His son Charles Wacheno received a fee patent for the remaining twenty acres on March 19, 1925. There is no record indicating what happened to Foster's 196.17-acre allotment after his death.[58]

Wacheno, Maria (1821c), wife of Clackamas husband	Native Name: None known by author
Alias: Maria Watchano	Allotment: None known by author
Mother: Unknown to author	Father: Unknown to author

Maria was once married to **Chief Daniel Wacheno** (Wachinu). By him, she had a daughter, Nancy, who married **John Dick,** a Klickitat Indian from the north side of the Columbia River near present day Washougal, Washington.[59]

In 1886, aside from other things, Maria owned two houses and a hack. Her son-in-law, John Dick, and her daughter, Nancy, were staying with her. John and Nancy had their two children, Eddie and John, with them. Maria's niece, Julia, was also staying with her.

In 1887, Maria was living alone, but the following year, she was listed as a widow living with an unnamed niece, probably Julia, and the widower, **George Whiney.**

Wacheno, Rosa (1879c–1919c), Clackamas, Tualatin band of Kalapuya, Wasco band of Chinook, Klickitat[60]	Native Name: None known by author
Alias: Rosie	Allotment 240
Mother: Philomene Mary Sutton, Tualatin band of Kalapuya	Father: John Wacheno, Clackamas, Wasco Chinook, Klickitat

55 National Archives, Salem, Oregon, Polk County Circuit Court Case Files, Index to Divorce Cases 1859–1909, Dan Wacheno vs. Vict Wacheno, File 3462.
56 Jacobs, Field Notebook 51, *Music and Ethnology*, 36.
57 1887 GRIC: gives Josephine's native name as "Sla-kin."
58 *Heirs to Deceased Indians*, Allotment Record 233.
59 Lynch, *Free Land for Free Men*. Jacobs, Field Notebook 53, *Texts and Ethnology*, 40–44.
60 Munnick and Beckham, *Catholic Church Records—Grand Ronde*, Register II, p. 5, B-15, p. 49, B-48, p. 68, B-6, p. 78, S-6, p. 77, S-3.

Rosa received an 80.25-acre allotment. The fee patent was issued August 5, 1907.

Wacheno, Salome (1881–1921), Clackamas, Tualatin band of Kalapuya, Wasco band of Chinook, Klickitat	Native Name: None known by author
Alias: Sallie	Allotment 241
Mother: Philomene Mary Sutton, Tualatin band of Kalapuya	Father: John Wacheno, Wasco band of Chinook, Klickitat, Clackamas

Salome received an 80.07-acre allotment. The fee patent was issued October 19, 1907.

Wacheno, Susan (1888–1903), Clackamas, Tualatin band of Kalapuya, Molalla, Wasco band of Chinook, Klickitat [61]	Native Name: None known by author
Alias: None known by author	Allotment 236
Mother: Victoria Wishikin, Molalla, Tualatin band of Kalapuya	Father: Marc Daniel Wacheno, Clackamas, Wasco band of Chinook, Klickitat

Susan "Susie" Wacheno (right), daughter of Marc Daniel Wacheno and Victoria Wishikin. Photo courtesy of Barbara Danforth Private Collection.

61 Munnick and Beckham, *Catholic Church Records—Grand Ronde,* Register I, p. 27, B-40.

On May 23, 1907, Susan Wacheno's eighty-acre allotment was sold to Wallace McCamant by her father, **Marc Daniel Wacheno** (Wadams), who was listed as her sole heir.[62]

Wacheno, Thomas, Clackamas	Native Name: None known by author
Alias: None known by author	Allotment: None known by author
Mother: Unknown to author	Father: Unknown to author

In 1872, Thomas was listed with his wife, Hapso, and his two sons. Also with Thomas's family was an "old woman" called **California Mary**.

Walker, Peter (1815c)	Native Name: None known by author
Alias: None known by author	Allotment: None known by author
Mother: Unknown to author	Father: Unknown to author

In 1885, Peter was listed with his wife, Nancy (1823c), sister, Charlotte (1825c), and his brother, "Old Jack (1813c)."

Wallace, Henry (1837c–1909), Columbia River band of Chinook, Tualatin band of Kalapuya, Clackamas[63]	Native Name: None known by author
Alias: None known by author	Allotment 244
Mother: Kalloka, Columbia River Chinook, Tualatin band of Kalapuya	Father: Cathorawish, Clackamas

In 1905, Henry testified that he was a Columbia River Indian who came to Grand Ronde under the treaty with the Clackamas and several other tribes. He said,

> My father was a Clackamas and my mother was a Columbia River. My father was Ca-thorr-a-wish, a Chinook Indian, who died when I was a baby. My mother's name was Kall-o-ka, who was a Chinook woman, who died since 1880.[64]

Both Henry and his mother spoke the language of the Gigwalat tribe.[65]

---

62 *Heirs to Deceased Indians*, Allotment Record 236.

63 1872 GRIC: listed under Chief Kawache's Oregon City band. O. Applegate, Testimony of Henry Wallace. Jacobs, Notebooks 67, *Texts Ethnology Clackamas & Jargon*, 134.

64 O. Applegate, Testimony of Henry Wallace.

65 Jacobs, Notebook 67, *Texts Ethnology Clackamas & Jargon*, 134: "Henry Wallace was in the gigualat tribe. Wallace's mother was kalayugax; she was gigwalat, as was diyalax."

In 1872, Henry was listed on the GRIC under **Chief John Kawache**'s Oregon City band with his wife, Philenia, and their children, Louis (1864c) and Madeline (1872c). His hayash mother, **Lillie Wallace** (Kalloka), was also living with the family.

In 1885, Henry was listed with his wife, Sarah, and their children, Pauline (1871c) and John (1873c). By his Klamath wife, **Rose Kiki** (Ilhikhsha), he only had one child, **Louisa Wallace** (Washtali).[66]

By 1886, Henry had a good house and barn on sixty fenced acres with a small garden, four horses and two head of cattle. In addition, his mother had a good house, a scythe, wagon, one horse, and two head of cattle.

Henry served on the Grand Ronde Police Force from 1890 to 1893.[67] He believed that the Grand Ronde Reservation was set apart for the Indians in place of land they gave up to the Americans. He was never in favor of adopting "outsiders."[68] He received a 257.60-acre allotment. He did not sign the Surplus Land Agreement in 1901. On January 30, 1907, Henry received a fee patent for fee patent for 219.39 acres of his 257.60-acre allotment. On October 10, 1928, his granddaughter, Lizzie (Theresa) Toto, received a fee patent for the remaining 38.21 acres of Henry's allotment.[69]

Wallace, Lillie (1816c–89c), Columbia River Chinook, Tualatin band of Kalapuya	Native Name: Kalloka /Kall-o-ka/[70]
Alias: Lily Wallace	Allotment 246
Mother: Unknown to author	Father: Unknown to author

Lillie Wallace (Kalloka) was **Tualatin William Wishikin's** sister.[71] She spoke the language of the Gigwalat tribe like her son and **Peter Bennett** (Diyalakh).[72] In 1887, Lillie was listed with her son, **Henry Wallace,** and his family. She continued to live with Henry and his family until her death in 1889.

---

66 1887 GRIC: Indian name as "Ic-lac-shill." Jacobs, *Clackamas Texts,* Part II, 514 -515: Rose's Indian name as Ilhikhsha. Michelle, *Just a Memorandum,* 5: Louysa's mother, Rose, was Klamath. Jacobs, Notebooks 67, *Texts Ethnology Clackamas & Jargon,* 106: "itixca (a Cl. Name), Mrs. Henry Wallace, was part Molale, part Clackamas, she spoke both languages."

67 Grand Ronde Agency Ledger Book, Records of Employees at Grand Ronde July 1883–September 1907, Confederated Tribes of the Grand Ronde Community of Oregon Archive.

68 O. Applegate, Testimony of Henry Wallace.

69 Heirs to Deceased Indians, Allotment Record 244.

70 1885 GRIC gave Indian name as "Caliape." O. Applegate, Testimony of Henry Wallace: Henry gave her name as "Kal-lo-ka." 1887 GRIC: gave Indian name as "Cal-i-la-ga."

71 Jacobs, Notebooks 67, *Texts Ethnology Clackamas & Jargon,* 134.

72 Ibid.

Lillie received a 119.60-acre allotment. Her heir, Henry Wallace, sold forty acres of her allotment to W. N. Jones on September 11, 1906. He sold the remaining 79.60 acres to Wallace McCamant on May 23, 1907.[73]

Wallace, Louisa (1873c–1913), Columbia River Chinook, Tualatin band of Kalapuya, Molalla, Clackamas[75]	Native Name: Washtali /wash-TA-li/ (washt'áli)*[74]
Alias: Louisa Wacheno, Louise Ferris[76]	Allotment 245
Mother: Rose, Molalla, Clackamas	Father: Henry Wallace, Columbia River Chinook, Tualatin band of Kalapuya, Clackamas

Louisa Wallace (Washtali) married **Coquille Jake Orton** (Meka Tseltsa) of the Siletz reservation November 19, 1890, at Grand Ronde in the presence of witnesses Frank Mercier and **Mary Petite**.[77] Jake Orton and Louisa were listed as husband and wife on the 1891 GRIC, but they were only together a short time.

In 1896, Louisa married **Dan Robinson**. She and Dan had Lizzie Robinson in 1902.[78] After Dan, Louisa married **Felix Wacheno**. She inherited his estate in 1906. On March 3, 1907, Louisa received a fee patent for her own eighty-acre allotment.[79]

Wankhpa, Tualatin band of Kalapuya[80]	Native Name: Wankhpa /WANK-pa/ (wánxpa)*[81]
Alias: None known by author	Allotment: None known by author
Mother: Unknown to author	Father: Unknown to author

When the Tualatin headmen fought over the horses Joel Palmer had given them as gifts after the signing of the Willamette Valley treaty, Wankhpa was described as an old man. He was the one who first broke the news to **Chief Kiakuts** (Kayakach) that **Dave Yachkawa** was planning to kill him.[82]

In 1872, he was listed on the GRIC as "Wah-wan-pah" with his son, **Samuel Cowl.**

---

73 *Heirs to Deceased Indians,* Allotment Record 246.
74 Ibid., 33.
75 Jacobs, Field Notebook 51, *Music and Ethnology,* 23, 24, 33.
76 Affidavit State of Oregon, County of Yamhill, taken from John Wacheno April 18, 1908, Yamhill Co Probate, file 1206, George Sutton.
77 Munnick and Beckham, *Catholic Church Records — Grand Ronde,* Register II, p. 65, M-3.
78 St. Michael's Catholic Church Records, 1902.
79 *Heirs to Deceased Indians,* Allotment Record 245.
80 GRIC 1872.
81 Jacobs, *Santiam Kalapuya Ethnologic Texts,* Part 1, 170.
82 Ibid., 169–70. Palmer, Agreement of April 4, 1855 between LeMedicene, Dave Yatzkawa, and Chief Kayakach.

Warren, Amanda (1887–1905), Rogue River, Umpqua, Iroquois, Spanish	Native Name: None known by author
Alias: Manda Warren	Allotment 259
Mother: Cecile Leno, Rogue River, Spanish, Iroquois	Father: John Warren, Umpqua

On July 30, 1905, Amanda Warren's eighty-acre allotment was sold by her heir, **John Warren,** to W. J. Jones.[83]

Warren, Ellen (1884–93), Rogue River, Umpqua, Iroquois, Spanish	Native Name: None known by author
Alias: Helen Warren	Allotment 257
Mother: Cecile Leno, Rogue River, Spanish, Iroquois	Father: John Warren, Umpqua

July 30, 1905, Ellen Warren's forty-acre allotment was sold by her heir, **John Warren,** to W. J. Jones.[84]

Warren, John (1859c), Umpqua[85]	Native Name: None known by author
Alias: None known by author	Allotment 256[86]
Mother: Mary	Father: Chief Charley Bogus, Umpqua

John Warren was court clerk and treasurer for the Grand Ronde Indian Court in 1879. He was also one of the representatives from the south precinct at the ninth annual session of the Grand Ronde Indian Legislature when it convened on November 1, 1880.[87] In 1905, he served for a year on the Grand Ronde Police Force with **Frank Quenel.**[88]

By his wife Jane, John Warren had Manda (1876–1905) and Janette. By his wife Cecilia Leno, he had Pauline, Helen or Ellen (1884–93), Martha "Maud" (1885c), Amanda (1887–1905), Manalda Mary (1889–96), Melicie (1891), Philip (1892–1928), Augustine Roy (1895–95), Florence (1896), George (1898), Edith (1900–02), Gladys

---

83 Ibid., Allotment Record 259.

84 Ibid., Allotment Record 257.

85 1872 GRIC: listed under the Umpqua as a cousin to Winchester Jos.

86 *Heirs to Deceased Indians,* Allotment Record 256: patent issued for 200-acre allotment on June 29, 1907.

87 National Archives, Seattle, Grand Ronde/Siletz, Land and Enrollment Program records, Field Notes and Land Survey 1875–1898, Land Description Book 1878, Box 115; Grand Ronde Justice Court.

88 Confederated Tribes of the Grand Ronde Community of Oregon Archives, Grand Ronde Agency Ledger Book, Records of Employees at Grand Ronde July 1883–September 1907.

John Warren with his wife, Cecile Leno. Joel V. Berreman Collection. Courtesy of the Confederated Tribes of the Grand Ronde Community of Oregon.

(1901–05), Cora (1905), and Nora (1908).[89]

John's daughter Maud married **Abraham Hudson.** His daughter Nora married Loren "Shorty" Kimsey. His son Philip married **Lincoln McCoy**'s daughter Evelyn.

In the 1920s, Philip was selling illegal whiskey. After two Prohibition agents working undercover bought some from him, he was arrested. Philip escaped, ran home, and got his rifle. There was a witness to the shots that were fired, but not to the actual killing of the revenue men. Philip was acquitted after John Warren mortgaged his place to pay for his defense and his lawyer was able to successfully argue that someone else may have shot the officers.[90]

When Philip was killed in a logging accident sometime later, there were those who claimed he was purposely killed by the white loggers because they were upset over the outcome of the trial.[91]

---

89 Munnick and Beckham, *Catholic Church Records — Grand Ronde,* Register I, p. 126, M-5, p. 128, B-3, p. 133, B-45, Register II, p. 45, B-32, p. 55, B-12, p. 68, B-7, p. 81, B-30, p. 84, S-4, p. 99, B-1, p. 101, S-8, p. 104, S-1, p. 107, B-15, p. 116, B-4.

90 Zenk, Grand Ronde Field Notebook #9, 1988, 11.

91 Berreman, Field Notes, 1934.

In 1934, John still had twenty acres of his original 200-acre allotment, but his wife, Cecilia's, health was failing and she was partially paralyzed.[92] They lived in an old, unpainted house furnished in part with many family portraits, chairs, a sewing machine, and many relics. Among them, John still had several baskets brought from the Umpqua by his parents.[93]

Warren, Maria (1886), Umpqua, Rogue River, Iroquois, Spanish	Native Name: None known by author
Alias: Maud Warren	Allotment 258
Mother: Cecile Leno, Rogue River, Spanish, Iroquois	Father: John Warren, Umpqua

On July 30, 1905, Maria Warren received a fee patent for her entire forty-acre allotment.[94]

Warren, William (1855c–1916c), Umpqua	Native Name: None known by author
Alias: Billy Warren	Allotment 255
Mother: Mary	Father: Chief Charley Bogus, Umpqua

In 1880, William Warren was appointed treasury administrator to the Indian Court.[95] Shortly after that, William married a white teacher, Edith Vedder, on October 18, 1880.

Their marriage was a great scandal not only because Edith was a white woman marrying an Indian man, but because she had originally come to the Catholic school at Grand Ronde preparing to become a nun.[96]

Billy and Edith had a daughter, Maud, on August 25, 1881.[97] **Alexander Day,** who had earlier created a similar problem for the Catholic Church, became Maude's godparent. According to **John Basile "Mose" Hudson,** Edith only lived with William about five years. Then she took their daughter and left.[98] On October

---

92 Ibid.

93 Ibid.

94 *Heirs to Deceased Indians*, Allotment Record 258.

95 National Archives, Seattle, Grand Ronde/Siletz, Land and Enrollment Program records, Field Notes and Land Survey 1875–1898, Land Description Book 1878, Box #115; Grand Ronde Justice Court.

96 Berreman, interview with J. B. Hudson, 1937, 16.

97 Munnick and Beckham, *Catholic Church Records—Grand Ronde,* Register I, p. 119, B-19.

98 Polk County Circuit Court Case Files, Index to Divorce Cases 1859–1909, File 1505: their divorce occurred in 1883. In 1888, William may have regained custody of his daughter as he was listed on the census for that year as a widower with seven-year-old daughter, Maud.

Polk County Jail, 1892c. Photo courtesy of Oregon State Archives (OAE0024).

25, 1890, William married **Joseph Dowd**'s sister, Annie.[99]

A few years later, on December 11, 1895, Billy was arrested for assault with a deadly weapon and tried in Polk County court before being sentenced to a term in the Oregon State Penitentiary.[100]

According to one report, while awaiting trial in Dallas, William, well liked by the town citizens, was made a trusty. The sheriff let him out of jail in the morning to earn his breakfast by cutting wood for some of the town folk. Then late in the afternoon before he was taken to prison, "his mother, old Kitty Warren," came to the front door of the jail.[101]

Given that William and his brother John were orphaned and raised by Winchester Jo, this woman could not have been William's mother. However, the woman known to the town residents as "old Kitty Warren," may have been **Kitty Tom** (Acattycon), wife of **Tyee Shasta Tom.**

Reportedly, when it got dark, the woman sat on the ground and began singing her mourning song. She sang it through the night until they took William away the following morning.[102]

Billy's wife, Anna Dowd, sued for divorce in 1904, accusing him of calling her

99 National Archives, Salem, Oregon, Polk County Circuit Court Case Files, Index to Divorce Cases 1859–1909, Annie Warren vs. William Warren, File 2229.
100 Oregon State Archives, Salem, Oregon, 1895, Inmate File 3564.
101 Cerny, *The Case of Polk County vs. Billy Warren*, 19.
102 Ibid.

**William "Billy" Warren. Photo courtesy of
Oregon State Archives (File 3561).**

bad names and leaving her for three or four days at a time with nothing to eat while he played cards with the other Indians.

Anna's brother, Joseph Dowd, testified that William abandoned his sister completely around 1903. Their parents now had to support her while "Billy lived among the Indians" and "partly hunted" but gave nothing to Annie's support.[103]

William Warren received a 120-acre allotment. He did not sign the Surplus Land Agreement in 1901. On January 30, 1907, he was issued a fee patent for his entire 120-acre allotment.

He married for the third time, on Valentine's Day in 1910. This time, he married **John Smith**'s widow, Julie Ann Smith who was much older than he. It was William's third marriage and her second.[104]

Washington, Adrian (1851c–69), Cow Creek band of Umpqua[105]	Native Name: None known by author
Alias: None known by author	Allotment: None known by author

103 National Archives, Salem, Oregon, Polk County Circuit Court Case Files, Index to Divorce Cases 1859–1909, Annie Warren vs. William Warren, File 2229.

104 National Archives, Salem, Oregon, Polk County, 2003A-029 Health Division Marriage Returns, William Warren and Julie Anne Smith, 1910. GRIC for 1911 lists "Louise Smith, now Julianne Warren, wife of William Warren, widow, age 69."

105 Munnick and Beckham, *Catholic Church Records—Grand Ronde*, Register 1, p. 56, B-5, p. 57, S-5.

Mother: Unknown to author	Father: Unknown to author
Washkeya (1830c–98), Clackamas, Kalapuya	Native Name: Washkeya /wash-KI-ya/ (washk'íya),* Kamalhamakh /ka-MA-hla-maih/ (k'amáɬamayx)*[106]
Alias: Governor Wood, Waskea Wood, Wasco Wood	Allotment 261
Mother: Kalapuya[107]	Father: Clackamas[108]

Washkeya (Kamalhamakh) was **Chief Daniel Wacheno** (Wachinu)'s cousin.[109] **Charlotte Wacheno** (Wasusgani) said Washkeya was born during one of the great epidemics. People passing by in a canoe found him on a river bank attempting to suckle at his dead mother's breast. He was raised by Kalapuyan parents.[110] Chief Wacheno brought him back to Clackamas country after he was grown.[111]

Washkeya's tamanawas was *itktctle*, a spirit in the air. With the power of itktctle, he could make three wooden dolls dance by merely singing his power song.[112]

He was also a canoe builder who had two canoes of his own: a coyote and a bear nose. Before removal, he would move his family each winter to a place near the mouth of the Tualatin River. He lived in a cedar bark lodge, but insisted the females in his household sleep in an "underground house." Chief Wacheno's people were the only ones who used this style of shelter.[113]

Besides his Clackamas-Molalla wife, **Watutamkh Wood**, Washkeya had a

---

106 1872 GRIC: "Waskea Wood." The 1887 GRIC: "Wasgher." Michelle, *Just a Memorandum*, 5, gave it as "Washqua Woods." *Heirs of Deceased Indians*, Allotment Record 261 gave it as "Waski." Jacobs, *Clackamas Text*, Part II, 547: when Old Wood was a very old man his name was Kamalhamakh. Jacobs, *Field Notebook 58, Texts and Ethnology*, 128, gave "Mr. Cold" as another Indian fun name for him and Victoria Wishikin-Howard recalled how Washkeya got that name: he slept with a woman and advertised the fact that her anatomy was cold, cold, cold all around. Then he was popularly dubbed with the English name "Mr. Cold." Even children who knew no better called him "Mr. Cold," though he howled back at them "*wik wawa kagwa*," do not say that.

107 Drucker, *Clackamas Notes*, n.p. (31–32 in transcript): John Wacheno said Waske was half Kalapuya.

108 Michelle, *Just a Memorandum*, 5: mother, Calapooia, father, Clackamas.

109 Jacobs, Field Notebook 51, *Texts and Ethnology*, 13.

110 Jacobs, *Clackamas Text*, Part II, 547.

111 *Heirs of Deceased Indians*, Allotment Record 261: give John Wacheno as Waske's nephew. Drucker, *Clackamas Notes*, 3–32: John Wacheno said Waske was a close relative to Chief Wachinu; "their fathers were brothers, he thinks." Jacobs, Field Notebook 69, *Texts Ethnology Clackamas & Jargon*, 74: "Old Wood, he was raised by the Kalapuya, but his o. brother (his cousin Old Watcino), he brought him back to Clackamas Oregon City. Watutam, a part Molalla woman, was his wife."

112 Drucker, *Clackamas Notes* (31–32 in transcript).

113 Ibid.

Washkeya Wood. Photo from Wilmer Gardner Collection. Courtesy of Clackamas County Historical Society.

couple of older female relatives living with him. He also had two or three slaves. One woman slave did the cooking. He sold her to a man from the Cascade tribe for a good price. After her husband died, she came back and stayed with Washkeya, "just like he was her own father."[114]

Washkeya, like most Clackamas men, was a fisherman. In June 1863, he and several other men contacted the superintendent of Indian affairs at Oregon City. They showed him a pass from Indian Agent Condon and a letter of reference from Mr. J. Campbell of Oregon City and asked the superintendent to give them a pass that would allow them to remain in Oregon City for the fishing season. Their request was denied.[115]

---

114 Ibid.
115 Huntington to J. B. Condon, June 24, 1863.

**Washkeya (Kamalhamakh). Photo courtesy of the
Oregon Historical Society (bb007367).**

Nevertheless, years later, **Victoria Wishikin** (Kinishi) could still recall the image of Washkeya on the Clackamas River spearing fish. She said others would stand on the bluff above him where they could see shoals of chinooks and steelheads. From this place, they would guide Washkeya's hand in throwing the spear. Using a spear pole some ten feet long, with a bone point and an attached rope, he would pierce one of the big fish every time.[116]

On January 22, 1882, Washkeya's son by his wife, Anna, sixteen-year-old Francis Wood, died at Grand Ronde. In 1888, Washkeya was listed as a widower living with his son **Joseph Wood**. Their assets were listed as three horses, two wagons, and a harness. Joseph died June 17, 1890, at Oregon City. His body was brought back to Grand Ronde to be buried.[117] **John Wacheno** (Tsinwalh) said Washkeya had lots of children, but they all died before they could get married.[118]

---

116 Jacobs, Field Notebook 59, *Texts and Ethnology*, 4.
117 Munnick and Beckham, *Catholic Church Records—Grand Ronde*, Register 1, p. 120, S-1, p. 62, S-8.
118 Drucker, *Clackamas Notes*, (31–32 in transcript).

Washkeya had a forty-acre allotment in trust at Grand Ronde. After he died April 4, 1898, his estate went to Chief Wacheno's son-in-law, **Eddie Dick**.[119]

Victoria Wishikin (Kinishi) recorded two of his power songs. She did not know all of Washkeya's tamanawas powers, but the second song she sang was that of his Grizzly power. Both songs were recorded by Melville Jacobs in 1929.[120]

Watson, John (1797c–1888c), Umpqua	Native Name: Geustic /Ge-us-tic/[121]
Alias: Old Man John	Allotment: None known by author
Mother: Unknown to author	Father: Unknown to author

In 1872, Old Man John was listed with his wife, Mary Jane (1797). They were still together in 1887.

Weston, James (1835c), Lower River Chinook, Clatsop[122]	Native Name: None known by author
Alias: Jack Weston	Allotment: None known by author
Mother: Mary St Clair, Clatsop, Lower River Chinook	Father: David Weston

James was the son of a white man named David Weston (1819c–76c) who was with Dr. White's expedition in 1842. David Weston took a land claim next to Robert Newell's place at Champoeg and worked as a blacksmith for T. J. Hubbard. He voted for the provisional government in Oregon and fought as an orderly sergeant with the 8th Division, Company F in the Cayuse War.

David Weston married a "Chinook and Clatsop" Indian woman named Mary St. Clair who was the daughter of Chief Cowhivalas. Besides James, David Weston and Mary St. Clair had three other children: Mary J. Weston-Jette, Louis and Inez. According to Mary Shangaretta, James Weston was a blacksmith at Grand Ronde for several years.[123]

He was listed on the GRIC for 1885 with wife, Lucy, and children, Benjamin, Louis, Monoh, Francis, and Janet.

James Weston was listed as one of the potential heirs to **Polly Nachan**'s allotment.[124]

---

119 *Heirs of Deceased Indians*, Allotment Record 261.

120 Jacobs, Field Notebook 51, *Music and Ethnology*, 13.

121 1887 GRIC: Indian name as "ge-us-tic."

122 McChesney, *The Rolls of Indian Tribes*, Statement 107, Mary J. Jette. Affidavit of Mary [Shangaretta] Mitchel Yamhill County, State of Oregon, dated February 1, 1917, Regarding Estate of Polly Nachan, Allottee 139. Affidavit of Mary J. Jette and James Weston, Grays Harbor County, Washington State, February 8, 1917, Estate of Polly Nachan.

123 Ibid.

124 National Archives, Seattle, Heirs of Deceased Indians, Allotment Record n. 139.

Wheeler, Bertha (1839c–87c), Luckiamute band of Kalapuya	Native Name: Tewimme[125]
Alias: Bellie Amos, Bertha Morufi	Allotment: None known by author
Mother: Unknown to author	Father: Unknown to author

Bertha (Tewimme) was **Jacob Wheeler** (Shwa)'s sister and the former wife of **Steve Morufi**.[126] A little girl named Anna was born to her a year or two after Old Steve died. Around 1862, Bertha married **Amos Kilya**.[127]

Bertha's tamanawas was a water power that had something to do with boiling water coming out of the ground. **Victoria Wishikin** (Kinishi) recorded one of her power songs for Melville Jacobs.[128]

Wheeler, Edwin (1876c), Luckiamute band of Kalapuya	Native Name: None known by author
Alias: Edmund Wheeler	Allotment 249
Mother: Grace	Father: Luckiamute Peter Wheeler

Edwin Wheeler married Mary around 1902. They had at least four children: Mabel Mary (1903), Furman (1904), Grace (1907), and Meda Agatha (1911).

On October 29, 1906, Edwin Wheeler received a fee patent for his entire 80 acre allotment.[129]

Wheeler, Frank (1844c), Luckiamute band of Kalapuya	Native Name: None known by author
Alias: Luckiamute Frank	Allotment: 251
Mother: Unknown to author	Father: Unknown to author

In 1885, Frank was with his wife, Sarah (1846c), and his children Bennie (1868c) and George (1870c). In 1886, he and Sarah were listed with their children Lilly (1879c) and George.

Wheeler, Frank (1870c), Luckiamute band of Kalapuya [130]	Native Name: Aiwai /Al-wai/ (áyway)*[131]
Alias: Luckiamute Frank	Allotment 251
Mother: Nancy	Father: Luckiamute Peter Wheeler[132]

---

125 O. Applegate, Testimony of Amos Kilya.

126 Oregon State Archives, Salem, Oregon, 1904, Yamhill County, Estate File 1176.

127 O. Applegate, Testimony of Amos Kilya.

128 Jacobs, Field Notebook 51, *Music and Ethnology*, 48.

129 *Heirs to Deceased Indians*, Allotment Record 249.

130 1872 and 1888 GRIC listed Frank as Luckiamute with his father Peter Wheeler.

131 Jacobs, Field Notebook 36, *Santiam Kalapuya Text*, 190.

132 Munnick and Beckham, *Catholic Church Records—Grand Ronde*, Register 1, p. 62, B-13:

Frank (Aiwai) was the son of **Peter Wheeler** (Kutskait). He married **Stephanie Howard** (Lhimiki) on November 3, 1890. After Stephanie died, Frank married **Sarah Johnson** (Waganwish), the daughter of **Eliza Johnson** (Khakhshni) and the widow of **Henry Winslow,** on October 25, 1897. **Andrew Hoffer** and **Rosa Wacheno** were their witnesses.

Caroline Sitton-Strong wrote that she could remember Frank and his cousin John Wheeler getting drunk and talking together in French, but, she said, they never claimed to be anything but Indian.[133]

Frank Wheeler (Aiwai) received eighty acres of allotment land.

Frank Wheeler, left, and Adam Wacheno.
Photo courtesy of Barbara Danforth Private
Collection.

Father Croquet listed Frank Wheeler's father as Luckiamute Peter and his mother as a woman named Nancy.

133 Danforth, Private Letter Collection, Letter 19.

Wheeler, Jacob (1839c–1903), Luckiamute band of Kalapuya	Native Name: Shwa /shwa/ (shwa)*[134]
Alias: Luckiamute Jake	Allotment 252
Mother: Unknown to author	Father: Unknown to author

Jacob (Shwa) was **Peter Wheeler** (Kutskait)'s cousin. Jacob had a lot of spirit songs and a fairly strong tamanawas but he never doctored.[135] According to the GRIC, he also had a wife, Mary Ann and two young sons in 1872.

He was elected to the Indian legislature as a representative of the west precinct in 1878 and re-elected in 1880. April 2, 1881, The legislature appointed him to fill a vacancy for road supervisor until the next election on April 11, 1881.[136]

In 1885, he was listed with his wife, Big Susan (Shamkhakh), and sister, Sallie.[137] Big Susan was married as a girl to an old Tualatin and Yamhill man called Gidina.[138] After he died, she was left a widow for a very long time. Jacob and Susan were still together in 1889. Then **Eliza Johnson** (Khakhshni) was with him for a short time, but she left him in favor of **Gay Cooks**.[139]

Jacob Wheeler received a 180-acre allotment. After he died on April 28, 1903, his estate was described as twenty acres of brush land valued at $2.00 per acre, sixty acres of timberland valued at $4.00 per acres, eighty acres of grazing land valued at $1.25 per acre and twenty acres of tillable land valued at $6.00 per acre. In addition, he held one promissory note from **Joseph Michelle** for $285, a rifle, a shotgun, a hack, and an assortment of farm tools. All his property was valued at $887.

While Jacob Wheeler left no widow or lineal descendants, two of **Bertha Wheeler** (Tewimme)'s grandchildren by her daughter, Anna, and **Sam Chantelle** placed claims against Jacob's estate. Felineze and Louis Chantelle testified that they were Jacob Wheeler's cousins.[140]

Wheeler, Jesse (1874c–1910), Luckiamute band of Kalapuya	Native Name: None known by author
Alias: None known by author	Allotment 248
Mother: Grace	Father: Luckiamute Peter Wheeler

---

134 Jacobs, Field Notebook 51, *Music and Ethnology*, 51.
135 Ibid.
136 National Archives, Seattle, WA, Grand Ronde/Siletz, Land and Enrollment Program records, Field Notes and Land Survey 1875–1898, Land Description Book 1878, Box 115; Grand Ronde Justice Court.
137 Jacobs, Field Notebook 51, *Music and Ethnology*, 51.
138 Ibid.
139 Ibid.
140 Oregon State Archives, Salem, Oregon, 1904, Yamhill County, Estate 1176.

On October 29, 1906, Jesse Wheeler received a fee patent for his entire eighty-acre allotment.[141]

Wheeler, Orton (1884–1938), Luckiamute band of Kalapuya	Native Name: None known by author
Alias: Orcein, Ordin, Osoline	Allotment 250
Mother: Grace	Father: Luckiamute Peter Wheeler

October 29, 1906, Orton Wheeler received a fee patent for his entire eighty-acre allotment.[142]

Wheeler, Peter (1834c–92), Luckiamute band of Kalapuya[143]	Native Name: Kutskait /KUTS-kait/ (qútsqayt)*[144]
Alias: Luckiamute Peter	Allotment 247
Mother: Samanthy, Luckiamute Kalapuya	Father: Unknown to author

In 1872, Peter Wheeler (Kutskait)'s wife was named Jenny. By Jenny, Peter had twin daughters named Sophie (1866c–1907) and Islick and an infant named Elizabeth. Peter was appointed sheriff for 1879 by the 1878 Grand Ronde Indian Legislature.[145] In 1885, he was herding cattle for the agency.[146] By this time, Peter was living with a wife named **Grace Wheeler** (Skenan) and his children: Isoline, Frank, Jesse, Ellen, Edmund, Harriet, and another set of twins, two-year-old boys, Louis and Lenard. In 1888, only their children Frank (1870c), Jesse (1874c–1910), Edwin (1876c), Ordin (1884c), and Agnes (1886c) were still living with them.[147]

Both Peter and Grace were Kalapuya.[148] They had a house and barn on sixty fenced acres with a garden. Grace provided Yoncalla language information to Frachtenberg in her elder years. At that time, Frachtenberg made note that her

141 *Heirs to Deceased Indians,* Allotment Record 248.

142 Ibid., Allotment Record 250.

143 Gatschet, *Texts, Sentences and Vocables,* 369. 1888 GRIC: listed his tribe as Luckimute band of Kalapuya. Oregon State Archives, Salem, Oregon, 1904, Polk County, Estate File1004: gave his death as May 10, 1892.

144 Jacobs, Field Notebook 36, *Santiam Kalapuya Text,* 190.

145 National Archives, Seattle, WA, Grand Ronde/Siletz, Land and Enrollment Program records, Field Notes and Land Survey 1875–1898, Land Description Book 1878, Box 115; Grand Ronde Justice Court.

146 National Archives, Seattle, BIA, Grand Ronde, Box 190, Book 10819, Cash Book, 1875–1907.

147 National Archives and Records Administration, Central Plains Region, Prison File 5333, Louie Savage: gave Frank, Jesse, and Orton as full Kalapuya and in the same file on an affidavit taken from Joseph Day, January 3, 1914, Jesse Wheeler was "(now dead,) Orten Wheeler (don't know where he is), and Frank Wheeler (now in Grand Ronde)."

148 Michelle, *Just a Memorandum,* 7, gave the tribe for both of them as Kalapuya and listed their children as Sophie, Engeline, Stephen, Frank, Jessy, and Edwin.

**Grace Wheeler (Skenan). Photo courtesy of the
Smithsonian Institution (No. 01134300).**

eyes bothered her a great deal.[149]

Peter Wheeler received a 240.79-acre allotment. After his death on May 10, 1892, his estate was valued at $600. His surviving heirs were listed as: **Jesse Wheeler**, residing at the Yakama agency, **Frank Wheeler** (Aiwai), at Grand Ronde, **Edwin Wheeler,** at the Yakama Agency, **Orton Wheeler,** at Bee, Washington, and his daughter, **Sophie Davis,** at Grand Ronde.[150] On April 9, 1907, his heirs Grace Wheeler, Frank Wheeler, Jesse Wheeler, Orton Wheeler, Edwin Wheeler, and Sophia Davis were issued a fee patent for his 240.79-acre allotment.[151]

---

149 Leo J. Frachtenberg, *Yoncalla Kalapuya Ethnology*, 1923-f, Notebook 6271, Information taken from Mrs. Robert Allen Yoncalla Kalapuya woman at Grand Ronde Reservation, December 17–18, 1914, (Bureau of American Ethnology, Smithsonian Institute, Washington, D.C): n.p.

150 Oregon State Archives, Salem, Oregon, 1892, Polk County, Estate File 1004.

151 *Heirs of Deceased Indians*, Allotment Records 247.

Wheeler, Samanthy, Luckiamute band of Kalapuya	Native Name: None known by author
Alias: None known by author	Allotment: None known by author
Mother: Unknown to author	Father: Unknown to author

She was the mother of **Peter Wheeler** (Kutskait). She was listed with the Luckiamute in 1872.

Wheeler, Susan	Native Name: Shamkhakh, /SHAM-hah/ (shámxax)*[152]
Alias: Big Susan	Allotment: None known by author
Mother: Unknown to author	Father: Unknown to author

Susan (Shamkhakh) was married as a girl to an old Tualatin and Yamhill man called Gidina. After he died, she was left a widow for a very long time.[153] Later, she was the wife of **Jacob Wheeler** (Shwa). They were listed together from 1885 through 1889.

Whiney, George (1802c), Clackamas	Native Name: Hwaini[154]
Alias: None known by author	Allotment: None known by author
Mother: Unknown to author	Father: Unknown to author

George (Hwaini) was a Clackamas man who received his tamanawas from *itcixien* (ichklyan), an old man water spirit who lived in the Columbia River and was responsible for making the whirlpools there.[155]

The Clackamas believed that if you did not take ichklyan spotted dogs or horses, he could grab hold of your canoe and drown your people. If you saw him and pointed him out, he would kill you. He was very powerful.[156]

To George, ichklyan gave the power to foretell whether or not a child would live to adulthood. Ichklyan told him where to find a certain type of rock from which he was to make a stone vessel for the child in question. From this vessel, George would come to know the fate of the child.[157]

Once, George hired an Oregon City man to help him take a canoe upriver. The canoe tipped over and the Oregon City man drowned. In those days, people believed if one invited someone into a canoe and he drowned, it was the fault of the person who had given the invitation. The person had to pay the same restitu-

152 Jacobs, Field Notebook 51, *Music and Ethnology*, 51.
153 Ibid.
154 Drucker, *Clackamas Notes*, n.p. (32–33 in transcript).
155 Drucker, *Clackamas Notes*, n.p. (32–33 in transcript). Jacobs, Field Notebook 53, *Texts and Ethnology*, 71, 78, 80.
156 Ibid.
157 Ibid.

tion as if he had murdered the drowned man.[158]

In this case, George argued that because the victim had been drinking, he should not be responsible for any more than the cost of his funeral. According to George, the water was not bad where the canoe tipped over. The victim could have gotten out if he had not been drinking.[159] Hopefully he won this argument because he was not a wealthy man. In fact, among his people, he was considered very poor as he did not charge much for his work and as a result did not own any horses or slaves.

George married a Warm Springs woman. They had a son called Tamiyogomux who lived with them until he married and built his own house. For the price of a big feast, everyone helped in building his house.[160]

With another Warm Springs wife, George had another son and a daughter. His daughter married a Watlala (Cascade) man, but their children all died.[161]

In 1872, "George Whiney" was listed under the Clackamas band with his wife, Nancy. In 1886, he and Nancy were living in a small house with a little garden; in addition, they had one horse, a wagon, and two hogs. Nancy died April 5, 1887. Although the 1888 GRIC listed George with **Chief Daniel Wacheno** (Wachinu)'s widow, **Maria Wacheno,** and her seventeen-year-old niece, church records state "George Whiney" died on December 10, 1887.[162]

White, William, Umpqua	Native Name: None known by author
Alias: Salt Chuck Bill	Allotment: None known by author
Mother: Unknown to author	Father: Unknown to author

In 1872, Salt Chuck Bill was listed under the Umpqua with his wife Jenny and their children, Emma, Charlotte, and an infant daughter. Around March of that year they had another child whom Father Croquet baptized as Stephany on June 11. On January 19, 1873, Father Croquet baptized Salt Chuck Bill's daughter Mary, who had been born ten months earlier to his wife Jane. Their daughter Elizabeth or Betsi died in Salem when she was about seven years old. She was buried at Grand Ronde July 14, 1883.[163]

In 1877, Albert Gatschet, in his attempt to record native languages, listed Bill White as a Coquille language informant along with **Short Charley.**[164]

---

158 Ibid.

159 Drucker, *Clackamas Notes*, n.p. (42 in transcript).

160 Ibid., n.p. (32–33 in transcript).

161 Ibid.

162 Munnick and Beckham, *Catholic Church Record—Grand Ronde*, Register I, p. 35, S-15.

163 Ibid., Register 1, p. 75, B-27, p. 79, B-3, p. 124, S-9.

164 Gatschet, *Texts, Sentences and Vocables*, 318, 367: listed under Coquille or Salt Chuck as "Bill White."

Whitley, George (d. 1874), Cow Creek band of Umpqua	Native Name: None known by author
Alias: Old Tootlog[165]	Allotment: None known by author
Mother: Unknown to author	Father: Unknown to author

In 1872, Old George Whitley's sister Ann was living with him.

On January 22, 1873, Father Croquet wrote in church records that he had baptized "Vincent Witley, grievously sick of the Cow Creek nation," probably the same man listed in 1872 as George Whitley. On December 24, 1874, Witley of the Cow Creek nation was buried in the mission cemetery.[166]

Wilder, Alice (1853c–86), Rogue River	Native Name: None known by author
Alias: Alice Norwest, Alice Samson	Allotment: None known by author
Mother: Marianne	Father: Sam Wilder, Rogue River

Alice was the daughter of **Sam Wilder** and his wife, Marianne. On October 1, 1862, when the manual labor school was organized at Grand Ronde, "Alice Samson," age nine, was one of twenty three students in attendance.[167]

On January 22, 1868, Alice married **Frank Norwest.** They had a number of children together.

In 1885, Alice was not listed. Frank Norwest was listed with his new wife, Rachel. Her father was listed with Frank's brother, **Thomas Norwest,** and Tom's son, **Thomas,** but no mention of Alice.

On June 23, 1886, her death was officially entered in church records.[168]

Wilder, Chief Sam (1801c–bef. 1877), Takelma band of Rogue River[169]	Native Name: Toquahear /To-qua-hear/, Kokokahwah /Ko-ko-kah-wah/ ["wealthy"][170]
Alias: None known by author	Allotment: None known by author
Mother: Unknown to author	Father: Unknown to author

---

165 1872 GRIC: aka "Old Tootlog."

166 Munnick and Beckham, *Catholic Church Records—Grand Ronde*, Register 1, p. 79, B-4, p. 90, S-33.

167 *Annual Report Commissioner of Indian Affairs*, 1863, 84-85.

168 Munnick and Beckham, *Catholic Church Records—Grand Ronde*, Register I, p.51, M-1, Register II, p. 5, S-14.

169 O. Applegate, interview with Applegate Jack, 1905: Applegate Jack testified that "he belonged to the Itchkadowa or Applegate band of Rogue River under Chief Sam." Carey, *Mission Record Book.*

170 *Annual Report Commissioner of Indian Affairs, 1857,* 361: Indian agent John F. Miller wrote, "The principal chief is Ko-ko-kah-wah, Wealthy, (or Sam,) an Indian whose principal object is personal aggrandizement." Douthit, *Joseph Lane and the Rogue River Indians*, 482–85, gave his Indian name as Toquahear and Chief Sam's brother as Chief Joe Lane.

Chief Sam Wilder (Toquahear) was the brother of **Chief Jo Lane** (Apserkahar). In addition to several sisters, he also had a brother at Grand Ronde named Tom.[171]

In 1836, Toquahear's father, a chief from the Rogue River valley, was determined that his son attend the Jason Lee mission school. Many chiefs were anxious in those days for their children to learn to read and write English in preparation for the day when the Americans would come to negotiate for their land. The opening of the Jason Lee mission school offered Indian children this opportunity.

Toquahear arrived at the mission in the spring, and on March 5, 1836, the missionary took special note of a Shasta native boy named Samson Wilder who was unwilling to attend evening prayer and was thought to be uncommonly rude. Of special annoyance to the missionary was the fact that the boy would often boast that his grandfather had been a chief, his father was chief, and one day he, too, would be a chief of his people.[172]

By the time Toquahear reached manhood, the opening of the Applegate Trail in 1846 and the discovery of gold had brought increasing numbers of whites into his valley and into violent conflict with his people.

A peace compact made in 1850 with the Americans barely lasted one year. It was broken when Major Kearney and a detachment of United States regulars, who had been ordered to leave Oregon, chose instead to attack Toquahear's band, killing eleven men and wounding even more.

A week later, with additional reinforcements, Kearney attacked the Rogue River band again. There was a short skirmish in the morning of June 24 and a four-hour battle in the afternoon. The Rogue River people suffered badly but defiantly refused to surrender. On June 30, Kearney's men advanced on their village. When they discovered the men were gone, they took their women and children prisoners. The captives were first delivered to Lane. After Lane transferred them to Governor Gaines, Gaines used the women and children as hostages to negotiate a new treaty of peace.

In addition to peace, the terms of the agreement signed July 14, 1851, required both sides to surrender any property taken from the other and return all prisoners of war. It also placed the Rogue River people within the jurisdiction of the American legal system.

About a year later, a company of seventy-five volunteers were raised at Jacksonville in response to an appeal from settlers who apparently believed their homes were in danger. The volunteers united with a posse from the Shasta Valley and surrounded Toquahear's band.

With his people encircled by this force of armed men, Toquahear signed yet another peace treaty July 21, 1852. This time, he agreed to have no communica-

---

171 Douthit, *Joseph Lane and the Rogue River Indians*, 482–85. Letter to the Editor, *Oregon Statesman*, December 2, 1856.
172 Carey, *Mission Record Book*.

tion with the Shasta band who were in particular disfavor with the whites at that time.

On August 7, 1852, the *Oregon Statesman* printed a letter from an American named J. R. Hardin that claimed the new treaty had a provision that stated:

> … if any property, of any kind or description, belonging to the Bostons, was stolen or destroyed by the Indians, and Sam, the chief, does not produce it in a given time, that he was to be surrendered up into the hands of the Bostons, to do with him as they think proper, even to the taking off of his head.[173]

The actual terms of the land cession treaty, as it was recorded, read that the Rogue River tribe of Indians would agree to "cede and relinquish, for the considerations hereinafter specified, to the United States, all their right, title, interest, and claim" to their homelands.

In exchange, the United States would agree that the Rogue River tribe would be allowed to occupy temporarily that portion of their territory on the north side of Rogue River, at the mouth of Evan's Creek that included Table Rock.

The treaty further stated that, in a effort to prevent the friendship between the United States and the Rogue River tribe of Indians from being disrupted by the misconduct of individuals, the parties would agree not to take private revenge or retaliation, but rather, any complaint would be taken by the injured party to an Indian agent appointed by the Americans. It was the duty of the chiefs of the tribe to deliver any person or persons against whom a complaint was made and see that this person was punished according to the laws of the United States.

Further, both parties would agree that the Rogue River chiefs would do everything in their power to recover any property stolen from American citizens and to deliver the recovered property to the Indian agent so that it might be restored to its proper owner. On this point, the Americans promised that the Rogue River would receive full indemnification if their property could not be recovered, but only if there was sufficient proof that it was actually stolen by a citizen of the United States.

On the part of the Rogue River, the chiefs were strongly committed to the pledges they had made to prevent further criminal actions. Tyee Jim demonstrated the strength behind their promise when he went to Toquahear's village at the head of the Rogue River in pursuit of some Indians who had been charged with killing hogs belonging to the Americans. After determining the guilty man was

---

173 J. R. Hardin, Letter to Editor, *Oregon Statesman*, August 7, 1852, stated it was Tyee Taylor's band of Rogue River (Graves Creek Umpqua) people who attacked the Jacksonville settlements in the Rogue River valley. Benjamin F. Dowell, *Autobiography of Benjamin F. Dowell* (Ms P-A 133): 3–4. Dowell claimed it was men in Tyee John's band at Applegate Creek who made the attack on Jacksonville. Apserkahar and Toquahear's sister, Mary's version, as recorded by Joe Lane, is the one accepted here.

the husband of Chief Toquahear's sister, Tyee Jim tied and shot him. He then took two rifles and one bundle of snares to give the white men as restitution for their stolen property.

Despite all efforts, eventually all the violence escalated into a state of war and Toquahear's people were evacuated from Table Rock to the Grand Ronde Reserve.

On the 1856 GRIC, Toquahear was listed as the chief of a band of forty Rogue River people. In 1857, that number had increased to sixty men, women, and children.

At Grand Ronde there was only one significant incident between the military and the Rogue River people under Chief Toquahear. It occurred in May 1857 after the death of a Rogue River medicine woman and was recorded by Lt. Philip Sheridan.[174]

Apparently, one of the doctor's patients died after being led to believe that the medicine woman could cure him. As was the custom, the grieving family set out to revenge the death. The woman doctor was chased just inside the limits of the garrison, where, on the parade ground, and in sight of the officers' quarters, she was shot to death before the military could intervene.

According to the post surgeon, sixteen gunshot wounds were found in the doctor's body; one for every man seen chasing her. The military authority at the post felt the killing of the woman "was a flagrant and defiant outrage committed in the teeth of the military authority" and "necessitated severe measures, both to allay the prevailing excitement and to preclude the recurrence of such acts."

Sheridan sent word to the Rogue River village requesting a council with them the following day. When they met, Sheridan took the position that all the men who had taken part in shooting the doctor had to be delivered to the military for punishment.

The Rogue River attempted to compromise, but Sheridan held firm until he remembered that he was alone except for a sergeant who held his horse. As the Rogue River gathered closer around him, Sheridan began to grow anxious, and unbuttoned the flap of his holster to be ready for any emergency.

Young and perhaps a bit arrogant, Sheridan held his position that the Rogue River needed to surrender the men involved in the shooting. When the altercation grew, he reached for his pistol, but discovered it had been stolen by one of the Rogue River men. Unarmed, he softened his stance and quickly retreated to where the sergeant held his horse.

In making his getaway, Sheridan called back from the far bank of the river that the sixteen men who killed the woman doctor had to be delivered to him and in addition, he wanted his pistol. In all probability, he cringed when his final words were met with laughter.

Humiliated, Sheridan hoped to get a second chance to gain back his self-re-

---

174 Sheridan, *Personal Memoirs of P. H. Sheridan*, Vol. 1.

spect. To successfully accomplish this task, he asked his superior for a force of about fifty men.

Now among the Rogue River there was a woman called Tyee Mary who, fearing that the situation would bring further trouble, came early that next day to see Sheridan. She told Sheridan that she had done all she could, but her people were determined to fight rather than deliver up the sixteen men. She also told him that they had taken up a position by the Yamhill River on the road between the post and village, where they were waiting to attack any military force Sheridan might bring against them.

This information was all Sheridan needed. His battle plan called for a circuitous route by ferry boat down the Yamhill River. At 11 o'clock that night his military party left en route to the Rogue River village. Just before daylight, they took a position at the rear of the village, behind the line occupied by the Rogue River men who were expecting them to be on the road leading directly from the post to their village.

Just at break of day, the military rushed the village and found Toquahear dressed for war and fully armed in anticipation of a fight. With the chief as hostage, Sheridan gave orders to kill him instantly if the Rogue River fired a shot.

When the Rogue River war party realized that the American military occupied their village and were holding all their women and children, they came out from their stronghold on the river and took up a line of resistance about sixty yards away from the soldiers.

At this point, Sheridan called for his men to bring Toquahear to the front where he could be seen by **Chief Apserkahar** and the Rogue River warriors under his command. He told them that Toquahear would be immediately shot if they fired. This knowledge and the cries of the Rogue River women who were opposed to any hostile action by either party soon turned the Rogue River men in favor of discussing peace.

After Apserkahar sent word that he wanted to talk, he and Sheridan met between their respective lines. Sheridan remained firm in his demand that they turn over the men who killed the woman doctor and return his pistol. Apserkahar did not think it could be done, but agreed to consult his people.

When Apserkahar returned, he agreed to surrender fifteen men and Sheridan's pistol. According to Sheridan, Apserkahar also said the military "could kill the sixteenth man, since the tribe wished to get rid of him anyhow, and added that he was a bad Indian, whose bullet no doubt had given the woman her death wound."

After this conversation, Sheridan selected a firing squad. At the same time, Apserkahar was making arrangements for the execution. The plan required sixteen men to stand on a line. All of the accused men except the objectionable one man were told to run to the right of the line at a predetermined signal. The sixteenth man was told to stand fast on the extreme left.

The operation was carried out as arranged. After the sixteenth man was left standing alone, he was brought down from a bullet through the shoulder. While all this was going on, the other bands of the reservation, several thousand strong, had been occupying the surrounding hills in hopes of seeing a good fight; instead they witnessed a failed execution.

At the end of the day, Toquahear was released. The fifteen men involved in the shooting surrendered at Fort Yamhill where their weapons and Sheridan's pistol were confiscated. Then the Rogue River prisoners were placed in ball and chain and forced to work. After he recovered, the wounded prisoner was similarly punished.

On March 15, 1861, Father Croquet baptized Toquahear as "Augustin Sam, about sixty years old, Rogueriver's Indians Chief, of this mission."[175] His exact date of death was not recorded.[176]

Wilder, Sampson (1822c–99c), Santiam band of Kalapuya[177]	Native Name: None known by author
Alias: One Legged Sampson, Michel Samson Wilde	Allotment 260
Mother: Unknown to author	Father: Unknown to author

Michel Samson Wilder of the Rogue River nation was baptized on February 26, 1873, three days after his wife, Elisa (1843c). They were married two months later, on April 22. Apparently, Elisa and Sampson had been married by traditional ceremony for some time before their marriage in the Catholic Church as they were listed together in 1872 as "Sampson Wilder (one legged) and wife, Elisa."[178]

Oddly, "One legged" or "Sampson Wilder" was listed on the 1872 GRIC under the Santiam band of Kalapuya. In 1877, Gatschet listed him again under the Rogue River tribe rather than the Santiam and noted that "one legged Sampson" had a Modoc wife named "Weiley or Wylie," a slave who had previously belonged to **Chief Daniel Wacheno** (Wachinu).[179]

After Elisa died in July 1878, "Samson Wild" married a woman named Susan on May 1, 1879. **Peter Kenoyer** (Kinai) and **Rosalie Kidno** witnessed the ceremony.[180]

---

175 Munnick and Beckham, *Catholic Church Records—Grand Ronde*, Register I, p. 9, B-26.

176 Gatschet, *Texts, Sentences and Vocables*, 189: "Sam, Rogue River chief, died since-."

177 1872 GRIC: "Sampson Wilder" aka "One legged" under Santiam Band of Kalapuya. Father Croquet baptized him as Michael Samson Wilde and gave his tribe as Rogue River on February 26, 1873. Gatschet, *Texts, Sentences and Vocables*, 366, listed him under the Rogue River tribe rather than the Santiam and noted that "one legged Sampson" had a Modoc wife.

178 Munnick and Beckham, *Catholic Church Records—Grand Ronde*, Register I, p. 81, B-11, p. 82, M-4, p. 108, S-17.

179 Gatschet, *Texts, Sentences and Vocables*, 366.

180 Munnick and Beckham, *Catholic Church Records—Grand Ronde*, Register I, p. 111, M-7.

In 1879, the Indian legislature passed a provision of law exempting a number of old men, including Sampson Wilder, from working on the reservation roads.

On May 10, 1881, the road supervisors were to put their crews to work on opening a road between Sampson Wilder's place and **Peter Checkaon** (Chikhyan)'s land. In addition, the legislature renewed a provision of law that made Sampson exempt from working on the road due to his age, but he was still required to pay taxes.[181]

In 1888, Sampson was listed again under the Santiam band of Kalapuya. His son-in-law, **Frank Norwest,** was also listed as Santiam. Frank's brother, **Thomas Norwest,** was listed as Luckiamute. According to the GRIC, the three men were living separately. Although Tom and his son, **Thomas Norwest,** had been living with Sampson, they apparently had moved into places of their own.

In 1888, Sampson's farm was described as a house and barn on forty fenced acres. In addition, the Indian agent reported that his assets included three hogs, three horses, a plow, and a harrow.

Sampson Wilder received an eighty-acre allotment. His heirs were Alexander Norwest, Susette Simmons, and Frank Norwest.[182]

William, Chief, Oregon City Band Chinook[183]	Native Name: Wyanashot /Wy-an-a-shot/[184]
Alias: Chief Bill	Allotment: None known by author
Mother: Unknown to author	Father: Unknown to author

On the 1856 GRIC, there were thirty-one people in Chief William (Wyanashot)'s band. In 1857 the number in his band had increased to forty-five people. Where food was scarce on the reservation, all five Oregon City bands were allowed to return to their home country to fish at Willamette Falls.[185]

In a letter from Oregon City, dated June 21, 1856, the special Indian agent wrote:

> The Chiefs **Thomas, John [Kawache]**, and Bill [Wyanashot] was down by permission of the U.S. officer in charge, as salmon was plenty and easily taken. I had some hooks made and set them to fishing for themselves, no

---

181 National Archives, Seattle, WA, Grand Ronde/Siletz, Land and Enrollment Program records, Field Notes and Land Survey 1875–1898, Land Description Book 1878, Box 115; Grand Ronde Justice Court.

182 *Heirs to Deceased Indians*, Allotment Record 260.

183 1856 and 1857 GRIC: listed him as chief of an Oregon City band.

184 1856 GRIC: "Chief William" under Oregon City Bands. 1857 GRIC: "Wy-an-a-shot" under Oregon City Band.

185 1856 GRIC: the five Oregon City bands were identified as Thomas' band under Chief Thomas, William's band under Chief William, John's band under Chief John, Clackamas band under Chief Wachinu, Molalla band under Gwayakiti.

objection being made by citizens, but met with a hardy approval. Enough fish might have been caught to have wintered the Indians on the reserve without any detriment to the citizens of Oregon City.[186]

William, Mary (1848c–98c), Tualatin band of Kalapuya, Lower Chinook	Native Name: Dinewa /DI-ni-wi/ (dúuniʔwiʔ)[187]
Alias: Mary Tebeau, Mary Teabo	Allotment: None known by author
Mother: Lower Chinook	Father: Tualatin William Wishikin

Mary William-Tebeau (Dinewa) married a French Canadian named Franklin Michelle Tebeau. They had four children: Edward, Joseph, William, and Agnes. However, only Joseph and **Edward Tebeau** were alive in 1906.[188] In 1914, Joseph Tebeau inherited his uncle, **James Foster**'s estate.[189]

Williams, Clinnie (1870c–1908), Yoncalla band of Kalapuya, Umpqua[190]	Native Name: None known by author
Alias: Plaini Tipton, Pauline Cook, Clarissa Cook	Allotment 222
Mother: Unknown to author	Father: William Williams, Yoncalla, Umpqua

In 1872, Clinnie and **Dick Tipton** were listed together as husband and wife. In 1887, she was listed as a widow, living with her son, **Cephas Tipton**. By 1888, she and Cephas were living with her father, **Calapooia Billy Williamson** (Hosa-nunda) and his wife, Mary. From 1896 through 1905, she lived with **Frank Cook**.

August 5, 1907, Clinnie Tipton-Cook was issued a fee patent for her entire 260-acre allotment.[191]

Williams, Johnny, Molalla	Native Name: Matiyas /ma-TI-yas/ (matíyas)*[192]
Alias: None known by author	Allotment: None known by author

186 B. Jennings to Joel Palmer, June 21, 1856.
187 McChesney, *The Rolls of Certain Indian*, Testimony of Edward Franklin Tebeau, 79.
188 Ibid.,
189 Oregon State Archives, Salem, Oregon, 1914, Polk County, Estate, File 1732.
190 Jacobs, Field Notebooks 58, *Texts and Ethnology*, 92: "Cephas Tipton's father (Dick Tipton) was Umpqua. Cephas Tipton's mother was part or full Yoncalla Kalapuya (Plaini, they called her—an English, not Indian appellative.)" Michelle, *Just a Memorandum*, 10: Dick Tipton had one son, "John Betice" or "Seno Tipton," by Yoncalla William's daughter, "Plina." Oregon State Archives, Salem, Oregon, Polk County Probate Court Files, Box 35, Folder 307, Estate 1900, File 1003: gave her name as Pauline Cook mother of Cephas Tipton.
191 *Heirs of Deceased Indians*, Allotment Record 222.
192 Jacobs, Field Notebook 51, *Music and Ethnology*, 4.

Mother: Molalla Kate	Father: Unknown to author

Johnny Williams (Matiyas) was the son of **Molalla Kate** (Musui) and Renaldo Matches. Lizzie Smith (1879c–1952c) was his half sister.[193]

Johnny was brought up in Wasco country. He married **John Kelly**'s granddaughter, **Nellie Frank,** around 1890.[194] At that time, it was the tradition for people from Siletz to come to Grand Ronde every Saturday night to put on a fun dance. Johnny Williams would participate in the dances wearing his quiver pouch.[195]

After Nellie, Johnny married Calousa Davenport. They had several children: Cecelia (1892) and Mathew (1897).

Williamson, Billy (1825c–1900), Umpqua, Yoncalla band of Kalapuya[196]	Native Name: Hosanunda /Hos-a-nun-da/[197]
Alias: Calapooia Billy, Billy Williamson	Allotment 253
Mother: Unknown to author	Father: Unknown to author

Calapooia Billy Williamson (Hosanunda) was one of those present at the September 14, 1871, council meeting with Commissioner Brunot and Superintendent Meacham. They apparently made no response when he reminded them that for fifteen years they had been talking about what was needed on the reservation and asked if previous records of council minutes had gone to Washington.[198]

Calapooia Billy always followed the ancient Dream Power religion. He was a Dreamer before the Warm House religion came to Grand Ronde. After Bogus Tom brought the new dream philosophy to Grand Ronde, Calapooia Billy ran the Warm House lodge on the South Yamhill River along with **Chief Joseph Hutchins** (Yalkama) and **Thomas Hutchins** (Liham).[199]

In 1872, Calapooia Billy was living with his wife, Molly. In 1886, he was listed with two wives. They were poor. Calapooia Billy had the following children: Elias (1859c), Adam (1870c), Jesse (1873c), and Lucy (1878c), and **Clinnie Williams.**

Like others, Calapooia Billy worked hard. In August and July 1875, he delivered 500 wagon spokes to the Indian agent. In payment he took $15 worth of merchandise from the agency commissary and received $2.44 in cash.[200]

---

193 State of Oregon, Lincoln County, Affidavit from Hoxie Simmons dated September 9, 1957.
194 Zenk, 1987, Grand Ronde Field Notebook 8, 10–11.
195 Jacobs, Field Notebooks 52, *Texts and Ethnology*, 34.
196 1888 GRIC: listed his tribe as Yoncalla band of Kalapuya. Jacobs, Field Notebooks 46, *Santiam Kalapuya Text,* 44: JB Hudson gave "Bill Williamson as (a Yoncalla-Umpqua)."
197 1887 GRIC: gave Indian name as "Hos-a-nun-da."
198 *Annual Report Commissioner of Indian Affairs,* 1871, Minutes of a Council with Grand Ronde Indians at their Reservation, Oregon, by Commissioner Felix R. Brunot, September 14, 1871, 149–53.
199 Du Bois, *The Ghost Dance,* 30.
200 National Archives, Seattle, Grand Ronde, Box 190, Book 10819, Cash Book, 1875–

Mary Williamson-Allen-Cook (Skampup). Photo courtesy of the Smithsonian Institution (No. 01134500).

The Grand Ronde Indian Legislature elected him on May 9, 1881, to fill a vacancy for Court Administrator. He served for the remainder of 1881 and for 1882.[201]

In 1888, Calapooia Billy's widowed daughter, Clinnie Williams-Tipton and her son **Cephas Tipton** were living with him and his wife, Mary (Skampup).

1907.

201 National Archives, Seattle, Grand Ronde/Siletz, Land and Enrollment Program records, Field Notes and Land Survey 1875–1898, Land Description Book 1878, Box 115; Grand Ronde Justice Court.

Their property was described by the agent as a house on four fenced acres with a half acre garden, two horses, and a cow.

Calapooia Billy received a fee patent on a 180-acre allotment on October 29, 1906. His heirs were **William Lashman** (Laishmin), Clinnie Williams-Tipton, and Betsy Williams.[202]

When he died on December 16, 1900, his real property was estimated at $900. In probate, his heirs were listed as his son, William Lashman, his daughter, Clinnie, and his widow, Mary Williamson. Clinnie died during probate.[203] His widow, Mary Williamson (Skampup), married Robert Allen. After Robert Allen died, she married Frank Cook.[204]

Wilson, Judge, Luckiamute band of Kalapuya	Native Name: None known by author
Alias: None known by author	Allotment: None known by author
Mother: Unknown to author	Father: Unknown to author

In 1872, Judge Wilson was listed with the **David Davies** family.

Winchester, Mary (1843c–1896), widow of Umpqua husband[205]	Native Name: None known by author
Alias: Winchester Mary, Mary Jondro, Mary Neal	Allotment 78
Mother: Unknown to author	Father: Unknown to author

Mary was first married to **Winchester Jo.** After Winchester Jo died and Jean Baptiste Gendron separated from his wife, **Julia Agnes Gendron, Jean Baptiste Gendron** and Mary lived together for several years.[206] However, in 1888, Mary Winchester was listed on the GRIC once again as a widow living alone.

Mary married a white man named William Neal on July 1, 1890. When she died on May 5, 1896, he was her sole heir. June 15, 1908, a fee patent was issued to Neal for the entire forty acres. He lived on the allotment until his died in 1917.[207]

Both William Neal and Mary were buried in the Grand Ronde cemetery. Mary rests in a grave next to Winchester Jo.

---

202 *Heirs of Deceased Indians*, Allotment Record 253–54.
203 Oregon State Archives, Salem, Oregon, 1900, Polk County Estate, File 1003.
204 Oregon State Archives, Salem, Oregon, 1916, Polk County Estate, File 1594.
205 1888 GRIC listed Mary Winchester's tribe as Clackamas.
206 1885 GRIC: Winchester Mary was listed as the wife of Jean Baptiste Gendron. Jean Baptiste's sons by his wife, Clara: Henry and Jonas are living with them. 1886 GRIC: Jean Baptiste, age forty, was listed with Mary, age forty, and the widow Mary, age sixty-five.
207 National Archives, Salem, Oregon, 1896, Polk County Estate, File 1032.

Winslow, Anastasie (1871c–1913), Clackamas, Molalla	Native Name: None known by author
Alias: Anastasie Lafferty, Anastasie Franklin	Allotment: 99
Mother: Pauline Montour	Father: Mark Winslow, Clackamas, Molalla

Anastasie Winslow was the daughter of **Mark Winslow** and his wife, **Pauline Montour**. In 1887, she married **Marshell Laferte**'s son, **Peter Lafferty**. Peter and Anastasie had two children, Harvey and **Paul Lafferty.**

Anastasie received 230.23 acres of allotment land. On October 29, 1906, she exchanged twenty acres of her allotment with **Edward Petite**. On March 13, 1907, she was issued a fee patent for the entire allotment.[208]

Winslow, Henry (1844c–97c), Clackamas, Molalla[209]	Native Name: None known by author
Alias: None known by author	Allotment 263
Mother: Clackamas	Father: Molalla

Henry's father was Molalla and his mother Clackamas. **Mark Winslow** was his brother.[210]

In 1872, he was listed with a wife, Melinda, under the Clackamas. In 1888, he was listed as one of the Oregon City band.

In 1877, he served with the Tualatin sub-chiefs, **Lame James Shiliqua** (Shilik-wa) and **Dave Yachkawa** on the Indian Board of Commissioners that controlled the Indian Court Treasury. In 1880, Henry was elected sergeant at arms of the Grand Ronde legislative assembly.[211] He served as sheriff at Grand Ronde from 1884 to 1888.[212]

In 1885, Henry was listed with his wife Sarah, her mother, **Eliza Johnson** (Khakhshni), a fourteen-year-old girl named Melonia, and a little boy named Ezra. Henry had at least four wives: Louise or Melinda, **Sophia Gendron, Sarah Johnson** (Waganwish), and Anna Dowd. By Louise, he had three children: Nancy (1873c), Melonia (1870c), and Olivia (1871c). By Sarah (Waganwish), he had four children: Andrew (1884–85), Jose (1885c), Tillie (1886), and LaRose (1889c–1919).

---

208 *Heirs to Deceased Indians*, Allotment Record 99.
209 Gatschet, *Texts, Sentences and Vocables*, 371: listed under the Clackamas.
210 Michelle, *Just a Memorandum*, 7.
211 National Archives, Seattle, Grand Ronde/Siletz, Land and Enrollment Program records, Field Notes and Land Survey 1875–1898, Land Description Book 1878, Box 115; Grand Ronde Justice Court.
212 Grand Ronde Agency Ledger Book, Records of Employees at Grand Ronde July 1883–September 1907, Confederated Tribes of the Grand Ronde Community of Oregon Archive.

By Anna Dowd he had Henry or Gussie (1881c) and August (1892).[213]

Henry was with Sarah Johnson from 1885 until he died in 1897; however, he was married to Anna Dowd at the same time. Both Sarah and Anna lived with Henry from 1892 through 1897 along with Anna's son, August, and Sarah's little girls, Tillie and LaRose.

Henry received a 240.23-acre allotment.[214] His daughter **Tillie Winslow** received an eighty-acre allotment and married **Fabien Quenel.**

Winslow, James (1834c–1906) Clackamas, French Canadian	Native Name: None known by author
Alias: None known by author	Allotment 265
Mother: Clackamas	Father: St. Pierre, French Canadian

James Winslow said he was the son of a French Canadian named St. Pierre. His mother later married a man named Winslow. They were brought under the Kalapuya treaty to the reservation when the Clackamas people first came to Grand Ronde.[215]

Mark and **Henry Winslow** were his cousins. Their mother was a sister to his mother. James was "raised by his aunt, Mrs. Winslow."[216] As was the custom among Indian people, **Anastasie**, Mark Winslow's daughter, knew James as a "half brother" rather than "a cousin" to her father.[217]

James Winslow married Polly of the Wakanasisi band of Clackamas, formerly the wife of Joseph Gendron, who was living at St. Paul. At that time, Polly had four children by Joseph Gendron: **Edward, Sophie, Rachel,** and **LaRose Gendron.** They all came to Grand Ronde to live with James Winslow.[218]

In 1877, James was working as the agency blacksmith.[219] In November 1879, **Tom Gilbert** (Kiyukiyush) paid six dollars for James to get a license to practice law.[220] In 1880, James was the agency carpenter. He was in charge of the carpenter shop at Grand Ronde until he died.[221] He never had any children of his own, but

---

213 Munnick and Beckham, *Catholic Church Records—Grand Ronde,* Register I, p. 68, B-20, p. 83, B-30, p. 97, S-2, p. 100, M-2, p. 105, S-26, p. 118, M-1, p. 132, S-11, p. 129, B-1, Register II, p. 6, B-17, p. 51, B-2, p. 112, S-8.

214 *Heirs of Deceased Indians,* Allotment Records 263, 264.

215 O. Applegate, Testimony of James Winslow.

216 Ibid.

217 Oregon State Archives, Yamhill County Probate 1907, File 1228.

218 Michelle, *Just a Memorandum,* 7.

219 Gatschet, *Texts, Sentences and Vocables,* 371: listed as "James Winslow, blacksmith, ½ breed, really is a Frenchman."

220 National Archives, Seattle, Grand Ronde/Siletz, Land and Enrollment Program records, Field Notes and Land Survey 1875–1898, Land Description Book 1878, Box 115; Grand Ronde Justice Court.

221 Michelle, *Just a Memorandum,* 7.

he and his wife helped raise Sophie Gendron and **Charlie Petite**'s children after their parents died.

In 1885, James was married to Louiza. His sister, LaRose, her son, **Henry Petite,** and two daughters were also living with him. His farm was composed of a house and barn with a garden and orchard on 100 fenced acres, with eighty acres in cultivation. In 1886, no one at Grand Ronde had more acreage in cultivation than James Winslow. In 1888, he was listed with his wife, Polly, daughter, LaRose, and grandson, Eddie.

James Winslow received a 240-acre allotment. His heir was Mark Winslow's daughter, Anastasie.[222] By the time he died in March 1906 his property was described as "rough and unimproved" and his total estate was valued at $500. Anastasie Winslow-Franklin inherited it.[223]

Winslow, LaRose (1853c–1923), Clackamas[224]	Native Name: None known by author
Alias: None known by author	Allotment 267
Mother: Clackamas	Father: Unknown to author

In 1885, LaRose Winslow was listed as a sister to **James Winslow.** They shared the same mother.

LaRose Winslow received a 120.35-acre allotment. Her heir was **Paul Lafferty,** the grandson of **Mark Winslow** and **Pauline Montour.**[225]

Winslow, Laws	Native Name: None known by author
Alias: None known by author	Allotment: None known by author
Mother: Unknown to author	Father: Unknown to author

He surrendered "one shotgun, 24 bows and 20 arrows of the Klamath" to the Indian agent at Grand Ronde on April 6, 1856.[226]

Winslow, Mark (1842c–77), Clackamas, Molalla	Native Name: None known by author
Alias: None known by author	Allotment: None known by author
Mother: Clackamas	Father: Molalla[227]

Mark and **Henry Winslow** were brothers. James Winslow's mother was an

---

222 *Heirs of Deceased Indians,* Allotment Record 265.
223 National Archives, Salem, Oregon, 1907, Yamhill County Estate, File 1228.
224 O. Applegate, Testimony of James Winslow.
225 *Heirs of Deceased Indians*, Allotment Record 267.
226 National Archives, Washington DC: This entry was in a different handwriting from that of the rest of the document.
227 Michelle, *Just a Memorandum,* 7.

aunt to Mark and Henry on their mother's side. [228]

Mark Winslow had a son, Joseph, by Susanne in 1860. Joseph was baptized on October 7. His godparents were **William Laurence** and Mary.[229]

In 1872, Mark was listed on the GRIC under **Chief John Kawache**'s Oregon City band of Clackamas with his wife, **Pauline Montour** (1853c–1873), and children, Roselie, Agnes, Margaret, and Anastasie. After Pauline died, Mark married Mary Laferte on April 5, 1875. Witnessing their ceremony were **John Baptiste Menard** and Mary Shangaretta.

Mark Winslow and Mary Laferte had Mary Angele in 1876. Mark Winslow died and was buried February 23, 1877. Mary Angele, aged "about a year," was buried two days later.[230] When Rev. Summers visit the Winslow home that year, it was probably Mary Angele whom he saw laid out in her native burial dress. Summers described her as lying "on her little white bier with candles at the head and foot."[231]

Even though the family was in mourning, Rev. Summers took the time to look around. In one large room, he saw two small homemade sofa-beds next to two large beds. He also saw two large woven sacks, a number of baskets, and some other relics, but Rev. Summers wrote "just now we had no heart to trade."[232]

Winslow, Matilda Clara (1887–1915), Clackamas, Molalla, Watlala (Cascade) Chinook, Klamath	Native Name: None known by author
Alias: Tillie Winslow, Tillie Quesnel	Allotment 264
Mother: Sarah Johnson, Clackamas, Watlala Chinook, Klamath	Father: Henry Winslow, Clackamas, Molalla

Matilda "Tillie" Winslow married **Fabian Quenel.** They had a number of children, including Franklin "Nooks," Leonard (1905c), Fabian (1906c), Rose Amanda (1907c) Clarinda (1909c), and Albert Victor (1914).

On February 8, 1907, she received a fee patent for her entire eighty-acre allotment.

Wishikin, Tualatin William (d. 1875), Tualatin band of Kalapuya[233]	Native Name: Wishikin /WISH-i-kin/
Alias: William Washington, Washington, Wishikin, Wapato Bill	Allotment: None known by author
Mother: Unknown to author	Father: Unknown to author

---

228 O. Applegate, Testimony of James Winslow.

229 Munnick and Beckham, *Catholic Church Records—Grand Ronde*, Register I, p. 4, B-7.

230 Ibid., Register I, p. 101, 102.

231 Cawley, *Summers Indian Journal*, 39.

232 Ibid.

233 Gatschet, *Texts, Sentences, and Vocables*, 77.

Wishikin and **Henry Wallace**'s mother, **Lillie Wallace** (Kalloka), were brother and sister.[234] **Antoine Metzkar** (Tamulch), **Jack Nancy** (Shimkhin), **Callo Bonaparte** (Kalukh), **and Tualatin William** were also related. Reportedly, they were "all brothers through a common father."[235] In addition Wishikin had a brother, Ichamulh, who had two sons, **Lame James Shiliqua** (Shilikwa) and **John Pratt** (Gwaimit).[236]

Tualatin William was married to **Chief Quaiquaty** (Gwayakiti)'s daughter, Sarah. They had at least five children: Aik, Victoria, Antoinette (1869c–75), Moses (1872–73), and Henriette (1874c–75c).[237] By another wife, Wishikin had a daughter named **Mary William** who married a French Canadian named Franklin Michelle Tebeau.[238]

Wishikin came with the Clackamas when they first arrived at Grand Ronde, but only stayed a few years at a time. The rest of the time he lived at a place on the Columbia where he always fished for salmon.

In 1872, Wishikin and **Sarah Gwayakiti** were listed with their two daughters and infant son. Out of the children, only **Victoria Wishikin** (Kinishi), the oldest daughter was specifically named on the GRIC, but Antoinette's death was mentioned in Catholic Church records.

Wishikin died at Grand Ronde on December 17, 1875.[239] After his death, Sarah and their daughter Victoria lived with Sarah's mother, **Wagayuhlen Gwayakiti.**

Wishikin, Victoria (1867c–1930), Tualatin band of Kalapuya, Molalla, Clackamas[241]	Native Name: Kinishi /*Kinishi*/[240]
Alias: Victoria Wishington, Victoire Wishikin, Victoria Wacheno, Victoria Howard	Allotment: None known by author
Mother: Sarah Gwayakiti, Molalla, Clackamas	Father: William Wishikin, Tualatin band of Kalapuya

---

234 Jacobs, Notebooks 67, *Texts Ethnology Clackamas & Jargon*, 22.

235 Oregon State Archive, Salem Oregon, 1909, Yamhill County, Estate File 1327: Testimony of Amos *Kilya* and Louise Selkeah.

236 Jacobs, Notebooks 67, *Texts Ethnology Clackamas & Jargon*, 22: Mrs. H's father's brother, (itcamut) had a son, cilikwa; he was *itciqacuc* [a cousin] to Mrs. H. [Victoria Howard].

237 Munnick and Beckham, *Catholic Church Records—Grand Ronde*, Register I, p. 83, S-18, p. 87, B-8, p. 92, S-8, p. 96, S-26, p. 96 S-26.

238 McChesney, Testimony of Edward Franklin Teabo, 79.

239 Munnick and Beckham, *Catholic Church Records—Grand Ronde*, Register I, p. 96, S-28.

240 1887 GRIC gave Indian name as "Kin-i-shi."

241 1872 GRIC: listed with the Wapato Lake/Tualatin. 1932 Federal Census: Victoria Howard, age 65, Tualatin tribe, and "died September 26, 1930 West Linn Clackamas Ore."

Victoria (Kinishi) was the daughter of **Tualatin William Wishikin** and **Chief Quaiquaty** (Gwayakiti)'s daughter, **Sarah Gwayakiti.** When she was born, in keeping with her class status, Victoria's head should have been flattened. In fact, her grandmother had the cradle ready, but Victoria's father objected and snatched it away.[242]

Among the Tualatin people, if one had a bad dream about their children, the next morning they sang a song and rubbed their children with ashes. When Victoria was small, a medicine woman named **Jack Nancy** (Shimkhin) gave Wishikin one of her songs to sing to Victoria all the time. Years later Victoria recorded the song from memory for Melville Jacobs.[243]

In December 1875, her father and her younger sister died. A few days after her father's death, his mother began taking Victoria every morning before sunrise for five days to an old lady who had a special power that granted long life to orphans and could cause mourners to forget the deceased.

The prayers the old woman gave over Victoria were called a *caucau* (*shaushau*). In a monotone chant, with the breath held, "so that the she nearly suffocates between breathes," the old woman called out to the earth, "You, long time ago, were good. You knew how to make things straight. You knew all things. You make this girl's life long."[244]

Then praying in the same way, she would addresses camas, asking it to make the child strong and healthy, to give the child strength, and so on.

Then she would address fish: "Long ago you used to be food for our people. You gave them strength. You made them grow up strong and healthy. You would go in their stomach and so on."[245]

Next, she would talk to the deer, saying, "You always stretched yourself. You are strong. The people use you for food. You stay in their stomach and make them strong. Do the same for this girl. Give her your strength."[246]

Then again, the old lady might plead with the earth. She would ask the earth not to think the girl was *tcmax* (*chmakh*) least the girl might grow sick and die. She would tell earth that when the girl pulled camas or berries out of the earth, she did not mean to hurt her, but was taking the food that earth raised for people to eat in order to grow up stout and healthy.[247]

The old woman would address the berries and the sun. She would ask the sun to send her own brightness soon into everything including the girl's heart.[248]

Later, Victoria and her mother moved in with Victoria's maternal grandmother, Wagayuhlen. The three of them lived together until Sarah Gwayakiti-Wishikin

---

242 Jacobs, Field Notebook 54, *Texts and Ethnology*, 132.
243 Jacobs, Field Notebook 51, *Texts and Ethnology*, 9.
244 Jacobs, Field Notebook 61, *Texts and Ethnology*, 30–31.
245 Ibid.
246 Ibid.
247 Ibid.
248 Ibid.

married **Foster Wacheno** (Inawalh) around 1875.

With her mother gone, Victoria found herself alone from early morning until late at night as her grandmother spent long hours out doctoring the sick, sometimes two or three patients a day.[249]

In those days, there was a woman called *wagalgal* who wore a carved wooden mask called a false face. Wagalgal would wrap herself in a blanket or hide and carry a large Rogue River–style basket on her back. The basket was used to carry off bad children who did not obey their parents. Apparently, Victoria was a mischievous child as she was scared by wagalgal three times.[250]

In fun, once she sang **Tanas George Sutton** (Sakalkhida)'s power song. When it suddenly started to rain, poor **Louis Kenoyer** (Pakhawatas) thought for sure she had caused it, but Victoria felt sure the rain was just a coincidence that time.[251]

When Victoria was sixteen, she announced her intention to marry her step-father's brother, **Marc Daniel Wacheno** (Wadams).[252] The news disturbed many members of the family as Daniel was a relative and as such not an acceptable mate.[253]

Victoria's uncle, **Moses Allen** (Shkayinch), who had helped Victoria in the past, threatened that if she went through with this marriage and things went bad, he would not help her again.[254]

Despite the families' objections, they were married and Victoria had her first child, a little girl, a year later.[255] As a young mother, Victoria objected to head flattening as her father had many years earlier. Fearing something would happen to her child, she loosened her baby's head band whenever her mother-in-law was not looking.[256]

Over the years, she and Marc Daniel had a number of children, including Dan (1880c), Henry (1882c), **Josephine,** Sarah (1884c), **Charles, Susanna,** Andrew (1891), Florentia (1894) and Clara (1898c).

After Victoria left Marc Daniel, she married **Eustace Howard** in 1903. She had a daughter, Agatha, by Eustace in 1904. Agatha married Joseph Howe, who was related to the Laffertys.[257]

In 1929, Victoria recorded two of her own power songs for Melville Jacobs.

---

249 Jacobs, Field Notebook 69, *Texts Ethnology Clackamas & Jargon*, 113.

250 Jacobs, Field Notebook 54, *Texts and Ethnology*, 30.

251 Jacobs, Field Notebook 53, *Texts and Ethnology*, 102.

252 Jacobs, Field Notebook 58, *Texts and Ethnology*, 118.

253 Jacobs, Field Notebook 59, *Texts and Ethnology*, 24: "Mrs. H.'s grandmother and other relatives growled awfully about it; her uncle warned her that if she were abused or poor he would never offer help. When she left this first husband then she went to her uncle, who helped her."

254 Ibid.

255 Jacobs, Field Notebook 58, *Texts and Ethnology*, 118.

256 Jacobs, Field Notebooks 52, *Texts and Ethnology*, 17: notes with a pencil drawing of the cradle made for Victoria's baby by her.

257 Danforth, Bernice Howe-McEachran family tree.

Victoria Wishikin-Howard preparing to make a basket; taken 1919. Photo courtesy of Barbara Danforth Private Collection.

Victoria Wishikin-Howard with basket material; taken 1919. Photo courtesy of Barbara Danforth Private Collection.

He wrote that although he was afraid to ask her details about them, Victoria did mention that she used a cane when dancing and singing with at least one of the songs. This would suggest rattlesnake power. If she had the full power the cane would turn into a snake, but Victoria's power "left her too quick."[258]

In her elder years, Victoria joked about life. She said,

What kind of a house full of people is this? Everybody sick or crippled or afflicted with something. I am rheumatic, getting old; soon I'll be bent over. I have a weak heart—and so on. Eustace has dropsy with legs like an elephant's. My daughter is borderline tuberculosis, weighs 98 pounds or so. The two little girls, my grandchildren, one has epileptic seizures; the other has this and so. Pretty soon Eva, (a Rogue River lady about 35 living there at this time) will be an old lady with this and so. Young Adam Wacheno (also living there at this time, aged about 30) has a bad sprained back, etc., John here (an old—about 60—Indian living there) is stone deaf

---

258 Jacobs, Field Notebook 51, *Texts and Ethnology,* 12.

**Victoria Wishikin's son-in-law, Joe Howe
(left), and Paul Lafferty, both cowboys
and trick riders. Photo courtesy of Barbara
Danforth Private Collection.**

and all smashed up from an accident a few years ago. And so on and so on. We're all hanged up.[259]

It would seem things did not get better for her. In 1930, she was hospitalized after being struck by a hit and run driver. A few months later, she died of heart failure. She was buried in the Mountain View Cemetery at Oregon City where a roughly made tombstone marks her grave.

---

259 Jacobs, Field Notebook 62, *Texts and Ethnology*, n.p.

Wolford, George, Molalla	Native Name: None known by author
Alias: None known by author	Allotment: None known by author
Mother: Unknown to author	Father: Unknown to author

In 1872, George Wolford was listed with his wife, Kate.

Wood, Joseph (1873c–93c), Clackamas, Kalapuya, Molalla[260]	Native Name: None known by author
Alias: None known by author	Allotment 262
Mother: Watutamkh, Molalla[261]	Father: Washkeya Wood, Kalapuya, Clackamas

Joseph Wood received a 42.60-acre allotment. His heirs, **Foster Wacheno** (In-awalh), **Marc Daniel Wacheno** (Wadams), and **John Wacheno** (Tsinwalh), sold the entire allotment to J. G. Cockerham on December 22, 1903.

Wood, Watutamkh, Molalla, Clackamas[262]	Native Name: Watutamkh /wa-tu-TAMH/ (watutámx)*[263]
Alias: None known by author	Allotment: None known by author
Mother: Unknown to author	Father: Unknown to author

Watutamkl was a sister or cousin to **Henry Kiki** (Lhkaihkai) and the mother of Joseph Wood.[264] In 1872, she was listed as the wife of **Washkeya**. She had been with Washkeya for many years. Two of their children, Julia (1857c), and Felix (1857c), were baptized by Father Croquet in November 1860.[265]

---

260 Michelle, *Just a Memorandum,* 5: Washkeya had two son's Ywayash and Joseph by his Klamath wife.

261 Jacobs, Field Notebook 62, *Texts and Ethnology,* n.p., "Watutamx name of a half Molale, half Clackamas woman; perhaps a Molale name, but maybe Clackamas. Laailaai was her brother or cousin; she called him itcalxt. She was married to Waskiya."

262 Jacobs, Field Notebook 62, *Texts and Ethnology,* 14: given as "half molale, half Clackamas woman, perhaps a Molale name, but maybe Clackamas."

263 Drucker, *Clackamas Notes,* 31–32. Jacobs, *Clackamas Text,* Part II, 659. Jacobs, Field Notebook 69, *Texts Ethnology Clackamas & Jargon*: Watutam, a part Molalla woman who was Old Wood's wife. 1872 GRIC: Wa-tu-tum. Munnick and Beckham, *Catholic Church Records—Grand Ronde,* Register 1, p. 6, B-32: gave her name as "Watotames."

264 Jacobs, Field Notebook 62, *Texts and Ethnology,* 14.

265 Munnick and Beckham, *Catholic Church Records—Grand Ronde,* Register 1, p. 6, B-32, B-34, p. 12, B-162, p. 43, B-5, p. 69, B-32, p. 92, B-10, p. 99, S-17, p. 120, S-1, p. 122, S-8.

Y

Yachkawa, Daniel Webster (1868c–89c), Tualatin band of Kalapuya	Native Name: None known by author
Alias: None known by author	Allotment: None known by author
Mother: Unknown to author	Father: Chief Dave Yachkawa, Tualatin band of Kalapuya

Daniel was the son of **Dave Yachkawa.** He was the young man Rev. Summers saw taking his blind father around to complete some unexplained business first with the agent and then with Father Croquet. Summers implied his business with them might have had something to do with the illegal alcohol sold to Dave Yachkawa on July 4.[1] Daniel Webster Yachkawa received the sacrament of confirmation July 22, 1885.[2]

Yachkawa, Dave (1832c–82), Tualatin band of Kalapuya	Native Name: Yachkawa /YACH-ka-wa/ (yáchk̲awa)*[3]
Alias: Wapato Dave, Chief Wapato Dave	Allotment: None known by author Mother: Unknown to author
Father: Unknown to author	

Yachkawa was Wapato Dave's grandfather's name before it was given to him.[4] Dave acted as interpreter for the Tualatins during treaty negotiations and signed the 1855 treaty with the Kalapuya as third chief of the Tualatin band.[5]

A problem with illegal whiskey caused a serious breach between him and the

---

1 Cawley, *Indian Journal,* 37.

2 Munnick and Beckham, *Catholic Church Records—Grand Ronde,* Register I, p. 131, C-30.

3 Gatschet, *Texts, Sentences and Vocables,* 371: listed under the Tualatin as "Yatchkawa, wife and son.; [?] man." Gatschet, *Texts, Sentences and Vocables,* 30: Gatschet wrote "blind fellow, Dave, legislature; Iatskaua mi." Jacobs, Field Notebook 51, *Music and Ethnology,* 32. Jacobs, Field Notebooks 46, *Santiam Kalapuya Text,* n.p., "Yatckawa, Wapato Dave; of the Wapato Lake; came with the Tualatin group rather than the Yamhills. The last woman he had was possibly part Yamhill—she was an old med. woman. Both were killed (heads cut off by an axe) by an old Molale fellow who was angry at Yatckawa—some boozing stool pigeon business pulled off by Yatckawa." Jacobs, Field Notebooks 58, *Texts and Ethnology,* 12. Jacobs, Field Notebooks 79, *Texts and Ethnology Santiam,* 79, n.p.

4 Gatschet, *Texts, Sentences and Vocables,* 229: "Yatskawa, his father's father."

5 Kappler, *Treaty with the Kalapuya, Ect., 1855.*

Tualatin chief, **Kiakuts** (Kayakach), just after the signing of the treaty and pushed Yachkawa into a lifelong battle with alcoholism. Despite his reputation for being a drinking man, Yachkawa retained a position of prominence among his people; in 1869, the Tualatins asked him to speak to Superintendent of Indian Affairs A. B. Meacham on their behalf.

On the day selected for the meeting with Meacham, the people dressed carefully in their finest clothes. Some of the people had wagons or horses to carry them to the agency council ground; others walked. Once they were all gathered in front of the agency, Meacham explained a new program he wanted to extend to the Grand Ronde people.[6]

After listening, Dave Yachkawa spoke up. He said they did not know if Meacham was telling the truth, but the people wanted Meacham to know they were all very poor. They did not have a good mill, wagons, harnesses, or plows. If they had these things, they would work. Yachkawa said that the government need not give these things to the people; they would buy them.[7]

As a result of this council, Meacham gave permission for the people to establish an Indian government and Yachkawa took part by serving as an Indian commissioner with **Lame Jim Shiliqua** (Shilikwa) and **Henry Winslow** in 1876.[8] During this time, he also provided information to a man named Albert Gatschet, who was studying the Atfalati dialect.

On November 4, 1878, the seventh annual session of the Grand Ronde Indian legislature convened with Dave Yachkawa representing the reservation's east precinct along with **Foster Wacheno** (Inawalh) and Lame Jim Shiliqua. Dave was appointed court administrator with **Chief Louis Napesa** that same year.[9]

Throughout this time, alcohol continued to plague his life. On July 4, 1876, Summers wrote:

When he [Kachkawa] pulled up a box to make a speech, he fell to the ground so drunk that several men working together could not make him stand up any more. Although there was a heavy penalty for furnishing whiskey to Reservation Indians, someone had sold him seven bottles. The Indian police are busy trying to find the culprit.[10]

---

6   Meacham, *Wigwams and War-path.*

7   Ibid.

8   National Archives, Seattle, Grand Ronde/Siletz, Land and Enrollment Program records, Field Notes and Land Survey 1875–1898, Land Description Book 1878, Box 115; Grand Ronde Justice Court.

9   National Archives, Seattle, Grand Ronde/Siletz, Land and Enrollment Program records, Field Notes and Land Survey 1875–1898, Land Description Book 1878, Box 115; Grand Ronde Justice Court.

10 Cawley, *Indian Journal,* 37.

Summers also recorded a conversation he had with a young Indian woman about "Cultas Dave" Yachkawa:

> He was blind when we saw him last and we supposed him harmless; but this past winter he had killed his wife—the one we saw taking care for him—and now he had another one.[11]

Yachkawa's Clackamas wife, Jane, died in March 1875. There is no evidence that Yachkawa was the cause of her death. Following Jane's death, Yachkawa married Sarah, the widow of Chief Kayakach and more recently the widow of **Chief Shlawin. Peter Checkaon** (Chikhyan)'s wife, Marianne (Bochean), and **Moses Apperson** (Wannexke) witnessed the ceremony.

Yachkawa's new wife, Sarah, was a medicine doctor best known by her Tualatin name Washkayak.[12] According to Yachkawa, her power was such that she could draw blood by singing from the chest to the head of the patient.[13] Like Sarah, Yachkawa was an old-time doctor. When someone with his whirlwind power was cut or stabbed, a great storm would shake the land, you would hear thunder roll, it would rain, and hail would pour down.[14]

Both Yachkawa and Sarah were murdered by a Molalla man named **Tom Gilbert** (Kiyukiyush) just a few days after Thanksgiving 1882. Upset with Yachkawa for turning him in for bootlegging, Tom took up an axe and killed them both.[15] Father Croquet made note of the incident in the Catholic record book by writing that they had died "at the hand of an evildoer."

Months later, on December 6, 1883, Tom Gilbert was arrested for manslaughter. He was released July 5, 1884 having served six months of a one year sentence.[16]

Victoria Wishikin (Kinishi) recorded one of Yachkawa's tamanawas songs for Melville Jacobs in 1929.[17]

Yalput, Clackamas[18]	Native Name: None known by author
Alias: None known by author	Allotment: None known by author
Mother: Unknown to author	Father: Unknown to author

Yalput had a full sister who was a minor doctor and married a Kalapuya at

11 Ibid.
12 Jacobs, Field Notebooks 58, *Texts and Ethnology*, 12. Jacobs, Field Notebooks 46, *Santiam Kalapuya Text*, 161.
13 Gatschet, *Texts, Sentences and Vocables*, 401.
14 Jacobs, Field Notebooks 58, *Texts and Ethnology*, 12. Gatschet, *Texts, Sentences and Vocables*, 4: Peter *Kinai* believed Dave to have the power of a "rainmaker." Jacobs, Field Notebook 79, *Texts and Ethnology*, 17.
15 Jacobs, Field Notebooks 46, *Santiam Kalapuya Text*, 161.
16 Oregon State Archive, Salem, Oregon, Polk County, Inmate File 1467.
17 Jacobs, Field Notebook 51, *Texts and Ethnology*, 32.
18 Drucker, *Clackamas Notes*, 32.

Grand Ronde. His first wife was Warm Springs. She left him for some reason, but he kept their two children. Their son died unmarried. Their daughter married a Kalapuya man from the Wapato Lake band. After his Warm Springs wife, Yalput had a Cascade woman living with him for a time.

An old man who had never been beaten in a foot race and was a good gambler also lived with him. He and Yalput were related somehow. The old man also had a woman for a time, but she left him.[19]

Yelkas, Henry (1848c–1913), Molalla	Native Name: None known by author
Alias: None known by author	Allotment: None known by author
Mother: Unknown to author	Father: Chief Yelkas

Henry's second wife was Nellie Beaver Trapper, the daughter of **Sam Beaver Trapper** (Shayum) and Eliza California.

In 1886, Henry and Nellie were living at Grand Ronde where they were classified as "poor." The Indian agent listed their total assets as two horses, a wagon, and a harness. They were not listed on any GRIC after 1886 as by this time they were living continuously in Henry's original country near Molalla.

Unable to have children, Henry and Nellie adopted Fred E. Yelkas when he was about four years old.[20] Several years later, they separated. When Nellie left, Fred stayed with Henry, who also remained on good terms with Nellie's parents. Henry's former mother-in-law, Lisa Clackamas, lived on Henry's place for a number of years after the death of her husband in 1893.[21]

Henry Yelkas was murdered in Molalla after a town celebration in 1913. His body was found by the roadside. Nellie's second husband, Harry Clark, was arrested, but released after the prosecutor could not properly demonstrate a cause of death.

In the end, Fred buried Henry in the Yelkas family cemetery next to Chief Yelkas.[22]

Yelkas, Chief, Molalla	Native Name: Yelkas /YEL-cus/ (yélqas)*[23]
Alias: None known by author	Allotment: None known by author
Mother: Unknown to author	Father: Natilkai[24]

---

19 Ibid.

20 Oregon State Archives, Salem, Oregon, Yelkes, Fred, January 19, 1886, Evidence, Clackamas, Health File 0649.

21 *Molalla Indians*, 5.

22 Ibid.

23 Drucker, *Molalla Notes*, information from Molala Kate Chantell on Monday, June 25, 1934.

24 Ibid.

Joel Palmer received a complaint about Chief Yelkas from an early settler named Robert Hull on November 17, 1853. In part, Robert Hull wrote:

I was on my claim some time before I knew that I was on the Indian's camping ground, but [with] the land bill requiring them to be removed, I remained satisfied thinking that government would soon take them away. I have continually had to suffer from them ever since. Every fall they have stolen some of my cabbages and potatoes. They tell me that I had stolen their land. A number of times they have thrown down my fence. Year after year has past and they are still among us. When we got a change of government, I thought then surely they will be taken away, but they are still among us. I am not the only individual that has suffered from them. A few days ago an Indian that is well known among the settlers by the name of Old Man Yelkes came to my house. I had just been getting supper. He had the ribs of a side of venison. He said he wanted to swap for some flour. I did not like the looks of his meat. I told him I did not want

Photo taken of Henry Yelkas, son of Chief Yelkas, just prior to his death in 1913. Photo courtesy of Oregon Historical Society (OHS OrHi 022578).

to buy it. He said I must either buy it or give him some flour. I told him I would do neither. He came toward me. He took my hat from my head and struck me. I got my gun as quick as possible thinking to shoot him down, but I did not know whether I would be justified or not. I want to know of you whether I shall take the law into my own hands and shoot them down or shall I wait a little longer expecting to have them moved. I want you to write and let me know. [25]

The American settlers had to wait another two years for the United States to negotiate treaties that would extinguish Indian title to their land claims in Western Oregon. Chief Yelkas was one of those present when the treaty was signed on January 9, 1855. As Second Chief of the Molalla band of Molallas, he made his mark on the document along with First Chief Gwayakiti and Third Chief **Kowkama** or "Long Hair."[26]

On the Grand Ronde Reservation, Chief Yelkas along with **Chief Quaiquaty** (Gwayakiti) and others surrendered their rifles on April 6, 1856. After the war, Chief Yelkas did not stay continuously on the reservation, but returned as often as he could to his former country.[27]

Like other men, Chief Yelkas had several wives. His last wife was a young Modoc slave girl. When he bought her, his high status as chief relieved her of the stigma of a slave. The two of them lived out their lives together.

Survived by his son, **Henry Yelkas,** the old chief was buried near present day Molalla.[28]

Yocum, Frank (1842c)	Native Name: None known by author
Alias: None known by author	Allotment: None known by author
Mother: Unknown to author	Father: Unknown to author

In 1885, Frank was listed with his wife, Sallie, Aunt Nannie and "Old Jennie."

Yocum, Nancy (b.1812c–92c), Rogue River[29]	Native Name: Tohokuhsah /Toh-ho-kuh-sah/[30]
Alias: None known to author	Allotment 269
Mother: Unknown to author	Father: Unknown to author

25 Robert Hull to Joel Palmer, November 17, 1853, *Correspondence and Papers of Joel Palmer.*

26 Kappler, *Treaty with the Kalapuya, Ect., 1855,* 668.

27 List of guns turned in by Indians April 6, 1856.

28 Jacobs, Field Notebooks 52, *Texts and Ethnology,* 20.

29 1888 GRIC gave her tribe as Rogue River.

30 *Heirs of Deceased Indians,* Allotment Record 269: gave her Indian name as "Toh-ho-kuh-sah."

Nancy Yocum (Tohokuhsah) was the same woman listed as Aunt Nannie who was living with Frank Yocum in 1885. On the 1887 census she was listed as a widow. She does not appear on any GRIC after 1892. She received 160 acres of allotment land at Grand Ronde. Her heirs were **Joseph Jeff Day**'s children.

Young, Jim (1841c), Santiam band of Kalapuya	Native Name: None known by author
Alias: James Kirk	Allotment: None known by author
Mother: Unknown to author	Father: Unknown to author

Jim Young was one of the Tufak people whose native village was just north of present day Brownsville. Born to a prominent family, his head was flattened at birth to reflect his high social status.[31]

When Jim was a boy, one of the early pioneers, a man by the name of Riley Kirk settled near the Tufak. After discovering Jim was a good worker, Kirk invited him to live with his family. Jim took his surname and lived with the Kirk family for a number of years.[32]

During this time, Jim had several encounters with the law. He was arrested for grand larceny July 2, 1870, and released January 14, 1871. He was incarcerated again for larceny on December 4, 1872, and released September 22, 1873.[33]

Sometime later, he returned to his people at Grand Ronde where he became known as powerful Indian shaman. Once at a winter dance, a number of people saw him change cedar bark into a rattlesnake. Reportedly, the cedar turned into a rattlesnake after he blew on it for a period of time while singing his spirit power song. People said its tail even made the sound of a rattle. Then he put it on the ground and let it crawl away.[34]

When Jim was arrested in 1882, prison authorities discovered a snake tattoo on his left arm. The tattoo was that of three snakes. The center snake stood in a prone position while the snake on either side lay horizontally.

This time, Jim was found guilty of manslaughter. He was sentenced to five years in prison, but served only twelve months. His wife, **Calapooia Eliza** (Chaishna), visited him regularly until he was released on November 29, 1883.[35]

---

31 Jacobs Collection, 1693-71-13, bx 90, file 9, University of Washington Archives. Oregon State Archives, Salem, Inmate Register, Vol. 3, 1877–1887, James Kirke, November 15, 1882, Inmate Lane County Penitentiary File 1287.

32 WPA Interviews: Kirk, Andrew Warren, transcribed by Patricia Dunn of Lebanon Genealogical Society from WPA Interviews by Leslie Haskins and published on http://www.lgsoregon.org/resources/wpa/kirkanda.htm.

33 Oregon State Archives, Salem, Oregon, Inmate Linn County OSP 421.

34 Jacobs, *Santiam Kalapuya Ethnologic Texts*, Part 1, 339-340.

35 Oregon State Archives, Salem, Inmate Register, Vol. 3, 1877–1887, James Kirke, November 15, 1882, Inmate Lane County Penitentiary File 1287.

In 1886, Jim was living on the Grand Ronde Indian Reservation with Calapooia Eliza (1836c) and his son, Albert (1870c). He was the shaman rumored responsible for **Stephanie Howard** (Lhimiki)'s death in 1890.[36]

Jim Young's wife, Calapooia Eliza Young, standing on the steps of her home in Brownsville. Photo courtesy of Oregon Historical Society (OrHi 29505).

36 Jacobs, *Clackamas Text*, Part II, 520–22.

Bibliography

Annual Report of the Commissioner of Indian Affairs to the Secretary of the Interior, 1851–1913. Washington: Government Printing Office. Kansas City, MO: Public Library. http://archive.org

Applegate, Jesse. *The Yangoler Chief.* Roseburg, OR: Review Publishing Company, 1907.

_____. *Recollections of My Boyhood.* Roseburg, OR: Review Publishing Company, 1914.

Applegate, Shannon. *Skookum: An Oregon Pioneer Family's History and Lore.* New York, New York: Morrow, 1988.

Baker, Dean. *The Last of the Yangolers.* Roseburg, OR: Review Publishing Company, 1907.

Bancroft, Hubert Howe. *The Works of Hubert Howe Bancroft. Vol. 29. History of Oregon, Vol. 1, 1834–1848.* San Francisco: The History Company, 1886.

_____. *History of Pacific States of North America. Vol. 25. History of Oregon, Vol. 2, 1848–1888.* San Francisco: The History Company, 1888.

Barker, Burt Brown, ed. *Letters of Doctor John McLoughlin Written at Fort Vancouver, 1829–1832.* Portland, OR: Binfords & Mort, 1948.

Barnett, H.G. *Indian Shakers, A Messianic Cult of the Pacific Northwest.* Carbondale, IL: Southern Illinois University Press, 1957.

Barth, Gunther, ed. *All Quiet on the Yamhill, The Civil War in Oregon.* Eugene, OR: University of Oregon Press, 1959.

Beattie, Judith H., and Helen M. Buss, ed. *Undelivered Letter to Hudson Bay Company Men on the Northwest Coast of America.* Vancouver, BC: USB Press, 2003.

Beckham, Stephen D. *Requiem for a People, the Rogue River and the Frontiersmen.* Norman, OK: University of Oklahoma Press, 1996.

Beckham, Stephen D., ed. "Trail of Tears: 1856 Diary of Indian Agent George Ambrose." In *Southern Oregon Heritage: The Magazine of the Southern Oregon Historical Society,* Vol. 2, No. 1, Summer, 16–21, 1996.

Berreman, Joel V. Collection of interviews and photographs taken from Native Americans at Grand Ronde in 1934. Cultural Resource Department Archives, Confederated Tribes of the Grand Ronde, Grand Ronde, 2005.

Binns, Archie. *Peter Skene Ogden Fur Trader.* Portland, OR: Binfords & Mort, 1967.

Boas, Franz. "Chinook in Handbook of American Indian Languages." Smithsonian Publication *in Bureau of American Ethnology,* Bulletin 40, part 1 (1911): 561–677.

_____. "Notes on the Tillamook." University of California Publication in *American Archaeology and Ethnology,* (20) (1923): 1–16.

Booth, Percy T. *Until the Last Arrow.* Coos Bay, OR: B & B Publishing, 1997.

Brooks, Van Wyck. *The World of Washington Irving.* Kingsport, PA: E.P. Dutton & Company, 1944.

Brown, James H. *Brown's Political History of Oregon,* Vol. I. Portland, OR: Wiley B. Allen, 1892.

Browne, J. Ross. *Report to Commissioner of Indian Affairs* dated December 4, 1857, "Indian Wars in Oregon and Washington Territories." Published in Executive Documents Printed by Order of the House of Representatives, First Sess., Thirty-Fifth Congress, 1857–58. Washington: James B. Steedman, Printer, 1858.

_____. *The California Indians: A Clever Satire on the Governments Dealings with its Indian Wards.* New York: Harper Brothers, 1864.

_____. *Indian Affairs in the Territories of Oregon and Washington.* Ye Galleon Press, Fairfield, Washington, 1977: 22–28. This work contains a history of the Grand Ronde Reserve, description of the military post, talks with chiefs and headmen, and commentary about the Rogue River Chief, Toquahear. In 1863, the author was a special agent of the Department of the Interior on the Pacific Coast assigned to investigate matters concerning Indian Affairs.

Buchanan, Robert C. Letter to Joel Palmer dated July 8, 1856, *Indian Affairs in the Territory of Oregon,* no. 94. Report to Commissioner of Indian Affairs accompanying the Annual Report of the Secretary of the Interior for the year 1856. Boston University, College of Liberal Arts Library, Washington: A. O. P. Nicholson Printer, 1857.

Carey, Charles H. *History of Oregon,* Vol.1. Chicago–Portland, OR: The Pioneer Historical Publishing Company, 1922.

_____. "The Mission Record Book of the Methodist Episcopal Church, Willamette Station, Oregon Territory," *Oregon Historical Quarterly,* Vol. 23, No. 3 (1922): 230–266.

_____. "Diary of Rev. George Gary." *Oregon Historical Quarterly* (24:1) (March 1923): 86–87.

_____. *The Journals of Theodore Talbot, 1843 and 1849–1852.* Portland, OR: Kessinger Publishing, LLC, 1931.

Cawley, Martinus. *Indian Journal of Rev. R. W. Summers.* Lafayette, OR: Guadalupe Translations, 1994.

_____. *Father Crockett of the Grand Ronde*. Lafayette, OR: Guadalupe Translations, 1996.

Cerny, Alta Savage. "The Case of Polk County vs Billy Warren." *Historically Speaking*, (3) (Aug. 1874): 19.

Clark, Ella E. *Indian Legends of the Pacific Northwest*. Berkeley: University of California Press, 1953.

Clark, Margaret L. *Reconstituting the Fur Trade Community of the Assiniboine Basin 1793 to 1812*. Winnipeg: University of Winnipeg and the University of Manitoba, 1997.

Clark, Robert C. *History of the Willamette Valley, Oregon*. Vol. 1. Chicago: S. J. Clarke, 1927.

Clarke, Samuel A. *Pioneer Days of Oregon History*, Vol. I. Portland, OR: J. K. Gill Company, 1905.

Coan, C. F. "The First Stages of the Federal Indian Policy in the Pacific Northwest, 1849–52." *The Quarterly of the Oregon Historical Society* by the Oregon Historical Society, (22) (1921), ed. Frederic George Young, Portland, OR: The Ivy Press.

_____. "Adoption of the Reservation Policy in the Pacific Northwest, 1853–5." *The Quarterly of the Oregon Historical Society* by the Oregon Historical Society, (23) (1922), ed. Frederic George Young, Eugene, OR: Koke-Tiffany Company.

Cooper, Edward S. *William Babcock Hazen: The Best Hated Man*. Madison, NJ: Fairleigh Dickinson University Press, 2005.

Danforth, Barbara. Private Letter Collection held by Barbara Danforth, Letters received by Agatha Howard-Bloom and Bernice Howe-McEachran from Mary Ann Hoffer-Michelle, Velma Hudson-Mercier, Amanda Jeffries-Riggs and Caroline Sitton-Strong, 1953–94, Tigard, OR, 2011.

Douthit, Nathan. "Joseph Lane and the Rogue River Indians: Personal Relations across a Cultural Divide." *Oregon Historical Quarterly, Special Issue: Aspects of Southern Oregon History* (95) (1994): 472–515.

_____. "Between Indian and White Worlds on the Oregon-California Border, 1851–1857; Benjamin Wright and Enos." *Oregon Historical Quarterly*, (100) (1999): 402–33.

Du Bois, Cora A. *The 1870 Ghost Dance*. Berkeley: University of California Press, 1939.

Dunn, John. *History of the Oregon Territory and British North American Fur Trade; with an Account of the Habits and Customs of the Principal Native Tribes on the Northern Continent*. London: Edwards and Hughes, 1844.

Drucker, Philip. Clackamas Field Notes, 1934. Bureau of American Ethnology, Manuscript 4516:82, Smithsonian Institute, Washington, D.C. Ethnographic notes taken in interview with John Wacheno, who gives personal information about Doctor Smith, Jack Nancy, Washkeya, Yalput, Hwaini, Judas, and others.

_____. Molalla Field Notes, 1934. Bureau of American Ethnology, Smithsonian Institute, Washington, D. C. Ethnographic notes taken from Kate Shantelle [Chantelle].

_____. "The Tolowa and Their Southwest Oregon Kin." University of California Publications in *American Archaeology and Ethnology*, 36 (1936): 219–99.

Dye, Eva Emery. *McLoughlin and Old Oregon.* Chicago: A. C. McClurg, 1903.

Fagan, David D., ed. *History of Benton County, Oregon.* Portland, OR: A. G. Walling, printer, 1885.

Faris, John T. *Winning the Oregon Country.* New York: Missionary Education Movement of the United States and Canada, 1912.

Fidler, Peter. Brandon House, 1817. Unpublished HBC journal, Hudson's Bay Company Archives, B22/a/20, Provincial Archives of Manitoba, Winnipeg.

Frachtenberg, Leo J. *Molala Ethnology.* MS 2517 pt., Information obtained from Stephen Savage 1910–11. Bureau of American Ethnology, Smithsonian Institute, Washington, DC.

_____. *Kalapuya Grammatical Notes.* MS 1923-d, Volume 1, Mary's River or Kalapuya Proper, information taken from William Hartless of the Mary's River Kalapuya at Siletz Agency, 1913. Bureau of American Ethnology, Smithsonian Institute, Washington, DC. Frachtenberg includes information from Grace Wheeler and one story, "The Origin of Death," from Mose Hudson taken August 30, 1913, at Grand Ronde.

_____. *Yamhill Kalapuya Ethnology.* MS 1923-e, Volume 1–3. Information obtained from Mrs. Louise Selkeah on the Grand Ronde Reservation in August 1913. Bureau of American Ethnology, Smithsonian Institute, Washington, DC.

_____. *Kalapuya Grammatical Notes.* MS 1923-d, Volume 2, Mary's River or Kalapuya Proper, information taken in September 1914 from William Hartless of the Mary's River Kalapuya at Siletz Agency, OR. Bureau of American Ethnology, Smithsonian Institute, Washington, DC.

_____. *Kalapuya Grammatical Notes.* MS 1923-d, Volume 3, Mary's River or Kalapuya Proper, information taken in September 1914 from William Hartless of the Mary's River Kalapuya at Siletz Agency, OR. Bureau of American Ethnology, Smithsonian Institute, Washington, DC.

_____. *Kalapuya Ethnology.* MS 1923-a, Vol. 1–13, Information taken September through December 1914 from William Hartless of the Mary's River Kalapuya, and Grace Wheeler of Kalapuya, Bureau of American Ethnology, Smithsonian Institute, Washington, DC. Volume 4 Includes William Hartless's version of

"Coyote Loses his Eyes" and the story of Panther and Weasel along with notes concerning John Skna'um, Susie Jim, and Maria Talzan as possibly "good Chehalis informants." He also noted that John Skna'um was "chief of the Shakers."

_____. *Kalapuya Ethnology*. MS 1923-b, Volume 1–3, Information taken from William Hartless of the Mary's River Kalapuya at Chemawa, OR in October and November 1914. Bureau of American Ethnology, Smithsonian Institute, Washington, DC.

_____. *Kalapuya Ethnology*. MS 1923-c, Notebook 6271, Information taken December 11 from William Hartless of the Mary's River Kalapuya at Chemawa, OR. Bureau of American Ethnology, Smithsonian Institute, Washington, DC.

_____. *Yamhill Kalapuya Ethnology*. MS 1923-e, Volume 3, Information obtained from Mrs. Louise Selkeah on the Grand Ronde Reservation December 15, 1914. Bureau of American Ethnology, Smithsonian Institute, Washington, DC.

_____. *Yoncalla Kalapuya Ethnology*. MS 1923-f, Notebook 6271, Information taken from Mrs. Robert Allen, Grand Ronde Reservation, December 17–18, 1914. Bureau of American Ethnology, Smithsonian Institute, Washington, DC.

_____. *Kalapuya Ethnology*. Found among papers in J. P. Harrington's Office, 1959. American Philosphical Society Library.

Fremaux, Sylvain, ed. *Memoires d'un Grand Brainois; Monseigneur Adrian Croquet. le Saint de L'Oregon*. Association of the Museum of Braine-l'Alleud, 1976. Translated by Jean Bosse, Grand Ronde, OR: Confederated Tribes of Grand Ronde, 1996.

Fuller, George W. *A History of the Pacific Northwest*. New York: Knopf, 1948.

Gatschet, Albert S., Leo J. Frachtenberg, and Melville Jacobs. "Kalapuya Texts." *Kalapuya Texts*, Part 3. University of Washington Publications in Anthropology, Vol. 11 (June 1945): 145–369.

Gatschet, Albert S. *Umpqua Texts*, Recorded From Chief Peter McKay and Winchester Jo, Grand Ronde Reservation, December 30, 1877, MS 76. Bureau of American Ethnology, Smithsonian Institution, Washington, DC.

_____. *Yamhill Kalapuya Vocabulary*, Vol. 1 & 2, From Peter Se'klia, Grand Ronde Reservation, December 8, 1877. Bureau of American Ethnology, Smithsonian Institution, Washington D.C.

_____. *Texts, Sentences and Vocables of the Atfalati Dialect*, MS 472-a-b-c, Grand Ronde Reservation, November and December 1877, From Peter Ki'nai and Dave Yatchkawa. Bureau of American Ethnology, Smithsonian Institution, Washington, DC.

A.S. Gatschet manuscript with additions and insertions from Dr. Leo J. Frachtenberg, 1913–1914 and Melville Jacobs, 1936–1937. University of Washington, Seattle, 1939.

Gibbs, George, *Yamhill Kalapuya Language Vocabulary*, taken from (illegible) and Antoine, chiefs, 1851, MS 475-a-b. Bureau of American Ethnology, Smithsonian Institution, Washington, DC.

George Gibbs graduated from the United States Military Academy in 1846. In 1864–65, he commanded a cavalry reserve brigade and served under General Phil Sheridan on several raids. An interesting letter from him regarding the causes of the Indian Wars in Oregon and Washington Territory can be found in the appendix of James Swan's book, *The Northwest Coast or Three Years Residence in Washington Territory*, 1857.

_____. *A Dictionary of Chinook Jargon or Trade Language of Oregon*. Washington: Smithsonian Institution, 1863.

Glassley, Ray H. *Pacific Northwest Indian Wars*. Portland, OR: Binfords & Mott, 1853.

Glisan, Rodney. *Journal of Army Life: R. Glisan*. San Francisco: A. L. Bancroft, 1874.

Gray, William H. *A History of Oregon, 1792–1849: Drawn from Personal Observation and Authentic Information*. Berkeley: University of California, 1870. Keeping in mind that Mr. Gray was an American missionary, his version of the Cayuse upraising against the Whitmans and the Indian war that followed is important to fully understanding the issues between the races during this time period. Colonel Gilliam's Battle with the Cayuse can be found on pp. 547–68. At least three French Indians and Iroquois mixed bloods who later removed to the Grand Ronde Reservation fought on behalf of the Americans in this war: Louis Vasselle, Frank Quenelle, and Joseph Shangaretta.

Gunther, Erna. "The Shaker Religion of the Northwest." In *Indians of the Urban Northwest* ed. Marian Smith, 37–76. New York: Columbia University Press, 1949.

Handsaker, Samuel. *Pioneer Life*. Eugene. OR, 1908.

Hines, Gustavas. *Wild Life in Oregon; Being a Stirring Recital or Actual Scenes of Daring and Peril Among the Gigantic Forests and Terrific Rapids of the Columbia River (The Mississippi of the Pacific Slope) and Giving Life-Like Pictures of Terrific Encounters with Savages as Fierce and Relentless as It's Mighty Tides Including a Full, Fair and Reliable History of the State of Oregon, It's Crops, Minerals, Timber Lands, Soil, Fisheries; It's Present Greatness and Future Vast Capabilities and Paramount Position*, Worthington & Co., 747 Broadway, New York, Reese Library of the University of California, 1889 Hussey, James A. *Champoeg: Place of Transition, A Disputed History*. Portland, OR: Oregon Historical Society in cooperation with Oregon State Highway Commission and the National Park Service, United States Department of Interior, 1967.

Houston, C. Struart, and Mary L. Houston. *"The Sacking of Peter Fidler's Brandon House, 1816."* Manitoba Historical Society, Saskatoon, Saskatchewan, *Manitoba History* (16) (Autumn 1988).

Irving, Washington. *The Adventures of Captain Bonneville.* New York: John B. Alden, 1886.

Itemizer Newspaper Extracts for 1878, Polk County, Oregon. Compiled by Clara Foster and Justine Jones. Salem, OR: C. Foster, 1990.

Work includes: Fatal Affray, A White Man and an Indian Killed on Salmon River, and Homicide on Salmon River, A Correct Statement of the Affair. Two reports of an incident involving Levi Bob and several white men at Salmon River. Another report of this incident can be found in Summers Indian Journal.

Jackson, John C. *Children of the Fur Trade: Forgotten Métis of the Pacific Northwest, Columbia River.* Norman: University of Oklahoma Press, 1970.

Jackson, Donald, and Mary Lee Spence, ed. *The Expeditions of John Charles Fremont,*

Travels from 1838 to 1844, Vol. 1. Chicago: University of Illinois Press, 1970.

Jacobs, Elizabeth. Field Notebook 105–6, Misc Ethnographic Notes, Tillamook (Nehalem), Personal Papers, Melville Jacobs Special Collection, University of Washington Libraries, Seattle, WA

Jacobs, Melville.Field Notebook 33, *Chasta Costa etc., Santiam, Kalapuya.* (Department of Anthropology, University of Washington, Seattle, 1928).

_____. Field Notebooks 35–36, *Santiam Kalapuya Text*, Department of Anthropology, translation taken from John B. Hudson on February 16, 1928. 101 Museum, University of Washington, Seattle.

_____. Field Notebooks 37–40, *Santiam Kalapuya and Molale Text*, Department of Anthropology, Text taken from Louisa Selky and Molalla Kate Chantell with Partial translation from John B. Hudson in 1928. 101 Museum, University of Washington, Seattle.

_____. Field Notebook 45, *Yoncalla Kalapuya Text*, Department of Anthropology, translation taken from Mrs. Laura Blackerty Albertson at Siletz, Oregon in October and November, 1928. 101 Museum, University of Washington, Seattle.

_____. Field Notebooks 46–47, *Santiam Kalapuya Text,* Department of Anthropology, Translation taken from Eustace Howard and John B. Hudson in 1928. 101 Museum, University of Washington, Seattle.

_____. Field Notebook 51, *Music and Ethnology*, Klickitat and N.W. Oregon taken 1929–30. Department of Anthropology, 101 Museum, University of Washington, Seattle.

_____. Field Notebooks 52–56 and 58–65, *Texts and Ethnology (Upper Chinook) Clackamas* and Notebooks 66–69, *Texts Ethnology Clackamas & Jargon* taken from Mrs. Victoria Howard at West Linn, Oregon City, Oregon, 1929–30. Department of Anthropology, 101 Museum, University of Washington, Seattle.

_____. Field Notebooks 76–79 and 81–86, *Texts and Ethnology Santiam* taken from Eustace Howard at West Linn, Oregon City, Oregon, 1929–30. Department of Anthropology, 101 Museum, University of Washington, Seattle.

_____. Collection 40, *Autobiography of a Tualatin, My Life by Louis Kenoyer*, 1936. University Archives, University of Washington, Seattle.

_____. "Santiam Kalapuya Ethnologic Texts," Part 1. *Kalapuya Texts*, University of Washington Publications in Anthropology, Vol.11 (June, 1945):17–82.

_____. "*Santiam Kalapuya Myth Texts*," Part 2. *Kalapuya Texts*, University of Washington Publications in Anthropology, Vol.11 (June, 1945): 83–142.

_____. *Clackamas Chinook Texts*, Part 1. Research Center in Anthropology, Folklore and Linguistics, 8; *International Journal of American Linguistics*, 24(1), Part 2. Bloomington: Indiana University, 1958.

_____. *Clackamas Chinook Texts, Part 2*. Research Center in Anthropology, Folklore and Linguistics, 11; *International Journal of American Linguistics*, 25(2), Part 2. Bloomington: Indiana University, 1959.

Jahoda, Gloria. *The Trail of Tears, The Story of the American Indian Removals 1813–1855*. Avenel, New Jersey, 1975.

Johansen, Dorothy O., and Charles M. Gates. *Empire of the Columbia: A History of the Pacific Northwest*. 2nd edition, New York: Harper & Row, 1957.

Johnson, Don. *The Journal of Captain Nathaniel J. Wyeth's Expeditions to the Oregon Country 1831–1836*. Fairfield, WA: Ye Galleon Press, 1997.

Johnson, Tony A and Henry B. Zenk. *Chinuk Wawa; As our elders teach us to speak it,* (2). Language Program of the Confederated Tribes of the Grand Ronde, Confederated Tribes of the Grand Ronde Community of Oregon, 2009.

Kappler, C. J. *Indian Affairs: Laws and Treaties*, (2). Treaties. U.S. Senate. 58th Congress, 2nd Session. Senate Document No. 319, pt. 2 (*Serial Set* 4624). Washington, DC: Government Printing Office, 1904.

Knudsen, T.G. *Warrior of the Mist: A Biography of Qualchan Chief Owhi's Son*. Spokane: Glen Adams, 1996.

Kruse, Anne Applegate. *The Halo Trail, Story of the Yoncalla Indians*. Drain, OR: The Drain Interprises, 1954.

Labonte, Esther. Personal interview by Henry Zenk, 1982 as transcribed by Abigail Pecore. Cultural Resource Department Archives, Confederated Tribes of Grand Ronde, Grand Ronde, Oregon.

La Mere, Cletus Edward. *Father Felix Bucher, S.D.S. Missionary and Mystic of Grand Ronde, Oregon*. Lafayette, OR, 1996.

Lampson, Evelyn Sibley. "Some Visitors From The Grand Ronde," *Historically Speaking*, (3) (Aug. 1974): 20–31.

Lang, Herbert O. ed. *History of the Willamette Valley, Description of the Valley and its Resources with an Account of its Discovery and Settlement by White Men and its Subsequent History; Together with Personal Reminiscences of its Early Pioneers.* Portland, OR: G.H. Hines, 1885.

This author gives an excellent account of the prejudices and hostilities that led to the Rogue River and Cascade wars, p. 353–403.

Lattie, Alexander. *"Diary of Alexander Lattee,"* March 1846. *Oregon Historical Quarterly* 64 (1963): 211n.

Alexander Lattie sold his house near Cape Disappointment to Thomas Pisk Kipling, the interpreter who lived at Chinook Point, for $150, which Lattie's widow received after his death.

Layton, Thomas N. "Traders and Raiders: Aspects of Trans-Basin and California-Plateau Commerce, 1800–1830." *Journal of California and Great Basin Anthropology,* 3(1) (1981): 128–31. Retrieved from http://escholarship.org/uc/item/3793q75r

Lee, Daniel, and J. H. Frost. *Ten Years in Oregon.* New York, 1844.

Lent, Geneva. *West of the Mountains: James Sinclair and the Hudson Bay Company.* Seattle: University of Washington Press, 1963.

Lynch, Vera Martin. *Free Land for Free Men: A Story of Clackamas County.* Portland, OR: Artline Printing Inc., 1973.

Mackenzie, Alexander. *Journal of the Voyage to the Pacific.* New York: Walter Sheppe editor, 1995.

Mackey, Harold. *The Kalapuyans: A Sourcebook on the Indians of the Willamette Valley,* 2nd edition. Salem, OR: Mission Mill Museum Association in Cooperation with the Confederated Tribes of The Grand Ronde, 2004.

Mackie, Richard S. *Trading Beyond the Mountains: The British Fur Trade on the Pacific, 1793–1843.* Vancouver: UBC Press, 1997.

Maloney, Alice B. "Campsites of Jedediah Smith on the Oregon Coast." *Oregon Historical Quarterly,* 41 (1940): 304–23.

McChesney, Charles E. *The Rolls of Certain Indian Tribes in Washington and Oregon.* Fairfield, WA: Ye Galleon Press, 1969.

McKay, Harvey J. *St. Paul, Oregon 1830–1890.* Portland, OR: Binford & Mort., 1980.

McKay, John. *Brandon House, 1808.* Unpublished Journal, Hudson Bay Company Archives, B22/a/15. Provincial Archives of Manitoba, Winnipeg.

McNamee, Sister Mary Dominica. *Willamette Interlude.* Palo Alto, CA: Pacific Books Publishers, 1959.

Meacham, A. B. *Wigwam and War-Path: or Royal Chief in Chains.* Boston: John P. Dale and Co., 1875.

Michelle, Mary Ann. *Just a Memorandum.* February 29, 1956 (typed version), Cultural Resource Department Archives, Confederated Tribes of Grand Ronde Community of Oregon: 1–12.

Mary Ann was the granddaughter of Oregon City Kawache (1814c–85), chief of the Clowwewalla or Willamette Tumwater band of Chinook at Oregon City. She created a list of Grand Ronde Indian people including their tribal affiliation, general genealogy and family histories from her personal knowledge.

Minter, Harold A. *Umpqua Valley Oregon and Its Pioneers.* Portland, OR: Binford & Mort, 1967.

"Molalla Indians." *The Clackamas Historical Society Publication in The Oregon Trail Pioneer,* (May/June 1995): 5.

Morrison, Dorothy N. *Outpost, John McLoughlin and the Far Northwest.* Portland, OR: Oregon Historical Society Press, 1999.

Munnick, Harriet Duncan, ed. *Catholic Church Records of the Pacific Northwest — Vancouver and Stellamaris Mission.* St Paul, OR: French Prairie Press, 1972.

_____. *Catholic Church Records of the Pacific Northwest — St Louis and Brooks.* Portland, OR: Binford & Mort, 1982.

_____. "Grandma was an Indian," in *Marion County History,* vol. 7, Statesman Publishing Company, Salem, OR, 1961, 6–9.

Munnick, Harriet and Stephen D. Beckham, eds. 1987 Catholic *Church Records of the Pacific Northwest — Grand Ronde.* Portland, OR: Binford & Mort, 1987.

Munnick, Harriet and Mikell Delores Warner, eds. *Catholic Church Records of the Pacific Northwest — St Paul.* Portland, OR: Binford & Mort, 1979.

Nash, Wallis. *Two Years in Oregon.* New York: D. Appleton and Co., 1882. In this work the author provides a description of a visit made to the Siletz Reservation in 1877. Of particular interest is the arrest of three men for the murder of an Indian doctor whose patient died, the Indian patrol, and the author's remarks concerning the power of the agent.

Nesmith, James W. "The Council of Table Rock, 1853, Reminiscences of Senator James W. Nesmith and General Joseph Lane." In *Oregon Historic Quarterly,* Vol. 7 (March 1906): 211–20.

O'Donnell, Terrence. An Arrow in the Earth: Joel Palmer and the Indians of Oregon. Portland, OR: Oregon Historical Quarterly Press, 1991.

Ord, Edward Otho Cresap. *Ord's Diary in Curry County, Oregon, 1856.* Wedderburn, OR: H. J. Newhouse, County Surveyor, 1970. General Ord was an American soldier. His diary contains important passages about the war with the Rogue River and descriptions of the people who fought on either side between March 13 and July 16, 1856.

Orcutt, Ada M. *Tillamook: Land of Many Waters*. Portland, OR: Binfords & Mort, 1951.

Palmer, Joel. *Correspondence and Papers*. Special Collection, Knight Library, University of Oregon.

_____. *Joel Palmer Collection*. The Lilly Library, Indiana University, Bloomington.

Parker, Samuel. *Journal of an Exploring Trip Beyond the Rocky Mountains*. Ithaca, NY: Andrus, Woodruff & Gauntlett, 1844.

Phosch, Thomas W. "Notes From: A Government Document on Oregon Conditions in the Fifties." *The Quarterly of the Oregon Historical Society* of the Oregon Historical Society, Vol. 8, edited by Frederic George Young and Willis R. Duniway, 191–200. Salem, OR: State Printer, 1907. Author was a German-born American who arrived on the Pacific Coast in 1855 and from there, journeyed to Washington Territory. A retired newspaperman and author of a number of articles and books about early history, he was killed in a car accident in 1915. In this article, he gives an excellent summary of reasons behind the natives respect for the men of the Hudson's Bay Company.

_____. "The Indian War in Washington Territory." *The Quarterly of the Oregon Historical Society*, Vol. 16, edited by Frederic George Young, 1–23. Portland: The Ivy Press, 1915.

Pollard, Lancaster. "Site of the Smith Massacre on July 14, 1828." *The Oregon Historical Quarterly*, Vol. 45, (1). Portland: Oregon Historical Society, 1944.

Rich, E.E., ed. *The Letters of John McLoughlin from Fort Vancouver to the Governor and Committee, First Series, 1825–1838*, Hudson's Bay Companies Series, Vol. 4. Toronto: Publications of the Champlain Society, 1941.

Richards, Kent D. *Isaac I. Stevens: Young Man in a Hurry*. Provo: Brigham Young University Press, 1979.

Rockwood, Ruth E., "Pastor's Book #3." *Oregon Historical Quarterly*, Vol. 41 (1940): 297–301.

Ross, Alexander. *Adventures of the First Settlers on the Oregon or Columbia River*. Cornhill, London: Smith, Elder and Co., 1849.

_____. *Fur Hunters of the Far West; A Narrative of Adventures in the Oregon and Rocky Mountains*, Vol. 2. Cornhill, London: Smith, Elder, and Co., 1855.

Ruby, Robert H., and John A. Brown. *The Chinook Indians Traders of the Lower Columbia River*. Norman: University of Oklahoma Press, 1976.

_____. *A Guide to the Indian Tribes of the Pacific Society*. Norman: University of Oklahoma Press, 1986.

_____. *Dreamer-Prophets of the Columbia Plateau Smohalla and Skolaskin*. Norman: University of Oklahoma Press, 1989.

Schlicke, Carl P. *General George Wright: Guardian of the Pacific Coast*. Norman: University of Oklahoma Press, 1988.

Seaburg, W. R., and J. Miller. *"Tillamook, Handbook of American Indians."* Vol. 7: Northwest Coast, edited by Wayne Suttles, 560–567. Washington, DC: Smithsonian Institution, 1990.

Sheridan, Philip Henry. *"Personal Memoirs of P.H. Sheridan."* Vol. 1: chapters 5–7. George S. Patton Historical Society Library, Nonguill, MA, 1888. Philip Sheridan was an American soldier who was involved in the conflict at Cascade Locks. Later, he was stationed at Fort Yamhill on the Grand Ronde Reservation. His memoirs mention the battle at the Cascade, the murder of the family of an Indian ally by American settlers, the Indian doctor, Sam Patch, and an incident on the Reservation where he lost his weapon to the Rogue River during an altercation.

Stern, Theodore. "The Klamath Indians and the Treaty of 1864." *Oregon Historical Quarterly 57* (September 1956): 57–231.

Sullivan, Maurice S. *The Travels of Jedediah Smith: A Documentary Outline, Including the Journal of the Great American Pathfinder*. Santa Ana, CA: The Fine Arts Press, 1934.

Swan, James G. *The North-West Coast; or Three Years Residence in Washington Territory*. London: Sampson Low, Son, and Co.; New York: Harper and Brothers, 1857.

Author provides excellent examples of differences between Hudson's Bay Company treatment of Indians and those of Americans suggesting HBC tactics might make the management of the Indian population easier, p. 372. Also makes reference to a letter from General Gibbs that accuses General Wool of "incompetency" and "willful and obstinate inefficiency," p.390. James G. Swan was an Indian agent in Washington Territory who became known for his work in collecting Indian heirlooms.

Swanton, John R. *Indian Tribes of Washington, Oregon, and Idaho*. Fairfield, WA: Ye Galleon Press, 1979.

Teverbaugh, Aeron. "Tribal Constructs and Kinship Realities: Individual and Family Organization on the Grand Ronde Reservation from 1856." PhD thesis, Portland State University, 2000.

The Executive Documents Printed by Order of the Senate of the United States, First Session, Thirty-Fifth Congress and Special Session of 1858, Vol. 12, No. 40. Washington: William A. Harris, Printer, 1858. This work contains the report of J. Ross Browne, Special agent of the Treasury Department to the Commissioner of Indian Affairs, concerning his investigation of the causes behind the late Indian Wars in Oregon and Washington Territory including the feud between General Wool and the citizens of southern Oregon during the Rogue River conflict and the Cayuse upraising at the Whitman Mission. The latter includes testimony from many of the men employed or former employees of the Hudson's Bay Company. Of particular interest is the court problem Browne describes between McLeod and "the Klickitats."

The Federal Reporter, Vol. 158, "Cases Argued and Determined in the Circuit Courts of Appeals and Circuit and District Courts of the United States," Permanent Edition, April–May. St Paul West Publishing Company, 1908.

The Pacific Reporter, Vol. 112, "Containing all the Decisions of the Supreme Courts of California, Kansas, Oregon, Washington, Colorado, Montana, Arizona, Nevada, Idaho, Wyoming, Utah, New Mexico, Oklahoma, Courts of Appeal of California, and Criminal Court of Appeals of Oklahoma," January 9–February 27, 1911. St Paul: West Publishing Company, 1911.

Trafzer, Clifford E. *The Chinook.* New York: Chelsea House Publishers, 1990.

Underhill, Ruth. *Indians of the Pacific Northwest, Indian Life and Customs.* Washington DC: Education Division, United States Office of Indian Affairs, 1944.

United States Congress. *Senate Documents, Otherwise Published as Public & Executive Documents.* William A. Harris, Washington DC., 1858.

Whitman Massacre, statements and correspondence from Protestant and Catholic missionaries, French settlers, Hudson Bay Company officers, and others regarding massacre and following actions, pp. 1–66.

Utley, Robert M., and Wilcomb E. Washburn. *Indian Wars.* New York: American Heritage Press Inc., 2002.

Victor, Francis F. *The Early Indian Wars of Oregon Compiled From the Oregon Archives and Other Original Sources With Muster Rolls Pacific Coast Indian Wars 1847–1865.* Salem, OR: Frank C. Baker, State Printer, 1894.

Walsh, Frank K. *Indian Battles Along the Rogue River, 1855–56.* North Bend, OR: Te-Cum-Tom, 1972.

Webber, Bert. *Indians Along the Oregon Trail.* Medford, OR: Web Research Group, 1992.

Whitlow, Leonard II. *Grande Ronde Indian Reservation, Yamhill County, Oregon: 1860 Census, 1888 Census, 1901 Family Register (Family Groups, Births 1902–1937, Deaths 1902–1937).* Portland, Oregon, 1988.

Winterbotham, Jerry. *Umpqua, The Lost County of Oregon.* Brownsville, OR, 1994.

Wilkes, Charles. *Narrative of the U.S. Exploring Expedition, During the Years 1838, 1839, 1840, 1841, 1842,* Volume 5. Philadelphia, 1849

Work, John. "John Work's Journal from Fort Vancouver to Umpqua River, and Return, in 1834." Introduction and comment by Leslie M. Scott. *Oregon Historical Quarterly,* 24 (1923): 238–268.

_____. *Fur Brigade to the Bonaventura: John Work's California Expedition, 1832–1833, for the Hudson's Bay Company,* Alice B. Maloney, ed. San Francisco: California Historical Society, 1945.

Young, F. G. "Financial History of Oregon—Finances of the Territorial Period, 1849–1850." *The Quarterly of the Oregon Historical Society* by the Oregon Historical Society, 8: 120–90. Salem, OR: Willis R. Duniway, State Printer, 1907.

Zenk, Henry. *"Chinook Jargon and Native Cultural Persistence in the Grand Ronde Indian Community 1856–1907: A Special Case of Creolization."* PhD dissertation, University of Oregon, 1984.

_____. *Field Notes and Interviews from Grand Ronde Tribal People,* Cultural Resource Department Archives, Confederated Tribes of Grand Ronde, 2005.

CPSIA information can be obtained at www.ICGtesting.com
Printed in the USA
LVOW111048061211

258062LV00001B/2/P